INTEGRATION AND COMPETITION IN
THE PETROLEUM INDUSTRY

INTEGRATION AND COMPETITION IN THE PETROLEUM INDUSTRY

Petroleum Monograph Series, Volume 3

by MELVIN G. de CHAZEAU

and ALFRED E. KAHN

Published under the auspices of the Editorial Board of

the Petroleum Monograph Series, established by a

grant from the American Petroleum Institute

New Haven: YALE UNIVERSITY PRESS, 1959

Preface

THIS is a long book, but it deals with an important, complicated, and rapidly changing industry, no aspect of which proved alien to the assigned topic. One cannot assess the organization and performance of an industry like petroleum with a few deftly selected statistics, nicely designed experiments, or cogently phrased paragraphs. This study has been long in the making, longer than might have been required had we not chosen to collaborate so completely both in research and in writing over the entire scope of the project. The qualitative nature of much of the analysis recommended such a course; and, quite possibly, had even more summers been devoted to the job the result would have been a longer, not a shorter, document.

More people than can be enumerated have helped out along the way; to all of them our sincere thanks. More specifically, we are indebted to the American Petroleum Institute and the Yale University Press for making the study possible, to the reader assigned by the Press, who so effectively criticized the completed manuscript both for substance and form, to the Editorial Board for its invaluable suggestions, and especially to Ray B. Westerfield, for support, encouragement, and gentle prodding. We thank the many members of the industry who spoke to us freely and patiently, and especially Albert J. McIntosh for guiding us through the maze of its statistics—copious, but seldom in precisely the form needed. We thank Boni, Watkins, Jason, and Company for help with some statistical compilations, and John G. McLean and Robert W. Haigh for graciously letting us study their monumental work while it was still in manuscript. Separate and special thanks are owed Joel Dirlam, who spent one entire summer helping to survey the voluminous literature on oil. We gratefully acknowledge the assistance of our graduate students at various stages of the manuscript—Peter Max, Wolfgang Schoellkopf, Richard Bower. And, for miscellaneous important reasons, not least their admirable forebearance through the long process, our thanks to Marian Holmes and Rachel Kahn.

M. G. DE C.
A. E. K.

Ithaca, N.Y.
September, 1959

v

Monograph Series on the Petroleum Industry

Statement of (1) the manner of control of the project; (2) the objectives of the project; (3) the degree of academic freedom to be accorded to the authors of the monographs and the considerations motivating the Editorial Board in the selection of authors.

CONTROL: The funds to be used in the preparation, manufacture, and distribution of the monographs have been supplied by outright gift to the Yale University Press by the American Petroleum Institute, and this sum is in the sole control of the Yale University Press, which will pay all bills connected with the project. Professor Ray B. Westerfield, of Yale University, was asked by the Press and the donors to organize and head an Editorial Board of six members—four of whom would be economists having no connection with the petroleum industry—which would select the authors, supervise the preparation of the monographs, and determine whether a manuscript was worthy of publication. Expense accounts and any payments coming under the items of honoraria, travel, and research expenses required the approval of the Chairman of the Press.

OBJECTIVES: It is the desire of the Yale University Press and of the donors of the funds that wholly objective and searching studies be made of the petroleum industry. The deed of gift stipulates that "the purpose in establishing this series is to enable well-qualified scholars to make a free inquiry into the industry without any censorship, subject only to the recognized scholarly standards that will be imposed by the Editorial Board or by the Press. The authors will seek to ascertain the facts that bear on the industry's problems of production and distribution, questions of prices and markets, and allied problems." It was further provided that the American Petroleum Institute, through the two representatives of the petroleum industry on the Editorial Board, "will use its best efforts to obtain the cooperation of the members of the Institute in providing the essential help and free access to the records that will be necessary for the basic studies that are contemplated."

DEGREE OF ACADEMIC FREEDOM TO BE ACCORDED THE AUTHORS: The Editorial Board, by express unanimous vote, has confirmed the understanding its members had at the time it was first constituted, when the aims and purposes of the deed gift were related by the Chairman, in the belief that a comprehensive, free inquiry is indispensable if the end results are to be significant. The Board further declares its policy as follows:

(a) both the Board and the authors shall be free from industry pressure, dictation, or censorship; it shall be the Board's province to determine the field of study and to insist upon a thorough, objective, accurate, workmanlike, and readable job;

(b) the Board shall take great care in selecting as the author of each monograph a man who commands the respect of the professional economists for his competence and objectivity, and then shall give him full liberty to develop his research and monograph free from Board pressure, dictation, or censorship;

(c) the Board shall serve in an advisory capacity to the authors, without interfering with the full liberty to be assured them, as specified in the preceding paragraphs;

(d) the manuscripts will be published only upon approval of the Editorial Board; but such approval shall depend exclusively upon the technical adequacy of the study and not upon the Board's agreement or disagreement with the conclusions reached; and

(e) no Board member's criticisms of a manuscript shall be printed in the monograph when published.

Contents

PART IV

INTEGRATION AND COMPETITION IN PRODUCT
MARKETS

Tables

xvii

PART I

*Introduction: The Structure of the Oil Industry
and the Problems It Raises*

CHAPTER 1

The Public Interest in Oil

MAN'S MATERIAL PROGRESS through the ages has depended and will continue to depend on the harnessing of extrahuman sources of energy. The total energy used in this country in 1900 was the equivalent of only about 300 million short tons of bituminous coal. By 1925 it was 800, by 1950, 1,300 million—the energy equivalent of the labor of 200 slaves at the disposal of every American.[1] The Paley Commission estimated the national total would double again by 1975.[2]

This slave-power we have on call is fueled principally by oil. In 1900 nine-tenths of our total energy requirements were supplied by coal. In 1954, coal provided only three-tenths; the share of oil and natural gas had risen, during the intervening period, from one-twelfth to two-thirds.[3] In 1900, this country produced only 64 million barrels of crude oil and natural gas liquids. Fifty-five years later, we produced 2,749 million barrels and consumed 3,072. By 1975, the Paley Commission has estimated, our annual consumption will reach 5,000 million barrels.[4]

1. Eugene Ayres and Charles A. Scarlott, *Energy Sources—the Wealth of the World* (New York, McGraw-Hill, 1952), p. 28.
2. The President's Materials Policy Commission, *Resources for Freedom* (Washington, Government Printing Office, 1952, cited below as Paley Report), *I*, 103–104. Later projections have produced similar estimates. See, e.g., Philip Sporn, "The Role of Energy and the Role of Nuclear Energy in the United States," in International Conference on the Peaceful Uses of Atomic Energy held in Geneva, August, 1955, *Proceedings* (New York, United Nations, 1956), *I*, 423; Wallace Pratt, "The Impact of the Peaceful Uses of Atomic Energy on the Petroleum Industry," in U. S. Congress, Joint Committee on Atomic Energy, *Peaceful Uses of Atomic Energy*, Report of the Panel on the Impact of the Peaceful Uses of Atomic Energy, *2*, Background Material, Joint Committee Print (1956), p. 89.
3. Crude oil alone accounted for 42 per cent, natural gas 25 per cent, in 1954. U. S. Bureau of Mines, "Petroleum and Natural Gas," a chapter preprint from *Mineral Facts and Problems*, Bulletin 556 (Washington, D.C., December, 1955), p. 18.
4. The 1955 figures are from American Petroleum Institute (cited below as API), *Statistical Bulletin* (April 17, 1956), Forms 1, 2, and 8; all others, Paley Report, *3*, 4. According to later projections, the Paley Report's estimate of

The great upward surge in oil production and use in this century has been geared to the demand for gasoline to fuel the automobile and the airplane. But the rising output of motor fuel, itself regarded at one time as an unwanted by-product of kerosene, brought as its by-product a flood of kerosene, distillates (the so-called middle fractions, used for home heating and diesel engines) and heavy residual fuel oils, that needed to search out markets in competition with other sources of heat and power. How successfully this aim has been realized is suggested by the fact that between 1929 and 1955, sales of fuel oils for heating purposes soared from 37 to 426 million barrels, while production of anthracite coal declined from 74 to 26 million net tons.[5] Petroleum-derived fuels other than gasoline have found such important uses—not merely in residential and commercial heating and in industry, but also in transportation by railroads, water carriers, and trucks—that it has for long been impossible to regard them merely as unwanted by-products.

To meet the needs of mid twentieth-century America, with its unprecedented energy requirements, our oil industry has grown to gigantic size. During 1957, it employed gross assets of about $58 billion, gave direct employment to more than 2 million workers, and sold $24.4 billions of products. In addition, American companies and their subsidiaries accounted for 56 per cent of the crude oil production and 41 per cent of the refinery operations outside of this country and the Soviet bloc.[6] At the end of 1957, the United States held only

consumption for 1975 would seem to be modest. Cf., e.g., Joseph E. Pogue and Kenneth E. Hill, *Future Growth and Financial Requirements of the World Petroleum Industry* (New York, Petroleum Department, Chase Manhattan Bank, 1956), p. 16.

5. *Petroleum Facts and Figures* (9th ed., New York, American Petroleum Institute, 1950), p. 69; (12th ed. 1956), p. 61; U. S. Department of Commerce, *Business Statistics, 1957* (Washington, 1957), p. 168. An indirect reflection of the same development is the fact that while the use of petroleum products for transportation more than doubled between 1929 and 1950, their use for residential and commercial purposes (primarily in the form of kerosene and distillates) increased eightfold. As a result the percentage of total U.S. consumption of oil going into transportation declined from 55 to 49, in this period, while the share of residential and commercial uses rose from 6 per cent to 19 per cent: Paley Report, *3*, 3.

6. These and other data in this paragraph are from Frederick G. Coqueron, *Annual Financial Analysis of the Petroleum Industry, 1957*, New York, Chase Manhattan Bank, 1958. Net investment figures would be lower by the $22.9 billion of reserves for depreciation, depletion and amortization. The data presented are "for the petroleum industry in the United States," and hence presumably exclude investments abroad. The book value of the net foreign assets of the

11 to 14 per cent of estimated total crude oil reserves outside the USSR and its satellites.[7] Still it continued to produce the lion's share (46.6 per cent) of "free world" output. Moreover, after producing an astounding three-fifths of the world's cumulative production of oil between 1857, when oil was discovered in this country, and the end of 1955,[8] it emerged at the end of 1956 with greater proved reserves [9] than ever before, and with a substantial unutilized productive capacity. This was a remarkable achievement, and a continuing evidence of the virility of an industry which the pessimists have had repeatedly on the brink of exhaustion.

But oil is an exhaustible resource, and American oil must be nearer exhaustion than that of the other leading producing areas. Fundamental to all public interest in it, and a basic criterion of and limitation on all public policies toward the industry, therefore, is the crucial importance of a continuing and expanding supply. Our rising standards of living and our military might are closely geared to liquid fuels; in the foreseeable future this means oil. Thus the first major area of public concern in an analysis of integration in the oil industry is suggested by the fundamental question: Is the industry's form of organization in some sense essential to the expanding supply of liquid fuels on which our future may hinge?

Within the framework of this critical need, the American people, by tradition and by choice, are committed to a freely competitive economy. We would search out our fate as an industrial power, to the fullest extent compatible with the realization of other essential aims, through the processes of free markets and the freedom of choice and

---

thirty-three leading oil companies surveyed by Chase Manhattan were $5.6 billion at the end of 1957. Their market value is undoubtedly much higher.

7. The Chase Manhattan Bank estimate is 14.1 per cent. This figure should probably be revised downward in the light of the estimates of Wallace Pratt, cited below, n. 13.

8. *Petroleum Facts and Figures*, 12th ed., p. 351.

9. These are the quantities of crude oil proved with reasonable accuracy to be recoverable under current economic and operating conditions. Proved reserves have increased continuously over the years, despite mounting consumption, as a result of (a) continuous demonstrations that known fields contained more oil than was previously supposed, (b) discoveries of new fields, and (c) increases in the quantities recoverable from known fields because of improved techniques.

Proved reserves declined by less than half of 1 per cent in 1957, but this was at least partially the consequence of an 8.5 per cent drop in the number of wells drilled, in turn the result of an unprecedented excess capacity. See below, pp. 161–163, 219–220.

individual self-determination that they afford. Almost from the discovery of oil in this country, the petroleum industry has seemed to violate these precepts in the judgment of many observers, interested and disinterested alike.

From the days of John D. Rockefeller, who with consummate enterprise, foresight and shrewdness, and by massive mergers and ruthlessly predatory tactics, forged the Standard Oil empire into the archetype of monopoly in American history,[10] oil has never shaken off the aura of monopoly. The dissolution of the Standard Oil Company of New Jersey holding company in 1911 may have been the greatest triumph of the antitrust laws, but it did not serve to cleanse the industry in the public mind for long. The continued concentration of control over the greater proportion of the business in the hands of a relatively small number of Standard Oil successor companies and their more successful rivals; the at least temporary and partial acceptance by the former group of something like their previous division of spheres of influence, and by the latter group of the price leadership of the Standard companies in their respective territories; and the growth of vertical integration, by virtue of which the dominant firms extended their influence through all phases of the industry—all suggested that the dissolution decree had merely substituted cooperative group monopoly for single-firm predominance. The institution of state controls over crude oil production in the 1930's, in the name of conservation, served to fan the smoldering embers of suspicion anew.[11]

The frightful waste that characterized America's exploitation of its precious oil resources decades ago convinced disinterested observers, otherwise wholeheartedly committed to a competitive economy, that government regulation was essential in this industry. One reason oil companies advocated and accepted regulation, though by no means unanimously, was that in this way they could hope to achieve

10. See, e.g., those classics in the literature of American dissent, Henry Demarest Lloyd's *Wealth Against Commonwealth*, New York, Harper, 1894; and Ida M. Tarbell's *The History of the Standard Oil Company*, 2 vols., New York, McClure, Phillips, 1904.

11. See, among others, Myron W. Watkins, *Oil: Stabilization or Conservation?* New York, Harper, 1937 (cited below as Watkins); William J. Kemnitzer, *Rebirth of Monopoly*, New York, Harper, 1938; the 3,100 pages of hearings and exhibits (out of 18,500) that the Temporary National Economic Committee devoted to oil in its *Investigation of the Concentration of Economic Power*, 76th Congress, 2d Session (hereinafter referred to as TNEC), *Hearings*, Pts. XIV–XVII A (1940); and Eugene V. Rostow, *A National Policy for the Oil Industry*, New Haven, Yale University Press, 1948.

market stabilization. Partly for this reason, partly because of the nature of the system adopted, production control has been violently attacked as a mask for monopolistic privilege.

Finally, the global expansion of five giant American companies, and their joint control, with a few foreign interests, of something like 90 per cent of the "free world's" oil reserves outside the United States, stirred the wrath of federal agencies into active prosecution after World War II.[12]

Here, then, is the second major area of public concern with oil and that with which this study is primarily concerned. Is the massive integration of the industry's dominant firms—vertically through its various stages of production, transportation, processing and distribution, and horizontally over many geographical areas and functions at each stage—compatible with socially acceptable competitive objectives?

These questions assume a unique importance and a vast perplexity today, more than any other time in our history, because we appear to be in process of passing, if we have not already passed, the Great Divide between those who have oil in abundance (and exploit their resources to serve others) and those who require more than they can find within their own confines. The growth of American consumption was already pressing so hard against domestic ability to produce by the end of 1947 that in the following year this country reversed its traditional role and became a net importer of crude oil and products. Since then domestic policy and comparative advantage have combined to maintain and to expand the net import balance. Over the next quarter century, it is generally predicted, the trend will continue, and it could be halted or reversed only at mounting cost.[13]

12. U. S. Senate, Select Committee on Small Business, *The International Petroleum Cartel,* Staff Report to the Federal Trade Commission, 82d Congress, 2d Session, Committee Print No. 6, August 22, 1952 (cited below as FTC, *The International Petroleum Cartel*); *U.S. v. Standard Oil Company (New Jersey), Socony-Vacuum Oil Company, Standard Oil Company of California, The Texas Company and Gulf Oil Corporation,* in the U. S. District Court for the District of Columbia, Civil Action No. 1779–53, filed April 21, 1953. In addition, the Mutual Security Administration sued the international oil companies to recover alleged overcharges on oil and products supplied European countries under the European Recovery and Mutual Security programs. The suit was dismissed in 1957. *U.S. v. Standard Oil Company of California et al.,* 155 F. Supp. 121 (1957).

13. Predictions of this sort have often been confounded; discussion of the imponderables involved is reserved for Part II. The most compelling basis for public concern is the dramatic decline in the United States' share of world proved reserves compared with its consumption. By the end of 1957, America's

Of course, the way of progress and ultimately of national security is continually to search out new sources and substitutes for resources that are in short supply. Given time, most of the furnaces and machines that now burn petroleum products could be converted to use other fuels now available and technically, though not necessarily commercially, feasible. Already, ways are opening up to expand our own domestic, continental, hemispheric, and free world reserves of crude oil; to tap the larger potential alternative sources of synthetic oil products in the processing of oil shales and the hydrogenation of coal; to develop the even more revolutionary nonfossil atomic and solar energy. It is generally believed that, in the absence of imports, we would very shortly—within twenty years—be relying heavily on shales,

---

estimated proved reserves were approximately ten times total consumption in that year; for the rest of the world, far less thoroughly explored, they were seventy-one times consumption. This country took 8.6 per cent of its proved reserves out of the ground in that year; the Middle Eastern countries took out less than one per cent. See Department of the Interior, "Impact of the Peaceful Uses of Atomic Energy on the Coal, Oil and Natural-Gas Industries," in Joint Committee on Atomic Energy (above, n. 2), *2*, 82–83; Paley Report, *1*, 107–111, and *3*, 2–10; Pogue and Hill, *Future Growth and Financial Requirements of the World Petroleum Industry*, pp. 18–29; "Signposting the Future," *Petroleum Press Service*, 29 (July, 1956), 242–247; "Slowing Growth of U. S. Oil Reserves," *ibid*. (April, 1956), pp. 121–125; Petroleum Industry Research Foundation, *United States Oil Imports* (New York, by the Foundation, 1958); and Coqueron, *Annual Financial Analysis, 1957*, pp. 21–23. Compare the more optimistic view of the National Petroleum Council, whose predictions are conditioned by the proviso that "reasonable economic incentives" must be offered. *Petroleum Productive Capacity*, A Report on Present and Future Supplies of Oil and Gas, Washington, D.C., National Petroleum Council, 1952.

Successive authoritative and apparently comparable estimates of the Middle East's crude oil reserves were 15.5, 33, 78, and 140 billion barrels at the beginning of 1944, 1950, 1954, and 1957, respectively—31, 43, 58, and possibly 65 per cent of the respective estimates of total world reserves at these times. In the same thirteen-year time span, estimated and proved United States reserves increased absolutely from 21 to 30 billion barrels but declined relative to the world total from 40 to approximately 15 per cent. *Petroleum Facts and Figures*, 9th ed., pp. 443, 449; 11th ed., p. 291. Coqueron, *Annual Financial Analysis, 1957*, p. 21.

In 1956, Wallace E. Pratt published a widely accepted re-estimate of proved reserves of crude oil (including natural gas liquids, which are not reflected in data thus far mentioned) as of the close of 1954, that raised the figure for the Middle East to 230 billion barrels, while leaving the United States figure roughly constant, at 35, thus further increasing the first area's share of the "free world" total to 75 per cent and further reducing the American to about 11.5 per cent (above, n. 2), p. 93. See also "The Incomparable Middle East," *Petroleum Press Service*, 23 (July, 1956), 239–242.

tars, and coal for our liquid fuels. Indeed, the world as a whole may be doing so within fifty years. It is only the timing of these developments that is uncertain.[14]

There is no reason to fear that the power age will falter to a halt for lack of fuel. Still the dependence of current technology on oil-derived energy and the trend in domestic supplies pose a third group of issues that impinge importantly on the subject matter of this monograph and revolve around the question: How far and on what conditions should the United States rely on foreign sources of oil? This is not merely a question of economics; public policy toward imports must be compatible with military strategy—imports even from nearby Venezuela are vulnerable in case of war—and it must be articulated with political and economic situations abroad which this country may hope to affect but does not control.

Thus we might follow the traditional policy of stressing domestic exploration and production, providing for emergency military needs with reserve production capacity shut in below ground, and holding imports to a minimum. For an increasing cost industry like oil, this policy would inevitably accelerate the upward trend of domestic prices, and incidentally the profits—more strictly the economic rent—of those who already own producing wells. But rising prices would serve the joint purposes of holding down consumption, by encouraging substitution and the development of alternatives, and of stimulating production, by encouraging exploration and making feasible the recovery of more of the oil that is now left underground.

Alternatively, we might choose to use our depleting resources as little as possible in peacetime and shift the emphasis to the less expensive imports. Such a policy, however, would have the corresponding effect of discouraging production from marginal wells and the exploration on which our total domestic supply depends. Military considerations do not argue unequivocally for either alternative, or preclude various combinations thereof. Shut-in capacity for emergency use could be reserved under either policy; and the volume to be shifted from civilian to military use in case of war (the only conceivable basic reserve) depends not on our own production alone, but on the production potential of areas within our sphere of influence.

14. Harrison Brown, *The Challenge of Man's Future* (New York, Viking, 1954), p. 185; see also pp. 163 and 149–186 *passim;* also E. A. G. Robinson and G. H. Daniel, "The World's Need for a New Source of Energy," in International Conference on the Peaceful Uses of Atomic Energy, *Proceedings, 1,* 47. Cf. Bruce C. Netschert, *The Future Supply of Oil and Gas* (Baltimore, Johns Hopkins Press for Resources for the Future, 1958), pp. 55–63.

Whatever disposition is made of the national security problem, the choice of an acceptable national policy toward oil and toward vertical integration in the domestic market cannot be intelligently reached without consideration of the effect on oil-producing nations and on American leadership in the free world of the role oil imports are permitted to play in our future. While this broad subject can be treated only peripherally in this study, the conditions that govern oil development abroad will be found markedly different from those at home: in the services and facilities available which the firm can procure rather than provide for itself, in the legal conditions under which oil is searched and produced, in the political-economic attitudes of foreign governments—the sole proprietors of mineral resources within their boundaries—toward its exploitation, in the consequent predominance of a few giant vertically integrated firms of international scope. And these conditions are not of our making, or effectively subject to our jurisdiction. If expanding imports are unavoidable, or desirable, our domestic policies toward oil development and organization must be compatible with the growth and aspirations of these quite differently oriented oil-producing nations, and appraisal of the integrated structure of our leading companies as a competitive or monopolistic force must take into account the possibly quite different implications of integration in the domestic and foreign environments.

The United States petroleum industry is composed of tens of thousands of separate businesses, covering an enormous range in size, influence, and breadth of operations. Its behavior is governed not merely by the profit-seeking activities of these private parties, but also in vital ways by a network of governmental controls, direct and indirect, state and national—regulating output, providing differential tax treatment in the way of special exemptions and levies, fixing prices, limiting international commerce, as well as merely persuading, threatening, or cajoling managers into one course of action or another. This aggregation of separate business entities, thus organized and controlled, is expected to safeguard the national defense, conserve scarce resources, reduce prices, improve quality, expand capacity, and protect the competitive status of thousands of private parties whose interests are often flatly opposed. The diversity of these influences on industry behavior and the complexity of these tests of good and bad performance preclude a simple verdict in assessing the charges and counterclaims of waste and monopoly, conservation and competition that have plagued the industry during the entire course of its history.

CHAPTER 2

The Structure of the Industry

THE PETROLEUM INDUSTRY comprises a wide range of activities, spatially separated and technically distinct, but all collaborating in getting oil from the ground to the ultimate user. The main stages in the process are finding and producing the crude oil; transporting it to the point of processing; "refining" it—that is, converting it into products; transporting the products to regions of use; and finally distributing them at retail.

As soon as one penetrates beyond this rather simple façade, one encounters increasing complexities that make it much more difficult to define or characterize the industry. In the search for oil, producing companies are inadvertently or contingently involved in the production, use, and sale of natural gas, whose processing and channels of distribution are so different from those of oil and its products as to justify regarding it as a distinct, though inextricably related, industry.[1] In seeking to assure themselves of future supplies, many refining companies have spent millions of dollars experimenting with alternative sources of oil or oil-like hydrocarbons; and they will almost certainly become increasingly involved in the chemical process of creating or

1. In recent years, something like one-third of total production of natural gas has been from oil wells, and roughly one-third of estimated proved reserves of natural gas are either in contact ("associated") with or dissolved in crude oil. See, e.g., *Petroleum Facts and Figures*, 12th ed., pp. 153, 161. Moreover, most of the balance of production apparently comes from wells uncovered in the search for oil. General Ernest Thompson, chairman of the Texas Railroad Commission, the body charged with regulation of oil and natural gas production, has testified: "nearly all gas discoveries in my experience have been found incident to the search for oil." U. S. Senate, Committee on Interstate and Foreign Commerce, "Amendments to the Natural Gas Act," *Hearings* on S. 712 etc., 84th Congress, 1st Session (1955), p. 55. The overwhelming majority of leading natural gas producing companies are oil companies as well. See the list of the thirty-five largest nontransporting producers compiled by Senator Paul Douglas, *Congressional Record* (January 23, 1956), p. 890. Rapidly mounting demand and price moreover have caused the prospect of finding gas to play a role of correspondingly increasing importance in motivating exploration and development in recent years.

compounding their basic raw material rather than merely finding and extracting it. Finally, the versatility of the complex mixture of hydrocarbons we call oil and the progressive development of refining technology have impelled refiners into the broad-scale production of organic chemicals and into chemical processing as well. Upward of 2,000 products, apart from the familiar fuels and lubricants, now issue from the "oil industry." The number and volume of by-product organic chemicals will be vastly increased by any future resort to synthesis of hydrocarbons.

Crude oil is produced in the United States by perhaps 7,000 companies,[2] operating over 563,000 wells in thirty states. Three-fourths of the total output comes from Texas, California, Louisiana, and Oklahoma, slightly over 40 per cent from Texas alone. It moves mainly through 74,000 miles of gathering lines and 79,000 miles of trunk pipelines, though also in ocean-going tankers, river barges, tank cars, and trucks, to some 298 operating refineries in this country.[3]

These refineries, operated by perhaps 170 companies,[4] processed approximately 7,900,000 barrels of crude per day (b/d) in 1957, 12.5 per cent of which came from foreign sources. Ignoring wide differences in individual performance and minor year by year fluctuations, and focusing only on principal petroleum products, they break down a barrel of crude roughly as follows: 44 per cent into gasoline, 4 per cent kerosene, 23 per cent gas oil and distillates, and 14 per cent residual fuel oil. The most significant trend in these proportions in the last ten years has been the sharp rise in the yield of distillates,

2. The latest available figure for the number of crude oil production companies is the 6,654 that reported to the Bureau of Old Age and Survivors Insurance in 1949. Later published BOASI figures are for establishments rather than companies. In addition to these 6,654, in 1949 there were 528 firms engaged in producing natural gas and natural gasoline, 4,544 supplying various contract services (well drilling, rig building, etc.) and 284 unclassified, making a total of 12,010. Harold Fleming, *The American Oil Industry—A Forty-Odd Thousand Company Enterprise*, Oil Industry Background Information Bulletin No. 4 (New York, API, undated, around 1953), p. 5.

3. These various figures must be taken as only approximately representing the current situation. The figures on production and number of wells are for 1957 and come from *World Oil* (February 15, 1958), pp. 165, 184. The pipeline figures are for the beginning of 1956 and come from A. T. Coumbe and I. F. Avery, *Crude-Oil and Refined Products Pipe-Line Mileage in the United States, January 1, 1956*, Bureau of Mines Information Circular 7796, November, 1956. The number of refineries as of January 1, 1957 is from the Bureau of Mines, *Petroleum Refineries, Including Cracking Plants in the U.S.*, an annual survey (cited below as Bureau of Mines, annual refinery survey).

4. See below, pp. 22–23 and 484 ff.

from 16 to 23 per cent, in response to their mounting use in home and commercial heating and as diesel fuel, and the sharply declining yields of the much less valuable residual fuel oil, from 25 per cent to 14 per cent, as new processes have permitted an upgrading of products into higher valued uses.[5]

It is not possible to supply a brief description of the distribution of refined products in this country without doing some violence to the complex reality. Apart from the variety of products requiring separate treatment, methods of distribution differ from one company to another and for a given company from one region to another. In addition, precise information is unavailable. However, a recent study gives a useful picture, though a very rough approximation only, of the average practice in 1950.[6]

The greater proportion of products move from the refinery to the final customer via one or more intermediate storage facilities. This is true even of residual fuel oils, which go only to industrial and commercial consumers; it is overwhelmingly true of gasoline, roughly three-fourths of which is sold through service stations, and distillate fuel oil, perhaps two-thirds of which goes to home consumers. Most of these products go first to large terminals, located generally at the outlet of a pipeline, or on river, lake, or tidewater, where they can take barge or tanker delivery. By far the most of these terminals are owned by refiners, though independent wholesaler-owned terminals take a substantial portion of the distillate and residual oils. Slightly over half of the residual fuel oils are sold directly from terminals to the businesses that burn them; so that direct refinery and terminal sales move about three-fourths of all this "sawdust" by-product to final user. Probably most motor fuel and certainly most home heating oils, in contrast, go next to still another storage facility, the so-called bulk plant—although some is sold directly to large commercial, industrial, and governmental users. The bulk plant is generally smaller than the terminal, and nearer the final customer. From it, in turn, the gasoline is transported to service stations, and the heating oils to the storage tanks of homes and commercial establishments. However, in the case of gasoline there has been a marked tendency in the last twenty

5. API, *Statistical Bulletin* (April 7, 1958), Forms 8–10B. There has been some continued increase in gasoline yields as well, from about 40 per cent in the 1945–48 period to 44 per cent in 1956–57.

6. James S. Cross and Robert F. King, "Channels of Distribution for Petroleum Products" (dittoed, Massachusetts Institute of Technology, 1953), reproduced in *Petroleum Facts and Figures*, 11th ed., pp. 239–241. For a more detailed presentation of these data see below, pp. 386–392, and Table XXI.

years for terminal operators—mostly within the marketing departments of refining companies—to bypass the bulk plant and ship directly
to the service station. This development was made possible by the
construction of large-volume retail outlets and the use of increasingly
efficient truck carriers.[7]

To carry on the enormous task of distributing petroleum products,
there are 27,078 bulk stations, 1,241 terminals and 181,747 service
stations, according to the 1954 Census of Business. These facilities are
operated by the 170 or so refiners, by 15,000 agents operating refiner-
owned storage facilities on commission, by very roughly 10,000 wholesale distributors, and by 180,000 service station operators.[8]

SIZE AND CONCENTRATION

The petroleum industry is enormous. Already noted is its almost
$60 billion of gross domestic assets, of which over $47 billion is in
property, plant, and equipment. Oil companies alone accounted for
almost one-fourth of the total assets of the 500 top United States manufacturing and mining corporations at the end of 1956.[9]

7. The Cross and King figures unquestionably underestimate the importance
of these direct deliveries of motor fuel; they indicate that industrial and commercial consumers buy only 4 per cent of their requirements direct from the
refinery, and that service stations obtain only 4 per cent of their supplies from
the terminal. The distortion probably arises in the differentiation of terminals
and bulk plants. Both are wholesale outlets for receipt of product in large
quantities, for storage, and for distribution in smaller quantities. According to
former API definitions, the terminal was a facility the major proportion of
whose products went to other intermediate storage; the bulk plant was one
whose sales were primarily to service stations and final customers. With the
by-passing of the bulk plants, an increasing proportion of the terminal's deliveries was going not to intermediate storage but to the final buyers; in consequence, until the terms were redefined around 1953, terminals came more
and more to be classified as bulk plants, in proportion to their success in by-
passing their former bulk plant customers. On this development see below,
pp. 390 ff.

8. See below, pp. 423 ff. Summaries of the Census figures, including an enu-
meration of no less than 412,000 retail outlets of all kinds handling petroleum
products, are given in *National Petroleum News Factbook* (mid-May, 1957),
pp. 165, 207.

9. See below, n. 11. This comparison in a sense overstates the relative
size of the oil industry because (a) assets in oil are extraordinarily high relative to sales: on other bases like contribution to gross national product or to
total employment, the oil industry would bulk considerably less; and (b) a

Of this huge investment (see Table I), almost three-fifths is in crude oil and natural gas producing properties. No less than seven-tenths of the industry's total capital expenditures in the preceding ten years (72 per cent in 1956) went into extending these properties.[10] This con-

TABLE I

Estimated Gross Investment in Domestic Property, Plant, and Equipment, December 31, 1957, and Expenditures Thereon, 1948–57, by Departments

	PRO-DUCTION	TRANS-PORTATION	RE-FINING	MAR-KETING	OTHERS	TOTAL
GROSS INVESTMENT						
DECEMBER 31, 1957						
U.S. TOTAL						
$ million	28,100	4,750 [a]	8,750	5,100	700	47,400
% distribution	59.3	10.0	18.5	10.7	1.5	100.0
33 LEADING COMPANIES						
$ million	18,536	2,929	7,523	3,895	613	33,496
% of U.S. total	65.9	61.6	86.9	76.3	87.5	70.6
INVESTMENT EXPENDITURES						
1948–57						
U.S. TOTAL						
$ million	32,475	3,165	6,175	3,295	615	45,725
% distribution	71.0	6.9	13.5	7.2	1.4	100.0

[a] Of this total, in millions, $3,400 was in pipelines, $1,000 in marine transport facilities, $350 in tank cars and motor transport.

Source: Coqueron, *Annual Financial Analysis, 1957.*

centration of financial weight and effort helps explain why five chapters of Part II are devoted to a discussion of production alone.

There is no good single indication of relative size and concentration to set against these industry figures. The data shown in Table I, for the Chase Manhattan Bank group of thirty-three companies, are only roughly indicative of the general situation. Although the nineteen largest companies, by total sales or assets, are included in the group,

higher proportion of total oil industry assets is accounted for by the members of the top 500 industrials than is true for most other industries.

10. These ratios would be higher if various exploration expenses which the Chase Bank compilations point out are charged to income were instead regarded as investment expenditures, as well they might be.

the thirty-three were not chosen according to any consistent criterion of size. Many are significant in some areas of investment only. Further, the actual size and relative weight of the industry leaders is understated by the exclusion from the table of their 7.9 billion of gross investment in fixed assets abroad; such holdings, concentrated almost entirely in a handful of the thirty-three, can obviously exert a powerful influence on domestic markets through imports.

Companies run to huge size in this industry. In *Fortune's* 1956 list of the 500 largest United States industrial (actually, manufacturing and mining) corporations,[11] twenty-one of the top one hundred, and no less than ten of the top twenty, by value of assets, were oil companies. The twenty-one oil companies had 32.2 per cent of the total assets of the top 100. The thirty-two oil companies in the entire *Fortune* list, 6.4 per cent of the total number, accounted for 23.4 per cent of the combined assets of the 500, and about 14 per cent of the assets of all United States corporations in mining and manufacturing.[12]

The fact that oil companies do not bulk nearly so large in sales or employment [13] indicates that it is as massive aggregations of capital, principally, that they achieve their impressive proportions. This is the most heavily capitalized of our manufacturing and mining industries: the oil companies on the *Fortune* list had the highest sales per worker ($37,000, compared with an average of $18,760 for the 500) and the highest value of assets per worker ($42,450, compared with an average of $14,200 for the 500) of all the industries represented.[14] A firm expanding either horizontally or vertically in oil has to make some sizable expenditures.

Because there are so many giant corporations in this industry, the concentration of shipments in the hands of the very few largest firms is only moderately high compared with American industry in general. The top four companies in petroleum refining accounted for 33.0 per

11. Supplement, July, 1956.

12. Standard Oil of New Jersey, Gulf Oil, Socony Mobil Oil, Standard Oil of Indiana, and the Texas Company alone accounted for 13.2 per cent of the total assets of the 500. The 14 per cent is computed on the basis of *Fortune's* estimate that their 500 firms accounted for 59 per cent of the assets of all U.S. manufacturing and mining corporations. See the accompanying article, "Biggest Year for Big Business," *ibid., 54* (July, 1956), 89.

13. The thirty-two oil companies on the list accounted for only 15.3 per cent of the aggregate sales and (the thirty-one which supplied employment figures) for 7.3 per cent of the employment of the 496 which reported their employment.

14. *Fortune* (n. 12, above), p. 89.

cent of total shipments in 1954 as compared with the 35.7 per cent (arithmetic) average of the concentration ratios of the sixty-five industries with shipments of over one billion dollars in that year. However the concentration in share of total sales accounted for by the top eight, twenty, and fifty firms rises faster for oil than for the average: the top twenty petroleum refiners accounted for 84.0 per cent of industry shipments compared with an average of 58.4 per cent for the top thirty-eight industries.[15] While the industry certainly cannot be regarded as a "monopoly," if that term is used with any precision— twenty firms are many more than one—it is just as certainly dominated by a relatively small number of companies. Whether such a market structure assures effective competition is a question for analysis, not something one can assume at the outset.

The degree of market concentration in the industry varies considerably from one segment to the next. Decisive, up-to-date figures for all branches are not easy to come by, though the figures for refining and production are reasonably accurate. However, Table II indicates the proper orders of magnitude involved—all that can be meaningful in any event since economics affords no basis for drawing precise conclusions from concentration ratios.

Concentration is clearly the most pronounced in the field of foreign production. The companies affiliated with Standard Oil of New Jersey alone account for some 50 per cent of total foreign production by American companies, and this amounted to about 28 per cent of the aggregate "free-world" production outside the United States. Addition of the activities of the Gulf and Socony Mobil Oil Companies brings the former ratio to something like 85, and of the Texas Company and Standard of California to over 90 per cent.

Within the United States, concentration tapers at either end of the industry: it is clearly highest in the transportation of crude oil [16] and in refining, less so (though still high) in production at the one end and marketing at the other. The fact that the top twenty companies probably operate less than 2 per cent of the service-station outlets in

15. Computed from U. S. Senate, Committee on the Judiciary, "Concentration in American Industry," *Report* of the Subcommittee on Antitrust and Monopoly, 85th Congress, 1st session (1957), pp. 220–223.

16. Product pipeline operations are at least as highly concentrated as crude, but whereas almost three-fourths of all the crude oil delivered to American refineries in 1955 came by pipeline, only about one-third of the products suited for such transport moved (in 1954) via product lines. *Petroleum Facts and Figures,* 12th ed., p. 229, and Bureau of Mines, "Petroleum and Natural Gas" (above, p. 12, n. 3), p. 17. See also below, pp. 333–334.

TABLE II

Concentration Ratios in the United States Oil Industry:
Percentages of Total National Operations Accounted for
by the Top Seven and Top Twenty Companies [a]

	7 COMPANIES	20 COMPANIES
Net domestic crude production [b] (1955)	29.1	47.5
Gross domestic crude production [c] (1955)	33.3–34.3	54.3–56.0
Production abroad by U.S. companies [d] (1955)	94	98
Crude oil carried in gathering and trunk pipe-lines (1948) [e]	56.7	88.2
Refinery throughput (1955) [f]	53.7	86.4
Sales of gasoline (1954) [g]	49.6	80.4
Terminal and bulk plant sales of all light products (1950) [h]	n.a.	55.8
Service station sales of gasoline (1950) [h]	n.a.	55.9
Number of service stations operated (1955) [i]	1	1.5

[a] The companies are the leading ones in each category; hence their membership is not constant from one category to another. However, the membership of the top seven companies in the first, second, fourth, and fifth groups is identical—comprising Standard of New Jersey, Socony Mobil, Gulf, Texas, Standard of California, Standard of Indiana, and Shell; the first five of these companies account for at least 90 of the estimated 94 per cent figure in the third group (foreign oil operations); and the seven leading gasoline marketers are the same seven with the single exception that Sinclair enters the group, in seventh place, and Standard of California departs.

[b] From below, Table III.

[c] Calculated from the net production figures to include royalty oil—the oil produced by the companies in question and in fact controlled by them but belonging legally to the royalty owners. The lower estimates are based on the general understanding that royalty oil is $\frac{1}{8}$ of the total, so that the net figures are raised by $\frac{1}{7}$; the higher uses the conversion factor of 118 per cent (rather than $114\frac{2}{7}$ per cent) implied by Leslie Cookenboo's figures of the net and gross production of the seven leading companies, all of whose gross figures, he states, differ from the net only by their inclusion of royalty oil. *Crude Oil Pipe Lines and Competition in the Oil Industry* (Cambridge, Harvard University Press, 1955), p. 74; see also pp. 72–73.

[d] Very rough estimates that cannot, however, be more than a few percentage points off either way. They are obtained from the *National Petroleum News Factbook* (mid-May, 1956, p. 99), summary of foreign production from the annual reports of the twenty leading oil companies, adjusted to include in the totals very rough but generous estimates of foreign production by U.S. companies not included in that group (notably the smaller U.S. participants in something under 5 per cent of Iranian production under the consortium agree-

the country grossly understates the degree to which they control retail distribution, however. As the table indicates, 55.9 per cent of national retail sales of gasoline in 1950 were made by service stations that the twenty leading companies controlled by ownership or lease.

VERTICAL INTEGRATION

Concentration in the various segments of the oil industry reflects in large measure the high degree of horizontal or geographic integration of its companies: they typically engage in numerous operations at each level that could conceivably be performed by a greater number of separate firms. They search for oil in many places; they operate many wells, pipelines, and refineries; they sell through many terminals and bulk plants in widespread geographic markets.

All of the largest companies and many of the smaller ones are integrated vertically as well. Though the physical flow of oil from well to user may be almost continuous, the sequence of operations is traditionally regarded as falling into a number of broad categories. Not only could each of these separate operations conceivably be performed by different companies; the categories do in fact correspond to the areas in one or another of which the preponderant majority of businesses in the industry specialize: exploration and production, transportation, refining, wholesale marketing, and retailing. Vertical integration occurs when the activities of a single company span two or more of these stages.

It is easy to point out the arbitrary character of any such precise

---

ment—see below, pp. 206–207; in the Kuwait neutral zone; and in Canada).

e Cookenboo, *Crude Oil Pipe Lines,* p. 34. The second figure is for the nineteen integrated "majors"; it is probable that a true concentration ratio for pipeline transport would include in the second total the share of a nonintegrated carrier, the Buckeye Pipeline Co.

f Computed from *World Oil, 142* (1956), 100.

g From below, Table V.

h John G. McLean and Robert W. Haigh, *The Growth of Integrated Oil Companies* (Boston, Harvard Business School, 1954), p. 47 (cited below as McLean and Haigh). The figures show the percentage of total national sales made through facilities owned or controlled through lease, but not necessarily operated, by the twenty leading companies.

i Very rough estimates that can not be more than a few percentage points off. Based on incomplete responses to the *National Petroleum News Factbook* (mid-May, 1956), p. 175, compared with the 1954 Census total of 181,734 service stations.

definition.[17] There are firms—like well drilling contractors, or fuel oil peddlers—that specialize in particular subsegments of the conventionally designated branches; there are others—like crude oil or product brokers—that operate only in their interstices. Virtually all companies in the industry are in a meaningful sense integrated, because they engage in more than one single operation,[18] though not spanning more than one of the above-listed stages of production. Conversely, firms, according to the conventional definition, may be classed as vertically integrated, even though segmented operations might really be economically unfeasible. An obvious case can be made, for example, for the proposition that certain kinds of transportation, or marketing, are by their very nature "plant facilities"—that is, inherent and managerially inseparable parts of the refining function. If operation in refining alone is economically inconceivable, it becomes meaningless to characterize as integrated the refiner who does the irreducible minimum of transporting and selling.

Finally, defining integration in terms of financial and managerial control draws an unrealistically sharp line through what is really a continuum. One company may exercise great influence over an ancillary operation, may in a real sense actively participate in it, without legally controlling or directly engaging in it. To take the most obvious example, effective integration may be achieved by minority rather than majority stock ownership. There are other financial arrangements between legally separate firms that partake even more remotely of the character of ownership, yet create a kind of integration between them. Notable instances are the loans and grants refiner-producers make to prospectors or drilling contractors, and the leases by which refiner-marketers turn the operation of their bulk plants and service stations over to distributors and dealers—contracts characterized by a rich variety of rewards and commitments, written and unwritten. Finally, even contracts of supply, freely negotiated between

17. For an elaboration of this point, contending that not only the concept but the occurrence of integration may be expected to change from time to time and to differ from place to place, see below, pp. 38 ff.

18. So the wildcatter who looks for oil in more than one place, and drills or arranges to drill more than one well, is really horizontally and geographically integrated. The smallest refiner and service station operator produces or sells a variety of products and services, and is therefore circularly integrated. The crude oil producer who engages in geophysical exploration, drilling, and operating wells; the barge operator who owns terminal storage; the wholesaler who carries products to and from storage in his own trucks—all are vertically integrated.

distinct and independent business entities so far as formal appearances go, may in fact reflect and convey a close managerial control by one party over the other. Who controls whom and to what extent, in all such arrangements, depends on the relative freedom of choice and bargaining power of the opposing parties, something difficult to measure but impossible to ignore.

Though its definition raises difficulties, the phenomenon of vertical integration is a real one, and the problems it creates are real problems. The familiar boundaries between this stage of production and that, the spanning of which is conventionally taken to constitute integration, do correspond broadly to industry practice and, in most cases, to firm specialization. And however arbitrary the definition of integration according to legal form may be from the point of view of identifying effective managerial influence, in fact only such a form conveys to the observer the assurance that complete control is being or can potentially be exercised. Moreover, the kind of financial stake that only ownership usually conveys will be shown to be an important aspect of the impact of integration on competition. The fact that any usable dividing line between integrated and nonintegrated operations must be in some measure arbitrary does not rob the concept of significance or usefulness, providing the qualifications are borne in mind.

Whatever its precise definition, vertical integration is an outstanding characteristic of the oil industry. Though the majority of the firms are specialists within one or another of the conventional categories, the striking fact is that the bulk of industry operations are conducted under vertically integrated business organization. This fact may be quickly grasped by looking again at the concentration ratios in Table II, above, with the additional fact in mind that with perhaps only two exceptions [19] every single one of the companies in the eight categories of twenty industry leaders (ignoring service-station operators), for which combined shares of total operations range from 50 to 98 per cent, is a fully integrated company, operating in all major branches of the industry. In every case, a substantial additional share of domestic

19. The two known exceptions are Amerada Petroleum Corporation, a nonintegrated producer accounting for 1.3 per cent of net domestic output of crude oil in 1955, and Standard Oil Company of Kentucky, an exclusively marketing company (originally integrated within the Standard Oil empire, of course), which sold an estimated 1.6 per cent of the nation's gasoline in 1954. If there are other exceptions they are very few and trifling. There are some nonintegrated producers now engaged in foreign operations, to which one might have to attribute a fraction of the difference between the 94 per cent of the top seven and the 98 per cent of the top twenty.

operations is accounted for by other integrated companies not included in the top twenty.

Though the dominant role of twenty-odd integrated companies has long been a source of legal and policy disputation, until recently no comprehensive statistical study had been made of the scope, depth, or intensity of vertical integration in the industry as a whole. With the publication of John G. McLean and Robert W. Haigh's *The Growth of Integrated Oil Companies*,[20] in 1954, the most important aspect of the phenomenon was comprehensively revealed [21] for the first time, namely the degree of integration of oil companies that operate refineries. McLean and Haigh's estimates are for 1950, but they are undoubtedly still representative in 1959.

The most striking fact disclosed by their inquiry is how widespread is the integrated form of organization among refiners, small as well as large. Of the 106 refiners who supplied the authors with usable information, eighty-seven—not quite one-half of the estimated 179 operating refiners in the industry as a whole—were represented also in at least one other sector (production, wholesaling, or control of retail outlets), seventy in at least two other sectors, and fifty-four in all four stages of production. Even if attention is confined to the smallest companies, who are far less uniformly integrated than the large, only seventeen of the sixty-one reporting refiners with less than 10,000 b/d capacity were in refining alone.[22]

Vertically integrated companies do most of the oil business—59.8 per cent of domestic and 99.6 per cent of foreign crude production,

20. Data in this section are taken from chap. 2 of this study; they were secured primarily from a questionnaire to the industry.

21. The data are necessarily minimal, for no account could be taken of integration effected through minority stock ownership or through contractual arrangements of the kind discussed above. However, the authors did adopt the reasonable convention of treating as integrated in wholesaling or retailing refiners who merely controlled bulk plant or service station facilities by ownership or lease, whether they operated them with salaried employees or leased them in turn to distributors or dealers. Also usable data were received from only 106, or 59.2 per cent of the estimated 179 operating refining companies. However, these 106 represented 74.3 per cent of the total number of refineries owned by the 179, 94.7 per cent of their operating and shutdown refining capacity, and 97.3 per cent of their domestic refinery runs. In other words, the seventy-three companies not covered in the returns had only 5.3 per cent of capacity and only 2.7 per cent of refinery runs.

22. Since the nonreporting companies were typically very small, and hence undoubtedly less uniformly integrated than those who reported, the foregoing data exaggerate the commonness of integration in the industry as a whole.

83.1 per cent of the delivery of crude oil by gathering and trunk lines, 96.2 per cent of domestic refining, and 61.4 per cent of terminal and bulk plant sales; also, 58 per cent of service-station sales of gasoline are by stations they control. These data of McLean and Haigh confirm what Table II has already suggested, that in general the percentage of the industry's total domestic facilities owned or leased by integrated firms is largest in the immediate vicinity of the refinery, including the pipelines that bring in crude oil at one end and take out products at the other.[23] Beyond the pipeline, the percentage control of industry facilities and output by integrated companies declines both backward toward the well and forward toward the consumer.[24]

Small refineries may or may not be integrated; large ones always are. The McLean and Haigh survey showed that at least half and possibly a considerably higher proportion of the country's operating refiners was integrated to some extent. But apparently all the thirty-five companies with refining capacity greater than 20,000 b/d in 1950

23. Thus according to their estimates (as always, for 1950), 68.3 per cent of all refineries, representing 93.2 per cent of all domestic crude charging capacity (refinery capacity being generally stated in terms of the number of barrels of crude oil it can process per day, even though actually this figure is an elastic one), belonged to integrated firms which also accounted for 92.2 per cent of product pipe line, 82.1 per cent of crude trunk line, and 85.4 per cent of the industry's crude gathering line mileage. This focus of integration around the refinery is not the deceptive consequence of the fact that McLean and Haigh's study is a study of integrated *refiners*. The only significant vertical integration in oil that does not touch refining is the joining of wholesale and retail marketing operations.

24. Integrated refining companies owned or leased 68.6 per cent of the industry's terminals and bulk plants; they controlled 51.6 per cent of the service stations, and operated less than 2 per cent of them. In the opposite direction, they controlled 35.4 per cent of producing oil wells and only 7.7 per cent of drilling rigs. It is worthy of note, however, that integrated companies typically seem to achieve a higher output from their facilities than other firms, so that the foregoing figures underestimate their participation in these branches of the industry. The 35.4 per cent of total producing oil wells they owned in 1950 produced over two-thirds of all domestic crude. (McLean and Haigh show that they accounted for 59.8 per cent of net domestic production, but since they produced the royalty oil as well, their gross production must have been at least 1/7 higher. See above, Table II, n. c.). The 51.6 per cent of the industry's service stations they owned or leased made 58.0 per cent of all service station sales. The lessee-dealers of the twelve major oil companies who supplied in 1955 some 94 per cent of all gasoline sold in New Jersey sold an average of 15,887 gallons monthly, as compared with only 8,226 for (independent) contract dealers. U.S. Senate, Select Committee on Small Business, "Gasoline Price War in New Jersey," *Report* No. 2810, 84th Congress, 2d Session (1956), pp. 7–9.

were at least partially integrated.[25] And, excepting only one of the smallest, all the twenty-four companies above the 40,000 b/d level— indeed the majority of integrated refiners, and those doing by far the greater proportion of the business—perform all the major functions from producing crude oil to owning (but not operating) service stations.[26]

At the same time, it is important to recognize also that no oil company is completely integrated, in the sense that its operations are self-sufficient from well to consumer. As a group, also, integrated refiners are far from perfect balance. They are far less self-sufficient in crude oil production [27] than in pipeline transportation. They rely heavily upon outside purveyors of transportation services other than pipelines—tankers,[28] barges, trucks—and on nonintegrated and only contractually affiliated marketers—branded distributors (a term used herein, with or without the adjective "branded," to refer to wholesalers who carry the refiner's brand), unbranded jobbers (a term used, along with "private branded jobbers," to refer to wholesalers who do not sell under the refiner's brand), and of course service-station operators.[29]

25. The only possible exceptions were the two companies with 25,000– 30,000 b/d and one between 35,000 and 40,000 b/d that did not report.

26. Integrated refining companies that did not own facilities in production, refining, wholesaling and retailing owned only 4 per cent of national refinery capacity, and comparably low or lower proportions of other facilities. They accounted for 3.4 per cent of national refinery runs and output of refined products, and less than 2 per cent of all other industry operations.

27. McLean and Haigh found that the net domestic production of refining companies who were integrated back to the crude level supplied on the average only 32.7 per cent of their refinery requirements. For the eighteen refiners with over 100,000 b/d capacity the ratio was 50.0 per cent. The latter situation was roughly similar in 1955, when the twenty refiners with over 100,000 b/d of refinery capacity, as a group, had a net domestic production equal to 48.7 per cent of the crude they used. See below, Table III, and, for more comprehensive statistics on crude-oil self-sufficiency of the leading companies, Table XII. Inclusion of imports of their own foreign-produced crude would raise this ratio almost to 60 per cent. Computations supplied by the Economics Department of a major oil company.

28. According to McLean and Haigh, integrated refiners owned 47.9 per cent of the country's tankers in 1950. They control many more under long-term charter. See below, Chap. 13.

29. E.g., according to the rough estimates of Cross and King, above, n. 6, 36 per cent of the national production of distillate fuel oils (which are used principally in residential and commercial heating) moved into the hands of nonrefiner marketers at the refinery; and 65 per cent of all shipments to final consumers from intermediate storage—terminals and bulk plants—were han-

Moreover, there are vast differences between integrated companies in the extent to which they rely on this or that intermediate market for supplies or services. For example, the net domestic crude production of the twenty refiners with over 100,000 b/d capacity in 1955 ranged from 8 per cent of refinery runs (for Ashland Oil and Refining, number 19 on the list) to 92 per cent (for Continental Oil, number 16).[30] At the other end, Standard of Indiana sold only 9.9 per cent of its gasoline and 3.8 per cent of its kerosene and distillates to wholesale resellers in 1950, while Sinclair sold 34 per cent of its gasoline and Texas 63 per cent of its kerosene and distillates to such nonintegrated marketers.[31] There are also differences in practice between products. The distribution of gasoline, for example, is typically carried on much more completely in integrated channels than that of home-heating oils.[32] And, finally, the balance of operations of various integrated companies has often shifted drastically, this way or that, over time.

Vertical integration therefore has by no means eradicated intermediate markets in the oil industry. Indeed, the attempt to assess the vitality of these markets, and the opportunities they offer for the entry of nonintegrated companies, is a major part of the analytical problem of this study.

The Combination of Size and Integration —"Majors" and "Independents"

It is the combination of relative (horizontal) size and (vertical) integration of the dominant companies that has generated so much con-

---

dled by independent marketers. Since, according to McLean and Haigh, at least 93.9 per cent of the total national production of kerosene and distillates came in 1950 from refiners who were also integrated into wholesale marketing, manifestly this forward integration was very incomplete for distillates. For the picture in gasoline, see below, n. 32.

30. See below, Table III. The next lowest self-sufficiency ratios were those of Standard of Ohio (21 per cent) and Sinclair (30 per cent); the next highest were Sunray Mid-Continent (90 per cent) and Union Oil (65 per cent). Humble Oil and Refining had a ratio of 145 per cent, but the consolidated ratio for Standard of New Jersey, which owns 87 per cent of Humble's stock, was only 53 per cent.

31. McLean and Haigh, pp. 691, 692, 695.

32. According to Cross and King, only 7 per cent of the national motor fuel output left the refinery in the hands of nonaffiliated marketers; and only one-third, at most, of all shipments from terminals or bulk plants were in independent hands. Even the latter figure may be an overestimate. See below, p. 386, n. 1. See the markedly higher corresponding figures for distillates in above, n. 29.

troversy about the organization of the oil industry. Neither the phenomenon nor the controversies are unique to oil. The structure of the steel industry is similar in these respects; but, partly because of the importance of its product, partly because of the very numerous, organized, and vocal nonintegrated competitors, suppliers, and customers interspersed throughout it, the oil industry provides the best-known and most controversial, if not also the purest, example of the problems that arise when size and market dominance are associated with vertical integration.

The companies which combine these only qualitatively definable attributes—size, substantial weight in the market, and vertical integration—are popularly known as the "majors," a term henceforth employed without quotation marks. Some persons associated with these companies bridle at the term, because to them (and indeed to many who use it) it carries invidious connotations. Whether one finds it preferable to use this term or another more euphemistic, however, the distinction between majors and other firms (whether integrated or not), which, following popular precedent, shall be termed "independents," describes a characteristic of the industry's structure with which any student must reckon.[33]

Thirty and forty years ago, the customary distinction was between the Standard Oil successor companies on the one hand, and the "independents" on the other. With the dissolution of the Standard Oil holding company in 1911, its properties and territories remained divided as before among its previously subsidiary companies, most of which carried the Standard Oil name. Many of these successor companies inherited little short of 100 per cent of the business in their respective territories. They therefore continued to assume the leadership role they had played when all were centrally controlled. Furthermore, for some time at least, it was generally suspected that residual concentration of ownership (especially by the Rockefeller group), continuity of management, and the complementary character of their business prolonged practices of cooperation and nonaggression among

33. McLean and Haigh justified their use of a similar distinction as follows: "We shall define a 'small refining company' as any firm not included among the top thirty in the industry in terms of refining capacity. This definition is necessarily an arbitrary one, but our research indicated that it was at about this point that refining firms changed in character with regard to such important factors as the nature of integration arrangements, the size and type of plant equipment, the geographic scope of operations, brand name advertising programs, and the breadth of stock ownership" (p. 519; see also their chap. 18, *passim*).

these companies that had been born of a less than competitive environment.

Whatever the merits of the suspicions, the original circumstances were subject to fairly rapid erosion. In a rapidly growing and changing industry, the Standard successor companies gradually drew apart, and began to compete with each other. Moreover, with the expansion of demand unleashed by the automobile and of supplies consequent upon dramatic new discoveries, the Standard companies could not maintain such dominating shares in their respective markets. Some unintentionally eased the lot of new competitors by holding their prices unrealistically high, in sluggish disregard of the changing competitive situation. By the middle thirties, their market shares had dropped precipitously, some to 20 per cent or less in their original home territories. Other companies (originally referred to as "independents") came to rival them in size and to challenge their market leadership. So, when the Temporary National Economic Committee (TNEC) listed the twenty "major companies" in the industry in 1938, it included eight former Standard companies and twelve of these interlopers, some of which had become prominent well before 1911.[34]

The majors, then, are separate business entities, financially, managerially, operationally. There are some likely exceptions: Richfield could be controlled jointly by Cities Service and Sinclair.[35] J. Paul Getty controls the Getty Oil Company (formerly Pacific Western Oil Company), which in turn, directly and through intermediate corpora-

34. Former Standard companies were the Atlantic Refining Company, Continental Oil Company, Ohio Oil Company, Socony-Vacuum (now Socony Mobil) Oil Company, Standard Oil Company of California, Standard Oil Company of Indiana, Standard Oil Company (New Jersey), and Standard Oil Company of Ohio. The non-Standard majors were: Cities Service Company, Consolidated Oil Corporation (now Sinclair), Gulf Oil Corporation, Mid-Continent Petroleum Corporation (now Sunray Mid-Continent), Phillips Petroleum Company, Pure Oil Company, Shell Oil Company, Skelly Oil Company, Sun Oil Company, Texas Company, Tide Water Associated Oil Company (now Tidewater Oil) and Union Oil Company of California.

35. As of December 31, 1955, Sinclair owned 30.6 per cent and a subsidiary of Cities Service owned 31 per cent of Richfield's common stock. Richfield claims to be completely free of domination by its two large stockholders. This may well be true administratively, but a Richfield Oil Corporation of New York, 100 per cent owned by Sinclair, markets Sinclair products in the East under the Richfield brand; the California Richfield has several officers and directors in common with Cities Service and Sinclair; and in only one state (Idaho) do both California Richfield and one of its large stockholders (Sinclair) both market. See marketing territories in *National Petroleum News Factbook* (mid-May, 1956), pp. 170–173.

tions, controls both Skelly and Tidewater.[36] The Rockefeller family still owns substantial minority interests in some of the various Standard Oil companies and there are a few minor financial interlinks between them.[37] However, no evidence has been found in either the managerial personnel or the policies of the Standard companies to contradict the latter's assertion of complete operational independence; there seems to be neither more nor less interdependence of, say, Socony Mobil and Standard of Indiana than there is of either with, say, Texas or Gulf.[38]

Thus the differentiation of majors and independents is erroneous if it seems to imply that the former companies act in concert. There can be no question that they compete against each other for business in such a way as to belie any implication that for any one of them it is a matter of indifference whether the business goes to one or to the other. On the other hand, this conclusion in no sense precludes the possibility that, bulking so large in the market, each of these companies, and therefore all of them collectively, may pursue its own interest in ways that fall short of effective competition from the point of view of the buying public. Size and fewness of sellers inevitably breed recognition of the fact that each can seriously injure and be injured by the others; and this recognition *may* produce policies ob-

36. As in the case of Richfield the financial control is associated with common officers and directors as well.

37. E.g., at the end of 1955 Standard of Indiana still held slightly over 2 per cent of the outstanding stock of Standard of New Jersey, which it received in partial payment for the sale of its foreign properties in 1932. For a brief summary of these financial data see Leslie Cookenboo, Jr., "Structure of the Oil Industry," in R. S. Brown, Jr., ed., *Readings on the Petroleum Industry* (mimeographed, New Haven, Yale Law School, 1950), pp. 74–75. Information about the Rockefeller interest in these companies is available only for 1938–39, the period covered by TNEC questionnaires. For a more exhaustive survey, comprehending the far more pervasive "indirect links" between oil companies, see FTC, *Report on Interlocking Directorates* (Washington, D.C., 1951), pp. 358–378.

38. Cf. Cookenboo (above, n. 37), pp. 74 and 83 ff., whose conclusion to the contrary is based on mere supposition. No way has yet been devised for an outsider to evaluate the influence that may or may not be exercised by minority stock interests over corporate policy. There is no doubt that such stock ownership can be sufficient to ensure working control of many corporations, especially where the remaining stock is widely held. On the other hand there are abundant illustrations of corporations in effect running themselves, with managements beyond the effective reach of minority stockholders. All the evidence inclines to the conclusion that the Standard companies fall in the latter rather than the former category.

jectively indistinguishable from conspiratorial joint action. Direct and indirect interlocking relationships, financial and managerial, could of course contribute to that kind of behavior.

Any classification of firms on the basis of size and integration, attributes with a variety of dimensions, will probably be fuzzy at least at the margins. Since there are substantial variations in the balance of integration among firms, the twenty biggest oil companies will have different ranking, and, at the lower levels (say numbers 15 to 20), different membership, depending on whether one selects this or that measure of size to separate the men from the boys. But by whatever test, the identities of the major companies come out much the same.

Consider the four lists of the top twenty firms in the industry (Table III) as ranked by domestic refinery runs, total assets, net domestic crude production, and estimated share of national sales of gasoline. With one peripheral exception, the top eight companies are identical, though their rankings vary.[39] It takes the names of only twenty-four companies to make up the total of eighty places. Two of the "odd men out" are strikingly successful specialists at either end of the industry's spectrum: Amerada sells its crude oil at the wellhead and Standard of Kentucky continues, as it did before 1911, to purchase its products from Esso Standard. One has to go down to number 13 on all four lists before one encounters a company (Ohio Oil, the number 13 producer) that is not among the top twenty in the other categories as well. There are only three refiners (Standard of Ohio, Richfield, and Ashland), all very low on the list, that do not appear among the top twenty producers; the first two rank as about 26 and 22 respectively among the producing companies. Of the three producing companies not on the refiners list (Ohio Oil, Amerada, and Skelly), all are relatively low on the list of producers, and the first and third rank about 24 and 21 respectively among the refiners. The unusual lack of balance of the two Ohio companies (like that of Standard of Kentucky) is the heritage of a functional concentration determined by their roles in the original Standard Oil trust and not yet fully corrected by subsequent integration.[40]

39. The exception is the replacement of Sinclair from the group of producers by Continental Oil, eighth on that list, a displacement subsequently reversed by Sinclair's acquisition of several large producing companies. See, along similar lines, above, Table II, n. a.

40. Differences between the lists reflect mainly divergent degrees of self-sufficiency in domestic crude. Some of these variations in rank are really misleading. Were the foreign production of companies like Gulf and Socony Mobil included in their crude output figures, their ranking in that column would more

TABLE III *The Major Oil Companies*

COMPANY	DOMESTIC REFINERY RUNS 1955 [b]		ASSETS DECEMBER 31, 1955 [d]		NET DOMESTIC CRUDE PRODUCTION 1955 [f]			ESTIMATED GASOLINE SALES 1954 [g]	
	THOUSANDS OF BARRELS PER DAY	RANK	$000,000	RANK	THOUSANDS OF BARRELS PER DAY	RANK	PER CENT OF REFINERY RUNS	PER CENT OF UNITED STATES	RANK
Standard Oil Co. (New Jersey)	784	1	7,164.1	1	415	1	53	7.8	2–3
Standard Oil Co. (Indiana)	576	2	2,332.4	3	241	5	42	7.7	4
Texas Co.	562	3	2,114.6	5	336	2	60	7.9	1
Socony Mobil Oil Co.	541	4	2,361.9	2	230	7	43	7.8	2–3
Gulf Oil Corp.	506	5	2,160.8	4	231	6	46	6.8	5
Shell Oil Co.	465	6	1,207.0	8	276	3	59	6.6	6
Standard Oil Co. of California	453	7	1,855.6	6	251	4	55	4.4	8
Sinclair Oil Corp.	408	8	1,250.1	7	119	10	30	5.0	7
Cities Service Co.	284	9	1,094.7	10	95	14	33	3.1	11
Phillips Petroleum Co.	229	10	1,201.9	9	125	9	55	3.3	10
Sun Oil Co.	227	11	536.9	13	102	11–12	45	3.6	9
Atlantic Refining Co.	196	12	611.5	11	86	16–17	44	2.2	13
Tide Water Associated Oil Co.	167	13	485.4	15	89	15	53	2.4	12
Union Oil Co. of California	157	14	546.5	12	102	11–12	65	1.8	15
Pure Oil Co.	155	15	457.0	17	67	20	43	2.1	14
Continental Oil Co.	146	16	503.9	14	134	8	92	1.6	17–18
Standard Oil Co. (Ohio)	129	17	322.3	19	27	[26] [f]	21	1.7	16
Richfield Oil Corp.	122	18	304.5	[21]	57	[22] [f]	47	1.5	19–20
Ashland Oil and Refining Co.	110	19	154.8	[24]	8	…	8	1.5	19–20
Sunray Mid-Continent Oil Co.	89	20	482.1	16	80	18	90	1.2	[21]
Skelly Oil Co.	47	[21] [c]	317.1	20	68	19	145	n.a.	n.a.
Ohio Oil Co.	42	[24] [c]	347.5	18	97	13	231	n.a.	n.a.

								1.6	17–18
Standard Oil Co. (Kentucky)	—	—	111.4	n.a.	3,230	6,807	47.5		80.4
								100.0	
Total of top twenty [a]	6,306	27,353.2						80.4	
Total United States	7,480	34,600 [e]					48.7		
Top twenty as a percentage of total United States	84.3	79.1			3,071				
Top twenty refiners (total)	6,306	27,310.2						80.0	
Top twenty refiners as a percentage of United States total	84.3	78.9					45.1		

[a] These totals are for the top twenty on each list; the membership of the group is therefore not constant from one category to the next.

[b] Source: Economics Department of a leading oil company, adjusted to include Ashland. The figures exclude crude run for others, and include crude run by others for the company's account.

[c] Skelly had an operating capacity of 53,650 barrels per day, Ohio Oil 44,000, at the beginning of 1955. Southwestern Oil and Refining Co. had a capacity of 53,000, Aurora Gasoline Co. 50,500, and Eastern States Petroleum Co. 47,000 barrels per day at the same time. Refinery throughput for the latter three companies being unknown, it may be that one or both of the first two of them actually surpassed Skelly's crude runs in 1955; Ohio Oil's rank is assigned on the arbitrary assumption that it was surpassed by two of the three.

[d] Source: "The Fortune Directory of the 500 Largest U. S. Industrial Corporations," *Fortune, 54*, Supplement, July, 1956.

[e] Source: Coqueron, *Annual Financial Analysis, 1955*, pp. 34, 41 (net assets of the entire industry in the United States, plus the net foreign assets of the thirty-four leading companies, the latter comprising all but a negligible fraction of the entire industry's foreign investment).

[f] Source: see above, note b. Ranking of producers necessitated reference to the lists in *World Oil, 142* (June, 1956), 100, 102. In addition to using sometimes net, sometimes gross production data, and sometimes including, sometimes excluding production of natural gas liquids, the *World Oil* lists are also incomplete. Additional adjustments in rank were therefore made for Richfield, and Standard of Ohio, on the assumption that Richfield's production of 20.7 million barrels was probably surpassed by Superior Oil Co., which produced 21.3 million in 1953 and 1954, and that Standard of Ohio's production of 11.5 million barrels (from its Annual Report) was probably surpassed by Signal Oil and Gas Co., which produced 16.3 million in 1954 and 15.6 in 1953, by the Honolulu Oil Co., which produced 14.3 million in 1956, and by the Seaboard Oil Co. (partially controlled by the Texas Co.), which produced 11.8 million in both years. The rankings for these lowest companies must be taken as approximate only.

[g] Source: see above, note b. Percentages for Ashland and Sunray Mid-Continent are based on their refinery runs (shown in the table) as a percentage of the national total. (This also required adjustment for Sunray's apparently substantial runs for the account of others.)

The lower boundary line of the majors is variable, depending on which list in Table III one consults. Still if attention is centered on refining, the heart of the industry and the essential link in the integrated operation,[41] the line is not at all indistinct. The bottom five companies on the list ran 89,000 [42] to 146,000 b/d of crude in 1955; the next largest refiner, Skelly, ran only 47,000. One might or might not choose as the TNEC did to include companies like Skelly or Ohio Oil among the majors.[43] In certain relatively restricted regions they, and even much smaller companies, may have a weight in the market comparable with that of the authentic majors. In any event, the dominant group is consistently identifiable by whatever test one chooses.

The twenty major companies can be clearly distinguished from the independents by their size. They are also typically integrated horizontally far more widely than their smaller rivals. As of January 1, 1957, these twenty major refiners had 126 of the country's 319 refineries; 165 companies owned the other 193.[44] And the average of twenty-eight states of the Union in which the majors marketed their products in 1957 contrasts with an average of only six states for seventy-seven other "important" marketers.[45]

In the degree and completeness of their vertical integration, how-

---

closely approximate their rank as refiners and in total assets. See below, Table XII. Other discrepancies reflect the fact that companies like Continental, Skelly, Ohio Oil, Sunray (even more clearly before merging with Mid-Continent in 1955) and Shell historically have been heavy (and even exclusively) producers, while others like Standard of Ohio, Ashland, Atlantic, and Standard of Indiana began or grew principally as refiners and/or marketers. In five of these cases the imbalance reflects specialization that originated in the Standard Oil empire.

41. See above, n. 23.

42. Sunray Mid-Continent actually ran 99,000 b/d in 1955, but apparently 10,000 b/d of this was for the account of other companies. See Table III, n. b.

43. The TNEC's omissions were Ashland, a small company as recently as 1947, and Richfield, the latter presumably because it already had established financial ties with Sinclair and Cities Service. Skelly, ranking 19 among the producers and about 21 among refiners, marketing at wholesale and retail in sixteen states, selling a widely known brand, and having direct financial ties to Tidewater and the other Getty interests, is clearly a borderline case.

44. Computations from Bureau of Mines annual refinery surveys.

45. Computed from *National Petroleum News Factbook* (mid-May, 1958), pp. 100–105. Subsidiaries are grouped with the parent company, with duplications of marketing territories eliminated. Leaders of the nonmajor marketers were the Hudson Oil Company (twenty-three states), Spur Distributing Company (twenty-one), Skelly Oil Company (eighteen), Kerr-McGee Oil Industries (sixteen) and twelve others selling in ten to fifteen states.

ever, the majors do not differ greatly from the ten to fifteen moderately large refiners with capacities of 30,000 to 55,000 b/d at the beginning of 1955. Few refiners with an investment in tens of millions of dollars apparently operate without assuming a substantial direct responsibility for providing their crude oil and marketing their products. On the other hand, majors and "minor majors" together are typically far more uniformly and thoroughly integrated than smaller refiners. According to McLean and Haigh, there were nineteen refiners at the close of 1950 with capacities of 90,000 b/d or more: these would have to be our twenty leaders minus Sunray Mid-Continent. There were ten more with capacities of 30,000 to 50,000 b/d, three of whom have since moved into the major category by merger; and some 150 operating and forty nonoperating refiners with capacities below 30,000 b/d.[46] All of the nineteen giant companies were in production, wholesaling and retailing, as well as in refining. The same was practically true of the next ten companies.[47] Although the greater proportion of the 150 smaller companies were probably also integrated in one way or another, they showed much greater variation in this respect.[48]

The eighteen major oil companies with refinery capacity of more

46. Of the operating companies, there were six in the 20,000 to 30,000 bracket, twenty-three between 10,000 and 20,000, and one hundred twenty-one below that level. The 30,000–50,000 group presumably included Mid-Continent (47,000 b/d) and Sunray (42,000), who have joined forces; Skelly (42,500); Globe Oil and Refining Company (34,000), which has leased its refinery to Pure Oil since 1954; Ohio Oil (49,500, of which 18,500 were shut down and thereafter partly dismantled); Crown Central Petroleum Company (32,500); Southwestern Oil and Refining Company (30,000); Petrol Refining Company (50,000, all shut down—now the Texas City Refining Company); Republic Oil Refining Company (34,000); and Eastern States Petroleum Company (40,000). Calculations from the Bureau of Mines, annual refinery surveys. The estimate of forty nonoperating companies comes from a comparison of the study of C. M. Furcht, Coordination and Economics Department, Standard Oil Company (New Jersey), "Growth and Structure of U. S. Refining Industry" (mimeo.), which lists two hundred twenty-three refining companies as of January 1, 1950 (p. 2) and McLean and Haigh's estimate of one hundred seventy-nine companies actually operating at the close of that year (pp. 19–20).

47. Of these ten, eight operated at all levels, one was in production, refining, and wholesaling but not in retailing, and one did not report.

48. McLean and Haigh, pp. 20, 24–26. By the same token, the geographically restricted operations of some small refiners are probably well integrated vertically. For example, of the sixty-one refining companies with less than 10,000 b/d capacity which reported to McLean and Haigh, forty-four were at least partially integrated, and eighteen were involved in production, refining, wholesaling, and retailing.

than 100,000 b/d in 1950 had net domestic crude production amounting on the average to 50 per cent of their refinery runs, again according to McLean and Haigh. Several among them also had very substantial foreign production, some of which they imported to meet
domestic refinery requirements, raising the crude self-sufficiency for
the entire group to over 60 per cent.[49] (Worldwide, the crude oil self-
sufficiency of the twenty major refiners [Table III] as a group was
almost 75 per cent in 1956, on the basis of net production alone.) [50]
The ten companies with capacities of 30,000 to 100,000 b/d which
reported to McLean and Haigh averaged 60 per cent in 1950.[51] In
contrast, the remaining forty-six reporting refiners who engaged in
production as well, all with capacities of less than 30,000 b/d, supplied
averages of only 21–26 per cent of their refinery runs with their own
crude. The remaining thirty-two reporting companies, and undoubtedly a large percentage of the estimated seventy-three operating refiners that did not report (all but one with capacity of less than 30,000
b/d), had no production of their own.

Tables II and III together indicate how large a share of the various
operations of the industry the majors account for. Concentration ra-

49. See above, n. 27, for the source of the adjustments for imports. As the
discussion there indicates, the situation in 1955 was substantially the same.
For nineteen leading companies (these apparently include eighteen leading
refiners in Table III, plus Ohio Oil), net domestic production amounted to
53 per cent of combined refinery runs in 1950, 50 per cent in 1955. The adjustment for imports would raise the composite self-sufficiency ratios to 62.8
per cent for the earlier year and 60.4 per cent for the later.

50. Computed from Table XII, below, p. 224, with Skelly and Ohio Oil
omitted. In terms of actual crude produced and controlled, gross rather than
net production should be used. Gross production would raise the ratio of self-
sufficiency to well over 85 per cent. See above, Table II, n. c.

51. This is their average ratio of net domestic production to refinery runs.
Significantly, several of these "minor majors" have moved by merger to bring
their production and refining into closer balance. The union of Sunray and
Mid-Continent in 1955 brought together two companies which were overbalanced in opposite directions—the one ranking 23 among the refiners and 19
among the producers in 1953, the other standing 20 and 24, respectively—
and thereby created a twentieth clear-cut major. Also, 50 per cent of the
stock of Republic Oil Refining Company, an independent refiner on the Gulf
Coast, has long been owned by the Plymouth Oil Company, a large nonintegrated producer; in 1949 Plymouth took over the remainder of the stock as
well. Eastern States is reputed to have financial ties with the Mexican Oil
Company (Pemex), whose crude it imports. The Wood River Oil and Refining
Company would have been included in this group of refiners but for the fact
that it sold its 30,000 b/d refinery to Sinclair a few months before the close
of 1950, in large measure because it was having trouble getting crude.

tios for the various industry sectors do not decline appreciably if they are computed for an identical group of twenty leading refiners; in each stage of the industry, the twenty leaders are virtually identical. Moreover, on balance the figures understate the actual market importance of the majors: as noted, the net production figures underestimate the amount of crude oil they effectively command; the marketing figures do not reflect the influence suppliers of nationally known, branded products may exert over formally independent distributors.

A study of the interrelations of integration and competition in the petroleum industry cannot be an analysis of the phenomenon of integration considered in isolation, whether horizonal or vertical or a combination of the two. Both horizontal and vertical integration *in some degree* are practically indigenous in an industry like oil with its unique risks of discovery, exploitation, processing, and distribution of a fluid that "flows" beneath the surface of the earth and above it from the wellhead to its final use in motor car, tractor, locomotive, industrial boiler, and home furnace. Complete vertical integration without horizontal integration (i.e. from a single well to a single retail outlet) is economic nonsense; and while the reverse situation is meaningful (and is often realized), the expectation that it would or should prevail generally in even approximately pure form is equally unthinkable. It would be inconceivable for a large refiner not to assume some direct responsibility for marketing his product or for seeing to it that his basic raw material was laid down as cheaply as possible at the refinery. Both efforts might well require some vertical integration. In the myriad combinations that this form of business organization does take, integration per se must be close to a neutral competitive force. It is only when it expands the size and limits the number of participants in the competitive process to the point of dominance or possible market control that it becomes a matter of public concern.

CHAPTER 3

Integration, Competition, and the Public Interest: Problems for Analysis

THE GIST OF THE CASE against the role played by the majors in the oil industry may be briefly stated, although with some violence to the richly divergent views of its critics. The contention is that these companies have a strong mutual interest in avoiding competition: because they are large in size and small in number, each realizes that any effort to improve its position by competing strenuously can only provoke retaliatory price-cutting with the end result that the profits of all will suffer. The companies are able to achieve their monopolistic ends, it is held, because they are few, and can therefore easily act— whether independently or conspiratorially—in concert; because they are vertically integrated and can thereby foreclose independent competitors, actual and potential, from supplies and markets; and because state authorities regulate production of crude oil in such a way as to limit its availability to independent refiners, and to insulate its price against competitive market forces. The small number of large companies at each level of the industry, according to this indictment, is the manifestation of the urge to monopolize, and the necessary condition of effective market collaboration; and vertical integration is the instrument for forging and maintaining this kind of market structure, substituting financial resources for the efficient service of the public as the prime determinant of profitability and the sine qua non of survival.

The answer of the majors—and here, again, different companies would reply in different ways—is both positive and negative. The positive defense is that such business size and integration as characterize the oil industry are essential if the risks of huge investments in facilities of optimum size are to be taken promptly, if the efficient flow of oil and products is to be maintained, and if current resources are to be conserved and future energy sources properly explored. In brief, they would contend that their market shares are a result and proof, their size and integration a necessary condition, of superior ability to compete in giving the public what it wants at the lowest

36

possible cost. Negatively, they would deny the charge of market collaboration. In contradiction, they would stress that, whatever their mutual interests, the leading companies compete strenuously against each other; that any one that fails to do so soon finds itself losing customers and profits; and that the industry presents ample opportunity for the competitive entry and stimulus of independent firms, provided they are efficient and enterprising. The pressures for and merits of state regulation of crude oil production, they would aver, have nothing to do with the size or integration of the majors, whose views with respect to prorationing and whose fortunes under its operation, as a matter of fact, diverge widely.

Within this framework of contradictory opinion lie the questions of primary concern in this study. Is massive vertical integration in any sense a necessary or socially desirable consequence of the economic and physical characteristics of oil production, processing, and distribution? Size of firm and degree of concentration in industrial markets will naturally vary widely with the governing economic conditions in each: Has the actual organization of such markets in oil surpassed the requirements of economic efficiency in ways calculated to depress competition and burden consumers? And though state regulation of crude oil production has undoubtedly brought a salutary stabilization to this potentially explosive industry, are there more effective ways of assuring the public interest in the conservation of oil, in its more economical production and in the more flexible adjustment of its supplies to consumers' demands?

Some of these broad issues raise questions of theory that must be further explored in this chapter before we can turn to their specific application to oil. The first question is this: Are there any general principles by which one can judge the necessity for vertical integration in a given industry—any tendencies for it to occur in certain institutional contexts and not in others? For example, it might be anticipated that vertical integration would prevail in an undeveloped economic environment which did not provide independent facilities and services adequate to the evolving needs of a new and growing industry. As qualified, specialized alternatives became freely available in expanding markets, one might expect that the original trends would tend to be arrested or reversed: that integration would give way to market specialization. No such result is apparent in the domestic oil industry; why might this be so? Secondly, it has been contended by some writers that vertical integration per se, far from creating monopoly, can only be expected to undermine and weaken it. Were this theory sound, there would be little point in the orientation of this monograph: it must therefore be carefully appraised. And finally, it is a necessary preliminary to examine the standards that may guide a study like this. Since most economists today recognize that even rough approximation to the atomistic market structure of pure competition is neither possible nor desirable in large segments of American industry, what are the elements of an acceptable or workable competition in oil; and can they be forged into useful criteria for this inquiry?

VERTICAL INTEGRATION AND MARKET ALTERNATIVES

Production may always be conceived as comprising an almost infinite succession of processes from the discovery, extraction, or growing of the raw material to the distribution of the finished goods or services to the ultimate user. In some industries, the typical arrangement is one of unified managerial control from beginning to end; in others the chain is forged by arms-length transactions between specialist firms at various intermediate stages. Why?

The social scientist is reluctant to accept explanations of social phenomena that run in terms of the vagaries of individual personality, talent, or motivation. For him the explanation of differences in industrial structure must be sought in such impersonal causal factors as the nature of the respective technologies, the conditions under which the products in question are supplied, the nature of the demand for them, the influence of other industries and of other social, political, and economic institutions, the stage of the economy's history in which each developed, and so on. To take a single illustration, it would be most surprising if one could not explain a very great deal of the organization and behavior of the American petroleum industry (in contrast with the industries of almost every other country in the world) in terms of a single legal institution—the "rule of capture." [1]

Like the rule of capture itself, these conditioning influences are subject to constant change. So the organization of an industry, like all other social institutions, is not a constant, independent variable, but one in process of evolution under the influence of changes in the forces, internal and external, that mold it. This does not of course mean that what is was inevitable, or that what will be is unchangeable: public

---

1. This is the legal principle, traditional in this country, that oil drawn from below ground belongs to the owner of the land surface, regardless of whose land it was originally under.

policy is itself an important determinant of business structure and behavior.

The importance of institutional arrangements and supporting economic activities in determining the pattern of integration may be indicated by contrasting the alternatives confronting a prospector for oil here in the United States with those he faces in a foreign land. The domestic prospector has a wide range of knowledge, assurances, and aids to support him. There is much geological information available covering many parts of the United States. He can tap this information through industry consultants; he can hire independent contractors to make particular studies; or he can negotiate with large firms for a likely location (including lease, information, and financial assistance) for a "farm out" or a joint drilling operation.[2] Alternately he may spy out areas in which the larger companies are conducting more intensive exploration than usual, taking up leases or options, or making drilling tests. Many individuals and many companies thus exercise their wits and their greater flexibility to acquire leases and options (often on better terms than the big company) on the edges of likely looking property. And since no one can foretell, despite improvements in scientific methods, where the strike may be made and what may be the direction of the field from the discovery well, the little fellow may hit where the big one misses, though the odds are the other way. Once a strike has been made in the general area, there is usually no problem of financing a drilling operation in this country. The independent may often engage a drilling contractor and crew during slack times at low, almost incremental costs. If a strike is made beyond the reach of existing transport facilities our prospector can usually sell out to a large company.[3] With luck and shrewdness (by playing large companies against each other for various allowances, for example), individuals are known to have brought in a well for practically nothing, indeed to have earned a net income with nothing but "dry holes" while still drilling for themselves.

In a foreign region like the Middle East (Iran, Iraq, Saudi Arabia,

2. See below, pp. 173–174.

3. Twenty years ago the lucky prospector had the additional alternative of building his own small refinery to salvage the more valuable components of the oil he found. Today, this would seldom prove feasible because refinery product standards require much more complex and costly processing. Forward integration of producers, except by merger with or selling out to established refiner-marketers, has therefore virtually ceased. The producer becomes, perforce, a specialist, selling to the pipeline or crude-buying subsidiary of the refiner.

Kuwait), in contrast, the prospector faces long and usually costly political negotiations for a concession before he can engage in any exploration. Before investing a dollar in exploration, he will find it only prudent to reach an understanding also about his rights and liabilities with regard to any oil subsequently discovered, to his future tax liabilities, and, in a world of exchange controls, his ability to repatriate profits. Highly specialized and rare talents are needed to establish satisfactory working relationships with one or more foreign governments. Under modern conditions suitable relations would have to be established also with our own State Department, with the military authorities, possibly with whatever agency was then administering our foreign economic programs and, as in the recent past, with American authorities concerned with procurement and export controls over steel or equipment.

This is only the beginning—the right to explore a vast wilderness of desert and sand with no available accumulation of geophysical or seismographical knowledge, no technical crews or special consultants standing by to be hired, no roads or transport facilities, no drilling rigs or drilling crews, no pipelines or railroads or tank cars, no equipment supply houses or steel supplies, no trained personnel, no local markets. If, finally, oil is found, a method of transporting it for shipment or a refinery to process it must be constructed and, often more difficult, a market must be developed. Not only will the operator abroad have to provide through his own investments the whole complement of equipment, facilities, and services needed to carry on the production and distribution of petroleum products, as these functions are traditionally defined. He must also provide all the "social capital" that businesses in a mature economy may take for granted—living accommodations for workers, utility services, medical facilities, medical personnel, recreation, access roads, schools, retail stores. Foreign exploration and production demand a combination of highly developed diplomatic talents, huge capital outlays, long waiting periods, and great risks. Expenditures of tens of millions of dollars over periods of several years are not uncommon before anything of significance is discovered, and a much longer time and a much heavier investment is likely before the product can begin to bring a return.

The domestic oil operator may trade with innumerable individuals and established firms, agencies that operate exclusively or partially within the industry, or indirectly to serve it. He may specialize in one or more of the broad stages of petroleum production and distribution, relying on other firms (the "market process") to supply him with materials and services, to dispose of his output or bring him business. Within each of these stages he may specialize very narrowly, or call upon the highly specialized services provided by others.[4] And serving him, whatever he does, and without his having directly to incur any of the costs of providing them, is a technically trained labor force and an institutional setup to provide for its needs.

Something of the inherent relativity of the idea of integration is conveyed by this example. It is easy enough to differentiate a combination of units of a single type like refineries, service stations, or oil wells as horizontal integration; to characterize any combination of different products like natural gas, carbon black, chemicals, and various final petroleum products as product (or "conglomerate" or "circular") integration; and to call a combination of different steps in the chain of production from raw material to finished products vertical integration—"forward" toward the ultimate consumer, "backward" toward the raw material. But neither the "steps" nor the "whole" can be defined except with some arbitrariness, and with reference to a particular time and place. It is not merely that there are functions supporting and essential to the production process at each stage that can only by convention be said not to be a part of it. It is rather that the very concept of different or separable steps in the production process, and the very concept of what is or is not a part of it, will change from place to place and time to time depending on the state of technology and the availability and efficiency of alternatives.

This comparison of the conditions facing the oil prospector in two institutional settings that differ markedly in economic maturity suggests a possible inherent historical tendency—for integration to give way to specialization. When an industry is young and new, particularly in an underdeveloped economy, its pioneers may find it necessary or expedient to perform most of its functions themselves. Necessity or opportunity may induce a refiner to develop his own service stations, or design oil burners, or build pipelines or oil tankers; or

---

4. In production, for example, geophysical and seismographic exploration, land surveying, leasing, well drilling, core analysis, well tool manufacturing, tool sharpening, and a host of other functions are performed as separate businesses. So is the provision of equity capital, by numerous investors all over the country seeking quick wealth, and attracted by the extraordinary tax benefits accorded ventures in crude oil. Transportation is provided through many common and contract carriers. Refiners themselves often call upon outside laboratories for testing and analysis of special problems and on equipment firms for work in process design. A host of manufacturing and maintenance businesses serve the retail station operator. And so on.

they may lead a producer to get into refining in order to create a market for his crude.

This resort to integration may come at the very outset of an industry's evolution. Or it may come only after a substantial period of growth. A young industry of a different character, or in a more mature environment, might find it not only possible but most expedient to rely initially on already existing distributive or productive facilities, perhaps not specifically or particularly adapted to its needs alone, but serving the purpose. At the outset the American oil industry utilized the services and skills developed in the drilling of wells other than oil; it used common carriers already in existence and serving other industries as well; it distributed its products through general stores and repair shops. With the expansion of the industry and of the businesses engaged in it, some of the latter began to supply some of their own requirements—to develop specialized techniques and products especially suited to their needs, to circumvent monopolistic positions, to do the job better.

In any event, as market volume grows, new institutions emerge and the relevant technical abilities come to be more widely dispersed, market alternatives to integration should improve. Opportunities should multiply for a "peeling off" of functions that can be more effectively performed by specialists. Services or products which earlier industry producers had to adapt to their purposes from other uses or develop for themselves could later become the focus of specially trained talents and specialized business organizations. In this manner, market economies external to the individual firm would be developed, making it cheaper to buy and sell than to "roll one's own." According to this theory, then, integration would be expected gradually to give way before market specialization.

On the other hand, there may be offsetting forces that tend to make integration historically cumulative or self-reinforcing. The theory that it should be self-limiting is based really on the assumption of general economic expansion on the basis of an unchanging technology, which specialists may learn and find it profitable to adopt. The progressive development of an industry's technology, however, reveals ever-new opportunities for profit. And it might be the "insiders" who would be in the best position to keep abreast of those developments, and to extend their operations to embrace and exploit them, particularly as innovation in modern industry becomes ever more expensive, time-consuming, and demanding of the collaboration of large aggregations of scientific and engineering skills, equipment, and capital.

Each extension of company facilities and specialized managerial interests broadens the scope of exposure to still further opportunities for profitable investment. Individual abilities and equipment capacities are seldom adapted perfectly to the job to be done or to the optimum capabilities of existing productive resources. Thus as personnel, equipment, and functions are added to existing organization, old needs may be met but new ones are revealed in unutilized capabilities created anew. The die is more likely to be cast for retention of integration and correction of emergent imbalances by further integration rather than by lopping off awkwardly protuberant parts, where the dominant portion of established costs seems to be sunk and the cost of additions is estimated on an incremental basis. Common costs may make it appear uneconomic to slough off functions that, standing on their own financial feet, could not support their own required investment. In this complex cost situation, real needs for growth to provide new opportunities for the advancement of promising subordinates, for the exploitation of new ideas, and for the improvement in efficiency may merge too readily with the personal satisfaction management derives from association with an organization that is not only big, but growing bigger all the time. The line between efficiency and inefficiency is blurred.

Integration also confers advantages of a purely strategic character, by giving a company more certain access than nonintegrated competitors enjoy to materials and markets, and by protecting it against the squeezes on prices and margins that may afflict firms confined to one particular stage of production. These advantages may be achieved merely by imposing corresponding disadvantages upon specialized competitors. Insofar as this is true, it follows that if no companies were vertically integrated, it would be less urgent for any of them to be. To the extent that integration narrows the alternatives intermediate markets offer to nonintegrated competitors, in brief, integration makes it necessary for them to integrate as well.

Integration may therefore breed integration. It is particularly likely to do so if it carries no offsetting disadvantages. If, for example, integrated companies are very large and at the same time operate with decentralization of management, they may enjoy the advantages of market specialization in their own departments while retaining the strategic benefits integration confers, of protection, assurance, and balance.

Despite improvements in market facilities, there is no evidence that the fully integrated oil company in this country has lost or is losing relative position to nonintegrated operators. This persistent flowering of integration in the face of probable decline in the need for it requires explanation before its consequences may be appraised. Chapter 5 attempts such an historical analysis, as a background for the attempt to ascertain whether the cumulative historical development of integration has reflected primarily a progressive exploitation of new opportunities for more effective service, or a quest for strategic advantage that, however real for the individual business firm, frustrates rather than enhances the effectiveness of competition. Neither these motives nor their consequences are mutually exclusive.

VERTICAL INTEGRATION AND MONOPOLY POWER

Since competition is the rivalry of separate sellers (or buyers) of the same or similar products for the patronage of customers (or suppliers [5]), it is a horizontal phenomenon: its success will depend on the intensity and effectiveness of the rivalry *within* any given horizontal stratum of an industry and between firms on the *same* side of the same market. Hence horizontal integration may bring together operations that might otherwise be competitive but vertical integration does not, at least at first blush. True, it takes transactions out of intermediate markets; and transfers between horizontal phases, otherwise accomplished by purchase and sale, will now be effected by managerial directive. It thereby reduces the number of sellers (and/or the volume of wares offered) in those markets below what they would otherwise be; but it does so only by reducing correspondingly the number of buyers and/or the volume demanded. In effect, therefore, vertical integration merely focuses the industry's competition on final sales in final markets; and there it does not, of and by itself, reduce the number of sellers, or the intensity of the rivalry between them.

Indeed, vertical integration may vastly increase the effectiveness of rivalry at any given stage. Firms often expand vertically because they feel they can perform the complementary function themselves more

5. In an ideally functioning competitive economy, such rivalry must be present on both sides of all markets. The ensuing theoretical discussion is framed exclusively in terms of competition between sellers, partly for convenience and partly because it is this competition above all that protects the interest of the consuming public against direct, monopolistic exploitation. However, public attention has often been directed to alleged inadequacies of competition among buyers, and this possibility in oil is examined, for example, in assessing the operation of crude oil markets. So-called monopsony power (the equivalent on the buyer side of monopoly power) can also pervert the functioning of markets, and be injurious not only to the sellers it exploits but also, indirectly, to the public at large.

efficiently than outside suppliers or customers. Or they may believe that the mere combination of operations will reduce costs, perhaps because of the closer dovetailing of supplies and needs and the consequent higher utilization of capacity that managerial control can achieve, perhaps because of the elimination of intermediate selling costs. Or, finally, they may feel that they can achieve a saving in cost or higher net realization on sales because integration will enable them to avoid monopolistic charges by suppliers or by those who would otherwise stand between them and the ultimate customer.

If vertical integration does not of itself tip the balance of power in favor of sellers or buyers in intermediate markets, or reduce the number of sellers at the final level; and if, on the other hand, it may well permit firms to reduce the cost of getting goods and services to the customer, it would seem never to be a proper subject of suspicion. Some economists have argued to this effect.[6] Vertical integration, they aver, does not impair competition and cannot enhance monopoly power. It can only serve the public interest to leave companies free to integrate vertically or not, as they choose: they will find it profitable to do so only if it reduces their costs or enhances their ability to compete for one or another of the reasons indicated above.

Manifestly, if integration conferred no additional monopoly power, a rational seller would integrate backward ("upstream") or forward ("downstream") only if he thought he could perform supplier or distributor functions more cheaply than they were previously being performed. If these hopes materialized both he and the public might benefit: with effective competition in final product markets, the integrating firm would be forced to pass some of the cost savings on to the consumer; if it were a monopolist instead, it would at worst pocket the cost savings, since it would presumably have already been exploiting its monopoly to the fullest. If, on the other hand, the hopes of lower costs or higher realization were frustrated, only the company itself would suffer. If the mistaken integrator were a monopolist who had failed to charge his optimum monopoly toll, he might find it possible to pass on some or all of the burden of his error to the consumer. The evil here, however, would be not vertical integration, but (horizontal) monopoly, which can penalize the public for its mistakes, whatever their source.

This theoretical defense of profit-seeking vertical integration is par-

6. See J. J. Spengler, "Vertical Integration and Antitrust Policy," *Journal of Political Economy, 58* (1950), 347; Robert Bork, "Vertical Integration and the Sherman Act: The Legal History of an Economic Misconception," *University of Chicago Law Review, 22* (1954), 157.

ticularly persuasive in an industry characterized by seriously imperfect competition in its various horizontal strata. A nonintegrated industry is subject to the pyramiding of monopoly surcharges through each of its successive stages of production and distribution. The levels that are characterized by seriously imperfect competition fix sales prices (and hence the cost prices for the next stage) that include either a supernormal return on investment, or costs that might have been lower had competition been more effective. The vertically integrating firm can avoid these exactions by making the product or performing the function itself.[7] It can obtain materials or have its forward functions performed at cost.

There is basic truth in the assertion that it is *horizontal* monopoly that is the major threat to a freely competitive economy. The theory under consideration here, however, minimizes unrealistically the threat that vertical integration, when combined with seriously imperfect competition in some segments of an industry, may itself pose for horizontal competition.

In juxtaposition with the view that vertical integration cannot impair competition may be set the somewhat more pessimistic theory that it is through the "countervailing power" organized spontaneously in opposition to "original" monopoly (or monopsony) power that society must hope to work out a reasonably acceptable market balance.[8] The big buyer, or an organized group of buyers, may exert significant pressure on the sales terms of sellers even if few and powerful, because the volume of their business is important enough to any single seller to make serious the threat of taking it to a competitor. It would seem

7. For a detailed argument to this effect, see Spengler, "Vertical Integration and Antitrust Policy." Of course, there is no advantage, necessarily, in avoiding payment of profits to suppliers or distributors; the cost to the integrated firm as well must include a necessary return on the capital committed to the upstream or downstream operations. The real gains from vertical integration must rest on one or more of the following advantages: superior efficiency, lower costs of capital, or circumvention of monopoly.

8. J. K. Galbraith, *American Capitalism: The Concept of Countervailing Power*, Boston, Houghton Mifflin, 1952. Also see, among others, the three essays and various comments discussing the Galbraith thesis, "Fundamental Characteristics of the American Economy," *American Economic Review, Papers and Proceedings, 44* (1954), 1–34; Walter Adams, "Competition, Monopoly and Countervailing Power," *Quarterly Journal of Economics, 67* (1953), 469–492; Simon N. Whitney, "Errors in the Concept of Countervailing Power," *Journal of Business of the University of Chicago, 26* (1953), 238–253; and Joel B. Dirlam and Alfred E. Kahn, *Fair Competition, the Law and Economics of Antitrust Policy* (Ithaca, Cornell University Press, 1954), 235–238.

to follow that to the extent sellers can preclude the emergence of countervailing buying groups or make themselves independent of them, by forward integration, they may be better able to cement their common front against the cracks that only a big, independent buyer can probe and widen.

A powerful buyer may also split or encroach upon the monopoly power of sellers by integrating backward and supplying his own requirements; or he may go only part way backward, by supplying capital and making long-term purchase contracts with an established manufacturer in exchange for something like a cost-plus arrangement. Why should a big buyer be better able to do this than an unorganized group of small ones? First, the volume of his business will enable him to offer a manufacturing subsidiary or affiliate the most convincing kind of guarantee of a market large enough to permit the achievement of economies of scale. Second, size is associated ordinarily with superior access to capital, a point to which we return in Chapter 11, below. The standing possibility that a big buyer will circumvent existing channels of supply places limits on the pricing discretion of suppliers, and provides stimuli to efficient operation, progressive cost-reduction, and product innovation similar to those exerted by competition itself.[9]

Therefore, size on one side of the market represents a threat to monopoly power on the other—a threat that is reduced if the organized suppliers either pre-empt the field downstream by operating in it directly, or join forces with the possessors of countervailing power. If a monopolist merges with a monopsonist downstream, two potential belligerents, capable of inflicting mutual injury, will have joined forces. Separate, their interests conflict, because they must divide between themselves such monopoly profit as the industry can extort from the ultimate customer. If either could have the complementary function performed at a price or margin more closely approaching cost, it could then arrogate to itself the greater portion of the industry's total potential monopoly profit. Separate, therefore, they are potential competitors, or potential sources of encouragement to smaller firms already in or that might be induced to enter the other's field of operations.[10]

9. See A. D. H. Kaplan, *Big Enterprise in a Competitive System* (Washington, D.C., Brookings Institution, 1954), pp. 184–185.

10. Of course bilateral monopolists on opposite sides of the markets may, like duopolists on the same side of the market, act as one, rather than risk the mutual injury of open conflict. However, where there are several parties on each side of the market, the possibility that one of them may try to inject some sort of competitive pressure on the other side is greatly increased.

It was precisely this kind of threat of reciprocal, dangerously competitive encroachment by vertical integration, each into the other's domain, that finally induced the Carnegie and Morgan interests to form the United States Steel Corporation in 1901. Vertical integration forestalled the threatened entry of new competition at both levels of the industry.

Were market position and power fixed and immutable quanta, vertical integration could do no harm and might do only good. It could not of itself enhance horizontal market power; and by causing complementary functions to be performed at cost, it might induce even monopolists to lower their ultimate prices. In fact, however, market positions are subject constantly to encroachment and market power to erosion in a dynamic economy. Every business in the real world, therefore, must devote a good deal of attention to securing itself against the inroads of competition. Vertical integration is one important and familiar way of trying to do this. Like others of the tactics companies use to protect or extend their market positions, it may be a competitive phenomenon, productive of social benefit. But it may also be a method of forestalling potential competitive or countervailing pressures.

Economists have placed increasing emphasis, in recent years, on freedom of entry as the hallmark of workable competition.[11] An industry dominated by a small number of vertically integrated companies is likely to be much more impervious to competitive entry than a disintegrated one, with an identical number of sellers at each level. With flourishing intermediate markets, a nonintegrated entrant enjoys fair assurances of ability to command supplies and find customers on equal terms with his rivals. The prices he pays for certain materials and services and the margins that are added to his product as it moves downstream may be subject to monopolistic manipulation; but his competitors are in the same position as he in this regard and must live within the same margins.

Widespread vertical integration, particularly if it encompasses strata in which competition is seriously deficient, eliminates these characteristics of a "fair field and no favors." The nonintegrated competitor lacks equal assurances of supplies and markets. He faces the possibility of active competition with companies that need not live within the same margins as those which limit his profits, because their activities embrace other, possibly more monopolistic, markets. He faces the

11. A leading exponent of this view is Joe S. Bain; see, e.g., his "Conditions of Entry and the Emergence of Monopoly," in Edward H. Chamberlin, ed., *Monopoly and Competition and Their Regulation* (London, Macmillan, 1954), pp. 215–241.

possibility, too, of being the victim of discriminatory applications of economic power by his integrated competitors, whether or not the latter are motivated by consciously predatory intentions. The integrated company is rarely in perfect balance. Ordinarily it will be buying from and selling to nonintegrated companies with which it also competes. If it enjoys substantial monopoly power in some of its markets, it may therefore be in a position to apply squeezes on its rivals —by transferring more of the function of processing its materials or supplying its requirements to its own affiliate, or by compressing the margin within which nonintegrated firms must operate by raising the price at which it sells to them relative to the price at which it sells in competition with them.

It is not unlikely, of course, that the pressures of the squeeze are in part at least the natural and inevitable concomitants of market change in an imperfect world rather than of deliberate policy. Even so, their impact would be concentrated on the nonintegrated firm by the partial insulation of its integrated competitors, whose losses or gains at one level of production are offset or modified by gains or losses at another. The important question is whether integration unduly constricts the competitive opportunities of independent firms, regardless of whether it is typically used deliberately to that end.

In the face of these uncertainties the potential entrant may fear to make the effort unless he, too, can enter in full integrated regalia. This means, however, that the capital requirements of entry are greatly increased, and the doors of opportunity are more tightly closed to all but the already established and the already wealthy. This may mean, in turn, that such companies as do still find it possible to enter will be the more likely, because of the necessity for integration, to be in "responsible" hands—hands that will reach for additional business only in ways that do not upset profitable markets.

Manifestly, vertical integration could not intelligently be subjected to attack in and of itself, either in oil or in any other industry. It is a legitimate method of pursuing profit, often highly beneficial to the consumer. If it does raise threats to nonintegrated competitors and to competition itself, it is only because it may be associated with (horizontal) monopoly power; the social ideal, in such cases, would be to attack that power directly, rather than the vertical integration that may possibly, in certain circumstances, make perverse use of it, or further protect it.

On the other hand, equally clearly, vertical integration associated with horizontal monopoly power may threaten excessively the well-being of competitors and customers. The contention that this has been the case in the oil industry is the subject of our analysis.

Standards of Acceptable Competition

There is no lack of competition in the oil business in the dictionary sense: "an act of . . . seeking, or endeavoring to gain what another is endeavoring to gain at the same time." Producers scramble for leases in a new or prospective field. In periods of shortage, buyers of crude oil—majors as well as independents—vie against each other with premium prices, special terms, or scarce drill pipe to keep their well connections or to make new ones. Refiners strain to keep transport costs down, and to adjust yields of products flexibly with differential changes in the market values of each. Qualitative improvements in products have left many an operator without a market. Price wars periodically wrack sections of the country. Whether in building or equipping newly designed and located retail outlets, in devising methods of cutting wholesaling costs of storage and delivery, in national advertising, or in the construction of new refining and new transport equipment, the petroleum operator, integrated or nonintegrated, large or small, will snort at the suggestion that something is lacking in the competition he faces daily.

This competition is not always in the price tag. But competition of other kinds may be no less pervasive and keen. The number of ways and the frequency with which oil men offer more to close a deal at the expense of competitors without altering the quoted price is limited only by their ingenuity and aggressiveness, both of which are considerable. Some such inducements constitute a turbulent real price competition beneath the placid surface of the posted price. Other offers may be more attractive than an altered price—perhaps a long-term, reliable supply or purchase contract. Competition is not less vital because an independent producer will not lightly sever a long-standing crude connection with a major oil company: the offer of a premium on the posted price by a small independent refiner will have little attraction if there is reason to doubt his ability to keep taking the oil as long as it flows. Nor is it necessarily a sign of ineffective competition if a distributor of home-heating fuels, aggressively undertaking commitments for the coming heating season, hesitates to desert his usual supplier in the event of a bargain offer, if an unusually severe winter might otherwise find his tanks empty and his doorstep crowded with irate—and cold—customers.

Again, competition may focus on product improvement rather than on price reductions on a standardized product. An obsolete refinery may be unable to sell its gasoline, except for reprocessing, because its octane rating is unacceptable for direct use, whatever its price. Under threat of being driven out of business the refiner must make one of several hard choices: to invest in new equipment; to acquire, probably at higher cost, special crudes from which to obtain higher quality product with existing facilities; to sell or exchange his products with other refiners for upgrading by them; or to have his crude entirely processed by others. Each of these alternatives has its examples, and each involves a species of real price competition. The petroleum industry offers rich documentation of the thesis dramatically stated by the late Professor Schumpeter, that the "creative destruction" of competitive innovation—as, for example, the revolutionary impact of the catalytic cracker—can be more devastating for the participants and contribute more to industry progress and consumer welfare than any amount of price competition.

This so-called new competition—with its origins in the research laboratory and its flowering in the merchandising of products often differentiated by nationally advertised brands—is concentrated on tactics that are more difficult than a change in price for rivals to meet: changes in product quality or packaging, changes in technology or processing, the development of entirely new ways of satisfying old or stimulating new wants. Consumer acceptance is captured and patronage weaned from rivals not through price, which is seldom strictly comparable, but by making rivals' goods, whatever their quoted prices, obsolete and outmoded. The protection afforded by distinctive product quality is at once the necessary condition and the objective of the large investments required for laboratory, pilot plant, and commercial establishment, for the exploration of new product uses and the creation of consumers' acceptance for the product in those uses, for building and maintaining effective distribution.[12] Market imperfection and management discretion are not merely transitory but permanent features of dynamic change and industrial growth in this twentieth-century economy.

It is this element of discretionary power in imperfect though competitive markets that undermines the assumption that competitive

12. For a skeptical appraisal of an oft-cited illustration of the heavy capital outlays and risks in introducing a new product, see Willard F. Mueller, "A Case Study of Product Discovery and Innovation Costs," *Southern Economic Journal, 24* (1957), 80.

self-interest of established firms will necessarily dictate the perform-ance compatible with the public interest. What makes the appraisal so difficult is that some measure of market power, with its insulation of stockholders' investment and workers' jobs and wages, may well be desirable; indeed, it may be the necessary condition, as Schumpeter stressed, of real economic progress through innovation. Economic ad-vance in this century is often associated with the large integrated firm.[13]

Modern industrial progress requires investments of great magnitude and duration; the savings, once risked, are sunk for a long time in their chosen employment. In the making or non-making of such in-vestments, therefore, anticipations of future market conditions neces-sarily play a central role. If private industry is to progress, investors must have reason to believe they can make reasonable guesses about the future; some assurance of stability or continuity of the relevant determinants of profit is required. Investors will and must take risks, but they will not and cannot be expected to do so if the risks are too great—if, to take an extreme example, revolution or invasion by hos-tile powers appears imminent. By a parity of reasoning, vertical in-tegration is not necessarily opposed to—in fact may contribute posi-tively toward—workable competition merely because it offers investors reasonable security against the big risks they may have to take.

By the same token, however, the amount and kinds of protection investors require will vary from time to time and place to place. If the security that vertical integration provides was necessary for industrial progress yesterday, that does not prove it is necessary today.

The fact that impurities of competition may contribute to innova-tion and may be inevitable by-products of efficient organization must not be permitted to obscure the social interest in competition itself. Competition is a total process; it involves rivalry in cost-reduction and product improvement as well as in price. It must be keen if it is to be workable. If its pressures are weak, both efficiency and industrial progress may fall short of the attainable. Moreover, competition in price is also required to insure that the benefits of technological ad-vance are widely spread. In imperfect markets, even where marked by technical progress, there can be no presumption that the public interest is best served.

By what criteria then are we to judge the effectiveness of com-petition in oil? It will be easy to show that it is seldom, if ever, "pure." But the only question relevant to public policy is: what can be done,

13. See Kaplan, *Big Enterprise in a Competitive System.*

if anything, to improve the functioning of the industry in the public interest? Some have advocated a breaking up of incumbent firms into units so small as to emasculate any probable effect on price through their independent action. The political and legal obstacles to this program are rivaled only by apparent technical difficulties at most levels of the industry. But, some have said, if pure competition is not feasible, let us at least try to make competition as pure as is practically possible. This easy acceptance of pure competition as the only test and goal of market structures represents an abdication by the economist of his true function, which is not to parrot his premises but to test and apply them against the facts. The problem is to show how business behavior and performance might be expected to change if the business structure were to be changed, and to evaluate such changes in the light of the industry's performance as it now functions.

Pure competition is not simply an unattainable ideal; it is not even an ideal. If we must leave that cozy harbor, yet also stay away from the opposite shore of monopoly, must we drift aimlessly in between? The navigational guide that economists have been evolving, the homely compromise with reality that J. M. Clark christened "workable competition," is not yet much of a guide, compared with its predecessor. It is as messy as the other was tidy, as fumbling and subjective as the other was incisive and objective. But it is nonetheless more useful because it is more relevant.[14]

Its primary ingredient, it would appear, is balance:

> sellers sufficiently few for efficiency and progress, yet numerous enough to give the buyer real alternatives and to prevent monopolistic exploitation and restrictionism; buyers big enough to offset the power of sellers yet not so powerful as to exploit them or the public; control over supplies and markets, whether by contractual arrangements or financial relationships, to permit desirable long-term investments and the risking of savings, yet not such dominance as excessively to restrict the competitive opportunities of new entrants; sufficient limitation of rivalry between competitors

14. We would by no means cast aside the pure competition standard entirely. It still provides one useful yardstick against which to measure the intensity of one kind of competition. The differences between it and "workable competition" are in some respects differences in kind—the latter embraces certain market imperfections as actually superior to purity. But other differences are those of degree only—workable competition is simply more tolerant of certain market imperfections and suggests only that if held to tolerably modest dimensions, they will not unduly obstruct the effectiveness of market rivalry.

to avoid cutthroat competition, yet not so much as to produce excessive monopoly power.[15]

How does one apply such a test to particular markets or industries? Some economists believe that the primary inquiry must be into the industry's structural characteristics. The main culprit is excessive monopoly power, and it must be the object of direct search. The assumption is usually that structure determines behavior and results; firms in an industry with an unworkable structure will not behave competitively, and will not give the public what it has the right to expect. But even if the behavior and results are apparently "good," these (indeed, most) advocates of competitive organization will not be placated; they will be satisfied only if "good" performance is *compelled* by the objective forces of the market—by external, competitive pressures on the businessman—rather than manifesting sheer *noblesse oblige*.

It is unnecessary at this point to discuss in detail the structural characteristics relevant to such an inquiry.[16] Obviously the number of sellers and their relative size and position, the ease of competitive entry, the characteristics of the product and its market, and the competition of substitutes are leading considerations. All we need point out is that while the structural tests of competition are important, the relation of the almost infinite possible number of combinations of structural characteristics to business behavior and results is still subject to enough doubt that it would be difficult to obtain widespread agreement among economists that this inquiry alone would suffice as a guide to policy in all but extreme cases.[17]

A second kind of evidence of the presence or absence of effective

15. Dirlam and Kahn, *Fair Competition*, pp. 13–14. "One cannot dispose of these new economic norms of workable or effective rather than pure or perfect competition merely by pointing out that they are vague, shifting, or pragmatic, or not much of a standard at all, unless one can point to some 'workable' alternative. An economist appraising the structure or performance of a market or industry cannot confine his efforts to demonstrating the ways in which either falls short of the purely competitive standard. The proponents of workable competition have made the case convincingly that purity is both unattainable and undesirable" (*ibid.*, p. 13).

16. For an elaborate and balanced discussion of structural and other tests, see the Attorney General's National Committee to Study the Antitrust Laws (cited below as Attorney General's Committee), *Report* (Washington, D.C., 1955), chap. 7.

17. For a critique of the market structure as well as the economic performance tests of monopoly see Kahn, "Standards for Antitrust Policy," *Harvard Law Review, 67* (1953), 33–42 and *passim*.

competition is the conduct or behavior of firms in the market. An examination of past conduct is essential if the present market structure is to be evaluated: both the antitrust lawyer and the economist regard differently the size of a firm that has reached its position by effective competition, by construction of new capacity, and by efficiency and progressiveness, on the one hand, and the size or market power that issue from mergers and the employment of exclusive tactics, on the other. In addition, the economist will want to see whether firms in the market at present act competitively, and may be expected to do so in the future. But here again, the objective record alone cannot be conclusive. Behavior that may in certain circumstances be competitive may in others be monopolistic in its effects: witness the difficulty economists and judges have, for example, in evaluating such practices as the accumulation and active prosecution of patents, or price-cutting, selective or general, or heavy advertising expenditures.

Finally, some have sought pragmatic evidence of the presence or absence of workable competition in the economic results an industry produces—the level and trend of costs and prices, the development of new and improved products and production processes, the adequacy of supply, the conditions of employment, and the like. All these are clearly relevant to the economist's appraisal of an industry. We would emphasize at the outset, however, that no definite conclusions could follow from them. It is not only that they are essentially qualitative criteria for which the evidence is likely to vary *inter se* with no clear basis for weighing one against another. More important, performance tests lack conclusiveness because the potential is unknown. The record may be good but not half so good as it should have been; it may be bad but twice as good as would be likely under any probable alternative. The rate of invention, for example, may well vary from industry to industry and from time to time without necessarily reflecting, and certainly not reflecting exclusively, the workability of competition.

Analysis of the workability of competition will, except in unusual situations, require the appraisal of all three—market structure, market behavior past and present, and economic results. None of these tests can stand alone, and even all of them together are not certain. For every industry we know or are likely to know represents a moving equilibrium of competitive and monopolistic elements, of fluid and stable market relationships, of external pressures on the business firm that yet leave a margin of managerial discretion, of constraints imposed on managerial decision-making by the actions of competitors, by the scrutiny and intervention of government, and by its own professional mores and motivations. In appraising the impact of integration on the competitiveness of the structure, behavior, and performance of the oil industry, we should not be surprised if we find that what we have to appraise is not purity but compromise and balance, whether in the situation as it exists today or in any feasible alternatives.

The public expects other things of industry than workable competition. Our discussion in Chapter 1 has already indicated how significant these other things are in oil; the preceding discussion of economic performance tests of monopoly suggests the same is true of industry in general. There are some who would make a comprehensive economic evaluation of an industry's performance the central test of antitrust inquiries—note the following selections from a list of criteria for such inquiries suggested by the Business Advisory Council to the Secretary of Commerce:

> Volume of production or services
> Quality of the services or goods
> Number of people benefited
> Incentives to entrepreneurs
> Efficiency and economy in manufacturing or distribution
> The tendency to progress in technical development
> Prices to customers and suppliers
> Conditions favorable to the public interest in maintaining American investments abroad and in defending the country from aggression
> The tendency to conserve the country's natural resources [18]

To this list, which could readily be elaborated or extended, we would add three more criteria, already implied by some of these already listed:

> A modicum of security, for workers, investors, and consumers against intolerable market fluctuations
> Compatibility with the broad aims of U.S. foreign policy
> Fair-dealing for competitors

Most advocates of the competitive economy, which is what the antitrust laws are trying to preserve, have recoiled at the implications of such tests of "competition," for reasons similar to those we have ad-

18. *Effective Competition,* Report to the Secretary of Commerce, Washington, D.C., Department of Commerce, 1952.

vanced above.[19] Entirely apart from the obstacles to effective antitrust enforcement that these tests would erect, there is a conceptual objection: to stretch the concept of workable competition to embrace such goals as the provision of incentives to entrepreneurs, securing the national defense, conservation, security, and equity is to stretch it to the point of meaninglessness. Such objectives have no necessary relation to competition at all; some of them may be better achieved by government decree, cartelization of industry, or single-firm monopoly. Yet they *are* results the public expects of its industry, and most of them are particularly relevant in the case of oil.

Particularly vexing problems, likewise of direct bearing on the oil industry, are created by the public interest in competitive "fair dealing." It is a commonplace observation, in the literature of antitrust commentary, that there may be a conflict between the preservation of competition and the protection of competitors. Some of our recent antitrust policies, it is alleged, have confused the two, and, under the guise of serving the first, have in fact been trying to protect individual businessmen against the socially beneficent force of competition itself. Defenses of these actions have been offered on two separate planes, seldom clearly distinguished. First, the preservation of opportunities for small business is held to be a socially legitimate goal in itself, even though it may require a modification of the intensity of competition. Second, it is maintained that competition alone cannot protect the public unless it is kept fair; that is, unless efficiency and progressiveness rather than strategic advantage (superior bargaining power, greater financial resources, controlled access to supplies and markets) determine business profit or loss, survival or disappearance.

Many economists, lawyers, and government agencies have grappled with the question of whether fairness is compatible with effectiveness of competition: much depends, of course, on how the respective terms are defined. The point to be emphasized is that imperfect competition must also be "unfair," so long as fairness is defined to exclude strategic advantage unrelated to efficiency and innovation. The mere fact that an industry's structure contains firms of widely divergent size and integration practically assures this result. Squeezes of one kind or an-

19. See, among others, Attorney General's Committee, *Report,* pp. 12–14 (price-fixing is illegal regardless of whether the prices fixed are high or low), 43–44, 50 (illegal monopolization does not require that prices be actually raised, competitors actually excluded, or profits be unreasonably high), 322–324; Walter Adams, "The 'Rule of Reason': Workable Competition or Workable Monopoly?" *Yale Law Journal,* 63 (1954), 348–370.

other are inevitable when the operations and financial stake of some firms span a number of markets characterized by competition of varying degrees of effectiveness.[20] Price squeezes in a vertically integrated industry will continue to occur as long as supply adjusts itself to changes in market conditions with varying rapidity at different industry levels, as will be abundantly illustrated hereafter. Yet vertical integration at the same time may make positive contributions to the intensity and effectiveness of competitive rivalry from the viewpoint of the consuming public. Similar problems arise in the evaluation of business practices like price discrimination and the insistence on exclusive dealing. Beyond a certain point, the demands of fairness cannot be subsumed under the heading of "workable competition" but must be regarded as a separate, though not necessarily inferior, criterion of the social performance of industry.

Fair competition is a goal in itself for the American people. It means the dispersion of private economic power and opportunity for private economic initiative. It is also prized because, in general, it is expected to conduce to economic efficiency and progress. This present discussion is not intended, therefore, to conclude that cost reduction, quality improvement, conservation, and equity for competitors are necessarily incompatible with vital competition. Yet beyond some imperfectly definable point, they may best be regarded as separate and possibly even contradictory goals. It is not the function of the authors to choose between this goal and that when they conflict; but they must be alert, in appraising vertical integration in the oil industry, to point out the implications of its present structure and behavior not only for effective competition but for these other social values as well.

THE APPROACH OF THE PRESENT STUDY

The preceding discussion has suggested the inherent difficulties that harass every student of the organization, policies, and practices of an industry that cannot be readily fitted to the Procrustean bed of traditional competitive standards. Despite an abundance of statistical and historical information about the oil industry, dismayingly little will be found to have direct relevance to the public policy issues posed by the inquiry, and conclusions must be based on an informed judgment in which the intuition of different observers may lead them to widely different views. Historical records are particularly suspect, for there

20. This point is considered at length in Kahn, "Standards for Antitrust Policy," pp. 43–47.

is no objective measure of what might have happened if market structure had been different—if, for example, vertical integration had not existed. Price and profit records are notoriously subject to many interpretations depending on the analyst's conception of how they would have behaved under alternative, but still imperfectly competitive, systems of organization—and how these alternative market structures would have altered other facets of industry performance. Where, as in petroleum, processes call for enormous capital outlays, involve heavy fixed costs, and yield a variety of common products whose costs cannot be properly differentiated, standards of cost, efficiency, and investment yield become as elusive as quicksilver.

When one turns to the actions of the individuals and companies who are themselves participants in the unfolding drama of the industry's evolution, the evidence they provide is even less manageable. First of all, their testimony is unreliable, once one seeks to probe beneath the surface for underlying tendencies, explanations, or interpretations. In any event, all the observer can gather from these sources is an accumulation of individual case histories, leaving him still to guess about how typical or representative they are. In particular, the significance for the industry in general, and for the broader issues under consideration, of lists of grievances, instances of power abused, and lengthy explanations, rationalizations, and counter-considerations—all faithfully recorded—remains elusive.[21]

Essentially, this study represents a search for judgment as to whether the combination of public controls, private policy, and competition in the petroleum industry has produced and is likely to continue to produce socially acceptable behavior and results. The judgment can only be qualitative and intuitive: no objective data could automatically produce definitive and inescapable answers to the questions raised here.

The breadth of these questions inevitably drove the inquiry into almost every facet of the industry's operations. Apart from the economic and historical interpretation of vertical integration in oil that comprises the subject matter of the remaining chapters in this introduction, the analysis falls under three major headings. The primary focus of public control in this industry is on the production and sale of crude oil. Largely because of this intervention of government, the most critical issues concerning vertical integration in oil revolve

---

21. This is the problem, of course, that confronts anyone who would assess the significance of complaints before Committees of the Congress. How real is the alleged abuse? What was its source? How characteristic is it? Congressional hearings and reports seldom provide good answers to these questions.

about the propriety and consequences of linking together operations in exploration and production and in other, less pervasively regulated sectors of the industry. In Part II the basic issues of national purpose and industry strategy in the development and conservation of oil resources are formulated and analyzed; and the elements of a consistent public policy toward domestic and imported supplies and toward a more effective organization of production are set forth.

Part III explores the alleged advantages of vertical integration in non-price areas, most prominently in the marshaling of financial resources and the planning and execution of investment projects and innovations at the various levels of industry operations. While attention must be given to the competitive aspects of investment practices, the analysis of the impact of vertical integration on competition in product markets, on price rivalry, and on the opportunities for efficient independent entry and survival—in many ways the core of this inquiry —is reserved for Part IV.

CHAPTER 4

The Economic Setting of Integration in Oil

THE STRUCTURE of an industry is not an historical accident. It is shaped by the interplay of objective, conditioning forces, internal and external to it, and must be regarded as the response to those circumstances, as well as an independent factor in turn affecting them. Since the United States oil industry is characterized by integrated business organization to an outstanding degree, explanation must be sought in forces peculiar to it—reasons inherent in the physical and economic characteristics of the product, and traceable in its own history. These reasons are the subject of this chapter and the next. The two chapters therefore represent an essay in the economic interpretation of integration as it has evolved in oil, presented as background for analysis of its operation today and its desirability tomorrow.

THE PHYSICAL PECULIARITIES OF OIL

The oil industry is what it is very largely because of the peculiarities of its raw material. First and foremost, petroleum is a fluid, both as "captured" from the hidden recesses of the earth and as it passes through processing into final uses.[1] Second, it is concealed in the earth: all the advances of modern science have been incapable of eliminating the high element of gamble in its quest. Third, it is a raw material of almost infinite potentialities—some will be lost forever if care is not taken, some can be secured simply, others only with costly special equipment—from which a varying pattern of final products can be procured at a price. And finally, oil is an exhaustible resource, dissipated as used, of which the quantity of ultimate supply is not known. No one of these characteristics is unique to oil; but their combination is truly unique, and it imparts an unmatched potentially explosive vehemence to competitive forces in the industry.

Oil lies concealed beneath the earth's surface, entrapped in porous

---

1. For a lucid account of the physical and economic characteristics of oil and their consequences see P. H. Frankel, *Essentials of Petroleum* (London, Chapman and Hall, 1946), Pt. II of which is entitled "Economics of a Liquid." Also Watkins, chaps. 2, 4.

rock and sands. Its presence is difficult to ascertain and easy to miss. Caught in stratigraphic traps by geologic faults, oil may elude the probing drill by only a few feet. Such margins of error may make the difference between a producing oil well, a water well, or a dry hole. Overhasty drilling through low-permeable sands may pass through oil without discovery; and finances or hope may give out just short of a strike. There is no certainty of the geologic structure deep in the earth; there is no surety that all oil-bearing structures have been identified. The presence of oil can still be determined only by the drill and its discovery remains importantly a matter of chance.

An underground oil pool is like a great natural engine, an equilibrium of the pressures of encircling rock, dissolved or overlying gas and underlying water. A well opening releases these underground forces, which propel oil, gas, and water upward to the surface. As a fluid in the earth, oil will move over wide areas as these pressures carry it through sands or permeable rock strata to low pressure points like the bottom of a well. This fugacious character subjects it to capture by whichever owner of the land surface above can draw it most rapidly out of the underground reservoir. Under the rule of capture, and in the absence of government control, each leaseholder can thus legally rob his neighbors and be robbed in turn by wells tapping the same reservoir. As long as reservoir pressures last, the actual lifting of the oil costs him nothing. The race, therefore, goes to the fastest. The physical and, under American jurisprudence, legal "capturability" of oil puts irresistible pressure on the individual leaseholder to take oil out of the ground as fast as he or his neighbors find it.

Parenthetically—though the fact is by now familiar—capturability has not only molded the character of the oil industry more than any other single factor; it has also given rise to the most striking aspect of the industry's performance over most of its 100-year history— waste, appalling waste. For, unhappily, the more ardent the chase, the greater is the dissipation of the natural pressures relative to the amount of oil recovered. When the pressures are dissipated, the oil may lie inert in its microscopically permeable tomb, perhaps beyond all hope of recovery.

Petroleum is a mixture of hydocarbons of varying degrees of volatility and usefulness, and impurities. The danger of losing valuable lighter fractions on exposure to the air, fractions which add to the threat of explosion and fire, argues for a minimum of storage and of rehandling. So the industry has an incentive to do what the fluid character of its product makes feasible—move the oil and its products in as steady a stream as possible, closed from the air, largely unseen by human eye and untouched by human hand, from well to final user. Thus oil, once produced, puts the same pressures on its owners to move it out into processing and consumption as the rule of capture imparted to them when it was underground.

Even more important, the ingredients of crude oil have a dazzling, potential versatility. These two characteristics, its variability and versatility, open the door to a large assortment of refining techniques and refinery sizes appropriate to different kinds of crude and different complements of products. Forty years ago, the complex hydrocarbons that make up crude oil were separated and reconstituted into products simply through vaporizing the crude and drawing off different fractions as the vapors condensed at different levels in a "bubble tower." Depending on the kind of oil available, these simple distillation or skimming plants could produce some high quality products but the single largest proportion of the crude was left in the form of the least valuable component, residual fuel. The growing demand for gasoline of improved octane rating, for diesel oils and for other light oils threatened a major unbalance in the industry until the art of chemical manipulation through thermal and, two decades later, catalytic cracking, isomerization, polymerization, alkylation, and the rest revolutionized the process of refining. Now hydrocarbons are literally broken up and reformed to specification, to yield thousands of tailor-made, synthetic, organic chemicals. It is no longer necessary to produce residual oil at all. The scope of potential operating sizes and product patterns in the modern refinery is the *bête noir* of those who would seek some counterpart to the economists' conception of optimum size.

Finally, petroleum is both an exhaustible resource of unknown ultimate supply and a product dissipated in use without "scrap" recovery.[2] As the proper functioning of the economy became more and more intimately meshed with the continued flow of petroleum products, the public interest could no longer countenance the wastes of unfettered rivalry in the exploitation of a petroleum reservoir. Eventually, therefore, and inevitably, the production of oil was subjected to the control of the state in the name of conservation. But effective regulation did not come until the industry had reached its seventy-fifth birthday —by which time the combined characteristics of fluidity, uncertainty, volatility, variety, versatility, and exhaustibility, under a legal system legitimatizing capture, had gone far to fix its current aspect.

2. A minor exception is the fact that lubricating oils can be reprocessed and reused to some extent.

THE NATURE OF DEMAND

To speak of the demand [3] for petroleum products, with their great variety of types and uses, is something of a misnomer. For some uses there are practically no substitutes; this is notably true for gasoline or lubricants. In others, like boiler fuel, many large customers have equipment designed to operate readily on alternative fuels, and shift readily from one to the other. Broadly speaking, oil products used for stationary heat and power are likely to be in close competition with other fuels: while there may be advantages in the use of oil, they are not overriding in most cases. Here then demand tends to be elastic —that is, the quantity sold varies inversely and more than proportionally with changes in its relative price. The immediacy of the response varies from product to product and market to market, depending on the versatility of the oil-using equipment, and the ease and expense of converting it to alternative fuels. Thus, with industrial equipment designed to burn a variety of fuels, a shift in purchases may occur quickly with a change in price. But where specialization to a particular fuel makes substitution prohibitively costly, as in the home furnace, the machine will be operated with the fuel for which it was designed as long as it is operated at all. Hence, demand tends to be elastic within quite short periods for residual fuel oil, but only over longer periods for home-heating oils. [4]

3. Throughout this section it is the aggregate demand for petroleum products, not the demand for the product of one firm as compared with that of another, to which attention is directed. Obviously, for example, the consumer's demand for gasoline of *some* kind might be very insensitive to changes in price, while at the same time he might shift very quickly from one brand to another at the appearance of even a very slight price differential between them. An intermediate segment of demand is that for the product of an individual country alone; to the extent that international trade is possible, it introduces an element of elasticity into the demand for domestically produced crude oil and products comparable to the situation facing the individual supplying company. This possibility figures importantly in our analysis of domestic crude oil markets, below, Chaps. 9 and 10.

4. While equipment owners are thus limited by the design characteristics of their furnaces, oil competes with other fuels on new installations every year. If there is no discrimination between new and old customers, this interfuel competition will affect the entire market. In an expanding economy, this competition for a home-heating market that has grown faster than national income may hold the price as low as if total demand were elastic. Competition for new users who have effective alternatives benefits equally established users whose short-run alternatives are blocked.

In transportation and other more special uses, however, liquid fuel has overriding advantages compared with potential substitutes. The demand for gasoline, in aggregate, as well as for lubricating oils, tends therefore to be highly inelastic, so far as the possibility of substitution is concerned.[5]

Apart from the possibilities of substitution, changes in price of oil products would have little effect on their aggregate purchases because the cost of fuel and lubricants is a minor part of the operating expense of most equipment in which they are used, including the family automobile.[6]

This somewhat complex situation may be summarized in essentially qualitative terms as follows: The demand for petroleum and its products, taken as a group, is quite unresponsive to changes in price in the short run. The dominant determinant of the volume of sales is the general level of industrial activity, the standard of living of the people, the level of employment and incomes, and the weather. In the longer run, however, the price of petroleum products is an important factor in the growth of sales. It will affect the design and the installation of equipment to use liquid rather than nonliquid fuels. The downward trend in the cost of petroleum products relative to competitive sources of energy has undoubtedly contributed to the astounding growth of this industry since the turn of the century. And the fact that the United States industry is part of a world market has undoubtedly contributed something to greater elasticity of demand for our own production.

An aggregate demand that fails to respond readily to price changes exposes the industry that supplies it to wide price fluctuations. A price rise, when supplies become scarce, is not held in check by a quick contraction in the amounts buyers offer to take; a price drop, in periods of surplus production, is not quickly cushioned by expansion

5. See the testimony of Captain Pettijohn on the superior "form value" of liquid over gaseous fuels, entirely apart from their relative b.t.u. content, *In the Matter of Tidewater Oil Company*, Federal Power Commission Docket G-9932, July, 1957. Also Ayres and Scarlott, *Energy Sources*, chaps. 7–8, 10, *passim*.

6. Cassady and Jones cite an estimate that gasoline represents about 20 per cent of the "total upkeep cost of an automobile." *The Nature of Competition in Gasoline Distribution at the Retail Level* (Berkeley, University of California Press, 1951), p. 21. This means that even doubling the retail price (which would mean an even greater increase in the unit realization of the seller, *ex tax*) would result in an increase of only 20 per cent in the total cost of owning and running a car.

of purchases. So, in oil, instability is threatened, unless the short-term inflexibility of demand is countered by a flexible supply—unless, that is, suppliers respond with reasonable promptness to scarcity and rising prices with increased output, and to gluts and declining prices by curtailing production.

THE SUPPLY SIDE

Until the government intervened to regulate the production of crude oil, the characteristics of the raw material which we have stressed above determined a method of production and a method of handling and refining that prevented a flexible adjustment of supply with which to counter the inflexibility of short-run aggregate demand. For this inelasticity of supply there were two principal reasons: first, each production stage was dominated by high fixed, sunk costs relative to the variable costs that might be saved by contracting output, and, second, the law of capture insured that the major supply of crude oil offered to the market would reflect neither the level of demand nor the level of costs but the chance of discovery. Thus the early history of the industry became a procession of periodic gluts and droughts.[7]

Within two years of the first commercial discovery of oil in 1859, annual production increased from 1,200 to 5,000 barrels a day, and the price dropped from ten dollars to ten cents a barrel. Reflecting increasing demand, the average annual price of Pennsylvania crude thereafter rose from $0.49 in 1861 to $8.06 in 1864, only to drop back, following new discoveries and surplus production, to $2.41 in 1867.[8] Much later the swelling production from Kansas and Oklahoma in the 1905–15 decade was again followed by five years of shortage, drafts on stocks, mounting prices and imports, and feverishly increased exploratory activity at home and abroad. The pattern was repeated in the "grand, all-round debauch" of 1920–23,[9] following unprecedented discoveries in the Southwest and California, and, after three succeeding years of only modest success with mounting fears for the adequacy of future supplies, a new and even more dramatic series of discoveries between 1926 and 1931. The posted price

7. "The problem of oil . . . is that there is always too much or too little." Watkins, p. 40.

8. McLean and Haigh, p. 59; George W. Stocking, *The Oil Industry and the Competitive System: A Study in Waste* (Boston, Houghton Mifflin, 1925), pp. 10–11, and, for the later period, 119–127 (cited below as Stocking).

9. John Ise, *The United States Oil Policy* (New Haven, Yale University Press, 1926), p. 124.

of Midcontinent crude, which had reached a high of $2.29 a barrel in middle and late 1926, ranged between $1.28 and $1.45 in the next four years, and dropped to $0.33 in mid-1931,[10] when oil sold in East Texas for as little as ten cents a barrel.

It was *not* the dramatic fluctuations in the fortunes of exploration, in themselves, that made for such violent changes in price. It has been a rare year, in this century, that did not see a net increase in national proved reserves—that is, an excess of discoveries over production; and the historical sweep of the industry discloses a broadly corresponding upward sweep of production and consumption.[11] The source of trouble has been the compelling pressures to produce as rapidly as possible whatever was discovered—the pressures of heavy fixed costs and the law of capture.

Exploration, discovery, and development of crude oil call for large capital expenditures unrelated to short range fluctuations in the volume of output. The search for oil involves substantial outlays for not only scientific equipment and personnel to search the hidden depths of the rock strata for favorable locations but, more important, the drilling of wells, deeper every year, to test the accuracy of the scientific guess. Drilling costs increase at least geometrically with depth, and the average ratio of one producing well to eight new field wildcats [12] means of course that a large proportion of the costs are sunk before the oil is even discovered. Thereafter, as well, it is self-evident that practically all costs of production for wells on natural drives will be sunk costs. In the development of a reservoir, additional wells must be drilled, but even their costs are not simply and directly related to output. Later, and sometimes almost from the start, state regulations or self-interest may call for methods of secondary recovery with reinjection of either water or dry gas into the field. At this point, there will be a rise in variable costs, but an even greater proportional investment in durable equipment may be required for this purpose, leaving the balance of fixed and variable costs still heavily weighted on the side of the former.[13] It is only for the so-called stripper wells that

10. First-of-month figures, 1913–50, in *Petroleum Facts and Figures*, 9th ed., pp. 364–366; see also McLean and Haigh, pp. 84–94.

11. See, e.g., McLean and Haigh, p. 88.

12. This ratio has been about constant since 1937, though with some tendency to decline since 1954. *World Oil* (February 15, 1958), pp. 119–121.

13. It was estimated by the Independent Petroleum Association of America in 1948 that discovery costs of oil approximated 40 per cent, development costs 40 per cent, and lifting costs 20 per cent of total crude oil costs. Paley Report, *3, 5*. This would imply that costs unconnected with the current level

actual lifting costs may be very close to market price, and supply therefore responsive to price changes. But while most of our producing wells fall in this category—almost exactly two-thirds at the beginning of 1955—the combined output of these marginal wells is less than one-fifth of the national total, and would be much less than that if it were not for state limitations on the production of flowing walls.[14]

In transportation the fluid nature of the raw material, coupled with the incentives to develop methods for low-cost shipment of gigantic quantities delivered in a steady stream, led to the perfection of the pipeline [15] through which, in 1955, 75 per cent of all crude moving to domestic refineries was delivered.[16] Pipeline costs vary of course with capacity, character of terrain traversed, and type of product for which the line is designed. But the fact that total system investment even in flat country is estimated at $60,000 per mile for 350,000 barrels per day supplies an illustrative figure for current conditions.[17] More important, since pipeline operations are almost entirely automatic, the preponderant portion of their costs, like those of crude oil

---

of production averaged 80 per cent of total costs. According to another set of estimates, lifting costs were in both 1948 and 1953 only about 29 per cent of total industry expenditures on petroleum production. The rest of the expenditures were for exploration, development, and "production overhead." *Petroleum Facts and Figures,* 12th ed., p. 133.

14. Stripper wells accounted for almost 19 per cent of national output in 1954, but this was an abnormal year because the output of flowing wells was unusually sharply curtailed in that year in the face of weak market demand. In 1953, stripper-well production was only 16 per cent of the national total; and even in that year the nonstrippers were still forced to maintain a considerable percentage of reserve production capacity. Computations from *Petroleum Facts and Figures,* 12th ed., pp. 103, 122, 139–140. See also Joe S. Bain, *The Economics of the Pacific Coast Petroleum Industry* (Berkeley, University of California Press, 1944), *1,* 39–41.

15. Actual transport of crude oil and products utilizes a wide variety of media, from tank trucks and tank cars to barges and tankers, and in different situations the balance of advantage may shift from one type of equipment to another. In general, however, only the tanker can better the pipeline as a low cost, mass transporter, and in most areas the two media are not in competition. See H. N. Emerson, "The Place of the Tanker in the Transportation of Energy," *Proceedings,* 32d Annual Meeting, American Petroleum Institute (November 10 to 13, 1952), Section V, pp. 69–78; McLean and Haigh, pp. 183–186; see also below, p. 334, n. 25.

16. *Petroleum Facts and Figures,* 12th ed., p. 231. Since this is the percentage of deliveries using pipelines as the terminating transport medium, and since boat shipments usually originate at the pipeline terminal, even the 75 per cent underestimates the pipeline's importance.

17. McLean and Haigh, pp. 187–188.

production, are independent of output. The major costs are for the installation of the capacity which in turn governs the costs of supervision, line inspection, maintenance, and most operating labor; the only significant cost that varies with the level of throughput, and can therefore be sloughed off with a cutback in "output," is the cost of power for pumping stations.[18]

Refining, like pipeline transportation and production, is characterized by high fixed costs, compared with the costs that vary with volume of throughput (excluding the delivered cost of crude),[19] and continuous operations at near capacity levels. A refinery today is a combination of processes in which the crude oil and various derived intermediate products are successively subjected to controlled heat (and distillation) under different conditions of pressure or vacuum or in the presence of a catalyst. Some materials are treated with chemicals, some are broken down molecularly and completely reformed, and some are further processed into specialized products like coke or asphalt. Products are withdrawn continuously by reason of the varying degrees of heat at which they distill. The processes are almost completely automatic, operated from huge control panels.[20] Even labor, mostly highly skilled for control and for maintenance, can be varied hardly at all as long as the plant operates.[21]

Refinery capacity, measured in barrels of crude oil throughput, is a definite quantity only with respect to the type of crude and the pat-

18. Cookenboo, *Crude Oil Pipe Lines*, p. 30. According to Emerson, "Place of the Tanker," p. 74, variable or direct costs run in the range of 15 to 20 per cent of total pipeline costs.

19. McLean and Haigh's estimate "for the conventional refineries ranging in size from 10,000 to 200,000 barrels per day and operating at 100 per cent capacity" shows fixed costs at 73 per cent of total processing costs. This includes among fixed costs all costs of operating and supervisory labor (10 per cent of total costs), on the assumption that the full operating force would be retained at less than capacity operations. Fixed costs may therefore be slightly exaggerated. (See M. and H.'s pp. 562–563, and esp. n. 9.)

20. See "The Computer Age: 1. Running Plants by Mathematics," *Business Week* (April 7, 1956), pp. 53 ff.

21. Reflecting the automatic character of refinery operations, as well as the high ratio of fixed to variable costs is the fact that, according to preliminary figures of the 1954 Census of Manufactures, the average value added per worker in all manufacturing was $7,200; the corresponding figure in petroleum refineries ("and coal products") was $11,800, an output exceeded only by chemicals among the twenty groups into which all manufacturing industries are classified. *Statistical Abstract of the United States, 1956*. We have already noted the extraordinarily high sales and assets per worker among the oil companies in the top 500 industrial corporations, above, p. 16.

tern of end products to which the capacities of the facilities in question have been balanced. There is much potential flexibility in the pattern of products that a modern refinery can produce; theoretically it could, for example, convert all crude oil to gasoline. This versatility provides a greater flexibility of supply of individual products than would otherwise be the case, and this in turn promotes a closer interrelation of product prices than was possible in earlier years.

However the potential flexibility of a modern refinery does not eliminate the potentially unstabilizing influence of its heavy fixed costs. For one thing, the flexibility is of the relative proportions of its product yields, not of its aggregate output. Second, the technical ability to alter product proportions is subject to grave economic limits. To upgrade the output—that is, to increase the yield or quality of gasoline appreciably above what the refinery complex was designed for—means not only a rerunning of the lower graded products to be upgraded (for example, a running of distillates through the cat cracker), but also a larger capacity for such further processes and an underutilization of other capacities already available (for example, thermal cracking). Thus, although a modern refiner may increase the yield of gasoline at one time and of home-heating oils at another, he will seldom rely on this potential flexibility alone to meet the seasonal surges in demand for these respective products. The added costs of shifting refinery output beyond normal patterns (through handling costs, processing costs, and idle capacity costs) rapidly overtake and pass the added costs of providing for additional product storage within the established design pattern of product mix.

Similar economic characteristics are found, somewhat less accented, in distribution; but there is no need to follow this matter further at this point. Here one can only repeat that the heavy capital investment at each stage of the industry, and more particularly the high proportion of operating costs that does not vary with output, stem from the physical characteristics of crude oil and the kinds of equipment and processing perfected to handle a chemically versatile fluid with minimum waste.

The consequence of a preponderance of fixed costs in all stages of the industry is a compelling emphasis on volume and continuity of operations. It is variable costs that put a floor under price: generally speaking, it does not pay to produce if revenues will not cover even current bills for labor, fuel, and materials—bills which can be avoided by a simple curtailment of operations. When, however, most of the costs are sunk, cannot be sloughed off, and can be recovered in whole or part only from current revenues, price can fall far before the producer finds he would be better off shutting down.[22]

These economic characteristics, implicit in a production process with a preponderance of fixed costs, are not unique to petroleum—they are much the same for the steel industry, for example, except that steel has no parallel to the minimal operating costs of an oil well on natural drive. Wherever heavy fixed costs and relative price inelasticity of demand obtain, they make competitive adjustment costly, and expose the industry to wide fluctuations of fortune. But, especially in concentrated markets, these unstabilizing forces have not usually been beyond the power of the industry itself to stay. Indeed, crude oil affords opportunities to avoid price instability by adjusting supply to changes in demand and price that ordinary manufacture cannot match. For the manufacture of reproducible goods, heavy fixed costs tend to make supply inelastic because capacity left idle today is lost beyond recall and contributes little or nothing to one's ability to produce tomorrow. Oil in the ground, in contrast, is like a stock—if less is used today, there will be that much more on hand tomorrow. Thus in the former case, it is foolish not to produce where the added

22. Since 70 to 75 per cent of total costs to the refiner are made up of the delivered cost of crude oil (a measure of out-of-pocket expense only for the refiner who must purchase net crude supplies) it may be thought that the economic significance of a high proportion of fixed costs in oil processing (and in product distribution) has been exaggerated. The supply of refined products, it would therefore appear, ought to be not at all inelastic but very responsive to price, at least in the absence of vertical integration, since any appreciable decline in their realizations would soon make it unprofitable for refiners to continue buying the crude. This might indeed be the case were it not for the overriding impact of the short-run urge to produce the crude oil irrespective of price, in the absence of production controls. Any tendency for refineries to shut down or marketers to curtail their purchases because of declining product prices could not go far without inducing declines in the price of crude sufficient to make its refining and distribution profitable. So, given an inelastic supply of its major input, the aggregate supply of refined products becomes highly inelastic as well. For a similar phenomenon influencing the prices of various processed agricultural products, see D. Gale Johnson, "The Nature of the Supply Function for Agricultural Products," *American Economic Review,* 40 (1950), 539. And since, among the *processing* costs alone at the refinery level fixed costs predominate, this means that the supply of refinery services might likewise be highly inelastic in the short run; thus refinery margins too would reflect in sharp fluctuations the inertia in transmitting a price change from finished product to raw material.

costs of added output are covered or more than covered by the price even though total costs are not. With oil, even a price higher than added (that is, variable) costs of output may provide inadequate incentive to produce today if there is reason to believe that price tomorrow will be so much higher that it compensates for the cost and the risk of waiting.[23]

Thus where oil reservoirs or fields are operated as a unit, under concession or voluntary agreement, excess capacity does not necessarily generate irresistible pressures to produce crude oil as long as price exceeds out-of-pocket costs. The rate and time pattern of recovery may readily be planned so as to maximize the net value of recovery over time: short-run supply is thus rendered potentially far more elastic than the relationship of variable to sunk costs alone would seem to permit.[24]

What has deprived oil producers of this stabilizing alternative has been the inevitably erratic fluctuations in annual additions to capacity; and what has exploded newly discovered oil out of the ground in the absence of effective public regulation has of course been its fugacious nature in combination with the law of capture.

In yet another respect oil is in some measure distinctive. Out of it and out of the same productive facilities there issue a great diversity of products. In consequence, a large part of not only the fixed but also the operating costs are joint costs, in the sense that they cannot be allocated between this product or that except by rules of thumb that

23. The consequence of this fact is also to make a higher proportion of production expenses variable than would appear at first glance. Depreciation charges constitute a significant proportion of book expenses at the wellhead. (E.g., no less than $15,000,000 of the $64,200,000 of total expenses of the Tidewater Oil Company associated with production and exploration in 1955 represented provision for depreciation and depletion, and most of it the former. Testimony of Samuel Joseph, Exhibit No. 58-A, Schedule G, *In the Matter of Tidewater Oil Company,* Federal Power Commission Docket No. G-9932, 1957.) In manufacturing, depreciation is generally recovered per unit of time: economic life is limited by obsolescence, not by production. But oil-producing companies frequently compute depreciation charges like book depletion, on a unit-of-recovery method—that is, capitalized development costs are written off over the estimated amount of the oil in reserve and charged in proportion to actual output. See, e.g., Presley Ford, Jr., "Drilling and Development Costs of Oil and Gas Wells—Accounting and Tax Problems," *NACA* Bulletin (August, 1956), p. 1500. In this case, such charges are clearly variable; if production is curtailed, the life of the wells is extended and the financial interests of the owner in recovery are substantially unaffected.

24. The implications of these considerations for a national public policy toward oil are developed below, Chap. 10.

are in varying degrees arbitrary.[25] (Obviously to the extent—and it is substantial—that particular products require particular investments and particular treatment, their individual costs can be traced objectively.) [26] Costs therefore provide only an uncertain basis for the pricing of individual products, and an unreliable floor under competitive price reductions. As in the familiar case of railroads, which can carry diamonds and coal, the pricing of joint products in both unregulated and regulated markets is inevitably geared to what the respective traffics will bear. But this depends largely on the intensity of competition for each traffic—the competition not only of rival fuels but of rival oil companies. The joint character of much of the costs of petroleum products thus presents on the one hand a threat, on the other an opportunity. The threat is what unrestricted competition can do to industry profits, when the cost "floor" under competitive pricecutting is nebulous and elastic. The opportunity is one of enhancing profits by selective price discrimination that extracts from the market for each product the largest feasible contribution to joint costs, an opportunity that is maximized to the extent that competition is minimized.

In the absence of regulation, public or private, the vagaries of exploratory success, the law of capture, and the heavy fixed and joint costs at the several stages of production all make the supply of oil and its products unresponsive to price in the short run. A fluctuating and inelastic supply, in the face of consumer demand unaffected by price,

25. See Thomas M. Kavanagh, Attorney General, State of Michigan, *A Report to the Governor on the Gasoline Price Investigation,* 1955–56, prepared by Stanton S. Faville (processed, State of Michigan, 1956), pp. 133–135 (cited below as Attorney General, State of Michigan). This inquiry asked the companies selling in Michigan to submit their figures for the "cost of producing a gallon of gasoline": "in no instance was it stated that the cost of refining a gallon of gasoline was or could be accurately computed. In each instance, where any attempt to compute cost was made, arbitrary assumptions were included in the calculation. Some of the companies submitted no figures . . . stating that manufacturing cost could be obtained only by making unrealistic allocations among the various products" (p. 134).

26. The foregoing discussion does not purport adequately to assess the possibilities of joint cost allocations in the oil industry. For particular purposes and in particular circumstances economically meaningful allocations can be and are made. For example, the general practice of assaying the costs of the middle distillates produced in refining in terms of their value as substitutes for crude oil as sources of gasoline—that is, in terms of their opportunity cost— makes excellent economic sense. For a description of this method see the testimony of Robert Wilson before the TNEC, "Investigation of Concentration of Economic Power," *Hearings,* 15 (1939), 8638–8639, 8646–8647.

constitutes a truly explosive economic force, which, were it not for the long-run surge of petroleum consumption and the steadying hand of the conservation authority on the volume of oil drawn from the earth, could shake the industry to its foundations, and has done so from time to time in the past.

CHAPTER 5

The Historical Setting of Integration in Oil

THE INTEGRATED STRUCTURE of the leading oil companies today cannot be understood except in terms of its own past. As a "way
of life" adopted by the men who shaped the industry, it has a vitality,
persuasiveness and impact of its own, and has played an independent
role in shaping the history and development of the industry.

INTEGRATION AS A TOOL OF MONOPOLY [1]

It is not important, in explaining oil company integration today,
to decide whether John D. Rockefeller and his colleagues are best
regarded as robber barons or industrial statesmen, predatory monopolists or efficient competitors. The significant facts are that they consistently sought and came very close to achieving a complete monopoly over the American petroleum industry, and that vertical integration played a critical role in that achievement.

The first step began in 1870 with the merging of refineries; by the
early 1880's the Standard Oil group of companies controlled perhaps 80 to 90 per cent of national refinery capacity. The profusion
of crude oil producers after the Drake discovery in 1859 had been
echoed in refining, then a very simple distillation process requiring only a small investment. Capacity multiplied as plants were set
up to take advantage of cheap oil: in distinct contrast with more recent times, refinery capacity was possibly twice or three times the
volume of crude production. The result was a sharp compression of
refinery margins. Although production of crude oil continued to expand between 1866 and 1872, demand kept up with it; therefore,
while the price fluctuated widely over short periods, it fluctuated
around a roughly unchanging average. At the same time the price of

1. This period is well and succinctly treated in McLean and Haigh, chap. 3,
on which the following paragraphs draw heavily. Both are indebted to Allan
Nevins, *John D. Rockefeller*, New York, Scribner's, 1940; and almost all accounts of the history and policies of the Standard Oil Company draw heavily
on the Bureau of Corporations, *Report of the Commissioner of Corporations
on the Petroleum Industry*, 2 vols., Washington, D.C., 1907.

refined products declined by almost one-third—a reflection in part of declining costs of operation, but in part of the increasingly violent competition at that level.[2] The vulnerability of refining investment was intensified by the struggles of the major East-West railroads (the Pennsylvania, the New York Central, and the Erie) for dominance in the oil traffic. They bought up crude-oil-gathering pipeline systems (there were as yet no trunk pipelines) and made liberal use of secret rebates and drawbacks to favor large shippers. Rockefeller's Cleveland refineries were dubious pawns in these titanic struggles. Around 1870 he conceived and initiated his plan to join refiners in a horizontal combination, in which less efficient plants would be closed, their combined power in dealing with the railroads increased, and competition among them diminished. As Stocking has described the episode: "An economic situation had arisen wherein competition threatened loss, and centralized control meant economies and increased profit. Such a situation awaits only the appearance of shrewd business acumen and judgment until monopoly will develop." [3]

Escape from the rigors of competition could not be found at the producing end of the business. Entry was too easy, producers too numerous, conflicts of interest between them too great, the lure of a lucky strike too irresistible for the affected parties to organize themselves and effect the necessary control over supplies. Though entry into refining was likewise relatively easy, at least a successful refiner had to have capital, organization, and technical and managerial skills.[4] But ease of access was the Achilles' heel of a combination of refineries as well, and it became necessary at an early stage to buttress its market position. This was the reason for the second step, vertical integration.

The key was transportation control. Here was a segment of the industry into which entry was necessarily limited; control over the most efficient means of transport for a bulky commodity like oil meant the ability, within limits, to dictate the price of crude oil at the wellhead and to limit the opportunities for entry and independent survival at the refining end. But a nonintegrated monopoly of transportation alone was not possible. This was so not only because there were

2. See Nevins, *Rockefeller, 1,* 452; Stocking, p. 13.

3. For another fair appraisal see Ise, *United States Oil Policy,* pp. 48–50, 239–241.

4. See the lucid discussion by Frankel of why the movement to market control began in refining rather than production, and why it could not stop there (*Essentials of Petroleum,* pp. 70–77).

several major railroads serving various producing fields and refinery centers: competing with one another for the business, themselves the victims of heavy fixed costs, they were susceptible of being played off, one against the other, by powerful groups of refiners. More important, combinations of refiners and/or producers would shortly be able to construct their own pipelines, and so circumvent anyone who tried to arrogate to himself merely through extortionate transportation charges whatever monopoly profits the ultimate demand would permit. It was only a vertical combination of powerful refining and transporting interests that could present a unified front against widespread small-scale entry and the competition it threatened; only an integrated refiner-transporter or producer-transporter could be free of the threat of exploitation by powerful railroad-pipeline interests.

In part, the necessary "control" over transportation was achieved by the application of bargaining power rather than by ownership. Indeed, it was a major purpose of the original organization of refiners to improve the combination's ability to put pressure on the railroads; the power was exerted to secure not only rebates on freight charges but kickbacks on the fares charged shippers not associated with the Standard group.

In the case of pipelines, ownership was necessary both to achieve the advantages of the lower costs they made possible, and to assure their fullest utilization as a bulwark of monopoly. It was early apparent that the ownership of crude-oil-gathering lines was essential to any railroad that hoped to participate in hauling the oil; and that the only way a combination of refiners or of producers could protect themselves against an entrenched railroad-pipeline system was to acquire its own gathering lines and join with competing railroad interests.[5]

Standard's moves in this direction followed those of competitors. The Company's position in refining was seriously threatened when the Pennsylvania Railroad, through its affiliate the Empire Transportation Company, sought to establish a formidable rival system by buying up and constructing its own crude-gathering lines and refineries. It was apparently in response to this threat that Standard commenced a program of competitive purchases of crude-gathering systems and the construction of new lines as new fields were discovered. The threat of Pennsylvania and Empire to go into refining brought a characteristically massive reaction. Rockefeller had won or forced an al-

5. See Arthur M. Johnson, *The Development of American Petroleum Pipelines* (Ithaca, Cornell University Press, 1956), pp. 12–48.

liance with the Erie Railroad and the New York Central; these lines were apprehensive in any event of the advantages the Empire-Pennsylvania alliance threatened to obtain over them in competition for the oil-carrying business. Abetted by these two systems and by the Baltimore and Ohio, he stopped shipments over the Pennsylvania, cut prices in all areas served by that railroad and cornered as much crude as he could. In this way he made the fullest use of his horizontal and vertical integration—the geographic spread of his markets, his control over pipelines and refining. In the fall of 1877 the Pennsylvania capitulated, dissolved the Empire Transportation Company, and sold its refineries, pipelines, oil terminals, and barges to Standard. With this victory a virtual monopoly of crude-gathering lines made easy the absorption of refineries that had formerly bucked the combination; and Standard was now in a position to dictate to the railroads.[6]

Standard's entry into the long-distance pipeline business, similarly, was in response to an earlier venture of this kind by a competitor. It was not Standard but independents who pioneered in transforming pipelines from feeders of the railroads to competitors of them. Just as, in the early 1870's, the Pennsylvania producers had made several efforts to escape the monopolistic exactions of the Pennsylvania Railroad by constructing their own pipelines to competing railroad terminals,[7] so, around 1875, promoters began to talk of building a 300-mile trunk line all the way to the sea, to circumvent the growing power of Standard in combination with the railroads. It was the flood of oil issuing from the newly discovered Bradford Field that finally brought action. Standard's facilities proved inadequate to the task of handling it all and, at the close of 1877, the company imposed heavy discounts on oil offered for immediate shipment from that field. Producers were angered by what they considered a monopolistic imposition, and, with the financial assistance of the Philadelphia and Reading Railroad, they set out within the year to build the first crude trunk pipeline from the producing centers over the mountains to independent refiners on the seaboard. Because of the interest of the Philadelphia and Reading in carrying the oil over its own rails, it was not until ten years later that the Tidewater pipeline actually reached the Eastern seaboard;

6. McLean and Haigh, pp. 63–64; A. M. Johnson, pp. 58–69. For an account of Standard's varied tactics in obtaining and cementing its virtual pipeline monopoly, based in turn on the *Report* of the Bureau of Corporations (above n. 1), see also Stocking, pp. 24–25.

7. A. M. Johnson, pp. 17, 20–23, 34–48.

but in May 1879 it began successfully to pump oil through a line from Coryville to the railroad's terminal at Williamsport, a distance of 108 miles.

The combined pipeline-rail movement to New York involved a lower cost than Standard and its railroad allies could hope to emulate. The railroads initiated a rate war against Tidewater and the Philadelphia and Reading, but it was soon clear they could not compete, and it was up to Standard to meet the threat on its own behalf and on the interlopers' own ground. Having failed to buy either the pipeline or its total product, the company set about with typical skill, thoroughness- and aggressiveness to construct and acquire a great trunk pipeline system of its own. By 1881 it had trunk lines carrying crude oil from the Bradford Field to Cleveland, Buffalo, Philadelphia, and New York. It also set out to buy up independent refiners in the East who might use the Tidewater oil. By 1880, the last of the important New York independents had been purchased; in 1881 Standard actually acquired a financial interest in Tidewater; and in 1883 the two companies came to terms, agreeing to a division of the pipeline transportation and refining businesses and fixing uniform rates for carrying oil.[8] Standard's vertical integration had not forestalled the entry of a rival that was also a vertically integrated combination of producing, transporting, and refining interests; but competitive aggregations of such size would necessarily be few, and if they could not be completely licked, they could be joined.

Standard entered very heavily also into the production of crude oil and the marketing of refined products. Its integration into production, however, was never strategically critical, like the monopolization of refining and transport. It was only after around 1885 that the company mounted a real program of acquiring producing properties; its output reached a peak of only about one-third the national total in 1895; and it declined thereafter, with the rise of the great Midcontinent fields, to approximately 14 per cent in 1911. Why was this so? Because, as we have already suggested, centralized control over production would have been extremely difficult to obtain and maintain, and, by the same token and much more important, it was unnecessary to the Company that dominated transportation and refining. Nonintegrated producers could be counted on to assume the hazards of wildcatting, and competition between them would hold down the price

8. See A. M. Johnson, pp. 54–58, 70–76, 93–108, 121–122; McLean and Haigh, pp. 64–65; Tarbell, *History of the Standard Oil Company, 2,* 3–30.

of the raw material, leaving to the monopsonistic transporter-purchaser the cream of the industry profits.[9] Significantly, one of the Company's first major series of purchases of production properties was to buy into—and in this way to forestall the threatened competition of—a group of Pennsylvania producers who were planning an ambitious program of constructing pipelines and entering into alliances with independent refiners and marketers in order to break the Standard monopoly.[10]

The very extensive development of kerosene marketing by the Standard Oil companies was certainly motivated, in part, by the purpose of more effectively blanketing and dominating the market. But it is really difficult to explain this forward integration as involving anything more specific than exploitation of a profitable opportunity. Left to existing agencies, the marketing of petroleum products had been slow to develop methods and facilities suited to their peculiar character. It remained inefficient, and subject to waves of violent price competition. The development (probably more rapidly and thoroughly than would otherwise have occurred) of efficient bulk plants to receive the product from tank cars, of the tank wagon as a substitute for obsolete local cooperage and barrel warehousing and handling, and of greater uniformity of product quality were advantageous by-products of Standard's undeniably ruthless entry into this

9. For a description of some of Standard's procedures in using its monopsonistic position to squeeze the nonintegrated producers see Ise, *United States Oil Policy*, pp. 241–243. Ise makes perfectly clear, however, that it was the lack of organization among producers and the law of capture, rather than the Standard company, that were their prime foes. *Ibid.*, pp. 253–255. See also *ibid.*, p. 239, and chap. 18 *passim;* Stocking, p. 20.

10. See McLean and Haigh, pp. 68–70. The foregoing analysis of Standard's backward integration into production is necessarily truncated and excessively simplified. The Company was probably motivated to make its first important purchases, of oil lands in the newly discovered Lima-Indiana Fields in 1886, by a simple desire to assure its expanding refinery-marketing investments adequate supplies in the future. Lima oil itself had a high sulphur content that gravely reduced its value. But the sweet Pennsylvania crudes were thought to have reached their maximum output. The prospects of a future dependent on less perfect raw materials may well have buttressed the company's determination to lick the problem of devising a process to refine these sour crudes. And perhaps Standard executives had so often wrested profitable stability from loss-ridden chaos in their own inimitable style that, as professional stabilizers, they might have come to regard the violent fluctuations in crude as not beyond their powers to allay at a profit. See *ibid.*, pp. 67–68; and Ralph W. and Muriel E. Hidy, *Pioneering in Big Business, 1882–1911* (New York, Harper and Bros., 1955), pp. 155–188.

field toward the end of the 1870's. By 1904, Standard's distribution extended into most states and, the Bureau of Corporations estimated, 88.7 per cent of all petroleum dealers bought from the group and its affiliates.

INTEGRATION AS A MEANS OF
CIRCUMVENTING MONOPOLY

Vertical integration evolved in the oil industry as an instrument of competition, as well as of monopolization, of defense as well as offense. The Standard group itself went into pipeline haulage in response to competitive threats, first by the Pennsylvania Railroad, later by the Tidewater venture. Standard had to obtain for itself the lower costs of pipeline carriage not just to support its monopoly but to compete effectively, not just to place independent producers and refiners at its mercy but to prevent its own exploitation—by the railroads, for example. So, correspondingly, the efforts of the Pennsylvania producers to construct first their own gathering lines and later their own trunk lines represented attempts to compete with entrenched monopolists. Integration became a part of the way of life of the oil industry, historically, in large measure as an escape from and protection against Standard Oil.

The fact that the construction of pipelines reduced the costs of transporting crude oil must not be permitted to obscure the essentially *strategic* character of these decisions to integrate. It was the monopoly and integration of Standard (and, earlier, of the railroads) that denied to independent producers and refiners the benefits of pipeline transportation, and thus forced them to build the lines themselves. So monopoly and integration bred countervailing integration, entirely apart from any possible efficiencies of combined operations.

The first outstanding example of this phenomenon was the case of the Tidewater Pipe Line Company. Although the producers who set it up were blaming Standard and the railroads for their depressed prices, certainly it was the flush, competitive production of the Bradford Field that was primarily responsible; so also their forward integration was at least as much an attempt to escape or moderate the inherent instability of a competitive petroleum industry, victim of the law of capture, as to get around John D. Rockefeller. However, Standard's own monopoly position, and its use of integration to reinforce it, carried an historical weight of its own. One of Standard's responses to the Tidewater menace, we have already seen, was to buy up the Eastern refiners who were its customers. In response Tidewater did the only thing it could do: it built refineries of its own. And to make the defensive forward integration complete, it undertook a program of marketing refined products in Europe.[11]

The organization of the Pure Oil Company in 1895 by a group of producers and refiners represented the culmination of a series of efforts, similarly motivated, by Pennsylvania producers and East Coast refiners to obtain independent, unobstructed access to markets and raw materials, respectively. The precarious nature of the undertaking in the face of Standard's ruthless attack is illustrated by the charter provision that experience had shown to be essential—the setting up of five trustees under bond to vote one-half of the stock only for men and measures that would preserve the company's independence. Pure, which became Standard's first determinedly independent and continuingly successful antagonist, owned and constructed gathering and trunk pipelines (including a long-distance products line, apparently the first of its kind), owned or chartered tankers, and marketed extensively both in the United States and abroad.[12] Vertical integration was the essential key to its successful challenge—entirely apart from any superior efficiency of integrated operations.

Even before the dissolution of the Standard of New Jersey empire in 1911, the shift of the center of oil production from Pennsylvania to Texas, the Midcontinent Field, and California opened opportunities for newly organized firms to challenge its domination. It was the gushing Spindletop wells in Texas that gave both Gulf and the Texas Company their real start, in 1901 and 1902 respectively. Both companies were lucky enough to move to Sour Lake before Spindletop began its dramatic collapse in 1903 and both became important producers in the Glenn Pool of Oklahoma in 1906, where they obtained a crude that made superior kerosene and gasoline. The significant point is that outside of California—where early discoveries of crude in comparatively close proximity to markets reduced the dominance of the Standard company at a relatively early date [13] and made forward integration into pipeline transportation, refining, and marketing less urgent defensively (so far as competing with Standard was concerned)

11. Tarbell, *History of the Standard Oil Company*, 2, 13–15; A. M. Johnson, p. 75.

12. McLean and Haigh, pp. 69–70; Allan Nevins, *Study in Power* (New York, Scribner's, 1953), 2, 334–337; A. M. Johnson, pp. 173–175, 179–183.

13. It is notable that of the eleven important independents organized prior to 1911, as listed by McLean and Haigh (p. 71), five were in California.

—the newcomers found it necessary to integrate forward in order to prosper, if not to survive, in an industry where Standard Oil dominated their access to market.[14] As a result, Standard's preponderant position in refining was slowly whittled away—from 90 per cent of the national output in 1899 to 85 per cent in 1906 and 80 per cent in 1911.[15]

INTEGRATION AS A WAY OF BUSINESS LIFE BEFORE 1911

The Tidewater Pipe Line Company first acquired refineries in order to protect against the aggressions of Standard the markets for the crude oil it carried. It was not long, however, before the rapid growth in demand for products on the East Coast had outstripped the capacity of the Pennsylvania fields. So in 1905 the Company began to acquire producing leases in Oklahoma, and to extend its pipelines westward: "The desire to control the major portion of the crude supply of the eastern refinery led to a rapid development of the producing end of the business in the Mid-Continent." [16] Integration had evidently become a basic commitment of company policy.[17]

Out on the West Coast the founders of Union Oil built the first trunk line to tidewater to avoid the exactions of the Southern Pacific Railroad.[18] But the thorough integration of this company, well before Standard did anything but market in the area, could hardly be explained in terms of circumventing monopoly. The only general "explanation" that emerges from the official company history is the conviction of Lyman Stewart that the company would be stronger and

14. This is not to say that forward integration was in all these cases forced upon the producers by the strategic position of Standard, although this was to some extent the case. Standard was not so interested or in so dominant a position in Texas as in Pennsylvania and the Indiana oil fields (on the reasons for this see Hidy and Hidy, *Pioneering in Big Business,* p. 394); the forward integration of the two great Texas producing companies cannot therefore be explained simply as efforts to bypass the Standard monopoly. See below, pp. 85–86.

15. Arthur R. Burns, *The Decline of Competition* (New York, McGraw-Hill, 1936), p. 103.

16. B. F. Smith, "Tide Water Associated . . . an American Saga," reprinted by the Company from *World Petroleum* (December, 1947), p. 2.

17. Standard's efforts to obtain control of Midcontinent crude oil (see below, p. 85) may well have helped to convince Tidewater of the advisability of obtaining production of its own.

18. Frank J. Taylor and Earl M. Welty, *Black Bonanza* (New York, McGraw-Hill, 1950), p. 44.

more profitable if it integrated; he fought for years with Thomas R. Bard before he was able to put this conviction into practice. The only specific explanation was the necessity of refining superior products from the unfamiliar California crude oil:

> Stewart wanted to expand not only in the field by buying and leasing new oil lands while they were cheap but by building new markets, pipelines, tankers, expanding refinery capacity, improving products. Bard's idea was that Union should remain a producing oil company, drilling wells, pumping petroleum, selling to outlets at wholesale and letting them have the headaches of refining and marketing.
>
> Stewart considered the refinery the key to the oil business. He argued that only by refining an illuminant as good as that produced from Pennsylvania crude could the Western oil producers compete on equal terms with their Eastern rivals.[19]

W. L. Mellon brought to the Gulf Corporation a conviction—born in large measure of his own experience as a producer in the Pennsylvania fields—that only by complete integration could the company avoid being, in his words,

> in effect, a part of the Standard Oil Company's production department. Whatever price was posted by the Standard Oil Company at the well-head was the price the producer got for his crude. . . .
>
> In saying this I do not mean to imply that the company took unfair advantage of the producers whose oil it bought. . . . Nevertheless, these producers were at the mercy of this company, which had a complete pipeline system.[20]

But he was influenced also by the general conviction of his uncle, Andrew W. Mellon, like that of Lyman Stewart, "that the real way to make a business out of petroleum was to develop it from end to end; to get the raw material out of the ground, refine it, and distribute it." [21]

And, indeed, the direct predecessor of Gulf, the Guffey Petroleum Company, apparently realized it would be necessary to build pipelines and a refinery simply to create a market for the Spindletop crude

19. *Ibid.,* pp. 66, 94.
20. Quoted by McLean and Haigh, p. 77; this account of the integration of Gulf draws heavily on pp. 71–80 of that work.
21. *Ibid.,* p. 74.

oil. As in the case of Union Oil, the peculiar characteristics of the local crude made the forward integration especially urgent: the producer went into refining in order to develop the techniques necessary to convert it into salable products. Neither at the outset nor when the Mellons joined the venture did the presence of Standard seem to have dictated the recourse to integration. Instead, as is suggested in Chapter 3, vertical integration was apparently essential in the early stages of the industry's development to create an industry where none had existed before: "Guffey had Texas oil but Texas had no oil industry." [22]

Once the commitment was adopted, it worked in either direction, just as in the case of Tidewater. By 1906 the Spindletop Field was petering out, and the Company began an intensive campaign of extending its crude production and its gathering and trunk lines in order to assure itself of supplies for its 12,000 b/d Port Arthur refinery.[23] In this program, competition with Standard's monopolizing tactics was an important factor: that company had already moved full-scale into the Midcontinent area, to take over to the greatest extent possible the purchase, storage, and transportation of the area's burgeoning production, and thus to limit the supply of oil to independent refiners.[24] The threat of the Standard monopoly was still a real one. In any event, however, it took only five years for the experience of Gulf to demonstrate that a commitment to integration, once undertaken, will impel a company in either direction, forward or backward, depending on which end of the shoe pinches.

The growth and integration of the Texas Company, the other giant

22. Craig Thompson, *Since Spindletop* (apparently published by the Gulf Oil Corporation, Pittsburgh, 1951), p. 10; see also pp. 15–17.

23. Compare the following two explanations of two crucial integration steps, separated by a very few years: (1) "By devoting its energies to manufacturing and sales, the refining company could, with good management, go far toward assuring the producing company of a fair price and a steady market—very desirable considerations under circumstances that often bounced the price of crude from 10 cents per barrel to half a dollar and back again in a few weeks' span. In 1902, Texas oil even fell to the all-time low of 5 cents a barrel!" (2) "when Spindletop slumped . . . the position was reversed. . . . To keep vessels, refinery and other facilities busy, the discovery of new oil became an immediate necessity." *Ibid.*, pp. 15, 21.

24. Although Standard's subsidiary, Prairie Oil and Gas, itself produced less than 6 per cent of the total Kansas and Oklahoma output in the 1900–11 period, it made a mighty effort to buy, store, and carry all it could "in order to keep producers satisfied and thus to discourage the rise of competition" (Hidy and Hidy, *Pioneering in Big Business*, p. 398), and kept up so well with the phenomenally rising output that in 1911 it was still buying about three-fifths of the total (*ibid.*, pp. 394–403).

that sprang from Spindletop, is even more difficult to explain in simple terms. Its founders were among the first to see that the prolific fields of the Southwest opened up vast potentialities for profitable operation beyond the oppressive reach of Standard. But J. S. Cullinan originally went into Texas to buy the cheap oil there and sell it at a profit to Standard and other Northern refiners.[25] He and his associates apparently invested heavily in production simply because of the huge profits that awaited the quick and the lucky, and the Texas Company proved itself both. However, there is some evidence that the drying up of its Spindletop source of supply for crude oil marketing operations was one important force impelling it into the quest at which it proved so successful. Like Gulf, it too built a pipeline from Oklahoma, in 1907, to supply the refinery and asphalt plant it first built at Port Arthur in 1902–03.

Though the company made its fortunes in production, it was heavily market-oriented almost from the start, first as a seller of crude oil itself, then as an alert and aggressive seller of the products issuing from its refinery. By 1908 it was selling in all but five western states; in 1910 it had 229 distributive outlets flying its colors. Its sales of gasoline exceeded its ability to refine as early as 1915. Undoubtedly one important consideration in these various moves was to find the way of best vying with Standard. The company early developed its own brands of illuminating and stove oils. Its early emphasis on gasoline was in part attributable to Standard's pre-emption of kerosene distribution. And its widespread marketing gave it maximum protection against Standard's policies of destructive local price-cutting.[26] But neither the existence of Standard nor the quest for efficiency or stability, nor any simple motivating force seems to explain the company's thorough integration. All one can say is that it aggressively searched for profits wherever they might be found.

THE EXTENSION OF INTEGRATION AND THE DECLINE OF MONOPOLY AFTER 1911

By 1911, integration had become a part of the oil industry's way of life, at least so far as the large, successful companies were concerned.

25. Marquis James, *The Texaco Story* (published by the Texas Company, 1953), pp. 6–7, 15.

26. See *ibid.*, pp. 15–17, 21–31, 42, 48; also McLean and Haigh, pp. 383–384.

At that point, the Standard Oil Company of New Jersey, certainly the most successful practitioner of the art, was required by antitrust decree to divest itself of the stock of thirty-three constituent companies. The dissolution left the parts of the Standard Oil empire, except for Standard Oil of California, with major gaps in their vertical integration. Ohio Oil and Prairie Oil and Gas were producers and pipeline operators; Continental and Standard of Kentucky were purely marketing companies and Standard of New York almost exclusively so; Standard of New Jersey and the Atlantic Refining Company found themselves left as refiners, primarily, though both engaged to some extent in domestic marketing. Standard of Ohio and Standard of Indiana were refiner-marketers;[27] the latter company was prevented by its charter from engaging in crude production.

Even more important than the dissolution of the Standard Oil trust in altering the aspect of the industry after 1911 was the violent transformation and expansion in demand, with skyrocketing sales of automobiles, and the corresponding vast increase in supply, marked by alternating periods of threatening shortage and dramatic new discoveries. To the very end the old Standard Oil Company was primarily a producer and distributor of kerosene. Burton's experiments in cracking at the Whiting refinery had been frowned upon by top management. Symptomatically, it was around 1911 that his pressure still, the earliest commercial application of thermal cracking, was finally perfected, giving the new Indiana company a boost in the exploitation of the rapidly expanding market for gasoline.[28] Companies which, like Texas, were unwilling to pay royalties on the Burton process had to develop their own cracking techniques; the declining demand for kerosene and the accelerating consumption of gasoline made it imperative that oil companies be able to convert a profitable proportion of their crude into the latter. Thus technological bars to the production of a greater yield of motor fuel were raised at the same time that traditional market controls and proprietary relationships were broken and managements were freed to search out a new competitive status in the

27. For a list of the constituent and successor companies and their spheres of operation, see George S. Gibb and Evelyn H. Knowlton, *The Resurgent Years, 1911–1927* (New York, Harper and Bros., 1956), pp. 8–9.

28. By 1918 the consumption of motor fuel was already twice that of kerosene. During the next ten years the former rose another 246 per cent, the latter only 5 per cent, while annual consumption of crude oil and products combined rose by 137.5 per cent. *Petroleum Facts and Figures,* 9th ed., pp. 2–3.

rapidly expanding markets of the motor age. Integration in various degrees and directions—geographic as well as vertical, forward as well as backward—was one of the techniques of competitive thrust, parry, and counterthrust.

These rapid changes after 1911 conspired to create conflicts of interest between the old Standard subsidiaries. The dissolution itself did not achieve this result. On the contrary, the properties and territories of the group remained divided as before among its previously subsidiary companies, most of which carried the Standard Oil title. Many of these retained not much less than 100 per cent of the business in their respective territories. They therefore continued the leadership role they had played when all were centrally controlled. Their structures were necessarily complementary rather than competitive, precisely because of their geographic and vertical specializations. Furthermore, for some time at least, community of ownership —the holding company was not required to sell its stockholdings to outsiders, but merely to distribute them to its own stockholders—and continuity of management prolonged practices of cooperation and nonaggression among these companies that had been born of a less than competitive environment. The function of dissolution was not itself to create competition between the successor companies but to set the stage for it; it was the rapid growth and change within the industry that forced the Standard companies more and more to behave like competitors. Relations between them, for many years familiar and cooperative, chilled under these impacts.[29]

The significant fact, from the present standpoint, about this drawing apart and incipient competition between the Standard successor companies is this: the way they did so was by integrating, each of them, vertically and geographically. Marketers like Socony moved into refining and production, unwilling to remain dependent on the others for their supplies. Conversely, refiners like Standard of New

29. On the effects of dissolution, immediate and remote, see Stocking, writing in 1925, pp. 53–82. After pointing out the limited effectiveness of dissolution, he felt it necessary to add: "Conditions in the oil industry have been changing with remarkable rapidity, however, and within the very recent past counter-tendencies may be noted. Economic forces have apparently quite recently engendered a conflict of interests between the various Standard companies themselves which seems to threaten a genuine dissolution of the Standard organization. . . . it seems not unlikely that the interdependence of the various Standard companies is approaching an end. It may be that the force of economic circumstances will yet make the oil industry genuinely competitive and free" (ibid., pp. 104–114).

Jersey moved forward into marketing to push their own differentiated product, and backward into crude oil.[30] In the process, each invaded the market area of one or another of its former partners. And the erstwhile source of Standard crude in the Midcontinent, Prairie Oil and Gas, was abandoned in 1923 by its best customer, Standard of Indiana.

Meanwhile, as demand soared and new supplies appeared, unpredictably and dramatically, additional independents appeared on the scene: Shell, Phillips, Doherty's Empire Gas and Fuel, Sinclair, Skelly, Marland. Each of them integrated vertically, and invaded markets that had been the historic preserves of Standard companies.

The most dramatic change in the structure of the oil industry after 1911 was the resultant dissipation of the virtual regional monopolies enjoyed by the Standard Oil successor companies. The decline was the result mainly of the competitive inroads made by the independents of the first three decades of this century—the most successful of which became the majors of the 1930's and thereafter—and also of interpenetration of each other's theretofore exclusive market preserves by the Standard companies themselves. These historical changes are summarized in Table IV.

Since the Standard Oil companies together controlled some 85 per cent of total national product sales in the first decade of the century, each one must have been comparably dominant in its own exclusive market territory, to which it in turn restricted its operations.[31] This gives us a benchmark against which to compare the far lower shares in their original markets enjoyed by these leaders in recent years: the median market share was 37.6 per cent in 1926, 23.8 per cent in 1938, and 19.4 per cent in 1954. In view of the fact that the 20 TNEC majors accounted for over 80 per cent of domestic United

30. "The history of Jersey Standard from 1911 through 1927 is essentially the story of a tremendous task of reconstruction. . . . These years witnessed a determined drive to preserve and strengthen the integrated nature of the business. Jersey Standard executives did not entertain integration as a conscious goal—the word itself was rarely heard—and yet it was to that end that their major policy decisions were pointed" (Gibb and Knowlton, *The Resurgent Years*, p. 10).

31. E.g., it was estimated that in 1911 Standard of New York had 90 per cent of the oil business in New York and New England. FTC, *Report on Distribution Methods and Costs*, 4, 50. Standard of Indiana similarly enjoyed an estimated 88 per cent of the business in its territory, Paul H. Giddens, *Standard Oil Company (Indiana), Oil Pioneer of the Middle West* (New York, Appleton-Century-Crofts, 1955), p. 83.

TABLE IV

Estimated Gasoline Sales in Original Territories by Original Standard Oil Companies and Other Majors,[a] 1926–54

	% OF TOTAL CONSUMPTION IN OLD TERRITORY			% OF TOTAL U.S. SALES OF COMPANY
	1926	1938	1954	1954
TERRITORY OF ATLANTIC				
Atlantic Refining Co.	44.5	21.9	19.4	48.8
Other majors (12) [b]				
Present in 1926 (5) [c]	40.4	28.1	—	—
Entering after 1926 (7) [c]	—	44.5	—	—
All others	15.1	5.5	—	—
TOTAL	100.0	100.0		
TERRITORY OF CONTINENTAL				
Continental Oil Co.	47.2	18.0	11.8	26.8
Other majors (8):				
Present in 1926 (3)	29.5	29.7	—	—
Entering after 1926 (5)	—	32.4	—	—
All others	23.3	19.9	—	—
TOTAL	100.0	100.0		
TERRITORY OF STANDARD OF CALIFORNIA				
Standard Oil Co. (Cal.)	28.7	17.7	22.3	73.1
Other majors (6):				
Present in 1926 (5)	54.5	55.4	—	—
Entering after 1926 (1)	—	6.9	—	—
All others	16.8	20.0	—	—
TOTAL	100.0	100.0		
TERRITORY OF STANDARD OF INDIANA [d]				
Standard Oil Co. (Ind.)	35.5	20.0	17.4	58.8
Other majors (13):				
Present in 1926 (5)	27.4	29.8	—	—
Entering after 1926 (8)	—	29.8	—	—
All others	37.1	24.0	—	—
TOTAL	100.0	100.0		
TERRITORY OF STANDARD OF KENTUCKY				
Standard Oil Co. (Ky.)	33.3	23.8	18.7	100.0
Other majors (9):				
Present in 1926 (5)	46.0	48.5	—	—
Entering after 1926 (4)	—	17.8	—	—
All others	20.7	9.9	—	—
TOTAL	100.0	100.0		

TABLE IV (Continued)

	% OF TOTAL CONSUMPTION IN OLD TERRITORY			% OF TOTAL U.S. SALES OF COMPANY
	1926	1938	1954	1954
TERRITORY OF STANDARD OF NEW JERSEY				
Standard Oil Co. (N.J.)	43.2	28.3	27.2	46.1
Other majors (12):				
Present in 1926 (6)	45.4	39.4	—	—
Entering after 1926 (6)	—	27.3	—	—
All others	11.4	5.0	—	—
TOTAL	100.0	100.0		
TERRITORY OF STANDARD OF LOUISIANA [e]				
Standard Oil Co. of La.	35.5	24.6	24.4	79.9
Other majors (10):				
Present in 1926 (5)	32.1	46.0	—	—
Entering after 1926 (5)	—	18.4	—	—
All others	32.4	11.0	—	—
TOTAL	100.0	100.0		
TERRITORY OF STANDARD OF OHIO				
Standard Oil Co. (Ohio)	37.6	23.9	31.4	99.1
Other majors (12):				
Present in 1926 (6)	34.8	27.4	—	—
Entering after 1926 (6)	—	29.5	—	—
All others	27.6	19.2	—	—
TOTAL	100.0	100.0		
TERRITORY OF SOCONY-VACUUM				
Socony-Vacuum Oil Co.	46.1	24.3	18.0	27.1
Other majors (10):				
Present in 1926 (6)	32.2	38.8	—	—
Entering after 1926 (4)	—	27.4	—	—
All others	21.7	9.5	—	—
TOTAL	100.0	100.0		

[a] The "majors" are apparently nineteen of the twenty companies listed by the TNEC. See above, p. 27. The 1938 data here are derived mainly from TNEC questionnaires. Standard of California and Mid-Continent did not supply the data requested, and the FTC *Report* has apparently attempted to supply estimates for the former company only.

[b] Figures in parentheses are the number of other majors represented.

[c] The majors listed as "present in 1926" reported sales amounting to 1 per cent or more of total sales in the area; thus the majors in the group "entering

States sales of gasoline in 1938,[32] obviously the greatest beneficiaries of the reduced shares of each of the Standard companies in its own original territory, and the companies mainly responsible for the declines, were other majors—independents from 1900 to 1930—and other intruding Standard successors: the median of the successor companies listed in the table did on the order of only one-half of its total 1954 gasoline business in its original market area.[33]

For example, between 1926 and 1938 alone, Standard of New Jersey and Standard of Indiana helped themselves to 10 per cent and 5.2 per cent of gasoline sales in Socony's market; both had no sales [34] there in the earlier year. The Jersey company did the same thing to Atlantic, taking over 14.5 per cent of that company's market by 1938; and Standard of Indiana invaded the territories of its former partners on an even more extensive scale after 1926, obtaining 9.6

---

after 1926" are companies whose sales, if any, were less than 1 per cent of the area's total in 1926, and 1 per cent or more in 1938. However, it appears that Cities Service Co. was not covered in the 1926 survey; hence its sales appear among "all others" in 1926 when in fact it was a significant market factor at that time, at least in the Midwest. Sun Oil was not covered in the 1926 study either; it, too, may therefore swell unduly the market shares of majors "entering after 1926."

[d] Separate information on Nebraska, the market territory of Standard of Nebraska, is omitted here because that company was exclusively a distributor for Standard of Indiana before the latter merged it in 1939. In the 1920's it distributed also the products of Standard of Kansas (exclusively a refining company, made independent in 1911), and the Midwest Refining Company, controlled after 1920 by Standard of Indiana. The latter company also had its own distribution in Nebraska after 1926.

[e] A subsidiary of Standard of New Jersey.

Sources: 1926 and 1938 estimates from FTC, *Report on Distribution Methods and Costs*, Pt. IV, pp. 51–54. (This report gives market shares for each major company.) 1954 data supplied by courtesy of the Economics Department of a leading oil company.

32. Eighteen of these companies (Standard of California and Mid-Continent Petroleum did not submit data to the TNEC) accounted for 75.85 per cent of national production and 79.94 per cent of national sales of gasoline. FTC, *Distribution Methods*, Pt. IV, p. 26, citing TNEC compilations.

33. The precise median of the nine companies listed is 58.8 per cent, but one of the nine is Standard of Louisiana, which is a subsidiary of Standard of New Jersey and does most of its business in its original territory.

34. See footnote c of the table. These data on the market shares of individual companies in 1926 and 1938 are taken from the FTC tables of which our Table IV is a summary.

per cent in Standard of New Jersey's, 8.5 per cent of Atlantic's, and 18.3 per cent of Continental's markets respectively in 1938. Standard of New York (later, Socony-Vacuum and Socony Mobil) and Continental reciprocated by taking over 7.9 per cent and 2.5 per cent of Indiana's territory by 1938. The former company also moved into Ohio, where it accounted for 5.9 per cent of sales; it had earlier become a dominant marketer in the Southwest (Texas and Oklahoma) and on the West Coast, where its market shares in 1926 were 18.1 per cent and 7.4 per cent respectively. A striking recent instance of the invasion of a new market by a Standard successor company has been the entry into East Coast markets by Standard of California.[35]

As for the encroachments of the former independents, as early as 1926 the names of The Texas Company, Consolidated (later Sinclair), Gulf, Tide Water, Pure, and Shell had assumed market prominence. Two to five of them were in each major market area, along with the Standard companies. In the years that followed, some of these same companies continued to expand their operations. Shell, which had begun American operations in 1912 and during the next sixteen years concentrated its refining-marketing operations on the West Coast and in the Midwest, thereafter became a large marketer all along the East Coast and in the Rocky Mountain area as well. By the end of 1929 it was marketing in every one of the forty-eight states.[36] By 1938 Gulf accounted for over 8.4 per cent of the Ohio market, and Texas had

35. Calso, which did not market in the East before World War II, had by 1954 appropriated 3.8 per cent of the Socony market and 2.4 per cent of the combined Standard of New Jersey and Atlantic territory sales. Estimates by courtesy of a leading oil company. It has also moved into Rocky Mountain states. In 1956, the Jersey Company took several important steps toward entry into the Midwest. For these and other plans see "Here's How the Oil Companies Are Jumping into New Markets," *Business Week* (June 2, 1956), pp. 145–148. These market interpenetrations might have been even more extensive had not the ability of an intruding successor company to use the Standard name and brands in the territory of another been legally questionable. It was unfortunate that the 1911 dissolution decree made no provision against this obstacle to competition. See, e.g., Giddens, *Standard Oil Company*, pp. 134–135, 708; Gibb and Knowlton, *The Resurgent Years*, pp. 185–187. As recently as 1956 Standard of Indiana succeeded in obtaining a court decree enjoining Standard of Ohio from using its Sohio brand in its efforts to expand marketing operations in Michigan. See "Battle of the Standards: The Prize Is New Market Areas," *National Petroleum News* (July, 1956), pp. 96–97.

36. See the brief history prepared by the Company, "Oil Is a Major Source of Power," hectograph, September, 1952; and Kendall Beaton, *Enterprise in Oil: A History of Shell in the United States* (New York, Appleton-Century-Crofts, 1957), pp. 296–297, 311–330.

invaded the West Coast to take 6.9 per cent of that region's sales. Among the newer majors, Sun brought out "Blue Sunoco" in 1927 and rapidly became a major market factor along the East Coast. A products pipeline, completed in 1931, helped to expand its area into western Pennsylvania and Ohio. By 1938 it accounted for 5.2 per cent of sales in Jersey Standard's territory; 9.75 per cent in Atlantic's; and 7.3 per cent in Ohio. In 1927 Phillips acquired its first refinery and its first service station, and introduced Phillips 66 to the public. As with Sun, products pipelines accelerated its dynamic market expansion thereafter.[37] By 1938 Phillips accounted for 8.2 per cent of gasoline sales in the vast midwestern territory of Standard of Indiana, and 3 to 4 per cent in Texas, Oklahoma, and the Rocky Mountain territory of Continental Oil; and by 1955 its crude runs to stills had grown to 229,000 b/d, 3.1 per cent of the United States total, making it the tenth largest refiner in the country. Since World War II Phillips has been extending its selling efforts in all directions, notably with an aggressive entry eastward into Florida and adjacent south Atlantic states, and northwestward into Utah, Idaho, and Washington.[38] The growth of Skelly has followed less dramatic but similar lines.

INTEGRATION AS A PROCESS OF CONSOLIDATION

Integration contributed to these important shifts in the market positions of the leading oil companies, and to the intensification of competition that they reflect.[39] However, it must also be emphasized, the

37. In 1930 construction of two lines was started: one was Phillips' own, extending northward from Borger, Texas; the other, the Great Lakes line, owned jointly with Continental, Mid-Continent, Skelly, Texas, Pure, Sinclair, and Cities Service, which extended from the Midcontinent refinery centers northward to the Twin Cities and Chicago markets. See the brief history of Phillips prepared by the Company, unbound, August 19, 1953.

38. The same FTC Report (*Distribution Methods, 4,* 48) has a table showing the states in which each major company marketed in May, 1939, taken, like the information summarized in our Table IV, from the TNEC *Hearings.* It shows that Phillips sold in none of the above-mentioned states in that year. Estimates supplied us by a major oil company credit Phillips with 6.5 per cent of the Florida, 11.8 per cent of the Utah, 7.8 per cent of the Idaho, and 3.0 per cent of the Washington gasoline sales in 1954. See "How Phillips Marched into Dixie," *National Petroleum News* (November, 1956), pp. 104–106.

39. It was largely on the basis of the above-mentioned changes that the FTC concluded as long ago as 1928: "During the past 20 years the petroleum industry has changed from one in which there was a high degree of monopolistic control to an industry in which there is generally freedom of competition" (*Petroleum Industry, Prices, Profits, and Competition*—cited below as *Petro-*

extension of integration after 1911 represented a process of consolidation as well as of competition; the structural changes it helped produce involved a drawing together, as well as a pulling apart, in the industry.

First of all, it is noteworthy that a very large proportion of the instances of market invasion and interpenetration reflected in Table IV, and of the vertical integration through which the Standard successor companies gradually drifted apart, was accomplished by merger or acquisition. While company growth by merger may well make for more effective competition, it nevertheless tends, *ceteris paribus,* to tighten up and concentrate the structure of an industry.[40]

Looking first at the major instances of geographic expansion by Standard successor companies after 1926, we find that the Jersey company entered Socony's market largely by acquiring control of the Beacon Oil Company (thereafter reincorporated as Colonial-Beacon) in 1929, with its 25,000 b/d refinery in Everett, Massachusetts, seventy-seven bulk plants and 354 owned or leased service stations in New England at the close of 1928; and it entered Atlantic's Pennsylvania market partly by the acquisition of another string of service stations.[41] Its recent, highly publicized "invasions" of the Midwest have been signaled by several acquisitions in 1956, the most prominent of them being the Pate Oil Company, an independent marketer with 136 service stations and over 20 per cent of the gasoline business in Milwaukee county.[42] Even more clearly, Standard of Indiana accomplished its extensive invasion of East Coast and Southern markets simply by acquiring control in 1929 of the Pan American Petroleum and Transport Company, with about 40,000 b/d refining capacity[43] and extensive marketing facilities throughout these states; the ac-

---

leum Industry, 1928—70th Congress, 1st Session, Senate Document No. 61, p. 264).

40. This observation is not rendered pointless by virtue of the fact that the *ceteris* obviously did not remain *paribus* in this rapidly growing industry and that the acquisition of a weak by a strong company often led on balance to more rather than less intense competition. For a discussion of the difficulties of measuring the relative contributions to company growth or to changes in market structure and behavior of mergers and internal expansion, see below, pp. 347–350.

41. Most of the foregoing information is from Moody's. Information on the Pennsylvania acquisitions was supplied by an officer of the company.

42. "How an Independent Beat the Majors," *National Petroleum News* (July, 1956), pp. 98–100.

43. C. M. Furcht, "Growth and Structure of U. S. Refining Industry," gives a figure of 38,000 b/d; Moody's, 44,000.

quired organization continued to market thereafter under its established brand names Amoco and Pan-Am. Similarly in Continental's territory, Indiana acquired control in 1921 of the Midwest Refining Company, which had four refineries with combined capacity of somewhere between 54,000 and 85,000 b/d. This acquisition apparently played a critical role in supporting the subsequent expansion of Standard's marketing operations in the territory.[44]

Socony Mobil has dispersed its marketing operations more than any other Standard successor company (except for Continental, which, however, can be characterized much less clearly than any of the others in its present form as a Standard Oil successor—see note 57, below), as Table IV shows. This dispersion was initiated apparently in every important case by a very large acquisition. The company went into the Southwest by acquiring Magnolia Petroleum Company,[45] the dominant marketer in Texas and Oklahoma;[46] in 1926 it took over General Petroleum Corporation, a company in Los Angeles with about 50,000 b/d refinery capacity[47] and an estimated 7.4 per cent of sales in the West Coast area in the year of acquisition;[48] and in 1930 it purchased White Eagle Oil and Refining Company, a fully integrated company with 15,000 to 20,000 b/d of refinery capacity and 1,261 tank and service stations throughout eleven midwestern and Rocky Mountain states.[49] In addition, Socony acquired some

44. Furcht gives a figure of 54,000 b/d; McLean and Haigh (p. 257) of 85,000. The FTC table summarized in Table IV above shows Standard of Indiana with less than one per cent of the gasoline sales in Continental's territory (Colorado, Idaho, Montana, New Mexico, Utah, and Wyoming) in 1926 and 18.33 per cent in 1938. According to McLean and Haigh, Midwest became, sometime after its organization in 1914, "one of the most important refining and marketing companies in the Rocky Mountain area" (ibid.). However, the marketing developments seem to have occurred after the control shifted to Standard of Indiana. According to Stocking, "this acquisition gave the Standard almost complete control of the production, pipe-line transportation, and refining properties in the State of Wyoming" (p. 59).

45. On the rather complicated steps in, this acquisition see FTC, Petroleum Industry (1928), pp. 92–93; Stocking, p. 58 n.

46. Magnolia accounted for 18.1 per cent of gasoline sales in these states in 1926, according to the FTC estimate, Distribution Methods, 4, 53. According to Furcht, it had 69,000 b/d of refining capacity when Standard took over complete control in 1925.

47. Here again the Furcht estimate is lower, 43,000 b/d; the 1926 Moody's Industrials shows 60,000.

48. FTC, Distribution Methods, 4, 54.

49. Data from Moody's. In 1926 White Eagle accounted for well over ½ of one per cent of total national sales of gasoline.

large marketers while it was penetrating the midwestern market: among these, in the 1930's, were the Wadhams Corporation (a very large marketer today in Wisconsin, Illinois, Minnesota, and Michigan), Mid-Western Oil Corporation (an Indiana marketer), the Lubrite Refining Company, and the White Star Refining Company. Standard of California began its turbulent history of marketing on the East Coast with the purchase in 1946 of the 15,000 b/d refinery of the Barber Asphalt Corporation.

In the case of the non-Standard giants who made major geographic moves after 1926, merger with large going concerns apparently played a less important role. However, Shell's entry into the East Coast area followed the familiar pattern: "Late in 1928, Shell Union purchased the New England Oil Refining Company of Fall River, Massachusetts to serve as the nucleus for a new marketing company on the Atlantic Seaboard." [50] Gulf eased its way into Ohio and Michigan in 1930 partly by buying the Paragon Refining Company, with an 8,000 b/d refinery at Toledo and 344 bulk plants and service stations and other marketing facilities in these states.[51] Texas became a major marketer on the West Coast in 1929 mainly by acquiring the California Petroleum Corporation, an integrated company with over 50,000 b/d refinery capacity in California and Montana.[52] A number of relatively small acquisitions marked Phillips' and Skelly's entry into refining after 1920 but these purchases do not seem to have been important factors in their substantial market expansion.[53] Sun Oil Company, the other new major singled out for comment, has purchased no other refiners, at least since 1920. All have undoubtedly bought

50. "Oil Is a Major Source of Power" (cited above, n. 35), p. 13. The New England Company had a large, 27,000 b/d, but antiquated refinery, which Shell promptly dismantled. The organization's real attraction was its marketing facilities; to get them, Shell had to outbid the Beacon Oil Company, which had already been purchased by Standard of New Jersey. See Beaton, *Enterprise in Oil*, pp. 318–326.

51. McLean and Haigh, p. 97.

52. Furcht, appendix 18. The rise in Texas' participation in the Standard of Indiana territory, from 3.8 per cent in 1926 to 6.9 per cent in 1938 was undoubtedly greatly assisted by its acquisition in 1931 of the Indian Refining Company, with a 16,000 b/d refinery in Illinois and "quite complete" marketing facilities in surrounding states, including an alleged 20 per cent of the gasoline business in Indiana. James, *The Texaco Story*, pp. 54–55; see also McLean and Haigh, pp. 106, 108, 386.

53. Possible exceptions were the four relatively small purchases of refineries by Phillips, all in 1947, in Idaho, Utah, Montana, and Washington (with combined capacity of 14,800 b/d). Furcht, appendixes 7 and 11.

out marketers as they have expanded their own distribution, just as have all other integrated oil companies.

Mergers played a critical role also in the vertical reintegration by the truncated segments of the Standard Oil group. The most important step in Standard of New Jersey's progress toward developing its own domestic crude-oil producing and purchasing arm was the acquisition in 1919 of the majority interest in Humble Oil and Refining. This company, interestingly, had "grown out of the intense dissatisfaction of small independent producers in the Gulf Coastal area with their relations with the major oil companies which controlled the pipelines and constituted the principal purchasers of crude oil in the region." [54] An important forward step into direct marketing was the acquisition of the Beacon Oil Company. The corresponding backward moves of Socony into refining and production were the above-mentioned mergers with Magnolia and General Petroleum, both fully integrated companies with a large production of crude oil. Standard of Indiana integrated backward by purchasing first some smaller producing properties, then, in order, Midwest Refining, a half-interest in the Sinclair Pipe Line Company and in the Sinclair Crude Oil Purchasing Company in 1921, and the vast Pan American Petroleum and Transport Company system in 1925.[55] Not until around 1932 did Indiana begin a really active program of exploration and development on its own account.[56] These are only the most prominent examples of the

54. Gibb and Knowlton, *The Resurgent Years,* p. 411; see also pp. 409–412. We do not imply that by joining with Jersey the Texas producers were selling themselves into the bondage they had hoped originally to avoid; on the contrary. See below, Part II. In 1918 Standard's affiliates supplied out of their own production less than one-fifth of their combined domestic or Western Hemisphere needs (see *ibid.,* pp. 47, 49, 73–74). This figure represented the fruition of a successful effort to expand output in the years immediately preceding, but it too was an expansion "by acquisition . . . of established producing properties . . . a conservative, legal, and relatively sure way." *Ibid.,* p. 75; see chap. 3 *passim.*

55. See FTC, *Petroleum Industry* (1928), pp. 83–87, 92–94.

56. Giddens, *Standard Oil Company (Indiana),* pp. vi–vii. Since Standard had been a heavy purchaser of gasoline as well as crude oil, from Midwest among others, the purchase of the latter company in 1920–21 constituted a backward integration step. Pan American was one of the largest producers of crude oil in the world, and the merger was the largest until that date in the history of the industry (see *ibid.,* pp. 217–220, 239–241, and 210–249 *passim*): "The transaction gave enormous strength to Standard in its weakest spot—the lack of crude. With Pan American's vast crude supply behind it, Standard occupied an impregnable position among the oil companies of the world. It was the capstone in [Colonel] Stewart's effort to acquire a crude supply for his

importance of mergers in the early reintegration of the Standard successor companies.[57]

The second reason for characterizing the extension of integration after 1911 as a process of consolidation as well as of competition is the remarkable stability of the industry's structure during the last few decades. Dramatic as have been the shifts in specific market positions just described, over-all the organization of the oil industry does not look much different today than it did, say, thirty years ago; and the integration of the major companies has contributed directly to this stability.

Table V presents estimates of the proportions of aggregate United States gasoline sales by the leading marketing companies in 1926, the earliest year for which we have been able to obtain such information, and in 1954. The data for the two years are not entirely comparable, as the notes to captions on the table indicate. Probably no meaningful

---

company" (ibid., p. 245). The company embarked on exploration on its own account in 1927 or 1928, but the major emphasis of its backward integration remained for several years on purchases of established interests—witness its acquisition in 1930 of the remaining half interests in the two joint Sinclair companies, and of the McMan Oil and Gas Company. See McLean and Haigh, pp. 254–261; Giddens, pp. 442–446.

57. In this process, the Prairie Oil and Gas Company, the major producing and transporting member of the Standard group, was left high and dry by defections of its former affiliates, including Standard of Indiana. It therefore integrated forward, in its turn, by exchanging its stock in 1923 for that of the Producers and Refiners Corporation, a fully integrated company with refining capacity in excess of its own production and very extensive marketing facilities in the Midwest and Rocky Mountain states (FTC, Petroleum Industry, 1928, pp. 87–91), and by merging into Sinclair in 1932. McLean and Haigh, pp. 191, 389. It would be pointless to outline the complex steps by which Continental Oil—the pure marketer of the Standard group—was converted into the integrated major of today. In effect, this was accomplished by a series of mergers, most prominent of which was its own acquisition by the fully integrated Mutual Oil Company in 1924 and by Marland in 1929. Though the Continental name bobbed up after each combination, actually the role of the original Standard company in the present combination is very small. See FTC, Petroleum Industry (1928), pp. 91–92, and Moody's Industrials.

Similarly, when Ohio Oil decided to go into refining, in 1924, it began by purchasing the small Lincoln Oil and Refining Company; and when, in 1928, it pushed forward into marketing, it bought up Lincoln's largest jobber customer, as well as a number of other smaller marketers (McLean and Haigh, pp. 100–101). Incidents like the latter emphasize the need to look further before reaching any conclusions about the net competitive impacts of mergers: the Lincoln Company was financially weak and its refinery outmoded and when the Ohio Company decided to move into refining in earnest it had to rebuild the plant and enlarge it on its own account.

TABLE V

Estimated Proportions of Gasoline Sales in the United States by the Leading Marketing Companies, 1926 and 1954

RANK	COMPANY	%	RANK	COMPANY	%
	1926 [a]			1954 [b]	
1.	Standard Oil Co. (Indiana)	11.8 [e]	1.	Texas Co.	7.9
2.	Standard Oil Co. (N.J.)	9.5	2–3.	Socony-Vacuum Oil Co.[e]	7.8
3.	Standard Oil Co. of		2–3.	Standard Oil Co.	
	New York	9.1		(New Jersey) [e]	7.8
4.	Gulf Oil Corp.	6.7	4.	Standard Oil Co. Indiana	7.7
5.	Texas Co.	6.3	5.	Gulf Oil Corp.	6.8
6.	Sinclair Consolidated		6.	Shell Union Oil Corp.	6.6
	Oil Corp.	5.7	7.	Sinclair Oil Corp.	5.0
7.	Royal Dutch-Shell Cos.	5.2	8.	Standard Oil Co.	
8.	Atlantic Refining Co.	4.0		(California)	4.4
9.	Standard Oil Co. of		9.	Sun Oil Co.	3.6
	California	3.3	10.	Phillips Petroleum Co.	3.3
10.	Standard Oil Co.		11.	Cities Service Co.	3.1
	(Kentucky)	2.4	12.	Tide Water Associated	
11.	Standard Oil Co. (Ohio)	2.3		Oil Co.	2.4
12.	Pure Oil Co.	2.3	13.	Atlantic Refining Co.	2.2
13.	Continental Oil Co.	1.5	14.	Pure Oil Co.	2.1
14.	Union Oil Co. of		15.	Union Oil Co.	1.8
	California	1.4	16.	Standard Oil Co. (Ohio)	1.7
15.	Associated Oil Co.	1.2	17–18.	Continental Oil Co.[e]	1.6
16.	Richfield Oil Co.	1.2	17–18.	Standard Oil Co. (Ky.) [e]	1.6
			19.	Richfield	1.5
	TOTAL, 16 companies	73.7 [d]		TOTAL, 19 companies	78.9
	All others	26.3		All others	21.1
		100.0			100.0

[a] "Proportion of total motor fuel consumed in the U.S. in 1926 sold by twenty-four large marketing companies through bulk stations," FTC, *Petroleum Industry* (1928), p. 59. The apparent ties for eleventh and fifteenth ranking result from our having rounded the FTC percentages.

[b] "Estimated percentages of total potential gasoline sales in the U.S. by various oil companies," courtesy of the Economics Department of a leading oil company.

[e] Tie.

[d] The FTC list is for twenty-four companies. The FTC itself compressed these into nineteen groups. E.g. it included the figures of General Petroleum Co. and Magnolia Petroleum Co. with Standard of New York, which controlled them. These groupings not only correctly reflect financial affiliation but also make the 1926 figures comparable with 1954. We omit three others, i.e. three Standard Oil successor companies, with market shares of 0.7, 0.3, and 0.1 per cent.

[e] The FTC includes the 2.09 per cent of the Pan American Petroleum and Transport Co. even though the two were not merged until 1929.

conclusions can be drawn from the absolute changes in percentage figures for each company; and even the apparent directions of change may be somewhat misleading. The FTC figures for 1926 are for the "Standard marketing companies and the larger independents." The figures for 1954 probably cover the nineteen leading marketers; but differences in coverage, accentuated by intervening mergers, exaggerate the apparent shifts in position between the two years. Thus the Associated Oil Company ranks too low on the earlier list relative to the later, because the earlier figures do not include the eastern sales of Tide Water, with which it merged during that year. Cities Service and Sun, both well up on the 1954 list, are missing entirely from the first even though Cities Service, at least, must have been an important marketer in 1926.[58]

Despite these qualifications, the comparison over a twenty-eight year period shows far more stability than change, in not only the identity but the relative positions of the majors. The top seven marketing companies in 1926 were still the top seven in 1954.[59] All of the sixteen leaders in the former year were among the top nineteen in the latter.[60] Of the three additional companies on the 1954 list, one at least was an important marketer, and very possibly among the top twenty, even in 1926.[61] The only really new entrants were Phillips and Sun, to the meteoric rise of which we have already alluded, and of these Sun had already reached its present relative position as a marketer by 1935.[62] There have been shifts among the top firms, partly because of

58. Sun had over $55,000,000 of assets in 1926, three refineries with 0.8 per cent of total national refining capacity; and by 1929, it sold more gasoline than Union Oil, Standard of Ohio, and Cities Service. See TNEC *Hearings*, Pt. XIV A, pp. 7801, 7805. Still Sun extended its retail marketing only gradually after 1920 and intensively only after 1927. See *History of Sun Oil Company* (multilithed), by the company, 1951, p. 2. Robert Wilson, Chairman of the Board of Standard of Indiana, identifies Cities Service as having become a competitor of his company in seven midwestern states before 1921, and in four more in 1922–25. *Oil Competition in the Mid-West, A Case History* (Washington, D.C., National Petroleum Association, 1950), pp. 14–16.

59. To take an intermediate year at random, they were also the top seven in 1935 as revealed by figures from the same source as those for 1954 in the table.

60. The only other company whose gasoline sales probably matched those of Richfield, number 19 in 1954, was Ashland; this company reported total product sales of 117,000 b/d in that year, compared with Richfield's 110,000 (see their respective *Annual Reports;* also above, Table III, pp. 30–31).

61. This would be Cities Service; see above, n. 58.

62. Statistics from the source indicated in n. b, Table V show that Sun accounted for 2.8 per cent of national gasoline sales in 1932 and 3.4 per cent in 1935—when it ranked number 9 nationally, just as in 1954.

mergers (these help explain the rise of Texas and Tide Water),[63] partly because some Standard Oil successor companies, which historically were marketers or refiner-marketers, continued largely to confine their operations to these levels in restricted geographic locations and hence did not grow as fast as the industry as a whole (note the relative declines of Standard of Kentucky, Standard of Ohio, and Atlantic).

INTEGRATION AS A SEARCH FOR SECURITY

The ensconcement of integration in the oil industry was heavily influenced by the Standard Oil Company monopoly: for Mr. Rockefeller and his associates it was used to create, protect, and extend monopoly power; for those who would challenge the trust it became the sine qua non of survival. But though these historical circumstances undoubtedly helped to give the institution a continuing vitality, they do not explain its extension and consolidation after 1911, when it can no longer be explained simply as an effort by a single-firm monopolist to protect his position or by competitors to circumvent it.

Behind all the machinations of the Standard group was the stubborn economic fact that continued to plague the industry after the 1911 dissolution until conservation and prorationing were imposed by the major producing states: there was no foretelling when a new well or a new field would be discovered and there was no way, short of monopoly, to curb the flow of oil once its presence had been revealed. There were but two ways to avoid calamity. The refiner-marketer might attempt to insulate producers by monopolizing transport and refining, and forcing the mavericks to bear the full weight of their profligacy. This was essentially Standard's policy. But even Standard found it difficult to bottle up producers in their own oil: one purpose of its early ventures into production, as we have seen, was to forestall competitive forward moves by disgruntled producers with more to sell than the market would take. These efforts did not, and even without dissolution could not, have prevented the emergence

63. If Ashland is entitled to position number 19 in 1954 (see above, n. 60), this too would be because of its numerous acquisitions since 1947. Both Socony-Vacuum and Sinclair owe something of their continued prominence in 1954 to intervening mergers, notably of Standard of New York with Vacuum Oil Company in 1931, and Sinclair with Producers and Refiners Corporation in 1932. (See above, n. 57.) The FTC listing credited Producers and Refiners with 0.71 per cent of national sales in 1926; and Vacuum with 0.5 per cent of national gasoline production in 1925. *Petroleum Industry* (1928), pp. 59, 77.

of competitors out of the gushing Midcontinent fields. Moreover, there was always the opposite threat: that feast for the refiner would be followed by famine. So, both to preserve the refining-transport monopoly in the face of mushrooming supplies and to guard against possible shortages, it was necessary to integrate backward, part or all the way: to cultivate the good will of producers and make continued exploratory efforts attractive by constructing gathering lines and storage facilities as rapidly as possible and in sufficient volume to handle whatever was offered; [64] or to go into production.[65]

The producers, in turn, could escape only by developing their own market outlets; only by integrating forward could they find the assured markets and the more stable profits that would always elude the scrambling prospectors, subject to the vagaries of nature, the rule of capture, and the ease of competitive entry. In both situations, vertical integration contributed to the stability of the integrating company, by providing some security against competitive duplication, and greater assurances than nonintegrated companies enjoyed of continuous utilization of capacity of producing well, pipeline, refinery, and marketing facilities, so urgent in the presence of heavy fixed costs. It is in this quest for stability in a potentially explosive industry that we begin to find a convincing explanation of integration which applies as well after the dissolution of the Standard empire as before.

This is not at all to say that these underlying circumstances inevitably compelled the major oil companies to maintain a roughly balanced vertical integration under the threat of otherwise suffering catastrophic losses; nor does it deny that in the absence of integration by some companies the pressures on others to integrate may have been much weaker. But the historical fact is that these companies have sought a degree of balance mainly, as we read the record, for protection against what they conceived to be the threatened dangers and

64. "If Rockefeller and his associates were to continue to maintain the preeminent position of the Trust in the American petroleum industry, and to use that pre-eminence as a profitable stabilizing factor, they must at least buy oil, lay pipes, and erect storage tanks in northwestern Ohio [to take care of the rapidly increasing output of the Lima-Indiana field in the late 1880's]. In addition, they would certainly have to connect the system in the Lima region by trunk lines to Cleveland, and probably to the long-distance lines running to the Eastern refineries." Hidy and Hidy, *Pioneering in Big Business*, p. 157. See also above, n. 24.

65. On the fears generated by the widely predicted decline in Pennsylvania production, and the influence of the desire for assured supplies on Standard's large ventures into production in the late 1880's, see *ibid.*, pp. 155, 176–182.

instabilities of complete dependence on uncontrolled intermediate markets.

In truth this analysis of the historical record is less an explanation than a description of integration. All it really says is that companies have sought managerial control over their raw material supplies and product distribution because they wanted the greater assurances that financial control brings. Attempts to supply narrower and more precise interpretations invariably lack conviction.

It is of course possible to identify a great variety of more specific or more immediate historical explanations of particular integration moves. McLean and Haigh, for example, lay very heavy emphasis on "the pressure of crude oil before prorationing" as an explanation, particularly during the period between 1920 and 1935.[66] The price of oil is low when production is flush and a local market or cheap outward transport is lacking; [67] producers have undoubtedly been tempted in such circumstances to construct pipelines or refineries and to market their superabundant crude oil in more finished form, partly in a simple quest for customers, partly in the hope of enhancing their net returns per barrel of oil sold. From the Bradford Field, which spawned Tidewater, to the cases of Gulf and Union Oil,[68] it is possible to find numerous illustrations of just this kind of pressure even in the early history of the industry, just as McLean and Haigh do for the 1920–34 period, because the tendency to overproduction of crude oil has been chronic.[69]

Actually, it is not at all clear that producers of crude oil might have expected to improve their profitability by integrating forward between 1920 and 1934; the "pressure of crude" is therefore not entirely convincing, even if understood as describing short-run influences on the direction of integration moves, rather than supplying a basic explanation of the phenomenon. The price of crude oil did not decline more sharply than that of refined products between either 1918–19

66. Pp. 71–80, and chap. 4.

67. Williston Basin crude for several years brought a low price because pipelines had not yet reached it. See Amerada Petroleum Company, *Annual Report,* 1953.

68. See above, pp. 83–85. Certainly the major force pushing Union into refining and marketing was "Lyman Stewart's mania for more and more acreage," and his "hunting outlets for oil from Union's wells," which, just as in the case of Gulf, necessitated, among other things, finding ways of converting that raw material into an illuminant of acceptable quality (Taylor and Welty, *Black Bonanza*, pp. 71, 113; also pp. 62, 91, 94–99).

69. See, e.g., Watkins, chap. 4; Stocking, *passim;* Ise, *United States Oil Policy, passim.*

or 1921 on the one hand and 1930 on the other, although it both rose and fell more abruptly during the two periods 1919–21 and 1923–27.[70] Refining margins dropped more or less continuously from 1920 to 1932, and until 1927 no less rapidly than production margins.[71] True, the substantial rise of crude oil inventories from 1919 to 1929 might have given rise to uneasiness on the part of companies without refining outlets. Yet the stocks of products were rising at least as rapidly, in the same period, and more rapidly after 1923. Expressed as a percentage of annual consumption, stocks of crude slumped rapidly after 1923, and were still below the 1923 levels in 1929–30. Only between 1919 and 1923 and in the 1926–28 period did they rise more rapidly than product inventories.[72]

Of course the gigantic discoveries of 1920–23 and 1926–31 put

70. Compare the statistics of the national average annual price of crude oil with the unweighted fifty-city average service station price of gasoline, excluding tax, and the BLS indexes of wholesale prices of petroleum products, *Petroleum Facts and Figures,* 9th ed., pp. 121, 367, and 378; see also the chart in McLean and Haigh, p. 86.

71. The wellhead price of 36° gravity Midcontinent crude oil averaged $3.42 in 1920, dropped to a low of $1.56 in 1923, rose again to $2.13 in 1926, then fell to $1.38 in 1927, at which point it remained roughly stable until it began its sharp decline late in 1930. The average margin received by refiners from the products produced from a barrel of such crude was $1.32 in 1920, dropped to a low of $0.48 in 1924, and, after a mild recovery, to $0.42 in 1927. In the 1927–29 period refinery margins recovered somewhat, while the price of crude oil remained low; but in 1930 refinery margins slumped to $0.35 while the price of crude remained relatively stable at $1.23. Monthly and annual computations for 1920–38 in Sidney A. Swensrud, "The Relation between Crude Oil and Product Prices," *Bulletin of the American Association of Petroleum Geologists, 23* (1939), 766, 780–787; the annual data are reproduced and extended through 1950 in Ralph Cassady, Jr., *Price Making and Price Behavior in the Petroleum Industry,* Petroleum Monograph Series, *1* (New Haven, Yale University Press, 1954), pp. 136–137 (cited below as Cassady); see also the charts in McLean and Haigh, p. 134. The relevancy of comparing these gross realizations is of course open to question on the ground that neither the true "production margin" nor the profitability of refining is disclosed by them. The cost of producing oil varies widely between fields, pools, and wells (see, e.g., Watkins, p. 126, n. 6), and may well have declined sharply with the heavy discoveries of 1920–23 and 1926–31. In Swensrud's opinion refining costs probably increased in this period with increased use of the more costly cracking processes (pp. 769–770); on the other hand the transportation costs that are included in the refinery margin computations undoubtedly declined.

72. See charts in McLean and Haigh, p. 86. The relative decline in gasoline stocks between the end of 1925 and 1928, from 1/7 to 1/11.5 of domestic output (computed from *Petroleum Facts and Figures,* 9th ed., p. 226), in the face of climbing crude oil inventories after 1926 may well have helped induce producing companies to seek protection by integrating forward.

great pressures on oil industry markets. The behavior of stocks and prices of crude and products *together* clearly reflect their influence. What is not clear from these statistics—which are, the reader should be warned, national aggregates or averages, and therefore may conceal a host of divergent individual situations—is why producers in these circumstances might have felt that integration would improve their situation.[73]

If the "pressure of crude oil" in and of itself were really an important explanation of integration, it would imply a broader principle, namely that integration can be explained by the divergent and fluctuating profitability of different strata of an industry. So, the theory would run, it happened to be crude oil that suffered most seriously in 1920–35 from overproduction and narrow profit margins; producers were therefore induced to integrate forward. In this light, it is not surprising that McLean and Haigh's second major explanation of integration in oil is "the ebb and flow of profit opportunities": "One of the most important explanations for the development of all types of integrated structures in the oil industry in all time periods may be found in the contribution which vertical integration makes toward stabilizing a company's profit position." [74] Their detailed examination of the behavior of gross margins between 1920 and 1952 clearly demonstrates both the marked differences in their relative stability

73. Of course, there may have been advantages that would not show up in the statistics: for example the ability to produce or sell crude oil that would otherwise have been completely wasted or have had to remain underground. Moreover, the statistics do provide some limited confirmation of the apparent benefits of forward integration, in the two or three years after 1926. Note the sharper break after 1926 in crude prices than product prices or refinery margins, the recovery of refinery margins in 1928, and the sharper rise in crude oil than product inventories in those particular years. Finally, the forward investments in refining by heavy crude oil producers, impelled by the pressure of new discoveries, would themselves cause the statistics to conceal that pressure, by holding down the accumulation of inventories and supporting the prices of crude oil, and transforming these tendencies instead into growing inventories and declining prices of refined products. However, the typical relationship in oil is for the price of products to lead the price of crude, and this was true throughout the 1920's; the "pressure of crude [was thus] . . . exerted directly upon refined product markets" (Swensrud, "The Relation between Crude Oil and Product Prices," p. 777; see also pp. 771–774), with crude markets reflecting it only belatedly and indirectly. Therefore, so far as the statistics of prices and inventories demonstrate, the pressure of crude was not a convincing explanation of forward integration. Instead, integration is part of the reason why the pressure of crude oil tends to affect product prices first! See *ibid.,* and below, pp. 414 ff.

74. P. 115.

and in the timing of their changes, and the contribution that integration in whatever direction would almost invariably have made to greater margin and profit stability.

But the general principle which they adduce from this demonstration is hardly more convincing than their specific contention with respect to the 1920–35 period. Integration of course cannot enhance the over-all return on capital merely by spreading investment over strata of divergent profitability: it can only average out differences and fluctuations. But investors can achieve this simple actuarial protection of investment straddling in an investment trust; it hardly calls for managerial integration of successive processes in a particular industry. Integration implies a certain unifying functional and managerial interrelationship of the various sectors of a company's financial interests; it makes sense only if management feels that investment at one level of operation will somehow reinforce, protect, or enhance the profitability of investment at another level—for example, by assuring a higher utilization of productive facilities at all stages. So it is no wonder that McLean and Haigh are later forced to admit that: "We found, in fact, only a few cases where it could be said that a company made a particular integration decision primarily because its management believed that the move would in general help to stabilize the company's profit position." [75]

It is certainly true that one oil company after another was induced to build its own crude oil and product pipelines in the past by the high nominal profits earned by the pipeline subsidiaries of other integrated companies. But they did so to increase their profits, not to stabilize them simply by spreading the scope of their operations. And their primary purpose was to cut the delivery costs on their own oil and products, not to earn profits as common carriers. This kind of effort by refiners was on a par with any other kind of investment that promised to improve efficiency; it would be misleading to interpret it as an attempt merely to participate by investment in the higher or more stable "profits" of some hitherto extraneous field of operation.[76]

To explain integration in oil in terms of a quest for stability or se-

75. P. 116. On the distinction between investment straddling and integration, see J. M. Clark, *Studies in the Economics of Overhead Costs* (Chicago, University of Chicago Press, 1923), pp. 136–137.

76. Of course, examples can be found of "integrated" companies whose investments seem to have been assembled on the principle of spreading the risk or earning separate profits from the individual operations, with little or no effort to operate them as an integrated whole. The Ohio Oil Company would seem to be the most outstanding case in this industry. See McLean and Haigh, pp. 101–102, 204–205, 224–226, 420–423. But such instances are exceptional.

curity, therefore, is not to refer to the mere averaging of risks that comes from putting one's eggs in many baskets. The stability comes not from diversification but from mutual reinforcement, not from scattering resources but from concentrating them. The source of mutual reinforcement is the greater assurance of continuous operations that integration confers. Changing market conditions, or divergent circumstances in which different firms find themselves, influence the *timing* and the *direction* of integration decisions; they may give rise to a recognition by management of the need for better balance, and provide the occasion for seeking it. But they do not provide the explanation of integration.

Thus it was certainly the shortages and threatened shortages of crude oil around the close of World War I that awakened Standard of Indiana to the dangers of not having its own production: for a time it was forced to operate the Whiting refinery at one-half capacity and less, and despite large purchases of intermediate and final products, it was unable to supply its customers' needs. These fears similarly inspired the Jersey Company to embark on a worldwide program of exploration and production around 1918; it acquired control of Humble, it will be remembered, in 1919, just about the time when Socony took over Magnolia. Atlantic made a hesitant start at the same time, and for the same reasons.

However, major steps in these backward integration programs were taken in the 1920's—the very time when the forward pressure of crude oil would seem to have discouraged them: witness Indiana's numerous acquisitions of producing companies throughout the 1920–30 period and the intensified exploratory efforts of its affiliate, Stanolind, beginning in 1932; and witness the Jersey Company's intense and far-ranging efforts to get foreign production during the 1920's. Jersey acquired the marketing facilities of Beacon Oil in 1929; but just the year before it had purchased a majority of the shares of the Venezuelan producing company, Creole Petroleum. Like Indiana, Jersey was apparently intent on pursuing the profits of successful production and the security conferred by a closer balance of its own producing and refining operations, regardless of the temporary conditions of the crude oil market.[77]

77. In the same way Standard took its first major steps backward into production, in 1886–87, "as a matter of long run policy rather than of immediate necessity . . . the oil producing regions were once again inundated with an over-supply of crude oil" (McLean and Haigh, p. 67). On the later activities of the Indiana and Jersey companies, see above, pp. 88 ff., and the sources there

Again, the early history of Tidewater and Gulf can be interpreted in terms of companies integrating forward under the pressure of crude oil production; but within a very short time both companies were intensifying their efforts to find more crude in order to keep up with the requirements of their refineries and market outlets. The commitment to integration endured; only the direction of efforts shifted.

The priority and cumulative character of that commitment is well illustrated by the Gulf case. Even at the outset, the investments in refining were not regarded simply as a means of finding a market for crude oil free of Standard. W. L. Mellon made it clear that he regarded production as much a support to the refining and marketing operations as vice versa: "I concluded that the way to compete was to develop an integrated business which would first of all produce oil. Production, I saw, had to be the foundation of such a business. That was clearly the only way for a company which proposed to operate without saying 'by your leave' to anybody." [78] Indeed, from 1905 through 1917, Gulf's crude production was less than its domestic refinery runs, and it was forced to intensify its efforts to find enough production both at home and abroad to keep up with the forward operations. It took not only greatly expanded domestic production but rapidly mounting imports of company-produced oil to move and hold the crude oil self-sufficiency ratio above 100 per cent in the years 1918–24. [79]

Between 1925 and 1929, Gulf's domestic production leaped from 31 to 50 million barrels, its foreign output from 6.6 to 28.2 million barrels. The company became so concerned with this overwhelming volume of crude that it launched a $90 million expansion of pipeline, refinery, and marketing facilities in 1929, largely to assure itself a controlled outlet. The shoe had once again shifted to the other foot. The discoveries of crude oil do not explain and they did not cause Gulf's integration. They simply provided the opportunity and occasion for a company long committed to balanced growth to expand its operations

cited; also Gibb and Knowlton, *The Resurgent Years,* chaps. 11–13. Only Atlantic, of the four above-mentioned successor companies who were short of production, was apparently induced to hold back on its efforts to get closer in balance by the softness of crude oil markets in the 1920's. See McLean and Haigh, pp. 234–236.

78. *Ibid.,* p. 77; see also p. 72. This statement immediately followed the one quoted above, p. 84, emphasizing the need for forward integration to avoid dependence on Standard as sole customer.

79. The statistical data on Gulf's production and refinery runs are *ibid.,* p. 682.

at other levels correspondingly. The experience was not a happy one. As a sequel, the Company's stockholders were presented with a "whopping loss of more than $23,000,000" in 1931.[80] Prorationing in Texas and Oklahoma hit Gulf with unusual severity because of the concentration of its production in those states. It was unable to compensate by acquiring new production properties because the recent overextension of its refining-marketing investments had left it critically short of capital. Domestic production plus imports of its own foreign oil consequently fell substantially below its refinery needs, fluctuating between 61 per cent and 84 per cent of the latter from 1934 to 1952. After 1934 the company was concerned primarily to obtain enough crude to meet its refining and marketing needs. Yet only for a brief period (approximately 1930 to 1935) did it try to contract other operations to the levels of its crude oil supply, running them substantially below capacity.[81] Today, some Gulf executives would prefer to see the company in its original role, primarily a producer rather than a fully integrated company continuously a little short of crude.[82] But they also recognize that it is not a free agent, it cannot abandon its refinery and its marketing investments. At most, it can discourage the overenthusiastic efforts of its marketing division to expand into areas which it is not well equipped to serve. Integration is a process that the integrating company cannot easily reverse; and even though it may provide other advantages the security it affords comes at a price.

In short, the big oil companies long ago undertook a basic commitment to integration, antecedent to and in large measure independent of the temporary influences of fluctuating market conditions in the various sectors in which they operate. If anything, this general policy has become more and more widely accepted.

Confirmation of the basic uniformity of the pattern and commitment is provided by McLean and Haigh's detailed analysis of the crude-oil-producing activities and policies of seven major companies during the 1930's. Interestingly enough, those authors emphasize the differences among the seven:

80. S. Swensrud, *Gulf Oil: The First Fifty Years, 1901–1951* (the Newcomen Society in North America, 1951), p. 18; see also Thompson, *Since Spindletop*, pp. 52–54.

81. See McLean and Haigh, pp. 95–99, 377–381, 682.

82. We refer here to the domestic position of Gulf. Largely because of the discoveries in Kuwait, Gulf's foreign production soared from 22 million barrels in 1945 to 248 million in 1956, with the result that worldwide the Company is well over 100 per cent self-sufficient. See below, Table XII.

It is apparent that the seven companies had arrived at quite different positions with respect to their ratios of crude oil production to refinery runs. . . .

In some cases the companies moved in quite different directions at approximately the same time. In other cases they moved in the same direction at about the same time and under about the same circumstances but for very different reasons. In only a few cases could it be said that they did the same things at the same time for the same reasons.

The decade from 1930 to 1940 provides a particularly good example of a situation in which several of the companies followed different courses of action . . .[83]

As we read the record the similarities were far more significant than the differences. The managements of five of the companies—Texas, Gulf, Atlantic, Standard of Ohio, and Standard of Indiana—were essentially in accord as to the desirability of bringing their producing operations up into closer balance with refining and marketing. Their *abilities* to do so diverged; and for this and other reasons, there were differences in the *timing* of their efforts. Both Gulf and Sohio found themselves unable to marshall the financial resources for an expanded production program until after the middle 1930's, though the management of Gulf was "anxious" to do so,[84] and "there was a growing sentiment among the Sohio executives that the company should engage in crude production." [85] The other three, all within a year or two of 1933, "decided that the company's efforts to develop crude oil production should be substantially increased," and embarked on "a very active program" to this end; and all succeeded in raising the self-sufficiency ratios of their crude-oil production to refinery runs.[86] So there was a

83. Pp. 376, 388.
84. *Ibid.,* p. 388.
85. *Ibid.,* p. 243. The Company began producing on a very modest scale in 1937. See pp. 248, 687
86. The first quotation applies to Atlantic, the second to Indiana, and both can be duplicated in the case of Texas (*ibid.,* pp. 236, 263; see also pp. 384–386, 683, 686–687). Texas had experienced a substantial decline in its self-sufficiency ratio, from 74.8 per cent in 1929 to 43.7 per cent in 1934—in large measure because it had become its definite policy in the 1920's to place major emphasis on refining and marketing. But this de-emphasis of production was a subject of sharp internal controversy; and when the company changed management in 1933 it reversed the policy and succeeded in lifting the ratio to 63.1 per cent by 1939. See also James, *The Texaco Story,* pp. 49, 55–63. It was sometime during the early thirties that the Standard of Indiana management

strikingly unanimous desire of all five for better balance in the middle 1930's—in no small measure, as we shall see more fully in Part II below, because after prorationing that desire coincided with the desire for higher and more stable profits after tax in recommending heavier concentration on production.

Even McLean and Haigh's two apparent exceptions, Sinclair and Ohio Oil, were not so exceptional as they seem. Ohio's policies were different for the compelling historical reason that until 1924 it had been exclusively a producer and transporter of crude oil, as it was before 1911. Thereafter it too moved to closer balance, adopting the "well established policy . . . to carry on a substantial refining operation as an adjunct to its producing operations." By 1931 it had acquired refining capacity of 6,500 b/d, and during the following decade its refinery throughput ran one-fourth to one-third of its crude production.[87] As for Sinclair, according to McLean and Haigh that Company deliberately soft-pedaled its exploration and development expenditures, and permitted its crude-oil self-sufficiency ratio to fall from 62.5 per cent in 1932 to 33.1 per cent in 1939, because its management felt that state controls were increasing the cost of production excessively.[88] Actually Sinclair's expenditures on production in the 1930's reflect no such de-emphasis.[89] In any event, the difference, if any,

---

adopted the general goal of supplying at least 50 per cent of the company's crude requirements from its own production. It lost considerable ground in this direction when in 1932, because of the imposition of a tariff on crude, it sold to Standard of New Jersey the huge foreign oil interests it had acquired from Pan American. But the above-mentioned "very active program" succeeded in raising its domestic crude ratio from 22.5 to 38.6 per cent, between 1933 and 1937; these efforts persisted, and between 1943 and 1952 Indiana approximated the 50 per cent goal. McLean and Haigh, pp. 262–263, 687; Giddens, *Standard Oil Company (Indiana)*, pp. 649–652, 702. A dramatic incident in Atlantic's program to improve its crude oil self-sufficiency was the purchase in 1956 of the Houston Oil Company, with a daily production of 17,000 b/d, at a cost of almost $200,000,000.

87. McLean and Haigh, pp. 100–101, 685.

88. *Ibid.*, pp. 381–382, 684.

89. It is true that the company's average annual expenditures for crude oil production fell from about $14.4 million in 1927–30 to $11.3 million in 1931–1939; but the *proportion* of total capital outlays going into production actually increased from 50½ to 54½ per cent during the two periods—to 56½ per cent if the latter period is confined to 1933–39, when Sinclair's crude oil self-sufficiency ratio dropped. Compared with the others (excepting Ohio Oil which spent much more and Standard of Ohio which spent hardly anything), the latter proportion was not out of line: Texas 57½; Atlantic 45½; Standard of Indiana 50 (years 1936–39 alone available); Gulf 60. (These are simple averages of the annual percentages shown *ibid.*, pp. 697–700; see also chart, p. 368.) Sinclair was apparently unique only in its lack of success!

proved to be one of timing only. In 1949 Sinclair embarked on an intensive program to bring its crude ratio up to a minimum of 50 per cent, for reasons very similar to those that had motivated the other five in the years preceding.[90] Meanwhile Gulf, recovered from the financial stringencies of the early 1930's, was able to manage more nearly the kind of production effort it felt desirable. Sohio found it possible and profitable after 1940 to devote its attention to doing the same thing; and Ohio Oil, out of balance in the other direction, resumed the expansion of its refinery operations after World War II and thereby reduced its crude ratio from 474 per cent, its high point during the war years, to 245 per cent in 1952,[91] at about which level it has remained since.

If one looks to the details of company policy, or to the precise timing of integration steps, one may well conclude with McLean and Haigh that, while "similarities can be found in the general efforts they made," "the differences . . . were somewhat more marked than the similarities." But if one is more concerned with the long perspective, and with the general character of the companies' attitudes toward integration, he will find a remarkable uniformity, and perhaps even a trend toward increased uniformity. One indication of such a trend is to be found in the tendency toward convergence, in the last fifteen or twenty years, in the respective percentages of total capital expenditures that these same companies have devoted to production.[92]

90. Sinclair, which had reportedly been negotiating for the purchase of Houston Oil (see above, n. 86), made a similar move in 1956, acquiring for a reported $47,500,000 about 30 per cent of the stock of the Texas Pacific Coal and Oil Company, with a production of about 21,000 b/d. New York *Times*, August 17, 1956. The year before, Sinclair had purchased all the assets of the American Republics Corporation for $108,000,000, adding some 14,000 b/d to its production. See "They Rush to Get on Balance," *Business Week* (September 1, 1956), pp. 46–50.

91. McLean and Haigh, pp. 382–383, 685, 697.

92. *Percentage of Total Capital Outlays for Production*

	1936	1940	1952	1957
Ohio Oil	87	69	56	80
Sinclair	68	49	42	57
Gulf	55	64	62	57
Texas	53	62	66	57
Atlantic	51	38	56	67
Standard of Indiana	42	45	51	59
Standard of Ohio	0	1	56	28

Sources: McLean and Haigh, pp. 697–700, for the first three years; *National Petroleum News Factbook* (1958), for 1957.

The range of variation in percentages for these years, selected at random, obviously has decreased. Even if the top and bottom companies are lopped

Apart from the special tax and profit incentives that made investment in production so attractive, the common element producing such uniformity was the commitment of all these companies to a certain measure of balance—that is, of integration—in their operations.

The following composite paraphrase represents a rough consensus of how the executives of almost all leading oil companies seem to think about this commitment:

> We certainly try, in general, to keep a balanced operation. We will not ordinarily make major investments in one level without seeing that we are pretty well covered at other levels. So we do not expect to make the same return from our investments in production, refining and marketing. As a general rule we will not demand as high a return from prospective investments that put us in balance as from those that put us out of balance. We have a going organization, with substantial commitments at all levels; we cannot shift from one to another with each short-term fluctuation of returns; we have to protect the positions we already have.

CONCLUSION: THE SHIFTING HISTORICAL FOCI OF STRATEGIC INTEGRATION DECISIONS

It is dangerous to supply simple explanations of complicated phenomena; the foregoing historical essay has demonstrated the variety of motives and circumstances that have made integration so prevalent in the American oil industry. Even for the Standard Oil trust, which used integration essentially to buttress a monopoly of refining, other purposes were clearly influential—reduction in transport costs, the opportunity to make a profitable conversion of sour Indiana crude, the aggressive service of expanding product markets. The abiding faith of Standard's successful competitors in the merits of integration with roots deep in oil production, similarly, was not the product merely of the ruthless tactics of the Standard group. Producers of unfamiliar California and Texas crudes had to find ways of refining them successfully, merely in order to give value above ground to what they were finding below. Subsequent fears of crude oil shortage in turn precipitated heavy expenditures by these same companies in search of more, while at the same time the rich promise of the automobile's demands shunted major refinery investment funds forward into distribution as well, in order to cut costs or secure a desirable market

off in each instance, the range declines from 26 percentage points in both prewar years to 11 and 10 points in the two postwar.

position. In these and innumerable other ways the search for cost reduction and competitive strength and the exploitation of profit opportunities have vied with sheer protective strategy in conditioning the extension of integration, both before and after 1911.

But the essence of integration, it seems to us, is the protection it offers or seems to offer against the uncertainties and instabilities of reliance on often highly imperfect intermediate markets. It is a means by which oil companies have attempted, in an industry that is potentially highly unstable, to stake out and insulate market positions by securing dependable sources of supply (of raw materials and products) and dependable market outlets (for crude oil and products).[93] The impulse to integration imparted by these inherent instabilities was accentuated historically by the Standard Oil empire's dominance over intermediate markets and, even after dissolution, by the continued constriction of intermediate market alternatives because of the vertical integration of the other major oil companies. The thrust, in short, has been market control, or its circumvention. To what extent it has reached the mark is the subject of the remainder of this study.

The generality of integration and similarity of major oil company attitudes toward it obviously do not preclude great differences between them. But these differences—in balance, in timing, in direction and occasion for major integration moves—can usually be explained in terms of divergent historical circumstances. They persist because they too constitute a kind of commitment, reflecting differences in attitude, experience, and ability, and because, except with extraordinary luck or by a disregard of costs and profits, they cannot be eradicated even over a period of many years.

Apart from the differences between companies, changing circumstances affecting the industry as a whole naturally have the effect of altering the emphasis over time and place of integration decisions and policies. We have suggested why the horizontal combination of refiners and the vertical integration of refining and transport were particularly strategic to the stabilization and monopolization program of Rockefeller and his associates, and why it seemed both fruitless and unnecessary to try to attempt similar combinations in the unruly small-scale production end of the business. The potential monopoly profits

93. For a generalized interpretation of the competitive process as consisting of just such attempts to stake out market "niches" and of the attainment of such positions contributing to market stability, see Richard B. Heflebower, "Toward a Theory of Industrial Markets and Prices," *American Economic Review, Papers and Proceedings, 44* (1954), 121, esp. 124–127.

could be locked in against the law of capture and the pressure of fixed costs, it seemed, without undertaking the risks of wildcatting and the burdens of selling crude oil.

Frankel points out how different was the strategy of Henri Deterding, the Rockefeller of the giant international company, Royal-Dutch Shell—and why

> with new fields discovered and developed, not in the heart of an urban civilization as that of the United States, but in far-away and climatically difficult countries, the "unit" of crude production had become much larger and, for the first time, it was possible to achieve semi-centralized control of essential sectors of crude production. . . .
>
> John D. . . . thought rightly that the supply of crude would look after itself if he could only control the marketing end.
>
> . . . Deterding and his English friends . . . saw that it was vital to possess the oil, and that whoever controlled the crude could almost let the disposal of the finished products look after itself.[94]

In contrast with the situation within the United States that faced Rockefeller, centralized control of production could be effected abroad. Consequently, backward integration was essential to anyone who would operate on a large scale in refining or marketing in the world oil industry, as W. L. Mellon put it, "without saying 'by your leave' to anybody." No mere combination of marketers, refiners, or transporters could resist monopolistic exactions and circumvention by whoever obtained control over the raw material.

The atomistic character of American crude oil production continued to make integration into that sphere seem less attractive and less necessary after 1911 as well as before. However, the dissolution and dissipation of the monolithic control of refining and marketing made a more complete backward integration seem necessary to the refining and marketing remnants of the Standard empire, particularly when shortages threatened. The only places where it seemed monopoly profits could still be locked in between, say, 1911 and 1935, were in pipeline transportation, where entry was not easy and an integrated company could at least for a time hold on to the difference between the pipeline costs and rail tariffs; in the adoption of thermal cracking, where patent control blocked access of independents; and possibly in undertaking distribution of one's own branded gasoline

94. *Essentials of Petroleum,* pp. 91–92. Author's italics omitted.

through the construction of one's own service stations. In each instance, as we shall see, the high promised returns materialized, but could not be preserved indefinitely. These areas became the new foci of integration and investment decisions because changing circumstances made these the operations a large company had to control for its own protection—if only temporary and partial—against the eroding influences of free markets.

Of the three strategic points, integration of pipeline transport with refining was probably the most important. Typically, control over the pipelines by the major refiners still forced producers as the best of available alternatives to sell their oil at the wellhead, and it confined the smaller, nonintegrated refiners, who were unable to build their own pipelines, either to location in the field or to the high charges of the lines that were willing to carry their oil. It was in the high returns from pipeline investment, above all, that the potential monopoly profits of the industry could be locked.

With the institution of effective state control over production, from about 1935 on, production became the strategic area for almost the first time in the history of the American industry. Entry remained free, and production control relatively unconcentrated; but for the first time the tyranny of a highly unstable and inelastic supply was curbed, the market was effectively stabilized, and monopoly profits might now be secured by the successful producer.[95] Integration of marketing, refining, and pipelines alone no longer offered the promise of market control. The pipeline thereafter found it far more difficult to give preference to its own producing wells in periods of excess supply; the nonintegrated refiner and marketer now faced the radically changed and highly uncomfortable situation of buying in a market where prices were far more effectively maintained than in the one in which they sold, by virtue of the sovereign power of the state and the strength and fewness of the companies controlling potentially competitive foreign sources of supply. It is not surprising, thus, that the major companies, already committed to and appreciative of the advantages of integration, almost unanimously determined to improve the balance between their producing and downstream operations. Four of the seven com-

95. The unusually successful producer has always earned supernormal returns, of course, even before prorationing. But those profits are economic rents, the consequence of supernormal efficiency or luck. Production control added the profits that come from limiting supply and, in consequence, holding price above marginal cost. See below, Pt. II, for corroboration of this and the other observations in this paragraph about the effects of state production controls.

panies subjected by McLean and Haigh to detailed analysis devoted an average of 55 per cent of their capital expenditures to production in the period 1936–40, when effective production control had been instituted, compared with only 32 per cent in 1928–31.[96] It is this critical position of the production end of the business in integration —as well as in other aspects of competitive performance—of the oil industry since 1935 that justifies our devoting the following entire section of our study to it, even though emergent excess crude-oil production capacity in the fifties may already be shifting the focus of strategic integration decisions forward once more.

96. The following are the relevant percentages for the six companies who were less than fully self-sufficient in production:

Capital Expenditures in the Production Department as Percentages of Company Totals

AVERAGES [a] FOR SELECTED PERIODS

COMPANY	1928–31	1936–40
Atlantic	19.9	44.1
Gulf	30.9	61.5
Sinclair	42.8	57.2
Texas	35.7	57.7
Average of the averages	32.3	55.1
Standard of Indiana	n.a.	49.0
Standard of Ohio	0.0	2.7

[a] Simple arithmetic averages of annual percentages. We present an average of averages for only the first four companies because 1928–31 figures are not available for Standard of Indiana, and because Sohio's ratio is so unrepresentative.

Source: Computed from data in McLean and Haigh, pp. 697–700.

PART II

Crude Oil, Integration, and Public Policy

CHAPTER 6

The Issues Raised by Integration in a Regulated Industry

BUSINESS INTEGRATION in oil was an attempt, among other things, to stay or isolate the instability that competitive exploitation under the rule of capture forced on the industry. But whatever order it had been able to evolve was shattered by events of the second and third decades of this century: dissolution of the monolithic Standard Oil empire; the world war, which etched in public consciousness the vital role petroleum was to play thereafter in military might; the revolutionary impact of the automobile; and the deluge of oil discoveries toward the end of the period.

In this new perspective the recurrent wastes in new field development and production over some seventy-five years of domestic private operation combined with oil shortages immediately after the war to breed a pervading fear for the continuity of supplies. Some big firms intensified the search for foreign oil and, abetted by an aroused Congress and State Department, pried open doors in the Middle East that had been shrewdly barred to American interests by the British. And though the early fears for the imminent exhaustion of our petroleum reserves at home were soon drowned in the gushers of new fields, most dramatically in East Texas, the profligate waste of these episodes eventually ended in the acceptance of public regulation of output.

Regulation of output inevitably involves determination of price; the level of crude oil prices thus determined is naturally a matter of public interest. This alone, however, would not bring the subject within the scope of the present study. It is rather because the large integrated firm spans all levels of the industry and extends its operations typically beyond the jurisdiction of any single regulating state, often beyond all of them, that issues of significance to this study clearly emerge. Both the crude oil prices themselves and the regulations supporting them are administered in an environment in which such firms exercise significant influence as buyers, as sellers, and more recently as importers. If this influence creates differential advantages for the major

121

oil companies which can be exploited for their own gain at other levels of the industry by reason of their integration, the effect on less privileged competitors and on competition itself at these separate levels cannot be a matter of social indifference.

Vertical integration among competitive strata of an industry creates no problems by itself. But vertical integration encompassing markets in which competition is seriously imperfect does. A more obvious instance of an inherently imperfect market would be hard to find in any industry than that provided by the production of crude oil. Abroad, it is controlled by a few giant international firms; at home, it is regulated by state authority. Thus the production, control, and pricing of crude oil become the crux of the perplexing issues posed by vertical integration in petroleum. Any consideration of integration in this industry which omitted an appraisal of its impact on the functioning of crude markets and of the implications of market control in crude on competition in the entire industry would be like a history of the harnessing of atomic energy without mention of the bomb.

The public expects more than effective competition from this industry. It expects something it calls "conservation"; here again, the role of the large, integrated company must be assessed. Although there are differences of opinion about the meaning of conservation, there are none regarding the need for it in petroleum in some significant form. Nor is there serious question about the necessity for the intervention of public authority to harness competitive self-interest in the cause of efficient, scientific recovery. The really controversial questions concern the approximate definition of the "conservation" that public regulation is supposed to serve and how, and by whom, it is to be implemented.

The production control system now used in the states producing most of the oil has never been free of criticism either in concept or as administered in practice. It defines the waste it seeks to prevent to include production in excess of market demand, and it therefore exercises pervasive control over production, field by field and well by well, to adjust the total aggregate supply of crude to what it is anticipated the market will take. The process, known as prorationing, begins with the Bureau of Mines, which provides a monthly estimate of anticipated demand for crude oils from the various states. The state commissions may choose to modify this calculation: Texas, for example, makes its own estimates, based in part on the sworn "nominations" of the principal refiners indicating the amount of crude each plans to purchase within the state. To reduce the resulting estimate to a statewide production allowable requires a series of sub-tractions: for production which cannot be curtailed without risk of loss or which it is otherwise deemed undesirable to limit,[1] and for the volume of supplies beyond the control of public authority like stocks in storage and imports. The Texas Railroad Commission, which con-trols more than 40 per cent of United States crude production and approximately half of estimated national proved reserves, has also found it desirable to make allowance in its estimates for anticipated production in states that do not control production or use other bases of control. By thus allowing for estimated supplies beyond its jurisdic-tion, Texas in effect brings total available supply, including imports, within the principle of prorationing to market demand. Estimated market demand less these uncontrolled additions to supply gives the total which is to be prorated among fields and wells in a manner cal-culated to preserve equity among producers and to prevent any well from producing beyond its Maximum Efficient Rate (MER).[2] Scheduled allowables are expressed in numbers of calendar days of permitted production per month at MER.

Prorationing to market demand is often alleged to violate the principles of both economy and efficiency. When production allow-ables are held below MER, the primary consequence is said to be not

1. Thus old wells operating on the pump (the so-called stripper wells) and wells operating in old fields under secondary recovery drives will be permitted to produce without limit or up to a fixed maximum output per day. See Erich W. Zimmermann, *Conservation in the Production of Petroleum,* Petroleum Monograph Series, 2 (New Haven, 1957), p. 329. Also special allowances are made for new wells that may be discovered—a reward for exploration by way of more rapid liquidation of drilling costs. In each case, estimates must be made to offset against estimated demand.

2. The Maximum Efficient Rate is an engineering-geological determination of the theoretically maximum rate of flow of crude oil from the well that will not endanger ultimate recovery from the pool by a too rapid release of under-ground pressures. MER will vary with the character of the oil-bearing structure and the nature of the natural drive—whether water pressure, a gas cap, or gas in solution in the crude oil. It will generally be guided by mechanical indices like the pressure at the bottom of the well ("bottom-hole pressure") or the ratio of gas to oil in the crude produced. Obviously MER has signifi-cance primarily for wells that are still producing on natural drives. When these drives fail, one must resort to artificial pumping with or without a reinjection of water or gas into the structure (secondary recovery) to propel the oil through the stratum to the well. While the proper determination of MER in-volves the application of the best scientific knowledge available, at best the range of competent judgment is broad, so that MER may represent little more than an informed guess.

so much a limitation of waste as a support for the level of crude oil prices. In practice, conservation's objectives are held further compromised for political expediency when wells are permitted to multiply in a field, in violation of minimum spacing for effective drainage, because of the peculiarities of surface ownership.[3] The alleged defects of administrative prorationing to market demand have stimulated the search for alternative methods of regulation that would at one and the same time more fully serve the purposes of conservation, and permit a greater measure of competitive adjustment of supply to market forces. Two alternatives have been strongly advocated. The first and ostensibly the simplest of these is mandatory unitization, a requirement that the development and production of each field should be conducted under the control of a single operator for the combined account of the owners and leaseholders. The basis of operation would be a cooperative agreement among all parties with an interest in the oil reservoir under which their respective liabilities for assessments and shares in output or in revenue would be determined. It is often urged that with this plan in force, further state control of production would be unnecessary. A single operational control for an entire field would assure economy in both drilling and secondary recovery for the exploitation of the oil reservoir; and the number of competing unitized fields (that is, sellers) would assure that the public was adequately served at a reasonable price. The attractions of such a situation are self-evident provided they are practically obtainable.

The second alternative (sometimes combined with compulsory unitization) is that the state confine its control of output to preventing production beyond MER. Up to the point where output threatens ultimate recovery from the reservoir, it would be free of regulation. Under this system production of most wells would be uncontrolled and only a few would be subject to maximum output limits. Again, the economy of control and the apparent scientific objectivity are appealing.

Prorationing has demonstrated its ability to bring order out of pre-existing chaos in the production of crude oil. It has successfully throttled wasteful production from flush wells in excess of MER. But it has been far less effective in preventing excessive drilling of wells in a given reservoir with a consequent rise in investment costs per

3. Too many wells tapping a single reservoir, besides involving a direct waste of capital, dissipate and unbalance underground pressures and may render sections of the producing stratum inert, thus reducing ultimate oil recovery.

barrel of oil and a reduction in ultimate recovery. It has protected the correlative rights of small and independent owners in an oil reservoir—that is to say, their right to a share in the total corresponding to the amount originally in place under their property—by sharply curtailing discrimination by crude oil purchasers in taking oil from affiliated at the expense of nonaffiliated producers. But it has also served—despite protestations to the contrary—to buttress the crude oil price level against undermining by new sources of supply. The accomplishments are not to be jeopardized lightly. But neither should defects, which an alternative approach may avoid, be disregarded.

Since the United States has now become a net importer of crude petroleum and products, the regulation of domestic production can no longer be practiced in isolation. The State of Texas can continue to insulate domestic price levels from the lower costs of foreign production by contracting production allowables at the expense of domestic producers and users of oil to offset the volume of imports. But such action can only make importation more profitable than ever, and it must fail eventually unless an effective means is found to limit the inflow of foreign oil. The federal government may come to the rescue of state authority by exerting its influence to hold down imports, but only at the risk of denying American consumers the advantages of cheaper foreign oil, and of freezing existing (and promoting new) discriminations between firms which have foreign oil and those that do not. In the existing mélange of uncoordinated public controls over oil, only the large integrated firm, as buyer and seller of crude oil in many jurisdictions—and particularly the few who control the bulk of world reserves outside this country and the USSR—would seem to have enough alternatives and to retain enough room for maneuver to protect its own interests.

It is this complex linkage between the size and integration of the major oil companies on the one hand and the pervasive, imperfectly articulated public controls in the arena of crude oil production on the other, with possibly adverse implications for competition in subsequent levels of the industry, that makes an examination and appraisal of those public policies imperative in this study. What is the differential impact of prorationing and import limitations on the comparative interests of majors at home and abroad and of independents? What are the objectives of conservation and national policy in the crude oil area, and are there alternative ways of realizing them more fully and in a manner more compatible with the preservation of desirable competitive forces in this industry? This exploration demands a grasp of crude oil price-making forces even though price policy per se is not our primary concern.[4] It also requires examination of conservation purposes and practices even though conservation as such is beyond the scope of this monograph.[5] Finally, it involves a brief look at foreign oil sources and the policies that condition their development even though this study is focused primarily on the domestic market.

4. In the first volume of this series, Ralph Cassady, Jr., focused his attention on price. See his *Price Making and Price Behavior in the Petroleum Industry*.

5. For a full-length analysis of this subject, see Zimmermann.

CHAPTER 7

Regulation of Production by the States

AGAINST the rising demands and the evolving national consciousness of dependence on oil associated with World War I and its immediate aftermath, domestic production seemed to falter after 1915. Crude prices in the Midcontinent area rose from 40 cents a barrel in the spring of 1915 to $3.50 in March, 1920; imports increased, especially from Mexico; and domestic crude stocks were drawn down.[1] This experience inspired fears that the country might be running out of oil.[2] The subsequent reversal of fortune when new strikes flooded oil markets did not quell public concern: the wastes of temporary flush production boded ill in the long run for an economy of soaring demands. Both experiences afforded ample evidence of the public interest in some sort of government regulation.

CONFLICTING INTERESTS IN THE EVOLUTION OF STATE CONTROLS

Private interests too were intimately involved in these developments. Expanding company investments at other levels of the industry were threatened by discontinuity of supplies, and some state governments soon became aware of the higher royalties, higher taxes, and higher wages that could be generated by higher prices and more stable output.[3] The violent instability and wasteful, discriminatory behavior of uncontrolled crude markets became increasingly intolera-

1. See Watkins, pp. 40–41. Also *Petroleum Facts and Figures*, 9th ed., pp. 3 and 365–366.
2. Thus J. E. Pogue spoke of "approaching exhaustion" of domestic supplies in 1918, and he was still apprehensive in 1921. See C. G. Gilbert and J. E. Pogue, *Petroleum: A Resource Interpretation* (Washington, D.C., Smithsonian Institution, Bulletin 102, 1918), Pt. VI, p. 1 (quoted by Kemnitzer, *Rebirth of Monopoly*, p. 57); and Pogue, *Economics of Petroleum* (New York, Wiley, 1921), pp. 351–352.
3. An excellent analysis of forces converging to bring about public control was written during the period by J. Howard Marshall and Norman L. Meyers, "Legal Planning of Petroleum Production: Two Years of Proration," *Yale Law Journal*, 42 (1933), 702 ff., esp. n. 119.

ble to the parties directly concerned. Both buyers and sellers had much to gain from greater stability: sellers, caught in time of flush production without feasible access to market; buyers, exposed by widely fluctuating raw material prices to unpredictable inventory gains and losses, and to product markets infected by the same vertigo. However, no unanimity of opinion was to have been expected with respect to the appropriate methods and levels of stabilization, in a market where some buyers were also producers and others were not; where some producers were transporters and users and others were not. The interests of buyers and sellers in crude oil markets naturally diverged (and continue to diverge) and not only because of the varying degrees of their vertical integration. Additional, and richly varied cross-currents of interest were dictated by differences in size and financial resources, production costs, geographic location, and market position of individual producers and refiners.

The first, basic, and most destructive conflict of interests was of course between the several property owners or operators, competing to capture vagrant oil and gas on their underground trek toward low-pressure points. They had a communal interest in seeking release from this competitive scramble, because it involved them in heavier capital expenditures, lower physical recovery, lower prices in the period of flush production, and ultimately higher lifting costs than would some more rational, regulated system of production control. The heavier capital costs were imposed by the necessity for drilling numerous off-set wells [4] as rapidly as possible, in order to deflect a part of the sub-surface migration, or to beat one's neighbor to the draw. No one operator could defer drilling or hold back production of his flowing wells; and the faster all drilled and produced, the more rapidly were the energy-giving drives—natural gas in solution or gas trapped in a cap or the surrounding water level—lost by release or neutralized and isolated underground by irregular, unbalanced production. In either case, natural drives subsided, free flow ceased with most of the oil unrecovered, and artificial lift and costly secondary recovery prematurely introduced the final period in the life of the reservoir.

However, while producers of crude oil had a strong community of interest in production controls, there were also wide conflicts of interest that kept them apart, and that have always defeated and

4. An offset well is one drilled as close to a producing well as property lines, or other regulations, will permit. Its purpose is to tap the same pool and thus protect one's correlative rights in the ill-defined reservoir by offsetting the rival's withdrawals by withdrawals of one's own.

would today still defeat any limitations on production within this country that depended simply on voluntary cooperation. These conflicts are perhaps too obvious to require elaborate description. The race in production goes to the first and the quickest: these (or any producers who hope to qualify the next time—and wildcatters are occupationally optimists) will naturally resist any regulations that threaten their freedom to drill and extract. Rank wildcatting is conducted preponderantly by independent producers, often men with relatively little capital, in quest of a quick pay-out. Operators like these have generally feared limitations of production—imposed in part under pressure by larger companies, financially better able to sit on their oil—that would extend the pay-out period, even if higher ultimate recoveries would result. Their interest has typically been on the side of increased production for the most rapid possible recovery of sunk costs.[5] They have earned their fortunes by a rapid turnover of cash, invested and reinvested as quickly as possible in continuous exploration and development. Marginal or stripper-well operators may have feared production cutbacks that would push their operations below the margin of profitability. Other producers have felt that limitations on what they may produce from individual wells only force them to drill even more wells to get back their investment in an acceptably short time. Finally, there are always enough belligerent individualists who want no part of either voluntary cooperation or government controls—and many especially have resisted the intervention of government out of fear it would end up in oppressive regulation of all aspects of their business.

Beyond these elemental sources of conflict between producers, crude buying and selling interests in the domestic market have been shaped most importantly by the development and administration of pipelines. Few of our oil fields have been discovered near adequate markets (Los Angeles is the classic exception) and few are immediately accessible to water transport (again California and the Gulf coast provide exceptions). The pipeline became the crux of efficient, long-distance transport of oil, and before effective public control of its operations and of field production it could be a lethal, exploitative

5. Although the goal is still a quick pay-out, the means of realization and therefore attitudes toward production controls have been modified in recent years by high progressive income taxes (up to 91 per cent) and the superior alternative of capital gains (at 26 per cent). Through discovery and subsequent sale on terms which reflect the stability imparted to prices by prorationing, the independent may escape much of the costs while reaping the benefits of regulation.

weapon as well. It was his grasp of this elementary truth that sparked
Rockefeller's strategy for the stabilization of the oil industry to his
own advantage. The ruthless integrated firm could use its own properties (both production and transport) to force crude prices lower or
even to exclude the independent producer or refiner from the market.
Such opportunities were not neglected in the pre-prorationing history
of oil.[6]

Even when the full monopsonistic potential of pipelines was not
exploited for the benefit of their owners, the conditions of their efficient use tended to generate a conflict of interests with independent
buyers and sellers of oil. Interstate pipelines are common carriers before the law; but they have been designed primarily to serve the
needs of their integrated owners. Furthermore, the pipeline is a model
of both high fixed costs and increasing returns. Decreasing unit investment and operating costs accompany larger design capacity at any
given rate of utilization; and with most costs fixed, unit costs of operation swing abruptly and inversely with the rate of utilization realized.[7] Thus early line capacities were geared to the programmed requirements of their integrated owners, and strong precautions were
taken to maintain high rates of utilization while avoiding fluctuations
in loading for outside parties, more especially those likely to require

6. The development of pipeline investments by the integrated majors is
discussed in greater detail below, Chap. 13. Little is gained by illustrative
documentation of the discriminatory use of pipelines; but it might be noted
that this was an important factor in Oklahoma's early move (in 1914 and
1915) to bring production under control. When the Healdton and Cushing
pools were brought in in 1913, one major with substantial field production
owned the only pipeline outlet. Field storage was quickly filled and most producers could only watch their output go down the creek. See Zimmermann,
p. 137 and chaps. 4 and 5.

7. Operating costs of pipelines vary with line diameter, horsepower, and
throughput. For a given anticipated throughput, costs will be minimized by the
best combination of line diameter and horsepower. Where anticipated throughput is relatively small, this optimum combination may be found with smaller
diameters even though the application of increasing power to a small diameter
line raises operating costs very steeply; but with larger diameters, cost curves
rise much less rapidly with added power and throughput. No limit has yet been
reached to the design economies that can be attained for huge throughputs by
larger line diameters.

Once a line is built, short-run costs per barrel per mile rise rapidly as
throughput falls below its design capacity. This is because practically all costs
are fixed except for the cost of power. For an excellent discussion of the costs
of operation of crude oil trunk pipelines, see Cookenboo, *Crude Oil Pipe Lines*,
chap. 1.

added investment. Such considerations undoubtedly conditioned high, early rate structures, high "minimum tender" requirements for independent shipment, and the continuing insistence that intended customers be prepared with adequate storage to accept delivery at predetermined terminals before tenders were accepted for shipment.[8]

The natural monopoly of the pipeline dramatized the vulnerability of crude oil producers in the absence of some form of control. To protect their correlative rights in the underground reservoir against the raids of integrated refiner-producer-pipeline transporters, some way of enforcing a proportionate or ratable taking of oil from the pool had to be devised.[9] Probably even more than the small producer, the nonintegrated refiner-buyer of crude was concerned about the availability to him of pipeline service on reasonable terms. Minimum tenders had to be set at reasonable levels and some way found to provide service to non-pipeline-owners, even when aggregate demand

8. Since crudes of different specifications are sent through the line without physical separation but under guarantees of delivery of like quality to that shipped, it is important that quantities of a given specification be large enough to hold the mixing of oils at cutoff points (transfers, withdrawals or new intakes into the line) to a small percentage of the total shipment. Thus, minimum tenders were set with a very conservative eye on the requirements of this kind of shipment, known as "batching." Where "common stream" specifications are acceptable to the parties, there are no such technical problems. In the latter case, independent shipments as low as 1,000 barrels (in contrast with minimum tenders of up to 100,000 barrels) have often been accepted.

The efficient loading of a line also demands careful preplanning, especially where transfers from one line to another are involved. Transfer tank storage must be available throughout the length of the line to permit proper cutting out and in of batched shipments, to fill downstream capacity as shipments are withdrawn, and to make room for new inputs at other points. Thus shipment schedules are usually frozen for a full month in advance.

These and other technical conditions of economic pipeline operation may require larger nominal tenders, longer shipping schedules and more adequate terminal storage than many independents can readily muster. Under easy circumstances, the practice is much less restrictive; under stress and when pipeline owners' interests are at stake, the administration of such requirements could become a frustrating obstacle to shipment by the independent.

9. Ratable taking is the process by which any cutback in total purchases of crude oil below supplies offered in a given field will be distributed proportionately (ratably) among all suppliers. Although many large buyers practiced ratable taking as a matter of policy, prorationing established the principle uniformly. An individual buyer may shift or curtail sources of supply; but if alternative buyers are not available to take up the slack, production allowables for the field will be restricted until ratable taking is re-established among all potential sellers.

exceeded pipeline capacity, before pipelines became common carriers in fact as well as name: the method was pipeline prorationing.[10]

Finally, the pipeline was responsible also in large part for the pattern of market forces that governed the price behavior of crude oil. It brought the market to the well of the producer.[11] It also helped consolidate the practice of price determination by the buyer. A few large integrated companies, which are also crude oil producers, "post" (that is, publish) prices for crude oil in each field. This posted price expresses a judgment regarding the derived value of a complex raw material, not too dissimilar from a valuation of cattle by the livestock buyer for a packing plant; it also sets the price at which the firm will sell its own oil to other majors and to independents.[12]

The published price of crude oil, however, more especially during periods of market stress, is an unreliable index of market forces. Major integrated firms and some important independents as well feel that they cannot afford to deal publicly at prices other than the posted buying price. Their contacts, both as buyers and as sellers, include both big and little sellers and buyers in many markets closely interrelated by pipelines. Further, it is customary in oil for both individuals and firms to participate, through fractional well ownership

10. Pipeline prorationing is the process by which requests for pipeline transportation (otherwise compatible with regulations governing acceptance for shipment) that in aggregate exceed the total capacity of the line are scaled back, among old and new shippers, to accommodate all who can meet minimum qualifications at a fair proportion of their desired shipments. Many pipeline companies followed the practice informally before they were required to do so.

11. Typically, crude oil purchases are consummated on the outlet side of the producer's lease tank which has been gauged very accurately to permit a close measurement of withdrawals by checking differential tank depths. Crude is withdrawn from locked connections into the gathering (small diameter pipe) lines of a refiner or a pipeline company. At the same time the gauger tests the oil for temperature, gravity, and impurities. All of this information is recorded on the "run" ticket, where volume and gravity are converted to equivalents at 60° F. The run ticket then becomes the basis for payment.

12. The crude-oil self-sufficiency rate (the ratio of a firm's own production to its crude runs to stills) is clearly no measure of the scale of the company's purchasing-selling activities. A firm's own oil may be badly located or of a type poorly adapted to its own use. To obtain the most economical raw material, it will engage in a variety of selling, buying, and bartering activities. The aggregate volume of these transactions will often exceed its own needs: many integrated firms buy and sell for independents as well and they often buy for the specific purpose of resale.

and multiple working interests, as suppliers in many fields—an elementary way of spreading the burden of capital outlays and the risks of loss. Communication is good among buying and selling representatives of integrated firms and among these diverse, fractional owners in many fields; and to change price at one point would bring direct reactions from many. Posted prices for a given kind and quality of crude, therefore, must be uniform in a given field and they will tend to be so over wide areas: broad economic and public relations values at stake for the majors breed inertia in the published price.

While changes in posted prices tend to be initiated by the majors,[13] the more typical price adjustment to a new demand and supply situation is said to be initiated by independent buyers (that is, refiners), who offer premiums above the posted price and thus lure "connections" from the majors when supply is tight, or negotiate discounts from that price when the volume of demand falls below the supply seeking a market.[14] The nonintegrated refiners, and the independents generally, are less bothered by the considerations that make the posted price relatively inflexible. Quite the contrary, since product prices are typically more sensitive than crude prices,[15] a change in prospective margins would force or induce the independent to search out a lower price or offer a higher one, to lower his costs and ease a margin squeeze, in the first case, or improve his volume, in the second. Unfortunately, there are no systematic, quantitative data available on transactions at premium and discount prices.[16]

It is impossible to draw from the foregoing account of the behavior

13. For the leading instances since World War II, see below, pp. 186 ff.

14. The actual physical connection of an oil well to the gathering system of a trunk pipeline is seldom changed until the field is exhausted, although there are instances to the contrary. More commonly, to "lose a connection" or to gain one will merely alter the ultimate destination of the oil. Except in California, where long-term contracts are more general, crude oil is usually sold by the producer in the field under contracts of indefinite term but subject to cancellation by either party on short notice, usually twenty-four hours.

15. This was the case even when crude prices were most free to change, i.e. before prorationing, as well as after. See below, pp. 414 ff.

16. Some data supplied by a "major oil company" showing volume of crude oil moving below posted price and volume and premium paid for crude above the posted price are shown for selected periods in selected markets in Cassady, pp. 121–122. While majors do not trade at other than posted prices, it is common knowledge in the industry that such firms have often used "non-price" inducements, such as scarce steel supplies, to gain or hold connections when crude was in short supply. On such transactions, again, quantitative data are lacking.

of, and conflicts of interest in, crude oil markets any simple classification of attitudes toward state control of production on the part of
the variously situated parties involved.[17] Many producers, large and
small, integrated and nonintegrated, undoubtedly saw in production
controls a promise of salvation from intolerable market instability;
others saw in them intolerable restrictions on their freedom of action.
Some, perhaps most, nonintegrated refiners undoubtedly were impressed by the dangers of transforming their suppliers from unruly
competitors to regulated monopoly, preferring to trust to their flexibility and acumen as buyers not only to protect them against the
wide fluctuations of uncontrolled raw material production and prices,
but to enable them to turn the disorganization of crude markets to
their advantage. Others, however, may have longed for the stabilization of their own branch of the industry that an elimination of crude
oil shortages and gluts might bring to pass.

The large integrated firm, with its own pipeline facilities, had available to itself important profit-sustaining and maximizing opportunities that were in varying degrees denied its smaller, less integrated
competitors at both producing and refining levels. In view of these
advantages, the major was better equipped to survive and possibly
even to prosper in the chaos of uncontrolled crude markets. But for
all their superior ability to take care of themselves, the majors had
very real interests in market stabilization even at some limitation on
their own freedom of action. Of course, these companies were integrated in widely varying degrees, and the structure of each varied
over time as well, so that generalizations are perilous. But, as investors
in crude properties, which were coming to represent the lion's share
of both their assets and their capital outlays, they had much to gain
from a scheme that would help to fix a floor for crude prices. Even
though most of them were not sellers but purchasers of crude oil, on
balance, a more rigid and higher crude-oil price floor, buttressed by
production control, promised them higher and more stable product
realizations, as well. If product prices might reasonably have been
expected to reflect changes in their crude oil component, an integrated
producer-refiner would only gain from the higher (and more stable)
aggregate return on its integrated production-refining operations,

17. An interesting, hypothetical summary was constructed by two analysts
during the early thirties, when authorities were straining to contain the flood of
oil from East Texas. See Marshall and Meyers, "Legal Planning of Petroleum
Production," pp. 137–139.

while losing nothing from the higher price of its purchased crude-oil requirements.[18]

In addition, production control might have promised a higher and more stable refinery *margin,* through its effect on entry into refining. As long as production was uncontrolled and majors were unable to bottle up producers in their own oil, entry into refining could not be limited and product markets could not be protected from competitive compression and periodic disruption on this account, as well as on account of low and fluctuating raw material prices. With product prices leading crude prices, it is just possible that the profit margins of large integrated firms were often more compressed than those of independents, who were more quick to alter crude purchase prices, and able readily to do so with production uncontrolled. Certainly as the crude oil problem came to be considered one of persistent surpluses, the advantages that the integrated firm might hope for from its own controlled supplies would be dissipated, unless the level of output could be limited to what the market would absorb at profitable prices.

The prospective effect of production controls in reducing the ease and fluctuations of entry into refining, hence in reducing the intensity of competition in that branch of the industry, would have seemed beneficial also to the established, nonintegrated refiner, with modern facilities and products enjoying consumer acceptance. This should have been especially true prior to the late thirties, when catalytic refining raised gasoline quality to levels that in any case severely undercut the economic threat of the small field teakettle refinery.[19] Before that technological change, crude oil production in excess of what pipelines and established refiners would take found its way to independent refiners, in one way or another—if only to the most primitive plants, hastily erected in the field to skim off the more valuable components and sell them for whatever they would bring. In the circumstances refinery margins, as well as end-product prices, were subject to sharp compression and fluctuation. After that technological change and the consequent reduction in the threat of disruptive, small-scale entry into refining, the established independent refiner must have become more aware of the dangers than the benefits to him of a regulated producing branch of the industry. The refiners who erected plants in the field to take advantage of cheap, surplus crude probably never

18. See below, pp. 221–225.
19. See below, pp. 496 ff.

were aware of any but the disadvantageous effects. So the interests of independent refiners in prorationing were not unmixed.

While there can be little more than uncertainty regarding the particular interests of a given operator or even of a class of operators in any given method of crude-oil market stabilization, there can be no doubt that all producers, as a group, had a very real interest in removing or modifying the inherent instability in their branch of the industry. It is also quite clear that no matter how much small independents might have had to gain from any scheme of control, their numbers were (and are) so great and their circumstances so varied that there would always be a great many who would oppose and frustrate any control system unless the full authority of the state were brought against them.

On the other hand, a big company with a large share of the market will usually take a more responsible view simply because it sees that a competitive race, prodded by the rule of capture, could not increase its market share but must inevitably depress its prices and profits. The small producer, with a lucky strike, can always hope to improve his market share; it may be in the interests of all to stabilize, but there will always be a maverick to start the competitive snowball. But the big firm, and especially the big vertically integrated firm, has heavy investments elsewhere, investments which cry out for the assurance of continued supplies over time, investments which make it certain that he cannot hope to drive his rivals, similarly circumstanced, from the market. The big firm has more at stake and that larger stake makes it more conscious of the need and more willing to shoulder the burden of doing something to stabilize crude oil markets. In the moral climate of this century it can neither box off the weak operators, who are the initiators of instability, nor absorb them with impunity. There was no other alternative than to seek the cooperation of the state, when conditions in the free market became intolerable.

CRUDE OIL MARKETS ON THE EVE OF REGULATION

Annual data for crude oil production in the Midcontinent area are compared with prices and stocks in the period from the end of World War I to the beginning of effective regulation in Table VI. Actually, annual figures are far too gross for detailed analysis of developments in crude oil markets. Especially in the period after 1929, monthly and sometimes even weekly figures understate the magnitude of the forces agitating supply. Figures for a given point in time (like stocks at

December 31) and aggregates for a wide and important region like the Midcontinent over a period as long as a year will inevitably miss significant fluctuations within that period and will cover up large but compensating changes that may have occurred at different locations at the same time.[20] The averaging of prices and price changes is a more obvious case in point.[21] However, for the present purpose, which is only to illustrate some general features of the period before prorationing, these data should suffice.

The industry's response to the high prices and shortages at the end of World War I was dramatic. The total number of wells drilled (excluding service wells) spurted from 14,157 in 1915 to 33,911 in 1920—a number not exceeded until 1948.[22] Dry holes were little more than 20 per cent of the total in those days, and almost 72 per cent of the wells drilled in 1920 turned out to be oil producers.[23] The important point is how rapidly production mounted.[24] Despite rising demands, prices tumbled and United States crude stocks—a rough indication of the aggregate supply-demand situation in the country as a whole—began to climb.[25] It is quite clear that whatever the early

20. Although the data refer to the Midcontinent only, this has been the most important producing region in the U.S. since 1914, and production there behaved in much the same manner as the national total. The direction of change from year to year, although not the percentage of change, was the same in all but four years: 1924, 1926, 1931, and 1934. In taking production for a region rather than for a given field or state or for the U.S. as a whole, the sensitivity of the smaller and the "averaging" stability of the larger area are compromised.

21. How inadequately indicative of the actual course of prices these averages may be is suggested by the number and range of changes even in *posted* crude prices within each year, noted in Table VI.

22. The 1915 total was a low point. Wells drilled had ranged between 13,768 and 25,687 in the preceding five years (*Petroleum Facts and Figures*, 9th ed., p. 121). In the five years ending in 1920, an average of over 27,000 wells a year were drilled.

23. *Ibid.*, p. 130.

24. The API series, upon which our Table VI draws, begins only in 1920; but it shows, in the sharp rise of output after that year, the fruition of the greatly increased exploratory efforts immediately before. The Bureau of Mines figures for net national production show an increase from 301 million barrels in 1916 to 443 million in 1920. And the gross annual additions to proved reserves (according to the extremely rough estimates made at that time), which had amounted to only 1.00 and 1.84 times annual output in 1917 and 1918, jumped to 2.32 in 1919, and remained above 2.00 in 1920 and 1921 as well. Computations by Boni, Watkins, Jason, and Company, from Bureau of Mines production data and API reserves estimates.

25. The sharp increase of stocks in 1921 doubtless reflected the relative stability of demand in that recession year—crude runs to stills nationally rose

TABLE VI   Crude Oil Production, Prices and Stocks, 1920–34

YEAR	UNITED STATES CRUDE STOCKS DECEMBER 31 (MILLIONS OF BARRELS)	MIDCONTINENT [e] CRUDE PRODUCTION (MILLIONS OF BARRELS)	AVE. ANNUAL (DOLLARS PER BARREL)	CRUDE PRICE: OKLAHOMA-KANSAS 36° GRAVITY [f] RANGE OF POSTED PRICES HIGH	LOW	RANGE AS % OF HIGH	NUMBER OF PRICE CHANGES	U. S. SERVICE STATION PRICE [g] (GASOLINE) AVERAGE (CENTS PER GALLON)
(1)	(2)	(3)	(4)	(5)	(6)	(7)	(8)	(9)
1920	149.45 [b]	250.11	$3.40	$3.50	$2.75	21.4%	3	29.74
1921	217.32	258.46	1.79	3.50	1.00	71.4	10	26.11
1922	306.81 / 295.71 [c]	310.99	1.72	2.00	1.25	37.5	4	24.82
1923	376.62 / 340.64 [d]	348.46	1.58	2.00	1.00	50.0	11	21.06
1924	361.66 / 360.48 [e]	375.48	1.60	2.00	1.00	50.0	7	19.46
1925	343.82 / 345.86 [e]	425.08	1.85	2.04	1.25	38.7	6	20.09
1926	315.03	424.89	2.13	2.29	1.79	21.9	3	20.97
1927	379.66	547.62	1.42	1.90	1.28	32.6	3	18.28
1928	391.87 / 392.63 [e]	553.51	1.31	1.36	1.28	5.9	1	17.90
1929	428.45	584.28	1.36	1.45	1.20	17.2	2	17.92
1930	408.81 / 411.88 [e]	531.45	1.25	1.45	0.95	34.5	3	16.16
1931	370.92 / 370.19 [e]	543.74	0.64	0.95	0.18	81.1	6	12.98
1932	339.72 / 339.88 [e]	493.03	0.87	0.92	0.69	25.0	2	13.30
1933	355.31 / 354.22 [e]	601.15	0.61	1.00	0.25	75.0	8	12.41
1934	337.25	584.73	1.00	1.00	1.00	0	0	13.64

[a] Through 1924, data from Petroleum Facts and Figures, 9th ed., p. 160; beginning 1925, from API Statistical Bulletin (April 23, 1957), Form No. 7. Prior to 1924, stocks somewhat inflated by inclusion of nonrefinable California crude, subsequently removed.

[b] Figure listed for January, 1921.

[c] These are revised figures, presented by the Statistical Bulletin along with the ones immediately preceding with the indication that the unrevised figures are in each case comparable with those for preceding years, the revised with data for subsequent years.

[e] Midcontinent region: Kansas, Oklahoma, Northwest Texas, North Louisiana, Arkansas, Mississippi, Southeast New Mexico. Petroleum Facts and Figures, 9th ed., p. 152.

[f] No gravity price scale used prior to 1922. Average annual prices are arithmetic average of first of month quotations. High and low prices reflect actual price quotations. Number of price changes is total absolute number reported during year, including instances in which several occurred in a single month. Columns 4, 7, and 8 computed. Ibid., pp. 364–365.

[g] Average U.S. service station price: average first of month prices

fears of imminent exhaustion, the practical problem soon became one of surplus.[26] From 1920 through 1929 the Midcontinent area paced the country with a net increase in annual production of almost 134 per cent, and the contraction thereafter through 1932 was a decline only in comparison with the record years immediately preceding.

Most surprising in this record, and probably calling for explanation, is the relative failure of Midcontinent production (even less of United States production, which actually declined in each year after '29 until 1933) to reflect the output of the great East Texas Field, the discovery well of which was brought in on October 30, 1930.[27] Although production allowables were not set for the East Texas Field until May, 1931, when drilling was already at fever pitch and open flow was characteristic, and although these orders (and many others to follow) were largely nullified by legal action and often ignored,[28] the Texas Railroad Commission was already involved in cutting back

---

only to 443 million barrels compared with 434 in 1920—as much as the expansion of production and imports. But the continued rise in inventories in the next two years occurred in the face of refinery runs of 501 and 581 million barrels respectively (*Petroleum Facts and Figures,* 9th ed., p. 119).

26. This is indicated by the fall in prices and by the increase in U. S. crude stocks. Through 1923, stocks of crude oil increased by some 227 million barrels—a net enlargement of more than 150 per cent; after rising slightly further in 1924 (when one takes account of the subtraction, noted in our Table VI, of the California crude in 1923), stocks were drawn down about 45 million barrels in the next two years; but in 1927 through 1929, they spurted upward again by 113 million barrels. (These computations from the data in Table VI do not take account in the intervening years of the revisions described in n. b of that table, and may therefore be regarded as subject to minor errors of noncomparability.) In each of the first three years of the thirties, in part because of more effective state controls, total U. S. production declined—by roughly 11, 5, and 8 percent, respectively—the national decline in 1931 occurring in the face of an increase of Midcontinent output, shown in Table VI. Despite falling total demand, it was possible to cut back stocks as well, as the table likewise shows.

27. The East Texas Field was favorably located toward the market, most of its wells were low-cost wells, and it was exploited primarily by small operators, many of whom were inexperienced in oil production. In the first ten months following discovery, 1,600 wells were completed. During the next twelve months, 5,101 wells were brought in and in the following two years, the total number of wells in the field more than doubled. See Watkins, p. 44, n. 15.

28. The frustrating legal turmoil that embroiled the Texas Railroad Commission when it sought to cut back excessive production after 1929 served to clarify and consolidate prorationing in the state. Though fascinating in its own right, this story exceeds the scope of our study. The interested reader is referred to Zimmermann, chap. 4.

production throughout the state to match declining demand. Oklahoma, the second most important producing state in the region, had effectively prorationed its entire output by 1930 to reduce production by 38.5 million barrels in that year and about 36 and 27 million in each of the following years. Texas had promulgated orders in most flush fields by early 1931. In the tabulation below, the contribution of Texas to year-by-year changes in output after 1929 is contrasted with that of all other states (as a group) within the Midcontinent and Gulf areas, respectively.

TABLE VII

Changes in Crude Oil Production Over Preceding Year, 1930–34

(*Millions of Barrels*)

| | | | MIDCONTINENT | | TEXAS [a] | | |
YEAR	TOTAL U.S.	GULF AREA	TOTAL REGION	EXCLUDING TEXAS [a]	IN MID-CONTINENT	IN GULF	STATE TOTAL
1930	−109.31	+12.57	−52.83	−36.56	−16.27	+9.85	−6.42
1931	−46.93	−12.08	+12.29	−40.31	+52.60	−10.62	+41.98
1932	−65.92	−4.13	−50.70	−34.87	−15.83	−4.13	−19.96
1933	+120.50	+22.84	+108.11	+37.47	+70.64	+19.49	+90.13
1934	+2.41	+7.64	−16.42	+4.62	−21.03	−0.06	−21.09

[a] Texas output was divided between the Gulf area, which also included Louisiana, and the Midcontinent. By excluding Louisiana output from the Gulf and subtracting the residual from reported production for the State of Texas, a rough approximation of the Texas component of Midcontinent production as distinguished from the rest of that area was obtained.

Source: *Petroleum Facts and Figures,* 9th ed., pp. 145, 147, 152.

It will be observed that fields within the Midcontinent region but outside of Texas reduced their aggregate production in each of the three years after 1929, as did the country as a whole. The State of Texas as a whole produced in 1931 almost 42 million barrels more than in 1930, while those Texas fields within the Midcontinent area, which includes the East Texas Field, actually produced almost 53 million barrels more. The difference (between the 42 and 53 million barrels) represents cutbacks in production of Texas fields other than East Texas.

Thus what first appears as a more or less orderly retreat in aggregate Midcontinent production from the peak of 1929, becomes a major break-through in East Texas, only partially compensated by severe reductions elsewhere in the state and region. With control orders in contempt, prices collapsed in 1931. This was the first impact of practically uncontrolled production in East Texas: posted prices plummeted to 18 cents a barrel during the last week in July (actual prices were said to have fallen to much lower levels) and output soared to almost a million barrels a day, nearly one-third of national requirements.[29] Had it not been for substantial cutbacks elsewhere in Texas and in other states, and for the Governor's use of the state militia to enforce restrictions of East Texas output during the second half of the year, the 1931 record of the Midcontinent region would have bulged even more. From the fall of 1931 throughout the following year, well-production allowables were cut consistently.[30]

Production zoomed again in 1933 as orders were enjoined by the courts or flagrantly violated. This oil produced in violation of orders (so-called "hot oil") was variously estimated around 50,000 barrels per day, and field prices were reported as low as 10 cents. It was not until November that the Texas Commission achieved a firm control, with a field allowable of 400,000 barrels per day, at which level of production well pressures were finally stabilized. It will be observed in Table VII that production increases were general in 1933, in all of Texas, in the Midcontinent region, and in the United States, although the lion's share was contributed by that one state; but that in the following year, Texas output was successfully cut back in all major areas while output elsewhere was permitted to increase. The 1934 pattern clearly presaged the new role Texas was in process of assuming, as a balance-wheel of national supply and demand.

Although the years covered by Table VI were generally years of mounting surplus supplies, it will be noted that crude oil prices held up relatively well after their drop from the 1920 peak. In terms of annual averages, they declined from 1921 to 1929 by around 24 per cent, while gasoline prices fell more than 31 per cent.[31] Nonethe-

29. In the week preceding the military shutdown of the field under martial law (August 17), official daily average production was reported at 738,000 barrels but unofficial sources indicated output of approximately one million barrels during the twenty-four hours before the militia moved in. See Marshall and Meyers, "Legal Planning of Petroleum Production," p. 717 and *passim*.

30. Daily per-well allowables fell from 225 barrels on September 2, 1931, to 28 to 31 barrels (depending on well pressure) at January 9, 1933; and the entire field was closed from December 17, 1932 to the first of the year, ostensibly to measure bottom-hole pressures. See *ibid.*, p. 717, n. 44.

31. Any comparison of this sort is seriously affected by the price level in the base year. We have taken 1921 rather than the much higher level of 1920 for this comparison because 1920 was so clearly an exceptional year. For example, in nineteen of the twenty-four months preceding 1920, the price of crude was $2.25 per barrel. The weighted average price (weighted by the number of weeks

less, average crude prices varied inversely with changes in inventories, as one would expect, until 1929; and inventories moved generally upward. The price improvement in that year was smothered in the two following under the combined weight of falling demand and high production out of the huge discoveries in the years immediately preceding.

The strikes of the early 1920's were followed by renewed fears of imminent oil shortages. Despite higher crude stocks in the three years 1922–24, new discoveries and new developments failed to match increased production, and (estimated) proven reserves declined 300 million barrels. Prices began to rise again—hesitantly and slightly in 1924, in the face of higher inventories, more surely and rapidly in 1925 and 1926 as stocks declined. But new discoveries and developments already rebounded to exceed production in 1925 and they spurted dramatically after 1926. Over the six years through 1930 these additions exceeded 11.3 billion barrels, of which some 6.1 billion (over 117 per cent of total production during the period) were added to proved reserves, a net addition of more than 81 per cent.[32] The loss of 1.6 billion barrels in proved reserves during the following three years (1931–33) could not reverse the judgment that the primary problem of the oil industry was surplus: with the depression curtailment in demand, wells drilled had been cut back almost 50 per cent.

CONTROL ALTERNATIVES, 1920–35

In the early twenties the foremost advocate of public control over crude oil production was H. L. Doherty, a director of the American Petroleum Institute and president of a company bearing his name that was fiscal agent for the Cities Service companies.[33] Doherty was convinced that the only solution of the production problem in oil was mandatory unit-pool operation under federal compulsion. Having failed on several occasions to gain a hearing from his fellow directors for his views, he appealed to President Coolidge in August, 1924. At

---

during which each price prevailed) in each year was $2.12 in 1918 and $2.275 in 1919. Computed from *Petroleum Facts and Figures,* 9th ed., p. 366. See also the reference to the behavior of refinery margins and the BLS petroleum product wholesale price indexes, above, p. 105, n. 71.

32. Computed from *Petroleum Facts and Figures,* 9th ed., p. 182. Gross finding (net additions to proved reserves plus production during the year) to production ratios, which ranged between 0.64 and 1.00 during 1922–24, jumped to 2.31 in 1925, and 1.39, 2.89, 1.55, 3.18 and 1.45 in 1926–30, respectively.

33. See Zimmermann, pp. 122 ff.

least partially in response to his letter, the Federal Oil Conservation Board was established to study production problems and conservation prospects.

The attitude of the industry, to the extent that it was fairly represented by the Board of Directors of the API, would have made sense only if it had been governed by an overriding determination to avoid federal regulation at any price. At the very time when serious students of the industry were decrying the terrible wastefulness of its operations, the Institute filed a report alleging that waste was negligible, and it hired Charles Evans Hughes to challenge before the Federal Oil Conservation Board both federal authority over petroleum production and federal or state authority that would permit a majority of pool operators to control a minority. Rather than governmental control, it plunked for antitrust exemptions to permit output restriction under voluntary agreements. The Federal Board was sufficiently impressed to confine its initial recommendations to interstate cooperation for voluntary curtailment.

Cooperation and voluntary agreement, preferably with antitrust immunity, became a guiding objective of the industry in its subsequent relations with government.[34] In the middle of 1928, the Institute sponsored a conference of the larger producing companies in New York to explore steps that might be taken to stabilize world markets against surplus. Six weeks later, Walter C. Teagle of Standard Oil (New Jersey) drafted the Achnacarry or "As is" agreement of Standard, Royal Dutch–Shell, and Anglo-Persian Oil Company, Ltd., providing for a stabilization of company shares, cooperative use of existing facilities and controlled addition of new, and protection of world oil prices outside the United States. In April of the following year, after extensive consideration by the industry and full approval by the Institute, there was placed before the Oil Conservation Board a very similar recommendation, which would have restricted future United States production to 1928 levels, and thus eliminated the major loophole in the Achnacarry agreement—the failure to provide against burgeoning American production and export. These plans were wrecked when the Attorney General, in response to a request for an opinion, denied to the Board or any other government agency

34. See statement of Donald P. McHugh, counsel of the Subcommittee on Antitrust and Monopoly of the Senate Judiciary Committee, *Petroleum: The Antitrust Laws and Government Policies,* Report of the Subcommittee on Antitrust and Monopoly, Senate Committee Print, 85th Congress, 1st Session (August 16, 1957), appendix, pp. 12 ff.

the ability to grant immunity from the Sherman Act.[35] Consequently, under urging of the Conservation Board, the industry was encouraged to work with the oil-producing states to effect a prorationing control system.

Prorationing production allowables to reasonable market demand was developed in Oklahoma and later applied in Texas but received its greatest impetus from the federal government under the National Industrial Recovery Act.[36] The code of the industry began the monthly forecasts of demand for petroleum products by the Bureau of Mines, which have continued to provide a basic guide for production controls; and it prohibited interstate commerce in oil and oil products produced in violation of state law—a provision extended by act of Congress (the so-called Connally Hot Oil Act) after NRA's demise.[37] The way in which the Texas Railroad Commission translates these Bureau forecasts into production quotas ("allowables") field by field and well by well, for those subject to control, has already been outlined in Chapter 6.[38]

35. See FTC, *The International Petroleum Cartel,* pp. 199–213, esp. 210–213. Because of the American antitrust laws, the Achnacarry agreement explicitly excluded U.S. production and trade from its scope.

36. Two somewhat different views of experience under NRA are given by Watkins, pp. 81 ff.; and Irene Till, "Gasoline: The Competition of Big Business," in Walton Hamilton and Associates, *Price and Price Policies* (New York, McGraw-Hill, 1938), pp. 164 ff.

37. An Interstate Compact to Conserve Oil and Gas was eventually established with Congressional blessing in 1935; but its teeth were effectively pulled by compromises required to placate opposing attitudes of Oklahoma and Texas authorities. The compact serves informational and publicity purposes but it exercises no controls and binds no one to any specific action or form of control. See the U. S. Department of Justice, *Second Report of the Attorney General* (cited below by title only), as of September 1, 1957, Pursuant to Section 2 of the Joint Resolution of July 28, 1955, consenting to an Interstate Compact to Conserve Oil and Gas (Washington, U. S. Government Printing Office, 1957), pp. 15–31.

38. It is a common experience in rationing a maximum production quota that the total assigned will not be produced because of breakdowns and other unanticipated interferences. To these ordinary sources of scheduling error, familiar to anyone concerned with material allocations during the war, petroleum regulation adds a few of its own: error in scheduled anticipated production of exempt wells (including added allowables for new wells expected to come in during the month); and, on occasion, inability of wells to obtain pipeline connections. The Texas Commission is said generally to figure this underproduction of scheduled allowables at around 7½ per cent and normal underproduction is said to be taken into consideration in the calculation of allowables. In some years, however, like 1956, the short fall may be almost

The method of unit operation, which the industry refused to support, focuses on the planned development of an oil field as a whole: the number and location of wells to be drilled as well as the rate of production from each can be adapted to the optimum recovery of oil from the structure. The emphasis of this method is on responsible field development. As such it encourages efficient and scientific development, as an engineer would determine; and it leaves the problem of market value either to competition or to further regulation. Prorationing, by contrast, focuses primarily on market demand at a given price level and the limitation of aggregate supply to that demand. The latter process is not devoid of conservation significance, but the initial, and primary, impact is economic: [39] physical conservation or efficient development of the reservoir will depend importantly on other supplementary regulations regarding the number and spacing of walls to be drilled.

The economic and technical advantages of the unit operation of reservoirs could not have escaped practitioners in the field, especially those with foreign experience; and indeed the need was recognized in the API's support of voluntary agreements free from antitrust supervision. Why then did industry leaders fail to support mandatory unitization under federal control? One can only speculate. They might well have shied from the political and administrative headaches that mandatory unitization promised. The already complex conflicts of interest among the various property owners and oil operators in the development of an oil field would surely have been further complicated by the task of determining comparative property rights in an ill-defined reservoir of oil. So long as there was hope for voluntarily negotiated industry agreements there was hope that both open conflict and unwelcome government regulation might be avoided. Once this hope was blasted, it must still have seemed that a simple imposition of production quotas by the several states, without basic rearrangement of property rights, would permit a less restricted opportunity than federal regulation for the flexible pursuit of private interest.

---

twice this amount. See Zimmermann, pp. 220–223; *Petroleum Press Service* (January, 1957), pp. 29–30; and below, n. 66.

39. It is not intended to contrast "conservation" with "economic" considerations. On the contrary (see Chap. 10), conservation is essentially an economic concept. The only point here is to contrast a production control policy directed explicitly at eliminating the physical wastes of exploitation under the law of capture—which wastes were the prime justification for government intervention—and a policy concerned primarily and explicitly with the adjustment of supply to market demand at some given price level.

THE IMPACT OF PRORATIONING

Table VIII continues for the period after 1934 the statistical series in Table VI. The contrast between the conditions and behavior of crude oil markets reflected by the two sets of data is striking. The most obvious change is in the behavior of price: it became far more stable after 1934; moreover, with one minor exception, the only way it ever moved was up.[40] The behavior of inventories and of prices relative to inventories also changed, though less obviously. First, although the average level of United States annual production in the last twenty years or so has been more than twice the level of the earlier period, both the absolute level and the range of change in crude oil inventories has declined substantially.[41] Second, the rough relationship be-

40. This generalization is based only on the posted Midcontinent prices summarized in the table. Actually posted prices in other areas have at one time or another been reduced in periods of recession like 1938, 1949, 1954, and 1957. Confining our attention to the series in Table VIII, on October 11, 1938, the price of crude oil was reduced from $1.22 to $1.02 per barrel. Over the entire period of twenty-four years, there were only twelve price changes. In contrast, during the fourteen years through 1933 there were no less than sixty-nine recorded changes in price and except for one year (1928), when the maximum change was 5.9 per cent, the range of prices in individual years varied from more than 17 to over 81 per cent of the high quotation for the year. In five years it was 50 per cent or greater; in five it was 25 per cent or more but less than 50 per cent; in four it was less than 25 per cent.

The conclusion derived is shown more definitively by analysis of monthly data. McLean and Haigh measure percentage deviations from thirteen-month moving averages from 1920 to 1934 and 1935 to 1952 for the Midcontinent area. Average monthly deviations from average prices of 36° gravity crude at the wellhead fell from 12.6 per cent in the early period to 1.4 per cent in the later.

The difference between crude prices and finished product prices at the refinery (i.e. the computed refinery gross margin) was also stabilized, with deviations falling from 24.2 per cent to 7.2 per cent during the two periods. This stability was carried forward into distribution: for wholesale margins, deviations dropped from 14.2 per cent to 4.6 per cent, while for retail computed gross margins, they declined from 6.1 per cent to 3.0 per cent. See *ibid.*, pp. 118 ff.

41. In the period 1920 through 1933, U.S. production averaged roughly 764.5 million barrels annually; in 1934 through 1955, 1,670.2 million barrels. In the earlier period, apart from 1920 and 1921 when they were still being built up after having been drawn down during the war, end-of-year stocks never fell below 300 million barrels. In the latter period, aside from the first two years (1934 and 1935), when prorationing was still getting firmly established and the high inventories being cut to size, they exceeded 300 million barrels in only one year, 1937. In fifteen of the twenty-four years in the later period but in only two of the fourteen years of the earlier one, end-of-year

tween crude oil stocks, crude prices, and the average retail price of the most important finished product, regular gasoline, suggests a less persistent correlation in the period after prorationing than before.[42]

That these changes in the behavior of crude oil markets have occurred since 1934 does not of course prove that they have been the consequence of the production control that became effective at about that time. The upward thrust of price has surely reflected secular changes in the relation of domestic crude oil supply to demand. Continuous recovery in domestic output since 1934 has been paced by a steady upward sweep of total consumption [43] that eventually outstripped this country's comparative ability to produce. Apart from the mid-1930's, the rise in domestic production of crude oil and products has been less rapid than of domestic consumption; in consequence, our traditional position as a net exporter was undermined and eventually reversed, apparently permanently. This growth in aggregate demand reflected not only the steady climb of an expanding economy under improving levels of business activity [44] but also the

---

stocks were less than 270 million barrels; while in only one of the later and in ten of the earlier years they exceeded 330 million barrels. A quick comparison of Tables VI and VIII will indicate also that the variations in inventories have likewise diminished since 1935.

42. In both periods, however, the relation is vague. If one considers end-of-year stocks as an indication of demand-supply conditions in that year, one finds eight instances out of thirteen possible in which average crude prices moved in an opposite direction to stocks (the expected change) in the pre-prorationing period. In the later period, in only four out of twenty-three possible were inventory and price changes opposite; in eight they changed in the *same* direction and in eleven instances stocks changed up or down with no change in the crude price. On the other hand, average crude and average retail gasoline prices moved in a similar direction (not necessarily with similar amplitude) in twelve out of thirteen possible instances prior to 1934 and in twelve out of twenty-three possible thereafter. The less consistent showing in the later period reflects ten changes in retail prices while crude prices remained constant.

43. Indicated aggregate U.S. consumption of crude oil, natural gasoline, benzol, and refined products, after allowing for imports and exports, first topped the 1929 peak of 2.577 million b/d in 1935 with an average of almost 2.7 million b/d. With only one slight recession in 1938 (of 89,000 b/d) and a wartime cutback in 1942 (98,200 b/d), total domestic consumption increased in every year after the low point reached in 1932. The anticipated relapse of demand after the war never developed; demand continued to soar in every year to an average in 1956 of almost 8.76 million b/d. API, *Statistical Bulletin* (April 23, 1957), Form No. 2.

44. Although recovery from the great depression was not fully achieved until the forties and there occurred setbacks of varying degrees in 1938, 1946, 1949, and 1954, improvement in levels of business activity was characteristic throughout this period.

TABLE VIII   Crude Oil Production, Prices and Stocks, 1934–57

YEAR	U.S. STOCKS [a] DECEMBER 31 (MILLIONS OF BARRELS)	MIDCONTINENT [d] PRODUCTION	POSTED CRUDE PRICES: OKLAHOMA-KANSAS 36° GRAVITY					GASOLINE: SERVICE STATION [f] PRICE (CENTS PER GAL.)
			AVE. ANNUAL (DOLLARS PER BARREL)	HIGH	LOW	RANGE % OF HIGH	NUMBER PRICE CHANGES	
(1)	(2)	(3)	(4)	(5)	(6)	(7)	(8)	(9)
1934	337.25	584.73	1.00	1.00	1.00	0	0	13.64
1935	314.86	608.61	1.00	1.00	1.00	0	0	13.55
1936	288.58	669.54	1.09	1.10	1.00	9.1	1	14.10
1937	306.83	774.37	1.21	1.22	1.10	9.8	1	14.59
1938	320.34 [b] / 291.43 [c] / 290.63 [b]	677.52	1.19	1.22	1.02	16.4	1	14.07
1939	253.31	665.72	1.02	1.02	1.02	0	0	13.31
1940	276.62	686.98	1.02	1.02	1.02	0	0	12.75
1941	257.68	716.54	1.11	1.17	1.02	12.8	2	13.30
1942	245.75	703.49	1.17	1.17	1.17	0	0	14.46
1943	251.80	736.49	1.17	1.17	1.17	0	0	14.56
1944	249.40 [b] / 226.97 / 226.77 [b]	818.68	1.17	1.17	1.17	0	0	14.62
1945	223.26	846.23	1.17	1.17	1.17	0	0	14.48
1946	230.18	871.08	1.36	1.62	1.17	27.8	3	14.69
1947	230.65	949.55	1.88	2.57	1.62	37.8	3	16.93
1948	256.63	1,063.64	2.57	2.57	2.57	0	0	19.54
1949	253.36	949.83	2.57	2.57	2.57	0	0	20.27
1950	248.46	1,065.70	2.57	2.57	2.57	0	0	20.08
1951	255.78	1,238.60	2.57	2.57	2.57	0	0	20.31

TABLE VIII (*continued*)

POSTED CRUDE PRICES: OKLAHOMA-KANSAS 36° GRAVITY

YEAR	U.S. STOCKS [a] DECEMBER 31 (MILLIONS OF BARRELS)	MIDCONTINENT [d] PRODUCTION (MILLIONS OF BARRELS)	AVE. ANNUAL (DOLLARS PER BARREL)	HIGH	LOW	RANGE % OF HIGH	NUMBER PRICE CHANGES	GASOLINE: SERVICE STATION [f] PRICE (CENTS PER GAL.)
(1)	(2)	(3)	(4)	(5)	(6)	(7)	(8)	(9)
1952	271.93	1,267.52	2.57	2.57	2.57	0	0	20.24
1953	274.45	1,294.21	2.70	2.82	2.57	8.9	1	21.28
1954	258.39	1,265.06	2.82	2.82	2.82	0	0	21.56
1955	265.61	1,360.82	2.82	2.82	2.82	0	0	21.42
1956	266.01	1,445.31	2.82	2.82	2.82	0	0	21.62
1957	281.81	1,442.82	3.07	3.07	3.07	8.1	1	22.11

[a] API, *Statistical Bulletin* (April 7, 1958), Form No. 5.
[b] Revision of prior figure, as described in above Table VI, n. c.
[c] Inventories of California crude formerly classified as Heavy Fuel Oil are reclassified and included henceforth as Crude Oil. It would appear therefore that neither of the 1938 figures is comparable with those of preceding years.
[d] Source, same as n. a, Form No. 3A.
[e] Through 1949, data from *Petroleum Facts and Figures*, 9th ed., p. 364; thereafter from 12th ed., p. 305, and monthly *National Petroleum News*. Columns 4, 7, and 8 computed. The 1957 increase came early in January and the $2.82 price is therefore not reflected in the midmonthly figures on which the highs, lows, and annual averages are based.
[f] Simple average of first-of-month prices in fifty representative United States cities, *exclusive of tax*. *Ibid.*, 9th ed., p. 367; 12th ed., p. 305; and *National Petroleum News Factbook* (mid-May, 1958), p. 181.

continued extension of our relative dependence on petroleum sources of energy. The failure of domestic supply to expand *pari passu* indicated, above all, long-run changes in the conditions of production.[45] Under these circumstances, the general direction of price changes revealed in Table VIII hardly calls for further explanation. The emergence and expansion of a net import balance after 1949 would naturally have had the effect primarily of moderating not of reversing the secular increase; and, as will be argued below, the removal of production controls would mainly have postponed, not prevented it.

Even the greatly increased stability of crude oil prices since 1934 might to some extent have come to pass in a maturing domestic industry, in the absence of prorationing. The rate at which demand has grown has been markedly more stable since 1933 than in the preceding thirteen years.[46] On the supply side, the fluctuations in discovery rates have become less extreme. During the 1920–33 period, considered as a whole, new discoveries and developments amounted to an estimated 1.495 times production. But the annual fluctuations in this ratio varied from a low of 0.18 in 1932 to a high of 3.14 in 1929. In five of the fourteen years, ratios were less than one, and in five others they were more than two.[47] During the next fourteen years, the ratio improved for the period as a whole to 1.61, while annual fluctuations subsided. Extreme variations ranged from 0.987 in 1943 to 2.91 in 1937; in only one year was it less than one and in only two was it more than two. Between 1947 and 1956 these annual gross additions to known supply never exceeded two times annual production and never fell below it, the extreme ratios being 1.99 in 1951 and 1.17 in 1956. For the nine-year aggregates, new discoveries and developments exceeded production in the ratio of 1.45 to one. In 1957, for the first time since 1943, gross findings failed to make good the annual depletion; the finding-to-production ratio was 0.94.

However, prorationing is the primary reason for the vastly reduced

45. See below, pp. 199 ff.

46. See, e.g., the growth charts in Pogue and Hill, *Future Growth and Financial Requirements of the World Petroleum Industry,* p. 6.

47. It must be pointed out that the extreme fluctuations in the ratio before 1934 may be in part apparent only, reflecting the greater roughness of the API's annual calculations of proved reserves (and therefore of net additions thereto) in the earlier than in the more recent period. Reserves until 1934 were estimated in rounded hundreds of millions of barrels, and twice, between 1916 and 1917, and 1922 and 1923, were published as unchanged. In such instances the estimated gross additions to reserves would be shown as precisely equaling annual production, for a ratio of 1.0.

number of crude oil price changes since 1933, as well as for the timing of those that occurred. Nor can it escape responsibility for holding prices at the high levels they have reached since World War II. In view of the supply inelasticity characteristic of competitive crude oil production, the smoothness of the transitions from one price to another and the long periods of intervening stability in the face of changing demand bespeak the presence of administrative control.[48] Only in this way could the emergence of a rapidly expanding, low-cost, world source of oil in the Middle East have rolled back United States sales in Europe and even penetrated domestic markets without creating more than a ripple in the domestic price. And only in this way could great new discoveries and developments of crude oil have been blended into national production without upsetting the short-run balance of supply and demand.

For example, the price increases in 1936–37 might well have occurred in a free market: demand was expanding, crude stocks fell, and new discoveries had been relatively small in the preceding five years. Similarly, the price decline of the next two years seems an orthodox reaction to overexuberant exploration and development activity and sharp increases in discoveries in the face of a drop in aggregate domestic consumption in 1938.[49] The remarkable thing is that the entire adjustment involved only *three* price changes.[50] Again, it is less notable that prices advanced $1.40 per barrel in six price moves during the first two years (1946–47) after price ceilings were removed —drilling and finding ratios having slumped during the war years and

48. This does not refer, of course, to the administrative controls which from time to time during this period were imposed with the specific and direct purpose of raising and stabilizing *price*. At the beginning, for example, federally sponsored controls under the NRA Petroleum Code helped establish and maintain a dollar price for crude; and price ceilings during the war years (1942 through 1945) and the Korean episode (1951 through 1952) prevented a rise, though they would not have forestalled a decline. The reference is, rather, to the general system of controlling *production* that has prevailed throughout the period.

49. Total wells drilled fell off from their peak of 26,356 in 1929 to lows of 12,432 and 12,312 in 1932 and 1933, then recovered sharply to a peak of 31,622 in 1937. Correspondingly, the finding to production ratio slumped from an extraordinary 3.18 in 1929 to 0.29, 0.11 and 0.67 in 1931–33. The recovery was again dramatic: to 1.60 in 1936 and 2.91, 2.52 and 1.90 in 1937–39 respectively.

50. The reader is reminded that the discussion here refers only to the posted price, which is always in some measure fictional. Were it possible to measure the extent of departures from the posted price, these observations could be more precisely qualified, but their validity would probably not be undermined.

total demand continuing to rise—than that they held their gains in the face of expanded and expanding production capacity and rising imports, while demand leveled off in 1949. The reason is of course that production was severely curtailed in the latter year—by state orders. And the increase of 25 cents in the crude price in 1953, while the rate of production increase and discoveries were sharply tapering off, is less significant than the failure of price to fall in the following year when demand again leveled off and both stocks and production were forced to contract.[51]

As for the long-term upward movement of price: considering the extreme price inelasticity of unregulated supply and the relative inelasticity of demand, it is unlikely that in the absence of production control the price of crude oil could have made good and held all its gains of 1946–48 and 1953 in the face of an increasing availability of cheap imports. Only a part of the gain in 1957 had to be surrendered in 1958 because of exceptional circumstances to be discussed later. However, as has already been implied, it is far more difficult to place responsibility on prorationing for the long-run than for the short-run behavior of prices since 1934, because it is not at all certain what would have happened to domestic exploratory activity over the last two decades in the absence of production controls. Prices would undoubtedly have fluctuated more often and more widely—as indeed they did before 1934. Whether over the long run they would have been higher or lower, on the average, is a question we need not attempt to answer.

It is not the adjustments of production and stocks shown in Table VIII, however, that suggest the power of prorationing in smoothing out the price of crude. It is rather the potential supply from new discoveries that the industry is not permitted to produce beyond the volume that can be absorbed by the market at going prices. This was a period of tremendous growth in exploratory efforts. Even the war and its steel shortages did not cripple drilling activity in this country. True, the total number of wells drilled (excluding service wells) declined from 29,687 in 1941 to as low as 17,884 in 1943, but the number of producing oil wells did not cease to grow and total exploratory wells (even more decidedly, the total footage of exploratory wells drilled) generally exceeded levels reached before the war.[52] With the close of hostilities, the 1937 all-time record of 31,622 wells drilled

51. For a fuller discussion of this episode see below, pp. 190 ff.
52. During the five years, 1941–45, total exploratory wells drilled averaged 4,179 per year as compared with 3,038 in 1940 and footage drilled in such wells averaged 16.54 million feet in contrast with the high point of 10.3 million feet

(excluding service wells) was quickly approached, and in 1948 far exceeded. Every year betweeen 1947 and 1957 established a new record of wells drilled, with the total exceeding 58,000 in 1956. The first break in the advance came with the disappointing demand and sharp production cutbacks of 1957.

Furthermore, excepting only 1943, proved crude oil reserves continued to increase throughout the war and afterward. Not only did they continue to rise absolutely, despite the sharply increasing levels of production depicted in Table VIII. They also held a remarkably constant relationship to those mounting annual drafts upon them: the Life Index (the ratio of end-of-year proved reserves to annual production) averaged 12.7 years in the 1920's, 13.3 years in 1934–40, and 12.3 years in the period 1946–54.[53] Similarly, gross finding ratios (the ratios of annual discoveries to production) were likewise relatively stable, though, as in the case of the Life Index, they ranged somewhat lower after World War II than before.[54] Since 1951 discoveries have been less dramatic: the finding ratio has slumped, and the Life Index dropped to 11.8 years in 1957. However, new strikes continued through 1956 to inspire continually expanding exploratory effort,[55] and the industry has suffered, and continued in 1957–58 to suffer, from grossly excessive production capacity.

---

in that prewar year. Data derived from *Petroleum Facts and Figures,* 9th ed., pp. 121, 127, and 130.

53. Ratios computed from *Petroleum Facts and Figures,* 9th ed., p. 182; 12th ed., p. 157. The Life Index rose sharply, to more than 15 years, in 1930–1932, as output slumped; it exceeded 14 years in the late thirties, because of the great discoveries of 1937–39. See above, n. 49.

54. The annual ratios averaged 1.8 in the 1920's, 2.03 in 1934–40, and 1.6 between 1946 and 1951, inclusive. Computations *ibid.* It should be pointed out that these data on discoveries or additions to proved reserves do not reflect principally the effects of new discoveries during the year in question. By far the greater proportion of additions to reserves take the form of extensions and revisions of estimates of earlier years. East Texas, the greatest field of all time, has already produced more than 3.2 billion barrels of oil. Yet the gross amount of oil estimated in 1930, the year East Texas was brought in, as having been discovered in that year was only 1.3 billion barrels, and in the next three years combined only 0.7 billion, for the entire country. In estimating proved reserves, a very limited area is assigned to initial wells and corrections are made only gradually as new wells establish the size and characteristics of the reservoir. Thus, only long established fields can reveal something of their potential; fields of a few years' standing may register neither in output nor in proved reserves the contribution they will make eventually to supply. See below, p. 176, n. 16.

55. 1953 was the only year after 1951 in which net additions to proved reserves approached a billion barrels: the smallest addition was the 423 million

The postwar development of domestic oil supplies was powerfully augmented by a combination of financial considerations. First, in the midst of inflation proved reserves of petroleum and gas have come to be regarded as an ideal hedge. Postwar growth of consumption confirmed, if confirmation was needed, the judgment that no basic material is less likely to suffer from contractions in demand; while the certainty of long-run depletion and of short-run protection against overproduction preclude a major erosion of value from new discoveries. Second, in an economy of high and rising corporate and individual income taxes, the federal government offers exceptional inducements to any one who will look for oil or gas. If the search fails all exploratory and drilling costs may be charged against income from whatever source; and even where the search is successful, intangible (that is, nonsalvageable) costs—which include some 50 to 65 per cent of total well-development expenditures: wages, fuel, repairs, hauling, and other drilling costs—are allowed as expenses against income for tax purposes.[56] Once oil or gas is produced, the owner is assured a substantial tax-free component of income, up to 27½ per cent of gross sales value or 50 per cent of net income, whichever is smaller, as long as his property produces.[57] If the successful explorer chooses instead to

barrels in 1956, and 1957 experienced a decline of 134 million barrels. Gross finding to production ratios slumped from the high 1.96 of 1951 (and the longer-run average of 1.5 to 1.6) to 0.9–1.24 (except for 1953, when it was 1.40). Still, major finds in South Cuyama, California, in 1949, the Williston Basin of North Dakota in 1951, Paradox Basin in Colorado-Utah in 1952, and Citronelle, Alabama, and offshore Louisiana in 1955, not to mention Canada, have served to stimulate imagination and keep the drill rigs busy. Currently, in the Four Corners area (where Utah, Colorado, New Mexico, and Arizona join), an oil-gas boom is under way—an outgrowth of Paradox Basin oil finds in 1954 and the San Juan gas fields, which date from 1950. Many believe that the Four Corners will better the potential of other postwar fields like Spraberry in West Texas, Williston Basin, or Northern Alberta in Canada. See *Business Week* (September 7, 1957), pp. 88 ff.

56. Intangibles may be capitalized and charged over a period of time or expensed in a single year at the option of the taxpayer. Tangibles like pipe and pumping equipment are capitalized and depreciated.

57. Prior to 1926, depletion had been limited in aggregate to discovery cost or discovery value. The shift to 27½ per cent of gross income was made to avoid the cumbersome, inaccurate computations of discovery value and still approximate the same result. The choice of percentage was based on extensive experience under discovery value. It should be observed that this allowance is independent of intangible exploration and development costs, which are separately allowed against taxable income as indicated above. Finally, although discovery value was dropped as a basis for depletion deductions, the taxpayer is always entitled to cost depletion, under a general rule provided for its computation, whenever it exceeds percentage depletion.

sell out to a producing company he is subject only to a lower capital gains tax on his profit, and the percentage depletion privilege passes to the purchaser. These allowances were of minor consequence during the early years of the prorationing period, when income taxes were low. But as personal income taxes began to bite in incremental brackets up to 90 per cent, as corporate income taxes advanced to 52 per cent, and especially as marginal rates under the Excess Profits Tax reached 82 per cent, income-tax savings became powerful inducements to exploration for individuals and for firms both inside and outside the industry.

With the abandonment of price control in 1946, prices of Midcontinent crude soared $1.40 or almost 120 per cent in less than two years. Even without special tax incentives, this higher price (and the less important, but growing, opportunities for profitable disposition of any gas that might have been uncovered in the search for oil) was probably enough to spark a drilling boom. But when success crowned these efforts, the new supply potential could no longer react on price as it had in the past. Despite the booming discoveries of 1948–49 and 1951, stocks rose little more than needed to accommodate larger transport and refinery operations, and prices did not weaken: when they eventually broke, they broke upward! Success in oil exploration is no longer mirrored clearly in the market.[58] This is the nub of the matter; prorationing is now able to keep a larger proportion of potential supplies underground.

To measure the effectiveness of prorationing in cushioning the impact of demand changes and new crude oil discoveries, one would need a knowledge of MER's over the period of study and possibly the open-flow production rate as well. Actual production allowables compared with open-flow production rates and with MER's would permit a rough quantitative gauge of prorationing policy contrasted with no public control at all or with a control limited only to protection of optimum physical recovery.[59] No such data are available, however, although estimates of shut-in production (the margin between actual production and output at MER) are given from time to time.

58. Indirectly, of course, large discoveries do affect price; the additions to national production capacity of 1948–49 and 1951 (with respective finding ratios of 1.8 and 2.0) undoubtedly helped prevent any general increase between December, 1947 and June, 1953, while finding and production costs rose. However, even more impressive, massive discoveries abroad failed to break the American price.

59. Direct comparison would be questionable even were such data at hand, since both open-flow rates and MER's vary substantially over time as oil is removed from a field.

In the absence of such information, the response of production to sharp contractions of demand will provide an inkling of policy.[60] During the period 1934 to 1957 there have been four instances of annual contraction in United States demand for all oils and in the production of domestic crude. A minor recession in 1938 brought a fall of 11.6 million barrels (only 0.9 per cent) in total apparent consumption and a contraction of 64.8 million barrels in production of crude oil (a little over 5 per cent). This contraction was preceded by a sharp advance in crude and product stocks during 1937, the first for the two combined since 1933. Wartime restrictions in 1942 caused only a slight ripple: consumption of all oils contracted 27.8 million barrels (1.7 per cent), and domestic crude production declined 15.6 million or 1.3 per cent. In the other two years, 1946 and 1949, requirements of all oils fell only about 0.5 per cent. Contraction of crude production was equally negligible (about 0.6 per cent) in the earlier year, but it mounted to no less than 178.3 million barrels, or about 8.8 per cent of the prior year's output in 1949, when imports added to the problems of adjustment. In every other year both total amounts demanded and total domestic crude oil output increased over the prior year; at no time during the period was the industry confronted with a huge and prolonged recession like that following 1929. The cutback in 1957 following the Suez emergency is discussed at a later point in this chapter.

Table IX compares, for the years 1934–57, annual changes in total stocks of crude oil, refined products, and natural gasoline (an indication of comparative ease of total supply) with changes in crude oil production for the United States as a whole, for the Midcontinent region, and for the state of Texas. Production changes in the Midcontinent and in Texas are shown as a percentage of changes in the national total, and the ratio of Texas to United States output is also shown.

It will be observed that crude oil production in the Midcontinent area took an opposite turn to that for the United States as a whole in three of these years (1934, 1939 and 1957)—in all of which the Midcontinent output declined while national output rose—and that the magnitude of change exceeded that for the nation as a whole in two other years, the contraction of 1938 and the expansion of 1946.

60. Here, as in the case of Tables VI and VIII and the discussions based on them, the use of annual data underestimates the magnitude of shorter-period adjustments needed to preserve balance and actually effectuated by governmental edict.

TABLE IX

*Crude Oil Production Changes: United States and Texas,
1934–57*

YEAR	INCREASE FROM PRECEDING YEAR				PRODUCTION ANNUAL CHANGES:	
	STOCKS: CRUDE OIL, REFINED PRODUCTS	PRODUCTION			ANNUAL TEXAS	MID- TEXAS CONTINENT
		U.S. [b]	MID-CONTI-NENT [b]	TEXAS [c]	TO U.S. [d]	TO CHANGE IN U.S.
	(MILLIONS OF BARRELS) [a]				%	%	%
1934	−37.8	2.4	−16.4	−21.1	42.0	—	—
1935	−22.2	88.5	23.8	11.2	39.4	12.7	26.9
1936	−22.7	103.1	61.0	34.7	38.9	33.7	59.3
1937	45.8	179.5	104.8	82.9	39.9	46.2	58.3
1938	−9.1 [e]	−64.8	−96.9	−34.4	39.2	53.2	149.5
1939	−41.9	50.6	−11.8	7.6	38.2	15.0	—
1940	38.7	88.2	21.3	9.7	36.4	11.0	24.2
1941	−10.9	49.0	29.5	12.4	36.1	25.3	60.3
1942	−58.5	−15.6	−13.0	−22.5	34.8	144.2	83.4
1943	−12.2	119.0	33.0	111.2	39.5	93.4	27.7
1944	−6.2	172.3	82.2	152.4	44.5	88.5	47.7
1945	−13.5	35.8	27.5	8.0	44.0	22.3	76.9
1946	43.5	20.2	24.9	5.5	43.8	27.2	123.0
1947	−5.0	123.0	78.5	60.0	44.2	48.7	63.8
1948	107.1	163.2	114.0	83.3	44.7	51.0	70.0
1949	−2.9	−178.3	−113.8	−159.5	40.4	89.4	64.0
1950	−20.4	131.7	115.9	85.1	42.0	64.7	88.0
1951	37.0	274.1	172.9	180.4	44.9	65.9	63.0
1952	39.6	42.1	28.9	11.8	44.6	28.1	68.0
1953	51.8	67.3	26.7	−2.7	43.2	—	39.6
1954	−10.6	−42.1	−29.1	−44.8	42.0	106.4	69.2
1955	−0.1	169.4	95.7	84.4	42.6	49.8	56.6
1956	65.5	133.0	84.5	49.1	42.3	36.9	63.5
1957	60.9	1.0	−2.4	−23.1	41.4	—	—

[a] API, *Statistical Bulletin* (April 7, 1958), Form No. 6. Includes natural gasoline.
[b] Computed from *ibid.*, Form No. 3A.
[c] Computed from *Petroleum Facts and Figures*, 9th ed., p. 147; 12th ed., p. 144; and *World Oil* (Feb. 15, 1958), p. 165.
[d] *Ibid.*, 9th ed., p. 150; and 12th ed., p. 144. Other percentages computed.
[e] But cf. above, Table VIII, n. c.

In all five years, thus, the direction of change in that area diverged from that of the rest of the country. In every instance the behavior of Midcontinent output had a stabilizing effect. But its contribution to stabilization was far more decisive when prices threatened to fall than when they threatened to rise. Four of the five above-listed instances of divergent trend were instances of weak or weakening markets. If it be remembered that the Midcontinent region accounted for roughly 50 to 60 per cent of United States domestic production throughout this period, it will be noted that in addition to the three years (1934, 1939 and 1957) when it reduced its output while the national total expanded, it also contributed more than proportionately to all four national cutbacks: 1938, 1942, 1949 and 1954. On the other hand, the region participated less than proportionately in three of the five recoveries *after* cutbacks—in 1934 (already mentioned), in 1939–40, and in 1943; in one of the other recoveries (after 1949) the region rebounded more than proportionally and after the other (1954), about to the same extent as the rest of the country.

The comparative record of Texas is even more instructive because it covers one jurisdiction only and because Texas, by reason of its heavy share in national production and its even heavier share of flowing wells,[61] has long assumed a disproportionate share of the function of keeping aggregate domestic supply in balance with prorationing objectives. The comparison with United States production changes assumes that when Texas shares less than proportionately in national production increases and more than proportionately in cutbacks as the nation's crude output is curtailed, the reason is policy, not necessity. It is not possible to prove the validity of this assumption: such behavior could reflect secular decline in the state's share of national production capacity. But the sharp recoveries of Texas output when national market pressures are removed (most obviously in time of war), together with the stability of the state's share in national production over the period as a whole, seem clearly to vindicate the assumption. Occasionally, there are also estimates of MER's by which to test this interpretation.

The policy of restraint that Texas instituted in 1934, when it cut back production to offset increases in more loosely controlled areas

61. E.g., in 1955 its 47,669 flowing wells were 73 per cent of the U. S. total. It is the flowing well, of course, which is the primary object of control. Computed from *Petroleum Facts and Figures,* 12th ed., p. 122.

that threatened the stability of dollar crude oil,[62] was continued if not intensified in the recoveries of 1935 and 1936, Table IX suggests, but Texas participated more than proportionately in the vigorous recovery of 1937. In the several years after 1937 it is apparent that the Texas Railroad Commission held the reins much tighter than MER's would justify, and when curtailment was called for in 1942 Texas again supplied more than the aggregate, thereby offsetting areas which could not or would not contract. That this was indeed a matter of policy is indicated by the more than proportional expansion of Texas output in the war years 1943–44, when the state supplied almost the entire increase in national requirements, thereby expanding its share of national production to its earlier 1933 level of 44.5 per cent. The prompt action of Texas in the face of massive discoveries (1937–39) and economic depression undoubtedly helped snub price declines at 20 cents per barrel in 1938 and, before weakness occurred, in 1942. And this shut-in production turned out to be a boon to the country in the two following years.

Restraint was apparently resumed thereafter until Texas removed all stops from October, 1947, through 1948 and output zoomed to take up about half of the nation's increase in boom demands during those years. In 1949 Texas accounted for no less than 92.1 per cent of the national retrenchment in output! This restraint was all the more remarkable because the state in this year had increased its proved reserves 1.026 billion barrels—a full 75 per cent of the entire nation's additions (1.369 billion) by new discoveries and developments. In both 1950 and 1951, Texas increased output more than proportionally, possibly again reflecting national emergency and the removal of market pressures. But even then it was exercising restraint. In the middle of the earlier year, the Commission reported shut-in capacity at an annual rate of over 317 million barrels, more than 38 per cent of the state's production in that year. At three times in 1951, production was reported below MER by amounts varying from 94 to almost 142 million barrels (annual rate), or approximately 9.3 per cent and 14 per cent, respectively, of that year's output. Since 1951, except for the boom year 1955, Texas has shared skimpily in increases and heavily in decreases, primarily because of the growing importance of imports—still another factor to be offset if prorationing would attain its objectives. On October 1, 1953, a year in which the state shared hardly at all in the expansion of national output, the Commission an-

62. See above, pp. 139–140, 146–150.

nounced sustainable reserve capacity of Texas wells at almost 229 million barrels annual rate, 22.2 per cent of its production in that year.[63] In the 1954 recession, Texas accounted for the entire curtailment of domestic production; and it did the same thing in 1957–58.

There can be little doubt that shut-in capacity under prorationing is substantial and characteristic; or that Texas has played a disproportionately important role in holding United States production short of capacity, whenever necessary to keep it within the limits of market demand at current prices. However, the data do not exist to prove these assertions quantitatively and systematically. The National Petroleum Council estimated domestic reserve capacity at 2,212,000 barrels daily as of July, 1954; at the time of the Suez stoppage, shut-in production capacity was placed between 1.5 and 2.0 million barrels per day; at the close of 1957, the general estimate was 3.0 million barrels.[64] It has periodically been questioned whether estimates like these are reliable, in the sense that they represent the amount by which production could be increased sustainably for any appreciable length of time without endangering MER. On the other hand, Richard J. Gonzalez, of Humble Oil, has vigorously defended the two-million figure as a measure of our unused capacity to sustain a greater output for three years or more even if new drilling were to decline.[65]

63. Without more adequate data for national shut-in capacity it is not possible to demonstrate conclusively that Texas was at such times carrying more than its fair share of the burden of restricting output. However, Cookenboo's estimates of national shut-in capacity in 1951 and 1953 (see below, n. 64) suggest that Texas shut-in capacity in the earlier year ranged from roughly 41 to 62 per cent of the national total, and in 1953 it was over 90 per cent. These percentages generally exceed substantially Texas' share of national output, 45 per cent and 43 per cent in the two years respectively, and certainly in 1953 its percentage of shut-in capacity also exceeds its share of flowing wells.

64. U. S. House of Representatives, Committee on Interstate and Foreign Commerce, *Petroleum Survey*, "Oil Lift to Europe," *Preliminary Report*, 85th Congress, 1st Session, House Report No. 314 (1957), p. 4 (cited below as *Petroleum Survey*). Cookenboo estimated domestic reserve capacity in each of the three years 1951–53 at 627, 801, and 696 thousand barrels per day respectively (*Crude Oil Pipe Lines*, p. 70, table 13). These estimates were based on a comparison of actual production of wells subject to restriction with projected MER's for each of the five years, 1951–55, as estimated by the U. S. Petroleum Administration for Defense in "Transportation of Oil," December, 1951. Since MER'S of existing wells and fields change as oil is withdrawn and new development wells are drilled, these projections would have very limited significance. On the close-of-1957 estimate, see below, p. 557.

65. Historically, the U.S. has never produced for long beyond 8 per cent of its proved reserves, and it was this fact that underlay some of the reservations

Texas alone was believed to hold almost three-fourths of this reserve capacity, despite its failure during 1956 to produce up to total allowables by some 13 to 15 per cent.[66]

The role of Texas as a governor of national production was most recently demonstrated in the adaptations of 1957, first to the emergency requirements of Europe during the Suez episode, next to the high level of imports and stocks after that crisis abated.[67] As a result of the closing of the Suez Canal and of the pipelines through Syria, it was estimated that Western Europe (and West Africa) would require 410,000 barrels per day of oil and products from the United States Gulf during the first quarter of 1957, as compared with the normal fourth-quarter 1956 requirements of only 50,000. In addition, it was estimated the Gulf would have to supply 190,000 barrels more than usual for the United States East Coast and Canada, to help make up for lost Middle East imports.[68] The response of Texas to this situation was restrained by widespread belief that stocks should be substantially lowered before more production was authorized—a typical response of the state authorities, as is suggested by the tendency for the state's production to participate but slightly in the early stages of recovering national production. Thus the Railroad Commission permitted a rise of only 75,000 b/d in December–January allowables over the October–November rate and it advanced the February allowable a mere 93,000 b/d after prices had risen in January. It was not until the middle of the month that production for March was authorized at a record figure of 3,733,000 b/d, some 200,000 b/d above February. But the back of the emergency was already broken, and on

expressed about the large estimates of reserve capacity. However, Gonzalez pointed out, there are good reasons to believe that production could exceed this ratio without threatening optimum long-run output. Among them are the larger proportion of relatively new wells drilled, the expanding number of pressure maintenance and secondary recovery projects in force, and the improved techniques of fracturing and perforation of wells to increase withdrawals. *Petroleum Press Service* (January, 1957), pp. 29–30. See also below, p. 233, n. 4.

66. Major sources of this short fall in actual production were revealed, through classification of the aggregate allowable for March, 1956, to be wells exempt from restriction (which fell short by 27 per cent of the output allocated to them) and fields for which allowables are based on well depth rather than MER (some 13 per cent under their allowables). Large fields accounting for the bulk of Texas reserves failed to produce their allowable in that month by only 1.2 per cent. *Ibid.*, p. 30.

67. For a more adequate analysis of this experience see below, Chap. 9.

68. See *Petroleum Survey* (above, n. 64), pp. 21–22.

March 19 Texas allowables were cut back 224,000 b/d for the following month; by July, they had fallen to 3,086,000 b/d. From the last
week in January through March, Texas allowables were raised 237,-
000 b/d, and by the end of the next three months they had been cut
back 647,000 b/d. Allowables continued to be tightly restricted during the summer and fall, because of the depressed condition of the
market.

These wide gyrations in the monthly Texas allowables are damped
in the data for actual average daily performance as shown in Table X

TABLE X

*Adjustment to Suez: United States, and Texas Production
of Crude, October, 1956–September, 1957*

	PRODUCTION OF BARRELS PER DAY				PERCENTAGES	
		INCREASE OVER PRE-		INCREASE OVER PRE-	TEXAS AS %	TEXAS CHANGE AS % OF U.S.
MONTH	U.S.	VIOUS MONTH	TEXAS	VIOUS MONTH	OF U.S.	
Oct. '56	6,996	—	2,933	—	41.9	—
Nov.	7,137	141	3,006	73	42.2	51.7
Dec.	7,376	239	3,059	53	41.5	22.2
Jan. '57	7,412	36	3,078	19	41.5	52.8
Feb.	7,516	104	3,131	53	41.6	51.0
March	7,784	268	3,324	193	42.7	72.0
April	7,525	−259	3,208	−116	42.7	44.8
May	7,457	−68	3,160	−48	42.4	70.6
June	7,231	−226	3,080	−80	42.6	35.4
July	6,907	−324	2,803	−277	40.6	85.4
Aug.	6,799	−108	2,790	−13	41.0	12.0
Sept.	6,822	23	2,763	−27	40.5	—

Source: Production from *World Oil,* monthly issues.

in comparison with total domestic output. Apart from the usual leak-
age between actual and allowable production, an indeterminate
amount of authorized output was estopped apparently for lack of adequate pipeline capacity. Nevertheless, the Texas pattern of adjustment was familiar: a much less than proportional sharing in production advances in November and December when stocks were still
heavy (about 33.1 per cent of the national increase during the two
months); a more than proportional share of increased output as stocks
were drawn down (65 per cent of the aggregate three months' increase

through March); and, most characteristic, a more than proportional share in the cutback during the last six months shown.[69] Taking the entire year covered by the table, it appears that Texas accounted for no less than 170,000 b/d of the 174,000 b/d net decline in national rate of output. And even this experience was only a pallid taste of what was to come; as is shown more fully in Chapter 21, Texas production was subjected to progressive constriction after September, 1957, to such a point that its share in national output was compressed from 40.5 per cent in that month to a monthly low of 35.2 in May, 1958. Here is the measure of that state's contribution to solving the industry's problems, only temporarily postponed by Suez, of mounting production capacity, discouragingly high inventories, and stagnation of demand.

Prorationing: A Preliminary View

Prorationing to market demand has clearly brought about more orderly marketing of crude oil with much fewer and less extreme price changes. This altered pattern of price and supply behavior has been gained by making crude oil markets economically more imperfect, an undoubted social improvement over the peculiarly destructive character of competition under the rule of capture. Prorationing has also greatly increased the ultimate recovery of oil and gas. In so doing, however, it has extended the period of recovery from new flush fields and from new wells further than would have been necessary merely to secure optimally efficient ultimate recovery, if one may judge by the sizable magnitude of shut-in production below MER. The national realization of this policy has depended primarily on the State of Texas. Because of its dominant position in production and especially in proved reserves and wells on natural drive, Texas has been able to impart a flexibility in oil supply that neither the market nor the efforts of other oil-producing states could approximate. And though the Texas Commission has often denied any concern for price, it is clear beyond cavil

69. Since Texas production in March fell substantially short of that authorized, the reduction in permissible production in the months immediately following was much larger than curtailment of actual output. Nonetheless, Texas accounted for 54 per cent of the national contraction in output between March and August, and its output was held to a further reduction in September, while national production recovered slightly, so that the state's share of the national total declined from its 42.7 per cent peak in March to 40.5 per cent in September.

that its exercise of control over supplies has had a major impact in snubbing crude-oil price declines.[70]

With effective prorationing, crude oil prices were not only stabilized; they also began an upward movement that has resisted the periodic contrary pressures of ample supplies. Rising demands and rising costs help account for this trend and might have produced the same results in a free market; but even if one cannot ascribe the long-run change entirely to prorationing it is apparent that substantial shut-in production, given price inelasticity of demand, contributed importantly to the observed performance.

Increased stability of crude oil prices, especially their rising trend and resistance to short-run downward pressures, and higher ultimate recovery of oil should raise the value of investments in producing properties. On the other hand, restriction of output from new wells operating on natural drives and the consequent extension of time for ultimate recovery either of cost or value—for which prorationing is also responsible—would tend to lower present value. Indeed, cut-backs in output per well have been known to force the drilling of more wells, and the consequent rise of investment costs per barrel of oil produced, in order to maintain a profitable output. What may have been the net impact of these opposing effects on large and small producers, integrated and nonintegrated, is very difficult to say. Logically, the small nonintegrated operator will discount future returns at a higher rate than the large, and especially the large integrated, operator. With better access to investment funds and with an indefinitely enduring commitment not only to production but to the downstream operations the production properties serve, the major oil company should place a higher present valuation than the small independent producer on a property that will yield revenues only over a long period of time.

To the extent that this reasoning is sound, prorationing would have tipped the scales in favor of the operator with the long purse and the long-run perspective. The available statistics do not disclose any such tendency. The majors did increase their share of national production

70. On the basis of an analysis of the orders of the Texas Railroad Commission and the behavior of stocks of crude oil over the period 1935 through 1949, one study concluded that the "oil industry clearly restricted production for at least nine of the past fifteen years." W. B. Nelson, "The Oil Industry: A Case Study in Imperfect Competition" (unpublished dissertation, State University of Iowa, 1950), p. 214. Nelson pointed to the two-week shutdown in Texas and Oklahoma following directly on the announcement of a reduction of the posted price in 1939 as an illustration of the determination of the regulatory authorities to preserve the market price for crude.

during the first fifteen years following prorationing, but their percentage control has declined markedly since 1948, leaving them apparently with a small net gain over the entire period.[71] It is not clear, however, exactly what these gross data may imply. With effective prorationing, differences in discounting the future would be maximized in the valuation of wells on natural drive, and the majors would be expected to increase their comparative ownership of such wells. This may well have happened even though absence of ownership distribution data for such wells over time prevents confirmation; the declining percentage of national production in recent years could reflect no more than the disproportionate impact of cutbacks below MER on

71. Cookenboo found that the gross production of the nineteen majors accounted for between 51.7 per cent and 63.1 per cent of annual U.S. crude output between 1929 and 1948 as follows:

YEAR	PER CENT	YEAR	PER CENT	YEAR	PER CENT
1929	54.1	1937	53.5	1945	62.0
1933	53.3	1938	51.7	1947	62.4
1935	55.1	1943	59.1	1948	63.1

For 1952, he found the same group's gross production responsible for 60.3 per cent of the national total. *Crude Oil Pipe Lines*, p. 71, table 14; Cookenboo's figures for some of the intermediate years are reproduced by Eugene V. Rostow and Arthur S. Sachs, "Entry into the Oil Refining Business: Vertical Integration Re-Examined," *Yale Law Journal, 61* (1952), 879, n. 86.

The share of national production by the thirty and the thirty-five (later reduced by mergers among themselves to thirty-four and thirty-three) large oil companies surveyed annually by the Chase Manhattan Bank shows a similar trend—the low coming in 1938, sharp upward breaks in 1943 and 1944, a peak in 1948, and a definite decline since. This group of course includes several large but nonintegrated producing companies. (*Report of the Attorney General*, pursuant to Sec. 2 of the Joint Resolution of July 28, 1955 consenting to an Interstate Compact to Conserve Oil and Gas, September 1, 1956, p. 91.) Between 1952 and 1956 the net crude oil production of the thirty-five (including their consolidated subsidiaries) declined further from 55.7 per cent to 53.2 per cent of the national total. Computed from the Chase surveys.

It has not been possible to obtain figures precisely comparable with those of Cookenboo for the 1952–56 period. Estimates of the *net* domestic production of the same nineteen companies for those two years, compiled for us by Boni, Watkins, Jason, and Company, show a decline from 47.9 to 46.2 per cent of the national total. The discrepancy between the 47.9 combined share in 1952 and Cookenboo's 60.3 per cent is clearly too great to be explained by the fact that his figures are for gross production, these for net. In some cases his figures seem to include production of natural gas liquids which are not in the national total. However, the estimates used are not precisely comparable company by company, either; it is impossible to compile a perfectly consistent series from the published data.

free-flowing wells. On the other hand it could be that the growing importance of tax incentives after World War II and of a relatively riskless and costless hedge against inflation has accounted for a greater volume of exploration and production among smaller operators, and by companies, large and small, theretofore outside the oil industry. This development needs further attention at a later point; for if this is indeed the explanation, it has a bearing on the necessity for integration to assure adequate discovery and development of crude oil supplies.

In conclusion, then, it is not possible to prove that prorationing created a differential advantage for the large integrated operator over the small or the nonintegrated producer. To the extent that it has raised and stabilized price against a fall, it will have advantaged both large and small producers. Moreover, in some ways it has differentially benefited the latter, who own the bulk of wells that are exempt from output restriction, and in whose favor exceptions from well-spacing regulations were all too frequently made. But the major oil company will no doubt glean advantage from the smaller crude stocks that prorationing permits; it can better afford than its smaller competitors to hold domestic supplies for future recovery at better prices; and it may enjoy a great strategic advantage by virtue of its ownership of crude in both regulated and unregulated areas, domestic and foreign. Through their purchase nominations and their control of alternative sources of supply, the majors can influence the determination of the domestic crude oil price, a price which has significance for some of them far beyond the volume of their domestic production. This influence is the subject of Chapter 8. By straddling domestic and foreign output they can enjoy the price benefits conferred by prorationing while, unlike their domestic competitors, enjoying also a partial escape from its drawback —the limitation of permissible production: this is an important consideration in Chapters 9 and 10.

The Pricing of Crude Oil: I. The Integrated Firm and the Domestic Market

THE MOST IMPORTANT economic impact of prorationing is that it destroys the nexus between oil discoveries and short-run price. Crude prices are not completely insulated from market forces. Failures of foresight or errors in administration of controls and unexpected shifts in product demand may continue to create situations in which short-run market pressures challenge the validity of the posted price. Thus a failure fully to anticipate an expansion of demand, as in 1946–47, can propel prices upward; and a failure to cut back production allowables promptly when demand for products falls off, as in 1954, can breed discounts from the posted price. But the preponderant effect of prorationing is to dampen the tendency for changing conditions in product markets to force crude prices either up or down. The existence of a substantial and variable shut-in capacity is ample evidence that the price level is importantly affected by policy considerations. It is the direct and indirect long-range influence of the majors in this administrative decision with which the present chapter deals. This subject is merged with a study of world market pricing and of imports in the chapter immediately following for the simple reason that it is impossible to analyze the one without considering the others; prorationing and the domestic price are both profoundly affected by and in turn profoundly affect world prices and the trend of imports; and both are importantly influenced by the phenomenon of business size and integration.

Economically, the long-run price level for crude oil in competitive markets would be expected to be governed by the costs of finding and exploiting new domestic sources of supply and by the comparative costs and availability of crude oil from foreign sources. But this familiar expectation among ordinary products cannot be realized here. Even in the foreign field, where production is uncontrolled and entire fields are operated under single direction, the uncertain connection between an added dollar's investment and the volume of additions to productive capacity, exaggerated by the lure of the big strike and the gap between added costs and total costs, attenuates the interaction of long-run costs and the level of price. In the more complex economic and political environment of domestic production, where these inherent uncertainties are dwarfed by the short-run compulsions of the rule of capture, the role of cost-price relations is even more obscure. Nonetheless, a brief look at cost factors and investment practices that bear independently on long-run price levels is needed to understand the role of the majors in this crucial stage of the industry's operations. For clarity of presentation, Chapter 8 is confined to the domestic market, reserving the discussion of foreign sources, where conditions are much different, for appraisal in Chapter 9.

This search for the contributions of integration to exploration, development, production, and pricing of crude oil centers around three questions. First, does vertical integration play an independent, important role in influencing the finding and exploitation of these resources? Second, do the practices of the large, integrated companies sharpen or dull competitive forces affecting crude prices over time? Finally, do these firms, as concurrent buyers and sellers of crude oil, have a predictable impact on the level and behavior of its price?

THE ROLE OF THE MAJORS IN FINDING AND DEVELOPING OIL RESOURCES

Considered historically, there is some basis for the presumption that the large integrated firm contributes importantly to the search for oil and to its subsequent production in a manner calculated to maximize ultimate recovery. This expectation stems from several possible distinguishing attributes of the major oil company compared with the typical independent producer: a greater ability to marshal the ever-increasing amounts of capital needed for expenditures on this activity; a greater willingness to risk such outlays even in the face of currently unfavorable circumstances; and a greater ability and willingness to hold back the flow of production in order to maximize total revenues over time.[1]

The large, integrated firm undoubtedly commanded a preferred access to funds in the past and it may still do so today. Some of these advantages stem from size, with which integration tends to be cor-

1. These possible characteristics are not necessary or even probable attributes of vertical integration per se. Rather, they are associated with size and variety of operations that are importantly correlated with integration (vertical and horizontal) and personified in the majors. The reader is reminded of the difficulties of precise classification of firms in this industry. See above, pp. 25 ff.

related, and some with the greater stability of earnings derived from operating in various functional levels and geographic markets. Operating income from the performance of diverse functions is a more reliable source of internal funds; and a well-established position in many markets gives greater access to external funds (debt or equity) at lower rates. The expectation that the integrated company would show a particular willingness to spend on exploration and to conserve resources for a future day is equally persuasive. A company with heavy investments in transportation, refining, and marketing does not explore merely for the profit to be made in the production of crude oil. The security and profitability of its entire investment require a continuing flow of crude over an indefinite period of time. A longer view with respect to the justification of expenditures for crude oil is not a matter of choice; it is forced on the firm by its existing and cumulating commitments to the integrated enterprise. In other words, the opportunity cost of using its funds for finding and developing oil is lowered by the crucial need to protect its investments elsewhere; and it might well make expenditures for this purpose at a lower level of crude oil prices than would stimulate firms free of this duress. Furthermore, with more stable income from its variegated operations against which to charge exploratory and developmental intangibles in computing taxable income, the integrated firm might be expected to spend more freely and on a more stable time schedule for this purpose than the nonintegrated producer.

That the majors do spend more stably than nonintegrated firms for exploration is often asserted with conviction, but the proof is hard to come by. To test this thesis, it would be necessary to compare their exploratory expenditures with those of the rest of the industry over a period of time long enough to test for changing market conditions. Unfortunately, industrywide figures that show separately the number of exploratory wells drilled go back only to 1937; and the years since 1937 are not too good for this purpose, since economic conditions and production controls gave an almost continuous lift to domestic exploration after that date. Indeed, only from 1937 to 1940, when the average price of crude oil fell and production was cut back, and again perhaps in 1949–50, when prices eased and output was sharply restricted, would it be possible to test the impact of adverse conditions on drilling investment.[2] It is probably not surprising, therefore,

2. Average prices for the U.S. fell from $1.18 per barrel in 1937 to $1.13 in 1938 and $1.02 in 1939–40. They fell again in 1949 to $2.54 from $2.60 in the preceding year (*Petroleum Facts and Figures,* 9th ed., p. 121), and to $2.51 in

that the number of exploratory wells drilled show almost continuous and dramatic increases year by year, from 1,140 in 1937 to 14,937 in 1955, broken only by very slight (less than 2 per cent) declines in 1942 and 1954 and a deeper one, finally, in 1957 and 1958.[3]

To obtain data for integrated companies that could be compared with the record for the industry, thirty-three leading oil companies were circularized—the thirty regularly surveyed (until a few years ago) by Pogue and Coqueron for the Chase National Bank, plus Ashland, Deep Rock, and Sunray. Of these thirty-three, eight companies are producers exclusively but the other twenty-five operate at all levels. Usable data were received on exploratory wells drilled (either from 1937 or from 1948 through 1953) from twenty-three firms: three nonintegrated producers and twenty majors. The findings do not support the hypothesis stated above. While exploratory drilling for the industry as a whole more than doubled in the face of adverse market conditions between 1937 and the average of 1938–39, only five major companies (in two cases negligibly, in only one as rapidly as for the industry as a whole) increased the number of exploratory wells drilled, and eight (in two cases negligibly) actually reduced such drilling. This record is far less buoyant than that of the entire industry.[4] The discrepancy is even more striking when one compares the 1949–50 average with exploratory wells drilled during the 1948 price-output peak. The industry total rose 20 per cent during this period. But only five of the majors showed an increase, while fourteen drilled fewer exploratory wells and one showed no change.

1950 (*ibid.*, 12th ed., p. 103). One might be able to test the thesis also in the weakening crude oil markets of 1954 and 1957–58; unfortunately the survey, which is described presently, was conducted before 1954 well-drilling statistics were available.

3. Data for 1937 to 1955 from *Petroleum Facts and Figures,* 9th ed., p. 127; and 12th ed., p. 119. The 1937–55 increase continued in 1956; wildcat well completions were 12,624 in that year, up from 11,601 in 1955. In 1957, however, came a definite slump: only 11,383 wildcats were completed. The slump continued in 1958, with total wildcat completions in the first eight months of that year running 16.7 per cent below the corresponding 1957 figure. *World Oil* (February 15, 1958), p. 119; (October, 1958), p. 28.

4. Figures were requested that could be compared with those reported by the API, which are in turn actually estimated by Frederic H. Lahee and reported regularly in the *Bulletin of the American Association of Petroleum Geologists.* The companies supplied data for wells drilled by themselves or in which they had a direct interest. Some supplied separate figures, not included here, on wells drilled for which they had made some contribution in money or acreage. The group of nonintegrated producing companies for which data were assembled is much too small to use for comparative purposes.

It would appear that the long-run prospects of exploration and other inducements to drill were so favorable during the period after 1937 that the strength of integration has not been needed to bulwark this activity against short-term market deterioration. If anything, integrated firms have responded more sensitively than the industry to softer markets.

Indeed, the data available hardly confirm the presumed importance of the large integrated firm in the search for domestic crude oil.[5] Table XI presents an analysis of the drilling record in 1957 for the seventeen major companies which published the necessary data, in comparison with aggregate United States drilling in that year. The data are not always fully comparable, as the footnotes indicate, but they are probably fairly representative.[6] The most striking thing they show is that the large, integrated firms as a group, and with important exceptions, tend to leave a disproportionate share of wildcat drilling to their smaller competitors. These seventeen companies accounted for approximately 39 per cent of net national production in 1956; but they accounted in 1957 for only 19 per cent of the total wells drilled and only 12 per cent of exploratory tests.[7] While exploratory wells made up 30 per cent of all wells drilled by the rest of the industry domestically, they accounted for only 17 per cent of wells drilled by these majors.[8] Only partially offsetting this showing

5. Data are usable for only fifteen companies—the thirteen whose experience from 1937 to 1939 is summarized in the text plus Ashland and Sohio for which exploratory activity in the 1930's was nil or negligible. These fifteen companies accounted for 33 per cent of industry exploratory wells in 1937, 15 per cent in 1938, 11 per cent in 1940, 13 per cent in 1948, 11 per cent in 1951, and 10½ per cent in 1953.

6. These results are no more than generally indicative of the relative activity of the named firms in drilling during 1957. Since data are largely taken from company annual reports, their comparability is uncertain, especially in the elimination of Canadian wells. But the relatively small role they show the majors playing in exploration accords with the general observations of others. See, e.g., the testimony of W. S. Farish, then president of Standard Oil Company (New Jersey) before the TNEC, Pt. XVII (October, 1939), p. 9687; see also testimony of Karl A. Crowley, *ibid.*, Pt. XIV, p. 7593. See also below, n. 11.

7. Computed from Table XII, below, p. 224.

8. Experience ranged widely from one individual firm to another. Phillips, Socony Mobil, Gulf, and Standard of California had only 5 to 13 per cent wildcats out of all wells drilled—a meager record in comparison with the average for the listed majors and for the industry excluding these seventeen firms, and quite insignificant in contrast with Union and Sohio, which had ratios of 32 and 33 per cent. The number of wildcats undertaken in a given

TABLE XI   Analysis of United States Drilling Activity of Selected Majors, 1957

17 MAJOR OIL COMPANIES	NET WELLS DRILLED [a]				SUCCESS RATIOS		TOTAL EXPLORATORY WELLS AS % OF ALL WELLS
	ALL WELLS		EXPLORATORY WELLS		All	Exploratory	
	Total	Successful	Total	Successful	$(2) \div (1)$	$(4) \div (3)$	$(3) \div (1)$
	(1)	(2)	(3)	(4)	(5)	(6)	(7)
Gulf Oil Corp.	1,754	1,464	208 [c]	70 [c]	83%	34%	12%
Shell Oil Co.	1,274 [c]	961 [c]	269 [c]	48 [c]	75	18	21
Socony Mobil Oil Co.	882	747	40	10	85	25	5
Humble Oil & Refining Co.	867	648	169	47	75	28	19
Standard Oil Co. (Indiana) [b]	841	624	195	59	74	30	23
Standard Oil Co. of California	781	636	97	28	81	29	12
Cities Service Co.	676 [c]	542 [c]	97 [c]	29 [c]	80	30	14
Continental Oil Co.	511	393	83	23	77	28	16
Skelly Oil Co.	464	378	84 [c]	26 [c]	81	31	18
Sinclair Oil Corp. [b]	496	361	108	23	73	21	22
Sunray Mid-Continent Oil Co.	326	229	82	17	70	21	25
Phillips Petroleum Co.	319	264	40	16	83	40	13
Union Oil Co. of California	284	204	90	29	72	32	32
Ohio Oil Co.	227	197	43 [c]	13 [c]	87	30	19
Tidewater Oil Co.	187	167	22	13	89	59	12
Pure Oil Co.	182	125	43	19	69	44	24
Standard Oil Co. (Ohio) [b]	70	43	23	5	61	22	33
Total, 17 majors	10,141	7,983	1,693	475	79%	28%	17%
Total, United States	53,838	33,137	14,707	2,810	62%	19%	27%
17 majors as a per cent of United States	19%	24%	12%	17%			
United States total, excluding 17 majors	43,697	25,154	13,014	2,335	58%	18%	30%

[a] Net wells include in number of wells a summation of part interests.
[b] Includes some Canada.
[c] Gross.

Source: Table compiled and supplied by courtesy of Boni, Watkins, Jason, and Co. from *Annual Reports*. United States totals are from *Oil and Gas Journal* (all wells) and the *Bulletin of the American Association of Petroleum Geologists* (exploratory wells).

is the fact that the majors have better-than-average success in drilling. Their higher success ratios in aggregate wells drilled is somewhat deceptive, since they are partly attributable to a higher proportion of developmental wells than the industry: developmental drilling naturally has a much higher proportion of successes. However, the majors were also comparatively more successful in their exploratory drilling alone, although here individual experience was much more diverse.

The figures in Table XI, which generally include only the wells in which each company had an operating or ownership interest, understate somewhat the proportionate contribution of the majors to the national exploratory effort. Through the "farm-out" [9] the large firm may maximize its aggregate drilling effort per dollar available by making various contributions to induce others to drill more speculative locations in return for the information about the underlying strata revealed in the core.[10] Such assistance makes up only a small fraction of the lead of independents in the drilling of wildcats and the making of important oil discoveries in this country.[11] It is further claimed that the leading producers, most of which are also integrated, do most of the scientific work and account for a much larger proportion of

---

year is likely to be quite a variable figure; it would be fruitless, hence, to draw generalizations from these variations.

9. Large integrated companies often assist independents where drilling is highly speculative. Leases may be turned over with or without reservation regarding minimum drilling depth; acreage may be transferred to permit the small operator to raise cash for drilling; a dry-hole allowance may be promised when the well has reached a specified depth without finding oil or a bottom-hole allowance may be paid according to depth whether or not oil is discovered. These and similar farm-outs are made in return for the information that a wildcat can provide in well-logs, cores, and samples; the major may or may not also reserve a royalty interest in oil that may be discovered. McLean and Haigh, pp. 392 ff., give partial data for selected companies.

10. With literally millions of acres under option or lease, the large firm is under constant pressure to develop or to release properties. In areas already producing oil the terms of the lease will usually force continuous development —offsets and extensions to prove out a field and maintain output—whether or not crude oil is in short supply. New field wildcats may be deferred, however, and it is here that the farm-out is useful.

11. Until 1954, the annual drilling surveys by Frederic Lahee, published in the June issues of the *Bulletin of the American Association of Petroleum Geologists*, contained an estimate not only of the new field wildcat wells drilled by "majors" but also of wells drilled by independents with 50 per cent or more financing by majors. In 1953, according to these figures, majors drilled 1,153, or 16.6 per cent of the national total of 6,925 new field wildcats (but 25.2 per cent of those that turned out producers) and contributed 50 per cent or

additions to reserves than is indicated by their share even of successful exploratory wells.

The major firm could play a more significant role in finding and developing domestic crude oil resources in the future than it has in the past because of rising costs and mounting obstacles to discovery of new reserves. We have neither the desire nor the competence to project ourselves into the statistical maelstrom that engulfs the question of actual and future costs and prospects of finding and exploiting oil in this country. Some understanding of the issues, however, may help to gauge the contributions that integration might make toward their solution.

The prospective future development of domestic crude oil supply will depend broadly on four groups of factors. First is the undoubted increase in the dollar cost of exploration, drilling, and production as labor and material costs rise and deeper wells are sunk in less accessible locations both onshore and offshore. More funds must be marshaled and more must be risked on the threat of a dry hole. Second is the prospect of higher *real* costs, of less hydrocarbons discovered per well sunk and per foot drilled, as new finds approach the ultimate limits in the oil still available to be discovered within United States borders. Third is the increased realization from *known* reservoirs as recovery methods are improved and their added costs are justified. This is strictly a matter of technology and economics—only the size of its ultimate contribution is moot. And last, of course, is the economic limit to all of these activities that competition or policy may impose through the importation of crude from foreign lands or the

more to an additional 916. Giving them credit for 75 per cent of the latter raises their share in the national total drilled to 26.6 per cent, and in total producers to 33.2 per cent.

Lahee classified companies as majors if they were integrated to at least three levels, operated in two or more states or major divisions thereof, and had current assets in excess of $20 million. It is obviously very conservative to surmise that the group was at least broad enough to embrace the twenty-two companies listed in Table XII, below. The net production of these companies amounted to approximately 51 per cent of the national total in 1953.

Incidentally, these annual figures seem to corroborate the finding that major company exploratory drilling is less stable than the national total, i.e. more susceptible to discouragement by temporarily adverse market conditions, at least so far as the 1949–50 experience is concerned. Allowing them 75 per cent of the wells to which they contributed 50 per cent or more, their share in aggregate wildcat drilling dropped from 29.2 per cent in 1948 to 23.6 and 21.9 per cent in the next two years; their share recovered to between 24.4 and 27.7 per cent in 1951–53.

development of alternative sources of petroleum products, like shale oil.

Of all the factors affecting exploration and production, rising money costs are best authenticated. As drilling techniques improve, wells are sunk deeper into the earth—Louisiana boasts the deepest producing well (17,900 feet) and the longest dry hole (22,570 feet) in the world—and drilling costs mount astronomically as depth increases.[12] Single test wells may easily cost more than a million dollars, more especially when combined with high lease premiums per acre (though the height of lease premiums is price-determined rather than price-determining) and the expensive preliminaries incidental to drilling in offshore locations on the continental shelf, regarded today as our most promising potential.[13] Industry expenditures on exploration, development, and production per barrel of net crude oil produced more than doubled between 1944 and 1953, rising from an estimated

12. Although drilling costs vary greatly from one formation to another, the results of an IPAA survey based on 30.29 per cent of all wells drilled in 1953 are indicative of the relative costs involved.

DEPTH RANGE (FEET)	AVERAGE DEPTH (FEET)	AVERAGE COST PER WELL ($000)	AVERAGE COST PER FOOT ($)	ADDED DEPTH (FEET)	ADDED COST PER ADDED FOOT ($)
0–1,250	849	5.6	6.63		
1,251–2,500	1,793	14.3	7.99	944	9.22
2,501–3,750	3,121	28.4	9.10	1,328	10.62
3,751–5,000	4,292	43.3	10.09	1,171	12.72
5,001–7,500	6,104	76.4	12.51	1,812	18.27
7,501–10,000	8,631	128.3	14.86	2,527	20.54
10,001–12,500	11,083	230.8	20.83	2,452	41.80
12,501–15,000	13,380	363.3	27.15	2,297	57.68
over 15,000	16,038	644.8	40.20	2,658	105.91
Average	4,035	50.2	12.43		

Source: *Petroleum Facts and Figures,* 12th ed., p. 133.

W. W. Keeler reported Phillips' experience with drilling costs in 1951–52 in West Texas and New Mexico on a slightly different basis. He showed that an added thousand feet involved an added average cost per foot of $11 as wells went below 3,000 ft.; $20 below 7,000 ft., $72 below 12,000 ft. U. S. House of Representatives, Hearings before the Committee on Interstate and Foreign Commerce, *Petroleum Study,* 83rd Congress, 1st Session (1953), p. 94 (cited below as *Wolverton Hearings*). Using IPAA data in approximate fashion, it appears that a 16,000 ft. well, four times the depth of a 4,000 footer, will cost almost fifteen times as much.

13. The average off-shore well in the Gulf has been recently estimated to cost around $450,000 (*Petroleum Press Service,* January, 1957, p. 10). In 1953, the average drilling cost of all U.S. wells was $50,200; for offshore wells only, $298,800. *Petroleum Facts and Figures,* 12th ed., p. 134.

$1.47 in the former year to $2.21 in 1948 and $3.16 in 1953.[14] Other data, purporting to cover the cost of finding and developing reserves per barrel of crude produced (a component of the total represented above), show the same upward direction.[15] These are simply total outlays divided by net production during the same period. Such data have very limited significance as a measure of exploratory incentives [16] but their trend is indicative of the rising pressure on crude prices.

14. *Petroleum Facts and Figures,* 12th ed., p. 135.

15. Cost was estimated at 85 cents per barrel in 1946 and advanced to $1.75 in 1954. Scott C. Lambert, "Percentage Depletion and the National Interest," in U. S. Congress, Joint Committee on the Economic Report, *Federal Tax Policy for Economic Growth and Stability,* 84th Congress, 1st Session (1955), p. 462. In 1955 and 1956, the Chase Manhattan Bank's thirty-three company sample spent for this purpose $1.83 and $1.90 respectively per barrel of net crude produced. Coqueron, *Annual Financial Analysis, 1956,* p. 13.

16. Since oil discovered is a stock to be exploited over some future period, the significant measure of unit costs of exploration and development would seem to be the amount of product (oil or gas) which has been added to reserves, not the amount of crude oil produced. A striking example of the misleading results one can obtain by dividing aggregate exploratory and production outlays by production is the widely cited estimate by Ira H. Cram, senior vice-president of the Continental Oil Company, to the effect that offshore oil to date had cost $14 per barrel (produced). "The Outlook Offshore," address before the 36th Annual Meeting of the American Petroleum Institute, November 14, 1956. The height of the figure merely represented the high initial costs of heavy investments thus far (estimated by Cram at $1.6 billion) that had established production capacity but had not as yet borne fruit in correspondingly large production. According to Cram these expenditures had proved out an estimated 620 million barrels of oil, and 4 trillion cubic feet of gas. If the underground gas were valued at 5 cents per Mcf, this would reduce the aggregate cost of oil *found* to $2.25 a barrel, a figure which would in turn be sharply reduced if account could be taken of the ultimate size of the reserves thus far only hinted at. On this finding cost offshore see also below, n. 26.

There is no satisfactory way, however, to gauge the magnitude of discoveries as they are made. The API, in estimating proved reserves, has adopted methods that consciously understate the probable size of the new reservoir. The number of wells drilled, the drainage area established by such wells, and the technical behavior of well flow determine the estimate of reservé; and the figure is revised only as the drilling of new development wells provides good evidence for change. See above, p. 153, n. 54. About four-fifths of the annual additions to proved reserves in recent years have been accounted for by extensions and revisions of previously reported discoveries. It is for this reason that the industry can say that the dominant portion of the oil produced today is lifted from fields discovered from five to fifteen years in the past. Nevertheless, as long as new discoveries and developments of crude oil must pace annual pro-

The rise in money costs of exploration and development during the recent past, however, does not necessarily mark an inexorable trend for the future, apart from the possibility of continuing inflation of money prices and costs in the economy at large. One cannot ignore the opposite influence of cost-reducing improvements in technology and in the development and application of geological knowledge and geophysical techniques, about which something is said in Chapter 12. Moreover, the mere fact that as more oil is produced, ultimate United States supplies are to that extent depleted does not necessarily justify the assumption that oil discovered in any given decade means a higher real cost of finding new oil in the next. Such a simple view flies in the face of past experience and of current knowledge. The drill is still the arbiter of the presence and volume of oil in an underground structure; and the discovery of oil in a new location or in a new type of structure, while in a purely physical sense reducing the quantity of oil yet to be found, may nonetheless improve the economic prospects of new finds.[17] Scientific exploration helps to narrow the probabilities of finding oil by more accurately gauging the probable occurrence beneath the earth of types of structures that experience has shown to be favorable for its presence; but it does not circumscribe or delimit the oil yet to be found.

Probably no country on earth has been as thoroughly explored and drilled for oil as the United States, and yet the National Petroleum Council could conclude in 1952 that only something on the order of 1 per cent of our probable oil-producing area had been explored. True, producing provinces covered as many as 200,000 of the aggregate 1,860,000 square miles believed to be favorable for oil deposits,[18] but even this producing area is being continually re-explored

duction and no major changes occur in tax or price inducements, the rising trend in finding and developing costs will herald a rising cost of future supplies.

17. The history of oil exploration, even in recent times, is studded with examples. The major find of the North Snyder Reef Field in Scurry County, West Texas, in 1948 set geologists and geophysicists searching out reef structures for new exploration. Oil had been found quite close to this new field twenty-five years before, but reef structures had not previously been considered favorable oil prospects. Similarly, thirty-three years elapsed between the first discovery at Turner Valley, Canada, in 1914 and the find at Leduc, about 190 miles away, that set off a whole string of important discoveries. Many other examples are given by the National Petroleum Council in its report, *Petroleum Productive Capacity* (January 29, 1952), pp. 8 ff.

18. This is the area of sedimentary formations—some 80 per cent of U.S. territory—as reported by the American Geological Society, *World Geography*

as new technology and new experience, revealed in new oil finds, sends geophysical crews and drilling rigs back over the same territory.[19]

The physical results of discovery do not necessarily justify the pessimistic foreboding that has colored United States supply estimates from time to time. Exact figures are not very meaningful here because of natural variations in results from year to year and from one group of years to the next, and because of the re-evaluation of proved reserves as new wells and new information come to hand; but it is pretty clear that crude oil reserves have increased over the decades in proportion to production and that the development of new oil per well has remained roughly constant.[20] On the other hand there has been a clear decline since World War II in the discoveries of new oil per exploratory *foot* drilled.[21] If one relates new oil developed to total wells completed, the ratio shows some decline in new oil developed in each of the past three decades, but the trend practically disappears if new oil is compared with *oil* wells completed.[22] It is true that the

---

of Petroleum, Special Publication No. 31 (1950), p. 21. See National Petroleum Council (above, n. 17), pp. 45, 54 ff., and Exhibit A, pp. 85 ff.

19. More recently, Richard J. Gonzalez has observed that even North Texas, with more than four wells drilled per square mile—one of the most intensively drilled areas in the world—is still the scene of active drilling and increasing production as new finds in old and new provinces provide more information for a more effective search for oil. See "U.S. Not Running Out of Oil," *World Oil* (March, 1957), pp. 65–66.

20. The National Petroleum Council found that with some 700,000 wells we had found about 13 billion barrels of oil in the sixty-three years through 1922; and with roughly the same number (some 696,000 wells), we had uncovered an added aggregate of at least 56 billion barrels, more than four times as much, from 1925 through 1951 (*Petroleum Productive Capacity,* p. 51). Gonzalez notes that the ratio of new oil (gross discoveries, extensions, and revisions) to production averaged 1.52 over the first sixty-six years and 1.96, 1.50, and 1.49 in each of the decades after 1925 ("U.S. Not Running Out of Oil," pp. 64–65). Cf. above, p. 153, nn. 54, 55.

21. In 1947–50 an average of 12.1 to 25.6 barrels of oil were discovered per exploratory foot drilled—the average of the four annual figures was 17.2 barrels. In 1953–56 the range was between 9.8 barrels in the first two years and 6.3 in the last, for an average of 8.2 barrels. The trend over these years was clearly down. Computations from *Petroleum Facts and Figures,* API annual estimates of crude oil reserves, and the June issues of the *Bulletin of the American Association of Petroleum Geologists.*

22. The figures given by Gonzalez in thousands of barrels are 79, 74, and 71 respectively for the former, and 137, 124, and 133 respectively for the latter, comparison. Indeed, cumulative oil wells completed are shown to have a linear relation to cumulative new crude oil over the period from 1936 through 1955 ("U.S. Not Running Out of Oil," p. 65). The reason for the discrepancy be-

ratio of dry holes to total wells drilled (excluding service wells) has risen substantially since the war, but this reflects the changing pattern of wells drilled. Neither exploratory wells as a whole nor new field wildcats, the riskiest class of wells, show any definite trend for the worse since the war.[23] Indeed, the number of feet drilled in dry holes for each foot in producers has actually fallen since 1943, although there is no clear trend in the figures.[24]

What apparent weakness may be found in recent records per well or in regional deficiencies like those in California may be more than countered in the future by the performance of off-shore exploration in the Gulf. Despite the hazards and the high costs of underwater drilling, it was estimated that by the end of 1956 more than $1,500,-000,000 had been spent on finding and developing reserves in the Gulf and some 1.3 billion barrels of crude oil and natural gas liquids and 10 trillion cubic feet of natural gas had been discovered on tested acreage.[25] More remarkable than the magnitude of discoveries has been the comparative record. To September, 1956, 41 per cent of off-shore wildcats, with 45 per cent of wildcat footage, made success-

---

tween the two showings is that an increasing proportion of all wells drilled have been dry holes. A computation of the ratios between oil, gas, and natural gas liquids added and total wells drilled likewise shows a decline for the period 1940–56, though not so great a decline, of course, as findings per foot drilled. John C. Casper, "A Long Look Ahead," *Oil and Gas Journal* (July 29, 1957), p. 149.

23. In striking contrast with the prewar, the ratio of dry holes to total wells has been below 30 per cent in only one year, 1945 (when it was 29.82 per cent), and it has ranged from more than 35 to almost 39.9 per cent since 1949. This result is accounted for by the rising proportion of exploratory wells in total wells drilled (from around 20 per cent before 1948 to over 25 per cent after 1950) and by the heavy weight of new field wildcats among exploratory wells. While all exploratory wells averaged 4.02 dry holes per producer (19.90 per cent successful) during the 6 years of 1944–49, and 4.06 dry holes per producer (19.79 per cent successful) in the following six years, new field wildcats averaged 7.85 and 7.83 dry holes, for success percentages of 11.29 and 11.34 in each of the two periods respectively. New field wildcats were 11.9 per cent of all wells (excluding service) in the earlier period and 14.2 per cent in the later. *Petroleum Facts and Figures,* 12th ed., pp. 118 ff.; 9th ed., pp. 126 f., 130. On the decline in success ratios since 1954, see above, Chap. 7, n. 55, and statistics in *World Oil* (February 15, 1958), pp. 119–121. All wildcat wells averaged 9 per cent of total wells drilled in 1937–40 and almost 22 per cent in 1951–57. *Ibid.,* p. 120.

24. See *ibid.,* 12th ed., p. 119; 9th ed., p. 127.

25. Coqueron, *Annual Financial Analysis, 1956,* p. 26. Ultimately recoverable reserves offshore are estimated around 16 billion barrels of crude oil, including 3 billion off California.

ful strikes: the comparable success ratios for the country as a whole are 11 per cent and 14 per cent, respectively. For every offshore well drilled there has been added to reserves nine times as many hydro-carbons as from the average United States well over the same period. Thus, despite the fact that the average off-shore well has cost eight or nine times as much as the average onshore well, these prospects add up to "lower than average-priced reserves, granting a reasonably fast pay-out." [26] It is probable that once the legal obstacles have been cleared away, new records of discovery are likely in the Gulf and, over a longer future because exploration has been more closely teth-ered, off the California shore as well.

It is beyond the scope of this study even to present, let alone choose from, the wide range of estimates for the ultimate reserves of the United States.[27] For reasons already noted, even the approxi-mate figure is essentially unknowable, depending as it does not only on the physical presence of oil but also on policy and economic varia-bles which cannot be predetermined. Important among the latter is the expected recovery factor which governs final production from both existing and new reservoirs. Proved reserves are estimated on the basis of recovery factors technically and commercially likely under conditions at the time the estimates are made. At the end of 1956, this factor was set at 32.7 per cent.[28] Manifestly, there is enormous

26. Ira H. Cram, "The Outlook Offshore," p. 8. All comparative data taken from this address. The Chase Manhattan Bank estimates just referred to per-mit a very rough indication of the comparative finding costs offshore and on-shore. Those figures were an aggregate expenditure of $1.5 billion, yielding proved reserves of 1.3 billion barrels of liquids and 10 trillion cubic feet of gas. Valuing the gas underground at 5 cents per Mcf—which is apparently the general, though conservative practice of banks in making loans to producers—this estimate produces a finding cost, which includes to some unknown extent costs of equipping for lifting as well, of about 77 cents per barrel of liquids discovered. In the case of onshore oil, Gonzalez estimates ". . . the current price of developed oil reserves . . . [at] . . . about $1.25 a barrel. . . . De-ducting $0.40 or $0.50 at most for drilling and equipment costs per barrel of reserves [some part of which is undoubtedly reflected in the 77 cents average for Gulf reserves], the indicated value of oil in the ground . . . is about $0.75–$0.85 a barrel" ("U.S. Not Running Out of Oil," pp. 68–69). Offshore costs are clearly comparable.

27. The entire range of these estimates is analyzed in detail in Netschert, *The Future Supply of Oil and Gas*. We have drawn on this source for some general comments as well as on Gonzalez ("U.S. Not Running Out of Oil"), who discusses the subject more briefly.

28. This is the estimate of the Interstate Oil Compact Commission Commit-tee on Secondary Recovery and Pressure Maintenance. It is used by Netschert,

scope for expanded output in estimated future recovery factors—
which can only go up with a continuation of the already impressive
technical progress in recovery, and with any tendency for oil prices
to rise.[29] Whatever the ultimate magnitude of oil in place [30] it is self-
evident that a major role in future production potentials will be played
by improvements, even by small improvements, in the percentage of
the oil in place that is recovered.

We are not technically qualified to combine the foregoing complex
and often conflicting considerations into some conclusive judgment
about the future course of domestic petroleum supply and the costs
thereof. It suffices to put the question in the following way: what if
the various trends of the period since World War II in oil discovery
and costs persist? Would they justify a conclusion that the role of the
integrated major in exploration and development might be expected
to become more important in the future than it has been in the recent
past?

Although the costs of finding and developing crude reserves per
barrel of crude *produced* has risen sharply since 1944 or 1946, the
rise was not, at least until 1953 or 1954, any greater than the increase
in the average wellhead price.[31] There has been a tendency for the

p. 16, who cites P. D. Torrey, "Evaluation of U. S. Oil Resources as of January
1, 1956," *Producers' Monthly* (June, 1956), pp. 26, 28.

29. Thus Gonzalez would correct some of the estimates that have been
made of our prospective aggregate cumulative oil production for the modest
recovery factors he implies they contain: "Estimates that ultimate production
will be 200–300 billion barrels of oil really indicate discovery of reservoirs
with 500–700 billion barrels of oil in place" ("U.S. Not Running Out of Oil,"
p. 66). See also below, pp. 233 ff.

30. Gonzalez quotes as possibly modest a recent estimate of the Department of Interior of 300 billion barrels as the ultimate reserves of the U.S. and
its adjoining Continental Shelves. This reserve assumes an improved but un-
stated recovery rate. Netschert finds a "resource base" for future oil production in this country from adjusted expert opinion of the magnitude of 500
billion barrels.

31. The increase in aggregate industry expenditures on exploration, development, and production, from $1.47 in 1944 to $3.16 in 1953 per barrel of crude
oil produced (see above, p. 175), was actually slightly less in percentage terms
than the increase in the average wellhead price, from $1.21 to $2.68 in the
same period. The expenditures on exploration and development alone went
from $1.04 to $2.14, a percentage rise markedly less than that of price. Aggregate income of operators from petroleum production, according to the same
survey, rose from $1.39 to $3.17 per barrel of net crude oil production. *Petroleum Facts and Figures,* 12th ed., pp. 103, 135; 9th ed., p. 121. On the other
hand, the estimated finding and development costs per barrel of production
rose somewhat faster than price in the 1946–54 interval: the former from

real costs of finding a barrel of oil to rise since the war; but the corresponding rise in the price of oil has been such as to keep the estimated drilling cost of finding a dollar's worth of oil still not markedly out of line with prewar costs, and only modestly above the level of the immediate postwar years.[32] Moreover, incentives to drill must be related not to oil alone but to the value of all hydrocarbons uncovered; in this connection the price of natural gas, rising more rapidly than that of oil, has given that formerly almost unwanted by-product an increasing relative importance.[33] And finally, tax allowances, which became more persuasive as revenues and taxes rose and postwar inflation set in, added to the exuberance of drilling during the postwar years.

There is little apparent reason, in the foregoing record, for any conclusion that the integrated companies may be expected to play a much more important role in financing domestic exploration in the foreseeable future. This judgment is necessarily highly tentative. But

---

$0.85 to $1.75 (see above, p. 176, n. 15), the latter from $1.41 to $2.77. The absolute height of these various measures of unit investment costs cannot intelligently be compared with the price for the reasons set forth above, n. 16.

32. The estimated aggregate industry drilling expenditure divided by the gross additions to supply of crude oil (valued at wellhead price) give a drilling cost of $0.38 for a dollar's worth of new crude oil in 1955 and 1956. The corresponding costs were $0.46, $0.33, $0.18, $0.20, $0.26, and $0.37 in the years 1935–40 inclusive, an average of $0.30. The 1955 and 1956 figures represent a postwar peak: the corresponding estimates were $0.33 and $0.32 in 1945–46, dropped (with the sharp increases in oil price) to a postwar low of $0.15 in 1948, then began a steady increase. From estimates explained and set forth in detail in the testimony of Kahn, *In the Matter of Phillips Petroleum Company,* Federal Power Commission Docket G 1148, Exhibit 390, Schedules 13 and 14.

33. It is possible to adjust the above drilling cost figures for the discoveries of gas only in the postwar period. The adjusted figures show the drilling cost of finding a dollar's worth of oil and gas combined at $0.28 and $0.27 in 1955 and 1956, compared with $0.22 in 1946 and 1947 (and a low of $0.14 in 1948). *Ibid.,* Schedules 15 and 16.

When the industry's exploration expenditures of 1944, 1948, and 1953 (see above, n. 14) are divided not by production but by new discoveries of oil (valued at average wellhead prices), it appears the cost of finding a dollar's worth of new oil amounted to $1.04, $1.08, and $1.23 in the three years respectively. When one adds in the value of gas discoveries (valued at average prices on new contracts; see testimony of John Boatwright, U. S. House of Representatives, Committee on Interstate and Foreign Commerce, *Natural Gas Act,* 1957, 85th Congress, 1st Session, p. 1176), which are available for the latter years only, the exploration cost of finding a dollar's worth of new gas and oil declines from $0.91 in 1948 to $0.86 in 1953.

it appears that prorationing and the tax structure have greatly diminished financial risks. Capital is readily available for purposes formerly assured only to the large integrated firm. Even without special inducements, a 4.6 billion dollar net book investment in United States refineries with a capacity of almost nine million barrels crude throughput per day [34] is a pretty adequate assurance to nonintegrated investors that markets will support whatever it costs to supply their needs. The risks of unproductive acreage, of the dry hole, and of displacement by lower cost supplies remain and the dollar tag rises as competition for favorable sites pushes options to premiums and deeper horizons force greater outlays. But if these risks and increasing costs per drilling venture are to be shouldered, they require size to muster the necessary capital, and multiple undertakings to spread the risk— not necessarily vertical integration. Where risk is high and capital needs are great, the cooperative undertaking, as the majors have already demonstrated, is a way of limiting possible losses without sacrificing opportunities. Despite rising capital costs of new exploration and development, current trends would not seem to preclude effective performance by independents, acting alone or in cooperative undertakings.

THE LARGE INTEGRATED FIRM AND THE FUNCTIONING OF CRUDE OIL MARKETS

There are several factors that tend to insulate the price of crude oil from the impact of changing market conditions, and some of them are only indirectly influenced by the policies of the large integrated firm. Above all others is the influence of prorationing, which provides the administrative adaptation of supply that is the primary explanation of price stability. Next to prorationing, the most important such influence is the vast network of pipelines, that creates something like a single crude-oil market in this country east of the Rockies [35] out of the widely dispersed sources of oil production, excepting the sweet

34. Coqueron, *Annual Financial Analysis, 1957,* pp. 28, 30.
35. Historically, the Pacific Coast states have been insulated from the rest of the country. Prices, structured on Los Angeles, the major market of the sole producing state, have often moved independently of prices elsewhere. This isolation is deteriorating as California output declines relative to West Coast demand and crude is imported from the Middle East, from Canada via the Transmountain Pipeline to British Columbia and thence to new refineries in the Puget Sound area, even to California itself, and in the near future, via pipeline from the Four Corners of Arizona, Colorado, New Mexico, and Utah.

(nonsulphuric) paraffin-based Pennsylvania crudes, which are channeled mainly into lubricants. Since its variable costs are almost negligible and its earnings are limited by decree,[36] tariffs are only roughly related to distance. Resultant posted prices are more uniform and more stable than would be probable with alternative transport media. And lacking the feasibility of small discrete shipments (in contrast to the tank car, for example), the pipeline narrows the range of price differentiation among particular kinds, qualities, and quantities of oil that would otherwise have developed in response to comparative values in use depending on refiners' equipment and product patterns. For the modern refinery, fine distinctions among crude qualities are less important, and its greater ability to vary the proportions of particular products refined from a barrel of input contributes to general price stability in the face of a shifting product demand. The effect of these influences on pricing has little to do with the practices of the majors. However, the fact that pipelines typically are owned by the majors, who also possess the larger and more modern refining equipment, further dulls the sensitivity of price to market forces.

Two other factors that limit the sensitivity and meaningfulness of crude oil prices are more clearly a consequence of the size, integration and policies of the leading oil companies. The influence of the first of these, the way in which prices are posted, has already been indicated in Chapter 7. The ownership of pipelines by the majors fortifies their practice of crude oil price posting in the field; and the interests of these companies, combining within themselves the roles of buyer and seller, dealing with hundreds of independent producers over wide areas as competitor and customer,[37] is to avoid flexible use of price as an instrument of policy.

36. See below, pp. 334–340.

37. This influence of the majors, even on a volume basis, much exceeds the output from their own wells: through buying departments or separately incorporated companies they service many independents as well. Thus, of the total crude purchases of Stanolind Oil Purchasing Company, Standard of Indiana (by which it is wholly owned) takes only around 60 per cent. The company serves some thirty-seven accounts, for which it acts as sole or major supplier. The company must know the crude requirements of each of its principals in detail over a considerable period in order to perform this function properly. Similarly, Humble Oil and Refining produced some 350,000 b/d in 1952, but it purchased an average of 427,500 b/d and sold 521,600 b/d including about 100,000 b/d of its own production. Its own crude oil runs in 1952 averaged 251,600 b/d. In addition to its parent, Standard (New Jersey), it sold to some twenty-five nonaffiliated companies, including a number of small refineries. H. H. Baker, *Wolverton Hearings*, p. 272.

The second factor is the practice of intercompany exchanges of crude oils or products in different locations or of different types. Exchanges, like integration itself, remove transactions from the public view and subject them instead to administrative direction and informal negotiation not registered in open markets. Agreements may be made for a single exchange, but it is not unusual for a particular arrangement to continue indefinitely subject to cancellation after thirty to ninety days' notice. Only one principle governs such arrangements: advantages must be mutual. The actual volume is difficult to estimate, since the distinction between exchanges and purchases and sales is extremely fuzzy; but one important company has estimated that it obtains at least 40 per cent of its aggregate crude oil supply (production plus purchases) through trading.

This resort to barter may accomplish various objectives. Primarily it avoids or minimizes transportation and related costs: a refiner's crude, remotely located for his own use, is traded for equivalent oil more accessible. Concurrently, it may permit the acquisition of crudes better adapted to a refiner's equipment: a modern catalytic cracker may procure a greater volume of low-gravity oil near at hand in exchange for a smaller quantity of high-gravity oil which is not essential to its own satisfactory performance; or a refiner with corrosion-resistant equipment may secure a similar volume advantage by trading sweet for sour (sulphuric) crude. And sometimes crude that could not be "batched" through a pipeline may be brought into use without loss of quality or value through equivalent trades. These and similar gains can be realized through trading with advantage both for producers and refiners.

The administration of this complex network of separately negotiated agreements does not save the costs of selling from one level to another: the crude oil buying and selling organizations of the companies involved still have to canvass the field and seek out profitable trades, just as they would in open markets. At times, indeed, the reliance on barter must increase the costs of exchange: sometimes one, or both, of the parties to a given agreement may have to make a series of supplementary exchanges—including resort to purchase or sale— before he obtains the actual quality of crude he seeks at the location at which he can use it.

What the exchange does, in contrast with open-market buying and selling, is to limit access to the benefits of the market to those with two qualifications instead of the usual one—a need for oil of a certain kind in a particular place *and* possession of a particular oil that the opposite party will accept. The majors must be able to meet this double requirement more frequently than small nonintegrated firms. Although examples may be found where exchanges have benefited an independent by apparently creating a demand for his oil (or a supply of grades of oil for which he had a special need), his alternatives must be generally narrower and more elusive than would be the case in a market conducted exclusively on a monetary basis.

It is true that trading tends to sharpen the differentiation of qualities, types, and locational values of particular crudes that the technical requirements of pipeline transport have helped to blur. But the same results could be achieved through purchase and sale without the side effects of removing offers and bids from the open market and constricting the competitive opportunities of smaller, less integrated companies. Whether in fact open market purchase and sale would be equally compatible with efficient scheduling of flows of oil and products is a question that applies to integration itself and is deferred to Chapter 11. Irrespective of this issue, the substitution of the comparative seclusion of informal trading negotiations for monetary transactions in open markets multiplies the prospect of concessions and discriminations and of real price variations without disturbing the posted price. Exchanges maximize the advantages which size and integration accord to the majors and minimize potential competitive influences on the structure of prices. Thus they must help to preserve the rigidity and decrease the significance of the posted price.

THE IMPACT OF INTEGRATION ON THE PRICE OF CRUDE

It has been noted that prorationing strengthens administered pricing of crude oil by elasticizing crude oil supply: "surplus" is kept in the ground when demand falls short of what unregulated producers would be willing to offer at the posted price. This support is not absolute. Production control reflects considerations other than price and the decision to restrict output does not rest with the firms that commonly post crude prices.[38] The majors may, and do, influence these decisions. They make recommendations to state regulatory agencies framing production orders, and their buying plans (nominations)

---

38. Quite the contrary, within the range of output established by production allowables, the major is under the same compulsions as the small, nonintegrated producer to maximize his withdrawals from the common reservoir, except where entire pools are unitized.

support these proposals. But administration of crude oil prices cannot exceed the margin of discretion that the market, as regulated, affords. This discretion of the price leader depends, also, on the willingness of potential competitors to follow. This is a common limitation on all price leadership; it is less significant in oil because of the critical role of public authority in circumscribing competitive mavericks.

The interplay of crude-oil price-making influences can best be studied in actual situations, four of which are analyzed in the following pages.

THE ESSO STANDARD CASE [39]

The fuel oil shortage that developed in the winter of 1947–48 was not unforeseen, although its intensity was augmented by severe cold. Standard Oil (New Jersey) had accelerated efforts to enlarge its supplies a year earlier; and Esso Standard, its wholly owned subsidiary and a leading marketer of petroleum products along the Atlantic and Gulf seaboards, warned its customers, as the boom following release of price controls made an oil shortage imminent, that they could expect no increase in heating oil supplies during the coming season. Two months later (June, 1947) it discontinued the sale of conversion oil burners and new installations. While there was some concern for the good will of the expanding home-heating market for fuel oil, the more basic reason for the company's announcement on July 24, 1947, that it would hold all petroleum prices seems to have been its conviction that a price rise would uselessly feed price inflation. Demand for petroleum products would not be importantly contracted by a rise in price and new crude oil production would not be significantly increased, because drilling was limited by the amount of steel available. Company profits were already unusually high; President Truman had appealed to large firms to help combat inflation by holding down their prices; and the company believed that a failure of the industry to make such an effort would undermine good public relations and hasten government intervention.

Despite the statesmanlike overtones of Esso's policy pronouncement and the favorable publicity earned, it is difficult to determine how seriously the company regarded its role of price leader in this episode. The crux of the shortage was in heating oil, apparently recog-

39. H. L. Hansen and Powell Niland describe this episode in detail in "Esso Standard: A Case Study in Pricing," *Harvard Business Review, 30* (1952), 114–132.

nized as early as April; but nothing was done to induce a larger output of such distillates from the limited crude supplies available.[40] Furthermore, when Esso withdrew its Gulf Port quotations because it had no product to sell on the open market, the effect was to shift the onus of holding the price line from independent refiners selling at the Gulf Port low (theretofore fixed by Esso itself) to competitive jobbers and dealers in Esso territory—far less able and less inclined to do so.[41] It is not suggested here that alternative policies would have been more successful in holding the price line. But if the announced purpose was recognized as hopeless under existing and anticipated circumstances and if the methods used did not support it in any case, the significance of the episode either as price leadership or as industrial statesmanship is moot.

The price of crude broke upward on October 15 when Phillips [42] announced an advance of 20 cents per barrel. Sun Oil followed on November 28 with a further posted price rise of 50 cents [43] which

40. The percentage of gasoline yield from crude was actually increased from May to July, 1947, over corresponding months in 1946 from 39.2 per cent to 40.2 per cent, thus narrowing potential output of distillates. A relative rise in the price of heating oils might have induced a larger output.

41. Purchase contracts for oil and products at Gulf Ports are generally governed by the low quotation in Platt's *Oilgram*. Esso quotations were the lowest on the market and, even though deliveries were made by Esso only to established customers in limited volume, these quotations would govern other contract sales and thus create a squeeze on the refiner unless he in turn could buy his crude oil at pre-established prices. These lower contract sales prices would have enabled the Atlantic Coast distributor to buy his products at prices equivalent to those given by Esso to its own customers. By withdrawing the low price quotation, Esso permitted higher contract prices for fuel oil to go into effect, and independent refiners were under no compulsion to try to hold down the price.

Independent distributors were not literally squeezed by this manuever because Esso could not possibly supply the demand for heating oil at its established price. They were fearful, however, that some of their best accounts might be captured by Esso marketing affiliates and they, and many Esso dealers as well, were disgruntled by invidious price comparisons and resentful of their inability to buy (or to buy more) Esso products at the official prices. Charges of rank discriminatory tactics were loud and shrill before the Wherry Committee of the U. S. Senate, but evidence of actual losses did not materialize.

42. In 1947 Phillips' net production of crude was 103 per cent of its refinery runs. In 1948 this self-sufficiency ratio had fallen to 78 per cent, still sufficiently important (see below, pp. 222–225) to make the higher price profitable, even if it were not reflected in higher quotations on products.

43. Sun Oil justified its action as having been dictated by a loss of connections—some 7,000 barrels per day to buyers who paid premiums and

was met within a week by more than 20 large buyers, including three Jersey affiliates. On December 8 Esso capitulated and met the new crude price.[44]

The Jersey management view that a price rise would not increase crude supply significantly seems to have been corroborated in 1947: the price rose 56 per cent and output expanded only 12 per cent.[45] Since Texas production was at MER, an increase in production in that state certainly could not have been expected immediately. On the other hand, supplies from other states and from the rest of the world might have been more price-elastic than Standard reckoned.[46] At least a higher price for heating oils might have induced the earlier shift in refinery yields that the shortage required. M. J. Rathbone, then president of Esso, estimated that Jersey incurred increased out-of-pocket costs of some $88 million in purchasing crude for its domestic affiliated companies during the second half of 1947. This figure may exaggerate the net cost of the firm's hold-the-line effort,[47] but it suggests the futility of one company, however large, trying to hold down the price of crude oil when supplies are really short. Rising product prices offer irresistible inducements to refiners to pull in their own

another 26,000 barrels per day to parent or owner companies who withdrew the connections for their own use. *Oil and Gas Journal* (December 6, 1947), p. 53, cited by Hansen and Niland (above, n. 39), p. 120.

44. On December 22, after several other important companies had announced product increases, Esso raised its product prices by selective amounts calculated to stimulate a larger output of distillates and fuel oil, the demand for which was then at its height.

45. See Committee on Interstate and Foreign Commerce, "Fuel Investigation," House *Report* 2342, 80th Congress, 2d Session (1948), p. 8.

46. Because of the time factor, the possible effect of an earlier price adjustment is only suggested, not proved, by the substantial rise that did occur in 1948 both in production and in imports. Domestic crude oil production in 1947 exceeded that in 1946 by 123 million barrels and in 1948 it rose another 163 million barrels, increases of 7 and 9 per cent, respectively. Imports also rose in the two years: 11.5 million and 31.6 million barrels, or 11 and 32 per cent, respectively, much to the disgruntlement of independent producers and refiners. Data from *Petroleum Facts and Figures,* 9th ed., p. 6.

47. The explanation of the losses offered was the fact that Jersey purchased 59.2 per cent of its crude from royalty owners and nonaffiliated or minority interest companies. This explanation does not necessarily conflict with the fact that in 1947 the Jersey company's ratio of net domestic production to refinery runs was 56.6 per cent; the company's affiliates both buy and sell crude oil, and they may have continued to sell below the prices at which they were forced to buy, and to sell products at prices that did not reflect the higher price of purchased crude. However, the 59.2 per cent exaggerates Jersey interests as a net buyer because it ignores the company's position as a worldwide producer.

oil if they own any and to pay premiums and steal connections if they don't.

THE ABORTIVE PRICE ADVANCE, 1948

Phillips Petroleum's unsuccessful attempt to advance crude oil prices in 1948 reaffirms the inability of a major company to effect a price policy at variance with the general assessment of the market situation by industry leaders. In essaying the higher posted price, Phillips was said to have been impressed with the higher costs of finding and developing new reserves, although data presented earlier in this chapter indicate that the price increases of 1947 were adequate to cover average cost increments. Phillips produced 78 per cent of its own refinery runs in 1948, and apparently had no difficulty in purchasing the additional supplies it required. Nonetheless, it posted an advance in crude oil prices of 35 cents per barrel in September of that year. A few companies met this price, but the more important did not and several managements took occasion to comment adversely on it.

While the need to check the inflationary spiral was still prominent in public policy announcements, the basic facts that scuttled the price advance were the substantial increases in production and discoveries in 1948 and the unusually mild winter of 1948–49. After the harsh shortages of the preceding year, heating oil stocks had been conscientiously accumulated during the spring and summer. Coupled with increased production, other majors like Standard of Indiana and Humble Oil were convinced that the requirements of a normal heating season could be met without a further price rise. In fact, by December a slacking off of industrial demands accompanying a quick onslaught of business contraction combined with a very mild winter to turn conservative into burdensome inventories. There was no fear of losing connections and it soon became self-evident that the market would not stand a crude price increase. The higher posted prices were therefore withdrawn.[48]

THE RISE IN CRUDE PRICES, 1953

The price increase in 1953 demonstrates the feasibility of a purely policy advance in oil prices when there is consensus among the lead-

48. Prices of some special types of crude were actually lowered; e.g. Humble Oil posted a 25-cent per-barrel reduction in heavy crude prices because of the decline in the demand and price of residual fuel oil.

ers and the Texas Railroad Commission is sympathetic even though supplies are adequate or more than adequate. In a sense, this episode provides the converse of the moral of the 1948 performance: the leading performer (Phillips) is the same; the leading argument—that higher costs call for a higher crude price—is also the same; and the principle in both cases is identical: the supporting cast must be willing to support and not contradict the star.

The postwar adjustment of crude-oil price levels had been completed to all intents and purposes by the 1947 advance to $2.60 per barrel. Added pressure was put on the new price level by industrial recovery in 1950 and by the invasion of Korea, but except for a few advances in California prices held firm until officially frozen by the Director of Price Stabilization from January 1951 until February 13, 1953. Immediately thereafter California crudes registered a slight advance but price enterprise in the east was impeded by a warm winter and by heavy stocks.[49]

The real break occurred on June 15 when Phillips Petroleum posted a general advance of 25 cents per barrel of crude and, on the same day, Humble ordered an equivalent average rise but on a more selective basis.[50] The Humble pattern was quickly followed, and on June 23 the company posted selective advances in product prices at the refinery, at the tank-wagon, and at its 307 company-operated service stations.[51]

Although demand was strong, there was no imminent shortage of either crude or major products. Stocks of both had risen with the growth in demand. They were larger in 1952 than they had been in 1951 and they were still higher at the beginning and throughout the first six months of 1953. Production had been increased to meet larger sales, but partly by reason of continued heavy imports, productive capacity exceeded domestic output and Texas allowables were substantially less than MER's. The decision to raise the price of crude, therefore, may be regarded as strictly a policy decision for the long run.

The basic justification of the price increase offered before the Wolverton Committee was the uncompensated rise in the cost of ex-

49. Socony-Vacuum essayed an advance in gasoline prices but retreated when competitors failed to follow.
50. Humble increases were 10, 22, 25, 30, and 35 cents per barrel for various grades and fields.
51. Industry representatives were immediately called to account before Congress. See *Wolverton Hearings*.

ploration and development since the last general price advance in 1947. Company earnings had declined markedly from their postwar peaks in the boom year 1948, but were still very satisfactory compared with industry at large.[52]

Whatever the long-run merits of the price rise, the interesting feature of the episode is that the year 1953 established new records in domestic output and new highs in proved reserves and that the new level of prices was brought about while supply was outrunning demand, as it had done in the two preceding years. Although product storage began to bulge in the spring of 1954 and Gulf refiners lost gross margin as finished product prices weakened (from March to June gross margins narrowed from around one dollar per barrel to 60 cents, one of the lowest points over the last twenty years), no major break took place in crude prices. Important companies like Humble and Esso Standard cut back on their refinery nominations; and state authorities, notably the Texas Railroad Commission, reduced production allowables to an estimated aggregate of some 1.5 million b/d below MER.[53] With a rising demand for petroleum products in the latter part of the year, stocks of crude and products were substantially lowered, and prices firmed in the presence of a continuing level of

52. The temptation to select data to prove a point was apparently too strong for Humble's statisticians. Below, the ratio of net earnings to average invested capital (book value of outstanding preferred and common stocks and consolidated surplus accounts) is shown for individual years for the total industry (121 to 139 firms during the years shown) and for producing companies (sixty to seventy-seven firms from the industry group). Data were provided through the courtesy of the economics department of a major oil company. The industry figures check quite closely with the ratio of net income after tax to net worth as reported for the same period by the National City Bank of New York.

Ratio: Earnings after Taxes to Average Invested Capital
Percentages

YEAR	TOTAL INDUSTRY	TOTAL PRODUCERS	YEAR	TOTAL INDUSTRY	TOTAL PRODUCERS
5-year average			1951	16.0	19.3
1943–47	10.8	16.1	1952	14.0	16.9
1948	20.5	33.0	1953	14.1	16.8
1949	13.3	21.9	5-year average		
1950	14.8	19.2	1948–52	15.5	21.2

It is apparent that 1948 was an exceptionally profitable year for both groups.

53. See articles by J. H. Carmical in the New York *Times,* June 27, July 18, 25, 1954. For more appropriately weighted gross margin data, see below, p. 415, n. 67.

production allowables, much below MER, trimmed back enough to nourish a concern for connections.

At this point only the process is a matter of concern. It is clear that the increased price of crude was neither forced by real shortage nor explicitly justified before public authority by actual or anticipated costs. Whatever the true force that initiated the higher posting—some oil men stress the growing inadequacy of internal cash flow to preserve established exploratory programs rather than the more usual emphasis on rising costs—it was initiated by a private policy determination and maintained by a combination of private and public actions related only indirectly to cost considerations. This precarious balance of public and private interests was about to be strained by still another aspect of private determination—the level of imports.

THE RISE IN CRUDE PRICES, 1957

After 1953, domestic crude oil prices remained generally unchanged despite rising prices of raw materials and rising hourly earnings of employees. The industry found itself in the invidious position of sitting on substantial unused reserves while imports of crude and products mounted; and through most of 1956, independents complained vociferously of discrimination and low prices while stocks of both crude oil and gasoline increased to quantities that threatened the firmness of even the existing price levels.

From this viewpoint the closure of the Suez Canal and the crippling of the Iraq pipeline in Syria in the fall of the year was an unexpected boon. It permitted deferral of the long hard look that government was expected to give to the problem of imports; it created an emergency need for Western Hemisphere oil to keep Western European refineries in action and homes and industries supplied with fuel oil; and eventually it provided the occasion for Humble Oil, Jersey Standard's affiliate, on January 3 to advance its buying prices for Texas crudes. Price increases varied by location: from 25 cents per barrel for West Texas sour crudes and 35 cents for East Texas to 45 cents for the Gulf Coast—roughly a 10–15 per cent rise.

Although some domestic product prices (especially distillates and residual fuel) had started to move up earlier, Humble immediately raised prices of its products to conform with the crude oil change. Other firms followed quickly, and it was not long before Creole (Jersey Standard) and Shell had posed Caribbean prices (already jolted upward even before Humble's action by European demands for residual fuel) to conform to the new level of Gulf quotations.

At this point analysis of the foreign situation that triggered this price increase as well as foreign pricing problems will be deferred because the issue here is the impact of the large integrated firm on domestic prices, and it is quite clear that this price advance was not so much caused as occasioned by the European emergency.[54]

The attempt of the Committee on Interstate and Foreign Commerce to plumb the reasons for the price advance elicited two familiar explanations. Basic was the rise in the costs of finding and producing crude oil. Since 1953 these costs were said to have reached a level compared to prices which was inadequate to support desired future exploration. Second, it was claimed that Humble was forced to post a higher price when it was unable to fill its existing orders at established prices. In brief, the justifications were that (a) the price boosts were forced upon Humble and (b) were in any event justified on grounds of cost.[55]

The rise in costs of exploration and development since the end of World War II have already been noted. Whether or not these trends actually justified a rise in prices, the circumstances of the advance forcefully illustrate the role of policy considerations rather than simple market forces in effectuating it. Throughout 1956, stocks of crude oil and gasoline were higher month by month than they had been during the preceding year, so high that they gave rise to widespread industry complaint because of their threat to hoped-for price increases. After October, when crude stocks peaked at almost 286.6 million barrels, foreign demand brought a gratifying reduction of over 20 million barrels by the end of the year. Comparatively, Texas did even better. During the four months (April through July) Texas had actually succeeded in cutting its crude oil stocks below those of comparable months in 1955. Thereafter, they broke above the earlier year, until in October, at more than 127 million barrels, they were almost 5 million above October, 1955. But the Texas Commission held a firm hand on production as demand mounted, and by the end

54. Mr. Rathbone, president of Jersey Standard, summarized the impact of the European crisis as affecting the timing but not the substance of the price increase. See *Petroleum Survey* (above, p. 160, n. 64), p. 39.

55. Apparently, Director Hugh Stewart of the Office of Oil and Gas, Department of the Interior, and General Ernest O. Thompson, of the Texas Railroad Commission, were agreed that the crude oil price rise was "overdue" while Mr. Walter J. Hallanan, president of Plymouth Oil Company, believed that the increase was inadequate by some 50 cents per barrel. *Ibid.*, pp. 35–36, 38, 41.

of the year it had reduced Texas stocks by almost 10.7 million barrels, to a level more than 8 million barrels below that of a year earlier.[56]

The orientation of the Texas Railroad Commission's policies is probably nowhere better shown than by its refusal to permit January production allowables to rise above those for December, despite the improvement in the state's crude oil stock position and despite an estimate of the Bureau of Mines that January demand for Texas crudes would rise 228,942 barrels.[57] The decision may have been influenced by a report from Interior Secretary Seaton, based on a special study of the nation's petroleum potential in connection with plans for emergency shipments from the Gulf to Western Europe, that we could step up production by 2.1 million barrels a day, if needed, but that we could move only about half the added output from the oil fields.[58] Humble Oil claimed firm tanker nominations for specific January loading dates for a total of more than 5.5 million barrels of crude for Europe; but it stated that it could supply only 600,000 barrels from its own sources and could arrange for an export of only 1,038,000 barrels.[59] At the allowable hearing on December 19, Humble is said to have made an open offer to buy all crude that could be delivered to seaboard up to 170,000 b/d in addition to the output of its regular Texas suppliers on the eighteen-day production schedule (as compared with the existing sixteen-day schedule) which it and other majors were urging.[60] Again, in January, buyers pleaded for a substantial increase in allowables, and Hugh Stewart, director of Interior's Oil and Gas Division, announced that he would be "overjoyed" to see an eighteen-day schedule in Texas; but the opposition of the independents had been very vocal and the Commission finally raised February allowables only 93,000 b/d.[61] Furthermore, either

56. API, *Statistical Bulletin,* April 23, 1957. Crude stocks from Form No. 5; Gasoline stocks from Form No. 8.

57. *Wall Street Journal* (December 31, 1956), p. 6.

58. The study showed that pipeline capacity from West Texas to the Gulf Coast was being used to the full under then existing and planned conditions and an added movement of this magnitude would require emergency transport mobilization using all excess pipeline capacity to Wood River, Chicago and Lima, tank cars on the eastward movement, and barges, trucks and tank cars from Texas and Louisiana Gulf coast producing areas to ports. *Ibid.* (January 4, 1957), p. 20.

59. "Disputes Hobble the Oil Lift," *Business Week* (February 2, 1957), p. 29.

60. Empire State Petroleum Association, *Special Report* (January 31, 1957), p. 3.

61. *Ibid.,* p. 5. The sharp reversal at the December 19 hearings of the

despite or because of the inadequacy of transport facilities, the Commission refused to grant larger allowables to wells near the Gulf on the grounds that such action would violate its traditional policy of "across-the-board proration." [62] And finally, Texas never lost sight of the height of gasoline stocks. United States end-of-month stocks of finished and unfinished gasoline were comparatively much more excessive than crude stocks throughout 1956, and they had not subsided at the end of the year, when they were almost 22 million barrels larger than 1955. The Texas Commission believed that domestic refiners were processing too much crude oil and consequently building surplus gasoline. The solution of the problem, it asserted, was not to increase Texas production but to cut back on refining operations and divert the crude to Europe, thereby at one and the same time meeting European demands and cutting into the high gasoline stocks hanging over and depressing the domestic market.[63]

A sympathetic interpretation of the actions of the Texas Railroad Commission during this episode would emphasize its view that emergency requirements of Western Europe for crude should not be permitted to upset the equitable balance of interest among large and small, coast and inland producers. Transport facilities prevented inland oil fields and a large proportion of the independent producers from participating directly in this temporary swell of foreign demand. The majors, with their interests in transport, their dominance in coastal refining and (more especially for the international firms) their commercial responsibilities in European markets, had alternatives not open to the independents. The orderly growth of the domestic petroleum industry called for a selection from these alternatives which would shore up the position of the independents and yet permit a reasonable discharge of commitments abroad and some assurance of orderly development thereafter. Thus refusal to grant special allow-

---

traditional demand of the independents for higher allowables than buyers recommended led the authors of this Special Report to comment, ". . . it was quite obvious that their real motivation was to create an artificial crude oil shortage to prepare the ground for a price increase" (pp. 3–4).

62. Independents claimed that some 8,500 wells in West Texas were without any pipeline connections and that this was a discrimination against them. "The independents want the railroad commission to keep tight rein on Texas production until pipelines can be extended and until gasoline stocks can be reduced." "Disputes Hobble the Oil Lift," p. 29.

63. *Wall Street Journal* (February 5, 1957), p. 3. In March, U.S. majors did cut back their refinery runs some 200,000 b/d to release crude for Europe. Reported in *Petroleum Press Service* (March, 1957), p. 105.

ables for coastal fields forced the majors to improve transport from inland areas, to cut back on their domestic refining, and thereby to free both crude oil and transport capacity for added exports without further contributing to excessive gasoline stocks, and/or to shift crude from foreign sources away from domestic toward European destinations. This twofold relief could not but ease the position of the inland refiner and consequently of the inland crude oil producer from whom he purchased. There is no doubt the Commission was trying in this way to protect nonintegrated producers from discriminatory treatment by major producer-transporter-customers.[64]

The actions of the Commission cannot be fully understood, however, except in terms of the general conviction in the industry (among majors and independents alike) of the need for a higher price of crude and for creating conditions under which it would stick. From this viewpoint, gasoline stocks were a menace throughout 1956 (over 13 per cent above 1955 at the end of the year), but total crude stocks had been reduced to approximately 1955 levels by December 31 and were actually less than the previous year relative to domestic consumption. The pressure of gasoline stocks had to be relieved before higher crude oil prices could be sustained at inland fields where markets were limited to domestic use. It is too much to assume that the Texas Commission did not weigh these considerations.

The rationale of the 1957 price increase, like that of 1953, is elusive. With surplus reserve capacity under public control, a higher price offer should effect primarily a redistribution of supplies; but a general price increase is not an effective way to bring about a redistribution [65] and there is no evidence that higher prices were needed to

64. In connection with the allegations about insufficient construction of pipeline capacity to the wells of independent producers in West Texas, noted in 62, above, in September, 1957, five associations of these producers charged before the Texas Commission that the crude oil purchasing subsidiaries of major importing companies "are restricting some Texas production by limiting pipeline capacity to make way for foreign oil in the domestic market. . . . Last February, the Commission ordered all crude oil common carriers to show cause why unconnected wells should not be connected. The Commission also ordered certain carriers to show why trunk line capacity should not be increased." *Wall Street Journal* (September 18, 1957), p. 16. The *Second Report of the Attorney General* (above, p. 144, n. 37) comments specifically and at length on the significance of the fact that the predominant East Coast importers of crude oil are at one and the same time the largest foreign producers and the dominant interest in Texas pipelines (pp. 105–118).

65. The latter was facilitated by the differential price rise at Gulf Ports higher than elsewhere in Texas.

induce increased output once the Texas Commission approved expanded allowables.[66] Indeed, only prompt retrenchment in production by the Commission a couple of months later prevented a boomerang as the rapid passing of the crisis after March eroded the advance in product prices and augmented imports sapped at the new posted values of crude.

It is clear, even at this point in the analysis, that crude-oil price changes since the war bear little relation to the competition for connections traditionally associated with them. True, buyers may have feared losses of connections in 1957, like those they suffered ten years earlier, because of actual and prospective increases in demand, but the increase, like that of 1953 when no such pressures were evident, could not have been sustained without the active intervention of public authority. It is still too early to try to assess the impact of the large integrated firms on the pricing mechanism. Their influence is complicated not only by their Colossus-like stance as simultaneous buyer and seller in domestic markets but also by the international interests of the more important. These interests must be sampled before an answer can be essayed to the last question posed at the beginning of this chapter.

66. As noted earlier (see above, p. 161) the Commission finally raised production allowables for the state by 200,000 b/d in March but, with U.S. production close to 7.7 million b/d (some 750,000 b/d above the previous October) and mid-March imports reaching the new and alarming high of 1.7 million b/d, the Texas Commission canceled the March advance and followed with further substantial reductions in subsequent months.

CHAPTER 9

The Pricing of Crude Oil: II. The World Market and the Role of Imports

TRADITIONALLY this country has been a net exporter of petroleum if crude oil and refined products are considered together. Following World War I, however, until 1932, when an import duty of 21 cents per barrel was imposed, our imports of crude oil generally exceeded our exports by upward of 100,000 b/d. It was only the volume of exports of refined products that preserved this net export position.[1] Crude oil imports were substantially cut back following 1932; but subsequent tax reductions under the Venezuelan agreement of 1939 and, more importantly, rising prices and the added requirements of war brought a renewal of the crude oil import balance in 1941. It became continuous after 1943, and in 1948 the physical volume of all petroleum imports (crude and refined products) outweighed the aggregate of exports. Since that time the volume of imports has grown persistently in contrast to the volume of exports. In 1950 an import balance developed even on a value basis for the aggregate trade, and beginning with 1953 the pendulum seems to have shifted permanently in this direction.

THE EMERGENCE OF CONFLICT

The initial import balance in 1948 came as a relief to an economy straining to satisfy the vast surge of postwar full-employment demands. In 1947, as already noted, there was real shortage despite new record output. In 1948 entirely new heights were reached in both productive and exploratory efforts. Domestic crude oil production spurted from an average of 5,088,000 to 5,520,000 b/d and at the same time new wells drilled, excluding service wells, jumped from

1. In three years of domestic oil shortage (1920–22), however, the import balance for crude oil was so large that a net import balance was generated for the aggregate volume of crude oil and refined products. See U. S. House of Representatives, Select Committee on Small Business, Subcommittee on Oil Imports, "Effects of Foreign Imports on Independent Domestic Producers," House *Report* 2344, 81st Congress, 2d Session (1950), pp. 15, 39.

30,842 to 37,508. In this all-out effort, there was little concern that total oil exports (including refined products) fell to an average of 369,000 b/d compared with the peak of 568,000 b/d reached in 1944.[2] And no great alarm attended the accompanying rise in total imports of crude and products to a new high of 513,000 b/d; the net import balance was a welcome contribution.

Industrial recession in the following year brought a sharp reaction for total imports continued to rise while domestic production allowables were cut back in each successive month for nine months and the margin between capacity and actual production widened. Output in 1949, excepting only 1948, was greater than ever before; but this was the first year since 1942 that it had fallen below levels of the preceding year. Misgivings were stirred not merely by the volume of imports (they had increased an average of 131,000 b/d while domestic production of all petroleum liquids was cut back 445,000 b/d) but also by the differential advantage that ownership of foreign supplies gave to a handful of giant integrated firms.[3] With domestic production allowables adapted to anticipated market demand after consideration of total available supplies (including imports), these few majors might not only avoid the full burden of cutbacks but also impose on other producers and refiners, integrated or nonintegrated, a new form of margin squeeze. Not even other majors could be assured that their interests would not be prejudiced, if, like Phillips and Standard of Indiana, their production operations were all domestic.

This concern of purely domestic producers, whose profits were curtailed by restriction of their output without a proportionate reduction in their costs, was echoed in the fears of inland refiners who saw their markets restricted by the heavy inflow of residual fuel oil. Practically all United States imports were accounted for by crude oil and residual fuel oil, and the latter increased in 1949 and the early part of 1950 at a more rapid rate than the former. Issues were confounded as the coal industry, already harassed in its losing battle with the domestic petroleum industry, joined the fray against this "dumping of foreign oil," while independent distributors of residual fuel oil in the East took

2. *Ibid.,* p. 15.

3. See FTC, *The International Petroleum Cartel,* p. 21, where control of the petroleum industry outside the U.S. was said to be divided for all practical purposes between state monopolies and seven large international companies. Five of these firms were American: Standard (New Jersey), Socony-Vacuum, Standard of California, Gulf, and the Texas Company; one was Dutch (Royal Dutch–Shell); and one was British (originally Anglo-Iranian Oil, now British Petroleum Company, Ltd.). Shell is also a major operator in the U.S. market.

up the cudgels for imports to protect their dwindling supply sources.

The available facts do not seem to support the contention that heavy fuel oil imports were seriously injuring any domestic industry, or that they are likely to do so. Both coal and heavy fuel oil had suffered from competition, but it was the competition of other fuels rather than of imports. In single home heating, natural gas and home-heating oil (one of the distillates) were making heavy inroads on coal; on the railroads, the dieselization of railroad tractive power was rapidly cutting into the importance of both traditional sources of energy. In other markets, coal continued to lose position relative to heavy fuel oil in the bunkering of ships; and neither of the two could maintain its share of the industrial market in competition with natural gas.[4]

It is significant that residual fuel imports did increase in the East Coast region, the area of its predominant use, and it is important that the trend should continue. Residual fuel oil is the lowliest fraction in the refinery product hierarchy; one of the major incentives to develop and introduce improved refining techniques and equipment has been, precisely, to reduce its yield in favor of more valuable products. Prices range below the level of crude prices; with few exceptions, supply is confined locally by low value and bulk; and United States refineries have drastically reduced its percentage yield since 1945. In this compression East coast refineries have taken the lead.[5] Thus, there was a serious reduction in the domestic output of heavy fuel oil after the boom year 1948. To make good this deficiency from production would have required a serious waste of crude oil, an overproduction of other petroleum products, and/or a deliberate down-grading of product—all of them uneconomical alternatives. Here, at least, imports are more likely to supplement than to supplant domestic production.

The Committee set up by the House to explore this episode of 1949–50 failed to reach a positive proposal regarding the future of crude oil imports. It was more impressed that 1949, a depression year, should exceed the preceding boom period in number of wells completed, footage of wells drilled, exploratory wells, and new proven

4. See Report of the National Petroleum Council, *Petroleum Imports* (Washington, D.C., 1955), p. 34, where U.S. consumption of competitive fuels in various uses is compared for 1946–53.

5. See above, p. 13. Refineries east of the Rockies reduced their percentage yields of residual fuel oil from 24.9 per cent in 1943 to 13.1 per cent in 1954 (*Petroleum Imports*, p. 31) while yields for the country as a whole declined from 29.2 to 16.4 per cent (API, *Statistical Bulletin*, April 7, 1958).

reserves, which were increased almost 1.4 billion barrels by the end of the year, than it was by cutbacks in United States production allowables.[6] Imports had not as yet seemed to impair the health of the domestic industry.

The Committee recognized a certain unfairness in the fact that major importers could not be expected to restrict their imports in proportion as domestic production was cut back. Independent producers might be disadvantaged but available policy alternatives were too baffling for it to recommend positive action. The State Department was outspoken against restrictions, especially in view of the general dollar shortage. American companies, in effect protégés of the State Department, were already harassed by dollar-hungry countries with little more than their crude oil potential to sell. Limitation of imports was felt, moreover, to be inconsistent with United States foreign policy and international interests, even though the Defense Department had a preference for oil development within the Western Hemisphere and within American borders. The Committee itself considered demand-supply conditions in oil too unstable [7] to recommend either an import quota or a stiffer tariff; and it would not contemplate administrative interference by a federal agency with "the rights of the respective states to control their own production." The most it was willing to suggest was some form of voluntary agreement, under the general auspices of the President, by which "to control the importation of foreign produced crude petroleum and petroleum products into the United States." [8]

6. General Ernest O. Thompson, Chairman of the Texas Railroad Commission, who early in 1949 had recommended quotas that would keep imports within 5 per cent of domestic market demand, pointed out in February, 1950, that Texas alone "could easily produce an additional million barrels of oil per day without harm to the wells or to the reservoirs." Speech delivered before American Institute of Mining and Metallurgical Engineers, Statler Hotel, New York City, February 14, 1950. For the same month, Edward B. Swanson, Assistant Director of the Oil and Gas Division, Department of Interior, reported total MER at 6,300,000 b/d and total national production at 4,953,650 b/d. See U. S. House of Representatives, Subcommittee of Committee on Interstate and Foreign Commerce, "Petroleum Study," *Hearings* on H.R. 107, 81st Congress, 2d Session (1950), p. 43.

7. E.g., in 1945 the Petroleum Industry War Council recommended with general approval a limitation of imports to those "absolutely necessary" to supplement domestic production under "good conservation practices"; and two years later a Committee of the Congress was demanding that the industry rush its import schedules to lessen consumer hardship. House Small Business Committee, "Effects of Foreign Imports" (above, n. 1), p. 124.

8. *Ibid.*, p. 147.

The suggestion of voluntary control of imports, like the issues that had initiated the Committee report, dissolved as a reinvigorated economy recorded new high levels of demand for oil. Rearmament in late 1950 and the withdrawal of Iranian oil by Mossadegh in the following year so dissipated the fears of oil surplus that a new agreement with Venezuela (October 11, 1952) could be effected, reducing substantially tariffs on petroleum imports from that country and, under the most-favored-nation clause of the Reciprocal Trade Agreements Act, from other contracting nations as well. A running fight for restriction on oil imports continued, but no success was recorded until after the recession of 1954, when imports ranged above a million barrels per day and the margin between productive capacity and allowed production was estimated in excess of two million barrels per day.[9]

The Trade Agreement Extension Act of 1955 (P.L. 86) sets up a mechanism whereby the President, duly advised that imports of any article threaten the national security, may take whatever action he deems necessary to remove the threat. With this leverage, a voluntary restriction program was inaugurated by the Director of Defense Mobilization. The program was initially so arranged as to favor Western Hemisphere sources by excluding from control all crude oil of Venezuelan and Canadian origin and all imports into District 5 (the West Coast). This was possible because production on the West Coast had waned, no adequate domestic transport facilities from east of the Rockies existed, and most Canadian crude entered the Northwest; and also because the Venezuelan government had showed a willingness to stabilize exports from that country to the East Coast. With these exclusions, crude oil imports in Districts 1–4, mainly from the Middle East, were to be restricted to a percentage of production not greater than the ratio of such imports to production in 1954—4.65 per cent.[10]

Only pervasive fear of federal control could make so cumbersome and inequitable a control system work for long in a dynamic industry. The large international companies, which probably had most to lose from such a denouement, might have been expected to cooperate

9. The disputed reliability of this figure is discussed on p. 160.

10. See Office of Defense Mobilization, Staff Memorandum on Oil Imports (May 7, 1956), p. 1. The ratio of total imports of crude oil from all sources to total domestic production in 1954 was 10.34 per cent; the lower percentage is the ratio of imports to be controlled (i.e. after exclusions noted) to domestic production in that year. After excluding imports of residual fuel oil for military use or for bunkering ships in foreign trade, the corresponding ratio for residual fuel oil imports was placed at 4.24 per cent.

scrupulously.[11] But companies like Sun, Atlantic, and Tidewater, not normally involved in foreign oil, were forced by Texas cutbacks on their own production either to buy a higher proportion of their needs in the domestic market or to find or negotiate the import of cheaper foreign crude. (How it became cheaper will concern us shortly.) But foreign purchase contracts were usually made on a long-term basis and the buyers had often engaged tankers for a comparable period to pick up the purchased oil. With companies so committed, it is surprising that the system did not crack earlier. During the first six months of 1956 Middle East imports grew to an average 300,000 b/d, several new refineries were built, or were building, on the East Coast for the specific purpose of using crude from this area, and the number of importers had grown to more than fifty companies.[12] Only the attack on Suez on November 1 forestalled submission of the entire matter to the President under the terms of the authorizing legislation. But the reprieve was short: imports were making new records in March, 1957, and they were certified as a threat to national security in the following month.

The consequence of this re-look at the problem was another compromise "voluntary" program. But apart from the deletion of limits on residual fuel oil and other products, and the imposition of limits nominally on the individual importers rather than on the country of origin—an improvement from the standpoint of foreign policy—no real progress has been made toward a rational, equitable control. A flat ceiling of crude oil imports has been allocated among old and new importers, based on historic shares of imports.[13] But such com-

11. Jersey Standard, for example, was reported in July, 1956, to have imported no Middle East crude for use in its own refineries for more than a year. See J. H. Carmical, "More Cuts Likely in Imports of Oil," New York Times, July 1, 1956.

12. See ibid. As early as February 12, 1955, Business Week highlighted the contract of Sun Oil Company, long an opponent of foreign oil, with British Petroleum Company, Ltd.'s Middle East fields to buy 20,000 b/d for one year. At that time Sun Oil was reported as "just about the last East Coast refiner" to buy Middle East crude. In June, 1956, these imports were reported at about 50,000 b/d. Wall Street Journal, September 27, 1956.

13. See Office of Defense Mobilization, Report of the Special Committee to Investigate Crude Oil Imports, July 29, 1957. This system failed to protect the industry to the satisfaction of domestic producers and the Administration, in part because some refiners flouted it. It was therefore superseded in 1959 by compulsory quotas allocated among domestic refiners, this time in proportion not to previous imports or import needs but to total refinery runs in 1958. The

pany quotas are certain to chafe worst the firm with the most rapidly growing commitments; and though compromises may mitigate "hardship cases," they cannot eradicate the incompatibility of quotas with dynamic change.

PROBLEMS OF IMPORT POLICY

Tariff history is made out of the competition of a cheap foreign supply and a higher-cost domestic industry. Something of this familiar situation is found in oil. While the true total cost of foreign oil, with its extravagant losses as well as its extravagant finds, is unknown, it is clear that production from many foreign sources—Canada, Venezuela, and pre-eminently the fabulous Middle East—can be expanded in much greater volume at much lower costs than United States production. The more important of these foreign areas are relatively minor users of petroleum themselves; their development will be geared to the consumption demands of industrial and industrializing countries. Unless barred artificially, then, their output may be expected to contribute increasingly to the energy requirements of an expanding American economy.

The challenge of oil imports is more significant than mere competition from a lower-cost supply source. Their prospective availability questions the soundness of long-established conservation policies; while at the same time the conservation practices actually followed have had the effect, because of imports, of subjecting the domestic producer and/or refiner to a "squeeze" by the importer in which public authority has unwittingly played the part of accessory. Thus producers have been forced to forego sales and refiner-producers have been forced to purchase a larger part of their crude requirements because production allowables were curtailed to offset higher imports. And the importers themselves—especially the American international firms that dominate this traffic—thus supplant high-cost, publicly controlled production (higher-cost in the short run than it would be in the absence

---

new system, which is more discriminatory than the old and brings the industry even closer to comprehensive, compulsory cartelization, contains the proviso that, in the event the domestic crude oil price rises, the O.C.D.M. "determine whether such increases are necessary to accomplish the national security objectives of the Proclamation." See the *Proclamation* by the President of the United States, "Adjusting Imports of Petroleum and Petroleum Products," March 10, 1959; and the regulations issued by the Secretary of the Interior, March 13, 1959.

of prorationing) with low-cost, privately administered output. Higher global self-sufficiency gives them a decided advantage over their less versatile rivals.[14]

The problem of developing a satisfactory and consistent policy has become more complicated as it has grown more urgent in recent years. Exploration and development in foreign areas until the last decade comprised the prototype of risk in this business.[15] The unique obstacles and huge capital requirements made the foreign area the province of a handful of giant, fully integrated international firms and a few state monopolies which controlled, and still control, the predominant share of the world's production and its proved reserves outside the USSR. While the basic situation has not been significantly altered, remarkable developments in recent years mark a trend that could have profound consequences even though no more than marginal quantities as yet are involved. The first breach in the "Big Five" alignment of American firms in the Middle East came in early 1953, when the American Independent Oil Company[16]—a cooperative, exclusively foreign-oriented venture of independents—brought in its discovery well in the Neutral Zone of Kuwait. Participating American com-

14. See Table XII, p. 224, where self-sufficiency ratios, the ratio of owned production to refinery runs, are compared for major firms on both a domestic and a global base.

15. See above, pp. 39–40. No proper accounting of the huge expenditures and massive losses to be set against the better-known successes seems ever to have been made. A few examples of investments with a long time-lag to commercial operation and of investments that did not pay out, along with a vivid description of the problems and risks of foreign operations, are given in Leonard M. Fanning, *Foreign Oil and the Free World* (New York, McGraw-Hill, 1954), esp. appendix 1, table series 3 and 4. A series of studies dealing with the social and political as well as the economic ramifications of company responsibilities and commitments in the opening up of primitive hinterlands and undeveloped countries have been published in recent years. Among them may be mentioned, in the National Planning Association series on United States Business Performance Abroad, *The Creole Petroleum Corporation in Venezuela*, December, 1955, and *Stanvac in Indonesia*, June, 1957.

16. Aminoil, organized in 1947, is wholly owned by eight oil companies (Ashland Oil and Refining Company, Deep Rock Oil Corporation, Globe Oil and Refining Company, Hancock Oil Company, Lario Oil and Gas Company, Phillips Petroleum Company, Signal Oil and Gas Company, Sunray Mid-Continent Oil Company) and two individuals (J. S. Abercrombie of Houston and Ralph K. Davies, president of the Company). The Company acted for itself and for Pacific Western Oil Corporation, part of the Getty interests. It had acquired the concession to the Sheik of Kuwait's half interest in the Neutral Zone between Saudi Arabia and Kuwait; Pacific Western Oil Corporation held the concession in the Saudi Arabia half of the zone.

panies in Middle East oil expanded to twenty-two two years later when, as part of the settlement of the Iranian dispute, nine United States companies secured the shares of Iricon Agency, Ltd., a new Delaware corporation established to hold a 5 per cent interest in Iranian operations.[17]

A similar break occurred in Venezuela in 1956 when, for the first time in ten years, new acreage grants were offered for bid and were obtained (often through joint arrangements) by United States companies relatively new to foreign undertakings. But a more dramatic breakthrough of United States companies of every size and degree of integration has been the opening up of Western Canada. The strike at Leduc, Alberta, in February, 1947, fired dreams of a "new Texas" in a region physically, politically, and economically much like an extension of our own frontier.[18] Here, too, is an area where production of oil and gas is limited only by what the market will take, and both resources and markets may be importantly integrated with the development of our own.[19] These are conditions that tempt the independent who has neither the capital nor the inclination to develop markets, and especially foreign markets, for the crude he may discover.

The really significant change from this viewpoint is that an important marginal increment of foreign supplies, existing and potential, is getting into the hands of a rapidly increasing number of erstwhile domestic firms. The search for oil has been intensified throughout the

17. The agreement transferred a one per cent interest in the consortium from each of the other five American companies, leaving the interest in Iranian operations split as follows: British Petroleum Company, Ltd. (40 per cent), Royal Dutch–Shell (14 per cent), U.S. Big Five Companies, each holding 7 per cent (35 per cent), Cie Française Des Petroles (6 per cent), Iricon Agency, Ltd. (5 per cent). Shares in Iricon are nontransferable for five years. The nine owners are Atlantic Refining, Hancock Oil, Pacific Western Oil, Richfield Oil, San Jacinto Petroleum, Signal Oil and Gas, American Independent Oil, Standard Oil (Ohio), and Tidewater Oil. Each firm owns $\frac{1}{12}$ interest except Richfield ($\frac{1}{4}$) and Aminoil ($\frac{1}{6}$). "Iranian Issue Finally Settled," *Oil and Gas Journal* (May 9, 1955), pp. 82 ff.

18. Through 1955 it is estimated that U.S. firms and affiliates accounted for about 54 per cent of the Canadian oil investment since Leduc—some $2.6 billion for drilling and a further $1.6 billion for transport and marketing. See Coqueron, *Annual Financial Analysis, 1955.*

19. A beginning has been made in trunk crude oil pipelines that stretch from Edmonton west over the mountains to Vancouver and Seattle (an export market estimated at 250,000 b/d by 1960) and eastward through Superior to Sarnia and Toronto. During 1957 both the Westcoast Transmission Pipeline for natural gas and the Trans-Canada Line to Montreal were to have begun operations.

world—under pressures by the country that has none but seeks the means of industrial advance and by the country that does or may have it but must induce foreign capital and technicians to find and develop it. Artificial barriers to exploration are giving way to special inducements, and the competition of foreign capital offers the governments of oil-rich countries progressively higher bonuses, royalties and shares in profits in exchange for exploratory concessions. Each year sees new domestic names venturing abroad.[20] Many of these are majors in the domestic market but many are independents, usually combined in a joint undertaking, often with majors, where the job is particularly large or costly.

The lure of the foreign bonanza is sugared by the extension to foreign operations of the same tax offsets that can be employed in domestic exploration and development—the expensing of intangibles, the handling of exploration costs, percentage depletion. And since 1950 American companies operating abroad have found a highly satisfactory offset to the ever more grasping demands of foreign governments for higher shares of their profits. Concession payments in the form of income taxes (the standard 50 per cent of net operating income established by Venezuela) have been interpreted administratively as true income taxes and allowed as credits against federal income tax. In consequence, some of the most successful foreign operators—notably the Arabian American Oil Company (owned by Standard of New Jersey, Standard of California, Texas, and Socony Mobil) with its monopoly of Saudi Arabian oil—pay no income tax whatsoever to the United States Treasury.[21]

20. Dahl M. Duff identified some 60 U.S. firms seriously involved in foreign wildcatting operations in 1955. See "More Independents Are Going Abroad," *Oil and Gas Journal* (May 30, 1955), p. 46.

21. Foreign income taxes paid by American companies are allowed as income tax credits by the Treasury. In 1950 the Internal Revenue Bureau ruled that a 50 per cent tax on petroleum companies, levied by Venezuela, could be treated in this manner. Following this, Ibn Saud, with American assistance, reformulated his tax laws to include an income tax on petroleum companies of 50 per cent of net operating income against which all other taxes and royalties were allowable. Thus payments to Ibn Saud were raised to 50 per cent of net income while Aramco could use such payments as credits against federal income tax liability. Similar arrangements were incorporated in the Iranian Oil consortium agreement in September, 1954, and Internal Revenue approved the Aramco scheme in May, 1955.

Presumably, this way of handling the mounting demands of foreign states for a larger share in the profits from their oil concessions without increasing the financial burden of operating companies has become standard practice. It

In this unrelenting drive of the oil countries of the world for increased revenue and for a higher proportion of the income earned from the exploitation of their oil there is a major threat to the stability of the global industry, a threat that accentuates the danger lurking in the multiplication of producing companies now operating abroad. The concessionaire is under continuing pressure to increase output in order to keep the host government reasonably satisfied with its royalty income. The concession itself does not last forever and heavy fixed investments, plus the threat of political instability, urge a reasonably rapid rate of exploitation. The Iranian and Suez episodes are sufficiently clear in memory to prevent complacency on this score. In the past the situation was generally well in hand. A few large firms, working in close cooperation and with extensive control of marketing systems outside the United States and the USSR, were in a position to regulate output and to hold down royalty payments with reasonable assurance. Within their own group they represented the important and feasible alternatives. It is this assurance that the market today no longer affords.

All kinds and sizes of producers and producer-refiners are reaching out individually and in groups for foreign oil, propelled in part by a need to compensate for production cutbacks of their own United States producing properties. And for the most part these new foreign operators are not committed to the development of foreign markets. Quite the contrary, the leading ones are American refiners oriented toward the United States market and the provision of their domestic requirements. Thus there are several kinds of weakness inherent in their activities. First, they do not have the investments abroad—in all phases of the industry—that would make them sensitive to the long-run impact of their negotiations with foreign states or their crude oil sales agreements on price and cost stability in foreign markets. For similar reasons they are probably less impressed with the leadership function of the giant internationals, especially when it demands unprofitable restraint on their own actions; and they are more likely to have to cut prices to find markets for their growing output. Second,

---

may not last. In the report of the Subcommittee on Antitrust and Monopoly to the Committee on the Judiciary, August 16, 1957, it is recommended that appropriate congressional committees review the legality and propriety of such arrangements with an eye to remedial or corrective legislation. It is further recommended that the 27½ per cent depletion allowance granted petroleum producers be limited to production within the U.S. and its territories. See *Petroleum: The Antitrust Laws and Government Policies*, Committee Print, pp. 6 f.

they are less likely than the Big Five to be sensitive to the need to make the "voluntary" restrictions on imports work. As newcomers enjoying but a small share of world markets, and as refiners pinched by domestic prorationing, they are less likely to benefit from the status quo that such restraint helps to preserve. And indeed, there are rapidly getting to be too many of them to do otherwise than press their own short-run interests.

For the large international firms, the stake in preserving comparative freedom of opportunity for foreign oil imports and a fair calibration of world prices with the domestic market is extremely high, certainly worthy of substantial short-term forbearance and cooperation with the whims of Congress. The core of this concern for statesman-like action is their interests in the largest known reserves of cheap oil in the world. No one really knows the cost of Middle East oil; but it is reasonably certain it is so low that the extent to which the expanding free world demand is met from this region will be governed by policy and not by either scarcity or comparative cost.[22] This oil must be exploited at increasing speed to satisfy the owner-governments, and a not negligible part should be sold in the United States market, not merely because the price here is high and the demand expanding but also because of the importance of dollar sales in a world of frequent exchange difficulties. The international firm would not want to jeopardize its access to, or the prices it realizes in, this growing market; but there would probably be much worse consequences if imports were quantitatively limited or protective tariffs imposed.[23] Either action would weaken the industry's defense of its tax allowances, in-

22. Developed from the beginning by a handful of closely cooperating firms under unitized operations, the drilling of development wells is scheduled to supply expanding markets from free-flowing wells. The consequences are dramatic. With only 1,500 wells drilled in the entire area, reserves have been proved at more than 13,000 barrels per foot drilled in contrast with 600 to 700 barrels in Venezuela and only 20 to 30 in the U.S. (*Petroleum Press Service,* July, 1956, p. 239). And with merely 625 wells in operation at the end of 1955, average production per well was 5,090 b/d in the Middle East; in Venezuela with 12,815 wells, it was 176 b/d; in Canada with 8,759 it was 42 b/d; while in the U.S. a total of 537,293 wells produced an average of 13 b/d. (*World Oil,* August 15, 1957, p. 197.)

23. The choice between quantitative limits—involuntary or voluntary—and protective tariffs is itself by no means a matter of indifference to the established importing companies. As Senator O'Mahoney (of the Senate Judiciary Committee) has pointed out, import quotas protect private monopolies with no public gain; a tariff, on the other hand, will at least divert some of the monopoly gain from importers to the taxpayer.

cluding percentage depletion, on foreign operations and it would prejudice its case for continuation of credits against United States taxes for foreign royalties paid in the form of income tax.[24] Moreover, the pressure for increasing sales of Middle East oil, especially if it resulted in strict protective action against them by this country, could finally sever the last weak link that ties world prices of crude oil to the Gulf coast price. Were this to happen—it is already happening to some extent—and if world prices were to sag below those prevailing in the United States, the profit picture for the international companies would be badly dimmed and their defense of existing tax advantages on their foreign business would be critically deflated. In a situation evolving in this direction it becomes ever more important, if crude price stability is to be maintained, that the supply of oil should be kept in strong hands; the prospective increase in the size of marginal supplies in clearly weaker hands poses new problems for the industry both at home and abroad, and places an ever-increasing premium on restraint on the part of those who stand most to lose.[25]

PRICING CRUDE OIL IN WORLD MARKETS

The United States was the early supplier of crude oil and oil products to Europe and to the world; it is not at all surprising that in those days prices in this country should govern those in foreign lands. Gulf Coast ports were the natural centers for bulk transfers to ocean-going tankers from pipelines tapping dominant fields in Texas and the Midcontinent. It was here too that growth of large refineries, drawing on a vast oil hinterland and serving worldwide markets, was favored. Crude oil and petroleum products destined for the United States East Coast or for foreign lands were priced in the Gulf cargo market, which became the keystone of pricing structures throughout the world.[26] The Gulf was the primary source of petroleum for Europe and the cheapest. Even before the war, primacy began shifting to Venezuela as the marginal increment was becoming the main sup-

24. See above, n. 21.
25. This is the prescription and prediction also of David Ovens, of the *Economist,* "Crude Oil Prices—the Next Five Years" (manuscript of paper to be presented at June 4–6, 1958, meeting of the Institute of Petroleum, London), pp. 12–14.
26. The Gulf Cargo product market will be discussed below, in Pt. IV; see pp. 394 ff. Far Eastern markets were first served by shipments from California, and, since the Pacific Coast was effectively isolated from the East, prices were substantially independent of those in the rest of the U.S.

ply, and the Caribbean price—itself the identical twin of the Gulf Port price—gradually became the price leader for both crude oil and for refined products. Meanwhile, still before the war, yet another great center of production, the Middle East, had opened up. But Middle Eastern buyers continued to pay the Gulf price plus transportation from that point even if their purchases came from local sources. During the war, at the insistence of the British, a Persian Gulf base price was established for bunker fuel; this practice was extended in 1945 to apply to other refined products and to crude oil. Prices accepted for the new base, after considerable haggling with the British, were United States Gulf prices.[27]

The reasons for this pricing pattern are inherent in the economics of the industry and the foreign-concession system of crude oil development. With large concessions, single company operation of an oil reservoir or field was the rule. With only a few firms operating in a given field or even in a given country, no management could possibly fail to be intimately aware of the impact of its pricing actions on its rivals, even if the various company officers were never in communication. Furthermore added costs of added output (marginal costs) do not provide a reliable brake on competitive pressures in the oil industry.[28] In these circumstances it would have reflected on the

27. The development of pricing is discussed in detail in FTC, *The International Petroleum Cartel*, chap. 10, esp. pp. 352 ff. While the British were apparently content to buy at the new Persian Gulf base prices, the U. S. Navy considered them excessive in terms of costs, and the prices therefore came in for a good deal of controversy before a Congressional investigating committee. See *ibid.*, pp. 357–360.

28. Several estimates of the cost of Middle East crude were made in the process of evaluating a contract price proposed by Aramco to the U. S. Navy for oil to be supplied the French Government under Lend-Lease in 1945. The cost of Saudi Arabian crude was estimated at 40 cents per barrel, including a 21-cent royalty, and Bahrein crude was put at 25 cents, including a 15-cent royalty. There had been earlier offers by Caltex and the Texas Company to sell products to the U. S. Government at prices substantially below equivalent Gulf Coast prices. A vice president of Aramco later testified that costs were compiled monthly for the directors and that they were reported at 40 cents per barrel at the time a price of $1.05 was quoted to the Navy (*ibid.*). For another series of estimates, indicating average costs of $0.25 to $0.35 a barrel, and a surmise and indication that incremental costs are even lower, see UN, Economic and Social Council, Economic Commission for Europe, *The Price of Oil in Western Europe* (March, 1955), pp. 15–16 (cited below as UN, ECE).

For any particular well or project one can derive "costs"—total actual expenditures (possibly prorated over some arbitrary time period or equally arbi-

competence of private management if these foreign properties had not been developed to exploit to the fullest the advantages of their costs, location, and joint control. The search for an acceptable basis for pricing under these circumstances must turn on consideration of good public relations and simplicity of administration. Base prices linked to the familiar United States Gulf prices, with United States Maritime Commission (USMC) tanker freight rates as standardized transport costs, supplied the most effective foundation for price administration. They also carried a plausible justification that the market price in even a freely competitive market would always have to be set at the level of the marginal or highest-cost supplies required to satisfy demand. As long as some supplies had to come from the Gulf, therefore, the cost of getting oil from there would determine price—so the argument ran.

During the course of the war and immediately after, Middle East crude production increased its share of world output rapidly, from under 5 per cent in 1940 to more than 12 per cent in 1948. The upward spiral of United States crude prices permitted a painless adjustment of Persian Gulf prices to this enlarging market prospect. As American prices climbed a full $1.40 per barrel from their war-set ceilings, prices at Ras Tanura followed only part of the way, advancing $1.17 per barrel, and the equalized area of delivered prices from the Persian and Mexican Gulfs, respectively, using USMC tanker rates, was moved westward from the Mid-Mediterranean area of France to the United Kingdom. But toward the end of 1948 and into 1949 oil began to move in significant volume (over 4 million barrels per month) to United States Atlantic ports, and domestic production was cut back to offset the impact on the American market. The consequent differential in net-back at the Persian Gulf between shipments to Western Europe and those to the United States demanded adjustment, especially as the Economic Cooperation Administration, which was dollar-financing crude oil purchases by European refineries, began to explore the oil-pricing structure. Under pressure from ECA, prices at Ras Tanura were reduced 15 cents in April, 1949 (a compromise that did not efface the differential) and a further cut of

---

trary estimate of reserves)—reduced to a unit figure per barrel of output or of reserves. Whatever internal use this average figure may have, it should now be clear that it is *not* the variable, out-of-pocket cost of output, which is much smaller, nor is it the "replacement cost" of crude oil, which could be either much less or much more. This is not to deny that Middle East crude is very low-cost compared either to its price or to costs in the U.S.

13 cents to $1.75 per barrel was made in July, 1949, to equalize Middle East with Caribbean crudes at New York.[29]

In subsequent crude oil price advances in this country in 1953 and again in 1957, the Middle East has participated but not fully, thus further strengthening the price advantage of Middle East over Caribbean crude. For example, the physical adjustments by which the Middle East Emergency Committee [30] strove to close the gap in Western Europe's supplies created by the Suez incident meant higher costs for delivered crude—longer shipping distances, higher tanker freight rates, and higher prices for United States oil. Higher crude and product prices in this country were accompanied by Venezuelan postings; Persian Gulf quotations for obvious reasons remained at precrisis levels throughout the period the Canal was closed. Finally, on May 28, 1957, British Petroleum initiated a general advance in Persian Gulf crude oil prices of 13 cents per barrel, less than the much earlier advance in United States prices and the rise of 23 cents per barrel for Arabian and Iraq oil at East Mediterranean pipeline terminals.[31]

The collapse of tanker rates since the end of the Suez emergency has further unsettled the balance of Middle East crude prices in world markets. At current posted prices and transport costs, Middle East oil would probably equalize United States delivered prices far inland from the Atlantic coast. Only policy and political considerations prevent absorption of a much larger share of the United States market and undermining of the domestic price.[32] However, the impact of tanker

29. FTC, *The International Petroleum Cartel*, p. 367. Since actual tanker rates were 35¼ per cent below USMC at the time, current freight rates were used instead of USMC in order to limit the price reduction. With actual freight rates fluctuating more widely than USMC, stability of destination prices would be achieved at the expense of a varying net back.

30. In preparation for the emergency, long foreseen despite the surprise in the manner of its coming, this committee had been organized in July, approved by the Attorney General from an antitrust viewpoint, and authorized by the President in November to put into effect its plans to redeploy tanker fleets in shifting supplies to Western Europe to make up for the stoppage of the Suez Canal. See *Petroleum Survey*, pp. 14 ff.

31. *Petroleum Press Service* (June, 1957), p. 237. Since these pipeline terminal rates are adjusted to the cost of alternative tanker haul around Arabia and through the Suez Canal, they were adapted to then existing (higher) tanker rates.

32. Incidentally, the collapse of tanker rates has also made it cheaper, using single voyage tanker rates to Britain, to load at the Persian Gulf than at East Mediterranean pipeline terminals. See "Eastern Mediterranean Out of Step," *Economist,* July 13, 1957.

rates, especially of spot tanker rates, on the level of base prices is difficult to forecast. Spot tanker rates have always been highly volatile compared with charter rates and especially long-term charters; and attempts to stabilize the spot market have not been too successful.[33] It is clearly impossible to administer a stable pricing system based on fluctuating spot tanker rates and it would be equally unfeasible to adapt pipeline charges to their gyrations. Indeed, it would be un-economic to do so, since by far the greater part of tanker transport is based on long-term arrangements.[34] Fluctuations in single voyage rates, nevertheless, could be unsettling to world posted price struc-tures if oil were not held in a few strong hands.

This general adaptation of Middle East crude oil prices to the de-livered cost of Western Hemisphere oil in the markets (progressively farther westward) which management found it necessary or desirable to serve is, of course, reminiscent of the evolution of steel basing-point prices in this country and especially the development of a second Chicago base from the original Pittsburgh-plus. The pricing system in the case of oil was less needed as a means of assuring identical de-

33. The problem, of course, stems from the relatively inelastic supply of tankers (it takes from two to three years to get delivery) and the large pro-portion of the world tanker fleet owned (around 43 per cent) and controlled through ownership and charter (around 90 per cent) by integrated oil com-panies. The 10 per cent or so of the commercial tanker fleet that competes in the spot market for a shifting tonnage volume will be able to command ex-tremely high rates when demand is strong and must take very low rates when it falls off. For the source of these estimates see below, p. 343, n. 43.

34. To provide a more reasonable basis for the incorporation of tanker transport costs in the pricing of oil, considerable use has been made of Average Freight Rate Assessment (AFRA) rates as announced quarterly by the London Tanker Brokers Panel since the spring of 1954. The AFRA rate is a weighted average of charter rates for three classes of tankers: oil-company-owned ships; independently owned ships on long-term charter (over twelve months); and independents on short charter (less than twelve months). Average charter (or in the third group, spot) rates in each class are weighted by the percentage of total tonnage in that class. Government owned ships, ships in layup, ships in U.S. coastwise trade, and ships under 10,000 d.w. tons are excluded from the computations.

Prior to the last quarter of 1955, AFRA rates commonly ranged *above* single voyage rates because of the continuing impact of long-term charters made at high rates during the period of tanker shortage immediately after the war. During the Suez emergency after mid-1956, spot rates far exceeded AFRA. It is likely that these high rates will govern much tanker transport through long-term charters for a considerable time after the collapse of single-voyage rates. See *Petroleum Press Service* (January, 1957), p. 14; and letter to the editor from P. H. Frankel, *Economist* (July 20, 1957), p. 207.

livered quotations from whatever source or supplier than had been true for steel. The very small number of sellers in the Middle East and the necessarily intimate relations between them which the method of development of much of the area necessitated made it easy enough to secure a united front in delivered prices at any important destination. It was not administration but the need for justification of the prices established, economic justification to customers and political assurance to governments, that induced the adoption and modification of the basing-point system in oil. From the beginning it was crucial to link Middle East prices to a standard that was hallowed by a long tradition of competitive action, more recently molded (and blessed) by public authority. And as market areas spread and volume expanded, it was equally important to avoid discriminatory net-backs from the prices received in different market areas at the same time.[35]

This practice of pricing to equate delivered prices from rival supply sources is a form of market competition of course. Its competitive aspect is generally overstressed, however, by those who believe that oil prices are made by competitive forces beyond the power of management to control. It is a sound economic principle that competitive market price must cover the highest cost increments of supply which are required within a given market area; and if this highest cost increment must be obtained from afar, its higher delivered cost will govern the market price. But the critical condition of such a competitive model is that market supply be not expandible at any lower cost. It is idle for the oil industry to parade Middle East prices as competitive in this sense as long as the expansion of supply from this area is limited by company policy rather than by cost.[36]

To hold that Middle East oil prices are not determined by competition alone is not to say that they are "unfair"; it is only to remind ourselves that they are policy determined in the same way that domestic prices are policy determined, but within wider limits of discretionary control over supply. At delivered prices equated at New York, Middle East crudes undoubtedly carry a substantially larger profit margin than domestic crudes. It is this fact that galled domestic firms with no such low-cost alternatives free of public control to which they could resort. When rising imports were offset by cut-backs in domestic production

35. This is not to say that all sales were made, uniformly, at the openly quoted price. Here, as elsewhere in this and other industries, the pressures of expanding output have been manifested in special discounts and concessions. See, e.g., Ovens (above, n. 25), pp. 3–5. But so long as output is concentrated in a few strong companies, accounting for their profits to concessionaire governments, price discrimination of this kind is likely to be minimal.

36. For a lucid and convincing analysis, see UN, ECE, pp. 11–20.

allowables that kept domestic prices from falling, domestic integrated firms were forced to endure a lower utilization of their own production investments and to forego the tax advantages of percentage depletion, while being compelled to buy a larger proportion of their requirements at the artificially sustained price. They naturally complained.[37]

The problem for the oil industry today and for the future is how this disparity in costs and the ever-growing volume of Middle East oil can be accommodated to the world and United States pricing systems without jeopardizing the substantial advantages in various tax allowances that the international companies have long enjoyed. With no arbitrary limit on the volume of United States imports, prices in foreign markets need never fall below levels governed by domestic quotations, and the fiction of the linkage with the Caribbean could be projected into the future. But with limits imposed on American absorption, it is inevitable that the pressures for increased output, abetted by a larger number of somewhat weaker oil producers, should force prices to break away from their Western mooring. The trend is marked by the recent posting of product prices in the Persian Gulf for the first time. Some of the hazards for the international companies of this unwanted freedom in the pricing of crude have already been noted. The logic of the United States taxpayer offering special inducements to exploration abroad, which benefits primarily foreign consumers and widens the gap between American and foreign price levels, can hardly go unquestioned. The consequences for crude oil prices, themselves, may even prove to be among the minor effects.[38]

37. Thus the Standard Oil Company of Indiana, with no foreign production and two-thirds of its production in Texas, where output was most severely cut back, protested the substantial increase in crude oil imports and called for "statesmanlike conduct on the part of major crude importers" (*Annual Report*, 1953, p. 12). Sun Oil, also without foreign sources, alleged a loss of $3½ million after taxes attributable to Texas cutbacks in production allowables which forced the company to purchase crude that it might otherwise have produced (*Annual Report*, 1953, p. 4). Consequently, Sun asserted its intention to increase imports in 1954 in contrast with importer-producers who declared for more modest programs in the interests of "statesmanship" (see "Four Majors Schedule Import Cuts," *National Petroleum News*, June 9, 1954, p. 18). Sun has continued critical of Texas cutbacks (New York *Times*, June 27, 1954, sec. 3), as was Atlantic Refining in 1948 prior to its own foreign production (McLean and Haigh, pp. 199–200, 686) and also Phillips and Deep Rock in 1953 (see their *Annual Reports*, 1953), with only a hope of foreign oil at that time through their participation in American Independent Oil Company.

38. With Middle East governments opposed to price reduction and individual operators quite certain that any lower price in Europe would be met immediately, there is little prospect that competition will result in wholesale crude oil

SUMMARY AND CONCLUSIONS

This examination of the pricing of crude oil in the domestic as well as the foreign area has revealed the predominant influence of administrative policy considerations in the shaping of price changes and the central role assumed by the large integrated firm. In the foreign area, where a few giants have pre-empted the great bulk of production and have controlled as well the other levels of the industry, even through retail distribution, these policies have been frankly to maximize revenues within the limits set by the level of United States Gulf prices, the measure of the availability of the only meaningful alternative source of supplies—the Caribbean. As the vast potential of the Middle East has soared and particularly as in the last few years foreign oil has come into weaker hands, this price structure has been modified; but the link with the Gulf has not been destroyed. It is quite impossible, therefore, to exaggerate the importance of the procedures and forces that have combined to determine the latter price, and through it the structure of petroleum prices throughout the world. In this determination, public authority, in scattered state jurisdictions but most weightily in Texas, plays a crucial part. Here converge all the conflicting interests in crude oil markets. How much will Sun or Continental or Atlantic be taking out of Texas? How much will they get via imports? How much will the independents be permitted to produce? How much will the international companies bring in? It is the Texas Railroad Commission that must make the marginal yet ultimate decision—the number of

---

price reduction. And with European product price maxima pretty effectively set by Caribbean prices plus transport, it seems unlikely that crude prices will be raised importantly until higher U.S. Gulf prices for crude and products ease the way. See UN, ECE, pp. 24–39, for an analysis of the structure of European product prices.

It is possible, of course, that Persian Gulf prices might be raised at least to a level corresponding with the pre-Suez emergency differential, perhaps somewhat higher to allow for reduced tanker freight charges. With an effective political limit on U.S. imports from the Middle East, there is little advantage in the lower relative price of Middle East oil except perhaps to solace American integrated importers with a lower contract price. On the other hand, prices may be held down by rising output abroad and competitive weakness associated with more independents in the Middle East, including the small U.S. members of the consortium, lacking international marketing facilities. It is claimed by American oil men that imported oil is available at significant discounts from going prices of U.S. crude oil. See "What Price Oil?" *Economist* (July 6, 1957), pp. 49–51, and, strongly emphasizing expectations of declining crude oil prices, "An Abundance of Oil," *ibid.* (October 26, 1957), pp. 327–329.

days Texas wells will be permitted to produce at MER. It is this determination from month to month that presages whether prices will weaken or firm both here and abroad.

It has been seen that these forces have generally converged to sustain or boost prices, even when current supplies were easy. Since production allowables are administered with no overt consideration of price, there is never a formal presentation of the case for and against a price increase before an impartial body, or a critical analysis thereof, before the critical decisions are made. The adequacy of the crude oil price should be judged in the total situation affecting demand and supply and in terms of what is happening and likely to happen to exploratory and development effort at home and abroad. Too often, instead, it is appraised casually in terms of domestic cost trends that have no necessary relevance for the adequacy of profit, even less for the adequacy of future supply.[39]

Consider the kinds of evidence relevant to determining the appropriate level of the crude oil price at the end of 1956, on the eve of the increase. Some indications of an upward trend in costs in the years immediately preceding were noted in Chapter 8. Despite these trends, there was no apparent insufficiency of drive to find and develop oil resources through 1956. Both total and exploratory well completions reached new records in that year and gross discoveries of liquid hydrocarbons were exceeded in only three years during the preceding decade, while gross discoveries of natural gas were exceeded in none.[40] Ex-

39. Only obfuscation results when, for example, President Rathbone justifies the 1957 price increase by showing that "total U.S. producing costs" had risen 72 per cent while crude prices were rising only 6 per cent between 1948 and 1956. See mimeographed copy of his statement to the subcommittee on Antitrust and Monopoly of the Committee on the Judiciary, U. S. Senate (March 6, 1957), p. 7. Had he selected 1947 as a base instead of 1948, he would have shown a crude-oil price increase of 42 rather than 6 per cent by 1956; and had he slipped the base back to 1946, the crude-oil price rise would have shown up as 95 per cent (Computations from U.S. average annual prices as recorded in *Petroleum Facts and Figures,* 10th ed., p. 101.) It is not suggested that either 1946 or 1947 is an appropriate base for a comparison of cost and price increases of crude oil; but it is suggested that 1948, when oil industry profits were at unprecedented levels (see above, p. 192, n. 52), is almost uniquely inappropriate in the absence of specific justification.

40. The pessimist, of course, can stress the relatively small discoveries of new fields and of new pools in old fields (especially for crude oil only, where the 1956 figure was exceeded by all but three years during this same past decade). From the viewpoint of drilling incentives, however, it is almost self-evident that both oil *and* gas discoveries must be assessed. Yet various industry studies purporting to estimate increasing costs of exploration, development, and

ploratory and developmental activity did slump in 1957, for the first time in fifteen years,[41] but this occurred *after* the price increase! The reason of course was the general excess capacity in the industry. This induced Texas to cut back production allowables sharply after March, a decision influenced by rising imports which were importantly induced in turn by the high level of domestic price compared with the delivered costs of foreign crude! In these circumstances and faced with diminished production and demand, it is not surprising that domestic drilling slumped, for the first year since 1943, despite the higher price. As one of the producers approached by the *Wall Street Journal* picturesquely put it: "If you've got your cellar full of potatoes, there's not much need of planting any more." [42] The economic justifications offered for the price increase were obviously of questionable validity.

Exuberance in the continuing search for oil despite rising costs no doubt owes a great deal to the special tax advantages that are available to this industry, whether it operates at home or abroad. As already noted these advantages are of two general kinds, and the two supplement each other. First, there is the privilege of charging against income from any source the entire capital cost of exploration and drilling where wells turn out dry, and all intangible exploratory and development costs. Second, without regard to such charges or whether or not they are capitalized in the company's books, the firm is entitled to offset against income 27½ per cent of the value of hydrocarbons produced so long as the allowance does not exceed 50 per cent of net income.[43] Since one always has the option of percentage depletion, which is unaffected by costs, the expensing of intangibles does not amount to a mere tax deferral as in the case of accelerated depreciation. The cash flow is continuing and substantial—an effective

---

production apparently divide estimated aggregate expenditures by the production of oil alone. Thus no part of the joint costs is allocated to natural gas, the sales revenue from which accounted for 10 per cent of aggregate revenues of crude and gas marketing by the thirty-three companies surveyed by the Chase Manhattan Bank in 1956. Coqueron, *Annual Financial Analysis, 1956*, p. 9. On the consequences of including gas discoveries in the calculation see above, p. 182, n. 33.

41. The last years in which total wells drilled dropped below the level of the year preceding were 1942 and 1943. Exploratory wells had dropped slightly below year-before levels in both 1942 and 1954, but the decline of more than 10 per cent in 1957 and again in 1958 was far deeper and protracted than either of these.

42. (October 9, 1957), p. 1. See, along the same lines, *ibid.* (November 5, 1957), p. 1; and *Oil in Canada* (September 30, 1957), p. 3.

43. See above, Chap. 7, p. 154.

way to build asset values free of tax and a mighty inducement to reinvest earnings in the business, increasingly important as incomes and taxes rise and inflation-proof hedges become more scarce.

It is not the individual wildcatter but the corporation, which, owning the lion's share of depletable properties, receives the preponderance of direct benefit from the depletion allowance.[44] Nonetheless, the wildcatter, who does most of the exploring,[45] benefits indirectly as well, and heavily so. With the combined option of expensing dry-hole costs and intangibles, of selling the properties on which his search has proved successful at a price reflecting the advantages of percentage depletion to the buyer, and of paying only a capital gains tax on his net receipts, the wildcatter too is provided a powerful inducement to look for oil and gas.

These tax inducements undoubtedly have the effect of enhancing the flow of capital into crude oil exploration and production and hence of holding the price of oil lower than it otherwise would be.[46] This would be true whether the industry were typically integrated or not. In the presence of integration, percentage depletion has another effect that may have significance for this analysis of price-making forces. In the markets for crude oil the integrated firm is both a buyer and a seller. As a buyer it would be expected to press for a low price. But as a seller the same firm might be expected to seek a high price. For an integrated firm that is both buyer and seller, as well as a taxpayer, where is the balance of these contrasting interests? Is there some measure of the probable weight of the firm's interests in the level of the price? [47] Clearly, such a measure must depend on the degree of crude-oil self-sufficiency of the firm: that is, on the ratio of

44. In 1950 the Secretary of the Treasury estimated from a survey that corporations made 80 per cent and individuals 20 per cent of all depletion deductions. Quoted in Lowell Stanley, "The Independent Producer's Position," in Joint Committee on the Economic Report, *Federal Tax Policy for Economic Growth and Stability*, p. 479.

45. See above, p. 172.

46. See the papers by Arnold C. Harberger, "Taxation of Mineral Industries," and James R. Nelson, "Percentage Depletion and National Security," in *Federal Tax Policy for Economic Growth and Stability*.

47. Although these questions are posed for a single firm, the subject at issue is the motivation of integrated buyers in the pricing of crude oil—a function in which a measure of discretion has been shown to exist, and motivation may therefore be expected to have an influence on results. Cassady in his only references to the effect of integration on petroleum pricing seems to assume that the integrated companies are always interested in keeping prices low. See pp. 123, 127.

owned crude produced to the amount used in its refineries. It will also vary with the extent to which a higher price for crude oil is passed on in the prices of refined products. Using oversimplified assumptions,[48] it appears that if the rise in the former is not passed on in the price of products at all, a balance between gain and loss from the rise in the crude oil price will be reached for income after taxes when crude-oil self-sufficiency is 77 per cent. Above that percentage, the price rise would increase after-tax income; below it, after-tax income would fall. Further, as the price rise in crude is reflected more completely in higher product prices, the percentage of owned crude needed to make the increase beneficial in after-tax income will fall: if as much as 50 per cent of the price increase can be passed on, anything more than 38.5 per cent self-sufficiency would make a higher crude price beneficial.[49]

48. It is assumed that (1) corporate income taxes are paid at 52 per cent; (2) the increase in realized deductions for percentage depletion is the full $27\frac{1}{2}$ per cent of the added price (in reality, the limit of maximum realized depletion would be somewhat less because it is allowed only against income from the specific property and never in excess of 50 per cent of net income); and (3) sales of products are not reduced in volume by any increase in price resulting from the change in crude prices (total demand is in fact generally price inelastic but certainly not completely so).

49. Let X equal the added price of crude in dollars per barrel; let Y equal the percentage of X that is realized in product sales per barrel of crude; let Z equal the number of barrels of owned crude needed for each barrel of purchased crude when gains and losses are equal.

Then: *Realized gain after tax* for crude oil *sold*
per barrel $= .623X$
i.e. $X - [(X - .275X) \times (.52)] = .623X$
: Realized *loss after tax* for crude oil purchased
per barrel $= .48X$
i.e. $X - .52X = .48X$
: Realized *loss after tax* on *non-integrated* operations
per barrel $= .48X - .48XY$
: Realized *gain after tax* per barrel on *integrated*
operations $= .623X - (.48X - .48XY)$

Therefore, gains will equal losses when
$Z [.623X - (.48X - .48XY)] = .48X - .48XY$ or
$Z (.623 - .48 (1 - Y) = .48 (1 - Y)$

If no part of the price increase is passed on ($Y = 0$), owned crude (Z) will equal 3.36 barrels (i.e. .48 / .623 − .48) or 77 per cent of total crude required (i.e. 3.36 / 3.36 + 1.00). With 50 per cent of the price increase passed on ($Y = .50$), owned crude (Z) will equal .627 barrel (i.e. .24 / .623 − .24) or 38.5 per cent of total crude required (i.e. .627 / .627 + 1.0).

It is apparent that the break-even self-sufficiency ratio will vary from 77 per cent to 0 proportionately as the percentage of the crude price rise passed

There are limitations in this arithmetical demonstration. To the extent that the firm is able to avail itself of less than the maximum depletion allowance, the self-sufficiency ratios shown as necessary to engender an attitude of indifference to a rise in the price of crude are somewhat too low. On the other hand, the calculated figure may be much too high because higher crude prices will improve the market appraisal of a firm's oil reserves, and hence its credit position, even though this does not show on the books. A rise in product prices can seldom take place without any restriction in sales and to that extent the benefits of higher prices are overvalued; but a rise in crude oil prices seldom occurs without some reflection in product markets, and the relative long-run constancy of refiner margins over the years [50] suggests that crude price increases are generally passed on entirely: so significant ratios of crude self-sufficiency for this purpose decline.

In Table XII self-sufficiency ratios are shown for each of twenty-two majors in 1956 for strictly domestic operations and for their global operations as well. The range among firms is very wide: at one extreme, one of the lesser majors like Ashland Oil and Refining, primarily a refiner, has a self-sufficiency ratio of only 9.6 per cent; at the other, Skelly and Ohio Oil are predominantly producers, with ratios of 155 and 228 per cent respectively. For the group as a whole, self-sufficiency ratios run lower in their domestic than in their worldwide operations. Looking at the five predominant international companies among the seven top refiners (that is, omitting Shell—even though it is the affiliate of a great international company it does not itself have large foreign production—and Standard of Indiana), self-sufficiency ratios range from 42 to 58 per cent in the domestic market alone and 70 to 144 per cent in global terms. In contrast, Standard of Indiana has practically no foreign production and a global self-sufficiency ratio of only 43 per cent. It is quite evident that for the international companies, if not for the majors generally, an increase in crude prices need be reflected very little indeed in product prices for them to benefit. Since depletion is equally applicable to operations of United States companies at home or abroad and since foreign crude oil prices have been closely tied to domestic levels, the international firms must be

---

on rises from 0 to 100 per cent. Thus the break-even self-sufficiency rate will equal the value of $(1 - Y) \times 77$ per cent.

We are informed that Serge Jurenev, of Continental Oil, has made similar computations and reached similar conclusions.

50. See below, pp. 414 ff.

TABLE XII   Production and Refining Operations and Crude Oil Self-Sufficiency Ratios: Twenty-two Major Oil Companies, 1956

COMPANY	NET CRUDE PRODUCTION (DOMESTIC) (000 bbls.)	REFINERY RUNS (DOMESTIC) (000 bbls.)	RATIO OF PRODUCTION TO RUNS (DOMESTIC) (1) ÷ (2)	TOTAL NET PRODUCTION (WORLD-WIDE) (000 bbls.)	TOTAL REFINERY RUNS (WORLD-WIDE) (000 bbls.)	RATIO OF PRODUCTION TO RUNS (WORLD-WIDE) (4) ÷ (5)
	(1)	(2)	(3)	(4)	(5)	(6)
Standard Oil Co. (New Jersey)	159,576	302,682	52.72%	739,320	896,334	82.48%
Standard Oil Co. (Indiana)	93,926	226,614	41.45	97,266	226,614	42.92
Texas Co.	126,484	217,055	58.27	317,982	358,352	88.73
Socony Mobil Oil Co.[a]	87,635	206,317	42.48	221,038	314,378	70.31
Gulf Oil Co.[b]	104,012	202,907	51.26	352,417	244,417	144.19
Shell Oil Co.	110,059	182,184	60.41	111,317	182,184	61.10
Standard Oil Co. of Cal.	100,869	177,329	56.88	269,434	275,657	97.74
Sinclair Oil Corp.	45,124	160,059	28.19	54,854 [b]	163,903	33.47
Cities Service Co.[c]	44,263	94,539	46.82	44,263	94,539	46.82
Phillips Petroleum Co.	48,720	89,584	54.38	54,825	89,584	61.20
Sun Oil Co.	39,031	89,395	43.66	40,579	95,068	42.68
Atlantic Refining Co.[b]	35,344 [d]	75,316	46.93	39,977	75,316	53.08
Tidewater Oil Co.[e]	33,302	65,413	50.91	33,765	65,413	51.62
Union Oil Co. of California	36,760	61,453	59.82	37,728	61,453	61.39
Pure Oil Co.[f]	24,554	55,507	44.23	24,554	55,507	44.23
Continental Oil Co.	50,388	51,596	97.66	56,508	51,596	109.52
Standard Oil Co. (Ohio)	11,178	51,286	21.80	12,292	51,286	23.97
Richfield Oil Corp.	20,743 [d]	44,479	46.64	22,816	44,479	51.30
Ashland Oil and Refining Co.	3,313	45,405	7.30	4,335	45,405	9.55
Sunray Mid-Continent Oil Co.	30,149	38,843	77.62	30,301	38,843	78.01
Skelly Oil Co.	26,168	16,930	154.57	26,168	16,930	154.57
Ohio Oil Co.	34,359	15,526	221.30	35,469	15,526	228.45
Median			51.08			61.15
Ratio of aggregates for the group			51.24			75.87

[a] Excludes from reported refinery runs 1,791,000 barrels run domestically for others, and includes in foreign runs 7,487,000 barrels processed by others for Socony account.

[b] Production figures include some natural gas liquids.

[c] Production figures include natural gas liquids and royalties re-

[d] Includes Canada.

[e] Includes in refinery runs 22,886,000 barrels processed by others for Tidewater account.

[f] Excludes from refinery runs 4,313,000 barrels processed for others.

importantly biased toward higher prices except as economic motivation is tempered with political prudence.

In general it will be found in Part IV that higher crude prices do end in higher product prices. Therefore the break-even self-sufficiency ratios needed for an integrated refiner to benefit from higher crude prices are much below the maximum 77 per cent and probably below even the 38 per cent figure indicated where half the increase is passed on. Within limits set by demand elasticity, thus, most majors—not just the international giants—benefit from higher rather than lower crude prices even though, as they frequently point out, they are typically only about 50 per cent self-sufficient in domestic production. And the converse of this proposition is worthy of note. When product prices are weakening, the greater the self-sufficiency ratio of the integrated refiner, the more it will be in his interest to have the crude price hold firm. His losses will be greater, the greater the responsiveness of crude to product prices; and the situation that spells margin squeeze for the independent refiner is preferable to the integrated firm than regaining normal refinery margins at the cost of a crude-oil price decline.[51]

Thus, there is reason to believe, a self-sufficiency well within the averages for all or almost all the majors in 1956 will effectively dissipate for integrated companies the interest in lower crude prices that one would normally expect of net buyers. Here then is independent reason to agree with Bain, who, in his comprehensive study of the Pacific Coast petroleum industry, found that large integrated firms tend "to establish a rather high level of crude oil prices to protect refined product prices directly and the ultimate imputed value of their own petroleum reserves indirectly." [52] Since majors often buy more than half of their crude oil needs, this conclusion was not self-evident. Indeed, Rostow has implied the contrary, arguing that pipeline control by integrated firms is typically used to hold down crude price levels.[53]

51. This is particularly the case to the extent a reduced price of crude, consequent upon a decline in product prices, would only have the effect of lowering the floor under those prices and permitting them in turn to come down even more.

52. *Pacific Coast Petroleum Industry, 3*, 43.

53. "The level of pipe-line rates is a measure of the forces required to keep posted prices for crude at an appropriate minimum." *A National Policy for the Oil Industry*, p. 65. See also Rostow and Sachs, "Entry into the Oil Refining Business: Vertical Integration Re-Examined," p. 882. Bain found no evidence of such an effect in California (*Pacific Coast Petroleum Industry, 3*, 46), but,

Price changes since the war have been much too few to permit firm generalization from experience alone; but the instances examined, saving only Phillips' abortive attempt to raise prices in the already phenomenally profitable year of 1948, serve to support this conclusion regarding the majors' interest in a high price level for crude. Thus the trade press in 1953–54 was full of exhortations and applause from major oil company leaders in support of production cutbacks that eventually approached 2 million b/d of shut-in capacity and had the effect of entrenching the price rise initiated by Phillips in the midst of a plentiful supply.[54] Phillips at the time was producing 52.8 per cent of its crude requirements. When, after repeated cutbacks in refinery runs had failed to buoy up a "sloppy" product supply situation, gasoline prices were cut in July 1954, it is consistent that the first important firm to post a lower crude price was Ashland Oil and Refining Company, which had produced only 7.5 per cent of its refinery throughput in the preceding year and was suffering from a serious margin squeeze.[55]

Typically it has been the large integrated firm, and especially the major with foreign oil sources, that has argued for production cutbacks before the Texas Commission in opposition to the independent producer. On the occasion of the Suez emergency the reversal of this general position of the parties, for reasons discussed, was so exceptional as to call forth particular comment.[56] With the cessation of

---

as we shall argue below, the conclusion seems to us by no means inapplicable to the period before 1940 or 1935.

54. The following were typical: ". . . president of Shell Oil Company . . . said he thought the recent cut-backs were 'a step in the right direction' . . . Oklahoma crude purchasers threatened to reduce purchases regardless of what rate of output the corporation commission permitted. As a result, a 65,000-barrel-a-day dip was ordered . . . The 10-day shut-down ordered in Kansas drew praise . . . 'Kansas did a magnificent job' said one major oil company head." See "Most Industry Leaders Agree Oil Production Cutback Must Continue for 2 to 4 Months to Avert Price Break," *Wall Street Journal* (October 8, 1953), p. 18.

55. New York *Times* (July 10, 1954), p. 17. In the Midcontinent area, a nonintegrated firm, Ben Franklin Refining Company, led the decline (*ESPA Weekly Letter,* July 23, 1954, p. 1), followed by Rock Island Refining Company, Sinclair (which produced only 28.5 per cent of its domestic crude oil requirements in 1954 and had a self-sufficiency ratio worldwide of 31.3 per cent) and only thereafter by Magnolia Petroleum, subsidiary of Socony-Vacuum. New York *Times* (July 29, 1954), p. 32. Product price weakness was quickly reversed in August; and these minor slippages in field price postings were not followed by major buyers. The price of crude remained firm.

56. See above, p. 195. For a similar development in early 1958 see below, p. 445, n. 42, and pp. 557–558.

emergency and continued weakness in product prices, it is the majors again, and especially the international majors, who are the support for serious restriction in production allowables, sometimes more than the Texas Commission is willing to order, and it is the independent refiner who is quick to seek a lower crude oil price.[57] Despite the weakness in product prices, the appearance of some striking "adjustments" and a few veiled discounts from posted prices, the trade seemed convinced as of late spring, 1958 that a general cut in crude prices would not occur, importantly because of the opposition of independent producers.[58] It would also have little served the interests of the major

57. "Leonard Refining Company has reduced its prices for Michigan crude 15 cents per barrel. This is the first move on Michigan crude since the price was upped 25 cents per barrel last January." *ESPA Weekly Letter* (August 30, 1957), p. 1. Significantly, the leaders in instituting cuts in posted crude prices in December, with product prices and refinery realizations compressed, were Standard of Ohio, Ashland, Sinclair, Southern Minerals Corporation, and Suntide Refining. The self-sufficiency ratios of the first three, shown in Table XII, speak eloquently for themselves. Southern Minerals is a joint subsidiary of the Pittsburgh Plate Glass and American Cyanamid Companies, which does however produce oil and gas; and Suntide, though owning no producing properties, is 50 per cent owned by Sunray Mid-Continent, which is highly self-sufficient in crude (see Table XII).

It is probable, as the Chase Manhattan Bank analysts asserted at the time, that the cutbacks in production after March 1957 were not drastic or soon enough. Nonetheless, it was estimated that production was cut almost three million b/d below productive capacity (J. H. Carmical, New York *Times*, December 1, 1957, sec. 3, p. 1). Texas alone cut back from allowables of 3,733,054 b/d in March to 2,964,062 b/d in October, with actual production of 10–12 per cent below allowables. From an eighteen-day schedule in March, Texas cut to thirteen days in July through September, and to twelve days in October and November—the lowest production rate in the state since the beginning of public control. See "Oil Cutbacks Pose Problem in Texas," New York *Times*, September 29, 1957. Yet Gulf urged a cutback to ten days and Humble Oil, Sun Oil, and Atlantic Refining recommended eleven days. The other majors wanted twelve days excepting only Sinclair which plugged for thirteen. In permitting a somewhat higher production allowable (though still only a twelve-day schedule) in November than during the previous month (when many independents complained that it meant an effective schedule of only ten days' production in many parts of Texas), Commissioner Thompson stated that the producers' plight could be relieved only by mandatory restriction of imports. "Texas Agency Boosts Oil Output Limits for State in November," *Wall Street Journal*, October 18, 1957.

58. As put by one, "A price cut would start a ruckus that would . . . mean some sort of legislation restricting imports." See "Crude Oil Producers See No General Cut in Prices," *Wall Street Journal*, November 12, 1957. The pressure apparently was strong enough to bring most oil importers into line with government-set quotas. According to Interior Secretary Seaton only two companies—

integrated firms. After more than a year's delay an unprecedented combination of failing demand, rising imports, and a violent compression of refinery margins has forced such widespread reductions in posted crude prices as to erase by February, 1959, *only* about half of the 1957 increase.

It is now possible to answer with more assurance the three questions raised at the beginning of these chapters. In exploration and production, not vertical integration but size is a crucial factor in continued growth. The absolute risk of total loss in drilling a single well is very great; but this risk can be offset by drilling many wells in many fields or alternatively through sharing in many drilling operations. The large integrated firm, the large nonintegrated firm, and groups of firms acting through joint agreements can reduce to a quite manageable cost increment the residual risk involved.[59] With respect to the second and third questions, the large integrated company with a reasonable degree of crude-oil self-sufficiency will have an economic interest in administered rather than competitive pricing for crude oil and in high rather than low price levels. Within limits set by considerations of public relations and the long-run elasticity of demand, the integrated firm, and especially the international firm, may be expected to throw its weight on the side of stability and of rising crude oil prices. Traditional attitudes toward the sanctity of posted prices, the substitution of exchange negotiations for transactions in the market, and the leadership and support of major companies in realizing price advances since the war all support this conclusion. Here it is vertical integration, not size, that puts a crude oil buyer-seller into the psychological position of the producer-seller.

In the absence of a strong bona fide crude buyer interest in the deliberations of public authority (e.g., the Texas Railroad Commission), the cutbacks in production allowables to market demand at a high domestic price threaten not only a vicious upward cycle between prices and costs [60] but also a decline in domestic exploration and de-

---

Sun and Tidewater—had refused to join the program while one other, Eastern States Petroleum and Chemical Corporation, had been unable to comply because of contract problems. *Ibid.*, November 21, 1957. On the crude-oil price "adjustments" in the first half of 1958, which, however, left the basic price structure essentially intact, see below, pp. 443–444, 557.

59. On the alleged high risks of production see the essays of Harberger and Nelson (above, n. 46).

60. The president of the Independent Petroleum Association of America recently estimated that because of fixed costs, unit costs of crude production increased 15 cents per barrel for every day scheduled allowables were cut back

velopment, the stimulation of which is supposed to have been the prime object of recent increases in the domestic crude price.[61] These somewhat paradoxical consequences owe their existence to the unsolved problem of crude oil imports, which the sustained domestic price has made highly attractive. Prorationing and the curtailment of domestic output have enabled cheaper production abroad and improved low cost tanker transport to capture a larger share of the United States East Coast market than they otherwise would; this in turn has induced state regulatory authorities to cut back production even farther. The basic assumption underlying prorationing is an inelastic market demand for domestic production: the opportunity to import vitiates that assumption. International firms, thus cut back at home, merely substituted their foreign production. Others, caught without such alternatives, were forced into foreign areas, not just to preserve their profit margins but also to survive. How this problem should be resolved depends pretty largely on one's attitude toward petroleum conservation, the optimum rate at which to produce domestic oil, and how best to approach it. This is the problem of the next chapter.

---

in Texas. See New York *Times,* September 29, 1957. We return to the two-way relationship between prorationing and costs of production in Chap. 10.

61. See above, pp. 219–220, where the decline in drilling in 1957 is noted and attributed to the simple inability of producers to sell at a sufficiently high rate from their already burgeoning capacity. It is reported that even the big push in the Gulf offshore drilling is beginning to ebb, importantly because the limitations on production allowables will not justify the investment sunk in production wells. These cutbacks in production allowables make the foreign field, where no such limits are imposed, look much more inviting. See "Gulf Offshore Oil Drilling Ebbs as Crude and Refined Stocks Rise," *Wall Street Journal* (November 19, 1957), p. 30.

CHAPTER 10

Conservation, National Defense, and Public Policy

THIS INQUIRY into the impact of vertical integration on crude oil production and marketing cannot yield firm conclusions until certain basic issues of national conservation policy have been analyzed. The problem seems to turn on three overlapping questions. The first concerns the goal of conservation itself. Much has happened since state production controls were imposed; should these changes alter in any significant way our conservation objectives? Closely allied to this question is a second. The purposes of conservation thus far have been sought through prorationing to market demand; in the circumstances confronting the industry today, is that the best way to realize whatever conservation goals now seem appropriate? And finally, does this discussion throw any light on the possibilities of a coordinated policy toward foreign and domestic crude oil, directed toward achieving an optimum balance between the purposes of economic use of resources and national security?

CONSERVATION IN A DYNAMIC SOCIETY

The objectives and rules of conservation are often stated in physical terms, like avoiding the flaring of gas, or preventing production of oil above MER. However, conservation can have no logic as a policy except in terms of making the optimum recovery and use of a scarce resource whose increasing scarcity or exhaustion is feared; and making the best use of scarce resources is an economic question. From this fact two important conclusions follow. First, where a conservation policy is called for, as in oil, the avoidance of waste in extraction is no more and no less important than the avoidance of waste in its processing, distribution, or ultimate use. The process of conservation is logically as broad as the process of economizing with which it is inextricably merged. As long as cost is exceeded by benefit, it may therefore call for many diverse kinds of action: not only the prohibition of "flaring" gas or producing oil above the maximum efficient rate, but also preventing open storage, which permits the more precious components of crude oil to escape into the air; perfecting refining processes to capture higher-valued components of crude oil at the expense of lesser products; developing more efficient agencies for converting fuel into energy, like diesel locomotives; and preventing the use of natural gas for the manufacture of carbon black. In each instance, a larger relative supply is made available for the essential tasks that oil (or gas) is best fitted to perform.

The second conclusion is inherent in the qualification we have already appended to the various possible facets of conservation policy: "as long as cost is exceeded by benefit." An intelligent economic policy —and, consequently, an intelligent conservation policy—can be formulated only in terms of the comparative benefits and costs of alternative courses of action.

It follows that physical loss is to be avoided in the name of conservation only if it also constitutes economic waste. Those who focus attention on the former as opposed to the latter are influenced perhaps by a desire to narrow the scope of public control to objectively calculable purposes, and especially to avoid the extension of state regulatory authority over market forces. This may be a laudable end for other reasons but it may produce economically nonsensical results. For example, it has been noted that the average recovery of oil from the reservoir runs currently at about one-third; and it cannot be doubted that improvement in this record of physical recovery is an object of conservation. But it is equally clear that the percentage of oil to be recovered could be pushed too high—that is, to the point where the added opportunity costs of scarce resources applied in recovery and frozen by a slower rate of extraction would exceed the added present value of the extra oil to be gained.[1] Thus even the maximum efficient rate can be given meaning as a guide to public policy only

1. A particularly difficult question is posed by the flaring and venting of casinghead gas for lack of a market—a familiar phenomenon in the United States before World War II, and in foreign production areas still. It is estimated, for example, that 500,000,000 mcf of gas—well over $50,000,000 worth at current U.S. average wellhead prices—is physically lost in this fashion every year in Venezuela. Obviously the physical loss of gas that could be cycled at lesser cost to increase the recovery of a greater value of oil constitutes economic waste as well, and could occur on a large scale only because of the rule of capture. But it would be economically questionable to forbid the physical loss of gas that it is profitable neither to cycle nor to sell, or to shut in the production of the associated oil for that reason. The cost of not producing the oil that involves such a physical loss of gas is, in effect, the resources that would have to be devoted to producing substitute fuels; not producing the oil may thus involve no physical loss, but it clearly involves an economic cost.

in terms of economic alternatives. Of course, historically, the losses of energy from physically inefficient recovery have been so extraordinary that the dictates of efficiency and economy have clearly coincided. The economic purist, however, may rightly point out that delays in recovery, in the interests of MER, involve an economic cost, a cost which conceivably may not be worth incurring. Alternatively, the MER rate may be uneconomically high: slower rates of recovery, saving oil for more valuable uses tomorrow at the expense of less valuable uses today, may maximize the net current value of economic benefits over time even though in no way changing the physical efficiency of recovery.

An economic criterion of conservation denies the adequacy of any unchanging physical rule, but it does not provide a ready-made alternative yardstick of objectively and irrefutably demonstrable superiority. What is considered an uneconomic loss of energy will vary from one time to another with the estimated real cost of available supply and the weight of opinion with regard to the adequacy of ultimate reserves in the light of future alternatives. If reserves and alternatives are believed to be severely limited, a plausible case could be made for the flat prohibition of certain product uses, like that of natural gas under boilers where an almost inexhaustible fuel like coal could be employed, and the preservation of the scarcer natural gas for purposes in which its cleanliness, convenience, and controllability are difficult to match.[2] An exaggerated view of the imminent exhaustibility of petroleum supplies undoubtedly affected attitudes toward conservation in earlier days. But improving technology has been able to match ever-mounting demands for petroleum in war and peace and proved reserves have continued to increase both at home and abroad.

This rising aggregate of proved reserves of course provides no measure of oil available for emergency use. Depending on the nature of the structure, it would take years—in some cases decades—to produce the amount of the proven reserve even if we neglected the requirements of efficient recovery. How rapidly and how steadily it may

2. See, e.g., the dissenting opinion of Justice Jackson in *Federal Power Commission v. Hope Natural Gas Company,* 320 U.S. 591 (1944), pp. 628 ff. The relevant point here is that stringently restricted prospects of future oil supplies would raise the discounted value of its prospective future uses and, correspondingly, the sacrifices of present uses that would be justified. The decision of whether such sacrifices would best be effected by the particular proposal mentioned, or might be effected by the market itself, invokes numerous considerations, economic and noneconomic, that do not have to be appraised here.

be drawn upon is a matter of conjecture in which the experts are not of one mind.[3] On the other hand, proved reserves are not the measure of our total ultimate oil potential either. They are little more than a protecting film between our satisfactions and our needs, a film that must and can be continuously renewed. It is rather in our continuing ability to add discoveries in excess of current production, not to mention the prospect of imports from the unstrained potential of foreign reserves, that promise for future domestic supply resides.

In the further development of our domestic crude oil potential, no improvement in technology promises more certain gains than the methods now being applied, sometimes at the very beginning of the development of a new field, to increase the percentage of the oil in place that can be raised economically.[4] Some of the newer methods are still in the testing stage and their full technical and economic effects have not been measured; but it is certain that they will mean a substantial boost in our proven reserves [5] and in the rate at which those reserves can be produced on a sustainable basis. Next, it is now claimed that only a few cents per gallon (remember there are 42 gallons in a barrel) at the refinery divide crude oil operations from the commercial processing of oil shales. Drawing on the pioneering

3. A. L. Nickerson, President of Socony Mobil Company, deflated national shut-in productive capacity of 2 million b/d in 1955 (as estimated by the National Petroleum Council) to 600,000 b/d on a sustained basis. See above, p. 160.

4. The Interstate Oil Compact Commission estimated that recoverable oil reserves could be boosted some 40 per cent by applying generally pressure maintenance techniques now used for only 19 per cent of domestic crude production. New methods vary from water flooding, the use of detergents to "wash" oil from reservoir rock, the "thermal recovery" of highly viscous oil through combustion of part of the oil to various kinds of "enriched gas" injection. From something like 50 per cent of the oil on the average in the case of water recovery, new methods promise up to 98 per cent recovery where reinjection of enriched gases like ethane, propane, and butane are used. See Netschert, *The Future Supply of Oil and Gas,* and the sources he cites; also *Business Week* (October 13, 1956), pp. 63 ff.; and *Petroleum Press Service* (December, 1955), p. 452. For an estimate that fluid injection techniques *economically feasible* as of January 1, 1958, would increase recoverable reserves by 42.3 per cent, see the authoritative paper by Paul D. Torrey, "Evaluation of United States Oil Reserves as of January 1, 1958," presented on June 23, 1958, at the midyear meeting of the Interstate Oil Compact Commission, Salt Lake City.

5. Remember that proven reserves are estimated at the average recoverable ratio of 32.7 per cent; i.e. the estimated oil in place, at the base of the proved reserves figures, is approximately three times the amount of the latter. See above, pp. 176, n. 16; 180–181.

work of the United States Bureau of Mines, the Union Oil Company of California has built a $7 million plant in Colorado, and if its expectations are realized, huge reserves of oil shales would practically remove any fear that this country will run short of oil.[6] Shale oil is but one instance in the ferment of technological change and experimentation in alternative sources of liquid energy. Some oil men believe that the commercial prospects of shale oil are less imminent than those of releasing the hundreds of billions of barrels of crude oil now frozen in the Canadian Athabasca sands. Unlike the product of shale oil processing (kerogen), which requires costly refining to convert into usable oil, the product of the tar sands is true oil and, once it has been separated by heating, it will continue to flow. Now under negotiation is a proposal to use an underground atomic explosion to "mine" the sands on a mass production scale. If it succeeds, a vast new source of crude oil will be released within the American hemisphere. Even neglecting more distant prospects of atomic power, these possibilities serve to suggest the near-future ceiling that a supply of synthetic oils will impose on rising costs of crude oil.

It is only in the light of these supply prospects that an intelligent conservation policy can be formulated. Complacency in this situation would be foolhardy; but what seems obvious is that conservation cannot be fruitfully regarded as the protection of a limited stock for future use. Even if it were true that the total stock of oil were known and fixed for all time, intelligent conservation policy would still involve an economic balancing of future benefits against present costs of a slower rate of use. But the one thing reasonably sure about the future is that its schedule of values and its pattern of scarcities will differ markedly from our own. And though this does not justify neglect of conservation, it does indicate that we cannot wisely sacrifice current freedom of choice in the use of oil against so uncertain a future contingency. Mere non-use, in order to have more tomorrow, seems particularly foolish. Furthermore, the prospective supply situation challenges the view that we cannot afford to risk the loss of such stripper production as might disappear with any reduction in price—a

6. Even at the present stage of technology, Union Oil estimates 67 to 70 billion barrels of shale oil recoverable from the richest formation; the U. S. Geological Survey estimates over a trillion barrels from ore containing over 15 gallons per ton in Colorado, Wyoming, and Utah. Problems and prospects of shale oil along with other synthetic sources are discussed in more detail in Chap. 11.

familiar contention whenever the possibility of price reduction is raised.

The proponents of prices high enough to keep strippers going have not demonstrated to our knowledge how high a price would be required to preserve how much ultimate production—that is to say, they have offered no basis for weighing the benefit to be gained against the cost of such interference with a free market. Rather they have implied a purely physical criterion of conservation: the avoidance of any physical loss of potential supply, regardless of cost. Some aspects of the cost to be considered are: slower rate of withdrawal from flush wells necessary to maintain price, the greater use of resources implied in sustaining stripper production that would be closed down if more economical sources of supply were permitted to take over the market, the lesser total use of oil at the artificially sustained price, and the greater consequent use of other fuels. The burden of proof of economic desirability surely falls on those who would interfere for this purpose.[7] Loss of production or reserves of stripper wells in the event of a crude price decline is a highly questionable magnitude.[8] In any case against the uncertain value of this marginal supply there must be set the heavy opportunity costs of assuring its preservation.

Conservation, then, is fundamentally an economic concept. It can mean nothing more than economizing itself—in this context, maximizing the present net value of a stream of income flowing over time from the exploitation of scarce resources. In this respect it is analogous to but far more difficult than the planning of investment, which likewise involves the balancing of present costs against future income.[9] Conservation policy with respect to a particular resource, whether reproducible or not, thus involves the balancing of all the variables implied in this definition. In the case of oil, it would be necessary to make the best possible estimate of the additional future flow of benefits from

7. On the relatively low proportion of national production coming from the two-thirds of all producing wells characterized as strippers, see above, p. 68, n. 14. These wells in 1954 drew upon an estimated 3.7 billion barrels (or about 12 per cent) of prime reserves, and an undoubtedly lower proportion of the national total counting ultimate secondary recovery from known fields. *Petroleum Facts and Figures,* 12th ed., pp. 122, 123, 139, 144.

8. Some such wells may operate on a subsistence basis insensitive to price change, some have a long-run potential that would justify capping without fear of loss, and some would certainly be lost; but estimates of how many and how much fall into the last category apparently have not been made.

9. For an elaboration of the thesis that the underlying economic calculations are identical, see Anthony Scott, *Natural Resources: The Economics of Conservation,* Toronto, University of Toronto Press, 1955.

the added supplies that particular conservation practices would make available—a calculation dependent in turn on estimated future availabilities and prices of oil and its substitutes, and the respective costs of appropriating them—and of the proper discount factor, reflecting the cost of waiting, to apply to those benefits. These discounted values must exceed the present costs of producing and using less oil and correspondingly more of the more expensive alternatives today. Fortunately, it is beyond the scope of this monograph to explore the ramifications of such a calculation; but the mere statement of the problem is enough to breed some tolerance for the rules of thumb on which administrators have relied in practice. It also serves to support a general disposition to leave these complicated calculations to the self-interest of businessmen in competitive markets except where the market process can be clearly shown to produce serious distortions.

THE ADMINISTRATION OF A CONSERVATION POLICY

Prorationing of production to market demand has brought stability where there was chaos, and it has forced on buyers a ratable taking of oil without which correlative rights of lessors in the oil of a reservoir would, and often did, succumb to discrimination.[10] In the process, public authorities have scotched many wasteful practices—the dramatic reduction of flaring gas in Texas to less than 5 per cent of production in 1955 is an example—but they have also buttressed rising prices by production cutbacks in the face of unused production capacity, and they have flouted both conservation and the efficient exploitation of oil resources at minimum capital cost by permitting the small surface landowner to prove his claim to oil with the drill. To keep oil in the ground that might otherwise burden storage and to assure balanced withdrawals from reservoirs in conformity with MER will contribute to conservation but it is not enough. Excessive drilling must be prevented if gas and water drives are to be conserved and these vital forces must be replaced, where economically feasible, through secondary recovery. This is in fact the trend. With added knowledge, more of science and less of compromise apparently goes into public regulation. Since 1945 the Texas Railroad Commission has held at least annual hearings in setting MER's in each producing field, and controls over the spacing of wells have been more effectively enforced.[11] Yet as late as October 1957 the president of the Standard

10. See, however, above, pp. 196–197, nn. 62, 64.
11. Throughout its history, the Texas Commission has been overcareful of the correlative rights of individuals and both the state well-spacing regulations and the field regulations have been repeatedly violated by exception, granted

Oil Company of New Jersey was able to talk about possible savings of $360,000,000 in capital costs and $10,000,000 in annual operating expenses through the drilling of fewer wells in Texas alone in 1956 —an estimated saving of thirty-five cents for each barrel of crude oil produced in that state in that year.[12]

Controls remain oriented to market demand, with consequences never more paradoxical than those observed in 1957: production was cut back substantially from MER's in order to bolster a shaky crude oil price, itself advanced allegedly to compensate for higher costs and thereby to stimulate domestic exploration and development; and domestic drilling fell off in favor of foreign drilling because domestic production allowables were so limited relative to the required production investment that development was rendered decreasingly compensatory. The regulatory agencies were not to be envied in the task they set for themselves—to protect exploratory incentives—in a situation where they were forced in effect to choose between reduced prices and painfully curtailed production. It is no wonder they urged restrictions on imports.

Among the critics of prorationing to market demand from the viewpoint of conservation, none has been more vigorous than Eugene V. Rostow, of the Yale Law School.[13] He believes that conservation is

---

especially to the small land-owner or lease-holder. The Commission has been criticized for the number of such exceptions and for its failure to insist on unitization where land ownership or leaseholds would not permit minimum well spacing. The tendency to allow at least one well to each plot without regard to spacing cannot but penalize those who do obey the law, since such individuals share in the field allowable in part on a per well basis. (Most frequently, however, the Texas Commission formula for well distribution of the field allowable is based on 25 per cent for the well, 75 per cent for the acreage.) In newer fields, wells are often as few as one for every forty acres, sometimes one for every eighty acres. See Hines H. Baker, *Wolverton Hearings*, p. 44, and Robert E. Hardwicke, "Market Demand as a Factor in the Conservation of Oil," reprinted in "Price Increases in Petroleum Products," *Hearings*, subcommittee of the Committee on Banking and Currency, U. S. Senate, 81st Congress (June 29–30, 1949), pp. 53 ff. Also Zimmermann, pp. 279–290.

12. "Our Untapped Oil Reserve—Greater Efficiency," a speech by M. J. Rathbone, before the annual meeting of the Independent Producers Association of America, mimeographed (October 29, 1957), p. 5. See, in a similar vein, E. B. Miller, Jr., "Do We Produce Oil as Cheaply as We Know How?" *Petroleum Engineer* (July, 1958), pp. B-44–46.

13. *A National Policy for the Oil Industry*, chaps. 5, 6, 13. Bain (*Pacific Coast Petroleum Industry, 3*, chap. 6) takes a more moderate view. For him, some form of public limitation of production to market demand is essential to conservation even under unitization, whose more extensive application he favors.

served only incidentally and secondarily by the prorationing laws. Real conservation, he concludes, can be realized only if each field is treated individually, with the number of wells and their spacing, and the flow of oil from every well, adapted to the geologic structure. Variability in these conditions makes impossible any uniform rule of thumb on a statewide basis; and the conflict of private rights of small landowners has in any event effectively prevented the application of such general rules as have been formulated by state regulatory agencies.

The goal of conservation is perverted, in Rostow's view, with any restriction in production allowables below MER; and it is flagrantly thwarted by the failure of public authority to devise and enforce regulations, with respect to the spacing of wells, that are scientifically adapted to the structure of the reservoir and its most efficient exploitation. Taking his examples from early court cases, he concludes that prorationing is no more than the "rationing of a quota" in violation of expressed limits on the acts of signatory states in the Interstate Oil Compact "to the purpose of conserving oil and gas and preventing the avoidable waste thereof within reasonable limitations." [14]

Rostow has used strong cases to prove his point. The reader will remember the early weakness of public authority to curb production, let alone the right of an owner to drill on his own land. He will also recall that controls had to be imposed on a situation both physically and psychologically very much out of hand. And he will recognize that much of the professional and engineering knowledge that goes into the designed development of an oil reservoir and the setting of an MER, still importantly an art and not a science, was to be developed after the Rowan and Nichols cases.[15] In the early days of control, equitable considerations necessarily compromised conservation objectives. The fact remains that prorationing to market demand has stressed the economic waste of produced oil (a legitimate but not an exclusive element of conservation as it is defined herein) while in

14. *A National Policy for the Oil Industry,* pp. 36 ff. The cases were *Railroad Commission v. Rowan & Nichols Oil Company,* 310 U.S. 573 (1940), and 311 U.S. 570, 614 (1941). Ninety-eight per cent of the field allowables in the first case and 75 per cent in the second were allotted on a flat per-well basis, and the Texas Commission had adjusted production allowables on exception from its general rules in 65 per cent of the cases. Thus equity and not conservation had predominated in these decisions. No wells were cut below 20 b/d, and wells with allowable production ranging above this minimum were scaled back by a uniform percentage calculated to bring aggregate field output within the aggregate allowable based on estimated market demand.

15. See Hines H. Baker, *Wolverton Hearings,* p. 43.

varying degrees condoning economic waste in competitive development of the reservoir. By allowing the market absorption of oil at established prices to determine production allowables below MER, it has, without conscientious consideration of the public interest in price, served to implement the price policies of the large integrated firms and to accommodate the import programs of international operators. In so doing it has run the risk of sustaining excessive prices, resulting in economic wastes along lines just described. In the light of supply alternatives that now confront us, it is necessary to inquire whether some other form of control more compatible with public interests should not be devised.

Implicit in the criticism of prorationing is a recognition of two alternative methods of regulation: one is simply to restrict production controls to prevention of output above MER; the other would require mandatory unitization of all fields on natural drive,[16] within which production above MER might or might not be proscribed but supply otherwise left to competition. It is proposed here to pay no attention to the first alternative for two reasons. First, since MER is only a partial guide to conservation, state commissions would be relieved of none of their present duties, including the critical one of regulating the spacing of wells. Second, in the absence of output control, the law of capture would virtually force withdrawals to the full amount permitted by MER, and ratable taking would be undermined in the event output exceeded transport facilities or current demand.[17] There seems little advantage in eliminating prorationing in order to restore, even if only within the limits of MER, the rule of capture that makes it impossible for individual well owners to exercise prudence in exploiting our national resources. The states now committed to prorationing to market demand [18] could argue with good reason

16. Unitization would presumably be useful for the same kinds of fields as are now subject to prorationing, and pointless for stripper wells. It should be possible to provide a basis for expert determination of the appropriate dividing line between the two categories.

17. The preservation of ratable taking is essential not merely in equity but also in the interests of conservation since unbalanced withdrawals create irregularities in the encroachment of gas or water in the reservoir that jeopardize potential recovery. Conservation is poorly served when producers are forced to produce and sell because of the rule of capture at prices much below their long-run average total costs, or below the value to them of holding the oil for future sale. Intelligent choice between present and future sale is essential for conservation. Unitization does and production control restricted to MER does not permit the operator to make a rational production-sales decision.

18. Of the first nine oil-producing states, Texas, Oklahoma, Kansas, Louisi-

against even this limited restoration of that discredited principle.

Rostow proposes that the law of capture be supplanted by mandatory unitization. The "organization of companies and cooperatives in which all surface owners would share on an equitable basis, either in proportion to their surface ownership or to the richness of underlying deposits," would be required by federal statute, with "technical inspection services" provided and administrative procedures prescribed for determining the boundaries of oil-producing units.[19] Once all fields were unitized, each would operate autonomously; over-all limitation on production within MER would cease, and supply would be left to free competitive forces. Single control over an entire field would preclude the vicious consequences of the law of capture and permit enlightened self-interest to assure scientific well-spacing and economical secondary recovery in the development and exploitation of reservoirs. Assuming feasibility, there is no doubt about the desirability of unit field development from the viewpoint of conservation.[20]

The proposal for mandatory unitization on a national basis would command the support of few and would stimulate the opposition of many.[21] Already explored is the conflict of interests that separates the

ana, and New Mexico operate under statutes that specifically define waste or expressly authorize production control in terms of reasonable market demand; Wyoming and Illinois specifically deny intent and authorization to use market demand; Arkansas is silent, and California has been unable to enact a general oil conservation law. Eleven states seem to fall in the positive group, three in the negative; and several states' conservation statutes do not mention market demand. See Hardwicke, "Market Demand as a Factor in the Conservation of Oil," p. 57.

19. *A National Policy for the Oil Industry*, pp. 119–121.

20. Where mineral rights are reserved to the state, this matter can be handled effectively in the grant of concessions; where (as in this country, except on government-owned lands) such rights are reserved to surface owners, unit operations could be upset by a dissident minority unless there were some provision for making it mandatory. Compulsory unitization authority exists on federal lands and is exercised by some state commissions like Louisiana and Oklahoma, but in most jurisdictions, including Texas, unit operation is merely permissive. In a survey of unitized oil-field conservation projects as of January 1, 1955, the *Oil and Gas Journal* reported 278 units with 1954 production of 208.4 million barrels and estimated reserves of almost 5.3 billion barrels (roughly 9 per cent and 17.9 per cent of comparable U.S. aggregates at that time). It was estimated that recoverable oil for these projects would be increased by unitization from 27.5 to 46.3 per cent of oil in place. Data reproduced in *Monthly Business Review*, Federal Reserve Bank of Dallas (April 1, 1956), *41*, 53.

21. Something of the furor to be expected hit California in 1956 when a proposal, submitted to public referendum, to create a three-man state commis-

small, nonintegrated operator from the large integrated firm and the suspicion with which the former generally views the latter. The majors are generally in favor of rationalization of oil production, for reasons almost self-evident, and almost every large firm is involved in some unitized operations—required on federal lands, negotiated on a voluntary basis where conditions were felicitous or jointly undertaken in foreign concessions. But even the large firm is likely to oppose a mandatory scheme rooted in federal law. The fear of federal control is no less today than it was when Doherty's proposals along these very lines were squelched by the Directors of the API back in the twenties. And finally, the state commissions and the state governments would almost certainly oppose such a surrender of authority. This formidable array of interested opposition casts doubt not on the validity but on the political realism of such a proposal; it also helps to emphasize why unitization must be mandatory if its potential benefits are to be realized.[22]

An important substantive problem in the unitization of a field is the determination of its limits, vertical as well as horizontal. The potential of a reservoir is never accurately known and its limits will be ascertained only by drilling over a period not of months but of years. There is no way known to science, other than the drill, to answer this question. More especially where the number of surface owners is large or leaseholds are minutely subdivided, the determination of who should and who should not become members of the cooperative group and on what basis they should participate becomes both complex and uncertain. Basically, of course, the problem of physical participation in the underlying oil can be determined in the same fashion it has always been—by drilling. If oil is struck elsewhere in the same structure, the unitization agreement must be enlarged to include the new area; if it is not, that particular property is excluded. The operation can never be as neat as it would be in the exploitation of a single concession such as characterizes foreign operations. But the unitized development of a reservoir need never be as cluttered with multiple

---

sion empowered to control well-spacing, to fix MER's, and to order unitization when owners and operators of 75 per cent of any pool favored it, split the oil industry of the state into two highly combative groups. See *Wall Street Journal*, October 25, 1956. The proposal was rejected by a large majority.

22. Were this not the case, a few well-placed surface owners could bar the setting up of a unitized plan, use their leverage for discriminatory advantage, or sap the resources of the pool from outside its boundaries. Instances where nonconformists have been able to draw first water and then oil to their properties from voluntarily unitized operations are not unknown.

offset wells as the development of our domestic oil resources has been under the law of capture, after as well as before 1935.[23]

It is late in the exploitation of oil in this country for the institution of so drastic a reform. During the hundred years of our oil history a multitude of rights and expectations have evolved with regard to ownership, investment, and development of oil lands. Mandatory unitization may well expect a rocky road in the courts, like prorationing before it. Moreover, a great deal of the damage has been done: the need for this reform may seem to have been greater twenty years ago than it is today. But the latter consideration is no warrant for further delay, if the proposal is sound. No one knows how long oil will continue to be found and produced in this country; but it is known that it will be increasingly costly and subject to progressively stiffer competition from foreign sources. It is the more important that nationwide unitization with its promise of smaller investment outlays and higher recovery rates should be initiated.

In his own defense of compulsory unit operation, Rostow emphasizes that under such a system the adjustment of supply could be left to competitive determination under the guidance of marginal costs. That is, each field would be produced to the point where the added costs of added output would equal added revenue; beyond this rate of production, net income would decline. While the nature of oil production costs makes such a simple cost-revenue adjustment less likely than Rostow assumes,[24] the possibility of injecting a stronger element of competition than now prevails into the determination of crude oil

23. The process of initial reservoir development under mandatory unitization would probably require a strict accounting of all oil withdrawn during the possibly lengthy period in which the limits of the reservoir were being punched out by drilling. The consequent delays could be serious for a small operator—a further inducement for the wildcatter to sell out—even though special allowance could be made for the discovery well. Mandatory unitization implies a limitation on development that might be expected to deter independent exploration; but such a deterrent need be no greater than that imposed by prorationing with the prospect of production allowables far below MER. In either case, new discoveries would need special dispensation in allowable output to compensate for drilling costs.

24. Unlike variable production costs of exhaustible minerals like iron, coal, and copper which are reasonably stable and determinable, the added costs of added output in a developing oil field are likely to be too uncertain and erratic to guide competitive supply adjustments free of destructive consequences. More important, operators of a unitized reservoir could be expected to hold back output if they anticipated a price sufficiently higher in the future to justify the costs of waiting: idle capacity for oil production is not the same as idle production capacity for reproducible goods.

supply demands sympathetic consideration. It has been argued in this study that vertical integration forestalls the impact of independent buyers with an interest in holding supply up and price down; and prorationing implements the integrated producer-buyer interest in a high price and restricted supply. The consequence is a cost-price spiral: higher prices, restricted production, higher costs through underutilization, higher prices. Only the firm with foreign supply is a sure winner. If unitization could break the circle, it might benefit domestic producers as much as domestic consumers.

While it is impossible to be certain, there is some reason to believe that the institution of unitization and abandonment of state production controls below MER would introduce a desirable competitive element into crude oil production and marketing. There is little reason to fear it would go to destructive extremes: each unit authority would be free from the compulsions of the law of capture; its determination not to sell would be a decision to keep stock underground for sale at a more propitious time. Indeed, even though unitized fields would probably be measured in hundreds, it seems unlikely that the managers of each could ignore their price impact on the market. Even apart from the possible interrelations of unit operators, widespread common ownership interests in many unitized fields and recognition of comparative price inelasticity of demand for crude oil might encourage restriction of production and high price levels. On the other hand, the national character of the United States market, the interests of small land-owners in production up to MER, and the inevitable increase in the pressure of imports, could undermine such tendencies toward restrictionism even though the same large companies operated several unitized fields.[25]

It is not necessary to choose between these two possible effects, for in neither case does it seem likely that the tendency toward higher price and underutilization of productive capacity could be stronger than it is under prorationing to market demand. Indeed, it would

25. This result could be better assured, perhaps, if no firm were permitted to operate more than one field; it could be made much more certain if, as Rostow recommends, integrated firms were forced to divest themselves of crude oil properties. In the latter event there would be a rebirth of buyer interests in crude markets, with refiners pressing for freedom to import, and large refiners at least would be both ready and able to play one unitized producer against another. Divestiture might prove necessary also if there remained a serious problem of discrimination by integrated companies in purchasing oil between unitized fields in which they have and those in which they have not important ownership interests.

almost certainly be weaker, once the use of the sovereign power of the state to restrain the divergent interests of independent producers —domestic and foreign, if import regulations are altered as recommended below—were abandoned. Similarly, it seems unnecessary to demonstrate that mandatory unitization would reduce the regulatory responsibilities of the states, even though this seems a likely consequence. The objective is not to lessen regulation per se; it is rather to focus both regulatory authority and private self-interest on the real objectives of conservation—the most economical development of a reservoir and the most economical recovery of its oil and gas. It would nevertheless remain for public authority to help constitute and enforce the unitization agreements, perhaps to compute and police the observance of MER's, to determine the conditions under which a unitized field might eventually be returned to its owners for individual operation, and, if need be, to make use of the antitrust laws if operators of the very numerous unitized fields collaborated with respect to production policy or price.

COORDINATION OF POLICY

There is a critical need for a coordinated, consistent policy toward this vital industry. No such policy now exists: what we have instead is a patchwork of interferences, concocted and administered piecemeal, pragmatically, under a variety of influences, by a variety of governmental agencies, directed to a variety of goals—none of them ever fully reconciled. The absence of such a policy is at least partially due to the bewildering complex of knotty issues with which the subject bristles. This concluding discussion will concentrate on four important aspects, notably from the standpoint of their interrelationships and currently inadequate coordination. First are the requirements of national defense, and the costs and benefits of alternative methods of satisfying them. Second is the problem of imports, the notable benefits they promise to our economy, and the thorny issues—economic and political, domestic and international—posed by any policy of restricting them. Third is the problem of conservation, and the consistency of various policies that bear upon it. And finally, there is the problem of administration.

National defense has been offered in recent years to explain and to justify the development of excess refining capacity and the restriction of crude-oil production allowables substantially below productive capacity. The presumed preference of defense officials for supply sources within our own continental borders has served to buttress production and import policies often stimulated by less patriotic motives. Under the indirect methods of control actually practiced, there is little evidence of a causal or systematically planned relation between defense needs, on the one hand, and the policies adopted, on the other. This is unfortunate. Obviously the real needs of the military program must be provided for. But in order to evaluate the indirect benefits for defense of policies adopted largely for other reasons it is pertinent to inquire for what kind of emergency we are preparing. World War II required a pattern of total industrial mobilization over a period of years in which combined military and industrial needs put a premium on the added crude oil production that shut-in capacity below MER made possible. But even here the real reserve capacity was in civilian uses from which oil could be diverted. The shorter the prospective emergency, the less sense it makes to incur the heavy costs of sitting on extremely costly excess production capacity (in contrast with necessary stocks), and the more sensible it would seem to be to call upon normal civilian supplies, as well as to assure the immediate availability of specialized refining capacity to convert into military fuels the crude released from civilian uses. Is either of these patterns relevant to the kinds of war we ought to prepare for—either the brush-fire, local, limited conflict, or all-out war in the age of missiles? In any event, whether for a protracted or for a short war, ought not Western Hemisphere, at least Canadian, production be counted as part of our strategic reserves? What recognition should be given to the fact that the tanker haul from Venezuela to the East Coast is no longer than from the Texas Gulf? And if East Texas crude offers the additional security that it may alternatively move eastward by pipeline, may not the relevant surplus capacity to be reserved for emergency be pipeline capacity rather than domestic, in contrast with Venezuelan, production capacity? We do not pretend to answer these questions; but point out only that the military arguments offered in defense of present policies do not answer them either.

The economic progress of this country is still so intimately dependent on oil that we cannot afford to burden our future with a high-cost domestically oriented program in preparation for military contingencies already made obsolete by scientific advances. Only as volume and timing of major petroleum requirements are related to the probable range of emergencies for which we prepare can oil policy be adapted in a manner designed to secure the optimum blend of strategic benefits and economic costs.

Already discussed at length are the comparative prospects of domestic and foreign sources of oil which, combined with the impressive expansion of our demands, make it inevitable that imports will account for an increasing proportion of our needs as the years go by. But it is important to stress the economic desirability of this trend. The oil that moves in from abroad is cheaper oil. If it does not force down the price of refined products (and this is unlikely as a permanent proposition, at least under current controls), it will certainly help to keep their real costs from rising as increasing consumption is satisfied from this source rather than by forcing more costly domestic production. If the potential benefits from imports are not completely emasculated, by quota controls on the one hand and prorationing cutbacks of domestic production allowables on the other, increasing imports will displace some of our high-cost marginal exploration and production.[26] Under the perverted schema of current conservation controls this is unlikely. In effect, the Texas Commission has brought imports under prorationing; and it offsets cheap foreign crude by withholding production of our cheapest domestic oil—the output of wells on natural drive—thereby taking the pressure off both price and high-cost producers.

This policy makes sense only if it be assumed that the prospects of finding future oil in the United States, or in areas like Canada or even Venezuela within the economic and strategic sphere of this country, are so dim that we must subsidize American exploration at any cost in order to prevent an overwhelming future dependence on "foreign" sources (i.e., the Middle East) which would prejudice our bargaining with such areas, either economically or politically. The prospects of future oil within the American sphere may need more considered evaluation in terms of the impact of freer imports on supply capacity. But the evidence thus far adduced does not warrant a presumption that the price we are now paying is justified for this purpose.

Apart from the possible results of such an evaluation, the policy now followed makes little sense. The oil is in the ground; it won't run away. The higher price (and higher incentive) today will not change appreciably its total availability; it will only hasten the uncovering of resources already held out of use below MER. Only some marginal increment of stripper output might be "saved," of inconsequential

26. Imports could prevent domestic prices from rising as rapidly as would be the case in their absence. In this way, strippers would be gradually squeezed and some might abandon operations. And the more costly exploratory efforts might similarly be discouraged.

(or of negative) value compared with the savings from relying on imports crying for admission.

The petroleum industry points with pride each year to the tens of thousands of wells it drills, at costs running in the billions. This advertisement of so profligate a use of our resources—profligate compared with what it would take to obtain the oil indirectly, by export in exchange for import—seems singularly strange coming from an industry that has made such strides in conservation.

The prospect of increasing imports also opens up new competitive horizons in petroleum which should not be foregone unthinkingly. It has been observed that foreign supplies of crude are tending to get into weaker hands. Through production or contract, American firms with no foreign marketing facilities or inclinations are coming into possession of oil for which this country offers the best outlet. Under proper auspices these supplies could be used to pace the growth of our domestic industry in a manner consistent with both conservation and restoration of competitive markets. It is for this reason that the adoption of unitization for the development of oil fields in this country seems so attractive. With no limit except MER on domestic output, United States and foreign producers could be freed to compete with one another. The result could be advantageous not only to American consumers but also to the efficient domestic producer—who would still enjoy the substantial protection of transport costs at least vis-à-vis Middle Eastern competitors, would be freed from the oppressive burden of discriminatory low allowables, and enjoy the benefits of greater efficiency in the development and utilization of his capacity.

Would this competition be destructive? There are several reasons for doubting it. First, domestic producers would have been released from the pressures of the rule of capture; this would tend to make domestic supply responsive to changes in demand. Second, the overlapping foreign and domestic investments of importers should suffice to prevent market disorganization through dumping or similar tactics. Third, an international trade in oil freed from quantitative restraints means a greatly increased elasticity of demand for the production of individual countries. Price competition between domestic and foreign sources of supply will mean that any tendency for the price of domestic crude to fall will encourage its increased sale and discourage imports: certainly the flight of American refiners to foreign sources of supply has been largely impelled by the artificially sustained domestic price and the discriminatory curtailment of their own domestic production. Thus American consumers would be placed in competition with consumers all over the world, and especially in Europe, for the oil of the Middle East. These higher price elasticities should reduce the dangers of wasteful overproduction of oil that the market is incapable of absorbing economically.

The alternative on which we seem instead to have embarked poses major difficulties. Oil, more especially Middle East oil, is a critical pawn in the cold war. By precept and example we have sought to forge a freer, stronger bond between Middle Eastern countries and the West than nineteenth-century imperialism envisaged. For these countries, long impoverished and underdeveloped, this has meant aid not so much in the form of gifts as in the rapid development of the fabulous resources that American oil men have tapped and an enlarging participation in the fruits of their exploitation. That this country, the professed leader in the new internationalism, should now impose arbitrary, discriminatory limits on the import of Middle East oil hardly strengthens the hand of our State Department. That even stronger considerations of international policy cry out against our limiting imports from Canada and Venezuela goes without saying.

Setting aside the principles involved, the method of curtailing imports likewise continues to be a source of concern. The use of a tariff, perhaps the least discriminatory alternative, has been eschewed largely because it was not feasible to judge the effectiveness of a reasonably low tariff, and the internal regulatory setup was not conducive to price competition over an indefinite front. With domestic unitization, however, a tariff could provide a buffer against excessive imports, if such be required, and at least some federal revenue for the protection allowed. In contrast, maximum import quotas give a more rigid protection, facilitate a more effective offset of imports through State Commission action, and provide greater assurance that the profits remain with the importer. Perhaps these profits help to solace importers for the arbitrary discrimination between companies which import quotas entail in a dynamic industry. Apart from such heart balm, only a deep concern about the alternatives could be expected to elicit compliance with so flagrant an interference with the processes of free enterprise. Since this method of control can only become increasingly burdensome and arbitrary as the number of firms in possession or potential possession of foreign oil grows, quotas must be regarded as no better than a stop-gap measure.

In any reconsideration of government policy toward conservation objectives and imports, attention needs to be given to the size and appropriateness of the special tax inducements now offered to United

States firms on both their domestic and foreign operations. The decline in domestic drilling activity in 1957–58, despite the price increase at the beginning of the former year, suggests that the profitability of finding and developing petroleum for this market are more rosy abroad than at home. To the extent that this is so because of low utilization of production investment in this country, it would be offset by mandatory unitization. To the extent that this is so because of higher domestic costs and smaller discoveries, it would remain partially true even with unitization. In either case, foreign prospects would be relatively even more attractive if there were no restriction on imports. In economic terms, and apart from considerations of national strategy, this means that it is under present conditions wasteful to devote so much of our productive resources to the increasingly costly quest at home. The time to make such heavy investments, if ever, will be when foreign supplies cease to be cheaper than domestic: that should not be for many years. It is precisely the resultant wasteful use of our capital resources that challenges the special privileges accorded this industry. Our tax policy encourages a more rapid exploitation of our oil resources than would otherwise occur. By holding down the net costs of capital in petroleum compared to other industries, it enables the search and production of crude oil to attract capital long after investment has ceased to promise returns before taxes—and therefore a contribution to the national product—as high as such capital provides elsewhere. Because of special allowances against taxable income from (or devoted to) oil, it takes a lower return on capital before tax in oil to produce the same return after tax as in other industries.[27] In the midtwenties, when these exceptional allowances were devised, the extraordinary risks of petroleum exploration and development and the needs of the economy may have appeared to justify such differential treatment. But since that time the trend of risks has been lower (especially for the large firm), while the tax preferences (with rising tax rates on corporate and personal income generally) have become increasingly valuable, and it is difficult to find economic justification for special subsidy to this particular industry.

If these special allowances make a questionable contribution to conservation in the domestic sphere, they are even more vulnerable to criticism when applied to foreign operations whose full benefits are denied United States customers by public authority. The transforma-

27. See A. C. Harberger, "The Taxation of Mineral Industries," Joint Committee on the Economic Report, *Federal Tax Policy for Economic Growth and Stability,* esp. pp. 439, 441.

tion of foreign royalty dues into foreign income tax assessments, which can then be applied completely to eradicate federal income tax liability, serves merely to emphasize the tax contribution that this government is making toward foreign oil development. In the face of a policy that seeks severely to limit our benefits from imports, it is difficult to see that these tax inducements accorded United States companies operating abroad make any sense at all. They become a kind of concealed and hence irrationally distributed foreign aid program.

Thus far no concerted effort has been made to develop and administer a coordinated policy toward the exploration and development of crude oil. The industry, mistakenly in our view, has continued to espouse or accept makeshifts—anything to keep the federal government out of the picture to the greatest extent possible. The Congress and the Executive stress the *ad hoc* arrangement—the most limited kind of temporary action needed to preserve relative quiet among organized dissident groups. The Railroad Commission of Texas, by virtue of its position and the default of others, continues to make room for imports by curtailing Texas output enough to prevent too much pressure on the domestic price which it scrupulously leaves out of formal consideration. These problems deserve and will ultimately receive more responsible consideration. The availability and the cost of oil and natural gas are so central to the realization of our economic goals, and the integration of foreign and domestic supplies of petroleum is so vital to the success of our defense and broad foreign policy objectives that they cannot be left to the chance determination of public bodies responsible for only a part of the problem, or to private managements, no matter how enlightened their self-interest may be. A reasoned solution demands a comparative weighing of alternatives, no one of which is an absolute good. Overemphasis on any one will bring marginal benefits purchased at excessive cost on other fronts. A balanced and coordinated approach is essential in the public interest.

SUMMARY

It would be presumptuous to claim that this analysis has conclusively resolved any of the issues with which the discussion began. But here are the conclusions to which it seems to point.

First, the crude-oil price structure, both within the United States and outside our borders, is artificial in the sense that it is set by policy and maintained by administrative action, rather than determined by competitive adjustment to costs. It is one of the fables of this industry that prorating production to market demand is not price control. This same semantic sophistry is extended to world oil price structures as well.[28] Within the United States, production allowables have ranged 15 to 30 per cent below what output might be without endangering maximum recovery. In the Middle East no one knows how much production might increase—except that it undoubtedly would be phenomenal—if development were pushed to the full limit of its physically optimum potential. In both cases actual prices are announced by individual companies subject to market acceptance. But it cannot be doubted that if public authority did not contract domestic supply to whatever extent required, the market would not accept that price. It is exactly because public authority takes no cognizance of what the price level should be that there is no proper economic appraisal of either its output decisions or the price it supports. For this reason prorationing provides neither the substance nor the scope of public control needed to protect the public interest today.

Second, crude oil markets are so organized and dominated that a dependable downward (that is, buyer) pressure on price does not exist. The vertically integrated firm dilutes the impact of independent refiners on crude price through its methods of price quoting, its control of pipelines, and its use of exchanges. Percentage depletion and the normal tendency for higher crude prices to be reflected in refined product realizations have apparently converted the economic interests of vertically integrated firms from those of buyers to those of sellers —the more so, the higher their crude oil self-sufficiency. Since the State of Texas itself has a substantial tax interest in higher prices, prorationing to market demand, with its ostentatious disregard of price and its denial of public responsibility for it, becomes a public vehicle

---

28. The industry's views were fairly well summarized in "The Sinister Oil Cartel," *Fortune* (October, 1952), pp. 113–114, which expands the argument of Walter Levy that "The price of Middle East oil will normally fluctuate between a high that will just permit Western Hemisphere crude oil to be shipped to Western Europe, and a low that will permit Middle East crude to move into the Western Hemisphere." What *Fortune* and Walter Levy overlook in arriving at this "normal" with its competitive overtones is that the situation described is no more compelling and no more stable than the common production policy that it reflects. The volume of Middle East oil production and the extent of its market share in the United States and abroad have certainly not been limited by comparative costs, although it almost certainly reflects a calculation of long-run comparative profits. For similar reasons it is quite impossible to predict the point at which potential tariffs on cheap foreign oil would become prohibitive.

for the implementation of policies initiated by private firms in their own interests. The search for alternatives to prorationing is a search for some means of reinvigorating buyer interests debilitated by vertical integration and restoring competitive pressures for more efficient crude oil development, presently frustrated by public regulation of output.

Third, despite probable widespread opposition and important administrative difficulties, we strongly favor mandatory unitization for all producing pools throughout this country under federal law. Production control should be limited to prohibition of output above MER and minimum well-spacing should be required of every unitized operation; conceivably, these goals might well be realized through self-interest without intervention of public authority. We advocate so revolutionary a break with the past reluctantly, but see no other alternative that would as fully encourage proper conservation objectives, remove the duress of competitive intrareservoir withdrawals, and revitalize self-interest in both efficient development and competitive production and sales within the limits of MER.

Fourth, then, and setting aside possible defense complications, the abolition of quota restrictions on imports of crude oil and refined products is urged. With the domestic industry organized in unitized fields and free to compete within the limits of MER, removal of arbitrary limits to imports should provide an envigorating and socially beneficial downward pressure on petroleum prices. As long as vertically integrated firms still dominate in both domestic and foreign production, both as operators of unitized fields at home and as importers and shippers of foreign oil, it is hardly to be expected that this new competition would ignore the lessons of a generation and that firms would abandon overnight the self-restraint they have demonstrated in importation and in the development of crude oil resources abroad. Nonetheless, shifting the effective control of total supply out of the hands of the Texas Railroad Commission to the operators of the various unitized fields means shifting it into weaker hands, no matter how large the operating firms may be. Since foreign supplies are likewise slowly shifting into weaker hands, removal of import quotas should provide the catalyst for a highly desirable reinvigoration of competition at home.

The possible abandonment of some marginal stripper production would be a small price to pay for these benefits. If some cushion is needed—the burden of proof must rest with the claimants—an import tariff of reasonable amount, or even a direct subsidy limited to those who require it is preferable to a quota. The main differences between a tariff and quotas, imposed by "voluntary restraint" or government threat, are that the tariff permits price competition to continue to operate, as the quota does not; does not freeze economic growth and change, as the quota does; and forces the importer to share some of his monopoly profit with the government. Lacking a reasonable and reasoned basis for import policy, the federal government has chosen the pusillanimous course of insisting on "voluntary" curtailment—a holding action that puts off difficult policy decisions, that abdicates to the several states the determination of national supply (and therefore price), and that equivocally calls on the large firm to play the role of statesman that our elected legislators are unwilling or unable to assume. Imposition of compulsory quota controls in March 1959 represented a more forthright course of action; but it makes no more economic sense than the policy it supplanted.

Fifth, the potential interference of defense requirements with the development of a coordinated program of domestic production and imports is so serious that it calls for careful and critical review at the highest levels. National defense has too long been used, by indirection, to justify the uncritical projection of the dominant policies of the Texas Commission.[29] Questions have been raised about whether the development of large shut-in capacity, along with a continuous encouragement of domestic in preference to foreign supplies, at the expense of every consumer of petroleum products in this country, represents a reasonable safeguard against emergencies we are likely to face; or whether it represents an unimaginative preparation for the *last* world war.

But if it is decided that national defense requires a margin of safety in domestic crude-oil production capacity in being, it is still necessary to seek the least costly method of realizing that goal. Only as a last resort should such a need be allowed to freeze out the competition of the most efficient available sources of liquid energy. Two alternatives are suggested, both of which depend for their effectiveness on a national policy. The first would impose on all wells operating on natural drives a restriction of maximum output to that percentage of MER that would aggregate for the nation the required reserve capacity. The advantages of such a proposal are clear. Responsibility for national

---

29. The rationalization is that the higher prices its policy protects encourage exploratory effort and keep in being the reservoir capacity tapped by stripperwell production, while the shut-in capacity of reservoirs on natural drive provide emergency reserves for national defense.

defense is a *national* responsibility to be borne by those wells which alone can share it wherever they may be located and without regard to the vagaries of state production controls. With maxima set in the manner described and under mandatory unitization, no other quantitative limit need be imposed on production or imports.[30] Without unitization, however, this proposal would fail to assure ratable taking and proper conservation as already indicated.

If, however, the current system of output and import limitations should be retained, it would still be desirable explicitly to determine and enforce the reserve capacity required for national defense. In this case some relief from the resulting burden on private operators could be provided by issuing them transferable import quotas, equivalent to the full amount of their cutbacks in allowable production below MER, over and above their normal allotments. The merit of this proposal from the consumer viewpoint would be that domestic production capacity would in this way be reserved for emergency military use without limiting current market supplies below the aggregate of domestic MER's, plus imports whose quantity would be determined by national policy. The merit from the standpoint of producers would be that they would be compensated for having to carry reserve capacity for a public purpose; their transferable import quotas would have some market value. And equity would be served by making the monopoly profits issuing from quantitative import limitations available to those who served this public purpose. Needless to say, however, failure to require unitization, and the retention of quantitative restrictions on imports, would still deny to the economy the benefits of efficient field development and competition promised by our preceding proposals.

30. It is an open question whether the owners of wells on natural drive can in fact bear this cost, if they are deprived of the indirect compensation that our present regulatory system gives them of a sustained price and a guaranteed share of the market vis-à-vis imports. The elimination of those additional quantitative restrictions on competition might make it unreasonably onerous for private operators to bear the burden of national defense requirements. Such a contingency would however be reflected in dwindling domestic exploratory and developmental activity, disappointing additions to proved reserves, and a tendency for the shut-in capacity therefore to vanish. If such trends became evident, if not before, it might well be decided to provide a direct subsidy to producers, in proportion as their production is reduced below MER. In this event the costs of national security would be placed where they belong—on the nation's taxpayers, who would for the first time more clearly see what they were paying for and what they were getting and perhaps they might then better decide whether the latter justified the former.

Sixth, the national importance of petroleum in war and peace demands a national solution to the problems broached in this part of the study—the problems of conservation, of efficient development of domestic supplies, and of prudent participation in the oil resources of the free world that American enterprise, American capital, and American tax inducements have largely made available. Some important aspects of conservation—restriction of flaring natural gas, better spacing of wells, pressure maintenance, secondary recovery—can be partially realized under state controls; and there have been real achievements along these lines, despite a lack of uniformity in the application of regulations from one state to another. Compared with the situation that prevailed before the adoption of effective production controls, what we have today is in many ways infinitely preferable. But the system that has evolved has played into the hands of companies whose scope of operations exceeds the jurisdiction of existing public authority. In consequence, the efforts of the Texas Commission to adapt production allowables to market demand for the nation has encouraged oil companies to develop supplies free of Texas control, while relying on this same Texas control to prevent these new supplies from undermining an administered rise in crude oil prices. Efficiency has suffered as capital investments in our greatest oil producing state have been partially idled by severe cutbacks in production allowables, and the burden has fallen disproportionately on producers so limited.

It is clear that state controls under prorationing have failed to achieve attainable standards of efficiency in the development of oil reservoirs [31] and that they discourage socially desirable elements of competition in the production and pricing of crude. It is even more evident that state authorities are not competent to deal with problems of national defense or with a national policy toward imports. In making good these deficiencies in public policy toward petroleum, every effort should be made to minimize government controls in favor of release of competitive pressures excepting only that of the rule of capture.

In our view, these goals stand a better chance of attainment if a uniform federal statute governing oil development is substituted for the present multiplicity of state regulations. Such a statute should require unitization of all pools and it should forbid any public regulation of aggregate production (beyond what is explicitly determined to be required for reasons of defense) or aggregate imports. More

31. See chap. 10 of Zimmermann, who on the whole defends the present system against its critics; and above, pp. 236 ff.

than anything else there is needed at the national level a body charged with the responsibility to think through these problems of government-industry relations, including the special tax inducements thus far extended, to formulate a coordinated policy toward crude oil and an effective method of realizing it.

PART III

Investment and Innovation

CHAPTER 11

The Criteria of Investment Decisions

INVESTMENT is crucial to the successful development and growth of the firm, so vital that more than any other function of management it is hedged about with administrative reviews and opportunities for veto.[1] It is difficult to conceive of a major business decision—whether to enter a new market, expand in an old one, or merely protect an established market position—in which investment does not play a central role. This becomes more self-evident when investment is interpreted in its economic sense, to embrace all expenditures made to enhance future earnings—advertising, research and development, personnel training, as well as the more familiar expansion of plant, equipment, and other facilities—no matter how they may be charged in the accounts. The decision to integrate is itself a decision to invest.

The petroleum industry is outstanding in the amount of capital required, to provide for growth and for the high rate of obsolescence attending many of its processes, and in the risk associated with many of its capital expenditures.[2] A prominent defense of business size and integration in oil is the view that they are necessary conditions of efficient marshaling of the funds required for growth and progress, for expansion of facilities, and for innovation, all in the face of unusual risks. A prominent criticism is that integration imposes capital requirements on potential entrants so much higher than would otherwise be needed that it sharply alters the character of competition in oil and

1. Central control of capital outlays has survived the decentralization of managerial responsibilities—one of the most distinctive characteristics of modern large-scale industrial organization. Even the top management of large corporations is often restricted to discretionary expenditures of only a few thousands of dollars without approval of the Board of Directors. After general approval and budget authorization, project expenditures may still face the ordeal of review and subsequent cutback before actual appropriation of funds.
2. Without prejudging the broader issue of whether the aggregate investment over an appreciable period of time by a large oil company runs a greater risk than a similar investment in other industries, it may be observed that individual sums of very great amount can be lost totally in a way that few other industries can duplicate.

product markets. In general Part III is concerned with the first contention, Part IV with the second.

PROBLEMS OF APPRAISAL IN IMPERFECT MARKETS

To some extent a capitalist economy may be described as a kind of automatic, self-governing mechanism, by which, under the guidance of a competitive price system and free capital markets, the rate of saving and capital formation and the allocation of savings between this investment and that are determined in such a way as to maximize total satisfactions. If such markets operated perfectly, it is often contended explicitly or implicitly, the influence of billion dollar corporations, generating almost all the savings they need out of their own profits, pushing ahead this or that investment project to maintain or protect their own market positions, would be unnecessary and capable of producing misallocation of resources. Economically desirable investments would be profitable for the independent, nonintegrated firm, and it would be able to finance them in the open capital market. From this viewpoint, if integrated companies made more extensive capital outlays than nonintegrated operators or outsiders, only because they generated large internal funds or because they had more favorable access to capital, or special incentives for self-protection, the result could only be wasteful overinvestment on their part.

Unfortunately, there is no such easy solution to the problem of evaluating the impact on investment of integration accompanied by size. Imperfect knowledge and imperfect competition are characteristic of all real markets, including capital markets. It is because of these imperfections that the planning and budgeting of capital outlays are such vital management functions, and integration may contribute to their more effective performance. Firm *A,* which integrates several levels of production and processing, may know better than firm *B,* which operates at only one level, what investments will prove profitable for private investment and will meet a continuing public need. Or both *A* and *B* may recognize a socially profitable investment opportunity but, because the market for loanable funds is imperfect, only *A* may be able to effect the necessary financing on acceptable terms. In these instances *A's* advantage would have stemmed from its superior access, because of its integration, to relevant information, and from blocked communications in capital markets—advantages that are real enough while they last, but possibly evanescent, to the extent they depend on temporary or remediable defects in market knowledge and communication. Others may be permanent, inherent in the difference between integrated and nonintegrated operations. Such an advantage would be *A's* superior ability to reduce the real risks or realize the full benefits of investment by fitting a particular project into its integrated structure with consequent mutually sustaining or reinforcing advantages at more than one level of operation. For example, it might pay an integrated oil company, but not an outsider, to turn petroleum by-products into synthetic detergents, carry them to market in its own trucks, and sell them in its own service stations, because the added costs of the project are slight and it already has facilities to do part of the job.

Some of these handicaps to the less fortunate nonintegrated investor may be the result of integration itself. If *A* had not integrated or were denied the opportunity to do so, they might disappear. The existence of integrated refining companies, commanding preferential access to crude oil and blanketing market areas with their own service stations, undoubtedly discourages investments in refining by outsiders. If *A* had to sell its by-products rather than make use of them itself, *B* might buy and process. If *A* had to turn to the market to fill its need for cheaper methods of transportation, an independent pipeline company might then see the profitable opportunity and satisfy that need. Some of the encouragement and stimulus to investment supplied by the fact of integration must therefore be balanced against the corresponding discouragement of independent capital formation. Yet even after this kind of correction, it seems impossible to doubt that because of superior access to knowledge, opportunity, incentive, or resources, or because they already have part of the necessary capacity and it takes relatively little added capital to perform the new function, integrated firms may make investments that would not otherwise be made—investments that may prove economically justifiable in the sense that they add to the social product a sufficient amount of goods and services to justify use of the savings here rather than elsewhere.

Conversely, this proposition means that nonintegrated companies will tend on the average to require some greater inducement than integrated companies—in higher prices, higher prospective returns, greater tax incentives—to call forth a given amount of socially productive investment. The free market guarantees that such additions to social capital as can be privately profitable (in contrast with those that may be socially productive but may not pay any individual to undertake) will be forthcoming; unsatisfied demand will raise the relevant prices until the appropriate amount of investment is made. But where knowledge is imperfect, this mechanism operates haltingly and prices may have to rise higher than would otherwise be necessary to secure a given investment effect. In such markets, integration sensitizes responses and diminishes the range of price inducements required. It introduces a kind of administered economy where the line is more nearly direct from anticipated demand to expanded supply with a lesser necessity for intermediate price fluctuations to induce the appropriate adjustments in the allocation of productive resources. To the extent that the integrated companies guess right, it would seem that they could accomplish the process more efficiently, with less delay, less price fluctuation, less possibility of alternating and wasteful under- and overinvestment than typifies free markets that depend more upon the lagging responses of investors to price movements.

Integration may find economic justification in imperfect markets; but this is by no means the equivalent of saying that it will. It may lead to wasteful capital expenditures. Each outlay may "pay" the individual company in the sense that it protects some other position, ensures a continuation of earnings that might not otherwise continue; yet like most of competitive advertising expenditures that "pay" in the sense that the company that does not advertise will lose sales to the company that does, the net effect may be a wasteful use of society's limited resources. The same is true of the financial self-sufficiency conferred by high profits only a part of which stockholders successfully insist on having distributed to them. This internal source of financing may seem a boon in that it makes possible investments that might not otherwise occur. But from the standpoint of society it may encourage waste. Distributed in larger measure to the consumer in lower prices, to the worker in higher wages, or to the stockholder in higher dividends, the profits could produce a higher level of consumer satisfactions. Adding to the social capital is not an end in itself. More especially in an economy of high productive employment, the public interest demands a lively concern for consumption alternatives to investment. Finally, one must be alert to the possibility that the cumulation of investments and of the power to make them by integrated firms may so leach the prospects of competition from independents as to threaten long-run stagnation for the economy at large.

On paper, no system of economic organization could be more efficient than a monopolistic or centrally planned one. It would be capable of taking the fullest advantage of the economies of scale, yet have no need to go beyond this point. It could eliminate all duplication of investment, selling expenditures, or cross-hauling. It would enjoy the fullest possible knowledge of all production and investment plans because there would be no competitors to keep secrets from it, and the fullest opportunity to dovetail one operation into another because no facilities capable of integrated operation would be beyond its reach. However, the fact that integration *may* produce the most efficient possible planning of investments and a more rapid calibration of expansion of capacity to estimated needs does not mean that in practice it necessarily does produce the economically optimum outcome. In the imperfect markets in which industry must operate, therefore, there are no certain criteria of the kind of industrial organization that will best serve public interests.

THE EFFECT OF INTEGRATION ON INVESTMENT DECISIONS

The unique feature of the vertically integrated firm is that it is an entity. It is comprised of properties of quite different character and location but these properties, especially in oil, are physically meshed to permit the flow of product from well to customer. In contrast, at one extreme, the nonintegrated firm is committed to a single kind of operation; at the other, the holding company may link together by purely financial bonds a conglomeration of quite different businesses, operated as distinct and independent entities. The vertically integrated firm has the unity of purpose of the one and the conglomeration of properties of the other. But in its integration it is different from both. It enters into the business of, say, transportation, or operation of terminals or bulk plants, or retail service station development not for the profit to be gained from each individually, serving outside customers at these various levels, but in the expectation they will enhance the single profit it can earn in the final sale of its own products. Thus while it may temporarily—indeed permanently—have capacity available for outside service at one or another or several levels of its operations, this is likely to represent unbalance—a by-product of growth— rather than a commercial commitment of the enterprise to serve such markets.

At the end of their detailed study, McLean and Haigh conclude that the process of integration is "akin to that which may be found at work throughout the entire world of living organisms . . . a progressive adaptation to the physical environment . . . to withstand the relentless pressure of business competition." [3] They emphasize that this organic and continually evolving response to divergent circumstances

3. McLean and Haigh, p. 672.

affecting each company should be "two-directional," involving decreases as well as increases in depth, extent, and intensity of integration from time to time and company to company. What stands out in the history of the oil industry, however, is the underlying *sameness* and unidirectional character of process—not in details of pattern but in the development of an ever-larger, more balanced, and closely articulated whole.[4]

This direction of evolution is, paradoxically, especially probable when, as McLean and Haigh concluded, management's concept of "balance" is typically somewhat tenuous, and "the integration patterns [are] shaped somewhat more by the individual decisions made on the continuing series of day-to-day problems than . . . by general management strategies." [5] It is exactly in the resolution of day-to-day problems that the incremental approach to decision-making —whether operations or investment—is more likely to be dominant; and where it is, there will be an inevitable bias toward additions of new functions and away from any substantial divestiture.[6] Here is the clue to the basic impact of vertical integration on the criteria of business decision.

In the planning and execution of investment programs, all business units suffer alike from uncertainty of the future and managements' consequent inability to project costs and revenues over the life of proposed assets, let alone to discount these prospective flows to comparable present values. Petroleum companies may suffer more than others in this respect, not from instability of demand—which is for them broadly based in the social and industrial life of the nation—but from the uncertainty of supply, where the best of science is none too good to gauge the presence and the extractability of crude oil. In any event, any firm, in deciding whether or not to make an investment, should seek to assure itself that additions to the future flow of revenues will exceed additions to anticipated costs by amounts that aggregate a present value equal to the installed cost of the capital asset at a discount rate greater than the cost of capital. In the best of circumstances this is not a simple computation to make and apply. But for the vertically integrated firm, there are two additional considerations that must enter into the computation, both derived from the fact that any investment it makes will usually affect more than one level of its operations.

4. See above, pp. 107–114.
5. P. 673.
6. Such a tendency was hypothesized in Chap. 3 (above, pp. 41–44).

An individual investment by a vertically integrated company does not stand on its own feet, and cannot be fully evaluated except in terms of its indirect effect elsewhere. This is the first consideration that integration adds to the investment decision. For example, if part of the justification for adding to facilities at one level of the business (say marketing) is the added income thereby made possible at another level (for refining, pipelines, or even for crude oil), the investment in marketing could prove very attractive financially even though it did not appear to add to nominal marketing revenues *alone* enough adequately to pay for itself. By a parity of reasoning, such a project, justified (or apparently justified) in this indirect way, could induce capital outlays that would not recommend themselves to a nonintegrated company.

Whether one regards this effect as strength or weakness of vertical integration depends on his viewpoint; but irrespective of accounting conventions the integrated firm in fact transfers its products from stage to stage without interstage profit surcharges characteristic of the market. Wherever the nonintegrated firm must pay prices that include a monopolistic profit, the integrated one may obtain a comparative advantage. If the added cost of providing coordination and planning of material flow does not absorb this difference and if the firm operates with reasonable efficiency and volume at each level of production, it might expect to make a higher profit on investment than would its nonintegrated competitors.

To protect itself against comparative inefficiency, the integrated company may set transfer prices between production departments at market prices or their equivalent; but to the extent that one operation really supports another or integration has seriously restricted open-market operations, the company can never be sure what it would actually have to pay for its supplies or could get for its products if it went to the open market. Furthermore, the firm is more than the sum of its parts; much of its costs, including all top management expenses, are incurred and justified for the business as a whole. Thus both nominal costs and nominal profits at intermediate stages are merely imperfect guides to departmental efficiency; real profits arise only when outside sales are made.

The second consideration, and possible source of confusion is the inertia of accumulating sunk costs with less than full exploitation of productive and earning capacities. In the growth of every firm the capacity of production units and of staff and operating personnel can seldom be perfectly adapted to the market requirements of a given function, product or group of products. Imbalances are characteristic and imbalance means sunk costs—costs that need not be increased to permit larger or different output; costs that cannot be avoided if demand should decline or existing functions be given up. For the firm that is not vertically integrated, variable expenses tend to bulk large —these are the costs of acquiring necessary materials or services from outsiders. Vertical integration converts variable into sunk costs: the major part of the cost of crude oil for the refinery has already been incurred by the producing affiliate and cannot be sloughed off by reducing refinery runs. By the same token, integration tends to minimize the incremental or added costs of taking on new functions that promise to complement or make fuller use of existing capacity—that is, to spread sunk costs over a larger volume of business. In this process of enlarging the scope and size of the company's aggregate investment, with each decision resting in part on favorable earnings impacts expected at other levels, the vertically integrated firm may soon attain a size and complexity from which there is no easy turning back. That is, with investments at *each* level of the industry so large that they cannot be liquidated without severe losses both at that level and at other levels mutually supporting, the firm becomes more nearly an organism than a business unit. It must drag its past with it into the future. The relevant issue is not whether to continue to grow, but how and in what direction. In this situation the time span of investment decisions must be lengthened. Ability to foresee the future is not necessarily improved, but the rate of discounting the future is lowered, and as the discount falls the weight of intangibles in the final decision is likely to increase.[7]

Thus vertical integration has a somewhat contradictory effect on

7. Although the following comment by A. D. H. Kaplan, Joel B. Dirlam and Robert F. Lanzillotti, prefacing their study of *Pricing in Big Business: A Case Approach* (Washington, D.C., Brookings Institution, 1958), applies to the analysis of pricing decisions, it seems equally apt in describing the problem of explaining investment decisions as well: "Economists, legislators, and the public generally would like to see pricing decisions by big companies analyzed in logical fashion, with historical comparisons of competitors' prices, cost factors, and profit margins given consistent and quantitative weight in detailed memoranda of officials involved. Unfortunately for those who would insist on fully ordered business behavior, such strategic memoranda summarizing the considerations at an important conference leading to a price decision are rarely found. Perhaps the presumed formal conference was never held. Even where the people doing the pricing tended to have certain staff information placed before them while making up their minds, whether and just how that information was taken into consideration often remained obscure" (p. 5).

the criteria of business decision-making. On the one hand, it may tend toward increasing industrial efficiency by bringing to bear on the process of deciding whether or not to make an investment at any one point its probable impact on costs and gains at all other points in the industrial process. On the other hand, this broadening of the range of relevant considerations, both in scope and in time, could reduce the accuracy of predictions and multiply the possibilities of double counting of benefits among investments at different, mutually dependent levels. Whenever the prospects of quantification are dulled, the door is opened to the irrelevancies of personal interest and bias and the inefficiency that accompanies them.

EFFICIENCY AND INTEGRATION

Because of the diffusion and vagueness of its impact internally and the absence of an objective external market standard, no aspect of vertical integration will remain more controversial and elusive than its "efficiency."

McLean and Haigh deal at length with the "managerial and operating gains" this form of organization makes possible.[8] The advantages they describe do not flow from a physical linking of processes like the saving in heat from a combination of blast furnaces, open hearth furnaces, and rolling facilities in steel. Instead they are primarily logistical: they arise from better planning and more efficient coordination of operations and investments. Superior knowledge of the final market at many points and managerial control of successive levels of operation certainly make possible significant economies of this kind. The nonintegrated refiner must depend much more on the estimates of final demand reflected back through the changing orders of his wholesaling customers. The integrated firm can act with greater assurance on the basis of its own estimates of the ultimate market situation. It can plan its respective investments in refining and seasonal storage so as to assure the most economical use of its combined capacity by producing to stock when demand is low. A nonintegrated rival might do the same. But the former, controlling transport as well as market outlets, need not accumulate its stocks at the refinery, where they will be subject to transport bottlenecks; it can spread them through the territory to correspond with anticipated sales volume. It need not rely on the willingness of independent marketers to stock up in the

8. See their chap. 11 and p. 674; also James S. Cross, "Vertical Integration in the Oil Industry," *Harvard Business Review, 31* (1953), 69, 77.

off season. The result may be lower capital costs and greater efficiency of operations through a more constant use of available capacity.[9]

These advantages are particularly attractive in an industry forced by the nature of its product and technology to place an unusual emphasis on continuity of flow. The fluidity of oil and its products, the enormous volume of their continuing movement, and the essentiality of smooth synchronization of its almost entirely automatic processes make it difficult to conceive of a business system that did not provide assurances of continuous supply of material and acceptance of product.

Before the benefits of integration are chalked up as evidence of superior efficiency, however, it is necessary to note an inherent weakness of any such calculus. There is no available objective standard of the relative efficiency of integrated operations: least of all would be the actual performance of nonintegrated companies in the limited markets of an industry dominated by the majors. The controls which the latter firms secure over supplies of crude, pipeline transport to refinery or market and market outlets are real advantages to them, but they may have been secured at the expense of others: vertical integration itself augments the risk which it then serves to neutralize.[10] The lower costs thus achieved are strategic, not social advantages; they reflect less the efficiency of this form of business organization than the disadvantages of nonintegration imposed by the pre-emptions of the integrated companies.

Furthermore, one cannot neglect the fact that many functions undertaken by the vertically integrated firm would be performed in its absence by market specialists. The elaborate paraphernalia of market analyzing and logistical coordinating machinery of integrated companies could be a burden rather than an advantage, a cumbersome substitute for the specialized services and information that a more freely functioning market provides all participants. And the financial strength which permits a Standard of Indiana or a Gulf or a Shell to weather important errors of management that might have forced the collapse of firms less well established at more than one level of industry operations, will equally tolerate waste and inefficiency that may be offset in earnings by favorable contingencies elsewhere.[11] The

9. See McLean and Haigh, pp. 312–318.
10. See above, pp. 44 ff.
11. See, e.g., McLean and Haigh's respectful account of the lengthy analyses that enabled Standard of Indiana to conclude that it had been losing business for several years because its prices were too high (pp. 211, 215, 217, 219); and

major oil company thus has a heightened survival potential bolstered by imperfect capital markets, entirely apart from its superior or inferior efficiency compared with its nonintegrated rivals.

STRATEGIC VERSUS PUBLIC ADVANTAGE

Imperfect markets inject into business activity an element of uncertainty that arises from lack of control (that is, the prospect of control by one's rivals) of raw materials, transportation, processing, or marketing. Vertical integration is both a cause and a response to this uncertainty. It seeks to achieve security, dependability, and assurance of supplies and markets by financial control of critical suppliers and distributors; and, to the extent it is successful, it narrows the market for others and places in jeopardy those rivals who have not done likewise. If no companies were vertically integrated, it would be far less urgent that any of them should be. Here is a possible wedge between private and public gain from investment. The pursuit of security and dependability of supplies and of markets is a strategic consideration. It may result in higher utilization of a firm's capacities and skills and lower costs of operation. But these ends may be accomplished by financial absorption of previously independent operators or by pre-emption of scarce factors—sites, materials, skills—effected through greater financial resources rather than greater efficiency. If this is true, the strategic advantage of the firm is not a net advantage for the public.[12]

On the other hand, society may well gain from activities which spring from the desire for strategic gain. The quest may lead rivals to uncover new sources of supply, to build new and more efficient media

---

Indiana's slow and clumsy response to its loss of market position throughout the twenties, thirties, and forties (*ibid.*, pp. 210–222). See Gulf's massive "carefully coordinated" (*ibid.*, pp. 96–97) expansion of marketing facilities in 1928–31 in order to "find an outlet" for its mounting production of crude, the serious strains it imposed on the company's resources and the losses resulting (*ibid.*, pp. 377–380).

Shell was another company that seriously overextended its marketing operations into areas it was ill fitted to serve. It suffered heavy deficits in the early 1930's and thereafter embarked on a massive withdrawal, rationalization and decentralization program. See, e.g., "How Shell Builds Oil Marketing Profits," *National Petroleum News* (May 19, 1954), pp. 28–36.

12. It is correct to say that integration becomes increasingly important as markets become less free; but it is not true that free markets would rob integration of all competitive value. E.g., real efficiency gains of combining operations would still force competitors to emulation.

of transportation and more modern refinery and marketing capacity. Idle capacity could result from investments so motivated, as when a refiner integrates into marketing by building a string of service stations and leaves his former distributor-customer's service stations high and dry. Quite generally, however, the expansion of capacity in oil has been so paced by growth in total demand that it would be difficult to lay at the door of integration any general tendency to wastefulness of this kind.[13] Even if the search for strategic advantage takes the form merely of acquiring former suppliers, customers, or competitors, the acquisition may result in a fuller and more productive use of society's resources in the service of consumers.

Difficulties in sorting out social from strategic advantages are well illustrated in Sinclair's purchase of the Wood River Refining Company in 1950, an acquisition cited by McLean and Haigh as an example of the "managerial and efficiency gains" from integration. They point out that Wood River was worth far more to Sinclair, because of the way it would fit into the latter's operations, than to its previous owners, so that its transfer enhanced "the economic value of the refinery."[14] The advantage to Sinclair was clear enough: an efficient processing unit for its Wyoming crudes at the terminus of the Platte pipeline, of which it was part owner, and near its marketing operations in the St. Louis area. But the handicaps of the Wood River Company, which made it anxious to sell, were essentially strategic: it was having trouble finding assured sources of crude oil and market outlets. It is a reasonable question, then, whether society would have been any worse off if Sinclair, instead, had sold its crude oil to independent refiners like Wood River and if the marketers in the area, whom Sinclair had bought up in the late 1920's, had been free to buy the products of independent refiners like Wood River. It is not clear, in other words, that the transfer increased the efficiency with which the oil industry satisfies the public except in the sense that it may have removed inabilities to serve the public attributable to vertical integration itself.

Had Sinclair not followed the path of integration, however, might not the reduced value of its investment in differentiated facilities and brand name involved public as well as private loss? Some would answer this question with a clear negative; but the case is far from certain. There is no compelling presumption of social advantage from the private gains of an imperfect market, of course, but the persistence

13. See below, Chap. 14, for a more detailed appraisal.
14. P. 310.

of price differentials between major and independent brands suggests some social value in established national brands of gasoline. Sinclair's pursuit of its own strategic advantage here served to increase the flow of Wyoming crude oil, to lower its transport cost (through construction of the pipeline) and to broaden the availability of a major brand in the market.[15] Even though this portion of its program displaced a weakly competitive independent, one would have difficulty in concluding that society was not benefited by the change: some would say that the effectiveness of competition had been improved rather than attenuated.

These alternative interpretations of the Wood River acquisition are really arguing on two distinct levels. The favorable interpretation looks at the individual merger in the context of a given industry. The unfavorable one asks whether such a merger would have been either necessary or socially beneficial if the structure of the entire industry were altered. The independent might not have been so weak and dispensable a competitor had it not been surrounded by integrated firms who could not be depended upon to sell it crude oil or market its products. The fundamental question, then, is whether the integration of its rivals represented simple pre-emption of existing facilities, with no net social advantage issuing, or, instead, a socially creative process. Had integration been prohibited, would the industry have expanded its production, pipeline transport, and marketing facilities for the promotion and sale of widely accepted products at the same or at a socially more acceptable rate, or at lower cost? We return, in brief, to our pending question: the impact of integration on investment.

There is no single or objective criterion by which to appraise the social consequences of investments or of investment policies of large integrated firms. The problem is much like that posed by the concept of workable competition, and conclusions must rest essentially on qualitative judgments. Nonetheless, there are some logically presumptive consequences of such investments that may assist in an appraisal of their social effects. First, integrated firms, especially if they are large, are exposed by their own operations to investment opportunities at all levels of the industry and over a comprehensive area. This

---

15. This particular program was but a part of extensive postwar rationalization of Sinclair's operations: converting obsolescent refineries to terminals, expanding efficient refineries, constructing a complex and flexible network of pipelines, expanding direct marketing in areas efficiently served and contracting in others. See *ibid.*, pp. 303–312.

breadth of exposure could not by definition exceed that provided to nonintegrated participants in perfectly competitive markets; but such markets do not exist in oil and, in their absence, the communication developed within the major oil company is not approximated elsewhere except by other major oil companies.[16] Second, opportunities for investment in the application of new ideas that may have been developed in the research laboratories of the firm or tried out anywhere in the industry are further promoted by the advantage which the large firm enjoys in adding to its staff highly skilled professionals that smaller rivals can muster only as consultants. And the fact that a company *is* integrated, horizontally (geographically) as well as vertically, creates additional assurances that improvements initiated at one level will be used at another. Theoretically perfect markets supply such assurances without any need for integration; but the appropriate standard of comparison here is the real, or the attainable.

Third, with the exposure to investment opportunities that greater communication affords may also go a greater sensitivity of response because of the prospect integration affords of corralling benefits generated by improvement at one level through controlled operations at another. The nonintegrated firm may lower costs by investing in improvements, but its success sets in motion emulative and protective actions by rivals that tend to pass on to customers a goodly share of its initial gain. The integrated firm is better equipped to capture the whole of the advantage at one stage or the next without even revealing its source. If integration accompanied by size may conceal inefficiencies, it may conceal and keep from competition and the public special efficiencies as well. This observation is a variant of the one popularized by Schumpeter, and long embodied in our patent law, that innovation depends on the innovator having some prospect for a time of keeping to himself the benefit of what he has developed; integration may offer similar guarantees, and to this extent induce socially productive investments that would not otherwise be made. But of course this tendency will conduce to social advantage only if administration or competition eventually passes on the resultant gain, in quality or quantity of product available to the consumer. This is only another way of saying that integration is no substitute for competition.

16. The flow of market information from this natural exposure of the integrated firm is augmented by its organization of buying and selling functions performed in part for nonintegrated operators as well as on its own account. See above, p. 184, n. 37.

ACCESS TO CAPITAL

So far as its impact on investment is concerned, vertical integration has been credited above all with conferring overwhelming advantages in the marshaling of funds. Risks at any level of production can be reduced by spreading operations over many fields. Thus an oil company can obtain a more stable rate of return by combining in a single enterprise the diverse margin and profit trends of different parts of the industry. But the remedy is not necessarily vertical integration. Exploration and production may be carried out in many diverse fields and pools; refineries may be widely separated in location; marketing may overlap areas subject to different economic conditions; diversification may be achieved with larger size of the enterprise and thus cushion the impact of loss at any one point. The small firm, whether producer or refiner, will often have difficulty in raising capital while the larger firm, able to spread its risk, has no problem in generating internal funds or raising capital outside. Among producers especially, large and successful companies like Amerada have been quite content to limit their investments in this way to a single functional level of the industry. And investors have been avid to purchase its securities at earnings: price ratios extraordinarily low even for this industry. That other large producing companies have been willing in recent years to sell out to major refiners like Sinclair and Atlantic reflects far more the pressures on the necessitous purchaser, seeking a better crude balance, than on the sellers.[17] The incentives for the latter were fabulous sale prices and the tax advantage of recouping their profits in the form of capital gains; but the wooers were the refiners.[18]

It is only the refiner who seems to find vertical integration a crucial

17. This was less true before prorationing, by strengthening and stabilizing crude oil markets, greatly increased the availability of capital to independent producers. One of the more dramatic examples of the early advantage of the integrated firm was the acquisition of a controlling interest in Humble Oil Company by Standard Oil (New Jersey) in 1919. Despite Humble's position as one of the leading producers in Texas, its own management indicated that when the firm needed funds for expansion into refining it was unable to raise the necessary capital at reasonable rates either in Texas or in Wall Street. It was therefore forced to give favorable consideration to Standard's offer. Information supplied by the company.

18. Note, e.g., Sinclair's estimated $262.5 million expenditures for the purchase of producing companies in 1955–56 and Atlantic's $200 million purchase of Houston Oil, for which it outbid Sinclair. See "They Rush to Get in Balance" (the "they" are the refiners), *Business Week* (September 1, 1956), pp. 46–50.

adjunct to the protection otherwise afforded by size and diversification. The assurances of crude oil supply and the stability of brand-name distribution apparently become critical in the planned operations of the refinery and of pipeline and other facilities associated with it. For the rest the greater stability of gross margins at *all* levels of the industry since prorationing, and the dominant upward secular trend in the consumption of petroleum products, have surely made integration less important from this standpoint than it used to be. The major company probably retains marginal advantages over even the best of the independents (or most of them) in the costs of capital; [19] but these are for the most part the consequences of size rather than of integration. Large income from several different functions would also tend to ensure full use of all deductibles for tax purposes; but, again, any large firm, even a nonintegrated oil producer, can secure the same by an active drilling program.

Nonetheless there are four possible residual advantages of the large, vertically integrated firm in marshaling and applying investment funds that may continue to have significance in the future:

(1) While it is possible to spread risks within any stratum of the oil industry by spreading operations over many fields, refineries, and markets, vertical integration does seem in general to provide an additional tendency to stabilize earnings.[20]

(2) In imperfect capital markets, the conjunction of resources, exposure to investment opportunities and investment decision-making power cannot be assumed. The fact that these investment forces are brought together in the major oil company should add up to a greater volume of desirable investment projects from the public viewpoint than would otherwise materialize.

(3) The opportunity of the vertically integrated firm to exploit an improvement made at one level of operation through several levels, when combined with the volumes characteristic of large size, should support investment at a lower prospective rate of return than would be required by the nonintegrated firm operating at any given level.

19. One can find individual crude oil producers like Amerada whose securities sell at such high ratios to earnings as to suggest they could raise capital more readily than the majors. However, the sampling of producers is not adequate to justify this generalization for producers as a group; and at other levels of the industry there is no doubt that the financial resources of the majors must exceed those of the independents.

20. See the exhaustive analysis by McLean and Haigh, chap. 5.

(4) The management of the vertically integrated firm, using facilities and performing functions common to more than one level of the industry, is likely to anticipate higher net returns and/or lower incremental costs for any given investment than would the management of a company confined to one level. Inevitably, the former will have common sunk costs representing capacities—in facilities, in personnel, in advertising—which it seems can be more profitably employed by expansion. Minimum efficiency in expanding markets will generally call for a scale of operations, a degree of organization and technical and managerial competence, a size of facilities that apparently permit and encourage greater volume with less than proportional increase in costs. Thus the integrated company is always tempted to enlarge the scope of activities under its own control.

APPRAISING INVESTMENT POLICIES

Society expects its industries to produce an adequate current supply of products at reasonable prices; continuously to improve and adapt their quality to meet new and evolving uses; to develop and provide a range of alternatives of product type, of service, and of price available to customers of different needs, whims, and fortunes; and to maintain continuity of supply proportionate with the dependence of the community on them. It is also concerned with the rate and direction of growth over time.

There are no specific standards of desirable or even of minimum acceptable behavior in these aspects of workable competition where economic characteristics of an industry like oil preclude the feasibility of purely competitive market organization. The presence of vertical integration serves particularly to complicate analysis and to invalidate the use of even the most familiar measures of comparative industrial performance. This is especially the case with the use of profits, which might suggest themselves as an appropriate test of the comparative performance—the efficiency or whatever—of integrated and nonintegrated companies as a group, or of the economic merits of integrated company investments at this or that level of the industry. Even from the viewpoint of management itself, alternative profits are defective as a guide to investment decision. But for outside observers, comparative profits are even more questionable standards. Possibly even more than integration, the special tax inducements extended to the production phase of the industry, and especially percentage depletion, further undermine the reliability of intra- as well as interindustry comparisons of net earnings data. It will be necessary to make some use of such information regardless, but it is well to hold clearly in mind the consequent limitations of these comparisons.

No company will generally make an investment unless management thinks it will prove profitable. But entirely apart from problems of forecasting, no measure of profit is any better than the measure of costs on which it is based. This measure of cost becomes more difficult as products multiply and costs common to all increase in importance. Difficulties are maximized when the firm blankets many levels and many markets of the industry. Since the vertically integrated firm is concerned with its over-all profit, a satisfactory measure of profit (or of cost) for particular projects may not be feasible.

Of course, many oil companies have expanded vertically for the specific purpose of reducing costs, and have continued to expand in integrated fashion because their managements believed this was the profitable course to follow. Nevertheless, it is unlikely that their investment decisions can have been made purely on the basis of objective comparisons of costs and revenues over the appropriate time span. Quantitative calculations of the prospective flow of costs and revenues become more elusive when expenditure is undertaken for more than one product and more than one level of production; and, as already observed in this chapter, in such a situation the firmer the general policy commitment to integration, the wider is likely to be the scope of intangible considerations and the tolerance for immeasurables.[21]

21. McLean and Haigh (pp. 137–148 and appendix to table 1, pp. 680–681) have made an heroic effort to wring significance from comparative profit records in the industry, computing rates of return after taxes on borrowed and invested capital for a broad sample of companies, which they classified into six groups depending on the level on which they operated and the extent of their integration. Even among these broad groupings it was not possible to reach definitive conclusions regarding the effect of vertical integration on the average level of oil company profits. In part, as the authors noted, this was because it was not possible to get adequate control groups for nonintegrated refiners, wholesalers and retailers, and producers, largely because published data could be obtained only for the more profitable companies in most of the groups. After prorationing in 1934, profits generally improved both in level and in stability for all but the nonintegrated marketing group; only the refining group, apparently, could have improved its profit situation by further integration backward into crude oil. But the major qualification on all such comparisons was the fact that net profits are strongly affected by many factors other than extent and type of integration—e.g. by ability of management, geographic

The consequence is that cost and profit data for individual operations or investments of the integrated firm are seldom meaningfully comparable with similar information for the nonintegrated company that performs that same operation or makes that same investment. For the former, segmented profits can be based only on essentially arbitrary interdepartmental billing prices. These prices may be copied from quotations in the corresponding open markets in which independent rivals buy and sell, but those quotations do not necessarily reflect the relevant costs or benefits to the integrated company: the single major, and certainly the majors as a group, could not possibly be sure at what prices they would be buying and selling if they were not integrated. For one thing, they would not be performing the same function; for another, if they shifted to the role of buyers or sellers in intermediate markets the markets themselves would be changed. So departmental cost and profit statements for integrated companies are likewise largely arbitrary. The economic advantage of the pipeline over alternative transport media for the (major) companies which usually construct them could be shown as logically in higher prices for crude, lower costs at the refinery, or lower transfer prices to service stations as in profits of pipeline operation. The "profits" shown for accounting purposes as having been "earned" anywhere along the line therefore necessarily offset, or are offset by, reduced book earnings or losses elsewhere. In this sense the integrated firm inevitably "subsidizes" competition at one point from operations elsewhere. But in this sense subsidization also occurs in all business situations, wherever investments or talents embrace more than a single product, service, or market.

A more disturbing difficulty with comparison of profits or net earnings within the petroleum industry and between it and others arises from the special tax inducements which government has seen fit to afford it. With these special offsets against taxable income, oil investments may tend to be pushed until earnings after taxes are comparable with opportunities in other industries; that is, before-tax returns on oil investments tend to fall below those in non-subsidized employments. Certainly the prospect of tax-free cash flow from depletion and the privilege of charging intangible expenses associated with exploration and development against income before taxes have helped to induce heavy investment in this stage of the industry. Furthermore, since oil companies typically charge as operating ex-

location of facilities, size of operations, availability of funds for expansion, and luck.

pense, rather than capitalize, all dry-hole costs and all intangible exploratory—and sometimes intangible developmental—expenses in computing the net income they report to stockholders, net income as recorded may be regarded as understating the tax-free cash flow from the business available for purposes of additional investment.[22] Accounting procedures like these distort comparisons of profits between producers, whether integrated or nonintegrated, and other nonproducer segments of the industry. Also, they distort comparisons between the petroleum industry and other industries not so favored. The nature of the distortion is difficult to characterize with certainty, hence difficult to correct for. On the one hand, reported profits of oil production companies before or after tax may be regarded as understated because current expenses have been increased by expenditures which might well be treated as investments elsewhere. On the other hand, these special tax inducements may have served to induce a condition of overinvestment in the industry with a depressing comparative effect on its earnings before taxes.

Economic theory has generally found the strongest case for market imperfection in the conditions needed for economic progress—new products, new processes, new services through innovation and technological change. Here, if anywhere, the security of established position, conferred by size and integration, might be needed to balance the hazards of long and costly experimentation, of long-term expenditures on research and development for new products and processes, and of explorations to reveal new sources of crude oil and new ways of developing synthetics to take its place. A logical case can be made for the proposition that the public benefits from these advantages of the large vertically integrated company—from its greater sensitivity to investment opportunities, ability to marshal funds, and willingness to use them at relatively low anticipated rates of return. On the other hand if these advantages represent merely sources of strategic private advantage, it is possible they may end by denying the public the benefit of a wide range of competitive alternatives, and in the end therefore undermine industrial progress instead of the reverse.

22. The comparability of net income reported by oil companies with similar data in other industries is discussed in Dirlam and Kahn, "Leadership and Conflict in the Pricing of Gasoline," *Yale Law Journal, 61* (1952), 831–832, n. 45; also McLean and Haigh, p. 253.

CHAPTER 12

Economic Progress and Non-Price Competition

NON-PRICE COMPETITION is a hallmark of imperfect markets and a necessary condition of dynamic change. This does not imply that price competition does not exist where individual participants must weigh the market consequences of their own policies; it means merely that price is the easiest competitive weapon to parry and in such markets businesses search instead for advantages that are not so quickly matched in the eyes of the consumer. Price competition, if it predominated, would seek out some basis of equilibrium, usually in costs. But non-price competition has no resting point (other than mutual agreement); it is inherently dynamic, and the changes it may produce in production processes, in services performed, in product form and quality—from artificial gadgets on which to hang a sales talk to revolutionary inventions that alter the course of our existence —are potentially without limit.

Analysis and appraisal of the contribution of vertical integration to non-price competition in oil is extraordinarily difficult for a number of reasons that are worth considering because they place the present inquiry in its proper setting. First and most fundamental is the conceptual problem of trying to compare a known or knowable—the technological progress and product improvement that has actually occurred—with an unknown and unknowable—the kind, rate, and direction of development that might have taken place under some alternative system of organization. Second, there is no demonstrably accurate way of measuring even the "known" element, comprising as it does a great variety of incommensurable variables, such as improvements in physical efficiency, improvements in this or that aspect of product quality, introduction of new products and services. For example, prominent in a list of major innovations in oil would probably be improved methods of exploration and recovery of crude oil (for example, seismographic exploration), thermal and catalytic cracking, pipeline transportation, improved quality of fuels and lubricants (octane rating, volatility, performance under varying weather conditions, corrosion-resistance), improved service in the marketing of final products, the development of petrochemicals. How does one add these up, or rank them in importance? How does one trace their origins, when each has been a product of piecemeal accretion and collaboration among a host of agencies, of inspired individuals and organized, collective effort? The process of innovation is organic and social; it is often impossible to single out individual, self-sufficient causes.

Furthermore, even if the significant innovations could be identified, measured, ranked, and their origins traced, there is no definitive way of separating out the contributing or impeding influence of vertical integration. The economist has tended, in his industry studies and his market theories, to assume a fairly direct causal relationship between market structure and economic consequences. In part, this is the heritage of the purely competitive assumption: given atomistic rivalry, certain effects can be predicted which do not depend on individuals —the collectivity produces a determinate result. The neo-classical economist's concern with the maximization of society's satisfactions through optimum allocation of a given complement of productive resources strengthened his conviction of the crucial role of market structure. In moving closer to the real world of imperfect competition and the exploration of dynamic results, the economist has perhaps carried this assumption about the crucial role of market structure beyond the range of its major significance.

In technological progress, other causal influences may be more important than the system of business organization. Stated conversely, a market structure characterized by a particular degree and kind of imperfect competition and business integration may be compatible with a wide range of results. One vital determinant must be the existing state and inherent potentialities of technology in the particular industry in question. It has hardly been a consequence of market structure that the textile industry has been among the first to take on the characteristics of modern factory production in most countries; or that in the twentieth century it has been the industries exploiting modern physical and chemical science that have exhibited the most dramatic progress. Conversely, it is hard to imagine a modern industrial country that does not push the application of organic chemistry or electronics, whether under centralized state planning or a more decentralized system of organization.

This is not to say that industrial organization is an unimportant factor. Both theory and experience demonstrate the greater potential progressiveness—at least of certain kinds—of a decentralized, competitive economy operating on a variety of market-determined fronts.

But the traditional market categories leave wide margins for variations. A complete monopoly, able to tax its customers, could conceivably support the most extensive and fundamental research and the most rapid commercial adaptation of its fruits; or, secure against competitive displacement, it might progress not at all. An industry dominated by a few firms might still have both the wherewithal to support substantial research and innovation and the added spur of competition to ensure realization of these possibilities. Instead, competition might be confined by tacit understanding to meaningless product differentiation, to the proliferation of "extra features" for which there might have been no public demand without industry stimulation. It is not unlikely, therefore, that the progressiveness of the American oil industry is more attributable to "external" circumstances like the rise of the automobile, the existence of huge domestic oil resources difficult to exploit because of their quality and location, the inherent potentialities of petroleum technology given the current state of chemical science, and the ready availability of risk capital and the enterprise to use it than it is to vertical integration or any other specific form of industrial organization.

Before trying to sample the mass of changes that mark the history of oil, three aspects of the process of technological change need to be differentiated. At one extreme, there is true invention—the radical new idea that departs from accustomed ways of thinking and doing. Next in time and logic comes the process of innovation—translating invention into commercially feasible technology, or adapting known ideas or methods in new combinations, in new areas, and with new results. And finally, there is simple rationalization or scientific management, the application of better methods and techniques to the production process. All three of these categories represent forms or aspects of technological progress, and all may involve the application of truly creative intelligence. In practice, all, but more importantly the first two, are usually interdependent rather than clearly separable. Every invention, however radical, is a rearrangement of prior knowledge. But at some point it is useful to distinguish the significant invention, conceived as a single "flash of genius" from, in sequence, the invention that is the end product of painstaking, systematic group research, from the closely related innovation that brings an invention to fruition or adapts it to new uses, and from the mere application of new techniques accessible to anyone "skilled in the prior art." [1]

1. These categories may or may not coincide with the shifting judicial standards of patentability. The courts have at times refused to validate patents on in-

The completely new idea issuing from the individual flash of genius is extremely rare; and there is little reason to believe that industrial organization has much to do with it. Indeed, the disciplines of an industry and the conventions of professional training make it more likely that someone quite free of these preconceptions of thought and action should hit on radically new approaches; and the really new idea, when it occurs, is more likely than not to come from outside the industry entirely.[2] Despite an amazing proliferation of ideas and techniques in the processing of petroleum that makes the modern industry all but incomparable with its counterpart prior to World War I, it is difficult to find unqualified examples of radical inventions. It does not reflect adversely on the present structure of the oil industry that it does not originate these ideas. The more radical a break they represent with an industry's accustomed ways of thinking and doing, the more they themselves represent in effect a new industry and the less reason there is to have expected them to originate from within. If some day peanuts become the prime source of motor fuels, this fact is more likely to be discovered by a farmer's son with a chemical education, by the United States Department of Agriculture, or by a professor in a land grant college than by a petroleum refiner, regardless of the business structure of the oil industry.

Within an industry, the process of innovation is, precisely, a process of "cutting and trying," [3] of borrowing, adapting, and experimenting with ideas already present in our fund of scientific knowledge. Such

ventions issuing from organized, corporation-financed research regardless of their contribution to progress in science or the industrial arts. But the considerations influencing judges to apply a strict, flash-of-genius definition of invention in such circumstances have less to do with an appraisal of either the novelty or the value of the contribution than with the desire to prevent a monopolization of technology through the accumulation of patents.

2. In his study of the *Development of Aircraft Engines* (published together with S. D. Heron, *Development of Aviation Fuels,* Cambridge, Harvard University Press, 1950), Robert Schlaifer points out that "all the developments of all types of reciprocating engines done after 1918 consisted essentially of progressive refinement of well-known basic designs" (p. 84). The only really radical innovation in aircraft power plants since World War I has been the gas turbine, especially the turbojet form of gas turbine. Regarding its development he says, "Undoubtedly the most striking single fact in the early history of turbojets is that nowhere in the world was the first development of this type of engine due to an established producer of conventional aircraft engines" (p. 85). See also P. Hennipman, "Monopoly: Impediment or Stimulus to Economic Progress?" in Edward H. Chamberlin, ed., *Monopoly and Competition and their Regulation* (London, Macmillan, 1954), p. 434.

3. See Heron (above, n. 2), p. 559.

a process is continuous in a dynamic industry like petroleum. The same idea may have been tried in a variety of forms many times before and in many other places. But, like the oil that lies underground somewhere, undiscovered, ideas such as these are of no economic value until they are visualized as potential solutions for a given problem. Innovation is the process that begins with this perception and —what is usually the more costly, risky, time-consuming enterprise— carries the idea through until it becomes part of the economically usable technology. Society itself hardly begins to share in the successes until a more general industrial application forces a significant dispersion of benefits in the quality or price of the final product. But it is in these processes—the technical borrowing and adaptation, the commercial development, and the general industrial application of innovations—that economic organization and institutions within any given industry can play a decisive part.[4]

INNOVATIONS

The history of petroleum technology that would enable an economist to try to analyze the relationship, if any, between innovation and integration has not yet, to our knowledge, been written. It is possible to offer a more or less systematic list of what seem to have been the major innovations at each level of the industry, but it is not possible —without undertaking a separate, major research project—to trace the responsibility for them from flash of genius to commercial application in such a way as to permit meaningful conclusions to be drawn.

Exploration and Production

In this area information is particularly scanty. Yet it seems sufficient to justify serious doubt that the process of innovation—in the sense either of the original application of techniques new to oil or of their widespread adoption—has depended to any important extent on vertical integration.

To be sure, many of the major companies or their official biographers have claimed credit for one or another important innovation

4. It may play a decisive role also in determining the third aspect of technological progress distinguished above—the application of essentially already proved processes and simple rationalization. The oil industry's record along these lines will not be treated extensively in this chapter, because it seems more appropriately considered as an incident less of innovation, which expands the fund of technology itself, than of investment, which draws upon that fund and makes use of it.

—Union Oil for the first cementing of wells,[5] Standard of Indiana for fracturing of producing formations, "the best general reservoir and well-stimulation process known," [6] and Gulf Oil, recently, for a chemical additive to improve the lubricating qualities of drilling "mud"— a "basic breakthrough in oil drilling technology" according to the company [7]—to mention only a few examples. However, most of the earlier techniques were simply borrowed from other industries, apparently by independent prospectors and producers. The first important innovation in production was the drilled well. This resulted from the decision by Drake (or his employers in Connecticut) to use a technique for the production of oil which was common in brine wells. It was not a radical innovation and it had nothing to do with vertical integration. The second major development was the introduction of the rotary drill; it is perhaps significant that no indication of who first adopted it has been found. Drake was also responsible for setting the first casing, which he inserted to keep soft material out of the first bore. This too was probably not a radical innovation: the Chinese are supposed to have used casing some 2,000 years ago.[8] Directional drilling was first used in diamond mining in the Transvaal in 1905, and in Ontario for nickel mining in 1919. Hole surveying, which permits the operator to know whether he is drilling in the direction he intended, was also first used in diamond mining in the early 1900's by Joseph Kitchin; its first application to petroleum is credited merely to "geologists, who, through their basic training, were more or less familiar with methods used by the mining industry." [9]

Of course, methods of drilling and exploration have been immensely improved and extended over time. But in the process the independent and the specialized service companies seem to have held the center of the stage at least as often as the integrated firm. The brothers Schlumberger, French engineers, devised the techniques for electric well-logging, and the Schlumberger concern was set up to exploit the method in this country.[10] As for the use of geophysics in exploration, *Fortune* attributes to E. E. DeGolyer the introduction of the torsion balance, and the first geophysical oil discovery with it. His assistant, J. D. Karcher, is credited with inventing the reflection seismograph. At

5. Taylor and Welty, *Black Bonanza*, p. 85.
6. *Annual Report*, 1953, p. 19.
7. *Wall Street Journal* (February 17, 1958), p. 7.
8. E. DeGolyer, ed., *Elements of the Petroleum Industry* (New York, The American Institute of Mining and Metallurgical Engineers, 1940), p. 206.
9. *Ibid.*, pp. 161, 171.
10. *Ibid.*, pp. 84, 196.

the time, DeGolyer was president of Amerada, which is said to have had such a monopoly of geophysical talent that it organized the Geophysical Research Corporation to do exploratory work for other companies.[11] Although most major oil companies have exploration crews and some do research in exploratory methods, a very large share of the geophysical exploration until very recently has been carried on by independent companies. The high level of training in physics and the intimate acquaintanceship with the elaborate equipment and techniques necessary to take and interpret observations encouraged the entry of independent professional personnel. The appearance of these specialists apparently dates from about 1929.[12]

It has not been the purpose of this sketchy account to minimize the innovational contributions of the major oil companies. It is probably true that they have adopted and developed modern exploratory and production methods more rapidly than the wildcatter and nonintegrated producer. But it is highly doubtful that their record in these respects has surpassed that of their larger nonintegrated rivals. The distinguishing element is not integration but size and the ability it carries to hire good technicians and management; in the case of the above-average smaller businesses, it is often the unusual ability of their owners.

It seems likely that the relations currently prevailing between the large manufacturers of oil field equipment, the schools of mechanical and mining engineering, and the production companies, both integrated and nonintegrated, are so close and interdependent that it would now be impossible in any case to fasten responsibility for a development exclusively upon any one firm. This is particularly true because of the highly developed procedures for speedy communica-

11. "Amerada Plays Them Close to the Chest," *Fortune* (January, 1946), pp. 129–132, probably overstates the case for the independent. On the earlier history see DeGolyer, *Elements of the Petroleum Industry*, pp. 63–64, 75–78. On the importance of the reflection method see *Petroleum Press Service* (April, 1957), pp. 131–133.

12. "With industry growth came industry diversification. Bit, tool and equipment companies made up the early specialists group. Later came geologists, geophysicists and petroleum engineers. . . . About 25 years ago . . . the oil industry service group appeared on the scene. The service company offered the industry products or tools requiring special skills in application. . . . The men who run and produce the electrical logs which prove the ultimate success or failure of million-dollar drilling programs are not employees of the companies whose fates are at stake. Rather, these scientists and specialists are members of a 15,000 man team which has become known as the Oil Industry Service Group." Rieke, "Logging Services Playing Vital Role in Exploration," *World Oil* (April, 1954), pp. 207–208.

tion through trade journals, the proceedings of the American Society of Mining and Metallurgical Engineers, and the technical sections of the American Petroleum Institute.

Synthetics

Indeed, some might contend that the presence of large integrated firms in the industry has actually retarded progress in one important direction in the field of production. In spite of the perennial fears of a shortage of crude oil, the industry has done less than it might have done had it been differently organized to push closer to commercial feasibility various processes for synthesizing petroleum hydrocarbons from sources other than crude oil. It is not claimed that synthetic processes are commercially practical today. Rather, it is alleged that the majors, with half or more than half of their total invested capital in crude-producing properties, have dragged their feet in developing alternative sources to the point of commercial feasibility, and have discouraged the experimental efforts of the government as well. On both these counts there is some supporting evidence.

The Standard Oil Company (New Jersey) first became interested in the hydrogenation of coal, one of the three basic potential sources of liquid synthetic fuels, in the early 1920's, when a worldwide shortage of crude oil seemed imminent. The process had been developed and the patents were controlled by the aggressive German chemical trust I. G. Farben, which had no vested interest in cushioning its potential impact on oil company investments. By purchasing worldwide control (with Shell) of hydrogenation for use in the synthesis of fuels, Standard's negotiating executive felt that he had eliminated the "most serious threat" that had "ever faced the company since the dissolution." [13] Standard's avowed purpose was to protect itself by keeping control of the process in friendly hands. It was not interested in developing it to commercial feasibility. Exploitation of the patents was entrusted to a patent pool, which was given a mandate to keep itself informed about developments but not to attempt to "stir up interest" in countries "where none exists." [14]

This negative policy undoubtedly was attributable largely to the well-founded belief that the process was not commercially feasible except in countries like Germany, where governments wanted to free

13. Letter quoted in statement of Wendell Berge before Senate Judiciary Committee, reproduced in George W. Stocking and Myron W. Watkins, *Cartels in Action* (New York, Twentieth Century Fund, 1946), p. 92, n. 67.
14. Standard of New Jersey summary of policy quoted *ibid.*, p. 492.

themselves of dependence on imported crude oil. Discoveries of new fields kept up with demand, dissipating fears of shortage and discouraging costly experimentation with dubious alternatives. But the policy of "guidance and restriction" [15] was attributable also to the fact that the interests of (integrated) oil companies in such developments were equivocal. As marketers, they wanted to assure themselves of future supplies of products to sell, from whatever source. But their heavier investments in crude oil and refineries of the traditional kind naturally inclined them to search wider horizons for crude oil rather than to seek alternative, synthetic sources of fuels and lubricants. Walter Teagle, one-time chairman of the Board of Standard, clearly implied that a hydrogenation patents pool dominated by companies not involved in the production of oil might have been more vigorous in pressing for the exploitation of these patents.[16] A similar defensive psychology seems to have governed the move by Standard and Shell subsequently to control the patent rights to the Fischer process for hydrocarbon synthesis of gases.[17]

It cannot be concluded that the oil companies, including Standard, put these processes to sleep. Apparently they spent tens of millions of dollars in subsequent research on them.[18] Part of these expenditures, however, were directed apparently to perfecting methods of catalytic

15. See below, n. 17.

16. "The IHP [International Hydrogenation Patents Company] has very large investment [sic] in hydrogenation on which, up to date, it has secured a very inadequate return. There is little doubt in our minds but what, if other than oil companies had dominated the situation, the management's conduct of the business would have been along lines better calculated to secure the maximum return on the capital invested." Stocking and Watkins, Cartels in Action, p. 493.

17. Frank Howard of Standard Oil wrote, ". . . if we are to do anything in the way of trying to guide or restrict the development of the Fischer process outside of Germany, the time to do so is now" (ibid., p. 494).

18. In "Creating Tomorrow's Oil," Fortune (November, 1951), p. 143, stated that Standard Oil Development Company had spent $12 million on synthetic fuels research. Socony-Vacuum is understood to have spent comparable sums on the Fischer-Tropsch process, and the Texas Company in 1953 wrote off $13 million sunk in the failure of Carthage Hydrocol to synthesize liquid fuels from natural gas (the Texas Company, Annual Report, 1953, p. 15). Standard Oil (Indiana), which owned petrochemical facilities adjacent to and supplied by the Carthage operation, took up the search where the Texas Company left it, investing large sums of money to rehabilitate the plant. Finally, in 1957, it too gave up, evidently having demonstrated clearly the technical feasibility and economic infeasibility of the effort. "Why Amoco Closed the Brownsville Plant," Petroleum Refiner (October, 1957), p. 241.

cracking rather than synthesis of crude oil: Standard's hydroforming and fluid catalysis seem to have developed from experiments with hydrogenation.

In the early twenties the prospects of hydrogenation of coal were exaggerated both by those who feared the competition of the new process and by those who were chafing at their dependence on crude oil. Subsequent developments have more than justified the judgment —even though it was not an unbiased judgment—that turned the oil companies away from this kind of experimentation into accelerated and highly successful searches for crude oil. Only in terms of possible national emergency could the required large-scale research have been justified. It could hardly have appeared attractive to private investors no matter how industry was organized; least of all to petroleum, which had much more lush alternatives, and not even to the coal industry, the apparent victim of oil's successes.

Under the circumstances, it is appropriate that postwar experimental work in this area (stimulated by Germany's large-scale production before and during the war) should have been carried forward almost exclusively in this country by the United States Bureau of Mines. In question was not the technical achievement of producing liquid fuels and chemicals from coal but the probable costs of producing these materials on a commercial scale. There was a wide dispersion among the cost estimates—by the Bureau and, on its invitation, by the National Petroleum Council and Ebasco Services, Inc. (a private engineering firm)—for full-scale production based on the operation of the Bureau's pilot plant at Louisiana, Missouri.[19] The pilot plant

19. The Council estimated 41.4 cents a gallon for gasoline after credit for by-products; Ebasco came up with 16–17 cents and the Bureau with 11 cents. The wide discrepancy stemmed from the valuation of by-product chemicals, the rate of return required, and the scale of investment including subsidiary facilities like worker housing and community facilities. (All but the first item were excluded from consideration by the Bureau, which was not concerned about private commercial operation.) As for the first, the Council argued, "It is readily apparent that for any large scale adoption of coal hydrogenation to supplant even a small proportion of the fuel now supplied by the petroleum industry would make chemicals available completely out of proportion to those that might be absorbed." *Interim Report* of the National Petroleum Council's Committee on Synthetic Liquid Fuels Production Cost (July 29, 1952), *Report* to the Subcommittee, p. 7. Cf. U. S. Bureau of Mines, *Synthetic Liquid Fuels, 1* (1954), "Oil from Coal," *Report* of Investigations 5043. As for the last, it was estimated that a $400 million investment would be required for a liquid fuels capacity of 30,000 b/d. This should be compared with an estimated cost of $150 million for a corresponding capacity of crude oil (including transporta-

was closed down by the new administration in 1953. Whether or not that decision was wise, it seems clear that the projected investment required for commercial operations was quite infeasible for private enterprise.

The experience of the South African Coal, Oil, and Gas Corporation (SASOL) since that time with the first full-scale, commercial oil-from-coal plant in the world generally confirms this judgment.[20] It was established by the Union Government as a state-controlled public corporation in 1950 and was scheduled to begin production by the end of 1954 and to develop a capacity of 70 to 75 million gallons of liquid fuels and chemicals per year and some 70,000 tons of miscellaneous other products. The situation was as propitious as could be —not far from Johannesburg, the major market, 400 miles inland in a country that produces no crude oil of its own, with adjacent large reserves of exceptionally cheap coal, considerable water supply, and ample cheap labor [21]—and expectations were sanguine. For years, the progress reports were most discouraging: the project had been plagued with breakdowns, redesigning, and reconstruction; capital expenditures per ton of over-all capacity were estimated early in 1956 at three or four times that generally required for the whole range of oil industry operations; and the corporation's chairman was commenting that coal might prove a more important raw material for chemicals than for gasoline.[22] Late in 1957, however, it was reported that the project had finally proved its feasibility for the South African or

tion and production investment). The industry's skepticism about the size of the investment and the character of the plant seems to have been not without merit.

20. Other full-scale operations have been established by governments for military or technical reasons or for emergency requirements: Germany's hydrogenation and Fischer-Tropsch synthesis plants produced almost 4 million tons of liquid fuels per year in the early 1940's; a coal hydrogenation plant was set up at Billingham, England, before the war and one Fischer-Tropsch unit was erected in France and another in Manchuria.

21. The problems were also enormous—the creation of a 2 million ton per year coal production as well as a massive chemical industry of unfamiliar type and expanding size in a series of major plants of novel design. See "SASOL—The Trials of Pioneering," *Petroleum Press Service* (February, 1956), pp. 57–60.

22. In other areas outside the Iron Curtain, all existing coal hydrogenation or synthesis plants were switched to chemicals manufacture after the war (or to operation on liquid feedstocks for fuels production). Throughout the history of SASOL, it has been the increases in chemicals, not fuels, that have required new facilities. See *ibid.*, pp. 58–59, and *Petroleum Press Service* (January, 1957), pp. 22–23.

comparable situations. For more than a year the plant had been turning out 10,000 b/d of products comparable in quality and quantity
with those of a modern petroleum refinery. The entire investment
cost, including development of the coal mine and housing of employees,
estimated at $112 millions, would still be probably twice the cost of
comparable crude oil production, transportation, and refining facilities in the United States, but it has proved low enough to make the
project competitive or not far from it in South Africa.[23] Even though
the experiment may at last have proved a successful one for South
Africa—and prolonged initial disappointments in so novel an endeavor were certainly to have been expected—for the United States
at least the competitive prospects of hydrogenation of coal continue
to confirm the negative attitude of the industry.[24]

The recovery of liquid fuels from oil shale is a much more nearly
practicable alternative to crude oil in this country. Here, again, much
of the early experimental work was done by the Bureau of Mines, until its pilot plant at Rifle, Colorado, was also closed down by the new
Secretary of the Interior after 1953. The work was strongly supported
by Union Oil Company, which is now constructing a commercial
plant of its own.[25] Both the claims of near-future commercial success

23. This report was made by the project manager for the company that built
it (M. W. Kellogg), an interested party. The $112 millions was contrasted
with approximately $17,500,000 for a modern 10,000 b/d refinery and the cost
of "several times that figure" for comparable crude oil production, transportation and the like. J. H. Carmical, " 'Gas' from Coal Is Held Feasible," New
York *Times* (November 24, 1957), sec. 3, p. 1. The National Petroleum Council's 1952 estimate of crude oil investment costs appropriately comparable with
a hydrogenation plant suggests that the figure for 10,000 b/d capacity would be
$50 million (see above, n. 20)—an estimate that probably should be raised
somewhat for 1957. For a still pessimistic report, on narrowly financial
grounds, see *Petroleum Press Service* (January, 1958), pp. 34–35. Compare, in
contrast, the earlier suggestion of the London *Economist* that "it is fair to say
that Sasol's contribution to the South African economy cannot be counted quite
so cold-bloodedly. . . . Technical adventurism is perhaps less dangerous than
overcaution." "Oil from African Coal" (April 30, 1955), p. 399.

24. Union Carbide Company has found sufficient promise of commercial
success for hydrogenation to have invested over $20 million in experimentation
and pilot plants over the last twenty years; but only as a source of chemicals:
"Chemicals produced by coal hydrogenation are worth five times as much as
synthetic fuels made by the same process." "Chemical Engineering's Role in
Coal Hydrogenation," reprint from *Chemical Engineering,* December, 1953.

25. The Bureau of Mines estimated production costs of gasoline from shale
in 1951 at 14.7¢ per gallon when ordinary gasoline from crude oil was priced
at the refinery at 12.0¢ per gallon (exclusive of tax). The National Petroleum
Council put the cost of shale oil gasoline at 16.2¢ per gallon. Although its own

and the vast potential reserves of shale oil in this country make this a memorable undertaking.[26]

In some ways more amazing is a recently announced private project to process a part of the Athabasca tar sands of Northern Alberta. This is an area already rich in natural petroleum and also some 300 miles northeast of existing crude oil terminals. Improvements in large-scale mining equipment, absence of exploration costs, valuable by-products, and freedom from prorationing are major incentives in a scheme estimated to require a minimum investment of $50 million.[27] Much less significant in potential but equally fascinating as a source of oil products has been the recent development of Gilsonite, originally used for asphalt. Standard Oil of California is said to own a half interest in the project and to have put up most of the money and technical resources for research on the material.[28]

---

costs have not been released, Union Oil Company officers were predicting late in 1956 that commercial shale oil was less than five years away. Union expected the capital investment in a complete oil shale plant including retorting and partial refining to a pumpable crude to be of the order of $3,000 to $5,000 per barrel of daily capacity, not too much out of line (at the lower figure) with total current costs of natural crude including exploration costs. Since cost of natural domestic crude is expected to rise while costs of shale production may fall with more research and since shale oil is rich in by-products like ethylene, olefins, ammonia, sulphur, and coke, commercial production is expected to increase rapidly after 1960. How rapidly will depend on the expansion of demand for oil, the future of domestic crude production and imports, and the possibilities of extending the depletion allowance to shale oil. In any event, an increasing number of important oil companies are becoming large holders of shale oil reserves. See *Business Week* (December 1, 1956), pp. 99 ff., and *Petroleum Press Service* (February, 1957), pp. 57 ff.

26. See Netschert's estimate that shales may place an upper limit on the price of oil from traditional sources not far above present levels: *The Future Supply of Oil and Gas,* pp. 60–63; also "Is Shale Oil Ready to Compete?" *Business Week* (December 1, 1956), pp. 99–103.

27. The Royalite Oil Company is reported to have begun work on a 20,000 b/d operation for mining the sands, separating the oil, reducing it to a pumpable crude by coking, and transporting it by pipeline to Edmonton. The company expects to be in operation by 1960. While the estimated potential reserves in the sands are figured in hundreds of billions of barrels, those economically accessible without the development of some new low-cost underground recovery method are estimated at some 5 billion barrels. See *Petroleum Press Service* (February, 1957), pp. 72–73.

28. Gilsonite is a solid hydrocarbon, actually discovered in Colorado-Utah in 1883 and used for a variety of fringe purposes until American Gilsonite Company developed a refining process which converts it into gasoline and metallurgical coke. With a pipeline to bring the product as a slurry some seventy-two miles to Grand Junction, Colorado, and a refinery, the company

Although integrated companies have not ignored the subject, the majors have not been in the forefront of the development of liquid fuels from sources other than crude oil. Considering the alternatives available to them, this conservatism on their part can hardly be subject to criticism. What may be questioned is their general hostility to efforts by government agencies to push research along these lines.

Transportation

Some of the pioneer builders of crude-oil pipelines were oil brokers, others were refiners. Within a few years, however, all important gathering lines had been captured by refiners or railroads and, shortly thereafter, most of them were gobbled up by John D. Rockefeller. Almost from the start, crude-oil pipeline transportation became an inextricable segment of integrated company operations. The same was true a half century later of product lines. Apart from a kerosene pipeline constructed almost sixty years before, the first product line was put into use when the Tuscarora, an Esso subsidiary, began shipping gasoline across Pennsylvania in 1930 by adapting an earlier crude line.[29] An integrated major built the first pipeline ever designed "specifically to transport a refined product." [30] The products pipeline was taken up in earnest by the Great Lakes Company, owned entirely by integrated refiners.

The expansion of pipeline transportation since 1870 and the continuous improvements in construction and operation add up to a proud record of dynamic investment by the industry. The development was essentially one of diffusion-by-imitation, of extending the use of a method whose technical and commercial feasibility had already been demonstrated. Nonetheless, as late as 1930, there was widespread conviction that the pipeline could not be made to carry light products effectively, and especially that it could not hope to handle several light products through the same line without gross contamination. Yet to describe the process simply as either innovation on the one hand or rationalization and expansion of capacity on the

---

began commercial operations in its $16 million plant in August, 1957. Known reserves of Gilsonite ore are modest—an estimated fifty-year supply for the refinery which turns out 1,300 barrels of gasoline and 275 tons of coke per day. The future of the plant may lie in petrochemicals rather than fuels. *Business Week* (August 10, 1957), pp. 66 ff.

29. McLean and Haigh, p. 207, n. 32.

30. *History of Sun Oil Company*, mimeographed (July 2, 1951), p. 2. Actually it is not clear whether Sun or Phillips deserves this recognition.

other, would do violence to the facts. Exploration of vertical integration's role in speeding the investment process and, through continuous learning and improvement-by-doing, thereby contributing to significant innovation as well is reserved for Chapter 14.

The impact of vertical integration on the development of other methods of transportation—truck, barge, and especially tanker—is less clear. The weight of transport costs in the value of product is large enough so that there is no mistaking the incentive of the integrated oil firm to develop more efficient transport than existing markets allowed. Oil company histories are replete with concern over services and costs of rail transportation which drove individual companies into the design and operation of alternative transport media. But truck, barge, and tanker are so adaptable in size and investment and so flexible in operation that they remain predominantly independent in ownership and substantially so in operation. And though oil companies have undoubtedly contributed something to design improvement of all of these media as they have contributed, directly in their own investments and indirectly through long-term charters, to their financing, we are unaware of any outstanding innovations, even the innovation of tanker size, that may be said to owe their origins or their evolution to vertically integrated oil firms.

Refining

The first strategic advance in refining technique was probably the development of the Frasch process for desulphurization of crude oil.[31] This process, patented by Frasch in 1887, was purchased by the original Standard Oil Company in May 1888, along with the Ontario plant in which Frasch had been successfully applying his patented methods to sour Ontario crude.[32] Standard, apparently, had very little to do with the initial development of the process. As a virtual monopoly, it was merely the most profitable outlet for the improvement. Rockefeller's casual reference to Frasch as "one of our German chem-

31. Sulphur was no problem with "sweet" Pennsylvania crudes, but it was an effective bar to the commercial exploitation of many other crudes. When Rockefeller bought up leases in the Lima Field of Ohio and began production, this high-sulphur, sour crude sold at only 14 cents per barrel (as residual fuel) in contrast with $2.25 per barrel for Pennsylvania oil. See Herman Frasch, Address of Acceptance of the Perkins Medal Award, *Journal of Industrial and Engineering Chemistry*, 4 (1912), 134 ff.

32. R. Wilson, "Oil Competition in the Midwest" (above, p. 101, n. 58), p. 4. Cf. McLean and Haigh, p. 68.

ists" suggested little recognition on his part of the importance of the advance.[33] It is not clear how much of a risk Rockefeller actually took in buying up Lima crude leases after oil was discovered there in 1885 or beginning production before a method was devised to purify the crude. Certainly, he was bolder than his competition and apparently quite convinced that in time a commercially feasible desulphurization process would be found.

Whatever Rockefeller's appraisal of Frasch, his company's role at a minimum was to accelerate this first advance in refining technique by providing the vision and the funds needed to build on a large scale what had already been proven in a small plant. This is a primary function of the business innovator. Standard's large holdings in the Lima-Indiana field undoubtedly spurred it to perfect processes of refining its petroleum. By 1890 the company was drawing 56 per cent of its oil from that area. The commercial impact of the Frasch process was immediate and explosive.[34]

Desulphurization vastly increased the effective petroleum supply. Years later, in 1913, Standard of Indiana took a second great stride in the same direction when it initiated Burton's thermal cracking process on a commercial scale and thereby doubled the yield of gasoline potentially available from a barrel of crude oil. The process was the first great step in converting refining from a primitive operation of physical separation to a process applying and developing complex techniques of modern chemistry and physics. But these potentialities were realized only gradually.[35] In fact, it was not until 1936, on the

33. See Nevins, *John D. Rockefeller,* p. 680. Frasch had been a Standard Oil employee from 1876 to 1885, working in Cleveland on various aspects of refining. Thereafter he moved to Ontario, founded his own company, and discovered, what oil operators in that region had sought more than twenty years, a way of converting the so-called skunk oils of Ontario into rivals of Pennsylvania crude. See C. F. Chandler in his presentation of the Perkins Medal Award to Frasch in 1912, *The Journal of Industrial and Engineering Chemistry* (n. 31, above), pp. 132–133.

34. Output in the Lima Field rose from 30,000 to 90,000 b/d, the price of Lima crude spurted from 14 cents to nearly $1 per barrel, the market value of Standard Oil Stock (in which Frasch had been paid) climbed from 168 (paying 7 per cent dividends) to 820 (paying 40 per cent), and Standard began to build large works using the process at Lima, Cleveland, Whiting, Olean, Philadelphia, and Bayonne (*ibid.,* pp. 133, 135).

35. After seven years of operation with thermal cracking (i.e. in 1920), only one barrel of gasoline in eight refined was cracked. Probably Standard's restrictive licensing policy was partially at fault. See Stocking, pp. 259–261. However, there were other reasons as well. The Burton process was non-

eve of a still greater forward step in refining, namely catalytic cracking, that production of cracked gasoline exceeded that of straight-run in this country.

Again, the most that can be claimed for Standard of Indiana in this substantial contribution to the development of refining is that it recognized the need and boldly pushed the commercial development and application of cracking. The conversion of crude oil into various by-products when heated above the normal boiling point was a familiar phenomenon, first noticed by Silliman in 1855.[36] In the years that followed, many variations of the process were devised and patented but with little commercial impact. One of them, patented by Dewar and Redwood for the manufacture of illuminating oil rather than gasoline, is said to have differed only negligibly from the Burton process.[37] Neither Standard's William M. Burton, who took out the patent for gasoline, nor Robert E. Humphrey, who carried out the experiments, seems to have had any foreknowledge of Dewar and Redwood's work. Their successful research was brought to a temporary halt when the parent company, with the dissolution suit pending, turned down a request for a million dollars to construct a hundred 8,000-barrel stills. Thereafter, however, Standard of Indiana provided the funds necessary to demonstrate the commercial feasibility of the process.

It is no detraction from Standard's contribution that the perfection of thermal cracking should have depended on other developments, independently and concurrently arrived at. One of the best of these was the Dubbs process, developed independently of the major oil companies. It eliminated the formation of heavy carbon deposits and thereby made it possible not only to use ordinary crude or even fuel oil as a charging stock (as compared with gas oil in the Burton proc-

---

continuous, and heavy carbon deposits in equipment made it useful only with a gas-oil charging stock. Furthermore, the odor, color, and lower gravity of cracked gasoline compared with straight-run were all obstacles to widespread acceptance that had to be overcome.

36. Raymond F. Bacon and William A. Hamov, *The American Petroleum Industry* (New York, McGraw-Hill, 1916), p. 554. See also Benjamin T. Brooks, Raymond F. Bacon, Fred W. Padgett, and Irwin W. Humphrey, "The Preparation of Gasoline and Kerosene from Heavier Hydrocarbons," *Journal of Industrial and Engineering Chemistry*, 7 (1915), 180 ff. This article presents one of the best factual summaries of the development of the cracking process.

37. Giddens in his *Standard Oil Company* (Indiana), p. 142, gives the patent date as April 22, 1890. See also Benjamin T. Brooks, who gives a later date, 1895, in "A Statistical Review of the Problem of Gasoline Supply," *Journal of Industrial and Engineering Chemistry*, 7 (1915), 179.

ess) but also to operate continuously over long periods of time.[38]

In the next important advance following thermal cracking it was General Motors, not an integrated oil company, that discovered the importance of tetraethyl lead in reducing knocking in internal combustion engines. General Motors contracted to have E. I. du Pont de Nemours undertake the manufacture of the additive, and turned the marketing over to Standard Oil of New Jersey. When Standard, which had also been experimenting with antiknock additives, managed by June 1923 to devise a superior method of making tetraethyl lead, the two companies pooled their interests in Ethyl Gasoline Corporation (now the Ethyl Corporation), which they set up for purposes of research and marketing, leaving to du Pont, which at that time owned 23 per cent of the General Motors stock, the exclusive manufacture on the North American Continent.[39]

It was Graham Edgar, first with General Motors and later with

38. Unlike Burton, who was a chemist by training, Jesse A. Dubbs was a pioneer refiner in California. Troubled with an emulsion of water and crude oil that would not respond to known dehydration methods, he devised a still and condenser arrangement that operated under pressure built up by its own generated vapors. The scheme worked, and he applied for patent in 1909. It was not until 1913, when he learned about the Burton patent, that he realized that in addition to dehydration he had been operating a continuous thermal cracking process, and amended his patent application accordingly. The patent was subsequently acquired by a group of men, among whom Chicago meat packer J. Ogden Armour was prominent, interested in Universal Oil Products Company. Universal Oil filed suit in 1916 against Indiana charging infringement of the Dubbs patent. When it finally won out, in 1931, a general peace was negotiated among six major oil companies, which purchased for $25 million Universal's 1,000 shares of stock. In 1944, after some of the basic patents had run out, the six owners placed these securities in a charitable trust. Thereafter, Universal's profits were dedicated exclusively to the financial support of fundamental research and advanced scientific education through the American Chemical Society. "Pioneers in Research," reprint from *Oil and Gas Journal* (May 27, 1937). See also, "Universal Oil Company Faces New D-Day in New York State Court," New York *Times*, July 15, 1956.

Three other basic cracking processes were developed between 1910 and 1925: The Texas Company's Holmes-Manley process; Standard of New Jersey's tube-and-tank process; and the Cross process, controlled by Gasoline Products Company. After extensive patent litigation, a pooling agreement was negotiated in 1923 between the Jersey Company, the Indiana Company, and the Texas Company providing limited exchange of patents with individual freedom to develop and license. See McLean and Haigh, p. 385, and chap. 19. See also *Standard Oil Company (Indiana) v. U.S.*, 283 U.S. 163 (1931).

39. *U.S. v. E. I. du Pont de Nemours and Company*, 126 F. Supp. 235, 301–313 (1954); also Schlaifer, *Development of Aircraft Engines and Fuels*, p. 588.

Ethyl, who discovered the antiknocking properties of the branched-chain paraffins and thereby started a line of inquiry that led into the all-important development of high octane aviation fuels, as well as, eventually, a vast area of petrochemicals.[40]

Sun Oil must be credited with introducing catalytic cracking in the United States. Sun invested the $11 million necessary to bridge the gap between inventor Eugene Houdry's pilot plant and a commercial model. Houdry had begun work on his process in France in the mid-twenties and was originally brought to this country by Vacuum Oil. By the time Vacuum was merged with Socony in 1931, the price of gasoline had dropped and interest in continued experimentation with cracking was flagging. Sun, however, was trying to build a reputation on nonleaded, high octane gasoline, and it looked on the catalytic process as a chance to forge ahead in the octane race. It was this difference in product objective that led Sun to finance the experiment when no other integrated oil company seemed interested in methods of increasing or improving gasoline output.[41] Close on the heels of its introduction of catalytically cracked gasoline in 1937 came other uses of catalysts in refining: Standard of New Jersey's important contribution of using a fluid catalyst;[42] the development of polymerization, alkylation, catalytic reforming, and so on. In these developments important contributions have been made by engineering firms like M. W. Kellogg[43] and independent research organizations like Universal Oil Products,[44] as well as by many large integrated firms.[45]

Vertical integration seems to have played a more positive and cre-

40. Heron, *Development of Aviation Fuels,* pp. 549, 587–590.
41. According to *Fortune,* Standard Oil Development began work on catalytic cracking in 1936. Sun itself claims to have begun production of catalytically cracked gasoline in 1936 in a 200 b/d unit at Paulsboro and in a 15,000 b/d unit at Marcus Hook in the following year. See Bates, "This Mystery Called GASOLINE," reprinted from *Our Sun,* 1950. The first date is sometimes reported as 1935. See McLean and Haigh, p. 542, n. 8.
42. "Creating Tomorrow's Oil," *Fortune* (November, 1951), pp. 143–144.
43. Kellogg appears to be the inventor of the combination refinery which, by eliminating pauses between refining steps, cuts costs substantially. See "Engineers of Energy," *Fortune* (November, 1948), pp. 107–113, esp. 109.
44. Universal Oil Products brought platforming into commercial operation in 1949. Using platinum as a catalyst, platforming converts naphthas into high octane gasoline, and it has also proved an important source of aromatics for chemical uses.
45. See, e.g., Standard of Indiana's claimed pioneering role in fluid hydroforming (*Annual Report,* 1952, p. 14) and Phillips' early work in polymerization (Bates, "This Mystery Called GASOLINE," p. 13).

ative role in the development of refining than of production technology. The Standard Oil Trust was willing to back Frasch because of its holdings of sour crudes. Sun financed Houdry because of its interest in marketing a unique, high octane gasoline, independent of the Ethyl Corporation. Phillips went into polymerization to find a profitable way of disposing of its natural gas. In Chapter 5 were cited several instances in the early history of the industry of producing companies going into refining in order to find ways of converting unfamiliar crude oils into marketable products.

On the other hand, the integrated companies which pioneered in thermal cracking, and perhaps in catalytic cracking as well, did so as refiners, not particularly as producers or marketers. Similarly, non-integrated organizations like Universal Oil Products and M. W. Kellogg have found adequate incentives to improve the art in the competitive necessities of refiners, whether integrated or not. True, the ownership of marketing facilities and possibly the stress on brand distribution may have encouraged major oil companies to make higher expenditures on refining research than they would otherwise have done. True, also, these developments undoubtedly took size and substantial financial resources, and the correlation of integration with size and financial strength is not simply coincidental. Still, they did not depend on vertical integration per se.

Marketing

The original introduction of the service station was probably a real innovation. Although nothing seems more obvious today than that special retail outlets should have been provided to satisfy the soaring demands of the automobile for gasoline, lubricants, and service, this view is strongly tinged with hindsight; it unfairly minimizes the break that the drive-in service station made with the past. It was initiated, most observers seem to agree, by an independent, then adopted and quickly extended into chains by major refiners.[46] Once applied by majors, there was no containing the expansion of this new marketing medium.

While there is some doubt about the time and place of the first multipump, self-serve station, and an even graver question whether it deserves classification as an innovation at all, it is clear in this

46. See, e.g., McLean and Haigh, pp. 268–269, attributing the first company-operated drive-in station in the East to Atlantic; and Beaton, *Enterprise in Oil, a History of Shell in the United States*, p. 272, crediting Shell with "the first chain of drive-in service stations" in the country.

case as well as with most important first steps in the reduction of distribution costs [47] that the change began with an independent marketer.[48] It gathered momentum around Los Angeles immediately after World War II, under peculiar circumstances. Major companies in the area, grossly underestimating the postwar demand for gas and frightened at the prospect of war-created excess capacity, had eagerly entered into long-term contracts to sell large quantities of what they believed would be surplus gasoline to jobbers for unbranded distribution. The latter, in consequence, were able to offer privately branded gasoline of the highest quality at five cents below prevailing prices. With this assured supply of high-quality low-price product, the risk of the experiment was largely eliminated, and the huge volume which developed permitted substantial further economies in delivery and in operations. The self-serve station seems already to have subsided in importance and it would probably never have been important were cheap "surplus" gasoline not available to it; but in the circumstances of the time its effect was explosive. The multipump feature has been widely imitated by the major companies themselves.[49]

Excepting these instances, there has hardly been a development in marketing that clearly deserves recognition as an innovation, in contrast with a mere rationalization of distribution techniques. The large integrated firms have done much to improve the design, size, location, and operation of service stations; they have also made very impressive strides in streamlining the whole distribution operation. But anything approaching true innovation has begun with the independent. In applying these novel ideas the integrated companies have made their contribution to progress by exploiting their possibilities more rapidly and on a grander scale than would otherwise have been the case.

PRODUCTS INNOVATION

The annual reports of any of the integrated oil companies will illustrate the industry's continuous research for new products. From the wide spectrum of hydrocarbons available in a barrel of crude, refiners are fabricating increasing numbers of marketable products, far removed in character from the traditional fuels and lubricants.

47. See Bain, *Pacific Coast Petroleum Industry,* 3, 97.
48. According to Cassady and Jones, self-serve stations were introduced in Indianapolis in the early thirties by an independent marketer. *The Nature of Competition in Gasoline Distribution at the Retail Level,* p. 122, n. 3.
49. "Urich Sells 25 of 31 Multipumps," *National Petroleum News* (November 4, 1953), p. 24.

High octane gasoline itself is unquestionably a product innovation, as different from the natural, straight-run gasoline as rayon is from cotton. Produced first from thermal cracking, then extended by the use of Ethyl fluid, it was given an additional impetus by catalytic cracking and now benefits from polymerization, alkylation, and innumerable improvements in the catalytic reforming of straight-run gasoline.

Motor oils and greases, too, have been constantly improved, but it is difficult to point to any readily distinguishable major innovation in their quality or type other than the feat of developing satisfactory lubes from noncongenial crudes. The small Pennsylvania specialists can produce as satisfactory quality from their local, paraffin-based crudes as the billion-dollar integrated firms; but it was the latter, anxious not to lose this profitable business within each of their bulk plants and service stations, which evolved ways to turn out a lube from asphalt-based western oils that rivals the natural Pennsylvania product.

More obviously a novel product is liquefied petroleum gas (LPG), which has been made a familiar household fuel within the past twenty years. The basic processes may be traced to a German, Hermann Blau, who extracted the gas by compression in 1904; two West Virginians produced a liquid petroleum gas in 1910. But it was largely Union Carbide and Phillips which were instrumental in developing the market.[50]

It is outside the fuel and lubricant field that the product innovations by integrated oil companies have been most dramatic. The progressive advance of refining technology and in particular the adoption of catalytic cracking have produced a flood of versatile by-product hydrocarbons, familiar ones capable of displacing or supplementing traditional sources of supply, unfamiliar ones awaiting further experimentation to uncover new uses. A survey by *Petroleum Processing* in 1954 counted 176 companies engaged in the manufacture of petrochemicals in the United States and Canada and operating 269 plants. Forty-one additional plants, representing an investment of $550 millions, were in the planning or construction stages. Of the 176, sixty-two were oil companies and twelve were joint oil and chemical company subsidiaries. Practically all of the seventy-four oil companies involved were vertically integrated—among the leaders were Shell, Texas, Esso, Standard of Indiana, Phillips, and Lion Oil.[51] It is

50. "Bottled Gas," *Fortune, 37* (1948), 121, 124–125.
51. *National Petroleum News* (September 15, 1954), p. 38. Lion Oil Company was subsequently purchased by Monsanto Chemical Company.

difficult to think of a major oil company that has not begun to market substantial quantities of chemical by-products as a staple output of its refineries.

It is not easy to assess the relationship of this dramatic growth to vertical integration. The very nature of modern refining, with readily available and widely known techniques for re-ordering the molecular structures of hydrocarbons, makes it almost inevitable. For oil companies to exploit the prolific by-products of the modern refinery requires size and capital more than vertical integration: few refiners (Lion Oil was a notable exception) with less than 100,000 b/d capacity seem to have had the chemists to spare for purposes other than product-testing or others directly auxiliary to producing the familiar fuels and lubricants. However, integration may also have contributed: it is possible that the ownership of an accepted brand and of extensive marketing facilities has encouraged the majors to manufacture and market such items as insecticides or even candles (the latter hardly a petrochemical) under their own name.

More important, petrochemical production itself represents a kind of forward and circular integration. Here is a clear case in which integration effectively intensifies interindustry competition: witness Lion Oil's and Shell's synthetic nitrogen and fertilizers, Esso's Butyl rubber and synthetic toluene (for TNT), Shell's successful synthesis of glycerine, Phillips' early work in synthetic rubber. Whether or not vertical integration *in oil* was their precondition, integration into chemicals was the method of their effectuation.

Perhaps, indeed, the major oil companies have failed to innovate and integrate as aggressively into petrochemicals and their derivatives as the proponent of competition would have wished.[52] The aromatic hydrocarbons can be combined by alkylation with olefins and sulfonated to form the elements of detergents. Oil companies like Continental perform these functions; but they do not sell the detergents as such. They supply the soap companies rather than compete with them. Butadiene and styrene, which are co-polymerized to make synthetic rubber, come from petroleum refineries; but the processing has until

52. "It is not easy to understand the research problems of an industry whose primary business is to produce tomorrow what it produced yesterday. Such an industry must practice what is called convergent research. While the oil industry also practices some divergent research, it is content to leave most research of this type to the chemical industry and others. Divergent research tries to make something totally new. Convergent research tries to make tomorrow's product better, cheaper, and more plentiful than yesterday's." "Creating Tomorrow's Oil," *Fortune* (November, 1951), p. 112.

recently been done almost exclusively by rubber companies.[53] Except
for fertilizers and insecticides (and even these are exceptions only in
the case of a few of the companies that produce them), the oil industry has generally become a supplier of raw materials or intermedi-
ates to other industries which often subject them only to minor processing before selling them in final form. Thus, in striking contrast with
their practices in selling gasoline, the majors show considerable forbearance in further processing and marketing chemical products and
their derivatives.[54]

This forebearance can hardly be attributable to fears that chemical
companies would retaliate by going into petroleum production or
refining. More likely, it reflects the absorption of oil company managements with their traditional operations. Certainly, heavy participation in petrochemicals attests their willingness to break through
traditional industry boundaries where the prospects of exercising their
special talents profitably are good. Perfectly good business reasons no
doubt account for their operating through joint oil-chemical subsidiaries like Jasco, Inc., and Jefferson Chemicals,[55] and tending to
serve rather than to compete with some of the dominant firms in the
new fields that petrochemicals open up. Certainly, refiners would en-
counter novel problems of processing and marketing as manufacturers
and sellers of drugs, detergents, synthetic rubber, paints and plastics.
Still the vision of an oil company capitalizing on formidable assets it
has developed with the public to shake the complacency of leading
firms in these chemical arenas is intriguing for the customer.[56]

53. Having apparently availed themselves of the opportunity afforded by the
government's disposal of its plants in 1955, oil companies have become important producers of the rubbers themselves. In the period May–December,
1955, they accounted for 18.6 per cent of national sales of GRS, and in addition participated with rubber companies in joint ventures accounting for an
additional 20.7 per cent. *First Report of the Attorney General on Competition
in the Synthetic Rubber Industry* (May 1, 1956), p. 7.

54. This attitude was foreshadowed in an agreement regarding the hydrogenation field between Standard Oil (New Jersey) and I. G. Farben in the late
twenties which was summarized in a letter from a Jersey vice-president: "I.G.
are going to stay out of the oil business proper and we are going to stay out of
the chemical business insofar as that has no bearing on the oil business" (Letter
from Frank Howard to E. F. Johnson, quoted in Stocking and Watkins, *Cartels
in Action*, p. 93, from Truman Committee Hearings, Pt. XI, Exhibit 372, p.
4590).

55. Jasco, Inc. was the joint Standard Oil (New Jersey) and I. G. Farben
subsidiary for the United States chemical market; Jefferson Chemicals is owned
jointly by the Texas Company and American Cyanamid.

56. E.g., one soap company alone has accounted in recent years for some
two-thirds of the national sales of detergents. It has a number of widely ac-

These reservations about the products innovations of the integrated oil companies are, obviously, not a criticism of integration itself. Quite the contrary. Large nonintegrated refiners might equally have moved into petrochemicals. But lacking their own marketing facilities and brands as widely accepted or promoted, they would hardly have moved further or faster in product development than the majors.

WASTEFUL ASPECTS OF NON-PRICE COMPETITION

Vertical integration tends to increase the oil industry's emphasis on non-price competition for reasons to be explored in succeeding chapters. In his study of the Pacific Coast petroleum industry, Bain identified four major aspects of this non-price rivalry: (1) the continuous improvement of the basic products—gasoline and lubricants; (2) the construction of retail service stations with apparent excess capacity; (3) the proliferation of free services in the stations; and (4) the emphasis on aesthetic satisfactions with handsome attendants at the service station and beautiful singing stars on radio and TV programs.[57]

Non-price competition is by its very nature more difficult to appraise than price competition, from either the private or the public standpoint. Its advantages to the firm, if any, are seldom immediate or exhausted within a short period of time. A large part of business expenditures on the competitive acquisition of facilities, on product differentiation, on "free" services and on advertising is almost certain to be mutually offsetting, canceled by similar outlays of rivals and effecting no net improvement in competitive position. Any benefits in increased consumer satisfaction will often be impossible to measure, and their value may be far less than the cost of supplying them. These difficulties will be apparent in the evaluation of the industry's record not only of product innovation but also of investment in marketing facilities, discussed in Chapter 14.

One of the industry's most important innovations, the building of ever-higher octane ratings into its gasoline, aptly illustrates both the benefits and the wasteful extremes to which non-price competition can

---

cepted brands, protected by heavy annual investments in radio dramatic programs for child-wives. It would be a worthy rival. But the oil companies on their side also have widely accepted brands. Transferring consumer acceptance is sometimes tricky, but it is not entirely improbable that existing popularity might be extended to cover their own packaged detergents without expensive ventures into the already overcrowded field of the soap opera. The oil companies already have an extensive, established distribution network, and a clientele which comes to them anyhow, brings its own shopping bag on wheels, and presumably a predisposition in favor of the firm whose brand it patronizes.

57. *Pacific Coast Petroleum Industry*, 2, 242.

go and the difficulties of objectively drawing the line between the two. The higher octane gasolines of recent years make possible an enormous improvement in engine performance and a net fuel economy. In aviation fuel, where the engine and vehicle are designed to take the fullest advantage of these potentialities, the super fuels have been crucial to performance, particularly of military planes. *If* these gasolines are used in cars with appropriately higher compression ratios and *if* the higher power per gallon thus provided is used to get more mileage rather than, for instance, more rapid acceleration, the energy utilized at the refinery in increasing the octane rating is more than justified by the improved engine efficiency it permits. Both efficiency and economy are served.[58]

The qualifications that must be met, however, if higher octane rating is to mean a net social gain, whether measured in engineering (such as engine efficiency in energy use) or in economic terms (comparing benefits and costs), indicate extensive possibilities of waste. As for the first requirement, only a fraction of the cars on the road makes fully effective use of the potentialities of the fuel: [59] society suffers a net loss of the energy used in raising the octane rating for the others.[60]

58. E. V. Murphree, J. P. Haworth, A. F. Kaulakis, and A. R. Cunningham (all of Standard of New Jersey), "Trend to High Octane Is Sound," *Oil and Gas Journal* (January, 1954), pp. 229 ff. The critical Eugene Ayres, Gulf Research and Development Company, would apparently accept this statement. See his "Conservation and Motor Fuel—What's Ahead?" *Petroleum Refiner* (September, 1952), pp. 83 ff.

59. ". . . early in 1950—so far as data can be found—Sun Oil set out to get more of the Detroit and middle western market by upping its single grade of gasoline to about 88 octane. To beat this, some of the competition raised their regular and premium gas to 84 and 91 plus, respectively. Then the war spread swiftly to the East. Exuberant advertising writers failed to point out that only about 10 per cent of cars on the road . . . could get maximum use out of 90 plus fuel; that in engines not designed and attuned to it, high-octane gas means little or nothing in additional power." "The Octane Squeeze," *Fortune* (May, 1951), pp. 114–115, 118.

60. *Fortune* (May, 1951), p. 115, cites an estimate that production of 96 octane gasoline in a 100,000 b/d refinery would cut the gasoline yield 20 per cent. Ayres calculates that thermal cracking dropped the thermal efficiency of refining (i.e. the heat value of products compared with that of the crude) from about 97 to 92 per cent, but that lower efficiency was compensated by higher gasoline yields. Catalytic cracking, whose compensation has been not higher yields but only higher octane ratings of gasoline, drops efficiency to 87–89 per cent. This he estimates as equivalent to a loss of 60 to 100 million barrels of crude a year. "Conservation and Motor Fuel—What's Ahead?" p. 87. The cost of raising octane ratings from 95 to 98½ in recent years has been estimated by a General Petroleum Corporation study at about 3 cents a gallon; the same

The second condition for efficient utilization of these new fuels illustrates both the ambiguity of the phenomenon and the difficulty of assigning responsibility for it. In part, high octane gasoline has been oversold by the oil industry itself: the public has bought out of ignorance and a lack of alternatives for which the industry must bear some blame, even though each individual company may have been powerless to resist the trend for fear of losing its customers. In part, the refiners have been the willing prisoners of the automobile manufacturers, with their insatiable mania for bigger, heavier, and more powerful cars.[61] And who is the economist to say that there is waste if the buying public demands that *possibility* of rocket-like power, 150 mile-an-hour speeds, and lightning acceleration even though the energy potential is not used all of the time or is not used at all? [62]

The implication of the question posed—that the manufacturer adapts his product solely to the needs and desires of customers—is far from an adequate reflection of what happens in real markets. The taste-molding powers of advertising have probably been exaggerated, but there can be no doubt that the forms of competition the automobile and oil industries have chosen to emphasize, the ways in which they have altered and developed their products, bear a considerable responsibility for the shaping of consumer demands; this is true even though no single company may have been able significantly to stem the tide or alter the direction. The economist, of course, enjoys no special prerogative as judge; but it is for him to point out that the industries here concerned cannot escape some responsibility for the course that competition and consumer demand have taken and for the cost implicit in it.[63]

---

study indicates a cost of 5¢ a gallon to raise the rating from 100 to 105. *Wall Street Journal* (March 11, 1958), p. 4.

61. And, again, who is to blame? the automobile industry with its competitive drive for power, ostentation, bulk, and cumbersomeness—or the buying public, which apparently would desert any manufacturer who dared to offer convenience in size, modesty in weight, economy in fuel consumption? This is a chicken-and-the-egg kind of inquiry for which evidence is hard to find and harder to appraise.

62. The engineer owes it to the public to point out, with Ayres, that the "potential fuel savings [of high octane gas] are [being] thrown to the wind by . . . automatic transmissions, weight, and horsepower," that a "poor thermal performance [of the automobile] is an inevitable consequence of our insistence upon big heavy cars with soft tires and overpowerful engines," that small cars are physically far less wasteful. And the social critics may urge that we are paying too high a price for "amenities." Ayres, "Conservation and Motor Fuel —What's Ahead?" pp. 96 ff.

63. Not only does this gasoline require more energy to produce, but, ac-

The recent additives race further illustrates the opportunities for waste implicit in non-price competition that involves rivalry in selling uncheckable performance. The typical buyer is flatly incapable of knowing or ascertaining which of the cabbalistically identified additives is superior to the others, or whether any of them is worth paying for; [64] the market therefore cannot efficiently and reliably check the possibilities of wasteful excesses.

These possibilities of waste do not of course suffice to condemn product differentiation itself. From both a private and a public viewpoint, the identification of brands and the forms of competition associated with it are crucial to continuous product improvement and a maximizing of consumer satisfactions. This is true even though the effect has been to eliminate observable differences among major brands; for it must tend to do so by leveling the qualities of rival products upward toward that of the best product available. Without brand identification (the key to repetitive patronage), the incentive to quality perfection and product uniformity is sapped by the temptation to lower cost. The consumer can hardly be accused of irrationality or of having been hypnotized by advertising if he too rates assurances of quality, convenience, and service more highly than differences in price. [65]

---

cording to Ayres (p. 87), over a million tons of lead have been dissipated through the nation's exhaust pipes over the last twenty years. See *Fortune* (May, 1951), pp. 116–117, for references to experimental engines promising ultimate release from high octane requirements.

64. See, e.g., the assurance offered the motorist by Standard of Indiana in 1954: "Many road and other tests have been run on new types of additives, including competitive products. Thus far, none of them have shown benefits—at least with our clean-burning gasolines and oils—which outweigh their disadvantages." *National Petroleum News* (May 12, 1954), p. 34.

65. A survey of motorists' buying habits revealed that 77 per cent had a favorite brand which they usually bought, and 66 per cent bought the same brand exclusively. Of the 77 per cent who preferred a single brand, only 5 per cent were influenced by price. "Service Station and the Motorist," Report No. 2 (April, 1953), pp. 10–13, a survey by E. I. du Pont de Nemours and Company. Here again, however, we are caught in the familiar chicken-and-egg circularity. The extent to which motorists are influenced by considerations of price in buying gasoline depends on whether or not they are offered meaningful alternatives along those lines! If the price differences between competing products are minimal, price naturally will not significantly affect buyer choices. The spread of price wars indicates that if such alternatives are sufficiently divergent many motorists will respond. The failure of buyers to respond significantly to smaller differences may reflect simple inability to judge the reliability

Whether the benefits of product differentiation and innovation are worth their costs is, fortunately, not a question this study need try to answer. Its task is rather to explore how far vertical integration is responsible and how, if at all, would the situation be altered under a different business structure? Forward integration shifts competition from price to brand, quality and service, more strongly when, as in oil, it is combined with large size and relative fewness of sellers. If forward integration of refiners were not allowed, brand and service competition would still take place. Large marketers would take over some of the functions and probably some of the methods of big refiners today. But there would probably be more of them, and in that event the emphasis of their competition could be expected to shift more to price. And with the refiner facing tougher, larger-scale marketers as his customers rather than an unorganized and largely irrational buying public through his own tied outlets, not only might he have to rely more on price concessions to make sales, but he might also be forced to lay more stress on real and less on imaginary quality differentials.

At the same time it must be admitted there is no way of predicting these outcomes with any real assurance. It may well be that the reduced stress on the refiner's brand, the reduced availability of producer-refiner capital for service stations, radio programs, and research might also sacrifice some of the real benefits of brand competition just mentioned. To prohibit forward integration by refiners is to close the door to an important check on the possibility of monopolistic exploitation of consumers by organized distributors—a drastic step to take unless the evils of the present system permit no other solution. The ideal competitive situation is one in which buyers have a fair range of choice between alternative methods of rivalry, by vertically integrated and nonintegrated sellers as well. It is only insofar as integration proves incompatible with a mixed system of this sort that its complete abolition might reasonably be considered.

CONCLUSION

The student of this industry cannot help being impressed with its record in finding crude oil and natural gas, its achievements in realizing the inherent potentialities of its basic raw material, its ingenuity in

---

of the cheaper but less familiar gasolines; the social advantage of having familiar brands is thus dependent upon the perpetuation of buyer ignorance. If there were developed alternative institutions for dissipating that ignorance, the usefulness of brand names would diminish.

improving existing products and proliferating new ones, its boldness in amassing the necessary capital, and its progressive efficiency, at least in the last twenty years. The over-all performance is impressive; is this not enough?

Unfortunately, it is not enough. There are no standards against which to measure the results achieved. There is no way of telling how much better or worse they might have been under a different organization. One cannot even compare the record with that of other industries —technologies are much too different.

The rapid progress of petroleum is often attributed to its "research-mindedness"; but if this attribute is appropriately measured by the ratio of an industry's research expenditures to sales, petroleum refining does not show up particularly well among industries that conduct research.[66] Of some $2.5 billion total private research expenditures (including those aided by government grants) in 1952, it was estimated that petroleum accounted for $150 millions or about 6 per cent. On the reasonable premise that most of this was spent in the refining branch, which accounted for only 3 per cent of aggregate value added by manufacturing in the United States, it would appear that petroleum refining was more research-minded than the ratio of expenditures to sales would suggest. Certainly, better figures are needed, because oil is more of an extractive than a chemical industry and a very large percentage of its sales reflects a raw material which must be searched, not researched. Unless this raw material core is eliminated (such as by taking value added), the statistical measure of research outlays to final value will grossly understate the importance of research in parts of the industry where technology most encourages it. On the other hand, the opinion is becoming widespread within the industry that oil companies have been spending far too little on research in exploration and production, the area where the heaviest costs and most dramatic possi-

66. The average expenditure by manufacturing industries on research in 1951 was about 2 per cent of sales. The petroleum refining industry spent 0.6 per cent of sales, being almost at the bottom of the list. Bureau of Labor Statistics, "Scientific Research and Development in American Industry: A Study of Manpower and Costs," Bulletin No. 1148 (1953), pp. 78–79, tables C-19 and C-20. Most industries that spent a higher percentage of revenue on research were aided by government grants, which provided roughly 50 per cent of the funds for manufacturing research but only 3 per cent of the cost of research by the petroleum refining industry. Research expenditures of the chemical industry, which amounted to 2.5 per cent of sales, were financed in somewhat more generous fashion by the government, but only to 7.1 per cent of the total.

bilities of cost-reduction would seem to lie.[67] In any event, comparative figures, whether they show research expenditures in oil higher or lower than other industries, bear little on the issue of integration. Technology may be the more important determinant.

Though cognizant of the absence of statistical proof, and of the impossibility of knowing what kind of progress might have occurred under some other institutional arrangements, we cannot avoid the conviction that vertical integration has contributed substantially to industrial growth and progress in the petroleum industry. There were very few new ideas or inventions that could be traced from their origin to integrated firms, let alone attributed to their form of organization. Indeed, many of the more important were conceived and in some cases developed by outsiders. In the process of innovation, however, in the borrowing, developing, improving, applying, and spreading of the use of ideas, the major companies have played an important role. And though these results undoubtedly reflect the size as well as the integration of those companies, and the mere fact that the firms who do most of the business might naturally be expected to have done most of whatever innovating has occurred, we believe that integration itself accounted for much of the stimulus.

The possible contributions are varied but the basic one is to be found in the nature of the *incentives* inherent in integration itself— arising out of the mutual reinforcement and support that a company's separate operations lend to one another. The ownership of practically unusable sour crude in large amounts gave Standard Oil an urgent reason to seek a desulphurizing process and to apply it widely once it was found. The low, precarious margins of refiners provided strong incentives to minimize the costs of laying down crude oil at the refinery and distributing its products: they were practically forced to develop pipelines, to expand their use, to improve the efficiency of their barge and tanker transport, and to push forward the rationalization of their marketing. Heavy investments in refining and marketing facilities plus declining California output of crude oil undoubtedly spurred Union Oil to acquire oil shale lands and to study methods of using them. The protection of a brand name and other marketing investments led Sun Oil to push forward its critically valuable work on catalytic cracking and exerted similar pressure on all integrated re-

---

67. See, e.g., M. J. Rathbone (president of Jersey Standard), "Our Untapped Oil Reserve—Greater Efficiency"; and Douglas Ragland, "Effect of Modern Drilling Technology on Well Cost," *Petroleum Engineer* (January, 1957), pp. B-33, B-36.

finers to better their methods. Possession of noisome, uncongenial crudes forced continued progress in refining and spurred the development of new products, including a satisfactory asphalt-based lubricating oil. One could go on; but the point is simply this: in a closely integrated operation, failure, irritation, need, or surplus at any one level or in any one process of the industry creates an imbalance which stirs up compensatory, socially beneficial activity at other levels. This would be true under any type of industrial organization; but with common management and ownership spanning the various levels, the financial stimulus to action is probably more powerful.

Behind these direct incentives of the integrated firm—the leverage of imminent loss as well as the prospect of possible profit—are considerations mentioned in the preceding chapter. Integration permits decisions to follow more directly on conception of need and action to follow decision without waiting for the response of suppliers and customers. It may offer greater opportunities for innovation. The larger the exposure-front of a firm's commercial operations, the greater the probability that experts within its organization will recognize the potentialities of a new idea or product in commercial application; and the wider the firm's commercial interests, the more likely it is to apply its resources for the development of such an idea. Furthermore, the integrated firm may have more financial resources to apply. And finally, integration may itself be the method of effecting an innovation: Phillips, embarrassed by too much cheap natural gas, integrated into the production of LPG; and refiners have integrated into petrochemicals.

But times change, and with them the appropriateness of institutions. Looking to the future rather than to the past, some would say that, in areas where vertical integration seems to have already made its major contribution, little would now be lost by excluding it. For example, there can be no doubt that refiners contributed importantly to the rapid expansion of the service station, to its improvement as a marketing device and to the establishment of high standards of service, personal and technical, in its performance. Today, with major brands firmly established in the public eye and with customers highly sensitized to good service, it is extremely doubtful if the continuing emphasis on investment in retail distributive facilities by the majors contributes to the public good, or perhaps even to their own. The ownership and operation of crude oil pipelines in the domestic market may be reaching a similar status. In earlier days the construction of pipelines could not be safely left to the market. This could still be the case; but the important market areas are so well defined, the needs so clear, and the technical problems so well understood that even independent financing and construction are not unthinkable.[68] Certainly, with more effective public control of operations, a more open policy toward participation of independents in joint ownership would cost major companies little and it could gain them much.

However, in a dynamic economy the greatest danger is to impose artificial prohibitions on new forms and directions of growth. The essence of innovation is that its direction can never be predicted with assurance no matter how inevitable past progress may appear to hindsight. Too little is known of the origin of new ideas and new applications of old ideas; of the potential innovations that are still-born and lost to society for lack of the imagination, resources, and courage needed to develop them; and of the conditions most likely to generate them. The future may develop opportunities and pressures for more vertical integration rather than less. In the present state of our ignorance, both routes must be kept free. Certainly, the opportunity to integrate vertically in order to make a profit or to solve a problem must not be denied. Many reasons have been advanced why vertical integration should be expected to quicken perception of, and strengthen the response to need for, change. These may not be adequate in themselves to assure progress, but they should not be lightly, certainly not needlessly, sacrificed.

68. Interestingly, it has been independent shipping magnates who have played the major role in developing supertankers: the market seems sufficiently assured to attract their capital. See, e.g., *Business Week* (August 25, 1956), p. 60.

CHAPTER 13

Investment Practices and Integration: Production and Transportation

TOTAL UNITED STATES consumption of petroleum products has expanded at a cumulative rate of 5.8 per cent per year since 1920; and including natural gas, with which oil exploration and discovery is typically associated, the combined annual rate of growth since World War II (figured in b.t.u.'s) has been 7 per cent. Expansion has been markedly resistant to cyclical fluctuations; even the economic collapse of the thirties produced a relatively slight decline before long-run growth was resumed. There is good reason to expect demand to continue to grow substantially faster than the gross national product in the future, although probably somewhat less rapidly than during the last three decades: [1] the Chase Bank analysts estimate that, in a high employment economy with average increases in energy requirements of about 3.8 per cent per year, the consumption of oil and natural gas might expand during the next ten years at about 5 per cent annually.[2]

Such a growth—it would imply United States domestic consumption of 14.3 million barrels per day by 1966—would require a huge

1. It seems unlikely that the *rate* of expansion in motor fuels can survive an approaching saturation of the automobile market with an incipient trend toward smaller, more economical cars, a transition into the jet age of air travel, and a maturing stage of growth for truck transport and motorized agriculture. As for distillates, the conversion to diesel locomotives is almost complete, and the competitive availability of natural gas must slow the expansion of home-heating needs. Still, all of these demands will continue to grow and some—jet fuel, motor boats, air conditioning (in which oil competes with natural gas), asphalt, and liquefied petroleum gas—should expand at an accelerated pace. Revolutionary fuels, like atomic energy, are far enough in the future economically to set no near-term ceiling. With high employment and an expanding population, industrial requirements will also grow, but displacement of energy sources like coal must meet increasing economic resistance.

2. See Hill, Hammer, and Winger, *Future Growth of the World Petroleum Industry* (April 25, 1957), pp. 11, 19; and Terry and Winger, *Future Growth of the Natural Gas Industry* (May 13, 1957), p. 19. Both pamphlets were published by the Chase Manhattan Bank.

capital investment by the American industry, its amount and character governed by the assumptions one makes regarding the proportion of domestic requirements we shall seek to produce from our own resources in contrast with allowable imports, the rate at which we can safely produce relative to our proved reserves, and the ability of the domestic industry to find oil in the volume required to maintain a minimum reserve production ratio. On their own projection of these parameters, the Chase Bank analysts anticipate aggregate capital expenditures by the domestic industry during the decade through 1965 of $73.6 billion, of which more than $50 billion (practically

TABLE XIII

Gross Investment of American Oil Companies in Fixed Assets Located in Non-Communist Foreign Countries, December 31, 1955

AREA	TOTAL INVESTMENT		U.S. COMPANIES % OF TOTAL
	INDUSTRY [a]	U.S. COMPANIES	
	($000,000)		
Canada	2,525	1,365	54.1
Venezuela	3,450	2,095	60.7
Other Western Hemisphere	2,440	750	30.7
Middle East	2,750	1,290	46.9
Africa	425	100	23.5
Far East	1,950	755	38.7
Western Europe	4,060	1,045	25.7
Foreign-flag tankers	5,300	575	10.8 [b]
TOTAL	22,900	7,975	34.8
DEPARTMENT			
Production	6,685	3,225	48.2
Pipelines	1,275	725	56.9
Tankers	5,300	575	10.8
Refineries and chemical plants	5,315	1,700	32.0
Marketing	3,695	1,335	36.1
Other	630	415	65.9
TOTAL	22,900	7,975	34.8

[a] Industry totals include foreign companies and governments.
[b] Of tank ships above 2,000 gross tons, American companies were reported to control roughly one-third of the world's deadweight tons as of this date.

Source: Coqueron and Pogue, Investment Patterns in the World Petroleum Industry pp. 47–48, and table 13.

69 per cent) will be required for production.[3] Over the same period, these authors project capital outlays of more than $41 billion in other countries of the world outside the USSR and its satellites, for an aggregate expenditure of $115 billion. These foreign expenditures are also importantly a problem for United States companies, which own a very high proportion of aggregate investments abroad, especially in the major producing areas—the Middle East, Venezuela, and Canada—as shown in Table XIII .

SOURCES OF INVESTMENT FUNDS

As a basis for projection of the industry's capital needs and the formulation of recommendations for their fulfillment, the Chase staff drew on its financial analyses of this industry over the period since 1934. The results are summarized in two accompanying tabulations, the first showing the sources of funds for thirty oil companies [4] over the seventeen-year period from 1934 through 1950 (see Tables XIV), and the second estimating the sources of funds for capital expenditures only for the entire United States domestic industry for each of the years 1951 through 1955 (see Table XV). These tabulations are not directly comparable; they differ obviously in coverage but, more important, the former includes among the uses of funds net additions to working capital and investments and advances to nonconsolidated companies—it is derived from a detailed study that comes near to showing the sources and uses of funds for the companies involved—while the latter is restricted to the major capital outlays and neglects the broader question of total requirements for funds and the sources from which they were derived.

These tabulations reveal several important characteristics of the industry. It is instructive that despite the growth in total capital expenditures, the thirty oil companies found little need to go beyond their own internal resources except during the three big investment years following 1946. During the seventeen years they increased their combined net assets from 7.4 to 18.2 billion dollars (including approximately $3.0 billion located in foreign countries), yet net total

3. Estimated capital expenditures include the cost of drilling dry holes and of lease acquisitions but excludes exploration expenses and lease rentals. See Coqueron and Pogue, *Investment Patterns in the World Petroleum Industry* (New York, Chase Manhattan Bank, 1956), esp. pp. 32–35, tables 13–14 and Exhibits 12–13. Also see Hill, Hammer, and Winger, *Future Growth of the World Petroleum Industry,* p. 23.

4. The nature of this sample was discussed in Chap. 2, pp. 15–16.

funds required from external sources, including sale of assets, was only $3,039 million.[5] To accomplish this result, company shareholders had to be content with a dwindling proportion of net earnings in the form of dividends.[6] And though funded and long-term debt almost tripled as prorationing and expanding demand made oil securities a more attractive investment for banks, insurance companies, and the general public, the aggregate of such securities was still less than 20 per cent of net worth in 1950. Finally, allowances for depreciation, depletion and amortization, and the cost of dry holes aggregated a major proportion of capital expenditures, and a total sum over the period roughly the size of all pretax net income from operations. The exact impact of these allowances on income tax liability cannot be estimated from these data; but they aggregated about 71 per cent of reported net income (after deductions) before income tax.[7]

5. Aggregate external financial transactions were greater of course, the bulk representing changes in financial structure. Thus over the entire period:
Total external capital from financing: $6.200 billion.

Sources		Uses	
Borrowing	$5.342 billion	$2.482	billion was used to refund long-term debt
Preferred stock	0.239 billion	1.822	billion was used to retire long-term debt
Common stock	0.619 billion	0.431	billion to acquire preferred and common stock
		(1.465	available for expansion)

Other Sources		Other Uses	
Added funds from sale of assets	1.574 billion	2.163	billion added to working capital
Capital extinguishments	12.468 billion	19.425	billion capital expenditures
Accrued minority income	0.693 billion	1.105	billion other investments
Net income	12.077 billion	5.584	billion dividends, including minority interests
Total sources	33.012 billion	33.012	total uses

See Coqueron and Pogue, *Capital Formation in the Petroleum Industry*, pp. 6, 10, 30, 31.

6. Dividends aggregated a shade under 4 per cent of net worth, excluding minority interests, over the seventeen years.

7. By lumping dry-hole expense (a cash outlay) with depletion, depreciation, amortization, and property retirements (non-cash charges), petroleum company reporting makes it quite impossible to trace the effect of tax privileges on the flow of cash available for investment. Nor can the effect of these taxes be gauged by comparison of net income before and after tax, because it cannot be known what net income before tax would be were these special tax provisions not taken advantage of. It is only suggestive, therefore, that tax liability of the thirty companies for the entire period amounted to only 24.6 per cent of computed net income subject to tax.

TABLE XIV

Funds Provided from Earnings: Thirty Oil Companies, 1934–50

($000,000)

	1934–39	1940–45	1946–50	TOTAL 17 YEARS
Total cash from operations [a]	5,156	7,494	7,326	25,238
Less: capital extinguishment charges [b]	2,950	4,256	5,262	12,468
Net income from operations [c]	2,206	3,238	7,326	12,770
Less: cash dividends [d]	1,329	1,612	2,641	5,584
Net income retained	877	1,624	4,685	7,186
Available for capital expenditures and other purposes [e]	3,827	5,880	9,947	19,654
Capital expenditures [f]	3,870	5,379	10,178	19,425
Net available for other purposes	−43	+501	−231	+229
Invest. and advances to non-consolidated companies	−220	−275	−610	−1,105
Net additions to working capital	−173	−772	−1,218	−2,163
Total funds required from external sources	436	546	2,057	3,039

RATIOS: %

	1934–39	1940–45	1946–50	TOTAL 17 YEARS
Dividends / net income from operations [g]	57.4	49.2	35.3	42.5
Net income retained / capital expenditures	23	30	46	37.0
Capital extinguishment charges / capital expenditures	76	79	52	64.1
External funds / capital expenditures	11	10	20.6	15.6

[a] Includes net income accruing to minority interests: $693 million over entire period.

[b] Includes depreciation, depletion, amortization, property retirements and costs of dry holes drilled. Also non-cash charges in the amount of $380 million over entire period.

[c] Including income accruing to minority interests.

[d] Includes dividends paid minority interests: $449 million over entire period.

[e] This equals capital extinguishment charges (except for dry hole outlays, these are charges against income which are not cash payments) plus net income retained.

[f] Includes expenditures on dry holes.

[g] Excluding income accruing to minority interests.

Source: Coqueron and Pogue, *Capital Formation in the Petroleum Industry* (Chase National Bank, 1952), pp. 9, 29, 30, tables 4, 5, 6, and exhibit 5.

During the subsequent five years, 1951–55, data estimated for the United States industry as a whole roughly approximate in total and confirm in proportions the observations already made about the thirty oil companies (see Table XV). Dividend payout continued roughly around 40 per cent of net income, and net income retained constituted about one-third of capital expenditures, somewhat less than the average of the earlier period. Capital extinguishment charges were the most important source of financing for capital outlays (more than 50 per cent); but the aggregate expansion of investment was so great (approximating total cash from operations after operating expenses), that combined capital extinguishment charges and retained net in-

TABLE XV

Capital Formation by United States Petroleum Industry, 1951–55

($ billion)

	1951	1952	1953	1954	1955	TOTAL
Total cash from operations	4.37	4.54	5.15	5.34	5.91	25.30
Less: capital extinguishment charges	1.98	2.21	2.46	2.73	3.06	12.44
Net income from operations	2.40 [a]	2.33	2.69	2.61	2.85	12.86
Less: cash dividends	.88	.91	1.03	1.07	1.18	5.06
Net income retained from operations	1.52	1.42	1.66	1.54	1.67	7.80
Available for capital expenditures and other purposes	3.50	3.63	4.12	4.27	4.73	20.24
Capital expenditures	3.63	4.40	5.03	5.35	5.60	24.00
Funds required from capital market and other sources to meet capital expenditures	0.13	0.77	0.91	1.08	0.87	3.76
RATIOS: %						
Dividends / net income from operations	36.6	39.0	38.3	41.0	41.5	39.3
Net income retained / capital expenditures	42.0	32.3	33.0	28.8	29.8	32.5
Capital extinguishment / capital expenditures	54.5	50.0	49.0	51.0	54.6	51.8
External funds / capital expenditures	3.5	17.7	18.0	20.2	15.6	15.7

[a] Figures are rounded.

Source: Pogue and Hill, *Future Growth and Financial Requirements of the World Petroleum Industry* (1956), pp. 32–33.

come fell short by more than 15 per cent over the five-year period. In contrast, these two items more than covered total capital outlays in the prior seventeen years. External funds in this context were merely the residual amount needed to meet capital outlays with no account taken of increases in working capital.

Indeed, capital expenditures in the postwar decade have outpaced physical expansion both at home and abroad, whether it be measured in crude oil production, in crude runs to stills, or in petroleum consumption. Over the decade 67.7 per cent of petroleum capital outlays in the non-Communist world were made in the United States, about 70 per cent of this total being directed toward exploration and production; and the domestic industry found 38,393 million barrels of crude oil and natural gas liquids (also 149.8 trillion cubic feet of natural gas). The rest of the world, with much lower capital expenditures and only 36.7 per cent of them in exploration and production, uncovered 136,683 million barrels of crude oil.[8] Outside the United States, investment prospects are certainly more lush.

In formulating their estimates of future financial needs and their policy recommendations, the Chase Bank analysts project the financial behavior of the industry as found in the twenty-two years prior to 1956 into the following decade. They anticipate a declining comparative role for outside financing, from 15.5 per cent during the first five years to 13.5 per cent thereafter, and allot retained earnings to a diminishing relative importance—27.4 per cent and 23.2 per cent respectively. It is to non-cash charges and cash charges against income such as intangibles and dry hole costs (57.1 per cent and 63.3 per cent respectively) that they look for the bulk of the $115 billion of capital expected to be required in the next decade. This conviction that growth in the petroleum industry will be geared strictly to the level of profits dictates a familiar industry contention: prices for crude oil and refined products must rise; allowances for depreciation and depletion must be increased to prevent the dissipation of low-cost productive assets (primarily crude reserves discovered many years ago and only gradually exploited over time) at less than compensatory rates as prices and costs spiral above original costs.[9]

8. U.S. data are gross additions to reserves for total liquid hydrocarbons and for natural gas (API, *Proved Reserves for Crude Oil, Natural Gas Liquids and Natural Gas,* December 31, 1956, p. 13, table 5B and p. 21, table 3). Capital expenditures computed from Coqueron and Pogue, *Investment Patterns,* pp. 37–38; see also pp. 49, 52.

9. See Coqueron and Pogue, *Investment Patterns,* p. 27; and *Capital Formation,* p. 20.

The assertion that the growth of this vital industry must be geared to the volume of internal funds is almost fantastic. In the days before prorationing, such a position was understandable. Loans based on oil properties during the thirties were seldom longer than a year or eighteen months and only an insignificant fraction of financing could be done through the banks. But with the stabilization of oil markets, terms were extended by the banks, eventually to ten years on some properties and even longer periods by insurance companies, which were reported to hold more than a billion dollars of oil company debt in 1954. With the development of organized oil departments of banks, serviced by engineers and technicians, credit on reasonable terms for producing properties is available to the smallest operator.[10]

What is true of the availability of credit is even truer of equity funds. The oil industry's predilection for internal financing is not unique among American corporations, but it is rooted neither in financial stringency nor in lack of profit. Indeed, in industry generally it is the smaller, less profitable undertaking that is often forced to seek external financing; the larger and more successful can afford the luxury of growth from earnings and the freedom of management it guarantees. The oil industry's special tax advantages also make a policy of growth through internal financing both especially attractive, by offering stockholders a chance for high capital gains in which the government bears an unusually large share of the costs of failure and an unusually small share of the fruits of success, and especially feasible, by increasing the tax-free cash flow.

The contention that tax allowances for depreciation and depletion in this industry are inadequate requires more evidence than it has received, more especially in the extraction of crude oil, which accounts for some 70 per cent of petroleum capital outlays in this country and over 50 per cent of gross capital investment. In both the drilling of dry holes and the intangible expense of development wells, allowances are complete: the entire expense may be charged against income in the year incurred.[11] And percentage depletion, unlike depreciation, is

10. For a striking example of an arrangement for extending credit and minimizing tax liability, see the description of the "oil payment" in Lyon F. Terry, vice-president of the Chase Manhattan Bank, "Petroleum Financing" (reprint) delivered at Financial and Accounting Group Session, 35th Meeting of the API, San Francisco, November 15, 1955.

11. Intangible costs include grading, labor, boring, testing, surveying, installing equipment—all costs that do not result in a tangible asset which could be sold or salvaged. The intangible portion of development costs may vary from 50 per cent to 65 per cent of the total. See Joint Committee on the Economic

not tied to a past dollar investment. It is based on market value and will therefore vary with important changes in production costs to the extent that they are reflected in price.[12] Actually, the cost of a given reservoir is a unique, historical incident with no significance for costs of replacement. The data do not exist that could transmute such financial facts into a meaningful measure of replacement costs. The adequacy of tax allowances, therefore, of which percentage depletion is but one, is a problem in incentives, and incentives can be measured only by results. In terms of results, incentives would seem to have been adequate, or more than adequate.

The heavy investment costs which confront the domestic oil industry argue less for more generous tax treatment than they underscore the need for more efficient use of capital. This is nowhere more important than in the field of production, where the cries for assistance are most persistent. An exploratory effort sustained by the lure of tax avoidance is likely to be socially wasteful. Special inducements to explore, drill for, and produce domestic oil; mounting capital outlays and higher costs in production; and prorationing restrictions on output that idle efficient production, lengthen the pay-out period, and reduce the return on investment. There is a vicious circle here that must be broken if our domestic oil industry is to meet the challenge of economic growth in the years to come. As long as we are tied to current practices, we must expect increasing demands for tax subsidies, increasing reliance on internal funds for expansion, and increasing dependence on giant vertically integrated firms that can merge the diseconomies of restrictive control with the advantages of more rational development outside this country. The solution of this dilemma requires that state prorationing be abandoned in favor of a national oil policy based on mandatory unitization, with an economically rational reliance on lower-cost foreign supplies to an extent consistent with a bona fide determination of the requirements of national security.[13]

Report, *Federal Tax Policy for Economic Growth and Stability*, p. 481. Tangible production equipment is capitalized and exploration costs like geological and geophysical expense and lease rentals can be allowed against income only when leases are surrendered.

12. On the other hand, petroleum is a high investment industry; the weight of depreciation of durable assets may well exceed the depletion allowance.

13. See James R. Nelson, "Prices, Costs, and Conservation in Petroleum," *American Economic Review, Papers and Proceedings*, 48 (1958), 502–515. And see above, Chap. 10.

Exploration and Production

The analysis of the economic, technical, and political forces impinging on the supply of crude oil in Chapter 8 led to the conclusion that under modern conditions of public subsidy and regulation there appeared to be no function in this area that could not be adequately performed by a large nonintegrated firm or a group of firms acting in a joint venture. As an integrated refiner, the major has special incentives to secure an adequate flow of crude oil, and these incentives may activate his own exploratory efforts, urge him to assist others through "farm-outs," bring about the acquisition of producing properties, or lead him to negotiate credit for an independent in return for first call on the oil.[14] But with stabilized crude markets and with financial agencies, equipped with technical staffs, competing for petroleum business, the essentiality of these and other ways of supporting crude oil development through the larger cash flows and superior credit standing of the majors is moot.

None of the information available is sufficient to prove beyond cavil a conclusion that vertical integration is unnecessary for a socially desirable rate of investment in production; but the presumption established for it is strong. In Table XVI the ratio of earnings after taxes to average invested capital is shown for eight leading producers as compared with a varying number of other producers as a group, and for twenty-two selected major integrated companies contrasted with a varying sample of refiner-marketers. Total industry averages are also shown for the period covered, 1933 through 1956. Excepting the war period (1940–45) and the single boom year 1948, the large producing companies consistently bettered the earnings record of other producers, very substantially in the last seven years. The combination of price control, shortage of steel for drilling, and intensification of production from existing wells probably holds the explanation for the wartime reversal of performance by these two groups. The reduction in the number of companies included, with the probable sloughing off of less profitable companies, would have worked in the same direction.

Much more startling is the comparatively drab performance of the

14. The major may be able to obtain a long-term insurance company loan at a low interest rate for an independent willing to give him a preferred position. Since such loans are made only on expert appraisal, they may strain neither cash position nor credit rating. McLean and Haigh quote an Atlantic Refining Co. memorandum on the subject (p. 201).

TABLE XVI — Ratio of Earnings to Average Invested Capital,[a] Petroleum Industry, 1933–56

PERIOD	PRODUCING COMPANIES — 8 LEADING COMPANIES[b] — RATIO %	PRODUCING COMPANIES — OTHER PRODUCERS — RATIO %	PRODUCING COMPANIES — OTHER PRODUCERS — NUMBER OF FIRMS	PRODUCING COMPANIES — TOTAL PRODUCERS %	REFINERS, MARKETERS, ETC. — 22 MAJOR INTEGRATED COMPANIES[c] %	REFINERS, MARKETERS, ETC. — OTHER COMPANIES — RATIO %	REFINERS, MARKETERS, ETC. — OTHER COMPANIES — NUMBER OF COMPANIES	REFINERS, MARKETERS, ETC. — TOTAL %	TOTAL INDUSTRY — RATIO %	TOTAL INDUSTRY — NUMBER OF COMPANIES
1933	1.0	0.8	38	0.9	1.3	2.0	29	1.4	1.4	97
1934	4.8	3.2	39	3.7	2.8	3.3	29	2.9	2.9	98
1935	6.4	5.8	45	6.0	4.8	3.7	32	4.7	4.8	107
1936	9.8	8.9	51	9.2	7.5	7.7	35	7.5	7.6	116
1937	11.6	10.8	53	11.0	9.8	7.5	36	9.7	9.8	119
1938	9.7	7.7	53	8.3	4.8	6.3	36	4.9	5.1	119
1939	7.6	7.0	52	7.2	5.2	8.1	36	5.4	5.5	118
5-year average	9.0	8.1	51	8.4	6.4	6.6	35	6.4	6.6	116
1940	5.8	6.1	52	6.0	6.2	7.1	38	6.3	6.3	120
1941	8.3	11.4	48	10.3	8.7	8.6	38	8.7	8.8	116
1942	8.9	11.8	44	10.8	6.5	8.8	40	6.6	6.8	114
1943	12.5	13.5	43	13.1	7.9	8.5	40	8.0	8.2	113
1944	13.1	14.9	41	14.3	9.6	9.1	36	9.5	9.8	107
5-year average	9.8	11.5	46	11.0	7.8	8.5	38	7.8	8.0	114
1945	12.5	14.3	46	13.7	8.5	11.2	40	8.6	8.9	116
1946	16.1	13.5	41	14.4	10.2	11.8	40	10.3	10.5	111
1947	25.4	22.6	47	23.6	14.8	18.2	44	14.9	15.4	121
1948	32.9	33.1	56	33.0	19.7	21.5	45	19.7	20.5	131
1949	22.6	21.5	53	21.9	12.7	15.2	44	12.8	13.3	127
5-year average	22.8	21.9	49	22.2	13.5	16.1	43	13.7	14.1	121
1950	22.0	17.6	55	19.2	14.4	15.6	40	14.5	14.8	125
1951	22.1	17.9	69	19.3	15.8	15.5	38	15.7	16.0	137
1952	19.7	15.5	74	16.9	13.8	13.5	35	13.8	14.0	139
1953	20.1	15.3	70	16.8	13.9	14.1	40	14.0	14.1	130
1954	19.6	13.2	70	15.3	12.8	12.0	30	12.8	12.9	130
5-year average	20.6	15.6	68	17.3	14.1	14.0	35	14.1	14.3	132
1955	19.2	12.4	63	14.6	13.4	13.6	23	13.4	13.5	113
1956	18.0	13.5	63	14.9	13.9	12.6	23	13.8	13.9	113

[a] Ratio of earnings after taxes to the average of the book value of outstanding preferred and common stocks and consolidated surplus accounts at the beginning and end of each year.

[c] In 1949 Plymouth became an integrated refiner. Thereafter, these ... Plymouth see n. c. In 1956 Houston was acquired by Atlantic, and drops out of this group.

twenty-two majors. In all but eight of the twenty-four years compared the integrated firms performed less well than the other refiners and marketers; in every year but four they earned less—often substantially less—than the group of smaller producers and consequently did even more poorly than the large producers. While the major integrated companies approximated, and sometimes equaled, industry average net earnings, they did not succeed, as a group, in excelling this average performance throughout the entire period.

But before too many tears are shed for the majors and their modest earnings record within the industry, it is well to recall the limitations of these data and particularly of the inherent bias in their selection. In the first place, the level of earnings of all the firms aggregated in Table XVI was not bad, apart from the first two, deeply depressed years. Dividends were held to a modest percentage of invested capital, but return on capital did not fall below 10 per cent in the postwar and reached 20.5 per cent in the boom year 1948, despite expansion that more than tripled the average invested capital from 1935 ($5.84 billion) to 1954 ($18.94 billion).[15] Second, the comparison made here is between two selected major groups which are held constant and a varying number of other firms classified as producers and other companies. In the two areas of the business where entry is easiest and number of firms highest—production and marketing—the smaller, and especially the less fortunate, operators cannot be represented. Many such firms are unincorporated and many, especially those that have failed, will leave no record for the analyst. This would be true even if a determined effort were made to represent them; in a compilation made from annual reports readily accessible, the selection of "other" producers and "other" nonproducers will necessarily be drawn from the larger and more successful members of the group.

15. The five-year averages for the entire group, from the same source, were as follows:

PERIOD	AVERAGE INVESTED CAPITAL ($ BILLION)	RETURN ON CAPITAL %	CASH [a] DIVIDENDS TO AVERAGE INVESTED CAPITAL %	DIVIDENDS TO EARN- INGS %	AVERAGE NUMBER OF COMPANIES
1935–39	6.22	6.6	3.8	57.6	116
1940–44	6.78	8.0	4.0	50.3	114
1945–49	9.39	14.1	5.0	35.7	121
1950–54	15.85	14.3	6.0	42.0	132

[a] Stock dividends in addition to cash dividends were paid amounting (in millions) to $157, $177, and $245 in 1952, 1953 and 1954 respectively. Previous years not available.

It will be remembered also that the somewhat lower percentage earnings of the major integrated firms will apply to a much greater capital base. One of the strengths of the integrated firm, and an advantage for the investor, is that it protects heavy investments by stabilizing earnings; the apparently equal stability in the earnings of the other groups of companies in Table XVI may well reflect their unrepresentative character and changing membership. Whether so huge an investment would otherwise have been made, or what rate of return it would otherwise have earned, in comparison with the far smaller aggregate investments of the remaining companies in the table cannot be guessed. Finally, the twenty-two majors have a large share of their assets in crude oil, carried in the accounts at the level of capital outlays, not value of reserves. While this fact may make their moderate profit record relative to other refiner-marketers more surprising, it also means that their nominal level of earnings, which tend to be depressed by the expensing of numerous cost items, also do not reflect the capital gains investors may obtain from the rising market value of their investments.

The security market's appraisal of the comparative risks and earnings of investment in large producing companies and major integrated firms is explored in Table XVII. After-tax earnings before interest charges are related to average borrowed and invested capital to avoid leverage differentials reflecting varying capital structures. On this basis, earnings of the nine producing companies substantially exceeded those of the twenty-one integrated firms in every postwar year, by almost 100 per cent in the early years. This showing corresponds roughly to that of the earlier comparison, in Table XVI. Not only have the producing companies tended to earn more than the majors on the average dollar of invested capital; as the last two columns of Table XVII demonstrate, investors have tended to place a higher valuation on a dollar of current earnings by the former than by the latter companies. In every year the earnings-price ratio of producer companies was lower (that is, the price-earnings multiplier was higher) than for the integrated group, and the disparity became larger as the period advanced.

Again, it is difficult to give these data a definitive meaning. Market valuation may have been importantly affected by the peculiar investment strength of the small number of producers sampled, more especially by the size and location of oil reserves discovered which do not show up in capital outlays or in average investment. Not actual earnings but anticipated earnings are what determine the market value of shares. Thus the size of cash flow generated from internal sources and the rate at which this cash is being converted into new crude oil assets may be more significant for market value than reported profits after tax. With spreading anticipations of long-term price inflation, and confidence in the ability of prorationing to restrain production, this comparative value of producing company investment should rise.

TABLE XVII

Comparison of Earnings and Market Evaluation of Earnings, Nine Producers and Twenty-one Integrated Firms, 1946–56 [a]

	EARNINGS AS A PERCENTAGE OF CAPITAL OUTSTANDING [b]		WEIGHTED AVERAGE EARNINGS PER SHARE OF COMMON STOCK [c]		EARNINGS-PRICE RATIO [d]	
YEAR	9 PRODUCING COMPANIES [e]	21 INTEGRATED COMPANIES [f]	9 PRODUCING COMPANIES	21 INTEGRATED COMPANIES	9 PRODUCING COMPANIES	21 INTEGRATED COMPANIES
	%	%	$	$	%	%
1946	15.69	8.34	0.73	1.19	7.50	8.38
1947	22.21	11.80	1.25	1.89	11.27	13.35
1948	33.44	15.65	2.28	2.92	15.78	17.74
1949	19.94	10.16	1.63	2.12	11.91	14.14
1950	17.76	11.74	1.65	2.67	8.70	14.47
1951	18.25	13.04	1.95	3.24	6.46	12.50
1952	15.40	11.58	1.90	3.13	5.15	10.22
1953	16.45	11.61	2.24	3.41	6.09	11.97
1954	15.67	11.02	2.37	3.52	5.12	10.09
1955	15.56	11.71	2.44	4.10	4.35	8.88
1956			2.49	4.64	3.58	7.96

[a] Sources: data derived from Annual Reports of respective companies; Standard and Poor's Corporation, Corporation Records and Standard Listed Stock Reports; Moody's Investors' Service, Moody's Industrial Manual. We are indebted to Boni, Watkins, Jason, and Co. for these computations.

[b] Earnings after taxes but before interest charges as applied to beginning and end of year average borrowed and invested capital.

[c] Earnings are weighted by the number of shares of common stock outstanding as of December 31, 1956.

[d] Weighted average earnings per share divided by weighted average price per share. Obviously, the lower this ratio, the higher the market price for any given earnings level.

[e] The nine producing companies are the six identified in Table XVIII plus Honolulu Oil Corp., Signal Oil and Gas Co., and the Superior Oil Co.

[f] Nineteen of the twenty-one integrated companies are identified in Table XVIII. The two others are Sun Oil Co. and Sunray–Mid-Continent. Cities Service Co. was excluded from the list because of its interstate gas transmission operations.

The prospect of capital appreciation may also have a particular attraction because of the lower tax rate on capital gains. These factors are not absent in the appraisal of shares of major integrated firms, some of which have a high proportion of their resources tied up in oil, but it is necessarily less concentrated than in the case of companies which are producers exclusively. It seems fair to conclude that among the larger nonintegrated producers at least, the traditionally higher risks of this stage of the industry have been so far and so successfully offset by spreading operations over many fields and many wells, and by all the other considerations that make investment in this particular area of endeavor particularly attractive, that they suffer no discrimination in the minds of investors even in comparison with major integrated firms.[16]

Further to test the relative importance of crude oil ownership in the market valuation of securities, six of the nine producers and nineteen of the twenty-one integrated firms analyzed above are listed in Table XVIII in the order in which the market value of their stock appreciated between 1947 and 1957. Arithmetic averages of the annual self-sufficiency ratios of each company, 1946 through 1955, are compared with the median value of these ratios, and inter-firm ranks determined by the degree of crude oil self-sufficiency are shown for 1947, for 1955, and for the computed medians. Five of the six producing companies head the list in investment appreciation during the period, and the sixth producer is bested only by Shell and by Continental. With an average self-sufficiency in crude of 64 per cent for the decade, Shell improved its comparative crude position substantially during the period.[17] Continental had an average owned crude

16. In view of the practice of the industry to finance expansion predominantly from internal funds and the consequent tendency for the stock of production firms especially to be closely held, this conclusion is only suggested by the data. The high price-earnings multiplier of this group of producers could fade rapidly in the face of a large stock issue; and for a proportionate public offering, it is consistent with the data shown that the multiplier for the integrated firms would stand up better than that for the producers. This observation does not deny the conclusion in the text; it merely notes its qualitative character.

17. It also apparently profited to some extent from its close association with international Shell when imports became a more important part of domestic supply; compared with net domestic production of 110 million barrels in 1956, Shell imported about 10.5 million barrels of crude oil that it had apparently produced itself. Import data and geographic origins are from Platt's *Oilgram*, Special Supplement, compiled by the Texas Railroad Commission, February 23, 1956–January 22, 1957; and Office of Defense Mobilization, *Report of the Special Committee to Investigate Crude Oil Imports*, July 29, 1957.

Appreciation of Security Prices, Oil and Gas Companies, 1947–57 [a]

COMPANY	SELF-SUFFICIENCY RATIO [b] RANKING		STOCK PRICES		PER CENT GAIN		SELF-SUFFICIENCY RATIOS, [d] ANNUAL, 1946–55		
	1947	1955	1947 [c]	1957	OVER 10 YEARS	ANNUAL RATE	ARITHMETIC AVERAGE	ME-DIAN	RANK OF MEDIAN
			$	$	%	%	%	%	
Getty Oil Co.	P	P	1.74	30.25	1638.5	163.9	P	P	
Texas Gulf Producing	P	P	3.19	44.87	1306.6	130.7	P	P	
Louisiana Land & Exploration Co.	P	P	4.37	52.50	1101.4	110.1	P	P	
Seaboard Oil Co.	P	P	8.71	69.75	700.8	70.1	P	P	
Amerada Petroleum Corp.	P	P	19.50	132.62	580.1	58.0	P	P	
Shell Oil Co.	9	6	13.65	90.50	563.0	56.3	63.86	63.7	8
Continental Oil Co.	3	3	10.28	65.50	537.2	53.7	109.19	105.0	3
Texas Pacific Coal and Oil Co.	P	P	5.90	37.25	531.4	53.1	P	P	
Skelly Oil Co.	2	2	12.13	76.50	530.7	53.1	149.21	147.9	2
Gulf Oil Corp.	11	13	23.88	147.00	515.6	51.6	51.68	50.6	13
Standard Oil Co. (N.J.)	12	10	11.04	63.12	471.7	47.2	54.35	54.0	11
Socony Mobil Oil Co.	17	15	11.36	58.25	412.8	41.3	40.59	40.3	17
Richfield Oil Corp.	16	12	14.50	70.00	382.8	38.3	45.87	47.2	15
Texas Co.	10	5	14.58	70.37	382.6	38.3	64.47	64.7	7
Tidewater Oil Co.	14	9	8.18	38.50	370.7	37.1	53.88	53.4	12
The Atlantic Refining Co.	15	14	12.00	55.37	361.4	36.1	48.50	49.3	14
Standard Oil Co. (Cal.)	6	7	11.86	53.62	352.1	35.2	73.88	76.4	5
Anderson-Prichard Oil Corp.	5	11	8.62	38.25	343.7	34.4	88.62	93.8	4
Sinclair Oil Corp.	18	18	15.49	66.50	329.3	32.9	30.31	29.1	18
Pure Oil Co.	7	17	12.06	46.12	282.4	28.2	63.51	63.1	9
Phillips Petroleum Co.	4	8	13.90	48.00	245.3	24.5	71.41	61.9	10
Ohio Oil Co.	1	1	11.94	40.75	241.3	24.1	300.33	255.1	1
Union Oil Co. of Cal.	8	4	18.18	59.62	227.9	22.8	66.73	64.8	6
Standard Oil Co. (Ohio)	19	19	19.14	59.75	212.2	21.2	27.35	26.7	19
Standard Oil Co. (Ind.)	13	16	20.35	54.37	167.2	16.7	46.52	46.1	16

[a] Basic data computed by Boni, Watkins, Jason, and Co. Rankings computed by us.

[b] The self-sufficiency ratio is the ratio of owned domestic crude oil produced to crude oil runs to stills. Companies are ranked among themselves in selected years from highest to lowest self-sufficiency.

[c] Price adjusted for stock splits and stock dividends.

[d] To test stability of self-sufficiency ratios over the ten years 1946–55, the arithmetic average of these ratios is compared with the median.

P = Producing Company. Hence no integration ratio.

production of around 109 per cent of its own needs, giving it the third position in crude oil self-sufficiency among the majors. These comparisons strongly suggest a connection between improving market valuation of securities and relative involvement in production. Nevertheless, it is also clear from the table that there is no simple positive correlation between the two, if one confines himself to the integrated companies and measures involvement in production by the comparative ranking of the firm in the ratio of its domestic crude oil output to its crude oil needs.[18]

Although this conclusion is not surprising for integrated firms, with their huge investments at other stages of the business and the possibility that much of their crude oil investment may be immobilized by production cutbacks, it would be surprising indeed if the extent of their involvement in production were found not to have an important effect on stock prices. Before attempting to see whether there was any such relationship, it must first be observed that the use of average self-sufficiency ratios in Table XVIII masks a decided trend: as Table XIX shows, there occurred a substantial reduction in these

TABLE XIX

Comparison of Crude Oil Self-Sufficiency Ratios: Nineteen Companies, 1946 and 1955

YEAR	1946	1955
Median ratio	64.57%	52.87%
Arithmetic average of ratios	89.71%	64.38%
Number of companies with ratios 70 per cent or greater	8	3
Number of companies with ratios under 50 percent	4	9

ratios during the period after World War II, probably a consequence of the rapid expansion of postwar refining as petroleum demands soared and also of an increasing emphasis on foreign oil sources that are not included in these data. The extent of the shift is more clearly viewed in a contrast of the extremes of the period. While the median ratio was falling some 12 percentage points, the arithmetic average shrank twice as fast, largely because of the collapse in the absolute

18. However the correlation is much better than Table XVIII suggests, since the self-sufficiency ratios are for domestic production only. It is significant that among the top eight integrated companies on the list, in terms of the appreciation of their security prices, two had ratios well over 100 per cent and four others had foreign production that expanded enormously in this period. See below, pp. 329–331, where this factor is taken into account.

size of ratios for the most self-sufficient companies (for example, the Ohio Oil Company's ratio fell from 416.72 to 249.02 per cent).

In order to check on the possible relationship between crude-oil self-sufficiency and profitability, Table XX divides the nineteen major companies into four groups at the risk of spreading a limited sample rather thinly. The first three groups are classified on the basis of their domestic self-sufficiency, the fourth consists of the five giant international companies, whose domestic ratios are a highly inadequate reflection of their stake in crude oil. Other firms among the nineteen here analyzed became owners and importers of foreign crude in varying degree during this period but it is neither feasible nor necessary to allow for it here.

Even among the three broad categories of domestic firms, earnings rates overlap considerably: obviously profitability is heavily influenced by factors other than the relative interest in production. However, these also confirm the judgment that percentage crude oil self-sufficiency is an important factor in profitability of an integrated firm. Average earning rates are consistently highest in the highest self-sufficiency group and, excepting 1946, they are higher for the second than for the lowest category, with less than 50 per cent owned crude.[19] It will also be observed that the high self-sufficiency group showed higher average earnings and a higher range of earnings rates than the five international companies, but that this discrepancy narrowed after 1951 and was reversed in the last two years of the period as foreign operations expanded relative to domestic.

With this background, the earlier Table XVIII reveals some interesting uniformities. First, with the exception of Gulf Oil and Union Oil, every integrated firm that improved its self-sufficiency ranking between 1947 and 1955 showed a percentage gain in stock appreciation during the decade greater than that of any integrated company for which comparative ranking deteriorated. Since Gulf added to its foreign oil during this period more than every other integrated firm but one, and since these resources are not reflected in

19. In 1946, because of the small number of companies, results were skewed by a single exceptional earning rate: Atlantic Refining in the second group came up with earnings of only 4.24 per cent. The differentials in average earnings between the three categories of self-sufficiency ratios would be considerably higher and clearer also were it not for the Union Oil Company of California which had high self-sufficiency ratios throughout—in the highest group during the first three years, in the second group during the last seven— but very low earnings. Its earning rate was the low point of the range in its group in every year after 1946 except 1953.

TABLE XX

Annual Crude Oil Self-Sufficiency Ratios Compared with Return on Borrowed and Invested Capital: Nineteen Major Companies, 1946–55 [a]

YEAR	DOMESTIC COMPANIES: 70% OR MORE		SELF-SUFFICIENCY RATIOS 50–69%		LESS THAN 50%		INTERNATIONAL COMPANIES [c]	
	NO.	EARNING RATE [b] %	NO.	EARNING RATE [b] %	NO.	EARNING RATE [b] %	NO.	EARNING RATE [b] %
1946								
Range	7	5.02–14.68	4	4.24–9.92	3	7.31–9.36	5	6.37–10.87
Arithmetic average		10.49		7.75		8.23		8.87
1947								
Range	7	8.59–21.51	3	8.76–15.06	4	6.16–12.95	5	9.67–14.91
Arithmetic average		15.99		12.73		10.91		12.42
1948								
Range	7	12.78–31.21	4	11.89–24.63	3	14.78–15.50	5	11.68–18.64
Arithmetic average		23.35		16.53		15.14		15.60
1949								
Range	5	9.16–18.38	4	7.52–15.37	5	8.09–14.23	5	8.04–13.81
Arithmetic average		14.85		11.28		9.94		10.51
1950								
Range	4	16.64–18.49	5	6.01–17.42	5	9.09–14.74	5	9.73–14.42
Arithmetic average		17.65		11.98		11.58		11.78
1951								
Range	4	16.08–18.71	6	8.79–17.46	4	10.22–12.14	5	11.32–15.43
Arithmetic average		16.85		13.35		11.36		13.36
1952								
Range	4	11.73–16.38	7	8.22–14.43	3	7.74–11.37	5	10.72–14.41
Arithmetic average		13.94		10.97		9.02		12.42
1953								
Range	3	12.98–16.45	8	8.26–15.28	3	7.55–9.17	5	10.61–14.60
Arithmetic average		14.30		11.68		8.39		12.66
1954								
Range	3	11.42–13.40	5	8.64–14.76	6	6.72–9.12	5	9.90–15.02
Arithmetic average		12.18		10.82		8.17		12.60
1955								
Range	3	11.62–13.53	4	7.16–13.83	7	8.01–11.73	5	10.54–14.96
Arithmetic average		12.34		10.30		9.53		13.24

[a] Integrated companies as listed in Table XVIII.

[b] Total earnings after taxes but before interest charges as per cent of average borrowed and invested capital (beginning- and end-of-year average).

[c] Included in International Companies are Gulf Oil, Socony Mobil, Standard of California, Standard Oil (N.J.) and Texas Co. With self-sufficiency ratios computed on domestic crude, these companies fell mainly in the 50–69 per cent class.

the domestic ratios employed in the table, Gulf is not really an exception at all; quite the contrary.[20]

Second, of the five integrated companies that retained their comparative ranking in crude self-sufficiency, Continental and Skelly, which were third and second respectively, enjoyed stock appreciation considerably above the median 38.3 per cent per year for the group as a whole; and Sinclair and Standard of Ohio, ranking at the very bottom in self-sufficiency, also fell well below the median in stock appreciation. This is what one would expect. The only apparent exception was Ohio Oil, with the heaviest relative production of crude oil and the highest earnings rate in its group in every year. Possibly the steady decline of its self-sufficiency ratio (from 417 per cent in 1946 to 229 per cent in 1955) tended to dampen the appreciation of its stock.

These comparisons do not carry definitive weight: there are too many factors, other than the proportion of needed crude oil that a firm produces for itself, that affect the price of stock in a given year or its trend over time.[21] On the other hand, they are consistent with and lend support to an observation commonly made in this industry: production is its most profitable branch, at least for those who succeed, and investors have shown increasing interest in the last ten to fifteen years in companies that have a large or increasing relative stake in that part of the business.

The situation in crude oil is almost a paradox. Over the years the risk associated with exploration and discovery has actually increased despite improved technology. This is indicated by the rise in the dry-hole ratio and the increasing costs of exploration, drilling, and production as wells must be drilled deeper and in more difficult offshore locations. But during the same period the willingness of investors to accept such risks has grown even more rapidly with the soaring demand for the product, an effective public policy designed to prevent excessive production or loss of value, income tax regulations building

20. See above, p. 100, n. 82. Union improved its relative ranking even though its own self-sufficiency ratio fell from 75 to 62.1 per cent during the years compared; but as just indicated Union's earnings were consistently low throughout.

21. Even if the investor were to confine his scouting to factors related to the firm's position as a producer, he would have to look to continuing and anticipated cash flows, to the location, amount, and quality of proved reserves (not merely current production), and to the prospective rate of finding and using such resources—factors not revealed in earnings records or in balance sheets or even in crude oil self-sufficiency ratios.

up the financial inducements of looking for oil as well as producing it, and joint ventures and multiple operations to average out the element of chance. Today bankers compete with one another to advance credit on crude oil assets. In consequence, there is less need than in the early days of the industry for vertical integration as a means of marshaling funds or increasing willingness to invest in exploration and production of crude oil.

It is doubtful that this would have been true before World War II. Although the major may still have advantages in this department, these advantages are more clearly related to size than to vertical integration, and they are no longer crucial, no longer a necessary condition of getting the job done. Even where costs mount to very high levels, as in offshore drilling, neither vertical integration nor giant size is indispensable: the joint agreement shows the way for smaller, less complicated firms to surmount these financial heights. Even though the services of the large integrated firm in the maintenance of crude supply may not seem as vital today as they were before prorationing, there has been no abatement of the majors' interest in their own crude supply. Quite apart from the need to protect their raw material flow and the cost at which it is made available, whatever the nominal price may be, it is only in crude oil that now-familiar tax allowances may be used to cut down, or avoid entirely, high income taxes and thus lock in profits both against the raids of rivals and against the tax collector. Vertical integration may no longer be needed for crude oil exploration and development; but crude oil is almost certainly necessary to a powerful vertical integration.

TRANSPORTATION

The efficient transport of oil and its products created serious problems for existing media, in the solution of which the oil industry itself was forced to play a leading part: in the development and improvement of the tank car, which the railroads regarded as a special facility to be provided by the shipper; in the evolution of oil barges and tankers and later the adaptation of the motor truck; and, most dramatic of all, in the perfection and construction of the pipeline system, which, more than any other, has determined the shape and character of the industry. In every one of these media, excepting only the trunk pipeline, independents have played a significant role. As truck fleet operators, contract and common carriers, they often supplant company-owned trucks entirely. On inland waterways, the independent has developed methods of operation, including the back haul, that often give him a clear advantage over oil companies themselves. Non-oil companies have even acquired tank car fleets, which they lease to refiners. And on the high seas the majors have conserved their capital while preserving their control over ocean tankers by using the long-term charter.

In pipeline transport, however, practically no one from outside the industry functions, and there are few independents except some remnants of the dismembered Standard Oil Trust. Chapter 5 describes early instances of producers essaying pipeline construction, but success in this field has been reserved for refiners. The domestic oil trunk pipeline is practically the exclusive preserve of the integrated firm.[22] For the most part, the typical crude-oil trunk pipeline (and the product line as well) has been built, owned, and operated by a refiner or group of refiners as a plant facility, for the primary purpose of procuring supplies for their refineries and servicing their marketing departments.[23]

22. "So far as we have been able to learn, only one pipeline has ever been built by interests unconnected with oil production or refining and for carrier purposes only. . . . It is also true that few, if any, important crude oil pipe lines have been built by producers who were not also refiners." Fayette B. Dow, "Petroleum Transportation," TNEC, *Hearings* (1940), Pt. XV, p. 8593. Producers have often constructed gathering lines to convey their oil to railroad or pipeline terminals, and railroads themselves constructed such lines in the early days to assure themselves the business of transporting the crude to refinery centers. (See above, pp. 76–79.) Refiners reported ownership of at least 86 per cent of crude-oil-gathering line mileage in 1950 and 82 per cent of crude-oil trunk mileage. Since approximately 12 per cent of gathering-line and 6 per cent of trunk-line mileage now owned by independent common carriers had been split off in 1911 from integrated facilities constructed by the Standard Oil Trust, these percentages should be raised to 98 per cent and 88 per cent respectively in terms of construction (McLean and Haigh, pp. 63–65, 181). In 1938 Roy Cook estimated that twenty majors controlled 85.4 per cent of national trunk mileage, a figure unchallenged by the industry (TNEC Monograph No. 39, p. 21, cited below as Cook). On a different basis, Cookenboo estimated that twenty majors carried 89.8 per cent and independent carriers created by the 1911 decree carried another 6.7 per cent of crude oil and product throughput in 1948. See Ralph S. Brown, Jr. (above, p. 28, n. 37), pp. 88–90.

23. Legally, all interstate crude oil lines are common carriers (though even now the law is still not crystal clear, cf. George S. Wolbert, Jr., *American Pipe Lines,* Norman, University of Oklahoma Press, 1952, pp. 111–132) and some products lines—like those of the Plantation Pipe Line Company from Baton Rouge, La., to Greensboro, North Carolina; and of the Great Lakes Pipe Line Company from Northeastern Oklahoma to Grand Forks, North Dakota, Minneapolis, and Chicago—were built and have been operated as common car-

Why should there be so profound a difference between pipelines and other transport media? Is the difference inherent in the economics of pipelines, or are there acceptable alternatives to the particular course their history has taken?

The Economics of Pipeline Investment

So essential has the pipeline been to the cheap, long-distance, overland movement of oil in this country that, rather than having displaced other transport media, it has really *created* a traffic and an industrial configuration that could not have developed in its absence.[24] From this viewpoint, the crude oil pipeline is more significantly in competition with the products line than with other methods of transportation. It moved the refinery from the continental oil field to the seacoast and the metropolitan area; the product pipeline could reverse the trend, making it much more feasible for crude-oil oriented refineries to compete with those located nearer the market.

Virtual pre-emption of pipeline ownership and operation by the vertically integrated firm may be ascribed basically to the economics of this revolutionary transport medium. This is not just a matter of the radical cost savings it promises in an industry where transport economies are crucial to profitability: [25] barges and, where usable, oil tank-

riers. But there are practically no crude lines built primarily to serve as common carriers (see *ibid.*, p. 111; although the Buckeye Pipe Line Company does build common-carrier lines typically with some sort of commitment from a refiner), and few product lines operate importantly in this capacity.

24. In the process the pipeline has become not only the primary carrier of crude oil (see above, p. 68) but a major element in the national transportation system as well. Of all freight transported in the U.S. in 1954, oil pipelines accounted for 16 per cent of estimated ton miles (up from 10.6 per cent at the end of the war). *Petroleum Facts and Figures,* 12th ed., p. 273. By the end of 1956 the gross investment of the domestic industry in pipelines (about $3.18 billions) was 7.3 per cent of aggregate investment in property, plant, and equipment. Marine investment was a poor second (2.3 per cent of the aggregate) and other transport (at $350 million) a mere 0.8 per cent. See Coqueron, *Annual Financial Analysis, 1956,* p. 41.

25. "The cost of transporting crude oil by pipe line is less than one-fifth of the cost of over land transportation by the next most economical means." See R. J. Andress, "Development of the Pipe Line Industry," in Paul J. Graber, ed., *Common Carrier Pipe Line Operations and Accounting* (Tulsa, University of Tulsa, 1951), p. 10, cited below as Graber. No one method of transport is always superior to another although, where volume justifies pipeline investment, the cost superiority of pipelines over rail is almost absolute. See above, p. 68, n. 15, and Dow, "Petroleum Transporation," pp. 8591–8592.

The following comparison of rail and pipeline rates will illustrate the latter's

ers are even more economical; it is rather in its obdurate, inflexible character as a transport medium. The pipeline does not yield its bounty lightly. It permits strikingly increasing returns with size, but economy in capital and operating costs will depend on proper design and stable operations close to designed capacity.[26] Since practically no costs, excepting power, can be varied with fluctuations in throughput, operations beyond a narrow range around design capacity will generally raise unit costs: lower volume being applied to costs that are almost entirely fixed; higher volume demanding more pump stations. To top it all, this transport mechanism is almost always unidirectional between fixed terminals and in contrast with other common carriers will accommodate only a single class of products. Power is applied directly to the cargo within the confines of the pipe: there are no vehicles to return, but there is no back-haul either.

For the firm contemplating a pipeline, therefore, design and location are crucial because the economies of larger size can be realized only if high utilization is maintained, and the oil to be transported in large volume cannot be stored except at excessive costs and high risk.[27]

---

advantage. The rail rate on gasoline from Tulsa, Oklahoma, to Fargo, North Dakota, was about 5 cents a gallon at the end of 1952. The pipeline rate was about 1¾ cents a gallon. Northwest Petroleum Association, *Annual Yearbook* (1953), pp. 35, 76. Evidence compiled by the ICC in the 1930's showed that pipeline rates on crude oil averaged 35.72 per cent of corresponding rail rates. "Reduced Pipe Line Rates and Gathering Charges," 243 ICC, 115, 123 (1940). Also the former afforded a far higher rate of return than the latter. Pipeline tariffs on petroleum products apparently compare even more favorably with rail than on crude oil. See the various estimates in McLean and Haigh, pp. 208–209.

26. Economy in pipeline construction and operation is a function of three important variables—pipe diameter, horespower, and throughput. Pipe size is influenced by volume and stability of volume to be moved, by type of oil, by need for batching, and by profile of route; and both pipe size and power are related to type of power available, to relative cost of fuel, and to operating and maintenance manpower. The interrelation of these factors is highly technical and beyond our scope except to observe that the larger the pipe diameter, the wider may be the spacing of pumping stations, with a consequent increase in investment but a fall in annual operating costs. Oil transportation costs per 1,000 barrel miles will vary inversely with the number of barrels to be delivered per day, falling along overlapping curves for larger diameter pipe with lower minimums. See T. R. Ande, manager of planning and economics, Service Pipe Line Company, "Design and Construction of the Typical Pipe Line System," in Graber, pp. 49 ff. Also, see Federal Trade Commission, *Report on Pipe-Line Transportation of Petroleum* (Washington, 1916), pp. 436–440; Stocking, pp. 217–224; McLean and Haigh, pp. 195 ff.; Cookenboo, *Crude Oil Pipe Lines*.

27. Minimum storage or handling capacity is required to insure continuity

Line capacity must be adapted both to the volume of crude available and to predictable refinery requirements at delivery points.

For a non-integrated pipeline carrier before prorationing, the risks of loss at either end of the line would have been staggering. Prorationing has extended the life of oil fields and stabilized their production, but in earlier days fields could dry up quickly and unexpectedly; the pipeline owner could assure supply only by keeping abreast of new discoveries with his trunk line and his gathering system. At the delivery end, unless he could negotiate firm long-term contracts, his risk was equally great. The refiner-customer might at any time withdraw his patronage in favor of building a line of his own, or he could threaten to do so and cut himself into the lion's share of any potential profits. No matter how golden the promise of gain from pipeline operations, gold could be transmuted into gilt at the will of one or a few self-interested customers. The threat was enough to bar independent capital from a highly lucrative field.[28]

Had refiners been barred by law from owning and operating them, pipelines would certainly have developed with independent capital; but they would not have been more competitive. The economics of their construction and operation would have been changed not at all: capital costs would still have been huge and efficiency would still have depended on performance near capacity. Pipeline service would still have been worth the cost of the best alternative transport available to serve the market. As long as capacity was substantially less than market requirements, pipeline rates adjusted to any lower level (for

of operations but will seldom exceed seven days' operations. See Graber, p. 26.

28. The ICC concluded in 1940 that "profits, or nominal profits, derived from transportation, reflected in dividends paid, were generally enormous. . . ." (Reduced Pipe Line Rates and Gathering Charges, 243 ICC 115, 140, 1940). It pointed out that these rates had been substantially reduced since 1933, but apparently for extraneous reasons ("That the reductions in rates in the past few years may be directly attributed to changes in the tax laws, is practically admitted on the record,") and it concluded that the rates and returns of many were still "excessive." Ibid., pp. 138, 141, 123–127. The ICC's figures for five "typical" pipelines owned by integrated companies, all with roughly similar earnings experience, showed that the five had a combined gross investment around 1938 of $305,833,000; had accrued depreciation of $167,090,000; and had paid out dividends of $420,267,000 during the preceding 9½ years (January 1, 1929 to June 30, 1938). Despite the depression, annual dividends had averaged about 32 per cent of net investment (computed ibid., p. 131). For other discussions reaching similar conclusions see Cook, pp. 21–23, 25; Wolbert, American Pipe Lines (above, n. 23), pp. 13–22; Roy A. Prewitt, "The Operation and Regulation of Crude Oil and Gasoline Pipe Lines," Quarterly Journal of Economics, 56 (1942), 189–199 and passim.

example, to costs plus a fair return on investment) would have discriminated against those forced to use the high-priced alternative. To put it less nobly, such favored shippers would have been cut into a share of the monopoly profits of innovation.

This was the rationale of early pipeline charges approximating tank car rates; the same argument would have served the independent operator, and with more reason, for he would almost certainly have faced higher costs and greater risks. Financial costs would have been higher because established oil business at other levels of the industry could not have been called on for cash funds or for credit; risks would have been greater because independent pipeline operators would not have had a direct stake in, and therefore an equivalent knowledge of supply probabilities and market potentialities. The operator would have sought the shortest pay-out possible; and the obvious dangers of price competition would have shielded him, more effectively than they could the integrated firm, from any temptation to overexpand pipeline investment. For, as has often been noted, the integrated company has unique incentives, and is subject to special additional pressures, to build pipelines.

With independent ownership and operation of pipelines, then, there would have been no more effective pressure on rates and on service than public regulation itself could have provided. To banish vertical integration from the field could have done no more than reveal more clearly the inherently monopolistic character of the service; and the requirements of administering a limited public monopoly could not long have avoided the imposition on common carriers of the requirement of obtaining certificates of public convenience and necessity.

It would have been an essentially anticompetitive solution to deny to producers and refiners, the most interested parties, the right to move oil and products by their own facilities whenever they thought they could do so more cheaply than outside common carriers. To make construction subject to certification by a governmental agency would certainly have exposed pipeline expansion to veto at the behest of existing carriers seeking to protect their own investments. To force producers or refiners to rely on voluntary common carrier responses or on ICC pressures to gain expansion or improvement of pipeline facilities, a new or more direct route, or a large diameter line to displace an accumulation of small diameter lines would invite rejection or delay in the interests of existing investment unless the refiner or producer were free to build a line of his own. The removal of this threat could serve only to slow the willingness of existing carriers to take risks and thus to entrench their monopoly power. The history of oil industry transportation offers strong indirect evidence that the development of pipelines would not have been so rapid had producers and refiners not been free to undertake the task.

The business of pipeline construction and operation is not, and could hardly become, a competitive one,[29] but in the hands of the vertically integrated firms it has served an essentially competitive purpose nevertheless. The pipeline has been used to create a market advantage over near rivals and to counter rivals' strength. The effect, however, was for a long time to place almost insuperable handicaps on companies too small to construct their own lines. So pipeline investment epitomized vertical integration itself: an instrument of competition among large companies, and a possible threat to the survival of small.

Appraising the Record of Pipeline Investment

The main purpose of pipeline investment by the integrated firm has been to save on transport cost.[30] Such savings are often part of a broader rationalization of company logistics: a new products line may serve to concentrate refining in a more efficient locale, or on a more efficient scale, and permit the shutting down of high-cost obsolete plant.[31] Presumably anticipated unit costs of these rearranged, integrated operations will be less than the out-of-pocket costs under the displaced system. If so, both the firm and society will benefit, even though the promised saving in cost may result from avoiding monopo-

29. This is also the conclusion of Stocking, pp. 224–237.

30. With these costs often accounting for around 25 per cent of the tank-wagon price (McLean and Haigh, p. 183), the saving from pipeline ownership could play a vital role in business success.

31. For example, in a series of interrelated decisions, Atlantic Refining in 1935–37 extended its Keystone products pipeline from its Philadelphia refinery into western Pennsylvania; closed down its archaic Franklin and Pittsburgh refineries, set up originally to refine lube-rich Pennsylvania crude; and built a new refinery on the Gulf Coast at Port Arthur, near the terminus of its crude pipelines from the West and East Texas fields, to make lubes (among other products) by the solvent extraction process and thus replace the production of the West Pennsylvania refineries. McLean and Haigh, pp. 208, 223. Sinclair made a similar decision to convert four small Midcontinent refineries to terminals while building a products pipeline system between its big Houston and East Chicago refineries. *Ibid.,* p. 306.

listically high transport rates charged by others.[32] Pipeline economics places so high a premium on full-capacity utilization that excessive rates to outside shippers are likely to reflect inadequate capacity, and a social need for additional investment.

Pipeline investments may have been made on expectations that proved afterward to have been mistaken; but examples are hard to come by. Often cited as such an instance is the Ajax Pipe Line, which was practically put out of business in 1938 after discovery of oil in Illinois had cut into the demand for the Midcontinent crude it carried.[33] However, the Ajax investment had already paid for itself. As the ICC pointed out, Ajax began operation on December 1, 1930, and by September 30, 1936, it had paid dividends of $17,450,000 on an investment at that date of $13,306,201, with accrued depreciation of $3,971,777. "So far as this respondent is concerned, all hazards have been amply provided for . . ."[34]

Speculation about possible waste through competitive integrated development of pipelines is not rewarding. First, much of the early risk could not have been dispelled by any acceptable approach to investment: oil men just didn't know as much as they know today either about underground reservoirs and methods of extraction or about pipeline economics. With improved knowledge and effective production controls, this source of waste is now greatly reduced. Second, there is no good measure of the true savings effected by pipeline construction of integrated firms; but the high nominal profits —however measured—of pipeline companies are hardly suggestive of wasteful investment. Third, as in any evolving technology, much early pipeline investment was on a smaller, less efficient scale than economics or technical knowledge would have justified. But some of this early obsolescence was created by the same force that has underwritten and supported the whole process of investment in pipeline construction in a manner calculated to minimize the inherent risks of the enterprise, namely the continued growth of the economy and the upward surge of its oil demands.

32. Thus Atlantic Refining is said to have built two lines in 1928–31 because rates charged by pipeline companies had unduly narrowed its own refinery margins (*ibid.*, pp. 195–199).

33. Between 1938 and 1939 the line is said to have lost 60 per cent of its traffic and 71 per cent of its net operating revenues. See Dow, "Petroleum Transportation," p. 8594.

34. *Reduced Pipe Line Rates and Gathering Charges,* 243 ICC 155, 122–123 (1940).

Indeed, both the high nominal returns earned by pipeline companies before the Consent Decree [35] and the recurrent complaints by independent refiners denied access to their service suggest under- rather than overinvestment, and consequently too slow a rate of extending to the public and the industry generally the benefits of this revolutionary transport medium. Criteria here are also slippery, however. Neither the level of the pipeline tariff charges nor the profit record of pipeline subsidiaries is a measure of the rate at which its gains are shared. Sharing of benefits could be indicated by the volume carried for non-pipeline owners on a purchase-sale (not an exchange) basis; but these data are not collected by the ICC. If outside shippers are ignored, little significance can be attached to pipeline tariff changes alone.[36] High nominal returns on this part of the business may in fact be passed on by the acceptance of low refining or marketing margins. Furthermore, as with all forms of rate regulation, control focused on the rate of return may be dissipated in higher costs. This is a very real danger where, as in pipelines, the economics of heavy fixed costs and the fewness of sellers preclude active price competition. The first impact of limitation on pipeline earnings could be to encourage as near to exclusive use of the line by its owners as possible: this would seal its profits into the integrated operation.[37] The second effect could be to conduct a more comfortable if less efficient operation, at tariffs that would provide a legal profit even at relatively low

35. The Pipe Line Consent Decree (*U.S. v. Atlantic Refining Co., et al.,* Civil Action No. 14060, District Court of the District of Columbia) entered in December, 1941, grew out of a case brought fifteen months before against most shipper-owner oil companies and subsidiary pipeline companies. It was charged that profits received from pipeline operations constituted rebates from tariffs filed with the ICC and therefore were subject to treble damages under the Elkins Act, 1903. The Consent Decree limited pipeline net earnings to 7 per cent of valuations approved by the ICC and froze excess earnings in a special surplus fund which can be invested in pipe line facilities but cannot be added to the valuation for dividend purposes. The effect of the Consent Decree on rate levels is unclear largely because the ICC had previously declared after a rate investigation that it would regard earnings above 8 per cent as excessive; and pipeline rates had already been reduced to a level approximating this rate of return. See Lloyd Wilson, in National Resources Planning Board, *Transportation and National Policy* (Washington, D.C., 1942), p. 466.

36. See above, pp. 276 ff.

37. For this reason, reduction in the size of minimum tenders required from prospective pipeline shippers and more equitable prorationing of pipeline shipments when transport requests exceed capacity are better evidence than reduction of pipeline tariffs that the economies are being shared.

rates of operation: break-even points as low as 60 per cent are reported.[38]

With the data available it is not possible to assess the proposition that pipeline investment has been too little rather than too much. But if this is the fact, it will not be solved by restricting ownership and operation to nonintegrated companies. The pipeline partakes of natural monopoly: this will not be altered by change in industrial organization. If earnings are considered excessive or public service inadequate, the solution must be found in better regulation, and in maximum freedom with respect to the construction of new facilities by whoever wants to do so.

Ocean-Going Tankers

Although the pipeline is pre-eminent in the domestic movement of oil, the ocean-going tanker is crucial for parts of the world like Western Europe,[39] and will inevitably play a more important role in the future supplies of this country as well. With huge investments in overseas production and refining, the large integrated firm has found it desirable to take a leading part in the development and operation of tankers.

When the closing of the Suez Canal emphasized the tenuousness of that link with the Middle East, it set off a strenuous program of building gigantic tankers, calculated to revolutionize the economics of crude oil transport. Behind the drive is the economic fact that both capital costs per deadweight ton of capacity and operating costs per ton-mile of cargo carried decline as size increases.[40] Despite the need

38. In a company memorandum (April, 1948), it is stated that "a 60 per cent rate of usage permits profitable operation of a pipeline system both according to experience and in the opinion of pipeline personnel" (McLean and Haigh, pp. 202–203). One of the incidental effects of so low a break-even was that the Atlantic Refining Company staff, in this memorandum, recommended that the firm build the proposed pipeline alone, since its primary function would be to serve as a purchasing agent for oil and the staff saw no gain in sharing this advantage with others.

39. The significance of tanker operations was underlined by L. C. Musgrave of Esso Petroleum when he estimated that combined gross operating expenses for a representative European importing, refining and marketing company during the period 1952–56, excluding the purchase price of oil, would be 56 per cent transport cost, 28 per cent refining, and 16 per cent marketing. *Petroleum Press Service* (April, 1957), p. 144.

40. Mr. G. Trypanis of Niarchos (London) Ltd., using German building costs and wage levels, twenty-year amortization, and 5 per cent interest on

for the less efficient twin-screw propulsion above 80–90,000 tons, despite the limit on tanker size of 43,000 tons (fully loaded) or 65,000 tons (partially loaded) set by the capacity of Suez, and despite the limited number of ports that can now load or unload tankers above 40,000 tons, the trend seems definitely toward the giant supertanker, limited only by a shortage of adequate shipyard facilities.[41] It is apparent that many oil companies are getting prepared to avoid Suez and to operate these huge new tankers like a kind of pipeline, at full load with maximum turn-around speed between fairly fixed terminals.

To design the fleet of tomorrow without tying up a disproportionate part of its resources, the integrated firm has used the long-term charter (up to twenty years, although five- to ten-year terms are more common) as a financing device. Hardly any tankers are constructed for permanent employment in the spot market anyway, because crude-oil-supply contracts in the foreign area generally extend over a period of years. With a long-term charter obtained before the vessel is built, and with charter rates fixed in the contract, an independent has often been able to raise funds from the banks at low rates and in amounts sufficient to finance construction with little outlay on his own part. Thus the oil company can shape the design and obtain control over the new vessel without committing its own capital or seriously impinging on its credit position.[42]

The large integrated firm has thus found it possible to guide the evolution and control the operation of the great bulk of the world's

---

outstanding capital, estimated that a 50,000-ton vessel would transport oil at about three-fifths the unit cost of a 12,000 tonner. Thereafter, his estimated cost curve flattens rapidly, with little change above 80–90,000 tons—the largest size that can be satisfactorily propelled by a single screw. *Petroleum Press Service* (June, 1957), pp. 209 ff. See also Musgrave, *ibid.* (April, 1957), p. 144.

41. As of January 1, 1957, the National Petroleum Council reported a world commercial fleet of 2,353 vessels above 6,000 d.w.t., totaling just over 41 million d.w.t., and a further 902 vessels (26.8 million d.w.t.) under construction or on order. These figures excluded all government ships and all USSR and satellite country ships. It estimated further that the commercial fleet would receive deliveries of 38 million d.w.t. by 1965, of which twenty-four vessels would be 100,000 tons or more, thirty-nine would be from 60–100,000 tons, 220 in the 40–50,000 ton class, about 320 from 30–40,000 tons, and almost 300 in the 16–20,000 ton category. *Petroleum Press Service* (April, 1957), p. 142.

42. The transaction is not without risk to the oil company. Long-term charter rates, fixed by contract, have come to exceed spot rates and have led to operation of charter ships while owned tankers were idle. The basic risk arises from extrapolation of world demand for petroleum and the rate at which efficient tankers are added to the fleet.

tanker fleet, unlike the pipeline, with a decreasing proportion of ownership. Independents, owning some 49 per cent of the prewar total, are believed to own about 54 per cent of the tonnage today and are expected to own 58 per cent by 1960. But oil companies are said to control through ownership and long-term charter from 72 to as much as 90 per cent of the commercial tanker fleet.[43]

Conclusion

In the development of specialized facilities for the mass movement of crude oil and petroleum products over land and sea, the oil company is not merely engaged in the business of transportation. More obviously with pipelines—but increasingly with ocean-going tankers as their flexibility in use is sacrificed to size and uniqueness of loading and unloading possibilities in the interests of efficient mass movement over long distances—these transport media are integrated into coordinated producing, refining, and marketing aggregates.[44] The size, location, and scheduling of these facilities becomes an integral part of the design and operation of an efficient production process, which includes the refinery and distributive organization. In this interdependent process, the consumers of petroleum products have much to gain from the incentives, knowledge, and capital that the refiner can bring to bear in the development of efficient transport facilities. Inherent monopolistic potentialities of the medium must be curbed by appropriate regulation; but the public interest will more likely be served in the long run if the right of oil companies to build and operate them is preserved.

It is easier to reach this conclusion at the present stage of industry

43. The figures on ownership are given by A. S. C. Hulton, Managing Director of Shell Tankers, Ltd.—*Petroleum Press Service* (May, 1957), pp. 189–190. L. C. Musgrave, *ibid.* (April, 1957), p. 144, reports oil company ownership at 43 per cent today, a figure confirmed by John I. Jacobs, London Shipbrokers—*ibid.* (March, 1957), p. 107—in a report which anticipates that one-third of ships now on order will be owned by oil companies and two-thirds by independents, mostly Greek. Exact figures on charters are not available but Musgrave reports 29 per cent of the commercial fleet under long-term charter to oil companies. This would leave 28 per cent available for short-term or single voyage charter. An industry source in this country estimates oil company control at closer to 90 per cent. An intermediate estimate was reported in *Business Week* (August 25, 1956), pp. 79 ff.

44. Some major American companies without appreciable foreign production have built or chartered tanker fleets to deliver foreign crude oil for which they have entered upon long-term purchase contracts.

development because the monopolistic advantages which the early pipeline secured for its owners have been largely eliminated. One important factor in this erosion process has been the fuller development of the capacity of the medium itself and the increased number and quality of alternatives it makes available. A striking example of this tendency has been the products line, which, whether common carrier or plant facility, has become a direct competitor of the crude line, by making it possible for refineries to be built in the field and compete with market-oriented refiners served by long distance crude lines. The advantages conferred on the integrated refiner by construction of a pipeline in turn forces other refiner-marketers, who have the strongest of all possible incentives, to emulate. The process of competitive emulation itself provides an important guarantee that in time the benefits of lowest-cost transportation will be extended to the ultimate consumer.

Prorationing, by increasing security of supply, and growth of metropolitan markets, by assuring demand, have undoubtedly simplified the problem of accessibility to capital markets for pipeline projects. The critic of integration, therefore, might urge divorce of these facilities from refiner control with greater assurance: little would be lost and much might be gained by scotching any residual monopolistic leverage wielded by the oil company owner. In addition, the advocates of divestiture see the possibility of a new kind of competition to spur common carrier pipeline investment, if only integrated companies were barred from the field—the competition for certificates of public convenience and necessity. Mindful of the experience in the federal control of interstate transmission of natural gas, Rostow and Sachs observe that the extension of these facilities has not been slowed by federal control. Independent pipeline companies compete strenuously with one another for supply assurances as new natural gas fields are discovered, and for permits to extend their lines. Franchise security has made high debt ratios feasible with low capital costs and comfortable earnings.[45] But the business of transporting oil differs critically from the transmission of natural gas. There is no counterpart in oil to the entrenched local gas distributor and the exclusive access to his patronage that the transmission franchise assures. Lacking an assured and rapidly expanding market, such as natural gas transmission companies have enjoyed, free of serious competition from alternative sources at points of delivery,[46] there is likely to be

45. "Entry into the Oil Refining Business: Vertical Integration Re-Examined," pp. 856, 896.

46. As best illustrated in the Standard of Indiana case (see below, p. 457)

considerably less incentive and less assured financial advantage to be gained in an oil pipeline public franchise than in similar franchises for transmission of natural gas.

There are certainly clearly defined routes where the proved presence of crude oil at one end and concentrations of refineries at the other would provide ample guarantees to investors in common carrier lines. But to bar oil companies from the field would place a heavy burden on public regulatory authority at the point where its effectiveness remains most limited—in securing adequate facilities and their prompt extension into new fields. From an economic standpoint, the integrated firm has inherently superior incentives and definitely superior knowledge, willingness, and ability to commit funds to the enterprise. The economics of pipeline and refinery construction and operation requires that the pipeline be effectively integrated into the refining and distribution plans of the oil company.[47] Integration lowers the risks and enhances the potential rewards of pipeline operations for the integrated firm, and it therefore promotes pipeline construction where a nonintegrated investor would hesitate to build.[48] And for the same reason, it lowers the risk, in contrast with independent common carriers, that a public policy of holding down pipeline tariffs will seriously impair the expansion of investment.

The historical record also indicates, however, that competitive emulation among the majors in the development of pipeline services cannot be relied upon to serve the market adequately. The market will not ordinarily support enough carriers so that one can rely upon

---

these alternatives arise from the emergence of new sources of supply and new methods of transport in a dynamic industry.

47. Contractual integration, through long-term commitments between a nonintegrated pipeline operator and refiners or suppliers of crude (as urged, for example, by Rostow and Sachs, "Entry into the Oil Refining Business," pp. 906–911), is definitely inferior. Indeed, it is dubious if a common carrier can bind itself contractually to give specified service to one customer in possible preference to other potential future shippers with all of whom it is required to deal equitably; and a contract subject to pipeline prorationing, in the event the limits of capacity are reached, would promise something less than an adequate *quid pro quo*.

48. This phenomenon may be illustrated in Gulf's decision in 1951 to build a crude pipeline system from four Mississippi fields to a terminal at Mobile, Alabama. In planning a pay-out of 4¾ years on the $7 million line, Gulf estimated a saving of $1.9 million gross per year on transporting its own crude (about 50 per cent of field production). Carrying for others was estimated to yield only $764,000 gross per year. It may be that the need to share that $1.9 million with an independent carrier would have left too little for Gulf to keep exploring and developing such marginal fields. McLean and Haigh, pp. 318–325.

competition among them to pass on the benefits to independent shippers and customers at reasonable speeds. Similarly, the rate at which connections are extended into new crude fields is seldom satisfactory to the independent producers operating there. The integrated companies, as the dominant producers and buyers of crude, may well be in a position to forestall any effort on the part of independents to solve their problem by building their own lines.[49] The power that resides in the large integrated firm, by reason of its large refinery throughput and its established product markets, to guarantee for long terms the traffic volume needed to assure the profitable operation of a pipeline or a tanker is an advantage that no independent can match. With it, a commitment to receive oil at the terminus of a pipeline or a charter of a tanker yet to be built is enough to assure availability of the bulk of the capital needed for construction from the financial fraternity at lower than normal costs. The terms are low not merely because the security is adequate but because the bank is assured that the commitment of the integrated firm can and will be carried through as written. A nonintegrated refiner, without its own production and gathering lines at one end and its controlled distribution at the other, could not give such an assurance; this ability to minimize risk is a real economy of integration.

Although the integrated ownership of pipelines may still permit the exercise of discriminatory power, it is our conclusion that the effect of integration on balance is to encourage rather than discourage desirable and speedy extension of pipeline investment. Independent operation under public certification of convenience and necessity would mean that not more but fewer pipelines probably would be built. The power that pipeline ownership conveys to the integrated firm, however, must be subject to public scrutiny and public control.

49. This was the substance of a public complaint by an executive of the West Coast Pipeline Company, a company set up by about fifty independent oil producers in West Texas who were seeking an outlet for their oil by constructing a pipeline into the Los Angeles Basin. According to his statement, after committing themselves for $22 million of equity capital (about 20 per cent of the total cost), the sponsors saw their project fall through when financial institutions, as security for their loans, required commitments from West Coast refiners to purchase a minimum volume of oil at the terminus of the line, and six of the seven majors refused to comply. Subsequent appeal under the Defense Production Act of 1950 for certification of the facility as essential to national defense, as a basis for a government loan or guarantee, was also turned down, allegedly on the representations of these same major oil companies. Statement of Lowell M. Glasco, before the Senate Committee on the Judiciary Subcommittee on Antitrust and Monopoly, March, 1957.

CHAPTER 14

Investment Practices and Integration: Refining and Marketing

REFINING

BECAUSE the industry's concentration tendencies have been largely initiated and had their fullest development at this level,[1] and (apart from transport) because independent entry is most difficult here, the growth of refinery investment through merger, as opposed to new construction, has been more controversial and may have consequences much more profound than in more peripheral areas like production or marketing. For this reason it is appropriate at this point to consider the role of mergers in the growth of the major oil companies and the implications of their expansion by this device.

The Role of Mergers

Over the thirty years to 1950, mergers contributed relatively little quantitatively to the growth of refining capacity of major firms, less than a fifth as much as the new capacity added by construction.[2] The quantitative insignificance of the net contribution of mergers tempts one to ignore their impact on present structure. A similar summary of the growth of the old Standard Oil Trust would probably have led to a similar conclusion. But it was through mergers that the Trust achieved monopoly position, that it was placed in a position to grow with the industry, that it became in effect the industry itself. It is impossible to measure the potential that is nipped by the merger, the

1. For a review of the evidence of concentration trends in refining see below, pp. 484 ff.

2. Of gross additions to capacity by the twenty majors identified by the TNEC, 23 per cent arose through merger or purchase in the years of the twenties, 28 per cent (although a smaller absolute aggregate) in the thirties, less than 5 per cent in the forties. With gross additions of 5,091,000 b/d over the thirty years, purchase and merger accounted for 769,000 b/d, 639,000 b/d were sold or scrapped, and 4,332,000 b/d were newly constructed. Of the latter, 2,077,000 b/d were built in the forties alone. See Furcht (above, p. 33, n. 46), p. 9.

independent competitive force that is stilled when one business absorbs another. What is certain is that mergers since 1911 have been much more important in the creation of the present organization of the petroleum industry than any toting up of relative capacities so acquired against those added by new construction would indicate.

From this viewpoint, it is significant that the bulk of mergers by major companies took place in the early part of the 1920–50 period: more than 61 per cent during the first decade.[3] Revolutionary changes in refining technology no doubt dampened interest in mergers during the thirties; the depression and the antitrust laws were probably also inhibiting influences. With World War II and the postwar boom, the twenty majors were able to increase their 1940 capacity by more than 60 per cent through new construction—in considerable measure, of course, with governmental assistance.

Very few of even the numerous mergers of the 1920's represented a direct union of competitors, and very few produced substantial increases in concentration in economically relevant market areas. Some of the most striking were part of a process of geographic integration: refiner-marketers in one region took over integrated organizations in other areas. The size and power of acquiring companies were increased; potential suppliers and potential purchasers for independents were snuffed out; the market structure of the industry became a little more compact, and the dominance of the majors a little more substantial.[4]

3. Mergers were often important in purely quantitative terms to the companies involved. Standard of New York acquired refinery capacity in this decade of not less than 133,000 b/d, compared with expansions of 84,500 b/d by other methods; Standard of Indiana acquired 92,000 by mergers and 106,500 by new construction; Continental 32,500 and 25,000 respectively; Tidewater 78,000 and 61,000; Texas 66,850 and 75,950. Additional strategic mergers early in the next decade include Vacuum, which brought 47,000 b/d capacity to Socony in 1931 while the latter's new construction for that decade added only 82,900 b/d. Solar Refining brought 18,000 b/d to Sohio in 1931 and that company added only 500 b/d in other ways during the 1930's. Sinclair's purchases between 1932 and 1934 amounted to 36,500 b/d compared with the 86,000 b/d it built during the decade. Standard of Indiana acquired 20,000 b/d from Standard of Kansas in 1932, not insignificant compared with the 91,000 b/d of new plant it built during the 10-year period. All computations from Appendices of Furcht.

4. Many majors made only negligible use of mergers with other refiners between 1911 and 1950. Notable in this group were Gulf (which, however, did acquire in the 1950's the Canadian company, British American, Ltd.), Shell, Sun, Union Oil, Mid-Continent (the last a product of several consolidations when formed in 1917), Atlantic, Standard of California, and Pure Oil. Partly

While concentration in refining capacity has increased only moderately since 1940, mergers help to account for a dwindling population. The twenty TNEC majors acquired fifteen independent refiners in the forties; Ashland acquired six more between 1948 and 1950; and, to mention only the more prominent, mergers between refiners absorbed Wood River in 1950, Kanotex in 1953, Globe Oil in 1954, Sunray and Deep Rock in 1955, El Dorado in 1958. Even this partial list of twenty-seven disappearances was 7 per cent of the number in existence in 1940, 12 per cent of the refiner population in 1950.[5] But neither merger nor internal expansion, which was far more important, could make little change in refinery concentration after 1936: the majors were already huge.[6] Interpretation of mergers in the petroleum industry since the middle thirties is complicated by the technological revolution that overtook refining about that time, and that was shortly to force most companies to modernize or go out of business.[7] In this process, many independents were unable to survive, and the merging of their properties with financially stronger firms can hardly be said to have weakened the competitive potential of the industry.

---

in consequence, the last five of these eight companies grew much less rapidly than the other majors and four (excepting Pure) less rapidly than the industry as a whole between 1920 and 1950. See table in Furcht, p. 5. Mid-Continent, of course, spurted forward in size as a result of its 1955 merger with Sunray. Mergers have been only moderately important in the cases of Phillips, Skelly, and Ohio Oil.

5. The trend here indicated for refining between 1940 and 1950 is comparatively unusual in American industry. Despite the furor over the 1940–47 merger movement, sparked by a report of the FTC covering this period, the net increase in number of firms in manufacturing in the U.S. during these years was fifty-three times the number disappearing through mergers; even in food and textiles, the two fields in which merger activity was greatest, the net increases were eight and twenty-nine times the number of merger disappearances. Only in "products of oil and coal," and in petroleum refining, was there a net decrease in the business population, though not, of course, mainly by merger. Disappearances by merger in 1940–47 were 1.4 per cent of the number of firms in textiles as of the latter date, 0.6 per cent of the number in food and kindred products; but in "products of coal and oil," they were 17.4 per cent. Summaries of data in Jesse W. Markham, "Survey of the Evidence and Findings on Mergers," in National Bureau of Economic Research, *Business Concentration and Price Policy* (Princeton, Princeton University Press, 1955), p. 175.

6. See J. K. Butters, John Lintner, and William L. Cary, *Effects of Taxation on Corporate Mergers* (Boston, Harvard Business School, 1951), pp. 267, 274–275, 278; also below, pp. 489–491.

7. In Chap. 12 we discussed catalytic cracking and other innovations which made a large fraction of refining equipment obsolete and forced refiners who survived into much heavier investment and larger capacity.

There was far less presumption of net social gain in the mergers of the twenties and early thirties. They significantly reduced the number of large refiner-marketers and unnecessarily increased industry concentration. Companies like Magnolia, General Petroleum, Midwest, Pan Amerian, White Eagle, Associated, Solar, Indian, California Petroleum, Beacon Oil, Standard of Kansas were in most cases absorbed by firms who operated in different markets, so that competition was not directly suppressed. But in the process there were eliminated powerful potential competitors who might well, in this dynamic industry, have invaded one another's market preserves; and, by the same token, the geographic interpenetration thus achieved by the acquiring companies was gained relatively painlessly, as it were.

Similarly, now that most of the weak refiners, debilitated by their failure to keep abreast of modern technology, have been eliminated, the mergers of relatively large and locally significant refiners continues a matter of serious concern. Although most of the more recent mergers can plausibly be explained and justified as strengthening the uniting companies, whose operations are typically complementary rather than competitive (as will be more fully discussed in Chapter 19), and although all of them together are incapable of greatly increasing the industry's concentration, many of them are eliminating established and potentially vigorous competitors.

An Appraisal of Refinery Investments

Next to production of crude oil, refineries and chemical plants are the most important objects of capital outlays in the industry. At the end of 1956, this category made up 18 per cent (or $27.85 billion) of gross investment in property, plant, and equipment. Capital equipment per man is at a maximum in refinery operations, where automatic processing has long been characteristic. In contrast with other stages of this industry, there is a marked dearth of complaints, either in the literature or by nonintegrated firms, against the integrated refiner as such. No one has charged that refining capacity has been monopolistically retarded: [8] such shortages as have occurred in supply have been more generally attributed to war emergencies and to state regulations.

Perhaps more surprising, no one has strongly asserted, except in very recent years, that refinery investment is excessive or wasteful.

8. On the phenomenal growth of refining capacity in absolute terms, see below, p. 486.

Throughout most of the twenties and thirties shut-down refineries were very numerous (ranging between 20 and 35 per cent of the national total), although their share in total capacity remained relatively modest—always below 13 per cent.[9] In the days before catalytic cracking and high octane gasoline, refineries were much more modest affairs than they later became, and shut-down capacity was a more normal and defensible adjunct of shifting supply sources, merger, or even price change.[10] With new refining techniques and the effective application of prorationing to production, this phenomenon disappeared. Not only has the number of shut-down refineries declined as a percentage both of all refineries and of total refining capacity but the rate of utilization of operating capacity has risen, running consistently around 90 per cent since World War II.[11] Rapid expansion in refinery capacity after the war and a slackening of the rate of demand increase in 1954 dropped average utilization to 88 per cent; but much of this apparent surplus was planned for military security and had been encouraged by accelerated amortization.[12] In any event, average usage rebounded to over 90 per cent in the following two years.

9. The number of shut-down refineries was especially large from 1922–27 and 1932–39. These early figures are not too meaningful, since this was the period when new oil discoveries spawned small field "tea-kettles" to skim the more valuable components from crude that would otherwise have been totally wasted. Computations for statements made in this and the following paragraphs were made from *Petroleum Facts and Figures*, 9th ed., pp. 256, 258; 12th ed., pp. 216–217.

10. The pre-prorationing practice of building simple skimming and topping facilities in flush fields to salvage a part of the value of cheap crude might be classed as socially wasteful. In the business sense, these investments often paid off handsomely; and in the physical sense of conserving crude they were also preferable to the only practical alternative, open storage or actual dumping. The system was wasteful, but the cause lay in the spewing of flush oil under the law of capture, not in the topping plants that saved a fraction of the loss. See Stocking, pp. 260–265, 313; and below, pp. 496 ff.

11. In recent years the number of shut-down refineries has been considerably less than 10 per cent of all refineries (in 1956 it was 7½ per cent) and it has usually constituted under 5 per cent of national capacity (2.9 per cent in 1956). Crude oil runs to stills had ranged widely from ⅔ to ⅘ of average operating capacity in the 1920's and from around 64 to 83 per cent in the 1930's; but since 1945 they have been around 90 per cent, except in 1949 and in 1954, when they were about 86 per cent and 88 per cent respectively. In 1955 and 1956 they were 93.1 per cent and 93.4 per cent (Coqueron, *Annual Financial Analysis, 1956*, p. 26). On the sharp cutbacks in 1958 see below, pp. 557–558.

12. See the statement by Bruce K. Brown, formerly Deputy Administrator of the Petroleum Administration for Defense, *National Petroleum News* (July 21, 1954), pp. 16–20.

Nonintegrated refiners do not generally lay their troubles at the door of "subsidized" competition from integrated refiners. They do complain of being "squeezed" from time to time; but their complaints are usually directed against government controls of production or against controls of transportation or of marketing facilities by the major refiners. They do not apparently find serious fault with the entry into refining by producers or by marketers, and they do not challenge the rate or amount of investment in refining facilities by the major companies in particular, although there have been general complaints about alleged excess capacity during periods of market weakness like 1954 and 1957–58. Both majors and independents seem generally to believe that refining since World War II is one of the less remunerative branches of this industry.[13] Over the entire period of 1920–52 computed refinery margins and apparently profits as well fluctuated more violently than margins and profits at other levels of the industry; [14] and very sketchy data suggest that, at least among more successful firms, those companies with a heavy investment weight in refining have been fairly consistently less profitable than those with greater concentration in producing and marketing.[15] Certainly, some integrated companies have been content to have independents do some of their refining for them on long-term contract.[16] And many successful

13. The theme was recurrent in interviews. See "The Oil Play," *Fortune, 48* (August, 1948), 74, for similar views.

14. See McLean and Haigh, pp. 122, 132–136, 143.

15. Earnings data are not conclusive evidence, as has previously been emphasized, but they are consistent with this generalization; e.g. compare earnings of producers and integrated firms (see above, pp. 321 ff.). McLean and Haigh studied returns on borrowed and invested capital for a greater number of classes of firms (pp. 680–681). Using medians over the entire period 1920–1952, their producing companies earned 8.5 per cent and their marketers (including a disproportionately heavy representation of larger and more successful firms) earned 10.3 per cent. Refining-marketing firms, however, earned only 6.8 per cent when crude-oil self-sufficiency ratios were under 10 per cent, from 7.6 to 8.0 per cent when they were higher. The group with the highest ratios (100 per cent to 500 per cent) showed the highest earnings rate.

16. Gulf purchased 11.5 to 18.7 per cent of its total products sold in the period 1946–52, predominantly from independents. McLean and Haigh noted this practice among all seven of the companies they studied intensively. Of the companies for which data were available, however, only Gulf showed a tendency to increase its purchases (pp. 427–436, esp. p. 428). Socony-Vacuum, an original marketing company of the Standard Oil group, still purchased about 18 per cent of its needs in 1949. U. S. Senate, Subcommittee of the Committee on Banking and Currency, "Price Increases in Petroleum Products," *Hearings,* 81st Congress, 1st Session (1949), p. 126. More recently, Socony-Vacuum

producing companies have continued to spurn refining despite favorable opportunities, during the shortages of the 1940's, to join with refiner-marketers who were short of crude. They justify this policy in something like the following terms:

> We have felt that over the years producing, if properly conducted, has been the most profitable branch of the industry. No marketer or refiner can do anything that his competitor can't imitate or duplicate. One marketer may give his customers free air or other free services, or he may build attractive new service stations in desirable locations; invariably his competitors will do the same thing, his advantage will be gone, and he will be left with higher costs. The products are essentially the same, at least for the large, reputable companies; everyone knows that. If you build the most modern, efficient refinery, anyone else can imitate you by hiring a competent construction company to do the same job. All you need is a checkbook. But in production, a company that succeeds in finding oil has something that twenty other competitors may not be able to duplicate. In refining and marketing by great effort you may reduce your costs and expand your margin by a fraction of a cent. In production we paint with a much wider brush.

This common attitude toward refining as compared with production seems to differentiate refining as a manufacturing process from production as the exploitation of a hoard. Sound as it may be for the nonintegrated operator at each stage, it seems most unlikely that the management of a vertically integrated firm should be so confused by its own accounting conventions of costing materials at various stages for control purposes. Crude oil is often, probably usually, transferred to the refinery at costs computed from posted prices and published transport tariffs. On this basis refinery margins and refinery "profits" can be computed even though they are arbitrary and can have no decisive weight in decisions whether to expand or to contract refinery investment. To consider these computed profits the measure of the contribution of refining operations would be to deny that the firm's integration has any net effect on the derivation of value from its crude

---

Exploration Company committed itself to supply the new independent Great Northern Oil Company refinery at St. Paul (20,000 to 25,000 b/d) with crude oil; and it was reported that Socony will market a substantial proportion of the output. "An Oil Empire Is Growing in the Midwest," *National Petroleum News* (March 17, 1954), p. 14.

oil; in other words, it would be tantamount to assuming that the firm in the absence of its integration could dispose of its crude oil in equivalent volume and value at the "cost" transfer price to the refinery. Were this indeed the case, and it could be in some particular instance, the integrated firm would do well to reappraise its competitive position.

Producers who belittle the profitability of refining as a prospective integrated operation for themselves may do so for purely personal reasons: the thrill of the treasure hunt for crude in contrast with the more prosaic job of manufacturing or the differential skills required in one or the other activity. But unless they, too, are bemused by computed margins, they are really asserting that aggregate refinery demand for crude is so ample, compared with the supply they are in a position to produce, that their profit position could not be enough improved by their entry into refining to justify the risk and the investment. This is probably an inappropriate assumption for the individual major company,[17] and it is almost certainly so for the majors as a group.[18]

The comparative acceptance of the integrated by the nonintegrated refiner, in contrast with the virulent attacks of the nonintegrated marketer, for example, despite refinery margins that often appear all too narrow may reflect either the unreality of posted prices of crude or the absence of political appeal among independent refiners. Certainly, their numbers are few and technological change has further weakened their bargaining position and claim to survive. Soaring demands for petroleum products and rapid technical advances in refining that have displaced (not just outmoded) equipment have served more rapidly than at other levels of the industry to efface what might otherwise have

17. Obviously a company as heavily and profitably involved in production as Gulf does not consider it appropriate. Else how, in the light of the high profit in crude oil, can one explain Gulf's investment of $120,000,000 in 3¼ per cent Union Oil convertible debentures—an arrangement apparently linked to the disposal of some of Gulf's burgeoning Middle Eastern crude oil to that West Coast refiner? See below, p. 366, n. 43.

18. See the appraisal of the effect of integration on the price of crude oil, above, pp. 218 ff. The assumption may be even less realistic in the future than it has been in the past. With the mounting pressure of crude oil supply abroad, and the dispersion of control over that supply in the hands of increasing numbers of producing companies, it may be increasingly important for a producer to have his own refinery and distribution: "the strongest oil companies over the next decade will be those that have the markets, rather than those producing crude oil." "An Abundance of Oil," *Economist* (October 26, 1957), pp. 327–329.

been excess capacity; while the continued willingness of major companies to modernize and expand have prevented prolonged maladjustments in the other direction.

Refinery Investment and Integration

In spite of contentions that refining is not very remunerative, the managements of integrated firms have continued to expand capacity in step with market demand and to expand dollar investment even more rapidly.[19] Company executives themselves explain these growing investments in terms of a commitment to integration and balance: the requirements of their marketing divisions must be met and the growth in their allowable crude oil production must at least be matched, though typically it is surpassed by product-producing ability. Paraphrasing a common response, "We have a substantial investment in marketing and in consumer good will. The only way in which we can take the fullest advantage of that investment is to count as a general rule on retaining our present market share, except perhaps in those areas where we are at a cost disadvantage. We cannot afford to slacken our selling efforts; and, conversely, we have to keep expanding our refinery investments to keep our customers supplied." Sometimes, the growth of refinery investment is explained as a kind of responsibility of the integrated firm to the industry to create and maintain a market for crude oil—a counterpart of the feeling that through the pipeline and the posted price for crude, the integrated firm has brought "an assured market for crude oil right to the wellhead."

However the matter may be phrased, the simple fact seems to be that those refiners who have been unable or unwilling to maintain the pace of refinery investment, on which product quality and comparative yields depend, have sunk to obscurity and disappeared. No integrated firm can expect to maintain the sale of its branded products and justify its investment in nationwide distribution if it cannot keep in the forefront of refinery improvements and know-how. Thus the

19. Thus between 1946 and 1955 total domestic demand for refined products increased 1,278.8 million barrels or about 71 per cent and average daily operating crude-oil capacity of refineries rose 3.015 million b/d or about 58 per cent; but capital outlays per year on refineries and chemical plants increased $575 million or 230 per cent and gross investment rose $4.175 billion or 139 per cent. Expressed differently, over the ten-year period gross investment increased from approximately $576 to $872 per *daily barrel* of crude oil capacity. Computed from *Petroleum Facts and Figures*, 9th ed., pp. 1, 258; 12th ed., pp. 1, 217; and Coqueron, *Annual Financial Analysis, 1956*, p. 42.

integrated firm has no choice: whether it would realize the potential profits of crude or maintain the business volume its existing investments require, it will continue to invest in refining no matter how narrow the nominal refining margin appears.

For management of the integrated firm to say that refinery investment is made to protect and support the market for its crude oil is undoubtedly to express part of the truth; and to regard this objective as its responsibility is equally cogent. But the responsibility is to its own interests, not to the industry, and the rationalization of refining investment implied is grossly oversimplified. Refinery investment is equally made to protect and to support its investment in distribution and in consumer acceptance. And it is also made either because the management believes the firm can do as good a job as its rivals, or a better job, in refining or because it realizes that if this is not now the case it had better become so soon or the firm may find itself a relatively hollow shell behind the façade of asset valuations in its balance sheet. It is the efficiency of vertical integration itself that is at stake in the quality and scale of refining.

It is not too fruitful to speculate on what might happen to refinery investment in the absence of vertical integration. The refiner would lose the cash flow, especially from crude oil, that now supports his operations, but he would also be relieved of the cash drain of investment in that sector. He would miss the security of material flow and product demand that his other investments provide but he would also be relieved of their investment weight. Uncertainty lies in the kind and degree of market imperfections that would persist. There is no doubt that a refining industry forced into arm's length bargaining for its raw material and for its distribution would require wider operating margins to cover its greater risks. Reduced assurances of continuous flows into and out of the refinery would probably raise capital costs. This alone need not prejudice consumers, however. Free of any ambivalent interest in higher crude oil prices that is now generated by vertical integration, the natural concern of materials users could bring relief in lower crude oil prices, limited however by the political influence of producers and the public policies with regard to production and imports.

It is probably true that a nonintegrated refining industry would find manufacturers' brands a weaker tie to consumer acceptance; and this could seriously imperil the kind of research and development that pushed Sun Oil and the industry into the perfection of catalytic cracking, for example. But here, too, it is difficult to predict. A heavy emphasis on product quality and brand does not necessarily depend on extensive investments in marketing facilities. Any consideration of the possible effects of dissolving financial ties between refining and marketing must await a survey of the record of marketing investment under integration.

So far as the record of vertical integration in the growth and improvement of refinery investment is concerned, it has been good. There is no clear presumption that a nonintegrated refinery industry would better it.

MARKETING

More than any other branch of the petroleum industry, marketing is the domain of small business. In no other sphere is it easier for new operators to enter—or exit. Here the integrated oil company must work through and alongside some 24,000 wholesalers and 180,000 service station operators.[20] Here, too, there has been tremendous growth; continual change in the character, location, and operation of facilities; and intense rivalry for customer patronage. It is not surprising that marketing should generate the most heated attacks on the investment policies and competitive behavior of integrated firms and that the issues posed should be easy to describe in general terms, difficult to put precisely, and almost impossible to resolve definitively.

It is generally recognized that excess capacity, more especially among retail service stations, has long plagued gasoline distribution; and it is alleged that this situation has gravely depressed earnings. The wastes of excess capacity are said to have their source in the investment policies of the vertically integrated firm, and in its proclivity for non-price competition, of which overinvestment in marketing is the manifestation and consequence.

The Prewar Development of Distribution Facilities

The distributive institutions of few modern industries are free from criticisms like these. The reasons are not hard to find. As soon as producers find some basis for differentiating their products, each wants to assure that effective selling efforts will be concentrated on his offering, that it will be placed before the customer in as many places, as conveniently located, and as attractively fitted out as possible, that it will be offered with a maximum of free services and assurances of quality as part of the sales package. In the case of gasoline, the con-

20. See below, pp. 423–427.

ditions were especially propitious for introducing this kind of sales promotion. An explosive expansion in demand for an unfamiliar product that had to be dispensed in a novel way, and whose quality could not be assured by inspection, induced the development of a completely new and specialized marketing institution, the service station. Here was a perfect vehicle for combining service and guarantees of quality with convenience, product differentiation, and advertising. These circumstances made the promise of excessive development very great. What converted this promise into a certainty were the forces on the supply side of the market that have already been briefly characterized in Chapter 5—the enormous, uncontrollable expansion of national crude oil production that led producing companies to do their utmost to stake out claims on the loyalty of the motorist at almost any cost. Large-scale programs of service station construction in ever-widening marketing areas were the way to do it.

Finally contributing to the mushrooming of service stations were the radical shifts in the configuration of demand—not just its rapid expansion in aggregate but the restless geography of a newly motorized population: the new highways and access roads, and the changes in zoning regulations that created the opportunity for new service stations and left old ones high and dry. Changes in demand of this kind are particularly acute in marketing because of their impact on capacity. In refining, new processes and new products (like high octane gasolines) have made many refineries obsolete; but capacity did not remain excessive, for long, because the old plants could no longer turn out a salable product. In contrast, an improvement in service station layout or location will outmode other stations; but in so doing it cuts primarily into their volume and net earnings; it does not usually force them out of business. The service station operator is a little like the farmer: he values his independence, and one of his main costs of operation is his own labor. Particularly in depression he is likely to stay in business even though the residual income that is his wage and return on investment is sharply compressed.

The growth of service stations after World War I was explosive: from 15,000 in 1920, they soared to 121,513 in 1929 and to 170,494 in 1933.[21] By the end of the thirties the number had reached 241,858, a rise of more than 99 per cent during the decade, while automobile registrations increased only about 22, and gasoline sales 45, per cent.[22]

21. FTC, *Report on Distribution Methods and Costs, 4* (1944), 61–62.
22. *Ibid.,* pp. 62–63. Thus, as the FTC points out, potential gallonage per station declined from 118,000 to 86,000 gallons in this decade. Atlantic Refining

Data on the number of stations actually controlled by integrated firms through lease or ownership during the twenties are not available, but they are believed to have been substantial, for this period coincided with the expansionary drive of firms like the Texas Company, Phillips, Shell, and various members of the old Standard group, into hitherto untapped sections of the market.[23]

Further expansion through the thirties was heavily weighted by the influx of individuals not otherwise employed, for the same reasons that drove them into setting up other retail establishments; [24] but they were encouraged by the integrated companies. Between 1930 and 1934, stations owned by integrated companies increased more than 40 per cent and the number of stations they supplied on a 100 per cent basis increased 30 per cent.[25] In 1928 a study of the situation had reached the conclusion that there "were six times as many retail stations as were needed to serve the public." [26]

Company estimated that average gasoline sales in company-operated stations declined from 302,000 gallons in 1925 to 205,000 in 1929 and 118,000 in 1934, while operating costs per gallon increased correspondingly from 4.47 to 5.55 and 7.04 cents in these years. See McLean and Haigh, p. 151.

23. See, e.g., the two cases summarized in Till, "Gasoline—the Competition of Big Business," pp. 134–135, and Wilson, "Oil Competition in the Mid-West" (above, p. 101, n. 58), *passim*.

24. A. A. Stambaugh (*Below Cost Selling of Petroleum Products,* testimony before the Ohio Senate Committee on Financial Institutions, Commerce and Labor, April 11, 1951, privately printed, p. 7) attributes the expansion to an increase in the retail margin from 1929 to 1939. The effectiveness of the one-cent margin rise in 1934, however, was exaggerated by poor alternative employment opportunities and overproduction. From 1945 to 1953 margins again advanced from an average of 4.13 cents to 5.35 cents; but at this time there was full employment, and the number of stations did not rise even though average station volume increased 59 per cent. See Stambaugh, *The Marketer's Role in a Free Economy* (duplicated by Standard of Ohio, 1949), pp. 18–19.

25. Data from *Report* on Marketing Facilities, supplement to "Petroleum Investigation," *Hearings* on House Resolution 441 (March 20, 1935), discussed in Watkins, pp. 27–28. The TNEC asked the major oil companies to report to it "the number of service stations owned, leased, operated, controlled and/or used as exclusive outlets" for each year, 1929 to 1938. The replies were not comparable, and so it is not clear how much reliance may be placed on them. For what they are worth, they show, for the eighteen companies who responded, an increase from 33,704 at the end of 1929 to a peak of 125,327 at the end of 1933, then a decline to 69,666 five years later. *Hearings,* Pt. XIV, p. 7429, Pt. XIV-A, pp. 7738, 7819.

26. This study was referred to with approval by A. A. Stambaugh, then chairman of the Board of Standard of Ohio, in *An Oil Man Looks at Distribution* (privately printed, 1951), p. 6. Standard of Ohio had suffered par-

The end result of this mushroom growth of service stations had to be hardship for some, the more certain when general depression slowed the expansion of demand. When recriminations were finally aired before the TNEC, three tantalizing imponderables made it impossible fairly to evaluate them. First, it became apparent that there was no objective measure of the alleged excess capacity. How could one reduce the intangibles of service station performance to a comparable profile from which to judge the appropriateness of current capacity? What of the hourly, daily, and seasonal fluctuations in the spacing of demand? What of the convenience to the motorist of always having a service station near, of never being forced to inventory reserve supplies of fuel and grease, of seldom having to queue up at the pump? In a high income economy, such luxuries may well be worth their cost: the test must rest with the impact of free customer choice on the rate of return on investment after costs.[27] But the attempts at measurement along this line encountered frustrations of two other sorts: data were not available on profit rates for a sufficiently representative sample of nonintegrated marketers;[28] and the now familiar impossibility of properly isolating either costs or revenues of vertically integrated firms by departments precluded an adequate earnings test of the charge of subsidized competition despite TNEC solicitations of departmental cost and net earnings data from the majors. Several companies replied that it was impossible to provide meaningful information; but

---

ticularly in the late 1920's from aggressive invasions of its market by other integrated companies, building their own marketing facilities and forcing upon Sohio and themselves sharply falling sales per service station and correspondingly rising unit costs. See McLean and Haigh, pp. 106–108, 240, 242. "The form that the [distributive] system has assumed is well adapted to its function, but its proliferation has gone to extreme and uneconomic lengths." Joseph E. Pogue, "Economics of the Petroleum Industry," in DeGolyer, *Elements of the Petroleum Industry,* p. 485; and for an excellent survey, Till, "Gasoline— The Competition of Big Business," pp. 129–140. See, finally, the criticisms by Bain, *Pacific Coast Petroleum Industry, 3, 95.*

27. See Sidney A. Swensrud, "The Marketing of Petroleum Products," TNEC, *Hearings* (1939), Pt. XV, pp. 8678–8681.

28. Standard Oil Company of Kentucky, solely a marketer, earned 7 to 8 per cent annually on its investment (stockholders equity; the company had no long-term debt) in each year during 1932–35, and in the next two years it earned 13 and 15 per cent; but the company enjoyed the advantages of a bulk purchase contract with Standard of New Jersey, cheap water transportation costs, and sales in a market territory where prices remained substantially above those in surrounding areas. Standard of Ohio, then a refiner and marketer only, whose market had been subject to much more strenuous marketing competition, lost money in 1932, 1933, and 1934.

twelve firms submitted data for assets and net income in each of the three years of 1936–38. The lowest rate of return for twenty-two of the thirty-six annual reports thus provided was shown by marketing departments, for eleven it was refining, and for three it was refining and marketing combined. Of the thirty-three differentiated observations, seventeen represented marketing as a deficit operation, fifteen reported refining to be so, and a deficit was shown in all three observations where marketing and refining were combined. Production and transportation were reported as moderately to phenomenally profitable in all cases.[29]

Since to the extent it is integrated the vertically integrated firm has but one level of real transfer prices—the sale prices of its marketing division to ultimate buyers—the significance of such a comparative record of profitability of any one department of the majors will depend on the nominal price at which that operation is billed for new materials and services received from other divisions and the price at which it is credited for product or service passed to another division. These prices and the criteria on which costs, common to more than one operation, are allocated among them are crucial to the meaningfulness of results.[30] The closer transfer prices approximate what the department could have obtained or would have had to pay in the open market, the more useful are the division results for purposes of management control and decision-making. Standard of Indiana alone specifically indicated to the TNEC that it attempted to base its interdepartment billing price "on the market." [31] On this basis its marketing department just about broke even during the period covered; its results are thus not out of line with the showing of the others.

The data submitted to the TNEC rather clearly reflected and in some sense corroborated a widely held industry opinion that marketing was not profitable. Paul Hadlick, perennial critic of integrated oil

29. TNEC, *Hearings* (1940), Pt. XVII-A, pp. 10040–10043.

30. Thus, the Pure Oil Company told the TNEC that it transferred its products between departments "at arbitrary prices and it is impossible to completely segregate all costs and incomes." Possibly illustrating the arbitrariness of its own reputed allocations (though possibly illustrating instead the effect on profits in a given year of random factors—emergency conditions or merely a decision to take a cumulative accounting loss or profit), Pure's statistics showed a loss of 42.78 per cent in refining in 1936 while marketing was credited with a profit of 4.12 per cent. Ohio Oil reported the opposite experience in the same year: i.e. refining profits of 28.6 per cent and marketing losses of 9.0 per cent (*ibid.*).

31. *Ibid.*

companies, marshaled before the TNEC a wide variety of indications that, as he charged, the big oil companies were subsidizing competition with independent marketers. He cited the Report of the so-called Blazer Committee, which concluded that the marketing costs of large integrated firms considerably exceeded the margins currently obtained by nonintegrated marketers. He quoted a *Fortune* magazine conclusion that Gulf's main profits were "locked in" production and transportation so that its officers "did not much care" whether refining and marketing showed a profit. The Texas Company's 1937 prospectus contended that its marketing division, with losses from 1930–35, had nonetheless served its purpose by providing assured outlets for other profitable divisions. Pure Oil Corporation's 1937 prospectus admitted that its marketing operations, billed at published wholesale market prices, would "show substantial losses," so that the company's earnings would have been much higher *"had it been possible for the company to sell its crude oil production as such at posted price or as refined products at full published wholesale market price."* [32] Colonial Beacon Company, a marketing subsidiary of Standard of New Jersey, and Standard of Nebraska, a purely marketing company, were both alleged to have shown losses consistently in the thirties until they were absorbed by Standard (New Jersey) and Standard of Indiana, respectively.[33] One major company, after analyzing its own marketing department's operations during the 1930's, concluded that it lost money in the first four years covered by the study and made negligible profits in the next three.[34]

These scattered bits of evidence are of some interest because they seem to corroborate the compartmental profits data. But in seeming

32. This catalogue appears in Hadlick's testimony, TNEC, *Hearings,* Pt. XVI, pp. 9152–9156. While the Pure Oil quotation may indicate why the company felt obliged to engage in "losing" operations, Hadlick's inference that "if the Pure Oil Company had not lost money in marketing they would have had a larger net income upon which to pay taxes and dividends" (*ibid.,* p. 9154), is clearly a *non sequitur,* since it implies that Pure Oil actually had the alternative it carefully specified.

33. *Ibid.,* p. 9164. See also South Carolina Oil Jobbers Association, *A Report from Committee on Divorcement of Marketing,* issued in 1952, mimeographed.

34. Information supplied by the company. In the best of the seven years just before 1939, profits did not exceed 2.5 per cent on investment. The Atlantic Refining Company has estimated that its returns on investment in company-operated service stations were 60 per cent annually before 1921, and declined steadily thereafter to 18.8 per cent in 1928, 7.5 per cent in 1930, and 2.1 per cent in 1934. These figures are before depreciation and interest. McLean and Haigh, p. 151.

to answer one question they merely raise another: if marketing operations were not deemed profitable in the thirties, why did vertically integrated firms continue to enlarge their financial stake in them? [35] The answer can only be that the major companies did not really accept the validity of their own interdepartmental transfer prices as a reflection of what they could obtain for their crude oil or products if they chose not to invest forward. *Fortune* magazine summarized the general philosophy in 1940:

> It is . . . clearly in the interest of large integrated companies to keep profits locked securely in the crude oil . . . and far away from the point where the refined products meet the pressure of the market. Under such a system gasoline price wars, touched off by dealers, are incessant; but the marketing companies usually cushion the shock before it gets to the crude margin. The general strategy of running an oil company might be defined thus: make big profits on the crude; protect the profits by owning pipe lines and tankers so that transportation earnings do not get siphoned off to others; and, finally, own sufficient refining and marketing equipment to dispose of your products at cost or better.[36]

While stress on the profitability of production seemed to be quite general in the industry in the middle and late thirties, it is characteristic that there were strong dissidents. J. H. Pew, for example, testified that he considered his production properties a drain on Sun's finances, tolerated only as insurance against some future supply squeeze.[37] In

35. Although three years is a very narrow basis for any kind of investment guidance, marketing losses were evenly distributed over the period even though two of the three years, 1936–37, were years of comparative prosperity. Refining losses, on the other hand, were disproportionately concentrated in 1938, when refinery margins were seriously squeezed by business recession, falling product prices, and fairly firm crude prices stabilized by public production controls. Most of the integrated companies did get out of the direct operation of retail stations in the middle thirties, under the immediate impact of chain store and social security taxes and for other, more basic, reasons as well. See Swensrud, "The Marketing of Petroleum Products," pp. 8682–8683, 8698–8699. But they did not, on this account, curtail their investments in service stations; they merely leased them to independent operators. See also McLean and Haigh, pp. 289–294.

36. May, 1940, p. 83. For citations of other statements by executives of integrated companies to the effect that they made no money on marketing as such, see Prewitt, "The Operation and Regulation of Crude Oil and Gasoline Pipe Lines," p. 200.

37. TNEC, *Hearings,* Pt. XIV, pp. 7206, 7226.

contrast, a president of a major company told one of the authors in 1952: "Marketing is a way of getting more for our crude than selling it to Standard of New Jersey."

The Postwar Shake-Down in Distribution

The major companies have probably not changed their basic policies with respect to marketing since they withdrew from direct operation of service stations in the middle thirties under the so-called Iowa Plan. But economic conditions and opportunities have so improved since before the war that both the direction and the impact of marketing competition have been importantly modified.

The integrated companies have achieved a dramatic rationalization of their wholesale marketing operations: they have by-passed and closed down bulk plants; they have built large terminals at the end of crude and product pipelines; and they have increased the size of tank trucks to ship products directly from terminals to buyers with larger product "dumps." In this field of wholesale distribution, which is more nearly than retailing within their own control, large integrated firms had realized very substantial cost reductions even before the war.[38] Construction of new retail service stations was halted almost completely during the war; and the drive since that time has been toward larger unit volume rather than greater numbers. Between 1939 and 1948 the number of service stations fell almost 26 per cent (from 241,858 to 179,647), while the domestic physical demand for motor fuel rose 58.6 per cent. Over the next six years service stations increased only to 181,747 in number, while the domestic physical consumption of motor fuel advanced another 40 per cent.[39] Generally, integrated companies have been building larger stations capable of handling a much greater volume of sales and taking much larger deliveries; and they have put pressure on their dealer customers to increase the amount of average deliveries. Sun Oil is an outstanding example: it has held down retail outlets, given more or less exclusive

38. E.g., Standard of New Jersey is reported to have reduced its wholesale marketing costs per gallon of gasoline by 46.7 per cent between 1932 and 1941. R. T. Haslam, F. M. Surface, and J. R. Riddell, "Petroleum Marketing Cost and Cost Reduction," Pt. II, *National Petroleum News* (March 10, 1943), p. 9 of a reprint of their series of three articles, March 3, 10, and 17, 1943. See also McLean and Haigh, pp. 272–281, for even more striking examples of cost saving.

39. See *Petroleum Facts and Figures*, 12th ed., p. 298; 9th ed., p. 342. Consumption of motor fuel taken from API, *Statistical Bulletin* (Apr. 23, 1957), Form No. 8. See also U. S. Bureau of the Census, *Statistical Abstract of the U.S.* (1951), p. 884.

territories, and concentrated on maximizing the volume of each.[40] More effective production controls of crude oil since the war and the mounting full employment demand for petroleum products have eased the pressure on the integrated firm to maintain realizations on its growing output through heavy investment in market facilities. The focus of investment outlays has shifted more than ever to expansion of supply, and especially of crude oil.[41]

In contrast with their attitude before the war, vertically integrated companies now generally claim that they make a good profit on their marketing operations. Paraphrasing,

> Our marketing division is billed at a price that reflects as accurately as we can estimate it what it would have to pay to make the same purchases in the open market. It must operate on the margin between that price and the price at which it sells its products —to service stations and to final customers. Operating within that margin, and bearing all the costs properly attributable to marketing—including advertising—our marketing division makes a good return on the capital invested in it.[42]

40. Willard M. Wright, general sales manager of Sun, described this policy in an address, *Keep Pace with Change,* before the Ohio Petroleum Marketers, mimeographed (September 15, 1952), pp. 8–9. Later Wright indicated that Sun had 26.5 per cent fewer stations at the end of 1953 than at the end of 1939, but each sold 281 per cent more gasoline than before the war. *National Petroleum News* (May 26, 1954), p. 28.

41. Between 1934 and 1940, investments in marketing ranged between 12 and 18 per cent of total expenditures for property, plant and equipment by the thirty major oil companies surveyed by the Chase National Bank. Between 1942 and 1945 this ratio varied from 2 to 7 per cent. Over the period 1946–55 marketing outlays by the industry are estimated at 7.5 per cent of total outlays. Since 1947 it has not been so high as 10 per cent and since 1951 it has been less than 7 per cent. See Coqueron and Pogue, *Capital Formation in the Petroleum Industry,* pp. 27, 33. Data since 1945 from Coqueron and Pogue, *Investment Patterns* (above, p. 314, n. 3), p. 37. Before the war, in contrast, a major cause of the overexpansion in the number of retail outlets was surely "the mounting pressure of the crude oil supply under the impetus of the rule of capture." Pogue, "Economics of the Petroleum Industry," in DeGolyer, *Elements of the Petroleum Industry,* p. 488.

42. See, among others, Sidney Swensrud (speaking for Gulf), *National Petroleum News* (May 21, 1952), p. 51; Herbert Willetts, director in charge of domestic marketing, Socony-Vacuum, address before Illinois Petroleum Marketers Association, March 11, 1953; Willard W. Wright, "Keep Pace with Change" (speaking for Sun), pp. 5–6.

Wright declared that Sun had operated since 1934 on a 1.6-cent margin or spread on motor fuel from the refinery to the dealer, including sales and training costs, maintenance of bulk plant, advertising, in fact all marketing costs including a profit (presumably on the marketing investment). "Sun Ex-

For service station investments the case is more tenuous; not that an integrated firm would continue to pour into such a venture money it knows it will lose, but rather that there is little evidence of the same rigorous testing of investments as in wholesaling. Logically one would expect the pressure on a major refiner-marketer to push branded distribution of its products or forestall market intrusions of rivals to soften its scrutiny of the profitability of investment in retail facilities. The small firm can afford no such luxury. The retailer who leases his service station to a major supplier at a higher rental than he pays the same supplier on a short-term leaseback, and who can use the long-term lease as security for a low-cost bank loan, may be able to construct a station that would be unprofitable for a retailer not enjoying such a subsidy. Furthermore, the project may be attractive to the major refiner who benefits from the increased volume of refinery sales.[43]

In this area the superiority of integration in raising funds and

plains 1.6¢ Gasoline Margin," *National Petroleum News* (October 1, 1952), p. 39; "Sun Tells Why It Won't Publish Cost Figures," *ibid.* (September 24, 1952), pp. 27–28.

In the study referred to above (n. 34), the major company's analysts concluded that the marketing department had made substantial profits since 1938: 8.8 and 18.7 per cent on total investment in 1939 and 1940; and in the four postwar years beginning with 1946, profits were reported as 16.1 per cent, 8.8 per cent, 14.4 per cent, and 28.0 per cent respectively. The gross margin or spread per gallon received by its marketing department on sales to stations not owned or leased by it was 3.45 cents in 1949 and 3.25 cents in 1950. From these margins (which include a reported profit of 1.33 cents and 1.06 cents respectively) one would have to deduct costs of terminal operation and transport between refinery and bulk plant before arriving at a figure comparable to the 2 to 2.75 cent margins received by independent distributors at the time. In this case, unit costs of the integrated company, plus the above-cited high returns on investment, seem to be within the jobbers' margin. On the comparability of the two operations, see below, pp. 368 ff.

43. At quite another level but illustrating much the same principle would seem to be the agreement between Gulf and the Union Oil Company of California. Gulf is half-owner of the Kuwait concession, now producing around 1,100,000 b/d, but it has little distribution on the West Coast. Union Oil is well established in the Pacific region—a deficit producing area in recent years—and it has been experimenting with shale oil refining. Gulf recently arranged for an advance of $120 millions to Union for capital expenditures in the form of a purchase of convertible debentures paying 3¼ per cent and maturing in twenty-five years. Union will "get access to Gulf's crude oil production at the market price." Though reported as an "investment," the low terms suggest that Gulf may be "buying" an advantageous market outlet for its Middle East crude in an area at that time free of import control and on terms of possible conversion to a more permanent basis. New York *Times* (April 5, 1956), p. 41.

stimulating their use, even where the projects undertaken pay their way by some private reckoning, may not accord with public advantage.[44] The inadequacy of data to permit even a rational guess about return on investment is a deficiency at least as old as NRA.[45] It is common for integrated firms to speak of a "target" rate of return on real estate investments of 6 per cent, a figure often conceded to be a maximum in practice. Too often the attitude appears to be that one's own company never invests in service stations unless it expects to make a reasonable return but one's competitors could not possibly be doing so.[46] Conversely, earnings of less than 6 per cent are condoned because "of course we are not in the real estate business, and don't expect to do much better there."

44. Haslam, Surface, and Riddell, in "Petroleum Marketing Cost and Cost Reduction," *National Petroleum News* (March 3, 10, and 17, 1953), defend such investments on the ground that this cost of brand differentiation is no more than a "fraction of a cent a gallon" but there is no way of appraising this estimate statistically. In 1952, Shell's Retail Department estimated the total cost of building a conventional service station at $30,000 and the cost of land at $20,000 in a typical city location. Annual depreciation, at 8 per cent for 12½ years, came to $2,400, taxes $600. "Station Price Tags," *National Petroleum News* (July 30, 1952), pp. 80–81. Assume that capital in this use should earn at least 8 per cent before income taxes (actual alternative earnings have been much higher since World War II), and a rough estimate of "costs" to be covered would be $5,896 per year (i.e. depreciation plus property taxes plus 8 per cent return on average station investment of $16,200 and average investment in land of $20,000). Average annual service station sales approximate 120,000 gallons of gasoline. Ignoring other sales but doubling this figure for gasoline at these relatively expensive locations, capital costs would still be about 2½¢ per gallon of sales.

In contrast with this rough guess, one integrated company (reference above, n. 34) has estimated its rental income from company-owned, dealer-operated stations at only 0.45 cents per gallon in 1950. Direct sales of motor fuel to company-owned, dealer-operated stations were said to be among the more profitable operations in which the company engaged, returning 15.2 per cent on sales in 1949, 12.5 per cent in 1950. This profit in 1950 was estimated at 1.06 cents per gallon, presumably including the rental of 0.45 cents, but capital costs were not indicated, nor was any information provided that would explain their estimate. If there was a profit in these operations, it must have been derived from sales, not from rentals.

45. See Petroleum Administrative Division, *Final Report of the Marketing Division* (Washington, D.C., 1935), p. 78. Although the Petroleum Administrator tried to collect marketing cost information from the integrated and other marketers, the diversity of the concepts employed and the inadequacy of the information forced the abandonment of the project of arriving at standardized marketing costs.

46. See, e.g., Wright, "Keep Pace with Change," p. 10.

Marketing as an Integrated Function

It should be quite plain by now that the difficulty in appraising charge and countercharge regarding subsidization of competition stems from the integrated nature of the decision to invest in marketing facilities. Without its own marketing, returns on the balance of the firm's operations might be lower: perhaps a lower price for its refined products sold to independent marketers; perhaps a less stable operating rate or a lower utilization of capacity for its refineries or for its pipeline investment. These marketing investments are made to sell product, only secondarily to earn a separately identifiable profit.[47] The "profit" data available do not reflect these broader considerations: they are unsatisfactory because they are partial and arbitrary with respect to transfer prices, to allocated costs, and to allocated benefits. The judgment of marketing investment by comparing what it adds to costs with what it adds to revenues is economically sound only if the analysis does take account of these integrated costs and benefits as well, the direct as well as the indirect consequences: arbitrary transfer prices may conceal rather than reveal some of the crucial benefits to the firm.[48]

47. A highly illuminating indication of the kind of broad influences converging on the marketing investment decision by an integrated company is provided in an article by Esso Standard's general manager of marketing, New York City:

"The primary objective of Esso's marketing department is to maintain a strong competitive position.

"Our marketing goals can be neither volume regardless of profit, nor unit profit regardless of volume. We must obtain an optimum balance between these two extremes.

"We know that we can 'buy' an increased share of the market. But we also know that volume secured on this basis is at the expense of profits.

"Conversely, if our sole objective is a big marketing profit, we can accomplish this too. We can turn down all business on which we don't get a fixed and satisfactory profit; we can cancel all plans for the acquisition of new outlets we can curtail all planned investment and maintenance expense. This would give us our profit for a year, or maybe two; but our marketing position would suffer immediately, and our profit position would deteriorate in the years ahead

"Is it possible, therefore, to accomplish both the objectives of a share of market and increased marketing department profits? The answer is yes. And the method can be simply stated: to earn a greater return on every dollar invested—in properties, in people and in plans." John A. Miller, "How Esso Applies Creative Thinking to Maintain Competitive Position," *National Petroleum News* (April, 1956), p. 114.

48. The procedure of Richfield before and after it was forbidden to require its lessee stations to handle its products exclusively illustrates the arbitrariness

We do not know how adequately prospective costs and gains are weighed in making investment decisions in marketing: the matters that are stressed are how many gallons of product can be moved, with what continuing assurance, and at what price.[49] Most integrated companies apparently transfer products to their marketing divisions at some approximation to "open market price." But this price is hardly an objective market fact with independent validity. Indeed, the integrated company engages in its own marketing in part to protect and support that market price. To the extent that the transfer price approximates what independents must pay, integrated company-marketing operations will approach comparability with independents; but they will not provide a basis for measuring the integrated value of marketing to the investing firm if, as is most likely, its own brand participation is greater than the company could command in the absence of its marketing activities.

In this area the major producer-refiner-marketer performs a unique function: only he can hope through forward integration both to protect his own price [50] and to help stabilize the market as a whole.[51] The

---

of any rule-of-thumb differentiation of refining and marketing profits in an integrated operation. After the adverse antitrust judgment, Richfield promptly raised its rental charge from 1 cent to 2¼ cents a gallon of gasoline sold (regardless of brand) and reduced its tank-wagon price—a clear indication that any appearance of low returns on marketing investment (via rental charges) neglected to reflect the effect of controlled outlets on the tank-wagon realization.

49. "In selecting locations for their owned stations the volume of business expected to be transacted through them was the object of prime interest. When the stations were sublet to individuals this still continued to be the lessor's prime interest rather than whether the rentals charged would return a profit on the real estate investments involved. The best information available indicates that the real estate operations of at least the major companies were carried on at a small profit, or even at a loss . . ." FTC, *Report on Distribution Methods and Costs, 4*, 87. The same observations apply to the practice of furnishing equipment to service station operators. *Ibid.,* p. 88.

50. It is not the sole purpose of forward integration, of course, to protect refinery prices. There can be no doubt that big refiners built service stations also to give better service to the customer, to provide superior assurances of product quality, and to reduce distribution costs. Moreover, substantial profits could apparently be earned in marketing until the middle and late 1920's. (See *ibid.,* pp. 87–88, and McLean and Haigh, pp. 101–102, 267, 282.) But to the extent that the provision of these services and these cost reductions did not produce a return on the additional investment commensurate with what the companies were obtaining elsewhere, the additional inducement must have been the protection of refinery markets and prices that these investments also provided.

51. That this is a consideration was clearly indicated in one company's

investment in the retail service station—in its design, its location, and in the service rendered—is much like advertising expenditures in other industries; it forms in itself an advertisement of considerable power and it breeds or forces emulation by rivals who would maintain their share of a market that is generally believed to be responsive to price in the aggregate. In this manner, stability is gained only at the price of increasing investment and increasing cost.

What then can be said of this competitive investment of vertically integrated firms in marketing facilities with their heavy advertising overtones? [52] Are we to find economic merit in the investment policies of integrated firms in production, transportation, and refining only to gag at their efforts to sell their products without which those other investments could hardly be justified? Such a view skirts the brink of the early fallacy that only activities devoted to physical transformation of goods are "productive." And it perilously approaches the morass of prejudice against competition itself, which must be rivalry in selling as well as in production. Still, one cannot avoid the need to differentiate wherever possible those investments that increase and those that diminish the range of buyers' choices, those that thrive on an informed public, and those that benefit from consumer ignorance.

Concern for social waste in the marketing of petroleum products by vertically integrated firms stems from several considerations that need to be aired. First, vertical integration in oil anchors in the value of the raw material which is importantly created by state regulation.

---

private analysis of its own marketing which noted the immediate and long range value of price stabilization to be gained through direct marketing. A. A. Stambaugh attributes to independent marketers the opinion that it is good for them to have integrated companies in marketing because "suppliers as a group are more apt to take a long range point of view in setting their own individual prices and policies than non-suppliers, and that a certain stability is contributed to the market by that fact." "An Oil Man Looks at Distribution," p. 21. The opportunity for market stabilization is one consideration that influences some large oil companies in keeping a surplus of marketing capacity over refining capacity; see below, pp. 431–434.

52. It is undoubtedly true that there is both social and private waste in competitive puffing and in the multiplication of service station "services" that for many may not be worth their costs. Many would agree with George Stocking that while demand may be "created" by advertising "the existence of such diversity of demand is, in the main, the result of competitive advertising, and this in itself from a social point of view is largely waste" (p. 270 n., 266–275). In a high standard of living economy, competitive advertising is not necessarily waste and no way has yet been devised to differentiate in advance that which is from that which is not. This does not mean that the thinking citizen cannot make his own aesthetic judgments, of course.

All integration permits a concentration of cash resources, derived from other parts of the business, at any given level of operations; but vertical integration in petroleum gives to the integrated firm a socially created unearned increment of crude oil value that colors its competitive relations with all other companies having no such resources.

Second, the social gain from non-price competition at the marketing level is more dubious than at other operating levels, where rational motives predominate. In research and the development of new products and processes, the protection afforded by imperfect markets has been a catalyst for the release of dynamic, creative forces which have made refining intensely competitive. There can be no doubt of the social gains that have flowed from this competitive activity, by any criteria of economic value that most of us would accept. Where consumer whim predominates, rivalry for patronage takes more questionable directions. And while no one person can say objectively at what point competitive marketing expenditures efface either private or social net product or at what point the services showered on the motorist cost more than they are worth, it is crucial that the market itself should be able to register a free choice in this matter. To this end, it is necessary that real buyer alternatives be preserved: we need them if market demand is to provide the guidance that private investment requires for effective use of our savings; and we need them even more in this instance if profits from social control of crude supply are not to be transmuted into private control of consumer choice.

It seems that vertical integration has undoubtedly contributed substantially to the economic development of effective marketing institutions and methods, both wholesale and retail, in oil. In marketing as at other levels in operation, vertical integration (and size) have also generated investment funds on better terms and at lower costs than nonintegrated operators could command. The advantage is strategic, but it is also economic in capital markets that continue imperfect. Nevertheless, there is no other level of this industry where the independent should be more able to hold his own and even to provide the funds for expansion, if freed of strategic handicaps. In view of the equivocal criteria for judging marketing investments, it is not at all clear that the readier availability of capital that integration provides in this area is socially advantageous.

Whether vertical integration has created social loss in oil marketing by encouraging and supporting excessive facilities and whether vertically integrated firms do "subsidize" their marketing operations in competition with independents, are not strictly determinable questions. The former cannot be resolved, for there is no reason to believe that excess capacity would not have characterized oil marketing, whatever the ownership; indeed, only monopoly or government control could bring rationalization to this segment of the industry—at what other costs has already been suggested. The second question will always create more heat than light because the integrated investment decision, if it is rationally taken, must always give weight to impacts elsewhere in the firm. Thus if marketing investment has any beneficial impact on flow of product and utilization of refinery, transport, and production investment, it can always be made to look like "subsidization" in comparison with the nonintegrated firm, except when demand is excessive and competition is lax. Stated differently, given the indirect benefits that importantly motivate major company investments in marketing, subsidization is an undoubted fact—in the sense that an integrated company can profitably make investments that an efficient nonintegrated competitor cannot afford. But to judge whether the net consequence is socially advantageous or not takes us back to the basic question that economics alone cannot answer: if an investment in marketing finds part of its justification in the higher price it permits a refiner to obtain from a customer who has freedom of choice, is the investment socially as well as privately justified? One must return inexorably to the test of the market: does integration so limit the range of competitive alternatives that the judgment of the market is not free? This is the subject of Part IV.

PART IV

Integration and Competition in Product Markets

CHAPTER 15

The Patterns of Competition Where Firms Vary in Size and Integration

COMPETITIVE strategy has many facets, especially in an industry as dynamic and turbulent as this one. Integration itself has been one of those facets. Investment, innovation and non-price competition are others. Yet historically and traditionally, the aspect of competitive *structure* that has received primary attention has been the number and relative size of firms—with a heavy emphasis on the importance of numerous small, independently acting buyers and sellers—and the aspect of competitive *behavior,* rivalry in price. The two are inter-related, although by no means uniquely or exclusively. The principal criticisms of integration in oil, as found in association with business size, have referred not importantly to its impact on innovation, or on output-expanding investment (with the outstanding exception of investments in marketing facilities), but to its alleged blanketing of the field against price-dickering, and the entry and survival of smaller, nonintegrated rivals. These contentions must now be specifically analyzed.

COST AND DEMAND INFLUENCES

The outstanding economic characteristic of petroleum production, transportation, and processing is low variable and high fixed costs at each stage of operation. But as oil passes through each of its stages of processing, these costs are transmuted into a price, and therefore into a variable cost from the standpoint of the operator at the succeeding stage. For the vertically integrated firm no such transmutation occurs, except as a fiction of interdepartmental bookkeeping. But costs for the nonintegrated operator beyond the crude production stage will be weighted heavily with the variable cost of the oil or the oil product itself, a very high portion of total costs at each individual stage of this industry.[1] Apart from any consideration of size or financial strength,

1. McLean and Haigh supply the following computations of gross margins at

this fact alone (the comparative weight of out-of-pocket expense versus invested cost) limits the range of the potential price competition of the nonintegrated firm compared with its integrated rival. In practice this limitation is importantly modified by two influences: the joint character of the products issuing from the refinery, and the conditions of supply of the crude oil or products to the nonintegrated refiner or marketer, respectively.

The commodities derived from crude oil are not strictly joint products in the sense that an increase in the output of one necessarily involves an increase in the output of the other in invariable proportions. Quite the contrary, a modern refinery will often increase the output of

---

each of the four levels of the industry, per barrel of crude oil refined and distributed in the Midcontinent region, December, 1950 (p. 117):

BRANCH OF INDUSTRY	SALES PRICES	GROSS REALIZATION PER BARREL OF CRUDE	GROSS MARGIN, OR VALUE ADDED
Production	Crude oil at wellhead	$2.57	$2.57
Refining	Weighted tank-car prices, at refinery gate	3.45	0.88
Wholesaling	Tank wagon prices, delivered	4.75	1.30
Retailing	Prices to ultimate consumers [a]	5.61	0.86
			$5.61

[a] This price is called the "retail price at service station." For reasons stated below, this $5.61 actually represents the total of the estimated realizations from the sale of all products from a barrel of crude at whatever point they are sold to the final customer.

The "refinery margin" includes the cost of transporting crude oil from the wellhead; the various refinery prices are weighted by actual respective realizations of each product, so that the price at the refinery gate reflects actual gross sales revenue per barrel of oil converted. The "wholesaling margin," similarly, includes the costs of transporting products (gasoline, kerosene, and distillates only) from the refinery to service stations or other customers. The retailing margin is based on sales of gasoline only. Both wholesaling and retailing margins represent the value added *not* per barrel of *product* bought and sold, but per barrel of crude oil refined: for example, the reason the indicated retail margin comes to only $0.86 per barrel, which is only about $0.02 a gallon, compared with a national average dealer margin on gasoline of about $0.05 a gallon in 1950 (*Petroleum Facts and Figures*, 10th ed., p. 197), is that $0.86 is all that the retailing function (confined exclusively to gasoline) was estimated to have added to the value of a barrel of *petroleum* (roughly 60 per cent of which was sold in other forms before it reached the service station level). The importance of the price of crude oil not only to the refiner but in the ultimate, weighted price to the consumer is evident. It is exaggerated, however, by the relatively low costs of transporting oil to refineries in the Midcontinent region. For example, the *national* average refinery gross margin was estimated by the economics department of a major oil company at $1.03 in 1950, compared with the $0.88 indicated above.

one of its products at the expense of another. By cracking distillate and heavy residual fuel oils, and polymerizing refinery gases, this process could continue until only gasoline and carbon emerged. Within limits, therefore, it is possible to measure the opportunity costs of individual products. Where this can be done, home-heating oils, for example, ought not to be sold for less than they are worth (after making allowances for additional processing costs) as substitutes for crude oil in the production of additional gasoline.[2] However, it may be economically impractical to shift substantially the pattern of products manufactured, especially in the short run.[3] Hence, it will not be feasible to obtain for the total production of each individual product differentiated cost figures from which the firm may fix a floor for acceptable prices.[4] Costs at the refining level, therefore, are generally regarded as common costs, and the costs of individual products (as well as their respective profitability) are recognized as arbitrary in some measure. These common costs restore to the product competition of the nonintegrated refiner some of the fluidity with respect to variable cost limits that out-of-pocket costs of purchased crude oil tend to delete.

The second factor enhancing the range of potential price competition offered by the nonintegrated firm is its availability and usefulness as a price-conscious outlet for surplus crude or product. Such surpluses may occur and persist because the supply functions of suppliers are made inelastic by the pressures of the law of capture and/or heavy fixed costs. For this reason, the buying price of raw material or product, generally bulking large in the total costs of the nonintegrated refiner or marketer and expected to set a high floor under the prices at which he can sell, may turn out to be more like the floor of an elevator than of a concrete bomb shelter.[5] Just as the ceiling of an elevator can be moved up and down with the greatest of ease, even though the space between ceiling and floor is narrow and unchanged, so the level of product prices may fluctuate within wider

2. See above, p. 73, n. 26.

3. For an argument that it is, in the longer run, sufficient for the alteration of refinery design, "theoretically, although not necessarily practically, possible to devise a unique method of allocating total refinery costs among various products on the basis of relative marginal costs of varying yields," see Bain, *Pacific Coast Petroleum Industry, 1,* 96–99.

4. In other words, while the opportunity cost of home-heating oils, insofar as it can be converted economically to gasoline, is the logical basis for determining the most profitable adjustment of the respective outputs of such mutually substitutable products at the margin, it does not promise a useful method for breaking down all the common costs of operation between them, because complete substitution is commercially infeasible.

5. See above, p. 71, n. 22.

limits than narrow refinery margins would seem to permit. By bolstering the floor, prorationing will of course have done much to bolster the ceiling.

The combination of these influences on the supply side—preponderantly fixed costs for the integrated company, heavy fixed and common operating costs for the nonintegrated refiner and marketer, combined with the possibility (heavily modified by prorationing) of fluctuating purchase prices—creates strong potential sources of price competition in product markets.

On the demand side of product markets a general unresponsiveness to price changes in the short run offers both a threat of wide price fluctuations and an opportunity for systematic exploitation. But two important influences moderate both the competitive danger and the monopolistic opportunity. First, petroleum products are at various points in active competition of varying degrees of effectiveness in the shorter or longer run with other fuels—the conversion of home heating to fuel oil and of locomotives to residual and diesel oil have been mentioned. Market growth will therefore depend on expensive initial investments less likely to be undertaken if burning-oil prices are high or very unstable. This factor alone would tend to raise price levels for gasoline and lubricants, for which there are no adequate substitutes, and to depress them for other products subject to readier displacement. This tendency in turn is modified by the ability of refiners, at a cost, to increase the yield of gasoline at the expense of other products.[6] Since it is costly to vary product proportions, re-

6. E.g., because of a disappointing demand for distillate and residual fuel oils in 1949, the national average percentage yield of gasoline rose from 40.1 per cent the year before to 43.7 per cent in 1949, while the yields of the other two products declined from 42.0 to 39.1 per cent (*Petroleum Facts and Figures,* 9th ed., pp. 252–253; 12th ed., p. 213). Another indication is provided by the fairly regular seasonal pattern in the percentage yields of motor fuel and home heating oils in recent years. The swings between highs and lows are not entirely smooth, but they are sufficiently so to indicate a regular pattern, corresponding to similar fluctuations in demand, appropriately anticipated:

Monthly United States Average Percentage Yields, Motor Fuel and Gas Oil and Distillate Fuel Oil, Highs and Lows, 1954–56

MONTH AND YEAR	MOTOR FUEL	GAS OIL AND DISTILLATES
February, 1954	42.8	21.7
May, 1954	44.7	20.0
February, 1955	42.4	24.2
July, 1955	45.0	20.8
February, 1956	42.5	23.8
May, 1956	44.0	21.4
June, 1956	44.3	22.0

Source: API, *Statistical Bulletins* (April 17, 1956, and April 23, 1957), Forms 8 and 10A.

finers permit most of the short-run fluctuations in the relative demands for the various products to be absorbed by storage rather than by changing refinery yields.[7] But refineries can be designed for different product yields, and they have been developed historically so as enormously to increase the relative output of gasoline.[8] These possibilities of refinery flexibility tend, to the extent that competition between refiners is effective, to prevent exploitation of the gasoline buyer.

Thus the question of the effectiveness of competition in oil under vertical integration is most clearly posed with respect to the pricing of gasoline, the industry's most important product.[9] It is the major product (apart, perhaps, from lubricants) with the least adequate substitutes; and the one for which refiners have undertaken the most comprehensive forward integration.[10]

7. McLean and Haigh summarized a study of the Esso Standard Company, indicating how significantly cheaper it is to build storage to absorb (a) seasonal fluctuations in aggregate demand for petroleum products, rather than alter refinery throughput, and (b) seasonally divergent trends in demand for this product as compared with that, rather than alter refinery yields (pp. 314–315). Monthly figures for stocks of finished gasoline in 1954 rose to a high of 173 million barrels at the end of March and were then drawn down to 141 million at the end of October; in 1955 the high of 172 million came at the same time as the year before, and the low of 140 million a month earlier—API, *Statistical Bulletin* (April 17, 1956), Form 8. However, altered refinery yields also made some contribution to meeting the seasonal peaks in gasoline demand, as the foregoing footnote demonstrates.

8. Before 1910, only about 10 per cent of a barrel of crude oil was converted into gasoline. With the introduction of cracking, average gasoline yield then mounted rapidly—to 18 per cent in 1914, 26 per cent in 1920, and 44 per cent in 1931, at which level it has remained (except for a drop of a few percentage points during World War II and the immediate postwar years). *Petroleum Facts and Figures,* 9th ed., p. 251; 12th ed., p. 213.

9. Of the total estimated domestic U.S. utilization of petroleum products of 3.1 billion barrels in 1955, motor fuel accounted for 1.3 billion, or about 43 per cent by volume. The wholesale value of motor fuel consumed in the United States in that year amounted to $6.8 billion, slightly over 58 per cent of the corresponding figure for all petroleum products. *Ibid.,* 12th ed., pp. 5, 292.

10. This concentration of Pt. IV on gasoline necessarily slights the rich variety of industry products and practices. Certain differences between the marketing of gasoline and of home-heating and residual fuel oils are touched on incidentally elsewhere. Lubricants probably pose distribution problems similar to gasoline because of their comparable demand inelasticity, lack of substitutes, and importance of integration. The hundreds of petrochemicals exemplify a full spectrum of marketing conditions. Some have close substitutes and correspondingly high demand elasticity; most are industrial raw materials transferred out of the petroleum industry at or close to the refinery, but a few (like refiner-branded insecticides, sold only in service stations) involve complete forward integration.

THE PRICE GOALS OF THE LARGE, INTEGRATED FIRM

An extensive literature attempts to characterize the impact of business size on the behavior of market prices. It is not easy to epitomize because of the broad variety of pricing policies found among big businesses, reflecting in turn, among other things, widely divergent elasticities of aggregate demand for the product in question, and wide differences in the degree to which business size is associated with market power.[11] There is fairly general agreement, however, that the bigger the firm and the fewer the number of sellers with which it competes directly, the more its pricing tends to reflect company policy, typically one of de-emphasizing price as an element of competitive strategy.[12] Excepting only where it is seeking an extended market for new products at low prices calculated to stimulate demand, the large company is more likely to stress the preservation of a relative pricing pattern between its products and those of its rivals than it is voluntarily to utilize changes in those patterns as a method of competing. The emphasis of price policy is on meeting, not beating, competition.

The essential motivation for the forward integration of oil companies into marketing has been a quest for security and high utilization of investment through a continuous flow of crude or of product, delivered at minimum cost, to a staked-out demand through controlled market outlets for a branded line of products. These heavy forward

11. See the purported disproofs of the influence of these factors on the basis of statistical studies of price changes between 1929 and 1933 by Alfred C. Neal, *Industrial Concentration and Price Flexibility* (Washington, D.C., American Council on Public Affairs, 1942), and Richard Ruggles, "The Nature of Price Flexibility and the Determinants of Relative Price Changes in the Economy," in National Bureau of Economic Research, *Business Concentration and Price Policy* (Princeton, Princeton University Press, 1955), pp. 441–495. But neither the theoretical assumptions nor the statistical demonstrations are entirely convincing. See esp. John R. Moore and Lester S. Levy, "Price Flexibility and Industrial Concentration," *Southern Economic Journal, 21* (1955), 435; the discussion of Ruggles' paper in NBER, pp. 495–505; and John M. Blair, "Means, Thorp, and Neal on Price Inflexibility," *Review of Economics and Statistics, 38* (1956), 427.

12. Although extensive references to the literature would seem out of place, the reader is referred particularly to J. M. Clark, *Economics of Overhead Costs,* p. 146; A. D. H. Kaplan, *Big Enterprise,* pp. 156–158; and, for a much more highly detailed survey issuing from the same studies, Kaplan, Dirlam, and Lanzillotti, *Pricing in Big Business.*

investments and long-term commitments counsel restraint in the use of price to obtain competitive advantage. Indeed the security they promise—though by no means uniformly deliver—is precisely the security of *not* having to offer a higher price for an additional barrel of oil, or a lower price to pick up additional sales of gasoline. In any market situation, price cuts are the form of competition most easily invoked and the most quickly and completely met—indeed surpassed, short of the distant bottom limit of variable costs. Thus the resort to short-run price competition in the face of an irresponsive aggregate demand is more likely to reflect market or financial weakness than strength on the part of the company that does so.

On the other hand the integrated firm has the widest range of any for invoking or resisting the play of price warfare. Within the limits set by the antitrust laws, a company selling in numerous markets can meet the lower prices of particular local competitors in good faith and, still earning profits in more peaceful markets, withstand the price war longer. Anywhere above the deep, bottom limit of cumulated variable costs for each successive stage of production, the vertically integrated company can reduce its ultimate product prices to preserve a market position without suffering out-of-pocket losses. A nonintegrated refiner or marketer, in contrast, is quickly pressed down hard against the variable cost floor set by the price at which he purchases. Superior ability of the integrated firm to compete in price poses the threat of unfair competition against the nonintegrated; it also creates an opportunity for lower end-prices to consumers. The greater the monopoly surcharges imposed on a product as it moves from one production stage to the next, the lower will be the costs of vertically integrated as compared with a nonintegrated operation, and the greater will be the promise integration offers of low prices based on actual, rather than monopolistically inflated, costs of production.

Manifestly, vertical integration may be compatible with widely divergent levels and behavior of final product prices. The actual outcome will depend in the first place on the vitality of competition between integrated companies. To judge this, the economist must look to their numbers, the extent to which they find it possible to price in concert, the ability of the dominant marketer to make its price policy and preferences stick, the pressure on each to pass on to the buying public any differential profits it may have been able to appropriate by vertical integration. The economist will look, secondly, for evidences of competition instigated by, or attributable to, nonintegrated business organization—by independent rivals on the same side of particular markets, and by centers of countervailing power on the other. Finally, the outcome may depend importantly, too, on the influences government brings to bear on the independence of competitive action and the accumulation and exercise of economic power.

THE SIGNIFICANCE OF THE INDEPENDENT

The more effective the competition between vertically integrated firms, the less the consumer needs the protection of nonintegrated sources of rivalry and countervailing pressure. Therefore it involves some anticipation of conclusions to say why it seems necessary, in assessing the effectiveness of competition in the oil industry, to look to the health and prospects of the independent.

The historical account in Part I showed not only that the major oil companies can be identified over years, indeed decades, but also that their continual maneuvering for market position has not produced drastic changes in relative position in the national market considered as a whole. This stability in the midst of flux undoubtedly mirrors the fact that giants of comparable economic strength do not kill each other off, even if they might want to. But it reflects the fact also that it does not pay them to try. As Stocking pointed out prophetically even while describing the "crumbling from within" of the old Standard Oil community of interest:

> It is scarcely to be presumed, however, that such free competition between Standard units would be directed primarily toward an increase in volume of business through competition in prices. The more modern and generally accepted principle of salesmanship directed toward the creation of good will and prestige would no doubt continue to dominate the situation. It seems not unlikely that a recognized "market leader" would continue to set the pace in matters of price.[13]

This prediction, coming on the eve of great new discoveries of crude oil, exaggerated the effectiveness of price leadership in a period of chronic oversupply like the fifteen years that followed. On the other hand it could scarcely have foreseen the stabilizing weight of prorationing and of centralized control of foreign oil resources and of limitations on its importation. It erred in underestimating the tendency for the struggle for markets and volume even among large, in-

13. Stocking, p. 114.

tegrated companies to hold prices down. Twenty major oil companies are not the same as one, or three; to the extent that mere numbers of financially and operationally distinct competitors with divergent market interests contribute to competition, the majors among themselves alone provide a conceivable basis for rivalry sufficient to pose severe limits on the power of any one of them to play fast and loose with its customers.

But each of the few hundred-million to billion dollar companies dominating individual market areas inevitably recognizes their mutual interdependence, realizes that by its own actions it could upset markets to the detriment of itself as well as its competitors, and, expecting to be in business for decades, has a strong interest in avoiding overhasty pursuit of the short-run main chance. The major company bulks large in most of the markets in which it operates. Its brands command wide and loyal public acceptance. It is disposed to channel its competitive efforts away from price variation both for crude oil and for gasoline. It inevitably feels a responsibility for market stabilization and for the reasonableness of price levels.

The smaller refiner and marketer is typically forced to operate much more flexibly in the market. Some have established stable connections with sources of crude oil, often by laying down gathering-line systems; others sell brands, often through their own service stations,[14] that enjoy consumer acceptance in limited market territories comparable to that of the majors. But they must be prepared to pay some sort of premium for crude oil when the market is strong, and they may pay less than posted prices when it is weak. And because they have neither the security nor the sunk investments of their larger rivals, they characteristically use price more willingly and flexibly to attract customers when demand is slack and to increase temporary profits when demand is strong. They may have to be more willing to experiment and to innovate, in order to offset the strategic advantages and possibly the superior efficiency of their bigger competitors. More readily able to move in and out of market situations in response to short-run profit considerations, the independent may play a role entirely disproportionate to its size in keeping markets competitive, flexible, and dynamic and in preventing a recognition of interdependence and the possible bureaucratic conservatism that go with size and quasipermanent life from stultifying competition.

Even if competition among the majors alone were adequate today fully to protect the public interest, one would still have to be wary of

14. See below, pp. 519 ff.

the possibility that a few of them—even ten or fifteen in each relevant market area—might be able progressively to entrench themselves in control of raw materials, market outlets, and consumer loyalties. The vitality of competition could deteriorate seriously if the market positions of the stronger suppliers were to become increasingly impregnable against competitive inroads of smaller firms. Lack of consciousness of community of interest between small refiners and their competitors, or the necessity to violate it, even when recognized, to overcome even graver handicaps, are a necessary continuing guarantee of competition. From this standpoint, the competitive impact of major companies' market interpenetration has been blunted when accomplished by the acquisition of firms already there. The replacement of a smaller marketer, incompletely integrated both geographically and vertically, by a major may well have weakened the forces making for price competition.

For effective competition to prevail, the market must provide the customer with real alternative choices in the satisfaction of a given want. The consumer will want to be offered convenience, service, product quality and reliability—all stressed by the majors; but he will also be very much interested in price. There is no a priori way to weigh price against non-price considerations; the choice is one for each consumer to make for himself, so that it will be free choices in the market that will preserve a proper balance among the various aspects of product value. It is not for the economist or the public administrator, therefore, to determine what shall be the desired bundle of services or its price in a competitive economy; on the contrary, the effectively competitive market will offer consumers a variety of bundles.[15] The market for gasoline, like that for any other good, comprises consumers with a wide range of preferences in price-service combinations: from the spartan, low-cost, high-volume, price-emphasizing type of distribution to the plush, convenient, quality and service-stressing variety. But it is the task of public policy to maintain conditions of entry and availability of supplies that will assure independent competitive rivalry in the proffer of alternative price-quality combinations. And it is the function of the economist to appraise industrial organizations and practices to see whether they tend unduly to constrict the range of choice.

15. As in the case of any other relatively low-price, convenience good, however, there are definite limits to the amount of choice it is feasible or desirable to offer the mass of gasoline buyers. Too wide a range may be offered only at the cost of inefficiency; standardization of product and sales at fixed price have been essential to efficiency and technological advance.

Thus the threat which integration in petroleum may hold for competition inheres in the tendency of size and integration to direct rivalry toward non-price objectives and the tendency of vertical integration to narrow the availability of supplies and market access for those who promote their self-interests primarily on a price basis.[16] It is conceivable, though not demonstrable, that an industry made up exclusively of vertically integrated firms would retain sufficient price rivalry to preserve a socially acceptable level of product prices: the more numerous the firms (consistent with efficiency) the more likely this would be so. While the sources and effectiveness of price and other kinds of competition among integrated firms cannot and will not be ignored, it is clear that in existing oil product markets it is mainly the independent refiners and jobbers who exploit opportunities for price competition—opportunities often created by the imbalance of major companies themselves; and the impact of integration on their effective functioning is therefore a matter of real public concern.[17]

16. Since what the customer and efficiency both require is a price that is reasonable over the long run, it may suffice that price competition be implicit rather than marked by extreme and rapid short-term fluctuations. But short term price maneuvering and flexibility, typically by smaller companies, may be essential instruments for keeping the long-run price level reasonable. The long-run and short-run aspects of price rivalry both need constant reflection in market processes if customers are to be best served.

17. The competitive status of the small, nonintegrated producer, already explored in Pt. II, is not relevant here; in any event, prorationing and ratable taking, effectively administered, protect his access to market from discriminatory tactics. Likewise, the problems of pipeline transporters are essentially matters of public utility regulation. At the other end of the industry, the service station operator, whose function like that of the crude oil producer is essentially complementary to that of the major, poses no critical issues of entry or survival in sufficient numbers to insure effective competition. The real question for concern in his case is whether his independence, in the presence of forward integration by refiners, is adequate to sustain his initiative in pricing, and to provide market access for independent refiners and marketers.

CHAPTER 16

The Structure of Product Prices and Markets

A ROUGH APPROXIMATION of the physical flow of major petroleum products from refinery to ultimate purchasers, drawn from Cross and King's systematic attempt at statistical measurement of average national practice, as of 1950, is summarized in Table XXI. The first column provides estimates of the aggregate flows through each physical channel (terminals, bulk plants, service stations, and, at each level, direct to final buyers), expressed as a percentage of national supply (refinery output plus net imports or minus net exports) of the product in question. The second and third columns indicate how those percentages were divided between marketing operations conducted, respectively, by integrated refiner-marketers and by distributors financially independent of refiners. Confining our attention first to the aggregates, it will be noted that most motor fuel goes from the refinery through three levels of intermediate handling before reaching the ultimate consumer—terminal (77 per cent), bulk plant (84 per cent), and service station (75 per cent).[1] Similarly, most distillate fuel oil, 65 per cent of which is indicated as having been sold to home consumers, goes through both terminal and bulk plant. Residual fuel oil, in contrast, is sold mostly to industrial and commercial consumers direct from refinery (22 per cent) and terminal (52 per cent).

It is the division of these flows between integrated and nonintegrated marketing channels [2] that is particularly important to this study. It

---

1. But see discussion above, p. 14, n. 7, regarding an apparent underestimate of direct deliveries from terminal to service station: the table shows only 3 per cent of supply following this route. A large part of the 22 per cent shown as going from refinery to bulk stations may also represent direct deliveries, some of those "bulk stations" really representing terminals, misclassified, as the above-cited note indicates, for the very reason that they did move products directly to service stations.

2. As the notes to the table make clear, integration is here defined in terms of financial affiliation with a refiner, since primary concern is with the impact of the integration of refining and marketing (and, correspondingly, with the competitive fortunes of the nonintegrated refiners and non-integrated market-

appears that over nine-tenths (93 per cent) of our national supply of motor fuel leaves the refinery in the legal possession of the refiner. In the case of distillates, the refiner still predominates, but by no means so overwhelmingly, in this first stage of distribution (64 per cent); independent wholesalers take 35 per cent of the supply at the refinery to (presumably their own) terminals and bulk plants. In the case of both products, the relative importance of the independent distributor increases as one moves from refinery to ultimate buyer, but here again more so in the case of distillates than in gasoline.[3] Of the 75 per cent of national supply of motor fuel sold through service stations,[4] an estimated 45 is carried to that point by (that is, with title still resting in) integrated refiners, the remaining 30 by independent marketers. Of the 65 per cent of national supply of distillates sold to home consumers (for heating and range use), only 22 is delivered to them by refiners or their agents; almost twice as much (the remaining 43 per cent of national supply) is sold them by independent distributors, mostly from independently owned bulk plants.[5]

Once motor fuel gets to the service station, independent marketers (either retailers or wholesaler-retailers) take over almost exclusively, so far as legal title to the business and products would make it appear. But these marketers are not necessarily independent of their refiner-suppliers in all respects: McLean and Haigh estimate for example that

---

ers). It is the extent of this integration that determines (inversely) the importance of intermediate product markets, in which nonintegrated buyers and sellers (as here defined) meet. Needless to say: (a) it is only to the extent that companies are incompletely integrated that they participate as net buyers or sellers in intermediate markets; and (b) integration of wholesaling and retailing operations alone is extremely widespread, and of considerable importance, as will be shown.

3. See also McLean and Haigh, pp. 441–446.

4. Actually, the Cross and King estimate, according to a communication from the former, is for sales through all retail outlets, and not merely service stations as defined by the Census. See above, p. 14, n. 8. The McLean and Haigh estimate of service station sales, for this and for other, undisclosed reasons, comes to only 53 per cent of national output (pp. 52–53).

5. Actually, these figures, which relate to the ownership of the product in transit, do not necessarily indicate who owns what proportion of the distributive facilities mentioned. For example, a very large number of nonintegrated distributors, especially important in the case of home-heating oils, are so-called peddlers, who own their trucks but buy from the bulk plants of refiners and other distributors. Their sales would show up as "nonrefiner-marketer" though the products they sell would in some cases originate at a refiner-owned bulk plant. On this point see also the following note.

TABLE XXI

*Channels of Distribution for Major Petroleum Products,[a]
1950*

A. MOTOR FUEL

	TOTAL	REFINER [b]	NONREFINER [c]
A. FROM REFINERIES (100%)			
to terminals	77%	72%	5%
to bulk stations (1)	22	20	2
to industrial and commercial users (2)	1	1	
	100%	93%	7%
B. FROM TERMINALS (77%)			
to bulk stations (3)	62%	33%	29%
to service stations (4)	3	2	1
to industrial and commercial users (5)	12	11	1
	77%	46%	31%
C. FROM BULK STATIONS (84%) (sum of 1 and 3)			
to service stations (7)	72%	43%	29%
to industrial and commercial users (8)	12	10	2
	84%	53%	31%
D. TO SERVICE STATIONS (sum of 4 and 7)	75%	45%	30%
E. TO INDUSTRIAL AND COMMERCIAL CONSUMERS (sum of 2, 5, and 8) [d]	25%	23%	2%
TOTAL (D plus E)	100%	68%	32%

B. DISTILLATE FUEL OIL

	TOTAL	REFINER	NONREFINER
A. FROM REFINERIES (100%)			
to terminals	82%	52%	30%
to bulk stations (1)	10	5	5
to industrial and commercial users (2)	8	7	1
	100%	64%	36%
B. FROM TERMINALS (82%)			
to bulk stations (3)	57%	39%	18%
to industrial and commercial users (4)	22	8	14
to home consumers (5)	3	1	2
	82%	48%	34%
C. FROM BULK STATIONS (67%) (sum of 1 and 3)			
to home consumers (6)	62%	21%	41%
to industrial and commercial users (7)	5	2	3
	67%	23%	44%

TABLE XXI (*continued*)

	TOTAL	REFINER [b]	NONREFINER [c]
D. TO INDUSTRIAL AND COMMERCIAL USERS			
(sum of 2, 4, and 7)	35%	17%	18%
E. TO HOME CONSUMERS			
(sum of 5 and 6)	65	22	43
TOTAL (D plus E)	100%	39%	61%

C. RESIDUAL FUEL OIL

	TOTAL	REFINER	NONREFINER
A. FROM REFINERIES (100%)			
to terminals	71%	50%	21%
to bulk stations (1)	7	3	4
to industrial and commercial consumers (2)	22	20	2
	100%	73%	27%
B. FROM TERMINALS (71%)			
to bulk stations (3)	19%	9%	10%
to industrial and commercial consumers (4)	52	35	17
	71%	44%	27%
C. FROM BULK STATIONS (26%)			
(sum of 1 and 3)			
to industrial and commercial consumers (5)	26%	12%	14%
D. TO INDUSTRIAL AND COMMERCIAL CONSUMERS			
(sum of 2, 4, and 5)	100%	67%	33%

[a] Quantities sold through the various channels indicated are expressed in all cases as a percentage of total national supply of the product in question: refinery output plus net imports in the case of residual oils, minus net exports in the other two cases.

[b] These represent the percentages of national refinery output moving through integrated channels—i.e. where the refiner conducts the marketing operation, retaining title to the product until it reaches the succeeding level.

[c] These represent the percentages of national refinery output marketed by distributors financially independent of the refining company.

[d] Commercial consumers also purchased 10 of the 75 per cent of motor fuel sold through service stations.

Source: Cross and King, "Channels of Distribution for Petroleum Products."

58 per cent of service station sales of gasoline were from stations controlled by refiners, by ownership or long-term lease.[6]

There is a vast complexity of nominally independent businessmen who carry on the marketing and distribution of petroleum products

6. P. 35. The Cross and King estimate of a 45:30 relationship of sales *to* service stations by refiner- and nonrefiner-marketers, which means that 60 per cent of total sales to service stations (i.e. 45 out of 75 per cent) were conducted by refiners, clearly coincides closely with, and is reflected in, the 58 per cent

in general and of gasoline in particular. It will clarify subsequent discussion if the main categories are identified at the outset; an appendix at the conclusion of this chapter presents a more detailed explanation and amplification of the information here summarized. Closest to the refinery are the products brokers; apparently they are few in number—a reflection of the preponderance of integration in this industry, whether achieved by financial affiliation or by long-term contracts. Next, there are at most 400 independent terminal operators; these are relatively big firms that purchase tanker or barge cargoes or take product in large quantities off the product pipelines, and either resell in smaller lots to other distributors, or carry it to the ultimate consumer through their own integrated facilities.

The most numerous and typical of what are generally termed independent wholesalers, jobbers, or distributors are the bulk plant operators, who buy their products from refinery or terminal, store them, and deliver them in smaller lots to service stations or customers. They vary greatly in the degree to which they are vertically integrated: at one extreme, a small but important minority own and operate terminals, and deliver their gasoline directly to service stations which they own or control, storing only their fuel oils in the bulk plant. In between, many own numerous service stations, though no terminals. At another extreme, they may operate a single, refiner-owned bulk plant and deliver only heating oils to customers' homes or gasoline to farm accounts. They vary, too, in the extent to which they handle a full products line. Among them three groups are differentiated, in descending order of independence. The least numerous, those who sell under their own brands, will be called "jobbers," "private-brand jobbers" or "unbranded jobbers." They are much less important in the distribution of gasoline than in home-heating oils: very often the same wholesaler sells gasoline under his supplier's brand and heating oils under his own. Next come the wholesalers who sell under their

---

of aggregate service station sales made by stations controlled by refiners. However, the correspondence is in part coincidental. Refiners undoubtedly also deliver a substantial proportion of total national gasoline sales to contractor stations, i.e. to service stations which they do not themselves own or control: the 58 per cent is too close to the 60 per cent to leave enough room for such deliveries, particularly since, according to a communication from Professor Haigh, refiners rarely permit stations they control to be supplied by independent distributors. The apparent incompatibility of the two figures is perhaps attributable in part to the fact that McLean and Haigh refer only to sales through service stations as defined by the Census, while Cross and King refer to all retail outlets.

suppliers' brand; these are termed "distributors" or "branded distributors." Jobbers and distributors together number perhaps 10,000. They typically own or control (by long-term lease) their own storage plants and trucks (although branded distributors sometimes lease from their suppliers), and, those who are in the gasoline business, their service stations as well. Last and least important among the bulk plant operators are the approximately 15,000 commission agents. Though technically independent wholesalers, these agents are even more closely tied to the refiner than the others, usually renting their plant from him, and selling his branded products on consignment, for a commission.

There are also numerous peddlers, who pick up gasoline or heating oils at bulk plants for delivery to service stations, farms or homes. They are generally confined to relatively remote, sparse markets (especially in sales of gasoline) and apparently are not an important competitive influence.

Finally, there are more than 400,000 retailers of gasoline, only 181,747 of which were classified as service stations by the 1954 Census. Of the latter group, very roughly 88,000 must have been dealer- or wholesaler-controlled and operated, another 83,000 dealer-operated but leased from refiners, 8,000 operated by commission agents, and about 3,000 refiner-controlled and operated.

Except for brokers at one end and service stations at the other, these categories of marketers cannot be identified unequivocally as wholesalers or retailers. Terminal operators are preponderantly the former, though some of them are integrated through the service station and some of them make fuel oil and heating oil sales to final consumers. Bulk plant operators typically deliver home-heating oils to the final buyer and make farm deliveries of gasoline as well. But they also wholesale both products to peddlers and service stations, and control if not operate the latter. Still, independent marketers may be divided into two groups: first, what may somewhat arbitrarily be called the wholesalers—mainly brokers, terminal and bulk plant operators; second, the retailers—peddlers and service station operators. Of those who belong in the first group no attention will be paid to the brokers, who are highly specialized intermediaries between refiner and marketer, and only incidental attention to commission agents, because, in terms of their competitive impact, they are scarcely to be regarded as independents. Of the second, the peddlers may be ignored for reasons already indicated.

Corresponding to these major categories of independent product marketers are of course the various intermediate markets and prices at which products are transferred to them by refiners and to one group of them by another, and the final markets where products pass to ultimate consumers, at refinery, terminal, bulk plant, peddler truck or service station. The remainder of this chapter is devoted to a description of these markets and an analysis of the interrelations of their prices, considered as always with particular view to the impact of integration, and with primary emphasis on gasoline.

REFINERY AND TERMINAL PRICES: THE SPOT MARKET

The market for petroleum products at the refinery is a rather narrow one. According to the Cross and King estimates, only 8 per cent of the motor fuel produced fails to move through integrated channels to terminals or bulk plants before sale, leaving a relatively small proportion of the output to be disposed of at the refinery: one per cent to industrial and commercial users, the other seven to resellers (see Table XXI). A larger share, about 35 per cent, of the distillate and light oils are sold at the refinery to wholesalers. Of course, refiners sell additional quantities of both these products to independent middlemen from their terminals. But the major proportions leave refineries and terminals together in integrated channels: according to the same estimates, of the 84 per cent of national motor fuel supplies going into bulk plants, 53 were brought in by refiner-marketers, and 31 by others; [7] and of the 75 per cent delivered to service stations, the corresponding division was 45:30.

The sales at refinery and terminal for resale (that is, setting aside direct sales to final customers) are of two kinds. The greater proportion is on long-term contract between refiner and marketer—invariably so in the case of branded distributors, frequently so for unbranded jobbers as well. A much smaller proportion are spot sales. So it is clear that by far the preponderant proportion of national deliveries of both gasoline and heating oils from refineries and terminals were through integrated or quasi-integrated channels—well over half through refiner-owned facilities, well over half of the remainder through distributors tied by long-term contract and flying their suppliers' brands.

The spot market at refinery and terminal has played an important

7. For distillates the relationships were not greatly different—an estimated 67 per cent of national supplies going into bulk plants, forty-four in refiner-marketer, and twenty-three in nonrefiner-marketer channels.

role in the history of oil industry pricing. With its relatively small modern dimensions—which obviously may vary widely from the particular national averages indicated from place to place and time to time—the precise character and significance of its function are matters of considerable uncertainty and controversy. The visible evidence of its activity is the quotation of "posted prices" or reported prices on spot sales, for current bulk shipments, by refineries in the Oklahoma ("Group 3" [8]), North Texas, East Texas, Gulf Coast, and other areas, and by terminals along waterways and product pipelines, that appear in Platt's *Oilgram* and other trade papers and reporting services. The buying and selling activity at most of these price-quotation points does not constitute an open market in the economic sense of a focal point of competitive bids and offers that determine a ruling price. But there are two important so-called spot markets for refined products —on the Gulf coast, for cargoes, and in the Midcontinent area—that come closer to the usual conception of an open, competitive exchange.

The composition of the Gulf cargo market varies from time to time, and the available information permits only the broadest generalizations about its operations. It is probably safe to say that by and large the main purchasers of gasoline in cargo lots are exporters or large independent terminal-operating marketers selling along the Atlantic seaboard, and the main suppliers are independent refineries. However there are from time to time purchases and sales by majors. The market is quite discontinuous. Sometimes sales are made in large volume; sometimes weeks go by with hardly any transaction reported —especially in gasoline. The majors probably appear there more often as spot buyers than sellers. Many of them purchase an appreciable proportion of their requirements; like integrated firms in other industries, they have traditionally kept their refinery capacity below the needs of their own marketing departments and of their regular customers as a matter of policy.[9] It seems to be more typical that their marketing expansion outruns refining capacity than the reverse, although it will be shown that the situation has changed somewhat since 1953.

The significant and controversial question about the spot markets,

8. This was a grouping of all Oklahoma refineries promulgated by the Interstate Commerce Commission, in setting for the Group a uniform railroad rate for tank car shipments to Midwestern markets. See Cassady, pp. 187–188.

9. See, e.g., McLean and Haigh, p. 429: "Some of the companies [of the seven studied] also made it a regular practice to purchase a small portion of their refined product requirements as a means of making sure that their own refineries always ran at capacity."

of which the Gulf is perhaps the most important, is whether or to what extent they assure competitive pricing throughout the industry. The interest shown by trade journals in the day-by-day transactions at the Gulf suggests that they exercise an influence disproportionate to their relative size. The price provisions in long-term contracts at this and other levels of the industry sometimes specify some relationship to the "low of the *Oilgram,* date of lifting," or to the low of the Group 3 spot market, when these spot quotations set a price that is more to the buyer's (that is, the marketer's) advantage. Such contractual provisions, it is maintained, merely reflect the inevitable fact that the entire price structure, whether contracts explicitly so provide or not, must bear some close relationship to those quotations. The Gulf price signifies to all marketers in the South and on the Atlantic seaboard the price at which their competitors can purchase. So, a short-term industry-wide surplus of supply over demand at current prices, for example, will be reflected in sales of distress cargoes at the Gulf or of added, price-depressing supplies at Group 3 to independent marketers; these, in turn, can set off a general price decline throughout the industry.[10] According to this view, the Gulf and Group 3 prices—necessarily interrelated because of the possibility of product movements between the two areas—are both sensitive barometers of industry-wide conditions of supply and demand, and the basis to which all prices must conform—in the one case, throughout the Southeast and all the way up the East Coast, in the other, throughout the Midwest and all the way East to the Appalachians.[11]

It is possible to argue, instead, that the Gulf cargo (and Group 3) market is less a focal point of price-making forces than a shadow market for the registration of price policy.[12] Such an argument would emphasize, first, how very thin these spot markets are, compared with the national total, or even with the total of sales in the relevant geographic regions.[13] Their effect on the price structures of integrated

10. Harold Fleming, "Oil Prices and Competition" (New York, American Petroleum Institute, 1953), pp. 25–26.

11. For an excellent description of these markets as well as an argument to the above effect concerning their influence, see Sidney A. Swensrud, "The Marketing of Petroleum Products," TNEC, *Hearings,* Pt. XV, pp. 8692–8695.

12. The former editor of *National Petroleum News,* after quoting Fleming's contention that prices in the "non-contractual market" have a great influence on the long-term contractual price structure, states flatly "the exact reverse is true" (May 6, 1953), p. 49.

13. Cassady emphasizes that even the Gulf cargo market, "perhaps the most important of all," "represents sales of marginal . . . quantities . . . by only a few refiners and involves only a small number of transactions and relatively small amounts of product" (p. 143).

companies can only be indirect. The strength of that indirect influence must depend on the potentially disruptive force of such sales;
and this must depend, importantly, on their volume. Second, and
related, is the often highly spasmodic character of the trading in these
markets. Days, even weeks may pass with no sales reported. In consequence, the quotations are not necessarily records of transactions
in which currently products are actually changing hands. They may
be unrealistically high, when demand is light, representing merely
offers to sell by refiners who are in fact not able to find buyers but are
still unwilling to cut their offer, at least for publication.[14] They may

14. Thus softness in the market is not registered immediately in changes in
the offering prices. There may be an increase in the number of published
lows; "discounts" from the lows, not given to the reporting services as prices to
be published, may increase; higher octanes may be made available at the published offering prices for regular or premium grades. During the winter of
1953 and spring and early summer of 1954, for example, the gasoline market
at the Gulf Coast was reported as extremely "sloppy." The following table
records the lows for 87 octane regular gasoline quoted in the weekly *National
Petroleum News* and the posted dealer tank-wagon prices for household gasoline
of the Esso Standard Oil Company at representative cities along the East Coast,
in cents per gallon, for the dates at which changes in each were reported. The
beginning prices are the high points reached as a result of increases in June,
1953, roughly contemporaneous with the increases in the price of crude oil
posted in that month. As for the Gulf prices, despite trade press reports of the
availability of 0.25¢ to 0.35¢ discounts below the reported lows, there was "a

DATE			GULF LOW	NEW YORK N.Y.	NEWARK N.J.	ALBANY N.Y.	CHARLESTON S.C.
1953	June	high	11.75	16.2	15.9	16.2	15.4
	Oct.	19	11.625				
	Nov.	2	11.5				
		10		15.9	15.6	16.0	15.1
		30	11.25				
	Dec.	7	11.00				
		11		15.7	15.4	15.8	14.9
1954	Jan.	11	10.75				
		30		15.5	15.2	15.6	
	Feb.	8	10.5				
	Mar.	15	9.5				
		29	10.2				
	Apr.	5	10.25				
	June	28	10.00				
	July	9		15.0	14.7	15.0	
		10					14.2
		14	9.75				
		19	10.00				
		26	10.25				
	Aug.	9	10.5				
		19		15.8	15.5	15.8	15.1

Sources: Gulf prices, *National Petroleum News;* tank-wagon prices supplied
by Esso Standard to, and reproduced in, Kaplan, Dirlam, and Lanzillotti,
Pricing in Big Business, p. 84.

be equally fictional in time of shortage, representing prices at which some refiners (notably Esso during the fuel oil shortage of 1947–48) actually do sell to their long-term contractual customers, while refusing to sell to outsiders.[15]

The spasmodic character of trading in the Gulf Coast market is partly attributable to the fact that there are very few refiners (perhaps not more than ten or eleven) [16] who sell there, even from time to time, on a "spot" basis. The ten major refiners represented on the Texas Gulf on January 1, 1956, because they had integrated marketing organizations, simply transported the preponderant portion of their gasoline to terminals by tanker or pipeline for eventual disposition through their own tank wagons or sale to distributors and large consumers. The independent refineries make a higher proportion of their sales on the spot market. But, first of all, independent refiners are more likely than majors to have discontinuous operations. Second, some of them operate under long-term processing contracts with other refiners, including the majors themselves. Finally, they too sell an undetermined amount of their gasoline on long-term contract, and through their own marketing outlets. Much more gasoline is sold, even at the Gulf and Group 3 refineries, on a contractual basis than gets to the "spot" market.[17] And there seems to have been a trend in this

---

dearth of cargo inquiry," a "lack of buyer interest," from August through October. Throughout the subsequent period until late July, excepting only a temporary revival in April, the Gulf low price was a hollow shell. Discounts were available to anyone who would bid, with few takers. An occasional cargo would be dumped, to register a new low, but the price was essentially nominal.

What is the significance of this experience? It clearly does *not* show that the Gulf market was able to resist the price-depressing influence of surplus supplies overhanging the market. A price decline even of 10 per cent in the face of a rigid price of crude was by no means negligible. But it does show how thin the market is, how much more it behaves like a barometer of the entire industry price structure than like a direct, price-determining force. Low price quotations at the Gulf cannot force down prices all over unless sales are actually made at those prices.

15. As the *Oilgram* quotations put it, "During periods of short supply, some sellers and at times all sellers, withhold quotations to new customers or the posting of firm prices but give OILGRAM the prices they otherwise would quote to the trade in general and which they confine to their regular customers only, and such prices appear in the price tables." *National Petroleum News* (October 13, 1954), p. 68.

16. Cassady, pp. 150–155, and esp. n. 23. On January 1, 1956, there were twenty companies with operating refineries on the Texas Gulf Coast, but ten were majors. However, sales are apparently made on the Gulf also by inland refiners from time to time.

17. See "The Open Spot Market—What It Is," *National Petroleum News* (May 6, 1953), p. 49.

direction; the independent refiners are becoming increasingly integrated.[18]

The Gulf cargo market and the Eastern seaboard terminal and tank-wagon prices do tend to move in step, although of course in areas where there are price wars, like Boston and Philadelphia, drastic upward and downward movements in tank-wagon prices occur without any change whatever in the Gulf cargo low. This correspondence is to be expected: the two prices must be related. And since spot sales, especially if made by independent refiners, are likely to reflect changing market conditions quickly, while the majors will naturally try to contain weakness in their administered, contractual price structure, it is not surprising that there has been some historical tendency for the spot prices to change more often than, and, in the directions of their changes, to lead the tank-wagon prices to tied service stations. What is in fact surprising is that the evidence of their leading is less clear than might have been anticipated; and that the amplitude of changes in tank-wagon prices seems to have been no less than in the case of spot market prices.[19] But a correspondence between the two prices

18. See below, pp. 523–525.

19. McLean and Haigh's comparison of the Group 3 tank-car price of regular gasoline with the average posted tank-wagon prices in leading Midwestern markets showed the former consistently leading the latter (pp. 152–154). Cassady's comparison of Gulf cargo lows and New York City tank-wagon prices on regular gasoline produced less clear-cut results; the figures sometimes indicate the Gulf price clearly leading, but very often it is impossible to say, and Cassady himself concludes that tank-wagon prices "often as not lead tank-car barge prices," which in turn by no means consistently lag behind the Gulf (pp. 306–310). Between 1928 and 1932, 1937 and 1942, and 1945 and 1950 it appears from Cassady's charts that the Gulf price had greater amplitude of fluctuation in percentage, but not in absolute terms.

The table above, n. 14, very clearly shows that open changes in Gulf lows were more frequent, and led changes in the posted dealer tank-wagon price. However, this behavior does not necessarily prove that the one price determined the other. For one thing, the Gulf prices fell more, even in absolute amounts, than did the tank wagon, between June, 1953, and mid-March, 1954. More importantly, both prices were in large measure nominal. The Gulf lows often reflected the offering of a single distress cargo; and if few transactions were actually consummated at the Gulf, even fewer were consummated at the single low quotation. And the tank-wagon price, which remained nominally stable all through the first half of 1954, reflected actual prices to dealers only in varying degrees from one city to another and from one time to another. Conditions of surplus supply in Eastern markets need not have been traceable to supplies from the Gulf; and when they arose, they very often took effect in local allowances below tank-wagon to dealers in price-war areas with tank-wagon price unchanged; conversely in instances of rising demand and improving prices. (See below, pp. 467–470.) For example, in July, Esso was openly giv-

tells nothing about the causal relationship between the two markets
—the small, sporadic, marginal one, and the huge, continuous, major
one.

There is no doubt that the spot market *could* and has in the past led
the contractual not only temporally but causally—the short tail has
wagged the huge dog. The pressures on independent refiners to produce to capacity will ordinarily outweigh any incentive to cut back
refinery throughputs in the interest of market stabilization. Given the
highly inelastic character of short-term demand for gasoline and heating oils, and the tightness of storage facilities all along the line to
market, it does not take a large percentage of price-cutting, open-
market sales to upset the market. Spot gasoline—distress sales of
which had so drastic an effect on the entire Midwestern price structure in the mid-thirties as to spark a concerted major company buying program in the interest of market stabilization—amounted to
only about 5 per cent of the total sales in the area at that time.[20]

On the other hand, whether or not it *does* so typically would depend on the length of the tail, the strength with which it wags, and
the vitality of the dog.[21] A single cargo in the hands of a small Gulf
refiner, seeking a buyer, is not going to upset an entire market. The
refiner will naturally avoid disposing of the distress cargo at lower
prices as long as possible. Some, perhaps most, majors on balance
tend to buy in the spot market just to avoid any such decline taking
place.[22] Some if not most of the leading independent refiners, in turn,
depend largely on the majors to take their products; others have been

ing its dealers throughout almost all of New Jersey 1.3-cent allowances below
tank wagon; and in August, a week before tank-wagon prices rose, the *National
Petroleum News* reported the majority of New Jersey marketers were "pulling
their dealer discounts."

20. See Rostow, *A National Policy for the Oil Industry*, p. 79, drawing upon
the record in *U.S. v. Socony-Vacuum Oil Company*, 310 U.S. 150 (1940); see
also below, pp. 435–437. On the role of the Group 3 tank-car price in undermining the market position of Standard of Indiana, see McLean and Haigh, pp.
211–213.

21. Fleming himself does not go to extremes in his statement of the case
for the influence of the spot market. Its prices, he says, "have a *large* influence
on prices made on long-term contract"; its small, independent, refiner-sellers
"often" lead the entire wholesale price structure. "Oil Prices and Competition,"
p. 25.

22. According to McLean and Haigh, some of the companies they studied
were well aware that by "maintaining a buying position in the refined products
markets" they "could occasionally absorb distressed cargoes" which, if they
had passed into the hands of cut-rate jobbers, might have precipitated price
wars (p. 430).

developing their own branded distribution in order to secure outlets for products that major companies have stopped taking, free of the price-depressing bargaining of private brand distributors.[23] And there are, after all, far fewer independent refiners today than there were in the Midcontinent and East Texas areas during the 1930's. Price wars require continuing, substantial supplies of cut-rate gasoline, not just a single cargo. These will ordinarily be sold on long-term contract, not in the spot market.

Whether the spot market leads and determines the pattern of wholesale prices is, then, not really the substantive issue at all. The real economic question is whether supplies in the industry tend to be adjusted readily to what the market will take, and at what prices. The determinant of the effectiveness of price competition is what kind of force regulates supply. In the presence of surplus product supplies, competitively produced and offered, both spot and contract markets will break. In the presence of supplies tightly controlled by public authority or private restraint, both markets will be strong.

THE PRICE TO JOBBERS AND DISTRIBUTORS

Some 33 per cent of our national supplies of motor fuel left the refinery, terminal, or bulk plant in the hands of independent wholesalers in 1950.[24] By far the greater proportion of these sales were under contracts formally or effectively long term.

The price governing these sales might be treated as a derivative of the spot refinery prices at Gulf coast or in the Tulsa area, plus transport and handling costs.[25] Certainly there must be some kind of relationship between prices in different parts of the country if products can move from one to the other. But, if the argument in the preceding section is correct, it is not clear in a highly integrated industry that one can "explain" the downstream price at which the dominant, integrated firms sell merely by adding intermediate costs to some upstream price at which only a relatively small number of market transactions occur. It is just as possible, a priori, to consider the upstream price a backward reflection of the downstream one.

---

23. "Southwest Trend: Independent Refiners Move to Brands," *National Petroleum News* (June, 1957), pp. 124–126.

24. See above, Table XXI. This is the percentage shown to have moved out of terminals and bulk plants taken as a group (i.e. eliminating flows from terminals to bulk plants, to avoid double counting) in nonrefiner channels.

25. See, e.g., the analysis by Swensrud, TNEC, *Hearings* (1940), Pt. XV, pp. 8694–8695.

Technically, since they are legally independent businessmen, the distributors of branded gasoline buy at a separate, bona fide, contractual price, and sell—since gasoline is seldom subject to a legal resale-price-maintenance contract [26]—at whatever price they choose.[27] However, refiners could not afford to bind themselves to contractually prescribed prices for long periods of time. Accordingly, the contracts provide for various sliding formulae. Essentially, whether or not the relation is formally specified, the price to branded distributors really depends in the first instance on the posted tank-wagon price that the major integrated refiner-marketers in the area charge their own service station customers. Usually the contract guarantees the distributor that the price at the time of delivery will be at least a minimum number of cents below the posted tank-wagon price in his vicinity. Even where it makes no reference to tank-wagon, but provides only that the delivered price shall be the one set by the supplier, the supplier and jobber both typically appraise and fix that price in terms of the margin it provides. Thus instead of building up their sales prices from some open market quotation like the spot tank-car price, refiners merely accept for the most part the going tank-wagon price established by someone else. There is no doubt that regardless of the formal contract, branded distributors believe they are being "allowed" a margin below the tank-wagon price, a margin they are intent on expanding in the face of a declining amount of gasoline available in the spot market.[28] The size of the margin is of course a price for the distributor's

26. On recent developments in this direction, which do not and probably will not vitiate this observation, see below, pp. 409–411.

27. So Cassady, emphasizing the independence of the prices charged to and by branded distributors from the prevailing tank-wagon price, states that "Many (if not most) of the present contracts make no reference to the tank wagon price or to any margin or to any trade publication quotation" (p. 182).

28. This attitude is so characteristic that we question Cassady's generalization on the subject, just cited. Indeed, Cassady's own footnotes 14 and 15 on the same page confirm this suspicion. A sales manager for a major concern whose distributor contracts make no mention of tank-wagon prices is quoted as saying that his firm establishes tank-car prices at levels affording the jobber a gross margin equivalent to those being extended by his competitors to their jobbers. And the price charged by a large integrated company operating "in the Indiana territory" whose contracts merely specify a delivered tank-car price, "actually . . . means the *Journal* quotation plus freight or the tank wagon price minus 2.5¢, whichever is lower."

The branded distributors interviewed by Marshall Howard in a central New York area did not think of themselves as paying any kind of tank-car price. They were paying a "distributor's delivered price," computed so as to yield a guaranteed margin—guaranteed, at least, as long as the tank-wagon price

services that is itself determined by all the market conditions influencing the supply and demand for those services.[29] But the absolute level of the price to distributors is most accurately conceived as a derivative of the tank-wagon quotation.

This is not to deny the necessity for some relationship between the price to branded distributors and the spot tank-car market price. A greater likelihood that these distributors might be enticed away from a major supplier by a sagging spot market probably explains a contract provision in the Midwest, customary at least until around 1949. The ruling contract (by Standard of Indiana) differed from central New York contracts in that it not only guaranteed the distributor a minimum margin below the prevailing tank-wagon price but also protected him against an undue spread between the delivered price of gasoline originating in Group 3 and tank-wagon: "Most contracts have provided for a minimum marginal spread below Standard's normal tank wagon price, with the low of the spot market prevailing when to their [the jobbers'] advantage." [30] Since 1949, Standard has altered its pricing policy in a number of ways which have made it less necessary to protect distributors against undercutting by competitors buying more cheaply than they. Some price protection is still provided by giving distributors the option of buying at Standard's delivered price to them, or at the spot prices at its own various refineries and terminals.

Branded distributors do not often shift to unbranded distribution, and they are unlikely to jeopardize their regular business by dipping into temporarily weak spot markets on the side. In most areas the difficulty of shifting supply sources has combined, historically, with the limited availability of cheap transportation and, more recently, with the thinness of spot markets, to keep the link between the dis-

---

actually prevails—averaging about 2 cents below "the" tank-wagon price. Howard, "The Marketing of Petroleum Products: A Study in the Relations between Large and Small Business" (unpublished dissertation, Cornell University, 1952), p. 312.

29. E.g., when Phillips was trying to mount a major new marketing operation in the southeastern coastal states and began to bid for distributors to handle its brand, the effect was to force other refiners to increase distributor margins a quarter of a cent throughout the area. Initially, at least, the increase took the form of a greater allowance off the tank-wagon price. Testimony of Otis Ellis, U.S. Senate, Committee on the Judiciary, Subcommittee on Antitrust and Monopoly, "To Amend Section 2 of the Clayton Act," Hearings, 84th Congress, 2d Session (1956), p. 356.

30. National Petroleum News (October 19, 1949), p. 15. To the same effect, see Cassady, pp. 180, 181. For further illustrations of "marginal" contracts see National Petroleum News (May 12, 1954), p. 59; (March 31, 1954), p. 20.

tributor's price and the spot market tenuous. To the extent the two tended to move together, until around 1940 at least, it was at a distance measured more nearly by the cost of rail shipment from the Midcontinent than by the much cheaper product pipelines actually used by the major suppliers, because the product lines in the area carried little or no gasoline for independents and their posted rates were roughly at the rail level.[31] Until a few years ago it appears that Standard of Indiana and other leaders in the area were still charging more than the low Group 3 spot quotations plus pipeline rates.[32] When open market gasoline has been available in large enough quantities to disrupt the market, it has more often done so by entering unbranded distribution channels and by feeding retail price wars, which in the end have undermined the established tank-wagon price. In such circumstances suppliers will often protect the jobber against being tied to a fictional tank-wagon price by allowing him half the price reduction allowed the service station operator. Beyond a reduction of one cent or so, the supplier may bear the entire burden of further allowances to the dealer. This kind of margin protection may serve aggressive, as well as defensive, competitive purposes of the supplying company.[33] But the jobber price remains essentially a margin.

Prices to wholly independent private-brand jobbers are more flexible than those to branded distributors, and typically less often tied to the tank-wagon price. The distributor is part of the integrated family, and interested in the stability as well as the size of his margins. The

31. See Wolbert, *American Pipe Lines,* pp. 17, 44–48; FTC, *Report on Distribution Methods and Costs, 4,* pp. 39–41; Cook, p. 44. Phillips reported to the TNEC that almost 20 per cent of the product moved on its line was for the account of other companies, but further inquiry elicited the information that practically all of this was for the Great Lakes Pipe Line Company, of which Phillips was part owner, and the remainder was for Pure Oil. *Hearings,* Pt. XIV-A, 7728, 8122.

32. See *Report of Economics Committee,* National Oil Jobbers Council (November 1, 1948), p. 4: "The jobber paid what he was directed to pay, usually an all rail rate from Oklahoma, whereas the gasoline and fuel oil came from the supplier by cheaper methods of transportation, either pipeline or water delivery." See also "Unbranded Gasoline Shakes Pricing Structure," *National Petroleum News* (October 29, 1952), p. 17. The mechanism for upping the minimum seemed to be that Standard added the pipeline rate to a higher spot price than was warranted, thus in effect carrying over part of the obsolete rail rate into the delivered price to the distributor. On the disappearance of this phantom freight in the major Midwest markets, see below, pp. 459–461.

33. In its invasion of the New Jersey market, Standard of California signed long-term guaranteed margin contracts with many distributors. U. S. Senate, Select Committee on Small Business, "Gasoline Price War in New Jersey," 84th Congress, 2d Session, *Report* No. 2810 (1956), p. 17.

unbranded jobber, on the other hand, is interested in getting gasoline for as low a price as he can, and will switch suppliers if he finds it profitable. A relatively minor factor in the national market considered as a whole, he is an important customer for open-market gasoline and, even more, heating oils, especially in the Midcontinent and along the Atlantic seaboard. He may operate terminals, and purchase largely on long-term supply contract from independent Gulf Coast or Midcontinent refineries; but he may also obtain supplies, on temporary or long-term basis, from major refiners. An East Coast major with refining capacity above its marketing facilities is reputed to sell large amounts of gasoline to independent price-cutting retailing chains.

It is more difficult to characterize the price to unbranded jobbers, precisely because the relationship to any supplier is more temporary and flexible than in the case of the distributor. The price is really ad hoc, negotiated in terms of the balance of market forces in general and the needs of each transacting party at the time. When long contracts prevail, the price specified is more likely to be the low of some publicly reported price, like the Group 3 spot market. Nevertheless, the jobber may have a contract not wholly dissimilar from that of the distributor, although in highly competitive areas he is likely to be given some additional concession—for example, a Group 3 rate plus a differential that is less than actual transportation, or a cent or two more discount below the tank-wagon price than the branded distributor.[34] He cannot charge as high a price in or to his retail outlets as the branded distributor, nor does he have the latter's assurance of supply; his more favorable price reflects these disabilities on his part, and from the standpoint of the refiner, the savings in marketing costs and/or the market pressures inducing him to sell in this price-conscious market.

TANK-WAGON PRICES

Some 75 per cent of national motor fuel supply is sold to service stations. These sales dominate the thinking and the economics of the oil industry, and their price, along with the price of crude, is the pivotal one.[35] It has been this tank-wagon price that has been the

34. See discussion in Cassady, pp. 188–192. Ashland Oil, on the other hand, sells to branded and unbranded marketers at a uniform price, perhaps reflecting the lesser availability of cut-rate supplies to private-brand marketers in its market territory.

35. The relative importance of the various prices naturally shifts with the changing structure and practices of the industry. For example, in the 1920's and early 1930's the spot, tank-car price was much more important than it is

focal point of pricing policy and leadership. It is a posted, openly quoted price. As such, it is more stable than what dealers are actually charged, largely because of its symptomatic value in price leadership and the importance to sellers of isolating areas of market disturbance. Thus company retailers afflicted by price "wars" are more likely to be aided by discounts, more or less covert, from the established tank-wagon price, and independent distributors by an adjustment in margin. In extreme cases the majors have tried to solve the problem at its source, the retail price, by shipping gasoline on consignment to re- tailers, and allowing them a three- or four-cent commission on its sale.[36] But if the disturbance is long continued, the tank-wagon quo- tation itself may be reduced.

Leadership in the tank-wagon price was most prominent in the years immediately following the dissolution, when the Standard com- panies continued to dominate their respective territories.[37] The drastic shrinkage of their market positions both reflect and explain a corre- sponding diminution over the years in the power of the market leader to lead. Responsibility for control over product supplies has come to be divided far more evenly, and so is the power to call the tune of market price. When opinions about what the market will bear vary today, the chances that the price of what is now somewhat euphemis- tically termed the "reference seller" will be cut are far greater than they were several decades ago.[38] When a single seller dominated the

today. Similarly, many refiners paid much more attention to the retail price of gasoline than they did after the thirties; and for them the tank-wagon price was of relatively small importance. Since 1950 there have been signs that the focus has been shifting back to the retail price, and away from tank-wagon. See below, pp. 407 ff.

36. "Majors Act in New Jersey Price War," *National Petroleum News* (January 27, 1954), p. 21. See also the discussion of price wars and tank-wagon quotations in Dirlam and Kahn, "Leadership and Conflict in the Pricing of Gasoline," pp. 818, 838–844.

37. The general counsel of the Texas Company told the FTC in 1916 that: "Now and then we take the initiative and make a price higher or lower, but as a rule we follow the Standard's prices, or the subsidiaries of the former Standard . . . I think the Standard Oil Company is the competitor who usually raises or lowers the price." FTC, *Report on the Price of Gasoline in 1915* (1917), p. 157. The general counsel for the Western Oil Jobbers Association testified that, ". . . we cannot have economic peace under the present con- ditions with a stronger competitor unless we try to meet their prices" (*ibid.*).

38. Differences of opinion tend more often to result in price cuts than in- creases because, as is typically the case in oligopolistic markets with high cross elasticities of demand between the various products offered, the man with the lowest price calls the tune for all. This is why the more dispersed the responsi-

market, the smaller competitors were likely to accept its lead out of a combination of fear of reprisal and a contented acceptance of the high profits this course ensured. When sellers did feel free to shade prices in hope of increasing their share of the market, the leader might still (as the Standard companies did for years) serenely continue to hold its price umbrella over the market, content with an increasing absolute volume though a declining relative share of the business. The passivity of some of the Standard successor companies in the face of competitive inroads by price-cutters undoubtedly reflected, in the past, simple conservatism and a slowness to recognize that times had changed.[39] It might also have stemmed from a belief that to drop their prices instead, in hope of retaining their preponderant market share, would only have reduced profits on balance or brought public censure. Today, with their market shares greatly shrunken, the traditional market leaders can far less easily afford to hold prices while rivals cut.[40] And for the same reason they cannot afford to fix their prices even tentatively very much above what they think the impersonal forces of the market will permit.[41]

In the sense that the price established today does try to reflect the impersonal determinants of the market, it may be said to be barometric.[42] This is not the same thing as saying that it is purely com-

---

bility for price-making, the farther price is likely to fall short of the single-firm monopoly level. Another reflection of this principle is the fact that in gasoline markets the market leader still leads more often on the upside than on the downside. He tends to assume responsibility for deciding when the market will stand an increase: no other seller can easily move up unless he does. But when he brings down the tank-wagon price, it is usually in recognition of the fact that the market has deserted him.

39. One gets this impression very strongly from McLean and Haigh's surveys of the cumbersome and tardy responses of Standard of Indiana's pricing policies to its drastic losses of business in the 1920's and 1930's (pp. 210–222).

40. The extreme limitations imposed by competitors on the power of the traditional market leader in a particularly competitive period and area is abundantly documented by Edmund P. Learned, "Pricing of Gasoline: A Case Study," *Harvard Business Review, 26* (November, 1948), 723.

41. For a fuller summary of these views and analyses of price leadership in gasoline, see among others Swensrud, "The Marketing of Petroleum Products," pp. 8700–8702; Cassady, pp. 86–108, 213–220, and *passim;* and Dirlam and Kahn, "Leadership and Conflict in the Pricing of Gasoline."

42. As Swensrud put it: "In summary, therefore, the so-called price leadership in the petroleum industry boils down to the fact that some company in each territory most of the time bears the onus of formally recognizing current conditions. Unless the so-called price leader accurately interprets basic conditions and local conditions, it soon will not be the leading marketer. Price

petitively determined. Given the state of demand, the prime "impersonal determinant of the market" that decides what price can be made to stick is of course the condition of supply—the state of inventories, current refinery throughput, and the offers of product by marketers. The condition of supply is not the simple outcome of independent competitive actions of individual producers and sellers, each paying no attention to the effects of his actions on the market. It is, instead, importantly governed by policy in the formulation of which companies and governmental agencies take explicit account of the effect of their actions on the market. The major policy decision is made in the fixing of crude output allowables. A second composite policy decision, not formally coordinated and therefore considerably less effective, is made by the major refiners in planning their levels of refinery throughput. Finally there is the policy implicit in a general practice of price leadership itself. The fact that the *same* firm, in each market, year in and year out is permitted by its competitors to assume major responsibility for serving as leader, even if only as a barometer, cannot be a tribute merely to its consistent sagacity.[43] It suggests a not completely ineffective—and far from purely competitive—mechanism for effectuating policy.[44] Where final price thus reflects a composite judgment, it may be a barometer not so much of impersonal, competitive demand-supply conditions as of industry opinion, an adaptation by a relatively small group of sellers to a policy of securing what seems to them an adequate return on investment. Actually, as is shown in Chapters 17 and 18, it is a mixture of both; to emphasize either aspect of the price of refined products at the expense of the other does serious violence to reality.

---

leadership does not mean that the price leader can set prices to get the maximum profit and force the other marketers to conform." "The Marketing of Petroleum Products," p. 8702.

43. Compare Standard of Indiana's apparently futile attempt to shed the burden in 1949 (Dirlam and Kahn, "Leadership and Conflict in the Pricing of Gasoline," pp. 837–838), with the policy of following the leader consistently pursued by a powerful seller like Gulf (Kaplan, Dirlam, and Lanzillotti, *Pricing in Big Business,* p. 206).

44. See a less critical presentation of the significance of "barometric leadership" in industries where supply is not subject to discretionary regulation, in Jesse W. Markham, "The Nature and Significance of Price Leadership," *American Economic Review, 41* (1951), 891, and the criticism it evoked: A. R. Oxenfeldt, "Professor Markham on Price Leadership," *ibid., 42* (1952), 380–384.

RETAIL PRICES

Twenty-five years ago the major oil companies not only owned but operated enough service stations so that their own retail price postings complemented and reinforced their price leadership at the wholesale level. Observations about the declining and limited effectiveness of leadership at the tank-wagon level would probably be equally appropriate in characterizing leadership in retail pricing, when it was still practiced.[45] Today, instead, only a few integrated firms like Standard of Ohio and Standard of California own and operate any sizable number of stations.[46] There are other ways—notable among them fair trading and consignment selling—by which refiners can exercise direct, legal control over the service station price; and there has been increasing resort to such methods in recent years. Also several states—notably Massachusetts and Michigan—have responded to price wars by enacting laws prohibiting retail sales "below cost," which in effect require retailers to add to the tank-wagon price some minimum margin. Still, it is generally the case that the retail price is set, above the level fixed by the tank-wagon price, by what might be termed (pending elaboration) competitive forces—by at least partially independent reactions of individual station operators to the prices charged by their competitors.

Actually there are so many informal influences brought to bear upon retailers in determining their mark-ups that the characterization of the process as a competitive one, while basically correct, tells only a part of the story. This inadequacy probably reflects in part the peculiar complexities of gasoline distribution; it also reflects the sparse content of the abstract concept of competition, which necessarily fails to convey the rich diversity of custom that characterizes any market. Only those influences most relevant to this inquiry will be mentioned here.

Prominent among the informal influences is the common practice for suppliers to "suggest" prices to their retailers, suggestions which

45. See Learned, "Pricing of Gasoline: A Case Study," whose discussion is relevant here as well as to wholesale price leadership, since Standard of Ohio is almost unique among the majors in the high percentage of its own stations it continues to operate.

46. See below, Appendix, and esp. nn. 98, 99. Other firms generally operate stations only for training purposes, or while they are in process of trying to find dealers to operate them. On the withdrawal from direct retailing, see above, p. 359, n. 25, and p. 363, n. 35.

carry unusual weight with dealers who are also lessees.[47] At this point two conflicting observations may be noted. On the one hand, price-cutting is said to be generally discouraged; majors do not like to have their retailers initiate price wars because they jeopardize the tank-wagon price.[48] But many major companies also put heavy pressure on their dealers from time to time to cut their prices sharply to meet reductions initiated by others. Complaints of dealers and Congressional committees in recent years have been directed far more at the latter than at the former practice, mainly on the theory that such pressures, often accompanied by allowances from the tank-wagon price to complying dealers, prolong price wars.[49]

Partly under pressure from dealers harassed by price wars and partly in their own interest, major company suppliers are tending to adopt more formal methods of controlling the retail price. Some have

47. See FTC, *Report on Distribution Methods and Costs, 4* (1944), p. 85. Cf.: "Most suppliers testified that it was a matter of company policy not to suggest prices . . ." but "the testimony indicated that some subordinate employees of the major suppliers continued to exercise unfair pressure by disregarding company policy. . . ." U. S. House of Representatives, Select Committee on Small Business, Subcommittee No. 5, "Distribution Practices in the Petroleum Industry," *Interim Report,* House Report No. 1157, 85th Congress, 1st Session (1957), p. 3; see also pp. 7, 15, and *passim.* See also, e.g., *U.S. v. Socony Mobil Oil Company,* U. S. District Court, District of Massachusetts, *Indictments,* Cr. Nos. 56-152 S through 56-157 S, filed June 28, 1956.

48. "It was the testimony of two oil company witnesses that where any of their brand dealers disturbed the retail price structure by reducing prices, the oil company supplier would grant discounts from the wholesale price to every other dealer in the trading area, while withholding such discounts from the dealer who had initially cut his prices." U. S. House of Representatives, Select Committee on Small Business, Subcommittee No. 5, "Alleged Coercive and Discriminatory Practices against Retail Gasoline Operators by Oil Company Suppliers," *Interim Report,* House *Report* No. 1423, 84th Congress, 1st Session (1955), p. 13; see also Cassady, pp. 244–246, 263–264; Bain, *Pacific Coast Petroleum Industry, 1,* 204–205; and Attorney General, State of Michigan, p. 152. The Department of Justice claims the West Coast majors "completely dominate and control the manner in which these independent businessmen operate their retail outlets. . . . Each . . . controls the price at which these independent operators resell gasoline and other refined petroleum products," to the end of eliminating all price competition between themselves. *U.S. v. Standard Oil Company of California et al.,* District Court, Southern District of California, Central Division, Civil Action No. 11584-C, *Amended Complaint* (1956), pars. 62, 64.

49. See, among others, House Small Business Committee, *Interim Report* (1955), pp. 13–17; Senate Small Business Committee, "Petroleum Marketing Practices," *Hearings,* 83rd Congress, 1st Session (1953), pp. 6, 26, 68.

openly established a policy of "suggested retail prices." [50] The purpose, recently at least, has been to induce dealers to meet competitively lower prices in price-war areas, and the suggestion has usually been accompanied by a provision of discounts from the tank-wagon price sufficient to make the retail price cut possible. Such a policy has long been practiced with varying mixtures of coercion (under threat of terminating leases) and inducement (offering discounts from the tank-wagon price) on an informal basis by many companies.

Other firms have begun to fair trade their gasoline. According to Cassady, fair trade has been infrequently used in the past.[51] In recent years it has appealed to dealers, Congressional committees, and suppliers alike—though one gets the impression that suppliers have been the most reluctant of the three—as a means of stopping price wars, that is, of *raising* retail prices. For a time, mainly in 1956, the adoption of fair trading by one marketer after another on the East Coast promised success. Since then its ability to hold retail price competition in check seems more dubious; and several companies have discontinued the practice. This has been hastened by a Federal District Court decision denying to Esso Standard the right to fair trade where the effect was to eliminate price competition horizontally between its own marketing divisions and its distributors—something explicitly prohibited by the McGuire Act.[52]

50. "In an attempt to lend strength to the Kansas City gasoline market, where retail prices for the past month or so have been 8¢ a gallon below the so-called 'normal,' Indiana Standard introduced its policy of 'suggested competitive resale prices.' Under this plan, retail regular-grade price of 13.9¢ gal. (ex tax) was 'suggested' to company's dealers as 'competitive,' with dealers being given a discount from the suggested price. Dealer tank wagon posting was discontinued. Standard has had similar policy in effect with its dealers in the Minneapolis–St. Paul area since early this year." *National Petroleum News* (July, 1956), p. 170. Continental adopted a similar plan on a county-by-county basis in Oklahoma, ESPA (February, 1958), pp. 5 f.

51. P. 244, n. 13.

52. An optimistic report, indicating that 98 per cent of New Jersey dealers were posting fair-trade prices or higher, was presented in *National Petroleum News* (September, 1956), pp. 177, 208. In a survey article, "Fair Trade: What Is Its Future as a Price War Peacemaker?" it was asserted that "fair trading of gasoline in the East is one of the most significant experiments conducted by oil marketers," although obstacles to its effectiveness were noted. See *ibid.* (December, 1956), pp. 90–94. Fair trading does not automatically eliminate the possibility of price competition: different major refiners may and have set divergent prices, and unbranded marketers may continue to undercut the fair traded major brands. See *ibid.* On the necessity for "cooperation" between major suppliers to make fair trade effective, see the frank interview, "Price

Several other majors—notably Sun and Union Oil—converted many of their dealer (that is, lessee) outlets in price war areas to commission stations, selling the refiners' gasoline on consignment. Many dealers have complained they were offered no choice but to accept this change in status. The purpose of the recent developments has been to enable suppliers more readily and flexibly to dictate retail prices, apparently in order to *reduce* them to meet (and possibly to stabilize) competitive prices. This method seemed attractive also because the Federal Trade Commission questioned the legality, under the Robinson-Patman Act, of suppliers offering concessions to selected dealers in order to permit them to meet price-war competition.[53] However, the Commission has recently charged Sun with violating Section 5 of the Federal Trade Commission Act, instead, in "coercing" its dealers to shift to commission operations, under an "alleged consignment" whose real purpose is "to dictate or fix and maintain the [retail] price." [54] Dealer associations have generally opposed the shift, on the ground that it eliminates their independence, constricts their margins (thereby reduced to guaranteed commissions), and prolongs price wars.[55]

These evidences of increasing refiner emphasis and influence on the retail price indicate a corresponding diminution in the focal importance of the tank-wagon quotation. In those areas where it publicizes a "suggested retail price," Standard of Indiana stops posting its tank-wagon price; the price to cooperating dealers is the suggested retail price less some minimum margin.[56] In fair trading, similarly, the focus of price policy shifts to the fair traded—that is, the retail—price.[57] Fair trade works, it is pointed out, only if leading mar-

---

Wars Can Be Curbed," *ibid.* (March, 1956), pp. 34–37. The apparent demise of fair trade is described *ibid.* (July, 1957), p. 136. The Esso decision is reported in the *Wall Street Journal* (May 6, 1957), p. 8. The precedent for that decision was *U.S. v. McKesson and Robbins,* 76 Supreme Court 937 (1956).

53. See below, pp. 477–482.

54. Docket 6934, Complaint, November 8, 1957. For a dealer's complaint against the practice, see Senate Small Business Committee, "Gasoline Price War in New Jersey," *Hearings,* 84th Congress, 1st Session (1955), Pt. I, pp. 18–24; also House Small Business Committee, *Interim Report* (1955), p. 17, (1957), pp. 6–7.

55. "Behind the Move to Commission Stations," *National Petroleum News* (July, 1956), pp. 93–95.

56. See above, n. 50. The same is true of the Conoco plan mentioned there.

57. In Pennsylvania, e.g., Atlantic, the price leader in that state, merely fixed the retail price, charging its dealers that price, *ex* taxes, less a 23 per cent margin. *National Petroleum News* (July, 1956), p. 106.

keters will follow similar policies and keep their fair-traded prices in line. Of course there is no tank-wagon price to consignment stations, only a fixed commission of so many cents a gallon. To the extent that refiner-marketers assume responsibility for the retail price, the tank-wagon charge becomes merely a derivative of the price to the motorist; and the dealer's margin, like that of the branded distributor, becomes a matter for negotiation (or dictation), an administered rather than an essentially market-determined price. In general, however, the assumption of this kind of responsibility by major refiners for retail pricing seems still to be regarded by them as a temporary, emergency action taken, largely under extreme pressure from dealers, in price-war situations, and applied only in the affected areas.[58]

Moreover, enough has been said about the character of price administration in this industry to indicate the unreality of any simple dichotomy between negotiated or administered and market-determined or competitive prices. Even when wholesale or retail margins are nominally administered, whether or not after negotiation, the influence of the market supply and demand for distributor or dealer services is never very far in the background. This is even more true in the case of these marketing margins than in the case of the tank-wagon price, because the latter is heavily influenced by discretionary control over supply; the supply of the services of gasoline marketers is far less subject to control, as will be shown. Therefore, although some qualification is needed, there is no reason to abandon the general observation that in the main what determines the margin that retailing adds to the tank-wagon charge is the essentially independent competitive action of a great number of service station operators. They cannot readily control supply because entry into their part of the business is so easy —and integrated companies make it easier—and because independence of action is typical.

Conclusion

Several questions remain: they involve the interrelationships of the various open-market prices, and the relationship between them and the price of crude oil; the significance of these open-market prices to

58. On an instance of apparent collusion to terminate a price war, with simultaneous instructions allegedly issued to dealers one evening to raise their prices to 31.9 cents a gallon effective midnight, see House Small Business Committee, *Interim Report* (1957), pp. 7–8, 23, and, growing out of that inquiry, *U.S. v. Standard Oil Company (Indiana) et al.*, indictment announced October 8, 1957.

the integrated company and to the prices it sets; and the effect of integration, in turn, on the operation of intermediate markets.

Integration and Intermediate Product Markets

To the extent that a company is integrated, it by-passes intermediate product markets; in reality it transmits crude oil and products from one department to another at cost, whatever the fictional interdepartmental billing price recorded in the accounts for the guidance of management. The only real price for the integrated company is the one at which it finally transmits its products to outsiders.[59] The more thoroughly integrated the industry, the less real is the significance for any part of it of intermediate markets.

But of course the oil industry is not completely integrated: independent producers, refiners, transporters, and marketers do have intermediate markets in which they buy and sell. The integration of the major oil companies is likewise incomplete, and in each of these markets they develop relations as suppliers, purchasers, or competitors with individuals or firms who operate only at that stage or in that area. The prices established in those markets are critically important to nonintegrated participants, and the majors influence those prices, wittingly or unwittingly, both by their own buying and selling policies on the transactions they bring to market and by keeping transactions out of them. The prices in intermediate markets would undoubtedly behave differently if every firm in the industry had to have full recourse to them for all its supplies and for all its revenues.

To what extent, in turn, do the intermediate markets influence the policies of the integrated companies? The most basic product price, of course, is the one at which the majors sell gasoline from their own trucks to service stations. This price cannot be explained adequately as determined by any open market. As the primary objective of price-making policy in the industry, it is more correct to say that other prices are related to it than vice versa.

The major branded distributor ordinarily follows the leader in his territory in fixing the price to his dealers, just as what he pays is, by and large, tied to the tank-wagon price. In some instances, as in Detroit in 1936–40, he may be a price-cutter; but as a general rule he does not deviate from the pattern that would be followed by the

59. Of course no company can be integrated in the sense that it has no recourse whatever to intermediate markets, for supplies, for labor, power and the like. So obviously even the "fully" integrated company will have a vital interest also in the prices that constitute its costs.

major's own wholesaling department in selling to retailers. This conservatism is not necessarily dictated by the supplier; self-interest suggests the same course. Should the distributor wish to tie more stations into his marketing system he will ordinarily do as the majors do—either build his own or offer to independent dealers one or another of the numerous kinds of indirect concessions that preserve the nominal tank-wagon price.

The price at which integrated companies sell to unbranded jobbers and to large industrial or commercial customers or governments bears a closer resemblance to a truly competitive, open-market price. These prices are sometimes related directly to tank wagon by a customary differential; but at other times they are made on a negotiated basis. The sales to large accounts are the easiest to use for disposing of surpluses, because they are not on a posted basis and, except for sales to jobbers, do not usually return to the market to undermine the tank-wagon price. In periods of plentiful supply they may therefore take place at substantial reductions, perhaps even approximating out-of-pocket costs.

This picture of product-pricing procedures and interrelationships, centering on the tank-wagon quotation, reverses the industry's traditional explanation. The more familiar description, which shows price as building up in the other direction—upward from the Gulf or Oklahoma spot markets via terminal and refinery posted prices through delivered tank-car and inland-terminal prices to tank-wagon—gives the process the appearance of an underlying auction. Such a description seems incompatible with the actual making of prices by the dominant integrated firms, and the actual, often ignominious, isolation of the spot market.[60]

But how then does the market leader decide on the appropriate level of the tank-wagon price? Although this question encroaches on the subject matter of the next chapter, it is clear at least that

---

60. "Because of the fact that most bulk gasoline contracts in the East are 'tied to tank wagon price,' quotations for gasoline have not eased along with falling rates for clean ocean tanker voyages from the Gulf." "Gasoline Prices Rise in Upper East Coast," *National Petroleum News* (June 17, 1953), p. 53. J. B. Smith, vice president and sales manager of Sunray, in a speech in January, 1954, objected to the practice of using trade quotations as a basis for refinery or tank transport prices, because "instead of having just one 'wholesale' market we now have hundreds of them. It is no longer possible for trade paper [sic] to reflect prices in effect at every one of these hundreds of markets." "Price 'Jitters' Plague Oil Industry," *National Petroleum News* (January 27 1954), p. 21.

the administered price is not administered in thin air. Its level depends on what the market will bear, and that depends in turn on conditions of supply. Since control of supply is highly imperfect, market leaders must look long and hard at the prices quoted and likely to be quoted by their competitors in deciding what they can or must do about their own. And they will also take into account conditions in the spot markets—not because those markets can or do typically dictate the tank-wagon price but because they may reflect most sensitively the over-all conditions in the industry that determine what tank-wagon price level can be held.

In any event, the prices in intermediate markets reflect the terms on which nonintegrated companies may be able to compete. Those terms therefore cannot be ignored wherever independents continue to have access to them; the tank-wagon price must necessarily fluctuate in reasonably close correspondence with refinery and terminal prices, on the one hand, and with retail prices on the other.[61]

The Relation of Crude to Product Prices

Sidney A. Swensrud, later president and chairman of the board of the Gulf Oil Corporation, made a detailed and convincing analysis of the relationship between crude and refined prices before World War II.[62] He first demonstrated that changes in product prices unmistakably led changes in crude prices, in both directions, during the period 1920–38. Cassady, carrying Swensrud's computations through 1950, generally corroborated this observation.[63] Confining attention to the experience under prorationing, the wholesale value of products produced from a barrel of Midcontinent petroleum moved up sharply above 1934 levels in 1935, while the (posted) price of that crude rose only at the outset of 1936. Refinery realizations began again to climb (after an earlier slump) late in 1936 and the price of crude responded early in 1937. Wholesale prices continued to climb until midyear, then late in 1937 started a long decline almost unbroken to early 1939 while

61. This is of course a striking oversimplification, ignoring all sorts of factors that make the course of these prices diverge over both short and long periods. But it remains sufficiently true for the present purpose (see, e.g., Cassady, pp. 306–311), which is to single out the crucial issues concerning the workability or unworkability of petroleum product price competition.

62. "The Relation between Crude Oil and Product Prices."

63. Pp. 134–140. While Swensrud supplied monthly figures through 1938, Cassady unfortunately did not.

the crude price did not break until October 1938. Through 1939 and 1940, refinery yields fluctuated but the crude price did not change.

The relationship becomes somewhat less clear after 1940, possibly because the fluctuations are obscured by wartime price controls (during the Korean emergency as well as World War II) and the sharp upward trend after 1945. It is not certain that product prices led crude in the next two jumps, early in 1941 and in 1946. There were several steps upward in the latter year, which continued on into 1947, but it is significant that refinery margins in 1946 were actually lower than in the preceding year, suggesting that product prices lagged.[64] Product prices seem definitely to have leaped ahead earlier and farther than crude in 1947, but their sharp slump in 1948–49 and recovery in 1950 are not reflected in the posted price of Midcontinent crude at all, for reasons already explained. In February and March 1953, when government controls on crude oil and product prices were withdrawn,[65] the only notable price changes that occurred were simultaneous increases in crude and products on the West Coast, a growing deficit area.[66] In the ensuing months markets remained stable to weak: only residual fuel oil recovered strongly in April. Socony-Vacuum tried to lead a general increase in tank-wagon gasoline prices on February 28; when other leading marketers failed to follow, it came back down on March 3. Finally, in May, prices of gasoline (and particularly of premium) began to recover notably with the seasonal recovery of demand, raising weighted average national refinery realizations to $3.92 a barrel from $3.90 the month before; but prices of kerosene and distillate slumped.[67] Strength in the gasoline markets (alone) continued

64. This may have been a reflection of the vagaries of price decontrol, however.

65. Crude oil and all products except home-heating oils were freed in mid-February, home-heating oils in mid-March.

66. Posted prices for Pennsylvania crude oil were also increased, but, significantly, the prices of lubricating oils remained weak. These observations are based on the weekly surveys of market conditions in *National Petroleum News*.

67. We have computed refinery realizations per barrel of crude for each month during this period. Average monthly prices for the four leading products (gasoline, kerosene, distillate and residual fuel oils) were weighted by the relative monthly production of each. Refinery margins were then obtained by comparing the resultant aggregate refinery price with the weighted national average crude oil price. Prices were those reported in the issues of the *National Petroleum News Factbook,* and production figures were taken from the issues of the annual API *Statistical Bulletins.* The refinery margins thus derived in-

into June, and on June 10 came the first general upward advance in posted prices on the East Coast, again led, this time successfully, by Socony-Vacuum. On June 15, Phillips posted a 25-cent increase in the crude oil price, and was promptly followed; almost at once several Gulf Coast refiners announced higher gasoline price quotations and, within the week, there was a wave of product price increases all over the country. Products still seem to have led, but (outside of California) the leader was mainly gasoline, and the lead only a month or two. The strengthening of the gasoline market may have sufficed to convince the major companies that the market would support the increase in crude oil that they believed long overdue. But it evidently took an administered increase in the crude price to buttress and generalize the improvement in product markets.[68]

Gradual weakening of product markets late in 1953 and through the first half of 1954 reduced refinery realizations from a peak of $4.19 a barrel in August to $3.94 at their low point in July.[69] Since crude oil

clude the cost of transporting crude oil from well-head to refinery. The resulting estimates for the period under present consideration (which, because they include the West Coast, do not reflect the market conditions described in the text as clearly as they might) are as follows:

DATE	WEIGHTED FOUR PRODUCT PRICE	WEIGHTED CRUDE OIL PRICE	REFINERY MARGIN
1953			
January	$3.78	$2.56	$1.22
February	3.83	2.60	1.23
March	3.88	2.63	1.25
April	3.90	2.63	1.27
May	3.92	2.63	1.29
June	4.10	2.73	1.37
July	4.19	2.83	1.36
August	4.19	2.84	1.35
September	4.18	2.83	1.35
October	4.18	2.83	1.35
November	4.17	2.83	1.34
December	4.13	2.83	1.30
1954			
January	4.10	2.82	1.28
February	4.10	2.82	1.28
March	4.05	2.82	1.23
April	4.06	2.82	1.24
May	4.04	2.82	1.22
June	4.03	2.82	1.21
July	3.94	2.81	1.13

68. Still, the fact that refinery margins were in June–November above the levels of the first half of 1953 would indicate the greater volatility and leadership of product prices.

69. See above, p. 395, n. 14; also below, pp. 468 ff.

prices remained almost rigid, refinery margins dropped from $1.35 to $1.13—9 cents below the regulated January 1953 level. Product prices led, in a sense; but crude prices scarcely followed.

Similarly, the recovery of product prices in 1955–56 was accompanied by only local readjustments in the price of crude oil, raising the national average merely from $2.82 in 1954 to $2.84 in 1956. Again, products led; but crude did not follow, with the result that weighted refinery margins rose from an average of $1.16 a barrel in 1954 to $1.26 in 1955, and (using a different series) from $1.29 in 1955 to no less than $1.40 in 1956.[70]

The rise in the price of crude oil in January 1957 could be regarded as the long-delayed response to the recovery of product prices in the two to two and a half years preceding, assisted by a slight shorter-term increase that began in November 1956. On the basis of composite, constant-weighted refinery realizations as reported monthly for four leading products in the *National Petroleum News,* it appears that product prices reached a peak of $3.95 per barrel in January–February 1956. They stayed within a range of $3.93–$3.97 until December, with the low point of the range reached in October under the pressure of mounting stocks. But major products other than gasoline recovered in October and gasoline prices gained somewhat in December, so that the composite moved upward to $3.96 in November and more vigorously to $4.07 in the last month. Products had once more led crude, but weakly, and probably futilely in the absence of active assistance by the State of Texas. However, as in 1953, the crude oil price advance of January 1957 was immediately followed by a slightly more vigorous rise in product prices to a new composite peak of $4.36 per barrel in February. Thereafter, product prices began a long retreat, still in process in June of 1958, when they aggregated $3.78 for the group; and, against a stable crude price, refinery margins were very sharply compressed. Product prices were again leading a downturn, but crude was scarcely following. Although a succession of reduced crude oil postings, beginning in the spring of 1958 and continuing on into 1959, obliterated about half of the January, 1957, increase, these cuts began more than a year after product prices had begun to fall.[71]

70. For the first-mentioned series see below, Table XXII. The second estimates were made by the authors.
71. Using constant weights to combine the four major products into an estimate of refinery realization, one derives a consistent but unrealistic measure of refinery margins, since actual margins will vary not only with prices but

Swensrud's conclusion about the chronological relationship between crude oil and product price movements in the period he studied would seem to require only slight modification for more recent years:

the time lag of crude price changes behind product price changes is greater on the down side than on the up side. In other words,

---

also with changing refinery yields. The estimated refinery margins based on such constant base-period weights are compared with computed margins for the same periods in which each period's percentage yield of each component product is used as a variable weight for its price, in the tabulation below. See above, n. 67, for a fuller explanation of the procedure followed. It will be observed that the trends of the two series are similar but the absolute size of the variably weighted series is substantially higher. Data are for $/bbl.

DATE	WEIGHTED FOUR PRODUCT PRICE (VARIABLE WEIGHTS) (1)	WEIGHTED CRUDE OIL PRICE (2)	REFINERY MARGIN (1)–(2)	REFINERY MARGIN CONSTANT WEIGHTS
1955	$4.09	$2.82	$1.27	$ .99
1956	4.23	2.84	1.39	1.12
1957	4.51	3.16	1.35	1.08
January	4.45	3.13	1.32	1.11
February	4.58	3.17	1.41	1.19
March	4.56	3.17	1.39	1.17
April	4.59	3.17	1.42	1.17
May	4.60	3.17	1.43	1.16
June	4.54	3.17	1.37	1.10
July	4.49	3.16	1.33	1.06
August	4.47	3.16	1.31	1.02
September	4.49	3.16	1.33	1.02
October	4.47	3.16	1.31	1.01
November	4.44	3.16	1.28	.97
December	4.41	3.16	1.25	.97
1958				
January	4.38	3.18	1.20	.90
February	4.19	3.19	1.00	.68
March	4.15	3.19	.96	.63
April	4.14	3.11	1.03	.70
May	4.11	3.10	1.01	.66
June	4.09	3.06	1.03	.72

Here, as in the case of the statistics in n. 67, the use of national data produces a somewhat deceptive picture. The sharp break in national average crude oil prices in the spring of 1958 was primarily the result of declines in two special markets whose oil had theretofore commanded premium prices for reasons no longer economically defensible. The price of 31-degree gravity oil at Wilmington, California, dropped from $3.41 to a range of $3.23–3.31, and of Bradford, Pennsylvania, from $4.65 all the way to $3.90 a barrel between January 15 and and September 15, 1958. In contrast, the price of 36-degree West Texas sour and 36-degree Midcontinent sweet crude remained virtually rigid, at $2.94 and $3.07 a barrel, respectively, from early 1957 to the latter date.

the crude oil price follows refined product price increases much more promptly than it follows product price declines. An examination of the timing of Oklahoma wholesale gasoline price changes, for example, and Mid-Continent crude oil price changes since 1924 showed that, on the average, the crude oil price declined approximately 6 months after declines in gasoline prices had begun. During the same period, the crude price increased on the average within 3 or 4 months after improvements in gasoline prices began.[72]

Product prices are still the more volatile, still reflect changing market conditions more sensitively, and therefore still tend to move first. But when general industry opinion holds that an increase in the price of crude oil is "justified"—an opinion *not* typically based on a consideration of demand and supply conditions in crude oil markets—product markets need strengthen ever so little to occasion the heralded advance, which is in turn entrenched, if need be, by public limitations on supply. The lead-time of products is either very long or very short. On the downside, product prices typically lead, but crude oil prices either do not follow at all, or, if they do, they follow only negligibly or after many months. Governmental limitation of supply supports and justifies this pattern of behavior: the sluggishness of crude oil prices on the downside, noted by Swensrud, is converted by production control into almost complete immobility.

Does this comparative flexibility of product prices have any causal significance? Here again Swensrud makes a shrewd observation:

> It is not intended in the foregoing discussion . . . to suggest that crude oil price changes are *caused* by product price changes. It is the writer's belief that the same causes are involved in both . . . for, except in a superficial sense, there is only one set of supply-demand factors in the oil industry . . . namely, the supply of crude oil and the demand for refined products. . . . In the oil industry, the highly integrated character of a large part of the operation makes it possible for the pressure of crude to be exerted directly upon the refined product markets.[73]

The changing forces of demand and supply operate more quickly on the relatively sensitive product markets; Swensrud offers a lucid explanation, along lines now familiar to the reader,[74] of why crude oil

72. "The Relation between Crude Oil and Product Prices," p. 771.
73. *Ibid.,* pp. 771–772, 777.
74. See above, pp. 132–133.

markets are less responsive. But comparative sensitivity does not in itself connote causality. On the contrary, it was clearly the fluctuating and inelastic production of crude oil that caused product price instability during most of the period Swensrud surveyed and it was prorationing that produced a change. The enormous increase in the elasticity of supply which it effected, in association with limits on imports and control of foreign supplies in strong hands, has tamed crude oil markets. This change is reflected in the greater stability of *both* crude and product markets since 1935;[75] it is also likely to mean that product price changes after 1935 owe more to the behavior of refiners, marketers, and ultimate purchasers than to the activities at the production end of the business.

If raw material prices scarcely follow products on the downside, yet often move up with them almost simultaneously, is there a long-run tendency for refinery margins to be squeezed? Table XXII presents a series of estimated refinery product realizations and margins for the last twenty years. In financial terms, it is clear, product prices have come to reflect the rising price of crude oil during the period: the calculated margin available to the refiner (which must cover also the cost of moving crude from wellhead to refinery) has risen from $0.71 in 1935–39 to $1.26 in 1955.[76]

Against these margins, however, must be set the more rapid rise over the same period in the "refiner's cost of living." The cost of refinery inputs (not including crude oil) rose more than 150 per cent, the estimated margin only 75 per cent, as the two indexes clearly indicate. This statistical evidence is consistent with two conflicting hypotheses: that refiners have so improved their efficiency that they have been able to absorb half of the increase in price of labor and materials; or that refiners have been gradually squeezed by their inability to pass on all of their rising unit costs.[77]

75. See McLean and Haigh, p. 123.

76. As above, n. 71, indicates, the margins moved up still farther in 1956 and early 1957—they averaged $1.35 for the entire year—then began a steady descent back to, and for a time at least, far below, the 1955 level. A strong recovery set in during the second half of 1958, however, and by March of 1959 average margins reached $1.46.

77. Unit costs might conceivably have increased by an even higher ratio than the price of inputs—for example because of the higher capital requirements and reduced physical product yields attributable to raising the octane ratings of gasoline. On the other hand, improved refinery efficiency in living within the margin is clearly indicated by the difference between the actual (estimated) spread of $1.26 in 1955 and what the spread would have been—$1.02—had relative product yields remained the same as in 1935–39. This point is further developed below, pp. 450 ff.

One way to decide which hypothesis seems the more valid would be to look at the profits of nonintegrated refining companies over the relevant period, to see whether they show any evidence of long-run deterioration. The data are far from satisfactory, but the profit records compiled by McLean and Haigh for as many companies as possible seem to demonstrate the following: first, that the refining companies in their sample have tended over the entire period 1920–52 to earn a lower rate of return on invested capital than producing or more

TABLE XXII

Refinery Spreads: Total United States 1935–55

YEAR	ACTUAL SPREADS [a]				PRICE CHANGES YIELD CONSTANT 1935–39 BASE [b]		"REFINERS COST OF LIVING" 1935– 39 = 100 [c]
	REALIZATION 4 PRODUCTS DOLLARS PER BARREL	CRUDE, DOLLARS PER BARREL	SPREADS, DOLLARS PER BARREL	INDEX 1935– 39 = 100	DOL- LARS PER BARREL	INDEX	
1935–39							
average	1.79	1.08	0.71	100.0	0.71	100.0	100.0
1945	2.00	1.19	0.81	113.7	0.87	121.0	129.4
1946	2.16	1.39	0.77	108.3	0.81	112.6	143.0
1947	2.84	1.93	0.91	127.4	0.93	130.2	175.2
1948	3.74	2.60	1.14	159.2	1.13	157.3	197.0
1949	3.43	2.54	0.89	124.6	0.82	114.3	200.7
1950	3.54	2.51	1.03	143.9	0.94	130.8	210.2
1951	3.73	2.53	1.20	167.1	1.10	153.3	228.4
1952	3.73	2.53	1.20	168.1	1.06	148.5	233.7
1953	3.92	2.68	1.24	173.1	1.04	145.2	239.5
1954	3.93	2.77	1.16	162.4	.94	131.5	243.6
1955	4.04	2.78	1.26	175.5	1.02	142.4	253.5

[a] Difference between realization from one barrel of four principal products and the price of crude at the well. The spreads, therefore, include the cost of transporting crude to the refinery. These are either from censuses of manufacturers or estimated by applying changing weights based on actual percentage yields of each of the four products (regular gasoline, kerosene, distillate fuel oil, and residual fuel oil) against price quotations.
[b] Estimates of what refinery net realizations or spreads would be if yields of the four products remained as in 1935–39.
[c] Index measuring price trends in direct labor, materials (not crude oil), plant, equipment, and indirect labor. In effect these are indexes of current (variable) costs and replacement capital costs. This index is not seriously inflated by the latter. Using book cost instead of replacement cost for the capital component, e.g., reduced the index number for 1950 only from 210.2 to 202.2.

Source: economics department of a major oil company.

fully integrated companies; second, that while essentially refining companies did about as well as more fully integrated competitors in the period 1920–34, they did less well, comparatively, during 1935–52. While these statistics suggest a possible secular squeeze on refining profits, a comparison of the profits of refining and of purely producing companies in the two periods denies anything of the sort. Refining company profits improved more than those of producers in the second period relative to the first; and, further, if one considers the trend of profits within the period from the early 1930's to 1952, there is no indication that profits earned by refiners have behaved less well than those of producers or integrated companies.[78] All in all, therefore, the profit records suggest that refiners have been able over the long run to pass on most of the rising prices of inputs over and above what they were able to absorb in increased efficiency, as well or almost as well as producers and integrated competitors. One important qualification of these observations is that available data probably summarize the experience of the more successful refiners only. The same qualification, however, would apply, even more strongly, to the producers and marketers. However, comparative reported profits of companies heavily involved in production may be understated in a period of rising exploratory and developmental activity by the practice of charging large proportions of such outlays as expenses.

Our interpretation of crude oil pricing strategy has drawn heavily on experience of the 1950's: how far have refiners been able to pass on the crude oil advances of 1953 and 1957 in higher product prices? In shorter periods like these the behavior of margins is probably more meaningful because less warped by changes in unit costs attributable to changing input prices and efficiency. As Table XXII indicates, refinery spreads averaged $1.20 in 1951 and 1952. In 1953 and 1954, despite the progressive margin squeeze after June 1953, they still averaged $1.20—$1.24 in the first year, $1.16 in the second. In 1955 they moved up to $1.26 and, according to our own estimate, in 1956 to $1.39. Despite sharp declines in 1957 the year's average was still $1.35.[79] In general, the increased cost of purchased crude oil has been passed on, with something substantial left over to take care of the continued rise in the "refiner's cost of living."

78. See esp. McLean and Haigh, pp. 140–141.
79. See the table above, n. 71.

APPENDIX

This appendix is in effect an extended footnote to the brief survey of the character and numbers of the leading marketers of petroleum products, and follows the classification set forth in that account. It may serve incidentally to indicate how inadequate, though copious, is our statistical information about this industry.

1. *Product brokers.* There is no basis for estimating either their number or the volume of business they conduct.

2. *Terminal operators.* In 1954, according to the Census of Distribution, there were 1,241 terminals handling petroleum products.[80] Cross and King [81] estimated that about two-thirds of these were in 1950 owned and in almost all cases operated by refiners or their agents; applying their ratio to the 1,241 suggests slightly over 400 terminals operated by independents. According to the *National Petroleum News* 1957 survey, only 2 per cent of the wholesale distributors of petroleum products own terminals.[82] Since their population may have been as high as 20,000 (see below), this too suggests a figure of 400. The relative size of the business of terminal operators compared with other wholesalers is suggested by the fact that the sales of the average terminal were almost $4,000,000, of the average bulk plant about $300,000 in 1954, according to the above-mentioned Census.

3. *Jobbers and distributors.* Estimates of their number used widely in the industry range as high as 15,000 but it seems unlikely that it could exceed 10,000. The 1954 Census tabulated 27,078 bulk plants and 1,241 terminals. Of these, taken together, 17,837 were owned by refiner-marketers, 10,482 by "others." [83] To the latter figure should be added perhaps another 1,100 or so—this was the number of unincorporated firms without paid employees in 1948, not covered by the 1954 Census—making 11,600 bulk plants and terminals owned by independent marketers, or 11,200 bulk plants alone (after deducting the estimated 400 independent terminals). According to the *National Petroleum News* 1957 survey, the average "jobber" (this means wholesale distributors as a group) owned 1.3 bulk plants; [84] a "jobber"

---

80. Department of Commerce, Bureau of the Census, *Wholesale Trade, Petroleum Bulk Plants and Terminals,* Bulletin W-2-8, 1957.

81. "Channels of Distribution for Petroleum Products," p. 2.

82. *Factbook* (mid-May 1957), p. 156.

83. Pp. 8–61.

84. *Factbook* (mid-May 1957), p. 156. The 1.3 is apparently the average not for all jobbers but for the 77 per cent who owned their plants.

survey by the *Petroleum Marketer* yielded a similar estimate, 1.4 stations, also in 1956.[85] This suggests that the 11,200 plants were owned by roughly 8,500 wholesalers. It is not clear how far this number should be increased to take account of branded distributors who lease from refiners, and whose bulk plants would therefore presumably be included by the Census as refiner-marketer owned. The Census says refiner-owned bulk plants are also refiner-operated; but McLean and Haigh found, for their seven companies, that while in "nearly all cases" distributors owned or controlled the bulk plants they operated, "in a few cases" they leased them from their suppliers.[86] The *National Petroleum News* showed only 77 per cent of its jobber-subscribers owning their bulk plants; again, it is not clear whether this means the remaining 23 per cent were peddlers, who should not be added to the foregoing 8,500-odd total, or lessees, who should.

Another approach is to begin with the Census' listing of 6,893 "independent" bulk plants in 1954—"independent" here means plants of jobbers who own and operate only one. Another 1,586 plants were owned by cooperative associations which could be part of integrated refining-marketing operations. Since, according to the same NPN survey, 80 per cent of its jobbers owned only one bulk plant, this suggests that the 6,893 plus some (probably small) part of the 1,586 ought to be increased by one-fourth to give the total number of independent bulk plant owners—perhaps 9,000, to which total one might again add the 1948 total of 1,100 small, unincorporated operations omitted by the 1954 Census.

These computations suggest that Fleming's total of 14,047 independent firms in terminal and bulk-station operation around 1953 [87] probably includes some commission agents as well. The same is perhaps true of other estimates, running between 12,000 and 15,000.[88] The *Petroleum Marketer's* subscription lists, which definitely exclude commission agents, contain 11,328 "jobbers." [89] However, these may include some peddlers, who are more nearly retailers than wholesalers; and this must be true of the 19,941 jobbers reported to NPN in 1957 by "96 important companies," including all the familiar majors.[90]

85. *ESPA* (March, 1957), p. 7.
86. P. 449.
87. "The American Oil Industry."
88. See, e.g., U. S. Senate, Committee on the Judiciary, Subcommittee on Antitrust and Monopoly, "To Amend Section 2 of the Clayton Act," *Hearings,* pursuant to S. Res. 170, 84th Congress, 2d Session (June–July, 1956), pp. 400, 495.
89. *EPSA* (March, 1957), p. 7.
90. *Factbook* (mid-May, 1957), p. 165.

There is no accurate indication of the relative numbers of the job-bers and distributors included within our estimated 10,000, except that it is clear the private-brand jobbers of gasoline are far fewer than those who fly their suppliers' colors. The *National Petroleum News* survey indicated that 22 per cent of its jobber subscribers (this means jobbers and distributors together, and perhaps some peddlers as well) handled a private brand of gasoline.[91]

The facts are hopelessly inadequate on the number of service sta-tions controlled by independent wholesalers—jobbers and distributors. The average jobber (this included branded distributors) surveyed by the *Petroleum Marketer* in 1956 operated 3.63 service stations, most of which were probably owned or controlled by long-term lease.[92] The NPN jobber survey, which, similarly, includes those handling both private and major branded products, showed an average of 3.2 stations owned. Apparently this was an average not of all the jobbers surveyed but of the 81 per cent who responded that they did own or operate stations.[93] The information provided by the latter survey is too skimpy and poorly presented to permit any decisive conclusion on the per-centage of wholesalers who own or control service stations. As in-dicated, 81 per cent replied that they own or operate stations. In another tabulation 93 per cent (which must be of the 81 per cent— that is, 75 per cent of the entire sample of wholesalers responding— since the two figures would otherwise be incompatible) were shown as owning one or more stations. On the other hand, the 1953 NPN survey states that 84.5 per cent of the jobbers reported they owned, leased, or supplied gasoline to retail gasoline outlets; and of that group only 14 per cent (this would be about 12 per cent of all jobbers sur-veyed) owned stations (they averaged almost 27 stations each!) and an additional 18 per cent (that is, 15 per cent of surveyed jobbers) leased them.[94]

4. *Commission agents.* The 1954 Census, cited above, listed 15,244 commission stations (bulk plants) selling oil products. The commis-sion agent typically conducts a smaller operation than the distributor or jobber. According to the Census figures, the average volume of sales of even the "independent" bulk plants—that is, of independent wholesalers with only a single plant—were double those of commis-sion stations: $364,000 and $180,000 respectively. The API's ex-

91. *Ibid.,* p. 154.
92. *ESPA* (March, 1957), p. 7.
93. *Factbook* (mid-May 1957), p. 156.
94. "Where the Jobber Sells His Products," *National Petroleum News* (August 19, 1953), p. 46.

tensive survey of consignees showed a median investment of $13,250, about half of it in trucks, and median gallonage of 836,000 a year; the NPN survey of 2,000 (probably larger than average) jobbers showed an *average* investment in fixed assets of $140,300 (the average investment even of its group of "small" jobbers was $53,700) and median gallonage of 2,152,000.[95]

5. *Peddlers* or *"tank-truck dealers"* operate no storage facilities, but own tank trucks. They play a minor role as wholesalers of gasoline to service stations, but are numerous—11,127 reported to the Bureau of Old Age and Survivors Insurance in 1949 [96]—in the retailing of fuel oil.

6. *Service stations.*[97] According to McLean and Haigh, refining companies in 1950 controlled by ownership or lease 51.6 per cent of the country's service stations, accounting for 58 per cent of industry service station sales, and operated less than 2 per cent of the national total.[98] The latter figure, at least, remains correct for 1957 [99] and the former is still probably roughly so. Another 8,000 stations at a maximum (most or all included in the 51.6, but not in the 2 per cent) are operated by commission agents.[100] Combining these various estimates produces the following rough breakdown of service stations: 3,000 refiner owned and operated, 8,000 commission stations, likewise re-

95. "Meet Today's Consignee," *ibid.* (August, 1957), pp. 111, 114; *ibid., Factbook* (mid-May, 1957), p. 158.

96. Fleming, "The American Oil Industry," p. 7. This is his figure for "fuel oil dealers," over and above those operating bulk plants. On the limitations of later OASI data, see above, p. 12, n. 2. Only firms employing one or more persons must report to BOASI, so there are probably many more than 11,000 peddlers.

97. See above, p. 14, n. 8, for reference to the Census figure and to the 412,000 total retail outlets reported to NPN by ninety-six petroleum refiners and marketers (a group that includes all the majors). To be classified as a service station by the Census, the retail establishment's major source of income must be the sale of gasoline and lubricants.

98. The six majors that supplied the relevant information sold 3.7, 0.1, 0.4, 1.0, and (Standard of Ohio) 31.3 per cent of their total service station sales of gasoline through company-operated stations in 1951 (pp. 46–47, 489).

99. Ninety-four companies, including all the majors, reported to the *National Petroleum News* salaried operation of only 2,933 stations. *Factbook* (mid-May, 1957), p. 165. Of the 2,139 stations reported by the twenty-two majors (including, among the borderline companies, Richfield, Ashland, Skelly, and Ohio Oil) Standard of California's Western operations alone accounted for 1,046, and Standard of Ohio for 350.

100. "Behind the Move to Commission Stations," *National Petroleum News* (July, 1956), p. 93.

finer controlled, 83,000 (51.6 per cent of 181,747, less the foregoing 11,000) refiner-controlled and dealer operated, and the rest, 88,000, dealer or wholesaler-controlled. How many of the last group were controlled by dealers and how many by distributors it is impossible to say with any precision. One indication of the possible order of magnitude is gained by applying the results of the above-cited jobber surveys: 81 per cent of the wholesalers responding owned stations, an average of 3.2 each; all distributors operated an average of 3.63 stations each. These factors suggest industry totals of roughly 25,000 wholesaler-owned and 35,000 wholesaler operated (or controlled) stations.

Simon Whitney [101] presents figures that diverge slightly from those arrived at here—he estimates 75–80,000 stations dealer-controlled, and 90,000 controlled by "suppliers" and leased to dealers. The discrepancy may be attributable to his including, among the 90,000, stations controlled by not only refiners but independent wholesalers, who also lease stations to some if not most of the dealers they supply. Whitney also breaks down the first figure between an estimated 60,000 dealer-owned stations, and 15–20,000 leased from third parties.

101. *Antitrust Policies: American Experience in Twenty Industries* (New York, Twentieth Century Fund, 1958), *1*, 126.

CHAPTER 17

The Impact of Size and Integration on Product Prices: I

THE PHENOMENON of vertical integration may properly be conceived in two almost diametrically opposing ways. On the one hand,
it may be regarded as the reflection of an essentially conservative,
anticompetitive strategy; its goal is security and its tactic is staking
out and insulating market position against the competitive uncertainties of open intermediate markets. On the other, it may be accepted
as an essentially competitive undertaking—to do more effectively
what the market seems to accomplish inadequately. The economist
who relies on static models of the theory of the firm might respond
that there is no contradiction between these two views, but only a
confusion of monopoly power—which is the consequence of relative
size and fewness of sellers at any given horizontal stratum of an industry and which alone may be conducive to conservative policy and
high price—and vertical integration, which in itself conduces to
neither. And in part this answer is valid; there is nothing incongruous
or contradictory about even a monopolist attempting by vertical integration to cut his costs and increase the intensity of his selling
efforts. But integration in this industry has developed to permit (horizontally) dominant companies to protect their market position against
dynamic competitive erosion by making it less necessary to raise
price to increase supplies, or reduce price to attract customers. In
the process, they have acquired a capacity to reduce sales prices that
goes beyond that of the nonintegrated firm, which acquires its supplies not at cost but at market price. The baffling question is, what
is the net outcome, on balance, of these potentially contradictory purposes—reduction in costs or entrenchment of market position?

The net effect of integration on price depends on how strongly it
has entrenched market position as measured at a given industry level.
The weaker this effect, the more likely it will be that the possible
benefits derived from obtaining supplies at lower cost will be shared
with consumers. The present chapter analyzes the tendencies inherent
in spreading integration to render market competition less intense,
and hence to increase the likelihood of higher prices through leader-

ship among a few dominant sellers. The following chapter assesses the counteracting competitive forces in the determination of product prices, both those inherent in and those external to integration.

INTEGRATION AS AN EFFORT TO SECURE HIGH AND STABLE PRICES: BEFORE PRORATIONING

There is no single key to price control of petroleum products but control over the supply of crude oil is crucial. Because it proved impossible to achieve such mastery without the help of government, effective prorationing marks a new era in the history of petroleum pricing, and it is the characteristics of the new era, now a quarter-century old, that are most pertinent. The thrust of integration itself, however, its motivation and influence, are more clearly seen before the industry shared the powerful assistance of the state.[1]

John D. Rockefeller and his associates demonstrated that it was not essential to limit the flow of crude oil, in order to gain effective control over the industry. With a monopoly of refining in their grasp, they were able, by vertical integration [2] back to but not necessarily including the wellhead, largely to determine the conditions under which independently produced petroleum could find its way to market.[3] In general this sufficed; but it could not completely control the aggregate flow of crude oil, and therefore it could not fully determine the level or prevent fluctuations in product prices. Even so, the monopolist who controlled refining and transport could extract an extraordinary profit at this bottleneck between production and consumption, at the expense of the unorganized producers who were left to bear the costs of their collective profligacy. To the extent that Standard's strategic position enabled it to curb the flow of crude oil to market, it could raise the price that consumers paid as well.[4] The power to squeeze cus-

1. This account draws on relevant portions of preceding discussions as developed in Chaps. 5, 7, 13, and 14, respectively.

2. It will be remembered that a kind of quasi-integration sufficed at the outset. By bargaining with the railroads, the organized Rockefeller refiners were able to obtain advantages similar to those of integration itself: the transport of their own crude oil at prices much closer to costs than independent producers or refiners had to pay.

3. "By the end of the year [1877] the entire pipeline system of the Oil Regions was in Mr. Rockefeller's hands. He was the only oil gatherer. Practically not a barrel of oil could get to a railroad without his consent." Tarbell, *History of the Standard Oil Company, 1,* 195.

4. When the New Jersey Corporation became the central holding company in 1899, stockholders' equity was $196.7 millions. In the twelve succeeding

tomers, however, was severely limited by substitute products, by the relative ease of field refining, and, most important, by Standard's inability to stem the flow of crude.

When Standard's monolithic control was dissolved in 1911, the need to regulate production for stabilization of product markets became more urgent. The monopolist had been able to exert some influence on the aggregate flow of oil to refineries: that power was now gone. Greatly diminished, too, were the massive obstacles Standard had constructed against independent entry into refining and marketing. In consequence uncontrolled and widely fluctuating production had a greater tendency than before to depress and upset not merely product prices but the refining and distribution margins included in them. While aggregate net profits before tax of a broad sample of 3,144 industrial corporations amounted to 10.5 per cent of combined invested capital in the period 1919–28, the return for the fifty-two petroleum refining companies in the sample was only 8.7 per cent,[5] despite soaring demand for the products of the industry.[6]

Nonetheless, vertical integration promised some insulation of profits against the eroding influence of, first, threatened crude oil shortage and, later, uncontrolled flush production. For the refiners who were big enough to undertake the investment, the pipeline provided the only solid basis for market power until the advent of effective production control. Pre-emption of the benefits of this low-cost medium provided a cushion both in the purchase of crude oil and in the sale of products against the rivalry of refiners without equal access to equivalent transportation. The economics of pipeline operations and the

---

years stockholders received dividends averaging just about $40 millions a year, and ended with an equity of $660.5 millions. Of total earnings in the 1891–1911 period, 41.6 per cent were ascribed to transportation, 23.9 per cent to marketing, 20.2 per cent to refining, and only 13.3 per cent to production activities. As virtually the sole pipeline transporter and the predominant refiner and marketer, there is no room for doubt that a substantial portion of Standard's profits, no matter how ascribed on the books, came out of the pockets of producers, and that a not insignificant portion reflected a monopoly surcharge in the price charged for products; but it is quite impossible to differentiate the one from the other. Hidy and Hidy, *Pioneering in Big Business,* pp. 628–629, 633.

5. Ralph C. Epstein, *Industrial Profits in the United States* (New York, National Bureau of Economic Research, 1934), pp. 40, 280, 619.

6. In 1919 what the industry calls aggregate demand for petroleum and its products (domestic plus export use) amounted to 438 million barrels. It increased steadily, with only the slightest dip in 1921, to 1,015 million in 1928. *Petroleum Facts and Figures,* 9th ed., pp. 2–3.

necessity for assured high level throughput to realize their potential effectively barred the entry of independents and confined investment to those few who could provide such enduring guarantees, the majors themselves. Throughout the twenties and thirties this advantage was partially reflected in the high level of pipeline profits,[7] a suggestion of the differential transport economies gained by the integrated pipe-line owner and of the differential handicap of the nonintegrated ship-pers privileged to use these facilities. More importantly, the control of pipelines by the majors tended to confine their independent competitors to market territories close to producing areas.

But if consumers were overcharged or producers underpaid because of high pipeline charges, was vertical integration to blame or was it rather the inherent horizontal monopoly of this new transport medium? The short answer is that a pipeline system lacking financial connections with suppliers at one end and refinery customers at the other could not have obtained or retained such monopoly power. Only large refiners or aggregations of refiners could supply the guarantees of patronage necessary to justify the heavy investments; and being in a position to supply the guarantees, or alternatively to build the pipe-lines themselves,[8] they would never have permitted independent lines to enjoy monopoly profits at their expense.

Secondly, integration promised some protection against competition in unstable markets by providing controlled distributive channels through which the refiner could promote both the sale and the recognition of his own brand. If the dominant sellers in an industry cannot regulate the aggregate flow of raw material and product, it is at first

7. The FTC found that in the years 1922–24 (relatively depressed for the oil industry) seventy-seven producing companies earned as a group from 5.9 to 9.7 per cent on their investment after upward adjustment to eliminate the depressing effect of special depletion and depreciation allowances taken for tax purposes (in 1925 the earnings were 18.6 per cent); fifty-eight variously integrated refining companies earned from 5.8 to 11.1 per cent after similar adjustment; and the pipeline companies surveyed earned from 17.6 to 22 per cent (*Petroleum Industry*, 1928, pp. 271, 284, 290). Twelve major companies which, at the request of the TNEC, submitted segregated investments and returns by departments for each of the three years 1936–38, reported highest rates of return for transportation in thirty out of the thirty-six observations. The medians were 2.0 per cent in refining and manufacturing, 9.5 per cent in production, and 20.8 per cent in transportation. See *Hearings*, Pt. XVII-A, pp. 10040–10042, and above, pp. 361 ff.

8. If producers or refiners were barred by law from such alternatives, the natural monopoly of pipeline service would become immediately apparent. Only public regulation could avoid monopoly pricing.

blush difficult to see how they gain merely by channeling that uncontrolled flow into strong hands or safe channels. If the volume of supply is fixed, it would appear that price depends entirely on the character of demand. Actually, however, successful brand promotion can affect the average level at which a fixed supply sells. It can insulate and charge a higher price to that part of the market that is willing to pay more for the familiar product, and for the kinds of service that major refiners historically have pushed their retailers to provide along with it.[9] By the same token, it may increase, as well as render less elastic, the aggregate demand for product. Certainly the increasing availability of gasoline of reliable quality, dispensed conveniently and courteously in service stations all over the country, added to the mobility of the American motorist in the same way as the construction of improved roads.

Neither the pipeline nor the massive forward integration into marketing during the twenties and early thirties were adequate to prevent the disruptive influence of uncontrolled, flush production of crude oil. As Swensrud indicates, the consequence was to transfer the pressure of oversupply of the raw material forward into product markets. But vertical integration cushioned the impact on the integrated firm, provided a differential advantage (or lesser disadvantage) in comparison with the independent, and promised through price leadership and controlled, branded distribution in partially protected markets a greater price and profit stability than nonintegrated firms could hope for.

Two further practices followed by the large integrated firms supplement the tendency of integration to maintain higher and more stable product prices: product exchanges and individual and cooperative programs of purchasing products from independent refineries for disposal through integrated marketing channels. Swapping products at different refinery or terminal locations [10] has much the same private advantages and social consequences as exchanges of crude oil, and

9. Analogously, pipeline control permitted exploitation of consumer demand in those geographic markets that independent refiner-marketers could not reach except at a severe cost disadvantage, even when it could not control the aggregate production of crude oil and products.

10. See the lucid descriptions of various kinds of exchanges in Cassady, pp. 169–174. According to information elicited by TNEC questionnaires, the major oil companies in 1937 received gasoline on an exchange basis which totaled 7.3 per cent of national consumption. Cook, p. 35. Sun Oil, alone among the majors, reported no receipts of gasoline on an exchange basis in the three years, 1935–37, but it supplied a small quantity, mostly to Gulf, in 1936 and 1937. TNEC, *Hearings,* Pt. XIV-A, pp. 7737, 7806–7811.

therefore calls for little additional comment. When a refiner with product at one point in excess of what his regular distributors can sell and a deficit at another finds a trading partner with corresponding and offsetting imbalances, it is clearly a real economy to trade providing qualities are appropriate. Competition may also be said to be improved by the practice, for it permits one company's refinery or terminal at one location to supply product at lowest possible cost to a number of competing sellers. A market too small to support several primary sources of supply may in this way enjoy the protection of a number of competing marketers.

The benefits, however, assume the continued existence of vertical integration of a given and unchanging depth and intensity.[11] If, instead, the surpluses at each point were to be sold in an open, intermediate market, and the deficit refiner-marketers were forced to purchase their added supplies in such markets, the geographic imbalances of integrated refiners would create expanded competitive opportunities for nonintegrated marketers.[12] As it is, the preponderant proportion of exchanges is necessarily between the large, integrated companies, which are most likely to have widely dispersed surpluses and deficits to swap.[13] In brief, the exchange is an extension and completion of vertical and geographic integration. It levels out imbalances without recourse to the open market. By excluding supplies and demands from these markets, it reinforces administrative (that is, integrated) control over a larger proportion of total product supply than would otherwise be the case. Like the exchange of crudes, it accomplishes by administrative negotiation and barter what imperfect, thin intermediate markets might not do as efficiently; but in so doing it keeps those markets thinner, less efficient, and less influential than they would otherwise be. It permits a single source to supply products at minimum cost to sellers in a given area, but the sellers served are more highly selected than would be true in cash markets and there-

11. See, e.g., W. S. Farish and J. Howard Pew, *Review and Criticism on Behalf of Standard Oil Company (New Jersey) and Sun Oil Company of Monograph No. 39 with Rejoinder by Monograph Author*, TNEC, Monograph No. 39-A (Washington, D.C., 1941), p. 44.

12. For the contention that exchanges among majors are conducted with the purpose and effect of excluding independents and cementing a general regime of market collaboration and dominance by the majors themselves, see *U.S. v. Standard Oil of California et al.* (1956), par. 58, 70a(5) and 70b(13).

13. Again according to the TNEC, in 1937 over 96 per cent of the gasoline received by major oil companies on an exchange basis was from other majors. Cook, p. 35.

fore are more probably those who are likely to be responsible in their pricing policy, to emphasize service and brand name rather than price in seeking customers. By thus emphasizing more orderly channels of distribution, exchanges tend to keep final prices more stable and, on balance, higher than they would otherwise be.

The extent of the practice of purchasing part or all of the output of independent refiners is not clear; but it is known to occur sometimes on an intermittent, sometimes on a continuing basis under sales or processing agreements. Almost all majors engage in such transactions to some extent, but it is not certain whether they are typically overbalanced on the marketing or on the refining side, making them net purchasers or sellers of products.[14] It is clear, however, that none of the seven studied by McLean and Haigh was fully self-sufficient in supplying products for its marketing operations. Their purchases, primarily from small refiners, customarily ranged between 2 and 20 per cent of their needs.[15] It seems that ordinarily the majors are on balance purchasers in spot markets. Such a policy helps to ensure fuller

14. As McLean and Haigh point out, the latter characterization would depend on whether such refiners purchase more product from other refiners than they sell to other refiners and marketers. But since, of course, they end by selling all their product, purchased and refined together, to wholesale and/or retail resellers, they are by such a test necessarily sellers on balance (p. 426). Even if sales to wholesalers could be segregated from sales to retailers, it would be questionable whether branded distributors should be characterized for this purpose as outsiders. The appropriate measure would seem to be whether the majors as a group are on balance net buyers or sellers in dealings with other refiners and unbranded jobbers: this would be the truer test of their net impact on freely competitive intermediate markets. There is no such information on a systematic basis. However, see below, n. 15.

15. The range of percentages for each company ran roughly as follows in a prewar (1935–39) and a postwar (1946–52) period not always indicated separately: Gulf 3 to 7 and 11 to 19 (the only company to show a definitely higher ratio of purchases after the war), Texas 1 to 4 (throughout), Sinclair 5 to 15, Ohio Oil 4 to 18 and 2 to 16, Atlantic 2 to 6, Standard of Indiana 14 to 33 and 8 to 14, and Sohio 4 to 11. Separate data available for individual products suggest that percentage purchases of gasoline generally ran lower than other products in the last years (roughly 1949–52, inclusive) except in the case of Gulf. *Ibid.*, pp. 428, 432–435. The percentage of total product sales supplied by exchanges was roughly comparable to the proportion supplied by purchase, excepting Ohio Oil, for which exchanges accounted for no less than 27 to 42 per cent of product requirements in the postwar period (*ibid.*). It also appears from McLean and Haigh's data that three of these companies sell about as large a percentage to jobbers as they purchase from other refiners, and three others certainly sell less, i.e. they classify as net buyers of open market product (cf. *ibid.*, pp. 432–433 and 461). Major company sales of gasoline to

utilization of their own refining facilities, and it helps to stabilize spot markets against upsetting distress sales by improvident independents.[16]

Sporadic purchases by individual majors were inadequate for market stabilization in the chaotic supply conditions of the early 1930's. A more vigorous and systematic attack with provision for a more equitable sharing of the burden was needed. So in the 1929–36 period the major companies organized a number of pools, partly under the aegis of NRA, to buy up surplus "distress" gasoline, often refined by independents from crude oil produced in excess of prorationing allotments. Most prominent was the one in the Midcontinent and East Texas, which became the subject of the famous Madison (Wisconsin) antitrust suit, brought in 1936.[17] This pool was an extension of a device initiated under NRA.[18] Constituted in March, 1935, it allotted to its members specific quotas of gasoline that each was to purchase from its prescribed "dancing partner." In this pursuit of a firmer and more stable tank-car market, the majors absorbed about 50 per cent instead of a more usual 12 per cent of independents' gasoline produced in the area.[19] A parallel activity was being followed on the Pacific Coast. It, too, led to a criminal indictment, which the defendants did not contest.[20]

The so-called "distress gasoline" in the East Texas and Midcontinent fields had its source in the weakness of controls over crude oil production, which had not yet become firmly established, especially in Kansas, and were still evaded in Texas and Oklahoma. Excessive supplies so weakened spot refinery quotations that the established

---

unbranded jobbers is small in percentage terms as late as 1950–53; see below, p. 538.

16. See above, pp. 393 and 398, and the discussion in McLean and Haigh cited there; also Cook, p. 34.

17. See *U.S. v. Socony-Vacuum Oil Corporation,* 310 U.S. 150 (1940), the Supreme Court decision on which this discussion is largely based.

18. See Watkins, pp. 160–166.

19. See Rostow, *A National Policy for the Oil Industry,* p. 79.

20. *U.S. v. General Petroleum,* Cr. 14149-M, November 14, 1939. Collaboration through buying pools on the West Coast preceded this case at least ten years. A consent decree in 1930 terminated an earlier collective purchase plan for independently refined gasoline, including direct price-fixing as well. *U.S. v. Standard Oil Company et al.,* Final Decree in Equity No. 2542-K, U. S. District Court, Northern District of California, Southern Div., September 15, 1930. The later pool apparently omitted explicit provision for price-fixing. See Bain, *Pacific Coast Petroleum Industry,* 2, 251, 261–271; Cook, pp. 34–35; Watkins, chap. 13 *passim.*

posted price for crude oil was jeopardized [21] and excess supplies of gasoline sapped at the tank-wagon price in the Midwest.[22]

Maintaining the spot price of gasoline, therefore, had a double attraction for the majors: It would bolster the price of crude and support selling prices to independent marketers throughout the Midwest. Without limitations on aggregate supply, such purchase programs might well have served merely to elicit an expansion in the output of independent refineries.[23] But to the extent that excess supplies were localized and believed to be temporary and the majors could compensate extra purchases in one market by greater restrictions in others—by curtailing their own refinery runs or by pressing for reduced allowables in states with effective production controls—the hope for greater stabilization could well have justified the higher costs (including higher transportation costs) implicit in such a purchase program. By preventing a fall in the contract price to jobbers and funneling distress, unbranded gasoline through their own marketing facilities (if need be, over a much wider geographic area than normal) as though it were their own—there to be subject to the disciplines of price leadership and brand-conscious promotion—the majors hoped to insulate final prices against the possibilities of price warfare.

In sum, these institutional arrangements and strategies of the vertically integrated firm undoubtedly contributed greater stability (and probably greater height) to petroleum product prices in general and gasoline in particular during the turbulent supply conditions of the twenties and thirties than the explosive character of competition under the law of capture would have led one to expect. Furthermore, the majors achieved their successes in a manner consistently to strengthen their position against independent rivals: sometimes blatantly, as mirrored in continuing high profits of their pipeline subsidiaries, sometimes more subtly, as by helping to bolster the price of crude oil—largely a nominal price for them but a real one for the independent refiner—or by diverting the flow of cheap excess product supplies

21. The high posted price was apparently fictional for two reasons: first, legally produced oil was being offered at discounts; and second, hot oil was being dumped on the market, at even greater discount, for whatever it would bring.

22. The reader will recall that the prevailing distributor jobber contracts in the Midwest generally set the price of product at the *lower* of two quotations: 2 cents below the normal tank-wagon price, or the tank-car price (that is, at Tulsa) plus freight from Group 3 (above, p. 400). Tulsa was a center of "distress gasoline."

23. E.g. see Bain, *Pacific Coast Petroleum Industry, 2,* 273, 284–285.

from price-cutting jobbers. In this process, the pipeline, price leadership in crude markets exercised through the mechanism of the posted
price, and forward integration into marketing played leading roles.
Not only did the posted price of crude follow spot markets for products
with a lag; but it tended to follow them downward with considerable
less alacrity than upward.[24]

There is some evidence of a progressive squeeze of refinery margins
in the late 1920's and early 1930's. The evidence is difficult to assess
because it is not clear what was happening to refining costs in these
years.[25] But refinery margins declined so far after 1923 that compensation through corresponding cost reductions seems improbable; until
the middle thirties the profits of companies engaged principally in refining seem to have been generally lower than those of producers or
more fully integrated competitors. Swensrud—who may not have been
entirely unbiased, speaking as he did at the time as an executive of
Standard of Ohio—claimed that from the beginning of 1927 to the
end of 1938 refining had been able "to stand on its own feet, on the
basis of full posted crude oil prices, in only three out of the twelve
years involved, namely, 1928, 1935, and 1936 . . ."[26]

This squeeze, and the shift of competition into product markets,
reflected less the price-supporting than the price-reducing aspect of
vertical integration. In the press of burgeoning production, integrated
companies were clearly conducting their refining and marketing operations and pricing their products not with an eye to the posted price
of crude oil, but with regard instead to their far lower out-of-pocket

24. See, in addition to Swensrud, "The Relation between Crude Oil and
Product Prices," FTC, *Petroleum Industry* (1928), p. 135 and chart facing
p. 170.

25. One element of the "refiner's margin," the cost of transporting crude
from wellhead to refinery, was undoubtedly declining throughout this period
for the integrated companies who were availing themselves increasingly of the
pipeline. Whether it was declining for the nonintegrated refiner is by no means
clear. As for the costs of refining proper, Swensrud expressed the opinion that
they had "doubtless increased," with the widespread introduction of cracking
("The Relation between Crude Oil and Product Prices," pp. 769–770). Cracking, of course, increased the yield and quality of gasoline, but these benefits
would be reflected in the refinery realizations on the basis of which the margins
are computed. McLean and Haigh state that the downward trend in the refining margin during the 1920's was "partially offset by the commercial development of the pipe still . . ." (p. 137).

26. Swensrud, pp. 770–771; see also pp. 777–778 for an explanation of the
development; also FTC, *Petroleum Industry* (1928), p. 175, and on the low
profits in refining, pp. 293–294, 301, and McLean and Haigh, pp. 140–141.

production costs. Competition and uncontrolled production were forcing them to pass on some of the profits normally "locked in" by the
posted wellhead price:

> The wide range which exists in the cost of producing crude pe-
> troleum enables refiners having low cost crude to offer gasoline
> at prices much below the market in times of overproduction or
> dull trade. . . . This situation is recognized by the larger refiners.
> For example, R. W. Stewart, chairman of the board of the Stand-
> ard Oil Company (Indiana) at a conference held February 23,
> 1927, made the following statement: "Before the crude cut to-day
> (February 23), no refinery, in our opinion, could make gasoline
> to sell for less than 10 cents per gallon, if they paid the posted
> price for crude, yet the price is actually 7¾ cents per gallon at
> Group 3 refineries." Colonel Stewart explained that the reason
> certain mid-continent refiners could sell at these prices was be-
> cause they had their own crude production.[27]

The fact remains that integration contributed to the *relative* sluggishness of crude oil prices on the down side and therefore to a relatively
higher floor under the prices of independent refiners.

Forward integration, likewise, strengthened the price leadership
of the majors during this period, but it is a very difficult influence to
weigh. As the 1920's progressed, the price leaders found their market
shares shrinking, their prices frequently undercut, and their policy
influence over the wholesale price tenuous. Nonetheless, the Federal
Trade Commission, after admitting that the industry had become generally competitive by 1928, stressed the sporadic character of price
competition: "While there is keen competition for volume of business
between the various independent marketers and the Standard Oil companies in the several territories, price competition is generally only
sporadic, local, or temporary." [28] Tank-wagon prices were generally
more sluggish than spot market prices.[29] As Bain concluded, from his
study of West Coast product markets in the 1930's:

27. FTC, *Petroleum Industry* (1928), p. 212.
28. FTC, *Petroleum Industry* (1928), p. xx; also pp. 214–255. Burns too
emphasizes the increasingly barometric character of price leadership, but nonetheless concludes that forms of competition other than price were the "more
important." *Decline of Competition*, p. 108; see also pp. 93–109, *passim*.
29. See, e.g., FTC, *Petroleum Industry* (1928), chart facing p. 156; and
McLean and Haigh, pp. 153–154, whose chart shows that changes in Group 3
tank-car prices tended to be more prompt and more extreme than in tank-
wagon prices.

Price leadership was evidently continued as a means of averting the normal instability . . . associated with a fully competitive market. . . . Given the degree of market concentration which had developed, some convention for restricting price competition was practically inevitable; the pertinent fact is that price leadership by Standard was recognized in fact and was followed consistently, with only minor defections, by other majors.[30]

Despite the efforts of the majors through vertical integration to stabilize product prices at high levels, they clearly fell far short of that objective, however much they may have improved markets from their viewpoint. Even before the Great Depression, the frequency and breadth of price changes at all levels of the industry are impressive evidence of the dominant influence of essentially uncontrolled market forces.[31] The tank-wagon price, a key price for integrated companies, fluctuated in close correspondence with the price of crude oil; and though both lagged, under the drag of price leadership, behind spot markets, both clearly responded to shifting competitive levels. When Prairie Oil and Gas in 1923 tried to stem the flood of crude oil by maintaining its own posted price, Standard of Indiana, whose tank-wagon prices were based on the Prairie price, soon found itself out of line—so far out of line that in August of that year its gasoline price broke 8.6 cents a gallon. Cheap crude oil had found its way to independent refiners, and cheap products produced therefrom and sold by price-cutting jobbers had left Standard high and dry.[32] It was in belated recognition of its incapacity to administer prices at the tank-wagon level in disregard of the prices at which crude and products were available to and from Midcontinent refiners that led Standard ten years later (and probably ten years too late) to anchor its prices throughout the Midwest on Tulsa quotations.

30. *Pacific Coast Petroleum Industry, 2,* p. 291. Bain also discusses at length the other measures pursued to hold in check the competition of price-cutting independents.

31. The FTC abundantly documents this conclusion in a detailed record of crude and tank-wagon prices at various centers. See *Petroleum Industry* (1928), pp. 168–175.

32. *Ibid.,* pp. 172–173; and Ise, *United States Oil Policy,* p. 252. This "distress gasoline" episode resembles that which led to the gasoline-buying program of 1934–36. It was not the force of commercial competition alone that broke down Standard's artificial price. The States of South Dakota and Nebraska actually went into the gasoline business, purchasing it in the tank-car market and selling it in their own service stations; Standard's first price cut, of 8.6 cents, was made in South Dakota.

In the period preceding prorationing, the objectives of vertical integration were only partially achieved: without control of crude oil production, it was impossible to steady the market for petroleum products. Even the cooperative buying programs had only limited success, at best.[33] Despite the leverage which ownership of pipelines placed in their hands, the majors could not stem the flow of cheap crude to independent refiners and the product supplies which they released to independent wholesalers at low prices.[34] Refinery and marketing margins narrowed under the impact and integrated companies were forced by competition to set their tank-wagon prices closer to delivered costs than to traditional posted prices of crude.[35] In their size and integration were opportunities—through purchase programs in distress areas and deeper cutbacks of their own production where circumstances permitted, and through a simple averaging of company performance over diverse market situations—to protect themselves against the severest vicissitudes of competition. But integration alone could not stabilize markets and in the worst years it could not prevent losses, either the nominal accounting variety based on internal transfer prices like the posted price or a real disappearance of profits from a competitive constriction of aggregate realizations.

33. Bain found buying pools on the West Coast useful in stabilizing product markets and raising refinery margins to the extent that crude control authorities failed to restrict supply effectively. However, success was marked only after crude production controls were established. *Pacific Coast Petroleum Industry*, 2, 180–182, 190, 207, 269–270, 293, 296–298. Differences of opinion regarding the effectiveness of buying pools usually turn on the possibilities of bolstering prices without controlling total supply. Compare Watkins, pp. 163–168, with Rostow, *A National Policy for the Oil Industry*, p. 80, and *U.S. v. Socony-Vacuum Oil Company*, 310 U.S. 150 (1940), pp. 219–220.

34. See the essays by Pogue and Swensrud in DeGolyer, *Elements of the Petroleum Industry*, pp. 384, 487–488. "Most of the Standard companies have reported to the commission that they will sell gasoline in tank car to anyone desiring to purchase; moreover, these sales are not limited to their respective tank-wagon marketing territories. . . . Independent wholesalers and brokers interviewed during the course of the inquiry were quite unanimous in stating that they had no difficulty in securing an adequate supply of gasoline." FTC, *Petroleum Industry* (1928), pp. 263–264.

35. "If the wholesale price of a finished product is so adjusted as to conform with changes in the cost of production of its primary raw material, instead of with changes in an arbitrarily maintained market price of the raw material which in no way affects approximately half the supply thereof entering the manufacturing process, economic laws have not been upset and there is no occasion for wonder." Watkins, p. 168.

INTEGRATION AS AN EFFORT TO SECURE HIGH AND STABLE PRICES: AFTER PRORATIONING

Effective prorationing after 1935 successfully throttled the violent eruptions of crude oil supply that the law of capture had engendered and vertical integration had been unable to tame. But it did more than that. By subjecting supply to policy controls, it opened up for the majors a positive, active role in price planning that they could never have achieved in former years. Their market power remained far more direct and complete in foreign areas, where monopolistic concessions, field-wide, gave the largest of them the power to regulate output in conformity with their own judgment of what constituted effective demand, subject only to indirect political pressures rather than economic compulsions. At home the situation was essentially reversed; it was the power of the state that was committed to the adaptation of aggregate supply to market demand, and private parties could exert a market influence mainly by persuading state authorities regarding the proper level of adjustment.

In this situation, nonetheless, the large integrated firm has gained new stature within the domestic market. As a refiner with modern facilities, it need no longer be harassed by a multitude of small cheap plants fed by cheap crude, legally or illegally produced. In the elimination of the small and largely primitive field refineries production controls were early abetted by catalytic processing and high octane standards of gasoline, which were eventually to make such plants obsolete. With cheap crude oil and products thus cut off, pipeline connections took on new significance in paring down the ranks of effective competitors among refiners in important markets. The integrated firm could better use its branded distribution to stabilize its operations at all levels of the industry; and, supported by the production controls imposed by prorationing, it could give range to its interests in a higher price of crude oil even at a comparatively modest ratio of owned to required supplies.[36] This does not mean that major buyers have always

36. The suggestion that vertical integration, as opposed to horizontal integration, could increase the price level of crude oil will raise hackles. On a strictly theoretical plane and assuming that all world oil producers were locked in an effective (horizontal) cartel to achieve profit-maximizing price levels, it is true by assumption that the monopoly prices set would owe nothing to vertical integration. Does it therefore follow that it is horizontal integration that is the sole source of price-raising forces and that vertical integration can have no part in such monopolizing behavior? We think not.

In the United States, where state prorationing controls under the leadership

pressed for higher prices—witness the Esso Standard attempt to hold the price line in 1947, and the refusal of most to follow Phillips in 1948. Pricing policy is never governed by strictly economic considerations, much less by profit-maximizing in the short run, and moderation is undoubtedly urged and practiced in deference to public opinion and the long-run interests of the firm and the industry. What it does mean is that it is difficult to believe major companies would so readily have increased prices in the market conditions of 1953 and 1957, to have their decisions then in effect supported by the production cutbacks which they were prominent in urging on the state of Texas, had they not very heavy interests in production themselves at home and abroad.[37]

The stabilization of crude oil markets under the aegis of the state has likewise stabilized refinery margins, but it has by no means eliminated their far greater sensitivity to fluctuating market conditions. Many products are sold in open, nonintegrated market channels for

---

of Texas give a semblance of such a cartelization of oil production, the objective is not a profit-maximizing level of crude oil price. Even if the authorities were more positively oriented toward such a goal, their constituency (i.e. the producer-owners) have far too diverse and conflicting interests (see above, pp. 128–129) in volume as well as price to permit administration on this basis. In short, the assumption of a profit-maximizing horizontal combination of producers is a gross oversimplification. In this situation vertical integration of large firms with a high self-sufficiency in owned production has sapped the normal buyers' interest in low price of their raw material and strengthened the pressure they bring to bear on regulatory authorities toward actions more likely to jog the production-price compromise in the direction of higher price. The *power* to raise the price still lodges in horizontal control; but its perpetuation and the manner of its exercise are importantly influenced by vertical integration.

37. It will be recalled that there are at least four important considerations that incline large vertically integrated companies toward higher crude oil prices, even though they produce at home only about one-half their domestic needs (see Table XII). (1) There are the provisions of our tax laws that make a dollar of earnings from the production of crude oil, *at home or abroad,* more valuable than a dollar earned from the sale of products. (2) World crude oil prices are geared to the American level, and price policies must therefore take into account self-sufficiency ratios worldwide. (3) Production is the stratum of the industry most effectively concentrated in global terms, and controlled under the auspices of the state in this country. Only domestic pipeline transportation was equally susceptible to concentrated control; but its advantages have been undermined by the expansion of water transportation, by Interstate Commerce Commission regulation, and competition among major, pipeline-operating refiner-marketers. (4) Production is the stratum that *must* be controlled if final product prices are to be stabilized above costs.

whatever they will bring. Business recession may sharply reduce demand for residual fuel oils, which are sold in direct price competition with coal and natural gas: between 1948 and 1949, for example, the average Gulf Coast price of Bunker "C" oil in cargoes dropped from $2.87 to $1.56 a barrel.[38] A warm winter, bringing a drop in demand for home-heating oils, will not, thanks to distributor affiliation with majors, cause a comparable dip in prices; but it will probably make more charging stock available for cracking, and the result may be bargain offers of gasoline on the Gulf Coast or at inland refineries and price wars in the Northeast and Midwest. It is unnecessary to elaborate the possible reasons for product price fluctuations; all reflect an articulation of supply with demand far less precise than in crude oil markets, and the result is that refinery realizations are subject to continuous variation, and periodic drastic compression.

It is an interesting phenomenon that this fate of the refining margin has aroused relatively little attack within the industry on the system of determining crude oil prices, particularly during recessions, when the inequities are most apparent. Even the partially self-sufficient refiner seems convinced that nothing is to be gained from a more nearly competitive behavior of the crude oil prices, presumably in the belief that final product demand is inelastic and that product prices would quickly follow crude oil prices downward. In short, having achieved the touchstone of crude oil production control, the leading firms and practically the industry as a whole behave like self-conscious oligopolists. This attitude is dramatically illustrated by the exhortations in the Chase Manhattan Bank's *Monthly Review of the Petroleum Situation* for January, 1958, a month of sagging product prices and cruelly compressed refinery margins:

> The deterioration of refined product prices is exerting ever greater pressure upon the crude oil price structure. And speculation is rife in industry circles concerning the possibility of a general reduction. It is quite evident that the current status of the refiner is untenable; he must have relief of some sort. *But we should weigh most carefully the prospects for lasting benefits to the refiner* in the event of a general crude oil price cut. And, in so doing, we can hardly escape the conclusion that relief to the refiner would be transitory. *For the industry's problems stem from physical supply rather than price.* If demand could be stimulated by reducing price, oversupply could be worked off. But such is

38. *Petroleum Facts and Figures,* 9th ed., p. 375.

not the case. Price cuts will not increase petroleum demand. *So reducing the volume of new supply is the sole means of liquidating the excessive inventories* which have been responsible for the deterioration of the refiner's product prices.

If there should be a general crude oil price cut while new supply and refinery rates continue excessive, it seems quite likely that erosion of refined product prices would not be halted. *And in a short time the refiner would again be no better off than he is today.*

The Bank's remedy: *"Clearly, the time is now at hand for a drastic cutback in the rate of new supply and refinery operations."* [39]

Thus the major oil companies typically urge on the State of Texas heavier cutbacks of production than the independent producers are willing to accept.[40] Even in the absence of vertical integration, of course, the larger and wealthier producers would be more likely to counsel curtailment than the smaller, since the two groups weigh differently the benefits of maintaining price at the expense of longer-delayed recovery of investment; but in that case the larger buyers might try to drive a wedge between the producers counseling sharp production cutbacks and those under stronger financial pressure to take their oil out of the ground rapidly.

When the demands of independent producers for larger allowables have prevented sufficient production cutbacks to stabilize product markets, the majors have also instituted on their own account and urged upon the industry generally a curtailment of refinery runs. To the extent that the latter stratagem is successful: (a) crude oil stocks tend to mount—a fact that will not escape the attention of state authorities in fixing allowables for the next month; and (b) the purchase nominations of the big purchasers submitted at the monthly meeting of the Texas Railroad Commission are correspondingly reduced. The declaration by the president of the Standard Oil Company (New Jersey) in February, 1958, when product prices continued to slump while the price of crude oil remained virtually rigid, is characteristic:

> "What we need right now," Mr. Rathbone stated, "is less refinery runs and consequently less product and the ability to work off burdensome stocks."

39. Released February 20, 1958.

40. See above, pp. 226–227. When independent producers took the lead in urging heavy cutbacks in the spring of 1958, in hope of relieving the mounting pressure on the crude price, the unusual character of their position was the occasion for comment. See below, n. 42, and p. 558.

Mr. Rathbone asserted that a general cut in the price of crude oil would not accomplish anything at this time.[41]

Simultaneously, Humble Oil and Refining was most prominently asking Texas to cut back allowables farther than the Commission seemed disposed to go.[42]

The significant question in the present context is whether this strategy of response to excess productive capacity is attributable to vertical integration. Certainly, cutting back refinery output in response to declining demand, even though prices remain above marginal costs, would be futile for a refiner who accounted for only a negligible share of the market: his reward would be lowered income. But if the refining branch were organized as it is, horizontally, would it not still behave in this fashion, whether or not it were vertically linked to production on the one hand and marketing on the other? The answer is —largely, but not entirely, yes.

In some degree, the financial link between production and marketing heightens and protects the crude oil price and therefore adds to the periodic squeeze on refinery margins. Capacity-expanding investments in refining are made by the majors with far less regard to the profitability of refining per se than is imperative for the nonintegrated refiner; and, for the same reason, their pricing of refined products without out-of-pocket loss is not confined by the variable costs of the refining process alone. The consequence clearly is to make independent entry in refining less attractive than it would otherwise be. To this extent, integration enhances the concentration in refining that is the prerequisite to a strategy of varying refinery runs in the interest of market stabilization. But it does so, it will be noted, by keeping refinery margins relatively *low*, as well as subject to periodic squeezes.

Similarly, forward integration between refining and marketing probably exerts some, though hardly a decisive, influence in favor of the strategy of varying output in the interest of price stabilization. To the extent that distributors are bound to a single supplier by ties of brand loyalty, or lessee relationships, they must be less price conscious, less able to shop around in buyers' markets, less capable of

41. *Wall Street Journal* (February 13, 1958), p. 5.
42. "Texas Oil Allowable for February Raised despite Protest by Big Buyer," *ibid.* (January 17, 1958), p. 7. Texas' unprecedented order slashing prorated output to nine days for March was one of the very few not accompanied by demands for even sharper cutbacks by major purchasers: "It was almost without precedent for several dozen independent producers to appear in Austin to ask the Railroad Commission to reduce production" (*ibid.*, February 21, 1958, p. 6).

bargaining with suppliers for price concessions. Correspondingly, demand created for a refiners' differentiated product through tied distribution channels is demand for his particular services, not a mere portion of national demand; and it enables him to pursue a price *policy,* rather than sell in the market for whatever his product will bring, and a corresponding production *policy,* rather than merely produce as long as price exceeds incremental costs.

Forward integration therefore plays some part in making price leadership effective—more effective, at any rate, than it would otherwise be. It is in sales to branded distributors and lessee dealers that the openly published tank-wagon price plays a major role; it is in company-controlled service stations, particularly, that retail price policy —whether effectuated by consignment selling, or "suggested prices"— is most effective.

Leading marketers seem to be guided by some conception of an "optimum" or "reasonable" rate of return that they feel investment ought to obtain over the long run. Whether as evidence of motive or of rationalization, Socony-Vacuum officials voiced such considerations when they said, "Socony's gasoline prices before this change (the increase of 1953) were at the same general level as they were in July, 1950. During this period of almost three years, gasoline quality has increased and large sums of money have been spent to accomplish this improvement. Wages, building, and other costs in distribution and marketing have also risen substantially." [43] And again, some four years earlier: "With fuel-oil storage filled to abnormally high levels for wintertime and fuel-oil prices softening and gasoline demand firm, we had to realize more for gasoline to help cover the undiminished cost of a barrel of products." [44] While administration is not always on the side of higher prices (remember Esso Standard in 1947), more often, as in April, 1949, April, 1950, and August, 1954, refinery prices of gasoline will be raised to maintain a "reasonable margin" even in the face of crude oil cutbacks.

The concern of the integrated refiner to shun price wars and to insulate his operations as far as possible from the competition of disorderly independents who have no good alternative to price cut-

43. Socony-Vacuum statement, as quoted by the *National Petroleum News* (July 17, 1953), p. 53.
44. "Price Increases in Petroleum Products," *Hearings* before Subcommittee of the Committee on Banking and Currency, U. S. Senate, 81st Congress, 1st Session (1949), p. 91. See also "What About Gasoline Prices?" *Lamp,* June, 1949.

ting hardly requires explanation. The customer loyalty built into a national brand through heavy expenditures in nationwide organizations of wholesale and retail marketers is a handicap that an independent nonintegrated refiner or marketer can hardly overcome even where his product quality is comparable, which it often is not. The sale of undifferentiated products through unidentified outlets means almost certainly lower prices and margins.[45] And when the independent refiner is confronted with a drastic decline in revenue from some of his products, his struggles to preserve a reasonable margin may undermine the entire regional price structure. Thus in 1949 the Midwestern price of gasoline fell substantially below the East Coast level because Midwest independents were making desperate efforts to compensate for a drop in residual and distillate oil prices. They re-ran these oils as charging stock in their cracking plants and actually bought up residual fuel, which was selling further than usual below the price of crude, for the same purpose.

There is no objectively valid answer to the enigmatic problem of evaluating branded (usually integrated) refiner distribution at higher as opposed to unbranded distribution at lower prices. But it must be re-emphasized that just as unrestricted price competition in this industry cannot be halted on the downward side at tolerable cost levels, in the face of excess capacity, so there is also no automatic, socially acceptable upper limit to the costs of competition in marketing expenditures. Snatching jobbers or dealers from competitors, making adjustments in rentals of stations or equipment, lending money, investing in strategic locations in order to prevent a rival from doing so,[46] may have widely varying effects. Through improving service and assurance of product quality, it may be equivalent to a real price reduction. Through increasing volume and improving the scheduling of deliveries, it may reduce costs and thus make possible explicit price reductions. By adding to marketing costs in order to achieve not so much efficiency as protection against price competition, it may necessitate a higher price to the consumer. By so diverting the course of

45. Actually, the private brand jobber may enjoy highly satisfactory margins, because his competitive handicap as a seller may (indeed will ordinarily have to be) reflected in corresponding concessions in his purchase price. But this is not an alternative available to the refiner, unless of course he successfully builds his own integrated marketing structure. See, e.g., "How Small Refiner Built a Retail Empire," *National Petroleum News* (October 20, 1954), pp. 26–34. Also below, pp. 523–525.

46. See the striking illustration of this practice in Stambaugh, "Below Cost Selling of Petroleum Products" (1951), pp. 14–15.

competition from price to non-price channels, it may make these higher prices possible. While some refiners have gone into wholesaling in the hope of cutting costs, there can be little doubt that most of them look upon their marketing facilities as a way of protecting and enhancing margins.[47]

The more widely integrated marketing is regarded and pursued as an essential defense of refinery investment, the less effective becomes any competitive check on wasteful practices in that area where only the test of competition can hope to differentiate wasteful and productive expenditure.

To the individual integrated company, even to the price leader, these observations will seem fantastically to exaggerate the range of its discretionary influence over price. Each feels above all else closely constricted in its decisions by the competition of its rivals, and sees only that what the market will take is determined not by it but by industry-wide supply which it is powerless to control. But here is an industry where, particularly for the integrated company, out-of-pocket costs directly assignable to an individual product are a tiny fraction of total costs, and where there has been fairly persistent excess capacity since around 1948.[48] How can it be that product prices nonetheless have been continuously above the incremental costs of additional output? Oil men correctly emphasize the potentially explosive or destructively competitive character of product markets; why then do not product markets explode all the time, driving prices down to marginal costs in periods of excess capacity for as long as is necessary to drive out the excess, then rising sharply as rising demand reaches the limits of capacity? It is surely not because the cost structure in oil is especially propitious to automatic adjustment of supply, or because demand is stable, or responsive to price changes. It is rather because supply is subject to discretionary determination. In this determination by far the most important influence is the control over production of crude oil, governmental and private.

Still, business size and integration have also played a role, though a less important one, in price maintenance and stabilization. Where large integrated firms have dominated product markets, prices have been sustained. This does not mean that competition *between* the

47. See above, pp. 363 ff. Also note the instructive case of Richfield Oil, above, p. 368, n. 48.

48. Consider, e.g., what must be the bare cost of supplying an additional barrel of gasoline in the United States from refiner-produced Middle Eastern crude oil, carried in refiner-owned tankers.

majors never breaks the price level. It often does, as will be shown. But in most cases when it does, it is because the disturber of the peace is incompletely integrated in marketing in the particular area of disturbance, and is therefore forced to use price as a means of inducing independent marketers or customers to take its products. Or it is in a market, like sales of gasoline or heating oils to large commercial or industrial accounts, where product differentiation and elaborate marketing expenditures to create it are of less avail. Where integration is incomplete, price becomes a more important factor in competition. Where independent jobbers, who must be price-conscious, can find large supplies of major or independently produced surplus gasoline, which as surplus is likely to sell on the basis of price alone, the entire price structure may be undermined. When this occurs, it occurs because of the incompleteness of integration.

CHAPTER 18

The Impact of Size and Integration on Product Prices: II

DYNAMIC CHANGE, an outstanding characteristic of the petroleum industry, is always a stimulus to competition, and a force tending to keep prices low and flexible. These changes have been translated into competitive results in part through integration itself, even more prominently through the incompleteness or imbalance of vertical integration as firms grow in size, under the influence of the competition of independents and the pressures of government.

COUNTERACTING FORCES: LOWER COSTS

Suppose that, in the absence of vertical integration, crude oil prices were monopolistically governed by state production controls, import limitations, and the concentration of foreign oil concessions in the hands of a few private firms; that pipeline transport were naturally monopolistic; and that there prevailed enough collusion among jobbers and retailers to maintain noncompetitive margins. The assumptions are not entirely unrealistic. In these circumstances, a single, vertically integrated firm *could* charge substantially lower final prices than could its nonintegrated rivals. Whether it *would* do so would depend on how responsive to the lower price it considered its demand to be. The more integrated companies there are, and the greater the rivalry among them, the more elastic each would consider its own demand to be and the more likely it would be to reduce or to be forced to reduce its price in correspondence with its lower costs.

There is abundant evidence of this particular consequence of competition between integrated oil companies, both before and after the institution of prorationing. The fact is that the majors have not been able historically to lock up all their profits in production and pipeline transport. As more and more of them obtained access to these profits or lower laid-down costs after 1911, one adventurer or another was sorely tempted to give some of them away in the hope of expanding his market.[1]

1. A recent example will suffice at this point. Work was begun in 1958 on

This price competition has not, as a general rule, taken the form of changes in interdepartmental billing prices, or overt reductions in the posted prices charged nonintegrated operators in intermediate markets. It has taken the form rather of accepting constricted margins, temporarily or over long periods of time, in refining, and of low nominal profit rates in marketing—a reflection in large measure of high and ever-improving standards of service to the final customer as well as concessions of one kind or another.

The tendency for the competition between integrated companies in product markets to force them to give away the cost reductions integration makes possible is the important element of validity in the persistent complaints by independent refiners and marketers that majors use their profits from production and transportation to subsidize downstream competition. The consequence of such price reductions (or their equivalent—for example, leases of stations to dealers at nominal rentals, the supply of equipment at nominal charge, and so on), impelled by competition, is a squeeze on the margins of nonintegrated competitors, and it is this differential impact of price competition that has recommended integration to disadvantaged independent competitors in an historically cumulative fashion. The Standard successor company without its own pipeline facilities or, especially after 1935, its own production operations found its profits shrinking compared with other majors more advantageously situated in these two respects [2]—and responded by attempting to remedy the lack of balance that was exposing it to a profit-price squeeze.

The selective price-compressing effect of integration is also suggested by the historic resistance of major marketers to fair trading, and similar methods of setting and protecting high distributive margins. A single monopolist refiner would have no interest in high distributive margins on products that had left his hands; on the con-

---

the construction of the Laurel Pipe Line, jointly owned by Gulf, Sinclair, and Texas, the first products line to use twenty-four inch pipe, to run westward from the Philadelphia–Marcus Hook refinery area to Pittsburgh and Cleveland. According to the *National Petroleum News* report (May, 1958, p. 123): "An Eastern major official puts it this way: 'Product is going to come into that area at such a low price that companies like Standard of Ohio will have only two choices. They'll either have to cut crude prices down to the bone, or buy product from us and other East Coast refiners. We'll be able to give a price that will lick current Gulf Coast rates silly.' "

2. See, e.g., the illuminating summaries of Atlantic's conclusions around 1934 about the reasons for its disappointing profit record in the preceding decade and the probable effects of prorationing: McLean and Haigh, pp. 195–197, 237.

trary, the lower those margins the larger the proportion of the profit-maximizing retail price he could keep for himself. The evidence, here as elsewhere, is conflicting. Independent marketers and retailers persistently criticize their suppliers' refusals to protect their margins by policing retail prices or by stemming the flow of product to price-cutting jobbers. Generally they allege that the retail price wars that fall so disproportionately on them could be stopped at any time if the majors would follow either course of action, or would simply stop making price concessions to dealers who meet the competition of price-cutters. The complaints suggest that the major companies do keep marketing margins, and to this extent final product prices, low, either by conscious policy or under pressure of competition.[3] The widespread adoption of the Iowa Plan, reducing the refiners' direct financial interest in the retail price, perhaps contributed to a willingness on their part to leave wholesale and retail margins to the play of competitive forces, to which they themselves contributed by encouraging entry of new marketers and dealers, constructing service stations, and selling surplus supplies at bargain prices.

The suggestion that the major oil companies might willfully instigate or prolong retail price wars in order to hold marketing margins low flies in the face of the competitive situation facing them. This might be intelligent policy from their standpoint if the tank-wagon price itself were immune to pressures originating in retail price competition. Thus a single refiner-monopolist might set his tank-wagon price as he chose, and happily permit distributors to compete as violently as possible, so as to minimize the mark-up passed on to the consumer, and maximize his own volume and share of industry profits. But when there are competing refiners, they often find it im-

3. Although this criticism is both biased and exaggerated, it is manifestly in the interest of the integrated firm to keep retail margins as *stably* low as possible. The House Small Business Committee put it another way: "the smaller the share that the retail dealer takes of the consumer's dollar, the greater is the share that can be taken by the oil company" ("Alleged Coercive and Discriminatory Practices," p. 17). While admitting that it had no evidence demonstrating that major companies fomented price wars with this end in mind, the Committee Report averred: "The evidence indicates, however, that . . . price wars, regardless of their origin, can and have had the effect of permanently reducing the margin of profit available to the retail dealer, while not lowering, but in some cases increasing, the wholesale price the dealer must pay. Moreover, reduced retail margins with no corresponding reduction in wholesale price may result in a greater wholesale profit to the oil companies to the extent that any greater volume of gasoline is sold because of a lower retail price" (*ibid.*, p. 16).

possible to quarantine price wars at the retail level and prevent their spilling backward to undermine the tank-wagon structure. In these circumstances, their frequent interventions to induce retailers to meet lower competitive offers are more likely to reflect irresistible competitive pressures on themselves, or attempts by disciplinary action to bring the wars to a close, rather than purposeful assaults on the dealer margin.[4] At the same time—and this is the relevant point in the present context—they often find themselves in this way *drawn into* price competition among themselves, and in the course of such competition they are often forced to give away large portions of the "profits" from other operations.

No one would expect any company, integrated or otherwise, voluntarily to give away any cost advantages it may have secured unless by so doing it could gain a more than proportional increase in sales volume or avoid a substantial contraction. With a general consensus that product demand is unresponsive to price change, cost savings will be passed on only as competition requires it. Thus, in setting price targets, a market leader will build its price structure (and hence its transfer prices between departments) on the basis of posted prices for crude oil, published tariffs for pipeline (or established charter rates for tanker) transportation, allocated refinery

4. "Inquiry among service station operators who do not own their own stations and lease from their suppliers will disclose that most of them feel there is a limit to the tolerance toward price-cutting that they can expect from the supplier. Maintenance of margins may therefore result in part from pressure by suppliers. . . . A fair generalization appears to be that by and large high retail prices to the motorist, and high margins, are found together; and they are associated with normal, or higher than normal tank wagon prices. . . . These relations merely reflect the fact that heightened intensity of . . . price competition . . . pushes down both tank wagon and retail realizations per gallon" (Attorney General, State of Michigan, pp. 152–153). This Report cites in support of the first observation the first declaration in Standard of Indiana's "Competitive Price Adjustment Plan": "We never aid a dealer who is himself responsible for the price cutting" (*ibid.;* see also above, p. 408). An illuminating indication that industry opinion supports the second observation appears in a hortatory letter from Atlantic's vice-president in charge of marketing: "I hope sometime I can convince enough important people that there is no solution for our troubles until each reputable company finds a way of protecting the retail price of its product. . . . When that system is established, some progress can be made into dividing up the pie fairly among retailer, jobber and supplier. . . ." (*National Petroleum News,* February, 1958, p. 9). No suggestion here that low retail margins are desirable so as to permit major suppliers to recoup in the tank-wagon price the maximum potential profits that can be extracted from the ultimate consumer at the point of final sale!

costs and desired terminal and bulk station margins.[5] But management is not bemused by such a statement of "costs." As the Esso
management observes, "Competition at times reduces or even eliminates this profit margin in the 'terminal price,' since it is at this point
that much of the 'give and take' of competitive marketing activity
occurs" and ". . . the only practical way to establish a realistic
refinery billing price is to . . . set our refinery billing prices in
line with the lower level of current market prices [frequently] below
our calculated costs." [6]

In the period before effective prorationing, the price of gasoline
was symptomatic of market determination rather than effective company administration. In the product price experiences of 1953–54
and 1957–58, as will be shown, similar conclusions seem to be justified. The sensitivity of final product prices to depressed market
conditions, despite rigidity of some crucial intermediate prices, has
been not just in spite of but in some measure because of the vertical
integration that helps make the prices in intermediate markets largely
nominal to the integrated competitors.

SOURCES OF PRICE DISTURBANCE: DYNAMIC IMBALANCE AND THE INDEPENDENT

The ideal of vertical integration is a smoothly calibrated flow of
material and product from one facility to another, with the respective
capacities at each level mutually adjusted so as to assure the fullest
possible utilization of each. In very general terms an approximation
to this sort of balance has been identified as the goal of the major
oil companies. However, there are both practical and substantive
reasons why even close approximation to perfect balance is neither
attainable, maintainable nor even desirable to the firm in a dynamic
industry. The pervasive and continuing lack of balance between the
almost continually expanding operations of the major oil companies
is the most important force that often impels them willy nilly into
price competition or its equivalent.

Major investment decisions are necessarily discrete, and expansions
of capacity are necessarily effected in lumps. The size of those
lumps is determined not solely by the need for perfect calibration of
capacity at varying levels, but also by other compelling considerations,

5. See Kaplan, Dirlam, and Lanzillotti, *Pricing in Big Business*, pp. 79–96,
for a description of Esso Standard and Standard of Indiana practices.

6. *Ibid.*, pp. 93–94.

like economies of scale. Moreover, in a rapidly growing and changing industry, capacities have to be constructed looking toward the uncertain future. It would be only the sheerest accident that this complex of determining considerations would produce a commitment to construct a crude oil pipeline to carry precisely as much crude oil as the company produced or its refineries required, or refinery capacity precisely in line with marketing requirements. And even if the accident occurred, the growth or decline of markets and exploratory successes and failures would soon upset the equilibrium.

This effect is also induced because a major oil company must develop a compartmentalized organization. The function of the marketing division is to sell products, without particular regard to the precise capacity of the refining department; if sales commitments outrun refinery capacity, so much the better from the salesman's standpoint. The transportation department will doubtless urge the most efficient size of pipeline within the limits of anticipated available supplies of crude oil; if necessary, crude can be carried for other refiners to keep it fully utilized. An exploration department is unlikely to call off a hot and promising chase for oil merely because the company's refinery capacity is temporarily—or promises indeed to be for a long time—too small to process what may be found and economical to produce.

It is the function of top management, largely through its control of the purse strings, to hold separate departments in some sort of desired relationship to one another. But given the uncertainties of discovery, the technical considerations, and the vagaries of markets, no control over budgets could assure balance, even if the company wanted it so. In fact, it may not even seek such equilibrium. One company may have particular aptitudes or more promising opportunities in one line than another; and every oil company is in part the prisoner of its past. Moreover, the majors often find advantage in encouraging independent producers and marketers to assume a share of the burdens of exploration and distribution respectively and, alternatively, they find it wise to buy some proportion of their product needs from independent refiners. The fact that major companies are, individually or as a group, net buyers in crude oil or product markets probably exerts a stabilizing influence: the more so since they do not typically exert the potential power they may possess to beat down the prices they pay. On the other hand, a major company with downstream facilities short of its upstream capacity is often a market-upsetter. Economies of wide-diameter pipelines and more effective common carrier regulation creates pressures to provide independent refiners and marketers with access to supplies and markets on more nearly equal footing. Major company refinery capacity that outruns the requirements of its branded distributors— and it does for some majors consistently, for others sporadically— exerts heavy pressure to extend direct distribution into new geographic markets, to bid distributors away from competitors, to sell products unbranded to independent jobbers at cut rates, or to bid on government, commercial, or industrial contracts at prices closer to incremental cost. This dynamic imbalance, combined with the pressures of fixed costs, impels major oil companies to compete with one another and to create opportunities for the competition of the independent.

The independent refiner suffers a number of competitive handicaps: he is relatively small, he often lacks a marketing organization, and he will often, though not always, have higher costs, a variable crude supply, an uncertain demand, an inferior or a less familiar product, a location further from important markets, and a short purse. He may sell a portion of his output to major marketers, but generally he must seek buyers outside their ranks at prices low enough to permit a profitable retail price some 2 cents or more below the prices of major brands.[7] Typically, the independent refiner is a price-shader who sells to independent jobbers—the most price-conscious operators in the most competitive markets in oil.

It is in these markets, when product flow is swollen by an abnormal supply of crude to independent refiners and/or by the product of major refiners out-of-balance on the long side with the requirements of their own branded distribution systems, that price wars find their source. The fuel for price-cutting competition may come from majors or minors,[8] but it must be fed ordinarily through independent marketers.[9] It is the large independent wholesalers, in possession of a

7. For exceptional cases, where independent local refiners and marketers have developed so high a reputation for quality and service that they can sell their brands at the same prices as the majors, see below, p. 466, n. 33.

8. When Standard of California invaded the East Coast, the urge for tied distribution led it to sign long-term contracts *guaranteeing* its distributors a fixed margin—an invitation to price-cutting that was promptly accepted. See Senate Small Business Committee, "Gasoline Price War in New Jersey," *Report* (1956), pp. 17–18.

9. "The sore point with many oil marketers in Memphis is that some of the private stations with low prices during the price war are supplied by the two majors." See "The Inside Story of a Price War," *National Petroleum News* (January 14, 1953), p. 52.

substantial low-priced supply of product, who seem to precipitate price wars.[10] Still the capacity of independents alone to upset markets is necessarily restricted within limits substantially narrower than those affecting the integrated firm.[11] And so it becomes almost impossible to separate the role of the independent in price wars from that of the vertically integrated refiner who often supplies him.

The pricing experience of the Standard Oil Company of Indiana, dominant marketer and price leader in the Midwest for more than thirty-five years, illustrates how the combination of major company imbalance and the independent makes prices flexible.[12] The Indiana company faced the burgeoning markets of the post World War I era with a pricing policy reminiscent of its origin as the regional marketing subsidiary of the old Standard Trust. The critical tank-wagon prices, based on its own Whiting refinery prices plus outgoing rail freight, were posted at each of its bulk plants through which most

10. Responsibility is traceable ultimately to an inelastic supply tending to outrun the demand at "normal" prices set by regular, ruly distributors. See, e.g., State of Connecticut, *Report of the Governor's Committee to Investigate the Gasoline Price War* (December 23, 1950), p. 6. This imbalance is transferred to the market through refiners' price concessions to independent branded and unbranded wholesalers (the marketing departments of the majors rarely start the price war). And the retailer who initiates the upsetting price reductions is usually a jobber with a string of stations who has found a bargain source of product. This does not necessarily deny Cassady's observation that "price wars in this day usually (if not always) originate at the retail level" (p. 275) or the similar flat assertion of the State of New Jersey's Gasoline Study Commission in its *Report* (February 16, 1953). But the more fundamental source is bargain product from some refiner, and it takes special concessions by other refiners to extend and prolong them (*ibid.,* p. 21). Independent Michigan refineries apparently supplied the gasoline that occasioned price wars in Detroit during the 1930's (although the FTC tried to tag Standard of Indiana with responsibility); independent refiner-marketers spearheaded Los Angeles price-cutters (Cassady and Jones, *Nature of Competition in Gasoline Distribution,* chap. 11); while service station chains, like Merit and Saveway, that have initiated price wars along the East Coast during the last ten years, apparently buy in volume from major East Coast refiners.

11. The capacities of the independent in this regard, however, are by no means negligible: the refiner can often buy his crude at sharp discounts from the posted price; he can sometimes avoid (e.g., in Los Angeles) the need to pay published transport tariffs; and the jobber can often obtain price concessions from the independent as substantial as those from the integrated firm.

12. Standard's experience is described in great detail for the period 1930–41 in McLean and Haigh, pp. 211–222, and in general outlines during its entire history in Wilson, "Oil Competition in the Midwest." See also Cassady, pp. 204–209.

of its gasoline was, and still is, sold. But the near monopoly it had formerly enjoyed was shaken as rivals set up new refineries or developed lower cost transport into its territory, most seriously after great new oil fields were discovered in East Texas and Oklahoma City. Standard's pricing system was an open invitation to new competitors, and the company responded sluggishly to their invasion, probably because its own business continued to expand even though its market share declined.[13]

In 1934 prices were belatedly shifted from Whiting-plus to Tulsa quotations—the major source of outside supplies had been the Midcontinent—plus Group 3 rail transportation to points of delivery.[14] But the new policy was soon undermined. A number of products pipelines were built into Standard's territory, increased use was made of barges, crude oil production took a substantial spurt upward in Illinois in 1939 and 1940, and in Michigan in 1935 and again in 1939. Refineries in these two states rapidly increased their gasoline sales in Indiana's territory, and the company's share of total sales continued to slide. Once again it was forced to change its pricing tactics. Special terminal prices were established in Michigan to meet the competition of independent refiners in this area.[15] But the competition from new transport facilities into other parts of its territory was more upsetting and more permanent. Finally, in 1949, a new policy was announced. Without price posting, Standard proposed to meet competitive prices as they might be established in local areas. The company's later policy of "suggesting competitive retail prices" in areas of active price competition was a logical further step in the abandonment of rigid and untenable posted pricing.

These revolutionary shifts in pricing policy well illustrate the dynamic forces in petroleum that will not brook a pricing formula as long as independents or integrated refiners out of balance can invade the market. Basically, the upsetting force was the pressure

13. Changes in Group 3 refinery prices invariably led and usually exceeded in both frequency and amplitude changes in Standard's Chicago tank-wagon price, 1922–27. FTC, *Petroleum Industry* (1928), chart facing p. 156. See also pp. 161–162.

14. The new policy was partly out of date when instituted. As McLean and Haigh observed, "The 'Group 3 plus' method of pricing adopted in 1934 was quite appropriate to conditions prevailing in the late 1920's and early 1930's" (p. 213).

15. Illinois, however, was a flash in the pan, and most of the small skimming plants in the flush Illinois fields disappeared before they could do much damage (*ibid.*, pp. 599–603).

of uncontrolled supplies: the great discoveries in Texas and the Mid-continent toppled the Midwestern price structure, not only by providing distress crude to independent refiners and distress products to independent marketers, but also by impelling majors to integrate forward and extend their marketing operations into each other's territories. The latter companies naturally attempted to channel the increased supplies of product through controlled distribution channels. But when supplies outran the capacity of their own branded distributors in the areas of their own greatest market concentration, and they tried to dispose of surplus product unbranded, the unbranded gasoline went to market at prices that eventually undercut them; and when instead they offered bargain prices to sign up new branded distributors in more distant markets, other majors were forced to retaliate by meeting the concessions that threatened to steal away their tied wholesalers or that, translated into retail price bargains, took business away from their dealers. The result was often price breakdown.

More recently, discoveries in the Williston Basin and Canada have further reoriented the traditional geographic pricing patterns. Gasoline in Midwestern cities like Chicago, Indianapolis, and the Twin Cities is said to sell at Midcontinent prices plus the Great Lakes Pipe Line tariff from the Group 3 area, *minus* ⅜ cents a gallon in deference to Montana refiners with excess capacity dumping their products eastward.[16] Actually, the decline of Group 3 pricing—the indications are that it is now practically dead throughout most of the Midwest area[17]—is attributable almost as much to transportation im-

16. The growing availability of Middle Eastern crude oil has put East Coast prices under similar pressure since 1949. For example, the output of Standard of California's Perth Amboy refinery, acquired from the Barber Asphalt Company in 1946 and expanded and modernized partly in the expectation of using these crudes of which Standard is a leading producer, has created continuous price disturbance in the area. As the price of Middle Eastern relative to Texas oil has progressively declined (accentuated by discounts from posted prices), refiners with little or no foreign production have followed Standard's lead. Since Tidewater's new refinery went on stream in late 1956, there is evidence that its gasolines have been selling at cut rates. Import limitations, which hit Tidewater with unusual severity, may therefore have the incidental effect of lessening product price disturbances in this area.

17. Cassady (pp. 202–204) states that surplus refining capacity in the Rocky Mountain Area has squeezed all remnants of Group 3 out of the pricing there and has pushed tank-wagon prices so low as to make freight absorbing sales from the Midcontinent unprofitable. Whatever this trend, it did not prevent a posted tank-wagon price in Caspar, Wyoming, of 15.70 cents per gallon

provements as to the discovery of new oil fields. True, the Great Lakes product line had tapped Standard territory as early as 1931 with Oklahoma products, but its rates in the thirties approximated rail rates, and its capacity was used exclusively by its owners. With increasingly effective regulation, the pressure exerted by expanding capacity to offer accommodation to nonowner-shippers,[18] the efforts of owner-shippers to expand market coverage, and the competition of supplies brought in by barge (as well as of locally refined crude), the "phantom freight" element in the pipeline tariff was gradually squeezed out. Standard remains the leading marketer, though its share has fallen from around 80 to under 20 per cent; but while its price leadership is by no means entirely dissipated, its pricing methods have been forced to conform with modern competitive realities.

It would be a mistake to characterize current Midwest product pricing as determined by freely competitive forces, however. Crude oil production is better controlled: production in the unregulated fields of Illinois and Michigan has declined and new Canadian output is not only prorated but also imported in strong hands. Apparently, the price of Alberta crude is equalized at Chicago; that is, it sells at the price of Midcontinent crude delivered at Chicago minus pipeline tariffs back to the Canadian wellhead. Cheap river transportation, where feasible, is available to majors and independents alike, and more product lines have been built; but many remain primarily plant facilities, to carry the products of their major company owners.[19] Not all markets where prices were formerly on a Group 3 basis are uniformly served by numerous sellers enjoying low-cost ingress. Also,

---

on May 1, 1949, when the corresponding rate at Tulsa was 14.00 cents and Wyoming was experiencing the surplus of refinery capacity that eventually led Sinclair and Continental to build the Pioneer Products line to take out surplus products (see McLean and Haigh, pp. 222–224). Despite surplus state refining capacity, the Montana Trade Commission alleges one of the highest tank-wagon prices in the country in "Gasoline Prices in Montana," *Preliminary Report,* and *Supplementary Report* (1957), answered by Continental Oil Company, *The Facts about Montana Gasoline Prices,* Company publication, 1957. These cases are possibly indicative of weak local competition of the kind that permitted the survival of Group 3 pricing in the past.

18. According to H. F. Horning, secretary of the Northwest Petroleum Association, unbranded gasoline sales in Minneapolis rose from 18.6 per cent to 42.45 per cent of the total, from 1935 to 1952. *National Petroleum News* (October 29, 1952), p. 17. This undoubtedly reflected the access of independent shippers to the Great Lakes line; many of them advertise their sales of common stream "pipeline gas."

19. Wolbert, *American Pipe Lines,* p. 48.

Standard's new policy of meeting competition quickly and selectively can have a very chilling effect on price competition. It poses the thorny phenomenon of price discrimination.[20]

THE AMBIVALENT IMPACT OF PRICE DISCRIMINATION

The widespread practice of price discrimination in the petroleum industry is by no means dependent upon or uniquely related to the integration of its leading sellers, and cannot therefore come in for thorough analysis in the present study. The preponderance of common costs in the refinery (including the costs of the delivered raw material) makes it inevitable that various refinery products will contribute unequally to them, depending on what the market for each will bear, a kind of price discrimination that would persist in the absence of integration.[21] Economies of scale in refinery operation require refiners to sell in several geographic markets and to a variety of classes of customers with differing elasticities of demand; under the pressure of heavy fixed costs, prices at varying mark-ups above out-of-pocket costs are therefore likely even in the absence of vertical integration. Independent distributors and retailers likewise would undoubtedly charge varying prices to different customers in the quest for increased volume.

20. The term "price discrimination" has invidious implications at law and in popular usage, which this use of it is not intended to carry. To the economist, it means only that a seller charges different purchasers of the same product different prices at the same time, price differences which do not correspond to differences in the costs of supplying them. Such prices are indicative of price discretion on the part of the seller; they may or may not be socially harmful.

21. See above, pp. 69–73. This is a *kind* of discrimination because different products are selling at different percentage mark-ups over direct cost. See Bain, *Pacific Coast Petroleum Industry, 2,* 159 ff.; Rostow, *A National Policy for the Oil Industry,* pp. 14–15. This latter kind of discrimination, however, insofar as it involves joint costs with invariable proportions, is compatible with pure competition, which would merely tend to force the price received for the bundle of products produced to equality with the marginal cost of producing the bundle. However, refinery product costs are not strictly joint: considerable change in the pattern of products derived from crude oil is technically permissible within economic limits of relative costs and relative values (see above, pp. 376–379). In these circumstances, there has been considerable discussion in the industry in recent years about the desirability of raising the price of home-heating oil, demand for which has been growing rapidly, relative to gasoline so as to help counter persistent undersupplies of the former and oversupplies of the latter (see the Chase Manhattan Bank, *Monthly Review of the Petroleum Situation,* September, 1956, pp. 3–4).

Price discrimination is nonetheless pertinent to our present inquiry because the larger the oil company and the wider its geographic and functional scope of operations, the greater are both the opportunities for and the impact of differential pricing. The accusation that the geographically integrated company uses profits from sales in less competitive markets to "subsidize" sales where competition is stronger is in effect a charge of price discrimination. The wider public acceptance is of its brand (and the more dealers it can hold to itself by owning the stations they operate), the greater will be the possibility that a refiner partially integrated into marketing can maintain its tank-wagon price on its branded products, while selling at a lower price to jobbers.[22] Peculiar to vertical integration is this practice of dual distribution—when the refiner sells both to wholesalers and, in competition with them, directly to service stations or final users through its own marketing division—which may have discriminatory effects.[23]

The possibilities of price discrimination, or something like it, in dual distribution are much like the familiar price and margin squeezes. Vertical integration, clearly, is not responsible for all divergent movements of intermediate prices that account for the variability of gross margins and profit prospects at different levels of the industry.[24] These rather reflect the differential ability of supply at the various levels to adapt readily to changes in demand and price. It is clear,

22. Here again the boundary lines of price discrimination become indistinct, in both the economic and legal sense. Is it discrimination to sell physically identical products at two different prices, the one for supplies carrying the refiner's brand, the other for unbranded? Economically the two "products" are not identical; yet even in economic terms, this may be a species of discrimination, with sales to markets of differing demand elasticity at different percentage mark-ups.

23. Again, the situation is often confused because the refiner may be selling two quite different bundles of services in two quite different economic markets. In the one, he may dispense the product alone at the terminal; in the other, he combines with the product itself transportation to the bulk plant, bulk plant storage, transportation to the service station, credit and other services. Yet here as well there may be a separation of markets, with price differences explainable by differences in their demand elasticity. If buyers are precluded from moving from one market to the other, if, for example, the refiner refuses to grant to retailers the same opportunity on the same terms of buying gasoline alone without the services attached, the probability of price discrimination is enhanced. These issues were inherent in but never seriously considered in the famous Standard of Indiana case (see below, p. 477).

24. See McLean and Haigh, chap. 6, for an excellent discussion of this subject.

however, that vertically integrated firms, being only imperfectly in balance, have an important influence on prices in intermediate markets; and that open-market prices would vary quite differently relative to one another in the absence of integration. Since there is a basic similarity in the relevant policies of most important integrated oil companies, it is not merely possible but probable that the majors by their combined influence, unconsciously or consciously exerted, do contribute to the failure of the various open-market prices in the industry to move in close articulation. In so doing they also contribute to margin squeezes on the independents who must derive their entire income from the difference between two of those prices.

Since integration tends to insulate the posted price of crude oil from the influence of changes in demand, especially against a reduction, these changes are concentrated on the refining margin, more particularly on refiners in inverse proportion to their crude-oil self-sufficiency. It is true, also, that integration of refiners into service station ownership tends to insulate the tank-wagon price, since the dealer who leases from his supplier is less able to bargain over the price he pays than the wholesaler who owns his own facilities. In consequence, the tied distributor or dealer is exposed to squeezes if, in periods of surplus supplies, jobbers succeed in obtaining price concessions and use them to cut the retail price. To the extent, in brief, that integration contributes to the lags in the adjustment of one intermediate price or another to changes in market conditions, it accentuates the difficulties of nonintegrated competitors who may find themselves compressed between the price that moved and the one that did not. And in a sense such squeezes represent a kind of conscious or unconscious price discrimination by the integrated companies as a group—they take varying "profit margins" over direct cost at the different strata in which they operate, under the influence of differential pressures of competition, and differential elasticities of supply. The discrimination is for them nominal, since the integrated firm does not earn individual profits at each level. But to the extent they buy and sell at those levels it is not nominal, and the differential impact on nonintegrated competitors is very real, precisely analogous to that of price discrimination of the more familiar variety.

The process by which some of these prices are made is actively competitive. Large commercial customers (bus, trucking, and industrial companies using large quantities of gasoline), for example, often buy on specification and typically have little interest in brand names and the paraphernalia of product differentiation. When markets are firm, they will buy at tank-wagon price or at some conventional differential above it.[25] But when distress or surplus gasoline is available in quantity, competing suppliers will bid for their patronage at prices much closer to out-of-pocket costs.[26]

Although wholesalers complain bitterly about the allegedly unfair competition practiced by majors in bidding for commercial and industrial business—especially when the transgressor is engaging in dual distribution and undercutting his own distributor—it is the practice of offering concessions to resellers that frequently has the more dramatic consequences. The oil companies undoubtedly practice price discrimination extensively in their arrangements with wholesalers and dealers. While the contracts follow a few standard forms, they are the products of individual negotiation, in the course of which suppliers may be moved to offer all sorts of terms for a desirable station or chain of stations. The contracts include agreements not only to supply product but also to lease (and sometimes to lease and lease-back) facilities and to provide a wide variety of services and assistance; there is room for pervasive and wide differences in the terms accorded to different distributors and dealers.

The negotiation of these contracts is part of a highly competitive rivalry for market outlets. This is the strong element of truth in the answers of Socony Mobil and Shell to a complaint issued by the Federal Trade Commission alleging the use of the following tactics in their sales of lubricants:

> the respondent has attempted to induce and has induced customers . . . to prefer respondent's . . . products . . . by engaging in various practices . . . including the following:
>   A. Said respondent has . . . furnished expensive lubrication equipment and other facilities . . . on lease, loan or sale with easy terms of repayment upon the condition . . . or understand-

25. See Cassady, pp. 156, and 284, n. 5.

26. See *National Petroleum News* (June 23, 1954), pp. 13–14, and Cassady, pp. 156–157. Although the dealer tank-wagon price of Standard of Indiana remained unchanged at 16.3 cents per gallon (excluding tax) from July, 1953 to July, 1954, large commercial customers in the Chicago area were getting gasoline for 12.8 cents per gallon toward the end of this period. See *National Petroleum News* (July 21, 1954), p. 57. The appropriate comparison in most cases is probably not with tank-wagon but with tank-car, barge, or distributor's prices. It is by no means clear that the discounts to big consumers, which often get big enough to exclude distributors from competing for the business, bring prices anywhere near out-of-pocket costs, or are unjustified by savings in direct costs of serving them.

ing, expressed or implied, that the prospective customer would thereafter handle, preferentially or exclusively, Socony petroleum products. . . .

B. Said respondent has granted to some customers substantial benefits, including gifts of cash, equipment, services, facilities, loans . . . coupled with different quantity, gallonage and other allowances . . . upon the [same] condition . . . or understanding. . . .

C. Said respondent has . . . furnished other facilities and benefits to prospective customers, including construction, painting, furnishing of paint, paving of lots and the installation and maintenance of lubrication equipment, without charge.[27]

Socony's reply asserts:

That free and fair competition under our economic system rests upon the major premise that each competitor will strive to gain custom and customers who will prefer its products . . . that in competing . . . it is necessary for respondent to . . . meet offers of competitors and to otherwise persuade said customers that respondent's products, terms and conditions of sale and the various aids and benefits offered by respondent are equal to similar offers of competitors, all of which is fair, honorable, legal and the very essence of free competition. . . .

That the principal practice complained of, namely, the furnishing of aids and assistance . . . is an historical one, long engaged in by the members of the industry . . . that such practice is a manifestation of and directly attributable to the existence of vigorous competition for said . . . business.[28]

Yet to a large extent the competition is non-price in character, just like the competitive acquisition and construction of service stations. Although the provision of paint, lube racks, advertising, and black-topping are in a sense the *equivalent* of price reductions, they are also in a sense a *substitute* for them. It is not inappropriate, indeed, to regard them, like integration itself, as a method of tying a dealer to a particular supplier without having to reduce or thereafter to dicker over the tank-wagon price.[29]

27. Docket No. 6915, Complaint of October 14, 1957; the Shell Complaint is in Docket No. 7044 and dated January 16, 1958.

28. Docket No. 6915, *Answer to Complaint*, April 22, 1958. Shell's answer is similar.

29. "The experience of one major company has been that when it was so

Still there are plenty of direct price concessions as well, especially when refineries are operating below capacity and storage tanks are bulging. Sometimes anticipated surplus capacity will be contracted out on long term;[30] more often surplus gasoline will be sold unbranded at what it will bring.[31] Such price rivalry, of course, may spawn or prolong price wars;[32] we have already traced the normal sequence of events, from unbalanced major or independent refiner,[33] through the independent wholesaler to the retailer.[34] Private brands generally come to rest at a differential around 2 cents at retail below major brands; but in the weak markets of 1958 some majors began to regard 2 cents as excessive.[35] Such differences of opinion can make for more things than horse races.

---

harassed by the high offers of competitors to provide equipment to customers, it was far better off to provide the equipment and then charge a price to cover its cost. According to an executive of this company, 'A sound equipment policy is one of the best methods of stabilizing the consumer tank-wagon price at an economic level above the dealer price' " (Cassady, p. 223, n. 5).

30. Several major companies on the West Coast, it will be recalled, fed the new cut-rate self-serve stations after World War II on such contracts. See above, pp. 298–299.

31. The method is hallowed by tradition. See Watkins, p. 163, n. 16.

32. John S. McGee, in his "Price Discrimination and Competitive Effects: The Standard Oil of Indiana Case," *University of Chicago Law Review, 23* (spring, 1956), pp. 398–473, gives a persuasive analysis of the Detroit market between 1936–40 from this viewpoint.

33. The *National Petroleum News* estimates that major companies "probably supply about 75% of the private brand gasoline sold today." See "The Private Brander: He's Confident" (February, 1958), p. 137.—This high ratio would seem to reflect the excess refinery capacities and product oversupplies of 1958. The private brand sellers who have apparently flourished in the Midwest since World War II have been supplied in large measure by incompletely integrated refiners; many of them—like Clark, Northwestern, and International Refineries, to mention only a few—are in fact integrated refiner-marketers. Not all are price cutters by any means; some, like Pate, in Milwaukee ("How an Independent Beat the Majors," *National Petroleum News,* July, 1956, pp. 98–100) —since acquired by Standard of New Jersey—and Leonard, in Michigan ("How High Octanes Pay Off for Independent," *ibid.,* June 9, 1954, p. 19), enjoy such strong local acceptance of their brands that they sell at or even above major brand prices. In Los Angeles, independent refiner-marketers sell their gasoline through different chains under different names at different prices (*ibid.,* May 5, 1954, p. 59). Sunset Oil has a "Thrifty" brand (cut rate) and a regular brand, Golden Eagle, sold through different stations.

34. See above, pp. 456–457.

35. See " 'Don't Tread on Me'—Anymore," *National Petroleum News* (May, 1958), p. 82, and "Is the Major-Independent Brand Spread Outmoded?" *ibid.* (June, 1958), pp. 8–9.

The verbal fireworks accompanying price wars are almost as tortuous as the complex personal and economic relationships involved. At one extreme, discounts to selected dealers in a price war situation are assailed as provocative and at best tending to perpetuate the trouble; price wars could not continue if majors would steadfastly refuse to grant concessions. At the other, the complaint is that such allowances are granted to discipline the independent and bring the war to a close; or concessions are defended as having been made in good faith to meet competition and retain the firm's business. Actually, in these highly fluid, imperfect markets it is neither possible nor defensible to choose between these contentions, which hinge largely on divergent interpretations of motives in situations where motives are inevitably mixed. What appears clear in most of these instances is that the major refiners do not start the price wars, although their gas may power it, and that they are drawn into the fray to meet competition. In doing so, they undoubtedly introduce a disciplinary effect, whatever the motive. The price-cutter is made to feel the consequences of his actions: he is forced to share proportionately in the lower margins that his action precipitated without the benefit of the volume he expected to realize. The important test for public policy is whether such tactics typically eliminate price competition in the end or are a continuing part of a continual process of price maneuvering. In general they seem to have been the latter— at least in the price war areas. Price wars have been chronic, because of a continuing problem of excess capacity.

It is easy and natural to overemphasize the dramatic price wars, and the price concessions that spark and fuel them, for it is these that stir controversy and command public attention. Price discrimination, however, involves a higher as well as a lower price. The concessions are by their very nature selective both in place and time; some, perhaps most, customers do not get them. The conduct of price competition in this selective fashion is, like non-price competition, a way of channeling and confining it, and minimizing its profit-eroding effect. It may act as a lightning rod, to protect the price structure in general. When concessions are made from tank wagon, the tank-wagon price itself usually remains unchanged—nominal as it is for the dealers immediately involved in price wars, it remains real and effective for the rest. The purpose of making them selective is in some instances avowedly to "localize the price disturbance." [36] The

36. This was the characterization by a vice president of the Texas Company: "At the same time, because of its application to dealers on an individual

"voluntary allowances" are ordinarily extended and terminable without notice on the initiative and responsibility of the supplier alone. They rarely make good the entire retail price cut; [37] the dealer and distributor margins bear the rest, and on their entire business, not just part of it. And when allowances have served their purpose, they are instantaneously withdrawn—often, it is alleged, simultaneously and mysteriously by all suppliers at once.[38]

Finally, whatever the motivation, there is the inevitable disciplinary effect when a large company reduces prices on a small part of its business to meet the lower price a smaller company is taking on a large part of its business. The imitation of price cuts is of course the essence of competition; this is how competition extends its benefits broadly to all buyers. The price-cutter cannot and should not enjoy protection against the natural response of his rivals. In imperfect markets, however, price cuts are more likely if the initiator can hope for at least temporary advantage; if they are certain to be met, quickly and hard, they may never be offered in the first place. The latter danger is greatest when the company doing the "meeting" is the dominant seller in a wide geographic area. Such a seller can hold the prices that determine the greater proportion of its income stable while reducing prices only in the area affected by the initial cut. If, in addition, the dominant marketer can force its tied retailers to bear part of the burden in reduced margins, the threat to a price-cutter is enhanced.

There is considerable testimony that several price wars were "initiated" by major companies when an independent exceeded the customary 2-cent price differential, that the explicit purpose was to bring the disturber of the peace into line, and that this was at times the effect.[39] Despite the ready access of jobbers in the Twin Cities

basis, the plan tends to help localize the price disturbance." Senate Small Business Committee, "Gasoline Price War in New Jersey," *Report* (1956), p. 19.

37. See House Small Business Committee, "Alleged Coercive and Discriminatory Practices," *Interim Report* (1955), p. 16.

38. "It is significant when the off-brand station is forced to raise its price to the 2-cent differential that the discounts are withdrawn, the price war ends overnight, and retail prices return either to their former or a higher level." *Ibid.,* p. 15. See also "Distribution Practices in the Petroleum Industry," *Interim Report,* p. 7, and Senate Small Business Committee, "Gasoline Price War in New Jersey," *Hearings,* Pt. I, pp. 4, 13: "Within a very short time, within a period of hours, the companies are all on or off the subsidy."

39. "The purpose and the effect of such discounts are to force the off-brand dealer to return to the 2-cent differential. . . . The evidence, therefore, is to the effect that the oil companies' concept of 'meeting competition' involves

area to independently refined gasoline from the Great Lakes Pipe Line terminal and from the local refinery, it was found in 1953 that private-branded gasoline typically sold at only a one-cent differential below the majors.[40] Interviews with independent refiners marketing there suggested that Standard's resoluteness in meeting local price cuts had made competitors fearful of attempting any deeper reductions and therefore had substantially stabilized the market. The new policy may explain the short-term stability in Standard's prices during 1953–54 in the face of extremely unsettled market conditions, accumulating product inventories, mounting inroads of natural gasoline, and price wars in other areas of the country.[41]

Nonetheless, Standard's margin of discretion in pricing seems to have been sharply compressed by competitive forces in its territory. Prior to its June, 1953, price increase, prices in its territory had ranged below both 1948 and Office of Price Stabilization ceilings despite substantial cost increases meanwhile. Not until crude prices were advanced in June was Standard able to lead prices upward. If the ultimate test of discriminatory pricing is whether it ends by intensifying or by suppressing competition, the evidence at hand is certainly no warrant for holding that Standard's new policy has had

---

a practice which results in the isolation and then the destruction of competition." *Ibid.*, p. 15; see pp. 13–15.

40. Independent stations, however, were giving away hospitalization policies and less extravagant premiums. See also Castle, "Unbranded Gasoline Shakes Pricing Structure," *National Petroleum News* (October 29, 1952), p. 17. Castle said that the independent marketers were very much afraid that a differential as large as 2–3 cents between major and independent brands (which is normal on the East Coast) would not be tolerated by the majors.

41. On June 22, 1953, Standard raised its Chicago dealer tank-wagon price from 15.3 to 16.3 cents a gallon, where it remained for over two years; in Minneapolis it raised the tank-wagon price from 15.9 cents per gallon to 16.3 cents, where it remained constant for a year and a half. The same stability (which is of course to some immeasurable extent deceptive, because of the varying meaningfulness of the formal, published price) characterized its tank-wagon price at virtually all points covered by the *National Petroleum News* between July, 1953, and July, 1954.

In contrast, the tank-wagon price in Washington, which was raised to 16.3 cents at the same time the Chicago price reached 16.3 cents, had fallen by July 14, 1954, to 15.1 cents (Esso); Harrisburg, which had been raised to 16.7 cents from 15.3 cents in the July, 1953, wave of increases, was at the later date enjoying a 14.9-cent price; in Philadelphia, Atlantic Refining, which had pushed the price to 16.7 cents in July from 14.7 cents in June of 1953, was then forced to retreat to 15.8 cents in November, 15.4 cents in February, and in the final cut in July, 1954, to 13.9 cents. *National Petroleum News*, various issues.

the latter effect. It seems quite clear that selling surplus gasoline at cut rates through independent marketers has powerful competitive consequences. What is not equally clear, however, is that competition would be more or less effective if major oil companies were forced, when they found it necessary or desirable to meet competition, to reduce their tank-wagon prices to all in nondiscriminatory fashion rather than being permitted, as now, to reduce price selectively to a few.[42]

One final point is worth emphasizing in concluding this discussion. Dual distribution, price discrimination, and the price competition they engender are a reflection and consequence of incomplete integration. They occur where major companies have to bid for the patronage of businessmen, in varying degrees independent of them and with whom they also compete. They result from the lack of balance in the developing productive capacity of the integrated firm, and from the presence and strength of independent refiners and marketers. They result also from an incomplete ability of the industry cooperatively to regulate supply. If the price wars that plagued the industry in the thirties found their ultimate origins in the flush, inadequately regulated flow of crude oil, those of the fifties are probably attributable primarily to surplus refinery capacity,[43] and also to the inability of state regulatory agencies even today to hold the supply of crude oil rigidly in check. Standard's experience demonstrates the important role played by independents—refiners and marketers—in squeezing the water out of prices, when they have the opportunity to do so. It shows also that an unregulated supply, in numerous hands, is what creates that opportunity. Similarly in Los Angeles, the basing-point for West Coast pricing, the independents have played a key role in what has been close to a thirty years' price war. The history of marketing in Los Angeles shows how fierce competition can be when the costs of integrating are negligible, and its strategic advantages correspondingly minimized. With crude in the same county and wholesaler-retailers ready to pick up product at the refinery rack for immediate sale in the metropolitan area, there

42. A major element of uncertainty is how such required nondiscriminatory action would affect a major oil refiner's willingness to create unbalance in the first instance and hence both the rate of adaptation of capacity to demand and the rate of growth. In short, it is conceivable that price discrimination in oil is the price paid for a dynamic industry.

43. This is clearly recognized by the Senate Small Business Committee Report, "Gasoline Price War in New Jersey," *Report* (1956), pp. 16–17.

is no need to concern oneself with outlets or with supplies. The emphasis is rather on price.[44] Conversely, the presence of abundant supplies of undifferentiated products provided the opportunity for adventurous large-scale retailers to use a combination of price-cutting and service innovations to attract business.

THE INFLUENCE OF GOVERNMENT: ANTITRUST AND CONGRESSIONAL INQUIRIES

Federal and state governments affect the pricing of petroleum products at so many levels and in so many directions that comprehensive treatment is much beyond the scope of this study. Among the more important direct interventions are the depletion allowance, prorationing, the voluntary import program, and the regulation of pipelines with which the reader is now generally familiar; but in addition there are the applications of the Sherman, Clayton, and Federal Trade Commission Acts, fair trade laws and statutes prohibiting sales below cost, which have been dealt with thus far only peripherally. The complexities and the ambivalence of the role of government are diminished but by no means obliterated when attention is confined to the kinds of intervention that have at least the avowed intention to ensure the preservation of competition.

Since 1911 there has been no successful government action to effect any basic change in the structure of the industry, although a major dissolution suit is in process [45] and periodically bills are introduced in the Congress to this end. Government, however, has tried in two ways to protect the public interest against the excessive accumulation or irresponsible exercise of power. First it has applied the antitrust laws. The Assistant Attorney General in charge of antitrust stated that in mid-1957 25 per cent of his lawyers were concerned with one or another investigation or suit in the petroleum industry.[46] Second, it has exposed the industry, its basic structure and its detailed policies, to continuous, often hostile, scrutiny. Exhaustive

44. For a survey of the Los Angeles market see Watkins, p. 231; Cassady and Jones, *Nature of Competition in Gasoline Distribution;* and Bain, *Pacific Coast Petroleum Industry, 3,* 97.

45. *United States v. Standard Oil Company of California et al.,* Civil Action 11584-C, S.D. Cal., Complaint, May 12, 1950; Amended Complaint, 1956.

46. Victor R. Hansen, "Antitrust and the Petroleum Industry," address before the National Congress of Petroleum Retailers, mimeographed (August 20, 1957), pp. 12–13.

survey or analysis of the individual cases or inquiries would be out of place here, but a general assessment of their nature and effectiveness is essayed.

There have been two important successful antitrust suits in the area of price-fixing. These cases involved the concerted buying pools, in East Texas and the Midcontinent and on the West Coast. There are differences of opinion about the effectiveness of these buying programs, but on the following points, which alone seem relevant to an analysis of the industry today, there is pretty general agreement. First, the buying programs could not provide a corrective for distress gasoline and weak prices anywhere nearly so effective as state control of crude oil production efficiently enforced. Second, these efforts at market stabilization required a concerted program, a combination. Without an actual agreement, express or implied, and a clear-cut meeting of minds if not of bodies among a substantial number of companies, effective wholesale purchases for stabilization purposes in a period of excess supply could hardly take place. Since the opposition of the law to any such cooperative ventures is now unmistakably clear and since the market now enjoys the far more important support of prorationing, the facts of the Madison case shrink essentially to historic interest.

This case (and its counterpart on the West Coast), however, focuses attention once more on the historic role of the spot market— the symptom of incomplete integration—and of freely flowing supplies of crude oil in the competitive behavior of the industry. The taming of this force, so rampant in the thirties, under prorationing and the subsequent dwindling of the strength of the spot market pose for the law another kind of threat. For the thinner the open market becomes, the tighter the controls over crude oil production, the more balanced the industry's integrated structure, and the fewer the number of firms: the less overt a combination must be to insulate product prices against competitive deterioration at the hands of independent refiners.

The impulse toward cooperative action against the nonconformist in pricing matters is no prerogative of the large integrated firm even though the latter gets most of the publicity. Indeed, more recent suits involving alleged price-fixing have shifted virtually to the retail level. Between 1953 and 1956 a number of complaints and indictments were handed down, all of them terminated with pleas of guilty or *nolo contendere* and settled by the payment of fines or by the entry of consent decrees, charging collusive price-fixing by local independent marketers enforced by group boycotts or similarly coercive tactics directed against outsiders and price chiselers.[47]

On May 29, 1958, an indictment was handed down charging twenty-nine companies, apparently all of the majors, with conspiracy in the increase of the domestic price of crude oil and products in January, 1957.[48] While it is impossible to pass on the merits of the charge with the very sketchy facts thus far available, the analysis in Chapter 8 led to the conclusion that this price increase, like that in 1953, forcefully illustrated the role of policy considerations in the pricing of crude oil. Despite the rise in demand, simple market forces did not require a price increase, no matter how legitimate and overdue on grounds of cost it appeared in the industry's consensus. The market circumstances, then, provided not the cause but the occasion for the rise, and the regulatory commission of the State of Texas, through its prorationing policies, first helped precipitate and then supported the price increase against eroding market forces that would otherwise have undermined it quickly. In brief, the way in which crude oil prices behave, though clearly not competitive, does not seem to depend upon conspiracy in any nonlegal, common-sense meaning of the term. Unless, therefore, the antitrust authorities find some way of altering the market structure—broadly defined to include the influence of prorationing and import limitations—it is difficult to see how they can significantly alter the market's behavior.

The same observation seems appropriate with respect to the alleged international cartel,[49] although here the record of formal collaboration, notably in joint ventures, is much more clear.[50] The entry

47. *The Federal Antitrust Laws, 1952–1956 Supplement* (New York, Commerce Clearing House, 1957), Cases 1167, 1168, 1169, 1238, 1239, 1240, 1287. Even more recently, a criminal indictment charges retail price-fixing by Standard of Indiana, eight other majors and four local distributors to terminate a price war in South Bend, Indiana. See above, p. 411, n. 58.

48. See New York *Times* (May 30, 1958), p. 1. Richfield seems to be the only major omitted from the charge, perhaps because it operates exclusively on the West Coast.

49. *United States v. Standard Oil Company (New Jersey) et al.,* U.S. District Court, District of Columbia, Civil Action No. 1779-53, filed April 21, 1953; transferred to Southern District of New York June 8, 1953, Civil 86-27.

50. Whether that record justifies legal condemnation is, of course, not our question. Joint ventures are not illegal per se under the Sherman Act even though they involve some limitations on competition between the participant companies; and perhaps the Courts will find that their organization in this case was forced upon the defendants by the policies of the countries in which they sought concessions.

of more and more firms into foreign production, and the mounting pressures of supply thus developed, would almost certainly prove far more effective competitive influences—if the American government would only devise a rational production-import policy that would let them operate on the domestic market—than any conceivable termination of the antitrust suit.

It is similarly difficult to see the need for conspiracy in the products price increases that very shortly preceded, but mostly followed, the crude increase of January, 1957. Prices would not have behaved precisely so in a purely competitive market, it is true; but the behavior of product compared with crude oil prices through most of 1957 and 1958 clearly identifies the major monopolistic element in the petroleum industry. If collusion was a factor in the behavior of product prices in early 1957, it would not seem to have been a necessary factor, and it was demonstrably ineffective in holding the line thereafter.[51]

There are other strings to the would-be price-fixer's bow where the leading firms are not strong enough to effect their will by individual action alone. The Ethyl case [52] illustrated a more effective and inherently more dangerous method of accomplishing the same purpose, although there were other purposes of the arrangement as well—notably the protection of product quality. Instead of imposing on an *ad hoc* group of majors the financial burden of neutralizing price-cutting refiners, it simply excluded the latter and their jobber customers from an increasingly crucial segment of the market. Very simply, the Ethyl Corporation, protected by its patents, refused to make tetraethyl of lead available to refiners selling to "unethical" (that is, to price-cutting) jobbers.[53] In this way the latter were confined to the market for third-grade, low octane gasoline, a market of diminishing size as engine compression ratios rose. Since independent refiners, selling gasoline without nationally known brands, often had to sell to price-cutting jobbers if they were to sell at all, the Ethyl policy threatened the survival of the whole nonintegrated segment of the industry. The Supreme Court upheld an injunction against the practices. With the decision of this case, jobbers buying from both major and independent refiners were assured that the

51. See below, pp. 557–558.
52. *Ethyl Gasoline Corp. v. United States*, 309 U.S. 436 (1940).
53. This is not to deny that some of the price-cutters were also product adulterators. But "ethics" was not defined simply in the latter terms.

Ethyl Corporation would not be able to cut off their supply of high-test gasoline by refusing a license; and cut-price marketers were thereafter able to offer such gasoline in competition with the majors.

It would not be appropriate here to consider the complex problems of reconciling the legal monopoly conferred by the patent law, and the unquestionable economic function it serves, with the competitive purposes of the antitrust laws. But it is clear that the Ethyl decision was essential to the preservation of price competition in the oil industry. It would have been intolerable to permit patent owners to seek their reward in a way that suppressed price competition in an entire market. And the principle has apparently been accepted by the industry; no complaint that patents have been so used since 1940 has been uncovered.[54]

Prominent among cases bearing indirectly on pricing policies are a number involving the practice of exclusive dealing.[55] A fundamental theory underlying these actions is that exclusive dealing is a species of integration (through contract) which permits the suppression of unsettling retail price competition. In fact there can be no question that the dealer who is free to shop around for supplies is more likely to be a price-cutter than the one who is tied to one refiner. Exclusive dealing is a kind of substitute for direct integration into retailing, with the same stress on service and brand loyalty but without the costs that integration may impose. To the extent that it impedes the access of nonintegrated refiners to the market and of nonintegrated marketers to supplies of unbranded gasoline, it definitely limits the open-market character of petroleum prices. It pushes the locus of

54. Rostow suggests that the decision is of slight value because any major refiner can still refuse gasoline to independent jobbers, and so still cut off supplies to price-cutters (*A National Policy for the Oil Industry*, pp. 86–87). Clearly, the Ethyl case did not solve all the competitive problems of the independents, but it did restore the possibility of competition that would otherwise have been barred when it got independent refiners out from under the thumb of the Ethyl Corporation. Once free of this central policy control the diversities of interest and supply position among major refiners and between majors and independents might be expected to forestall a united front against price-cutting independent wholesalers. Whether this is enough to maintain workable price competition in the industry is in a sense the subject of this study.

55. The Government has already won its suits against Standard of California (337 U.S. 293, 1949) and Richfield (343 U.S. 922, 1952); the FTC has reached a consent resettlement with Shell (Docket No. 6051, March 17, 1953), and the suit against Sun Oil (Civil 10483, U. S. District Court, E.D. Pa., Complaint, 1950) has gone to trial and is at the time of writing still awaiting decision.

competition forward to the pump, and so diminishes the competitive influence of intermediate markets.

On the other hand, this kind of control has not been strong or complete enough to come anywhere near suppressing either price competition at the retail level or the implicit competitive influences limiting the price-making discretion of the dominant firm. Furthermore, because of apparently mutual advantages to refiner and retailer of something like an exclusive arrangement, it is extremely doubtful if these cases can seriously alter the character of retailing methods, at least so far as the principal product, gasoline, is concerned.[56] While its possible obstacle to independent refiners cannot be ignored —and this will be considered in Chapter 19—exclusive dealing is in itself a relatively unimportant contributor to major-company influence over the retail price compared with refiner construction and financial control over service stations.

Although the theory underlying exclusive dealing cases is somewhat ambivalent, there is no question whatsoever about the principles decided in the Socony-Vacuum and Ethyl cases. To have approved cooperative action to stabilize markets, whatever the level of prices at which it was effected, would have seriously debilitated competitive forces in the industry. Certainly the temptation to use direct collaborative action to stem the weakness in product prices that followed the 1957 advance would have been strong, if not overpowering. In the domestic behavior of crude oil markets and prices, on the other hand, the reach of antitrust is necessarily limited when other government policies operate at cross purposes to it.

Conceptually most difficult to evaluate are the increasing number of suits that have been brought against individual major oil companies for price discrimination. This well-trodden ground need not be

56. Economically and psychologically, the service station that carries the "colors" and the name of the major refiner not only shares in the benefits of the latter's sales efforts but also, by its service and the quality of the goods it purveys, helps to mold the consumers' opinion of the integrity and the reputation of the refiner. These mutual benefits and stakes probably ensure preponderantly exclusive relationships. Suits like those against Socony Mobil and Shell in 1957 and 1958 (see above, pp. 464–465), because of the offer of inducements like lubricating racks and paint to secure from automobile dealers a preference for the refiner's oils and greases, are based on a theory similar to that of exclusive dealing cases. But judging only from the bare complaints, their economic consequences seem even more questionable. The provision of such goods along with the sale of product is so close to the essence of competition—even of *price* competition—that it is difficult to imagine what public interest would be served by prohibiting it.

retraversed,[57] but it is desirable to point up the ambivalent implications of these cases in the light of earlier analysis of the role of price discrimination in products pricing. The cases really fall into two groups. The first of these consists apparently exclusively of the action against Standard of Indiana under the Robinson-Patman Act; and the nature of its final resolution by the Supreme Court in 1958 seems to ensure that the class will remain small. The case hinged on dual distribution: Standard sold its Red Crown gasoline at the tank-car price to jobber-retailers while at the same time and in the same market it distributed directly to service stations at its tank-wagon price. The Supreme Court held first, in 1951, that it would be an absolute defense for Standard to demonstrate that it had offered the lower price to the jobber-retailers "in good faith to meet an equally low price of a competitor"; and second, in 1958, that Standard had in fact satisfied this requirement, and so enjoyed the protection of the good faith clause within the meaning of the Act. Each of these findings overturned decisions to the contrary by the Federal Trade Commission. In the competitive situations in which major refiners sell gasoline at cut prices to large distributors, it seems likely that they will always be able to make a sufficient demonstration of competitive necessity to satisfy the good faith defense;[58] there is no evidence that they do so except under such pressure.[59]

The second group of cases involves grants of voluntary allowances

57. For a discussion of and citation to other discussions of the most famous of these—the *Standard of Indiana* case—see Dirlam and Kahn, *Fair Competition*, pp. 121–133, 245–256, and McGee, "Price Discrimination and Competitive Effects." For the final outcome of that case, see 78 Supreme Court 369 (1958).

58. This may not be necessary if the refiner is not engaged in dual distribution. Only in the latter case could it presumably be attacked for selling at different prices to competing retailers and jobbers.

59. That this was so in the *Standard of Indiana* situation is persuasively demonstrated by McGee, "Price Discrimination and Competitive Effects." The boundaries of the good faith defense, however, are by no means clearly established. For one thing, the *Standard of Indiana* precedent would seem to require that the concession be defensive, that it be made to hold customers against competitive offers rather than to obtain new customers. Conceivably, therefore, the FTC might still be able to identify the *first* allegedly discriminatory offer and take action against it, more readily where the price-cutter is an interloper and offers unequal concessions to different customers. Again, the Commission might still successfully attack concessions that go farther than merely meeting competitive offers. However, the slowness with which antitrust moves makes it highly unlikely, especially in the light of *Standard of Indiana,* that it can cope with these highly dynamic market phenomena.

by major refiner-marketers to their dealers in price-war situations. These cases are in varying stages of development and the facts are not yet completely available, but it is alleged that the grant of allowances was always accompanied by pressure on the dealers to reduce their prices to meet competition. The suits instituted by the Federal Trade Commission against Texas,[60] Sun,[61] and Pure [62] have all been brought under the Robinson-Patman Act, on the ground that the allowances to selected dealers were discriminatory against other dealers, and further that the good faith defense does not permit a supplier to offer a differential concession to a selected dealer or group of dealers in order to enable *them* to meet price cuts by other dealers.[63] Violation of Section 5 of the Federal Trade Commission Act was also alleged on the ground that the individual suppliers had illegally agreed with their favored dealers to fix retail prices. The Department of Justice instituted similar suits in 1956 against Shell [64] and Socony Mobil [65] for allegedly combining with their dealers, in violation of Section 1 of the Sherman Act, to fix the retail prices of their respective gasolines and offering them concessions from the posted price to induce or make it possible for them to do so.

While the evidence developed in these proceedings may help to sort out the competitive consequences of voluntary allowances in price wars, the theories underlying the complaints seem to be partially contradictory. On one hand, the selective proffer of discounts by

60. Complaint 6898, October 10, 1957. In a similar private suit, filed by a service station operator who had been denied voluntary allowances that Texas had granted others of its dealers in his area, the Court of Appeals, overturning the District Court, held that the plaintiff had failed to prove damages and had not been in close competition with the favored Texaco dealers. *Enterprise Industries v. The Texas Company,* 136 F. Supplement 420; 240 F. 2d 457; Certiorari Denied, 77 Supreme Court 1049 (1957).

61. Docket No. 6641, *Initial Decision* (by the Hearing Examiner), April 30, 1958. The FTC's action against Sun in 1957 for "coercing" its dealers to become commission agents (see p. 410) is similar in intent.

62. Docket No. 6640, Complaint, September 28, 1956.

63. This represents a shift from the Commission's position prior to 1956 when it had held that such price reductions also enjoyed the protection of the good faith defense. See the testimony of Chairman Gwynne, Senate Committee on the Judiciary, Subcommittee on Antitrust and Monopoly, "To Amend Section 2 of the Clayton Act," *Hearings,* 84th Congress, 2d Session (June–July, 1956), pp. 229–232; and cf. *ibid.,* pp. 89–92.

64. Cr. 5675-W, Boston, Massachusetts. Defendants pleaded *nolo contendere* and were fined, March 28, 1956.

65. Five indictments numbered Cr. 56-152-S through Cr. 56-157-S and one Cr. 56-157-M, Boston, Massachusetts, June 28, 1956.

a company to particular dealers in exchange for a commitment to reduce the retail price is claimed to be unfairly injurious to its other dealers in the area who either lose business or find their margin further compressed between the declining retail prices of their competitors and their own established tank-wagon prices. On the other, this kind of vertical price-fixing [66] is alleged to be a way of disciplining the competitors who initiate price cuts. Here are the familiar divergent criticisms of major-company interventions in price wars: that they instigate and prolong them, and that they use their power to bring price-shaders and price-cutters to heel.

The ambiguities inherent in these practices are further clouded by the partially divergent purposes of regulation. The objectives of government in these cases (and in most Congressional inquiries of supplier-dealer relations) are mixed, and correctly so: they seek to preserve vigorous price competition, but they also seek to ensure fair treatment of the individual small competitor. Obviously, fairness is not solely economic. Just as clearly, the inequalities of bargaining power in petroleum marketing, arising largely out of differences in the size and degree of integration of the firms engaged in it, and the inevitably differential impact of price discrimination, make it almost certain that price competition in imperfect markets will expose some businessmen to pressures that may rightly be regarded as unfair. In these circumstances the fortunes of individual firms do not reflect merely their relative efficiency in serving the public.[67]

In its understandable solicitude for the fair treatment of the small retailer, however, the Federal Trade Commission has given inadequate attention to social advantages in permitting large marketers to meet competition in good faith in the popular meaning of the term; and it has not properly weighed the probability that these instances

66. Shell was also accused of horizontal price-fixing, which is of course illegal per se, on the ground that the company itself operated one of the service stations in the area in which it allegedly agreed with its other dealers on the prices they were to charge. This is perhaps why Shell pleaded *nolo contendere;* but most of the suits do not claim any price-fixing agreements between direct competitors. Socony, instead, pleaded the protection of the fair trade laws for its vertical price-fixing and won a favorable decision on these grounds. Commerce Clearing House, *Trade Regulation Service,* par. 68,679 (1957).

67. For example, Sun's discount of 1.7 cents a gallon to one dealer in Jacksonville, accompanied apparently by an understanding that he would reduce his price by 3 cents, seems to have resulted in a very marked increase in his sales and some substantial diversion of business from other Sun dealers who were not, for slightly more than six weeks, granted a similar concession. See *Initial Decision* (above, n. 61), pp. 4–10.

of differential pricing have more often invigorated than they have sapped the vitality of price competition as a continuing force in the markets affected. Most of the evidence seems clearly to demonstrate that a company offers discounts because its dealers are losing business to price-cutting competitors; since the major suppliers compete among themselves and with independents primarily *through* their dealers, the concessions are made in a very real sense in good faith to meet competition.[68] Furthermore, there is little evidence—and certainly none so far in these cases—that the discriminations complained of put a halt to price competition, or even threatened to do so.[69] On the contrary, dual distribution and discriminatory price concessions seem to have contributed on balance to the intensity of price competition, where their effects have been visible.

68. In the Sun case mentioned in the previous footnote the dealer had asked for assistance when on several previous occasions a private brand station across the street had increased the spread between their prices beyond the customary 2 cents and he had lost gallonage, before Sun finally gave him the 1.7 cents allowance. The Trial Examiner held that this allowance was not in good faith, within the meaning of the law, for three reasons: (1) under the new FTC interpretation mentioned above, the Act permits a company to give discounts only to keep *its* customers, not to help its customers hold *their* customers; (2) the cut enabled the dealer not merely to meet his competition but to beat it: his 3-cent price reduction narrowed the gap to only one cent above the private brand rather than the customary 2 cents (the competitor then came down another cent a week later, restoring the 2-cent difference); (3) a concession cannot be in good faith when it is contingent on an illegal agreement to fix prices. *Initial Decision*, pp. 11–16. It is difficult to see how a supplier could respond to a dealer's pleas for assistance in meeting the prices of a competitor without some understanding between them about what the dealer would do with the discount!

69. The *Initial Decision* in the Sun case permits a laconic calendar. *Prior to Dec. 27, 1955:* On several occasions, Super Test (the private brand station across the street) had cut prices, taken gallonage, and then restored the 2-cent differential. McLean (the favored Sun dealer) had requested an allowance from Sun to meet the price but to no avail.—*Dec. 27, 1955:* Super Test cut price from 26.9 to 24.9 cents; Sun granted McLean a 1.7-cent allowance; and he cut his price 3.0 cents to 25.9 cents per gallon.—*Jan. 3, 1956:* Super Test cut price to 23.9 cents to re-establish the 2-cent differential.—*Feb. 16, 1956 or thereabouts:* Price war broke out in entire area and Sun reduced its tank-wagon price to all its dealers in the area who until this time had been maintaining the original 28.9-cent-per-gallon price.—*Feb. 18, 1956 or thereabouts:* McLean went out of business. This is the end of the official record.

In the Standard of Indiana situation as well, the discounts failed to bring the price wars in Detroit to a close; indeed, they remained chronic throughout the period examined in the case—a major reason why the FTC found "injury to competition" within the meaning of the Robinson-Patman Act.

On the other hand, the effects of price discrimination are sufficiently invisible, and those of its possible alternatives sufficiently uncertain that it is often impossible to say whether the Federal Trade Commission's interpretation of the Robinson-Patman Act conflicts with the long-range interests of the ultimate consumer. These selective concessions, accompanied by pressures on retailers to reduce their prices to meet those of price-cutters, undoubtedly have as one purpose, and may well at times have the effect, of subduing an unruly independent if not driving him out of business.[70] The threat may forestall price competition that would otherwise take place. Its exercise may in the short term intensify price wars but in the longer run bring them to a close—one simply cannot be certain. It is simply not always clear that price rivalry would be any less effective if major suppliers were forbidden to discriminate.[71] Conceivably, price wars in this event would be diminished, or prove self-limiting rather than cumulative. But price wars are themselves a highly selective, unstable, and impermanent form of price competition. They may be the best one can hope for within the oil market structure. On the other hand, to prohibit price discrimination in these circumstances could improve competitive opportunities for independents, and, if so, it could ensure a wider and more stable distribution of the benefits of price competition. But this is a very "if-y" proposition because a prohibition of price discrimination, depending on how it is interpreted, strikes at one of the important competitive advantages of integration:

70. In the Sun case, again, McLean apparently would have been fully content to restore the 2-cent differential between his own price and that of Super Test (*Initial Decision*, pp. 12, 14–16). In the Pure case the concessions were allegedly accompanied by adoption of a so-called "Chicago plan" or "one-cent policy," involving a commitment by the Pure dealers to keep their retail prices at no more than one cent above private brands. There is nothing sacrosanct about the 2-cent differential, especially as private brands gain increasing reputation for quality, and it would be inappropriate for the government to tell individual sellers what relationship they must maintain between their respective prices. Still, "meeting competition" in this fashion can end by destroying it.

71. It is not always clear precisely how they can avoid discrimination and still compete. Sun cut its price to a single dealer to meet the price of a competitor across the street, and (at least in the *Initial Decision*) was condemned because Sun dealers a mile or so away lost business. It later cut its tank-wagon price to all dealers "in the area" and apparently thus ceased the condemned practice. But Pure gave its 120 dealers in Birmingham 1½ cents off its own tank-wagon price, and is apparently under attack under the Robinson-Patman Act for not having extended the allowance to its other dealers in Alabama and in other states. See "Oil Companies on the Carpet," *Business Week* (October 6, 1956), pp. 146–154.

horizontal and, conceivably, vertical as well; and its consequences might therefore be much more far-reaching than the regulatory agencies apparently envisage.

The foregoing discussion may appear needlessly inconclusive. This much can perhaps be said by way of summary. First, whether price discrimination serves the public interest can only be determined by the specific examination of individual cases. Second, the definition of the "public interest" is as much a political as an economic problem—that is to say, a problem of conflicting group interests and social values. Third, the assessment of even the "purely economic" consequences is extremely difficult, but that is probably because the issues are much closer than one would gather from most of the literature on the subject. The practice of price discrimination or its prohibition, of course, may have a very great effect on the fortunes of the individual businessmen concerned, but the interests of the ultimate consumers are not so heavily or so seriously involved in most of the difficult cases as is usually contended by the interested parties. Where supplies are out of control, one is likely to find both price discrimination and strenuous price competition; in those circumstances the prohibition of the former is not very likely to prevent the latter.[72] Where supplies are closely geared to demand and in strong hands, both price discrimination and price competition are less likely to be present; in those circumstances, to permit the former is by no means to assure the latter.

In addition to antitrust prosecutions, the government has exposed the oil industry during the last twenty years to almost continuous public scrutiny in innumerable hearings before various committees of the Congress. Beginning with the lengthy testimony and studies of the TNEC, Congress has concerned itself with a long series of pricing and marketing problems in petroleum: increases in the price of crude in 1947; the fuel oil shortage of 1948; the gasoline price increase of 1949; the effect of imports on the domestic price of crude; the problems of independent refiners in 1949; the crude and products price increases of 1953 and 1957; the New Jersey price wars; as well as a great variety of distribution practices.

---

72. McGee's analysis ("Price Discrimination and Competitive Effects") of the Detroit gasoline market between 1936 and 1940 makes it perfectly clear that the price discrimination at issue in the *Standard of Indiana* case was dictated by, and part of, the process of competition, and that it certainly did not destroy competition; what it does not make clear is that the price discrimination was essential or even the major factor in bringing prices and margins down.

It is impossible to supply an authoritative appraisal of the effect of these hearings. Considering their varying subjects and purposes, it would be surprising if they did not reflect all the ambivalences of other government policies bearing on the industry. They are frequently anticompetitive in tone, whether consciously, as in the hearings on the "import problem," or unwittingly, as in the hearings on price wars and the problems of small business.[73] Nonetheless one has the strong impression that this publicity serves a useful and important function. It is enough that the investigations are virtually current with the event subject to complaint, that they follow any significant change in policy as surely as income taxes follow the receipt of income, and that they are public. They cannot help imposing on management a constraint and a consciousness of areas of public concern that imperfectly competitive forces alone are unable to muster. They help to assure that pricing will be governed by considerations of fairness and cost-justification. Even if fully effective, these pressures could not be an adequate substitute for competition. "Just price" is never a dynamic, risk-taking, innovating price. But given the present market structure in oil, these pressures seem to serve the public interest.

73. "Senator KEFAUVER. . . . my question was, sir, whether you think it is fair, when you get to be a jobber, to be a retailer also, and take your larger discount and operate service stations of your own at a price which the other little fellows, because they are just retailers, cannot meet.

"Mr. CITRIN [of Citrin-Kolb, one of the jobbers in the Detroit case]. I will restate that the jobber's margin . . . is a separate part of the business which is to take care of the bulk plant and equipment and painting and servicing of the dealers.

"Senator KEFAUVER. . . . What you were doing was substantially injuring competition. That is right, is it not, Mr. Citrin? . . . You gasoline jobbers, if that is what you classify yourself as, cannot have your cake and eat it, too. You cannot be a jobber and run retail stations. . . . I would suggest when you are a jobber that you get out of the retail business, and sell to all of your customers at the same price and that you not get into the retail business and unfairly compete with your own retail customers."

Senate Judiciary Committee, "To Amend Section 2 of the Clayton Act," *Hearings* (1956), pp. 405–408.

CHAPTER 19

Vertical Integration and the Independent Refiner

THE READER will remember that there is no definitive distinction between major refiners—say the top thirty companies in the industry, which are completely integrated vertically but seldom in balance— and the independent refiners, the smallest of which are not integrated but which, as a group, are typically integrated in some varying degree. Nevertheless, the independent is so different from the major, and plays so distinctive a role, that it is important to consider his competitive prospects.

CONCENTRATION TRENDS IN REFINING

The most significant fact about petroleum refining in the last forty years has been its enormous growth. Refinery capacity in the United States expanded from 1,186,000 b/d of crude oil throughput on January 1, 1918, to 9,123,674 b/d on January 1, 1957.[1]

The second fact is that the average size of the physical refinery has been growing very rapidly. There were 267 refineries in the United States at the earlier date and 319 thirty-nine years later. Average refinery size thus increased from about 4,500 b/d to more than 28,600 b/d during the period.

Third, there has been a tendency for the number of refining *companies* to decrease. There were an estimated 274 such companies in this country on January 1, 1920, 223 at the beginning of 1950, and 185 at the start of 1957.[2] Of the 1950 figure, some 179 at most were actually operating at the end of that year,[3] only about 170 in 1957. The average capacity then of each refining company has been increasing even more rapidly than that of each individual refinery.

The trends just described conceal two opposite intermediate changes. The expansion of national production capacity until 1935

1. Bureau of Mines, annual refinery survey. Data on number and size of refineries and refining companies used henceforth are based on this source unless otherwise indicated.
2. See Table XXIII.
3. McLean and Haigh, p. 19.

484

or 1936 was associated with a very substantial increase in the population of refiners as well. Between January 1, 1914, and January 1, 1935, the number of refineries increased from 176 to 631 (despite an intermediate loss of 138 refineries between 1925 and 1930). Average size, therefore, rose only to about 6,400 b/d during this period from around 4,500 b/d at the beginning of 1918. Concurrently, the number of refining companies in the United States also increased very rapidly, though it failed to pace the number of refineries because of multiplant operations and numerous mergers.[4] After 1935 the number of refiners declined continuously and drastically along with the number of refineries, while the national refinery capacity rose and the apparent size of the average refinery and of the average refining company shot upward.[5]

Despite the dramatic character of these changes in numbers of firms, concentration in refining as usually measured (the share of capacity or output in the hands of some specified number of leading companies) has increased only moderately for a number of reasons. (1) The industry was a virtual monopoly in the first decade of the century; one could hardly expect an increase in concentration since then. (2) Dissolution left the major proportion of refining capacity with about eight leading Standard successor companies. Between 1920 and 1957 the share of two of these companies, Atlantic and Standard of California, and of some of the large independents as well, notably Union Oil,[6] has actually declined. Conversely, there has been a relative rise of most of the other majors, although their combined share has risen only moderately. (3) Most of the majors of 1957 were already majors in 1920.[7] (4) The predominant proportion

4. Data on the number of refining companies are not readily available, although they could be compiled for all years since 1918 from Bureau of Mines reports, which identify the owners of each refinery. The Furcht memorandum (see Table XXIII) estimates the number of refining companies and their capacities at ten-year intervals. Beginning January 1, 1920, he shows 274 refining companies and 383 in 1940, by which time the number of refineries had already declined to 547 from their all-time peak of 632 four years earlier. There must have been well over 400 companies in existence at the peak of the thirties.

5. These arithmetic averages are grossly exaggerated by the gigantic refineries and refining capacities of the biggest companies. The arithmetic average refinery at the end of 1950 had 19,500 b/d capacity; but the *median* size refining *company* still had less than 5,000 b/d, even though many companies had more than one refinery. See table in McLean and Haigh, p. 20.

6. The share of Mid-Continent also declined until its merger with Sunray in 1955.

7. Of the twenty leading refiners at the later date, Phillips, Continental, Rich-

of new refineries constructed in the upsurge of the twenties and thirties were small, some extremely so; their subsequent disappearance had relatively little effect on the concentration ratios of an already concentrated industry.

Table XXIII pictures the distribution of refineries and refinery capacity between the twenty TNEC majors [8] and the rest of the industry at selected dates since 1920. The apparent increase in the

TABLE XXIII

Growth of United States Refining Industry by Decades: TNEC Majors and Independents, 1920–57

	NUMBER OF COMPANIES	NUMBER OF PLANTS	CRUDE OIL CAPACITY (M B/D)	PER CENT OF INDUSTRY PLANTS	CAPACITY
Major Companies (As of Jan. 1st)					
1920	16	71	810	19.1	52.9
1930	20	134	2,711	32.5	72.0
1940	20	138	3,365	25.2	72.7
1950	20	131	5,262	35.8	78.6
1957	20	123	7,207	38.6	79.0
Independents (As of Jan. 1st)					
1920	258	301	721	80.9	47.1
1930	230	278	1,055	67.5	28.0
1940	363	409	1,264	74.8	27.3
1950	203	235	1,434	64.2	21.4
1957	165	196	1,917	61.4	21.0
Total Industry (As of Jan. 1st)					
1920	274	372	1,531	100.0	100.0
1930	250	412	3,766	100.0	100.0
1940	383	547	4,629	100.0	100.0
1950	223	366	6,696	100.0	100.0
1957	185	319	9,124	100.0	100.0

Source: 1920–50 data, C. M. Furcht, Coordination and Economics Department, Standard Oil Company (New Jersey), *Growth and Structure of U.S. Refining Industry,* mimeographed, p. 2; 1957 computations from Bureau of Mines.

---

field, and Ashland are significant exceptions. Sun and Standard of Ohio, now within this top group, ranked twenty-first and twenty-ninth in refinery capacity in 1920. For 1920 data see McLean and Haigh, p. 528.

8. See above, p. 27, n. 34.

share of those twenty companies over the entire period from 52.9 per cent to 79.0 per cent of national capacity, and especially the sharp advance to 72.0 per cent in 1930, however, is misleading because the companies identified as majors were selected on the basis of their status at the time of the TNEC inquiry—that is, late in the period studied. Selection of companies which have *emerged* as leaders inevitably exaggerates the appearance of increasing concentration over the period in which they have emerged.[9]

In Table XXIV the foregoing error is avoided by computing the

TABLE XXIV

Percentage Control of Total United States Refinery Capacity by the Leading Oil Companies [a] in Selected Years, 1920–57

PERCENTAGE CONTROLLED BY

	THE TOP FIVE	THE TOP TEN	THE TOP FIFTEEN	THE TOP TWENTY
January 1				
1920	30.9	48.2	58.8	65.0
1925	34.5	50.0	59.0	64.3
1930	39.4	61.1	70.4	75.4
1935	36.0	56.9	67.7	74.0
1940	38.1	58.6	70.3	75.8
1950	40.8	62.2	73.8	79.8
1957	38.7	61.3	73.5	80.4

[a] The companies falling in each group are the leading companies as of the year in question; thus the composition of the "top five," e.g., varies somewhat from one year to another.

Sources: 1920–50 from McLean and Haigh, p. 701; 1957 percentages computed from Bureau of Mines.

percentage of national capacity in the possession of a specified number of the top companies at each date without regard to continuity of company identity between dates. Apart from damping considerably

9. As a matter of fact, four of the TNEC's leading twenty firms had *no* refining capacity in 1920—Continental, Skelly, Phillips, and Ohio Oil. They must therefore have supplanted four other companies in any list of leading refiners in the earlier years and thus exaggerated the increase in concentration measured, as it is in Table XXIII, by grouping the top companies on the basis of their ranking in 1940. This technical error produces much less serious distortion in the oil industry than it might in others because the composition of the majors has been so stable over the last few decades and because almost all the leaders of 1920 which disappeared were simply merged into majors. See below, nn. 11, 12.

the relative rise of the top twenty between 1920 and 1957, and especially up to 1930,[10] the general picture is unchanged: their share rose from 65.0 per cent to 80.4 per cent of the national total during the entire period, with the biggest jump coming between 1920 and 1930, and another in the 1940–50 decade.[11] The substantial contribution of mergers to the 1920–30 change was noted in Chapter 14.[12] As Table XXIV shows, virtually all the increase in concentra-

10. The net increase in shares of national capacity held over the entire period is reduced from approximately twenty-six to about fifteen percentage points; from 1920 to 1930, the net increase falls from about nineteen to slightly over ten percentage points. Cf. Tables XXIII and XXIV.

11. Just as a selection of leading firms at the terminal date would show a more rapid increase in concentration, a selection of leading firms at the initial date should show a slower one. It is an indication of the relative stability of concentration patterns in the oil industry since 1920 that the differences between the results of these varying inquiries are not substantial. E.g., the top five refiners in 1920 had 30.9 per cent of the industry's capacity; those *same* five firms had 36.9 per cent in 1957, compared with 38.7 per cent held by the five who were in fact leaders in the latter year. Obviously the identities of the leaders could not have changed much (in fact four of the five were the same companies). The top ten in 1920 had 48.2 per cent of national refinery capacity; those same ten companies (Magnolia, No. 10 in 1920, is included with Socony Mobil in the later year) had 60.0 per cent of the total, compared with the 62.3 per cent controlled by the ten actual leaders in 1957. Eight of the companies in the earlier list were among the top ten in 1957.

Again, the top fifteen in 1920 had 58.8 per cent of the national total; if one takes those same companies, now dwindled to thirteen because of mergers among themselves, and adds to them the next two from the 1920 list (actually one must move down to numbers 19 and 21, since intervening companies have likewise been merged with firms higher on the list) in order to make a corresponding fifteen companies for 1957, one finds their market share increased to 72.0 per cent of the national total. This figure is scarcely lower than the 73.5 per cent share of the actual fifteen leaders in the latter year; only one company on the 1920 list of the top fifteen was not among the top fifteen thirty-seven years later!

12. Of the thirty leading 1920 refiners, fourteen are still among the twenty majors; sixteen have disappeared as corporate entities or as truly independent companies. These sixteen and their rankings on the basis of refinery capacity in 1920 were as follows: Magnolia (10), Midwest Refining (11), Associated Oil (12), Ohio Cities Gas (15), General Petroleum (16), Pierce Oil (17), Cosden and Co. (19), Vacuum Oil (20), Standard of Kansas (22), Indian Refining (23), American Oilfields (24), Midco Gasolene (25), Pan-American Petroleum (26), White Eagle (27), Constantin Refining (28), and Solar Refining (30). From McLean and Haigh, p. 528.

Magnolia was absorbed by Standard of New York and Midwest by Standard of Indiana, and Associated was merged into Tide Water Associated; Ohio Cities changed its name in 1920 to Pure Oil; General Petroleum was absorbed by

tion, so far as the leading five and the leading ten refiners are concerned, took place before 1930. Only the group between the 11th and 20th rankings increased its share of the industry substantially as compared with 1930, a reflection of the tendency for leadership to become somewhat more evenly divided among the major companies.

The indications of increased concentration in national refinery output are less clearly marked than in refining capacity. For its twenty majors (and subject to reservations already noted), the TNEC reported an increase from 71.2 to 82.6 per cent of total runs to stills between 1926 and 1937 with almost the entire rise occurring by 1931.[13] Since that date no significant increase in concentration is evident. Cookenboo's computations for nineteen of the same twenty companies (Mid-Continent alone omitted) for selected years show a slight increase from 79.1 to 81.2 per cent of the national total between 1930 and 1937, but thereafter hold roughly constant at 82.5 per cent and 81.7 per cent in 1948 and 1952 respectively.[14] The leading nineteen refiners accounted for 82.5 per cent of refining runs in 1956; the unchanged TNEC list of nineteen ran 80.5 per cent.[15] Even more striking, the Federal Trade Commission reported data which permit an estimate of "crude oil consumed" by the ten leading companies in 1925 at 64.1 per cent of the total in that year.[16] The ten

Standard of New York and Pierce Oil by Sinclair; Cosden was a predecessor of Mid-Continent; Vacuum and Standard of New York were merged in Socony-Vacuum; Standard of Kansas was absorbed by Standard of Indiana; Indian and American Oilfields by Texas Company; Pan-American by Standard of Indiana; White Eagle by Standard of New York; and Solar by Standard of Ohio. This leaves only two companies, Midco and Constantin, which went out of business; all the others were absorbed by companies that were already majors—all of them, except Standard of Ohio, among the top twenty refiners in 1920 before these acquisitions.

13. *Hearings,* Pt. XIV-A, p. 7735.

14. Using a changing group of the ten leading refiners, there is no increase in concentration whatever: the top ten accounted for 66.9 per cent of national runs to stills in 1930, 66.6 per cent in 1937, 65.7 per cent in 1948, and 66.3 per cent in 1952. Computed from Cookenboo, *Crude Oil Pipe Lines,* p. 44. The corresponding 1956 figure would be 64.0 per cent.

15. Computations from *National Petroleum News Factbooks.* The 1957 figures show a slight decline in concentration, 81.4 per cent of national refinery runs for the top nineteen and 79.3 per cent for the TNEC group. This followed policy cutbacks in refinery runs by the major companies in that year of declining prices while the runs of the rest of the industry actually increased.

16. *Petroleum Industry* (1928), p. 77. Actually the FTC gives figures for eighteen reporting refiners. But since it nowhere indicates that these were the eighteen largest—on the contrary, it is clear they were not—one must deduct

leading refiners in 1956 accounted for 64.0 to 65.6 per cent of national crude runs to stills.[17] No appreciable change appears from this comparison over a period of thirty-one years.

The preponderant majority of the refineries, the capacity of which has disappeared from national totals especially during the last twenty to twenty-five years, were extremely small—well under 5,000 b/d. Springing up in flush producing fields, operating on oil when they could get it and shutting down quickly when they could not, their actual refinery throughputs probably never approached magnitudes that reflected their nominal share of national capacity. A large part of their plant was not even being operated in the years in which it was still entered in the national totals. A disproportionate share of the capacity of the small refineries has always been listed as shutdown; but that proportion has been decreasing in recent years as obsolete refineries have been dismantled or for other reasons removed from the national totals. Thus, the share of the major refiners in national *operating* capacity has increased markedly less—though still significantly—than in aggregate capacity, as compared both with 1925 and 1935.[18] In addition, and for much the same reasons, small

---

the eight smallest (Standard of Kentucky, Galena Signal Oil, Standard of Kansas, Solar Refining, Continental Oil, Prairie Oil and Gas, Vacuum Oil, and Standard of Ohio—all included in the list of eighteen only because they were Standard successor companies. Even the largest of these, Sohio and Vacuum, had far less refinery capacity than Pure Oil and Union Oil, which were not included in the FTC survey). The remaining companies, Standard of New Jersey, of New York, of Indiana, and of California, Atlantic, Sinclair, Tidewater, Texas, Gulf, and Shell probably did comprise the ten leaders, with the probable exception of Atlantic, whose refinery capacity in 1926 was less than that of Union Oil. See capacity figures for each of the twenty majors, 1926–38, in TNEC, *Hearings,* Pt. XIV-A, p. 7801.

17. The higher figure includes Richfield with its owners, Cities Service, and Sinclair (see above, p. 27, n. 35). Comparable 1957 figures, depressed for reasons already indicated (above, n. 15), are 62.9 to 64.4 per cent.

18. Percentages of national operating capacity controlled by the five, ten, fifteen, and twenty leading refiners at selected dates were as follows:

JANUARY 1	TOP 5	TOP 10	TOP 15	TOP 20
1925	38.6	56.2	66.1	71.9
1930	40.4	62.3	71.9	77.0
1935	40.0	62.5	72.6	79.5
1940	39.7	59.8	72.0	77.2
1950	42.0	64.8	76.8	82.0

Source: McLean and Haigh, p. 701.

Comparing this table with above, Table XXIV, it appears that while the top twenty companies increased their share of total national capacity from

refineries typically operate at a lower percentage of their operating capacity than large. This was especially true of the smallest refineries of twenty-five to thirty years ago, most of which have disappeared from the scene.[19] As they were removed, the major companies' share of national operating refinery capacity would therefore rise more than their share of refinery runs.

Finally, the observed absence of secular trend in the concentration ratios of the top ten companies after 1925 and the continued comparative growth of the top twenty, merely underscores the expansion of this second group of majors, among which are counted several that were relatively small at the beginning of the period.[20] As noted, the top five or the top ten refiners accounted for about the same proportion of capacity in 1957 as in 1930 but the changing population from eleventh to twentieth largest rose from 14.3 per cent as a group to 19.1 per cent over the same period.

In sum, the last thirty-eight years have witnessed a substantial increase in the size of the average refinery and of the average refining company; a sharp decline in the number of refining companies, especially since 1935; some increase in concentration of refining among the major companies, whose dominant market position owes much to mergers in the 1920's and before; relative stability in the position of the very top firms since 1925 or 1930, but a con-

---

64.3 to 79.8 per cent in the 1925–50 period, their share in operating capacity rose noticeably less, though still markedly—from 71.9 to 82.0 per cent. The sharp decline that occurred between 1930 and 1935 in shares of national capacity of the top five and ten companies and their subsequent recoveries are both practically obliterated in the data for operating capacity: obviously the 1935 figure of stated capacity was heavily inflated by a large amount of shut-in refineries among the smaller members of the industry.

19. On the other hand, low reported operating ratios of small refineries in the 1930's may have been more apparent than real: many small field plants operated to a considerable extent on hot oil, and it is likely that much of their throughput was never recorded in the national statistics. This fact, too, would cause their disappearance to produce a greater impact on national capacity than on national output figures.

20. Over the period 1920–50, McLean and Haigh found that the top thirty refiners increased their share of national capacity from 71.6 to 85.1 per cent; but the original thirty had been compressed mainly through merger to a mere sixteen by 1950 which together accounted for only 73.3 per cent. Thus they observed that "a large part of the decline from 28.4% to 14.9% of the industry refining capacity experienced by small refiners over the 30-year period may be explained by the fact that 14 small companies moved into the large company group and thereby added 11.8% to the capacity of the large company group" (p. 529).

tinued expansion in the relative position of the newer majors and the larger, more fully integrated independents as well.[21]

SOCIAL EFFICIENCY AND THE STATUS OF THE INDEPENDENT

Two theories of the apparent decline of the independent refiner have been clearly articulated; each is or can be made to be internally consistent, convincing, and apparently adequate. Each has its partisans. And neither has ever been adequately reconciled with the other, assimilated into the other, or proved by objective evidence superior to the other. The task of choosing between them, or of formulating some combination that represents a nearer approximation to the truth, is perplexing; but it cannot be avoided.

The one theory regards the competitive handicaps of the independent refiner and the exit of so many of them as an incident of economic progress, resulting from a combination of inexorable forces whose existence and operation accords with the social interest. These forces are in part technological, in part institutional, but the consequences for society are efficiency and conservation, and for the business community, survival of the fittest. The other attributes the decline of the small refiner less to technology and the genuine requirements of conservation and efficiency than to the strategic handicaps imposed by the vertical integration and sheer size of the majors and to state production controls less in the interest of conservation than of price maintenance. According to this view, survival in the oil industry is not necessarily survival of those who serve society best; and the consequences threaten subversion of the public interest for the benefit of the few.

The issue is deeper than a mere conflict of evidence or of interests among opposing parties; it will arise among observers who try sedulously to be impartial and who have no direct economic interests that might keep them from doing so. Involved here are radically divergent conceptions of feasible institutional alternatives to the present system and of quite different conceptions of what kinds of social and institutional incentives and organizational arrangements are required to take the fullest advantage of the physical potentialities of the

21. While many small refiners have been dying off, many others have been prospering and holding their own with modern, expanded refineries. This is indicated generally in Table XXIII above, where the substantial decline shown in the number of refineries and companies other than the TNEC's majors from 1940 to 1957 is accompanied by a rise in capacity for this group of more than 650,000 b/d.

chemistry or the geology of petroleum compared with alternative sources of energy. In some essentials both theories are substantially correct. The respect in which both are wrong must therefore be their claim to exclusiveness as an explanation.

The Life Cycle of the Independent Refiner

The long-range decline in the numbers of independent refiners in the United States began around 1935. So did effective prorationing of crude oil and the introduction of catalytic cracking. It cannot be doubted that these phenomena are causally related.

The small, relatively nonintegrated refiner has thrived, historically, on cheap and plentiful crude oil. The history of the American industry before prorationing (and since then, as well, in areas lacking effective production controls) is a saga of the dramatic mushrooming of independent refiners in the fields where new discoveries had uncorked unmanageable flows of crude oil and forced its field price to a fraction of its former level. Eventually, these flush flows of cheap crude would dry up as pools were exhausted and pressures fell, as governmental production controls were established, or as pipelines were built into the surplus area to siphon the oil into more profitable markets. Whatever the cause, the net price at the wellhead would ultimately rise and soon thereafter most of the crop of refiners that a cheap and irrationally overproduced raw material had spawned would disappear.

McLean and Haigh provide a detailed documentation of this process in their careful description of the life cycles of two producing fields. Most phenomenal (in national and in world experience) was the period ushered in by the discovery of the great East Texas Field in 1930. Although records are not complete, about 100 plants were constructed in or very near that field in the following six years. But at the beginning of 1936 there were only seventy-six plants listed in the area and only twenty-seven were operating. By January 1, 1940, there were only fourteen plants, including those operating and those shut down as well.[22] This experience has been duplicated on a less grandiose scale time and again as other fields were discovered.[23]

Even today small refiners are concentrated disproportionately in

22. Pp. 587–599 *passim*. The discovery of the first commercial oil well in this country had induced a similar boom: between 1859 and 1863, sixty-one plants sprang up in the new oil fields; within fifteen years only a few remained. *Ibid.*, pp. 586–587.

23. For their story of the Illinois refinery boom of 1938–40 see *ibid.*, pp. 599–605.

and near the major producing fields. For example, at the beginning of 1957, when the average size of all domestic refineries was about 28,600 b/d, inland Texas had thirty with an average capacity of only 10,500 b/d, the Midcontinent states (Oklahoma, Kansas, Missouri, etc.) had thirty-four refineries averaging 22,200 b/d, the Rocky Mountain area had forty-four with 7,600 b/d, and inland Arkansas and Louisiana had fifteen with 7,200 b/d.[24] All of these areas except the Rocky Mountain have declined sharply in relative importance as refining centers since 1930 or 1935. In contrast, the big refineries, owned principally by the major companies, tend to congregate nearer the major markets and/or within ready reach of water transportation. The thirty-eight refineries on the Texas and Louisiana Gulf Coast averaged 77,800 and the twenty-five on the East Coast 54,500 b/d, on January 1, 1957.[25]

Technological Handicaps of the Small Refiner

The average size of the ninety-one operating inland refiners in Texas was 3,600 b/d on January 1, 1936, when all other operating refineries in the United States averaged over 10,000 b/d. The additional ninety-six Texas inland plants, already shut down, averaged under 2,000 b/d.

Considering only the costs of production, a refinery of 2,500 or 5,000 or 15,000 b/d was in 1936 and is today less efficient than one of several times the larger figure, assuming all were of the same type. There is little definitive information on the matter of economies of scale in refining, and much of what is available is to some extent conflicting. It would therefore lend a specious appearance of precision to the varying estimates to discuss them at length. But all authorities seem to agree that there are very substantial economies of scale up to a fair size—some would say 15,000 b/d might suffice for "reasonable efficiency," others would say a refinery ought to be twice that size to be competitive. Beyond this somewhat vague range, unit

24. Computations from Bureau of Mines, annual refinery survey. McLean and Haigh supply similar computations for selected years 1920–50 (p. 535). They show also that in the latter year, when national average refinery capacity was over 18,000 b/d, the Southern Great Lakes Region, covering the producing fields of Kentucky, Illinois, Indiana, and Ohio, but excluding the urban centers of those states, had an average refinery capacity of 10,241 b/d; the refineries in Michigan (outside of Detroit) averaged 4,367 b/d; those in the Appalachian area (western New York, western Pennsylvania, West Virginia) averaged 5,862 b/d.

25. Computations from Bureau of Mines, annual refinery survey.

costs continue to decline as the refinery gets bigger but at a much lesser rate. The tendency appears to have no apparent limit: a 60,000 b/d refinery will have lower unit costs than a 30,000, a 100,000 b/d than a 60,000, and a 200,000 b/d than a 100,000—although the margin of superiority becomes less and less. Both investment costs per barrel of capacity and unit operating costs fall as size increases.[26]

Independent refineries as a group have been not only inefficiently small but generally lacking in modern equipment and processes. In 1935, all refiners below the top thirty had 21.6 per cent of the nation's total crude oil throughput but only 9.3 per cent of national cracking capacity; that is, they had only twenty-three barrels of cracking for every 100 barrels of throughput, whereas the top thirty refiners had sixty-three for every 100.[27] This average was seriously depressed by the great number of simple topping or skimming plants, some of them hardly more than boilers, that had mushroomed in the flush fields of the thirties. The inadequacy of these plants is indicated by McLean and Haigh's estimate that "many" of these units in East Texas in the early thirties represented a total investment "well under $25,000." In contrast, they estimate elsewhere that a 25,000 b/d refinery in 1935, using the best processes available at the time, would have cost over $8,000,000.[28] Only seventeen of the seventy-six refineries listed by the Bureau of Mines in East Texas on January 1, 1936, had any cracking facilities, and of those only a few were modern.[29]

26. One set of estimates to which almost all studies refer was presented by Robert E. Wilson, then President of Pan-American Petroleum and Transport, to the TNEC. Citing three hypothetical refineries, of 5, 15, and 60 thousand b/d capacity, he presented estimates of investment costs per barrel of throughput capacity of $400, $333, and $267, depreciation and other overhead charges of 11.7, 9.9, and 8.1 cents, and direct refinery operating expense (including also "miscellaneous charges") of 22, 16, and 12 cents a barrel, respectively (*Hearings,* Pt. XV, p. 8636). See also the detailed studies by McLean and Haigh of the cost advantages of large refineries over small (pp. 558–567). More recently, Bain places the optimal scale of a single refinery at 120,000 b/d, but notes only a very slight rise in average cost as one moves back to half this level, and a moderate rise—about 5 per cent—at one-quarter optimal size. *Barriers to New Competition* (Cambridge, Harvard University Press, 1956), pp. 233–235.

27. McLean and Haigh, p. 533.

28. Cf. *ibid.,* pp. 554, 595. Simple arithmetic would suggest $320,000 per 1000 b/d capacity, actually an understatement because investment costs per barrel of capacity decline for larger plants.

29. *Ibid.,* p. 595. Similarly, the average crude throughput capacity of the

The rudimentary character of facilities does not enhance production costs compared with larger rivals as importantly as it forces lower realizations from the sale of products.[30] Lacking cracking installations, small refiners were unable to get anything like the percentage yields of the higher-priced lighter distillates from their crude oil, or anything like the quality of gasoline obtained by their better equipped competitors. The location of small refineries has tended to aggravate this disability. Competing in constricted market areas where demand was invariably too small to absorb the region's burgeoning output, typically forced to use tank-car or truck shipment to get their gasoline into consuming markets, and usually finding an inadequate local demand for the high yield of residual fuels left by their refineries, their construction could have been justified in the first place only by an absurdly low price of crude oil.

Historically, crude oil that was cheap enough and available in sufficient quantity could offset almost any other competitive disadvantage as long as it lasted.[31] During 1932 the estimated gross refining margin in the Midcontinent area averaged 37 cents a barrel, while the posted price of a barrel of 36-degree gravity Midcontinent crude ranged during this same year between 77 and 92 cents, an average of 87 cents. Since the cost of the raw material laid down at the refinery was a major part of the sales price of products,[32] the field refineries, despite their inefficiencies, were able to make very substantial profits for a while.[33]

---

eighteen refineries constructed in Illinois immediately after the discovery of local crude in 1938 was under 2,000 b/d, and only two of them had thermal cracking facilities. By January 1, 1941, only six of these plants were operating. *Ibid.,* p. 599.

30. See the detailed estimates by McLean and Haigh of the effect of varying refining techniques on profitability, *ibid.,* pp. 567–575.

31. Though technically the statement is a virtual truism, it is of far less significance today than even fifteen years ago. Without cracking facilities, it is almost impossible to produce gasoline of commercial quality today, although such plants may produce intermediate products for further processing by modern refineries.

32. Between 1927 and 1929, the average annual wholesale value of refined products typically obtained from a barrel of Midcontinent crude oil ranged between $1.80 and $1.94 a barrel and the average price of the crude oil was $1.31 to $1.38 at the wellhead—roughly 70 per cent of the final price. The respective values in 1935 and 1936 were $1.55 and $1.69 for product realizations, $1.00 and $1.10 for the crude oil. Reported by Swensrud, "Relation between Crude Oil and Product Prices," pp. 766, 783–786.

33. McLean and Haigh estimate roughly that an East Texas refiner could have earned profits of $5,700 *a month* on an investment of $10,000 to $25,000,

The profitability of the small, inefficient plant in flush fields was transient, and survival was closely geared to the possession or acquisition of improved facilities. As early as January 1, 1936, thirteen of the twenty-seven refineries listed as operating in East Texas had thermal cracking facilities; by the beginning of 1939, all of the eight plants still operating were so equipped. From January 1, 1940, to October 1, 1946, 140 refiners without cracking equipment went out of business, compared with thirty who had such facilities.[34] Surviving small refiners showed continuing improvement in facilities; by 1950 in the country as a whole, independents had almost 86 per cent as much cracking capacity per barrel of crude throughput capacity as the thirty largest firms.[35] The situation of smaller refineries, however, is still critical as revealed in Table XXV.

TABLE XXV

Cracking and Crude Charging Capacities of United States Operating Refineries, by Size Groups, January 1, 1958

CRUDE CAPACITY BARRELS PER DAY	NUMBER OF REFINERIES	% OF U. S. TOTAL CRUDE CAPACITY	CRACKING CAPACITY		
			THERMAL	CATALYTIC	TOTAL
			AS % OF CRUDE THROUGHPUT CAPACITY		
Less than 1,000	7	—[a]	0.0	0.0	0.0
1,000–4,999	75	1.9	17.0	2.4	19.4
5,000–9,999	53	3.6	19.2	5.3	24.5
10,000–19,999	46	6.5	18.6	40.4	59.0
20,000–49,999	61	20.5	25.0	48.2	73.2
50,000–99,999	27	18.9	19.0	45.8	64.8
100,000 and over	27	48.5	25.9	45.4	71.3
TOTAL	296	100.0	22.6	43.5	66.1

[a] Less than 0.1 per cent.

Source: Computed from *Oil and Gas Journal* (March 24, 1958), p. 162.

These data suggest the technological pressure under which the small, independent refiner must operate in modern markets even

merely from sales of topped gasoline, i.e. assuming no realization at all from their larger yields of residual oil (pp. 594–595). Crude was available at extremely low posted prices and/or at substantial discounts from those prices in East Texas and later in Illinois.

34. McLean and Haigh, pp. 533, 595, and 597.

35. *Ibid.* Similar improvement in relative technology on the West Coast is noted by Bain, *Pacific Coast Petroleum Industry, 2,* 219–220.

though, compared with any earlier year, the position of the average has been markedly improved. During the last five years, for example, there has been a sharp decline in the population of refineries with less than 10,000 b/d capacity, especially in the smallest category,[36] and a technological upgrading of facilities in the 10,000 to 19,999 b/d group. This upgrading has involved a significant diminution of thermal cracking in both absolute and relative terms, as catalytic cracking and catalytic reforming capacity have soared.[37] Catalytic processes, virtually indispensable in meeting quality requirements of modern gasoline, are still the greatest, albeit a diminishing, deficiency of smaller refineries.

The technological problem of the small refiner is usually pictured as primarily financial in origin, but the evidence is far from clear. Before the war it was possible for an independent refiner (one who has survived and expanded) to boast a modern type refinery of 12,000 b/d capacity with cracking facilities, constructed for $800,000 to $900,000.[38] After the war the rule of thumb was $700 to $1,000 per

36. While there are still far too many refineries in the smallest categories, the seven in Table XXV with less than 1,000 b/d capacity and no cracking capacity are remnants of a population of fifty-seven twelve years earlier; and the seventy-five in the 1,000–4,999 b/d class compare with 157 in 1946.

37. Cat-cracking capacity of refineries in the 10,000 to 19,999 b/d group amounts to 40.4 per cent of crude distillation capacity in 1958; the figure five years before was only 23.4 per cent, when the corresponding ratios for larger refineries in the earlier year ranged from 37.2 to 39.1 per cent. The shift from thermal to catalytic processes has been national in scope. As of January 1, 1953, total national thermal cracking was 31.5 per cent, total catalytic cracking 34 per cent, of national crude throughput capacity, as compared with the 1958 ratios of 22.6 and 43.5 per cent respectively, shown in Table XXV. In absolute terms, thermal cracking capacity declined from 3.0 million b/d in 1946 to 2.6 million in 1953 and 2.2 million in 1958 while catalytic cracking increased from 1.0 million to 2.4 million and 4.2 million b/d in the three years respectively. Catalytic reforming capacity was only 136,000 b/d in 1953 as compared with 1,533,000 b/d in 1958. See *Oil and Gas Journal* (March 23, 1953), p. 169.

38. Testimony of Louis J. Walsh, vice-president of Eastern States Petroleum, TNEC, *Hearings,* Pt. XIV, p. 7336. Walsh did not indicate the details of his plant. It first appears as 12,000 b/d capacity in the Bureau of Mines listing on January 1, 1937. Without specifications, it is not possible to compare the figure cited by Mr. Walsh with the $8,100,000 given by McLean and Haigh as the investment cost of a modern 25,000 b/d refinery in 1935. Eliminating from the McLean and Haigh construct the cost of utilities and general refinery off-sites and tankage probably not included in the Walsh figure, and reducing the estimate for process equipment to 12,000 b/d on a proportionate basis, would still give a figure of more than $1,800,000—more than twice the investment Mr. Walsh claimed.

It is also to be noted that after adjusting investment costs to a 1950 base,

barrel of crude throughput for a modern, balanced refinery—or possibly $10,000,000 for the aforementioned 12,000 b/d plant. There are tremendous variations in the estimates of the minimum cost of catalytic cracking facilities which must veil substantial differences in equipment specifications. Some small refiners have managed to make highly successful installations that were reported adequate to serve their purposes for under $1,000,000, and great progress has been made in recent years in designing efficient small-package catalytic units. General opinion in the industry, however, places minimum investment in the millions of dollars.[39]

Typically, independent refiners as a group have operated their plants at substantially lower percentages of capacity than their larger, integrated competitors, more especially when crude oil was in short supply.[40] Estimates of the percentage utilization of capacity—operat-

---

McLean and Haigh show no appreciable rise in investment costs of a "representative refinery" between 1915 and 1950, despite their repeated concern for the crushing effect on independent refiners of the rising investment costs of modern refining operations (p. 554). The handicap of the independent refiner would seem to reside rather in his increasing inability to utilize a less than "representative" refinery.

39. A Department of Commerce study in 1947 cited estimates supplied small refiners that catalytic cracking equipment (of unspecified capacity) would cost them $750,000 to $1,500,000 (*U. S. Petroleum Refining, War and Postwar,* p. 31). Humble Oil supplied a figure of $5,000,000 to $12,000,000 to the Wolverton Committee, capacity again unspecified (House Committee on Interstate and Foreign Commerce, 80th Congress, 2d Session, *Fuel Investigation,* Progress Report, House Report No. 2342, 1948, p. 48). Estimates of $2,500,000 to $8,000,000 were proffered Aetna Oil and Allied Oil for catalytic units to go with 10,000 to 20,000 b/d refineries after the war (McLean and Haigh, pp. 611, 623).

40. Among the reasons for this phenomenon, strictly locational disadvantages may or may not reflect strategic considerations. Location in or near the oil field may be *chosen* by the refiner as a means of compensating technological inferiority by the accessibility of cheap crude; or field location may be *imposed* on the refiner by strategic barriers to entry elsewhere and his technological inferiority may rather reflect the market limitations of his location. The removal of the latter deficiency is clearly in the social interest.

Whether the comparative disabilities of the independent rise during periods of crude shortage is not easy to document, in part because this phenomenon is difficult to define. The discrepancy in rates of utilization between majors and independents, however, narrowed markedly from 1947, a year of undoubted shortage, to 1949, a year of admitted surplus. This could mirror the greater availability of crude to all, and it could also reflect the greater willingness of majors in 1949 to cut back refinery runs in the hope of strengthening the market.

Divergent rates of operation do not explain the disabilities of the independent refiner; rather, they prompt a search for the more fundamental explanations.

ing capacity and total capacity—are shown in Table XXVI for the majors, the rest of the industry, and for the industry as a whole. Uniformly, the majors better substantially the record of the independents. Table XXVI also illustrates the effect of several developments in refining that have already been discussed. It will be observed that the discrepancies between major and independent rates of utilization are much greater when related to total capacity than to operating capacity, but that these differences narrow considerably in the postwar years as compared with those before the war, both between the two groups of firms and between the two measures of capacity for each group. These data are too scant to establish a trend, but the differences between prewar and postwar are so great that they could hardly be ascribed to the peculiarities of the limited prewar sample.[41] They seem rather to reflect the heavy weight of obsolete capacity in the earlier years, especially the disproportionate concentration of shutdown capacity among smaller refiners,[42] the squeezing out of such capacity after the war by majors and independents alike, a marked relative improvement in operating

---

E.g., differences between operating ratios of integrated and nonintegrated firms of the same size class turn up consistently greater than those between different size classes (see the questionnaire analysis of McLean and Haigh, pp. 40–41). This discrepancy, however, is compatible with two quite different interpretations: (1) lower operating rates of nonintegrated refiners result from strategic advantages of their rivals; (2) uneconomic refinery location and design are more characteristic of nonintegrated than of small refiners. The latter interpretation is suggested by the fact that McLean and Haigh's sample showed integrated companies with a very much higher yield of gasoline than the nonintegrated firms.

41. Thus ratios based on operating capacity for the majors exceeded those based on total capacity in the prewar by 5.7 to 7.7 percentage points, in the postwar by only 1.4 to 2.8. Similar ranges for "all other" were 12.4 to 16.6 percentage points before the war and 5.4 to 13.0 in the postwar with the difference clearly narrowing after 1950. Similarly, the rates of majors exceeded those of "all other" on the basis of operating capacity by a range of 15.8 to 17.9 percentage points prewar and (excluding the crude shortage year, 1947, when it was 23.2) from 5.1 to 13.6 after the war. In terms of total capacity, for which a longer span of data is available, the comparable figures were 19.0 to 36.0 prewar, and 8.1 to 22.2 percentage points during selected postwar years.

42. Similarly, Bain shows average annual percentage of idle distillation capacity of 18.7 per cent among minor companies on the West Coast between 1930 and 1941 as compared with 7.9 per cent for the majors, a gap that would have been larger had it not been for the gasoline buying programs of the majors in the interests of market stabilization, Pacific Coast Petroleum Industry, 2, 216–220.

TABLE XXVI

Crude Runs as Percentage of Refinery Capacity,[a] Major Refiners and Rest of the Industry in Selected Years

YEAR	PERCENTAGE BASED ON OPERATING CAPACITY			PERCENTAGE BASED ON TOTAL CAPACITY		
	19 MAJORS	ALL OTHERS	INDUSTRY	19 MAJORS	ALL OTHERS	INDUSTRY
1926				81.	62.	75.
1931			66.9	67.	48.	61.6
1935			71.8	73.	43.	64.7
1936			75.1	81.	45.	69.4
1937			79.9	85.	49.	75.
1938	84.5	67.9	80.8	78.4	53.7	71.3
1939	87.1	71.3	83.4	79.4	58.9	74.2
1940	88.4	70.9	84.4	82.4	56.3	75.7
1941	93.1	75.2	89.0	87.4	58.6	79.8
1944	n.a.	n.a.	93.0	93.9	66.9	87.6
1946	n.a.	n.a.	91.0	92.0	69.0	87.1
1947	95.8	72.6	90.9	n.a.	n.a.	87.5
1949	88.2	74.6	85.5	85.9	63.7	81.1
1950	90.5	81.3	88.8	88.2	68.3	84.0
1953	93.6	83.8	91.7	92.2	78.4	89.5
1954	89.7	79.3	87.8	87.6	73.0	84.7
1955	93.1	81.6	90.9	90.8	75.2	87.7
1956	94.5	84.5	92.6	92.3	78.9	89.7
1957	89.8	84.7	88.8	87.0	78.9	85.3

[a] All data relate refinery runs to the average of beginning and end-of-year capacity; the shares of the two groups—major refiners and all others—in national end-of-1957 capacity had to be estimated.

Source: 1931 figures and breakdowns between majors and independents for 1926–37 from Cook, p. 76, using the TNEC's list of twenty majors. Data for 1938–50 are compilations by the economics department of a major oil company; its "majors" are 19 companies—the TNEC's 20 excluding Skelly and Mid-Continent but including Richfield. The figures for 1953–57 are our own computations from Bureau of Mines and *National Petroleum News Factbooks*. Our nineteen majors are the nineteen leading refiners in those years; the list does not change in that period.

rates compared with the majors by those independents who succeeded in staying in the refining business, and perhaps the disproportionate burden of cyclical stabilization assumed by majors when markets are weak.[43]

The competitive problems of an inefficient refinery center in its inability to get the highest possible yield of more valuable fractions from its crude oil throughput. Refinery margins may be squeezed because of the disappearance of cheap supplies of crude oil,[44] because of a decline in product prices unreflected in crude oil prices (as in 1938, 1949, 1954, and 1958), or because of technological progress in refining. It is technological change in refining and a fuller use of refining capacity that has preserved the level of profits since 1935 despite a much more rapid rise in prices of the labor and materials a refinery uses than of the products it sells.[45] The contrast of margins actually realized with those that would have been gained had proportional product yields remained as they were in the base period is a partial indication of the pressure on the small refiner to modernize his equipment.

The most important change in refinery yields since the war has been the spectacular reduction in residual fuel and the substantial increase in the increasingly more valuable distillates. Between 1935 and 1947, the average percentage yield of the less valuable residual fuel oil refined from a barrel of crude in this country was roughly constant; a slight prewar tendency to decline from about 27 to 24.5 per cent was reversed by the war, and it was not until 1946–47 that the lower figure was again reached. Then began a sharp decline: from 24.2 per cent in 1947 to 14.4 per cent in 1957. On the other

43. The last point is only suggested in the data for 1938, 1949, and 1957, when ratios for "all other" improved at the expense of those of the majors. Unfortunately data are lacking for 1948, the peak year immediately preceding the 1949 recession. Also the relationship does not show up in the 1953–54 downturn.

44. Producers lacking pipeline connections must accept temporarily a lower price for crude at the wellhead, a purely transient advantage for the local refiner. In 1957, e.g., producers in West Texas were absorbing the 15 to 30 cents a barrel it cost to get their oil to market by truck. *Second Report of the Attorney General* (September 1, 1957), pp. 96–98.

45. In Table XXII these changes in the "Refiners Cost of Living" were compared with the spread between refinery realizations and crude oil prices, both the actual spread and the spread that would have been realized if proportional product yields had remained at their average 1935–39 levels. The reader should refresh his memory of this comparison as a background for the discussion in the text.

hand, the yield of distillate fuels rose substantially with the rapid increase in home heating with oil: from 10.4 per cent in 1935 to 13.1 per cent in 1939 and then, after a wartime halt, from 14.5 per cent in 1945 to 23.1 per cent in 1957. Yields of gasoline have been remarkably stable, running between 43.5 and 45 per cent during the entire period, except for sharp cutbacks during World War II. The long-run rise of distillates has therefore been accomplished at the expense of residuals.

What this shift in product yields meant to refinery margins is indicated by the fact that the average refinery price of distillate fuel oils was about 3.5 cents a gallon and of heavy fuel oils approximately 2 cents in 1940; their respective average prices in nine refinery markets were 10.05 cents and 6.15 cents per gallon in 1957.[46] The refinery that still obtained average 1935–39 product yields from a barrel of crude oil would have had to live on a $1.02 margin in 1955, less transportation costs of crude to its gate; the average refinery in 1955 actually had instead a margin of $1.26.[47] The more flexible refineries obviously did much better than the more poorly equipped from 1948 on, at least in gross income; and the fact that so many of them did make the shift in yields (and that so many who could not went out of business) indicates that the changes must have paid off in net income as well.

Flexible refinery equipment may be important also in cushioning the impact of the short, sharp squeezes to which refinery margins are often subject. The methods used to adapt operations to sudden changes in demand (or supply) conditions, like the unexpectedly warm early months of 1949 when home-heating oils were a drug on the market, depend on the nature of equipment in use. For example, a company with a vacuum still that can be used to make lubes or can be run

46. Yield data from API, *Statistical Bulletin,* April 7, 1958; prices from *Petroleum Facts and Figures,* 9th ed., pp. 373, 375, and *National Petroleum News Factbook,* mid-May, 1958. At 1957 prices, the change from 1935 means that the average refinery took in almost 4 cents a gallon more on about ⅛ of the 42 gallons in each barrel of crude oil—a gain of 21 cents per barrel.

47. See p. 421, Table XXII. Because the yield of residual fuel in 1945–47 was still approximately at 1935–39 rates on the average, the gain in distillates to that point had generally been primarily at the expense of the most valuable product, gasoline. Refinery realizations, therefore, increased somewhat less between 1935 and 1947 than the prices of the various products the refinery sold. After 1948, however, more valuable displaced less valuable products at a rising pace and refinery realizations moved up sharply compared with product prices. Actual spreads increased 37 cents per barrel of crude between 1949 and 1955; without these substitutions, they would have risen only about 20 cents.

on residual fuels to produce feed stocks for cracking units, and with cracking units that can run either crude or distillates, may make substantial changes with advantage. Crude purchases may be reduced while units formerly on crude are shut down or shifted to heavy naphtha or second cracked gas oil from the firm's own stock (thus increasing the yield of high quality gasoline and reducing the net yield of surplus heating oils), or, as many did in 1949, the refiner might purchase supplies of depressed residual fuels in preference to crude. In this manner a company with modern cracking facilities, or only vacuum distillation units,[48] might obtain considerable protection from a violent refinery squeeze like that of 1949.[49] While details of adjustment vary with a wide variety of specialized units of equipment, the principle is the same—to upgrade products within cost limits into a more valued pattern, making fuller use of the more costly equipment like the cracking units, at the expense, if necessary, of less specialized processing equipment.

So, on January 1, 1950, the amount of crude distillation capacity listed as shut down by the Bureau of Mines was more than twice what it had been a year before, while shut-down cracking capacity increased only about 15 per cent.[50] In addition, crude runs to stills fell from almost 93 per cent of operating capacity in 1948 to about 86 per cent in 1949; [51] but runs to cracking capacity were undoubtedly much better maintained. If the figures were available they would certainly show an increased proportion of cracked, and a smaller proportion of straight run, gasolines produced in 1949 compared with the preceding year.[52]

48. It is estimated that the capacity for reduced-crude distillation under vacuum is about 29 per cent of the basic crude capacity in the U.S. *Oil and Gas Journal* (March 24, 1958), p. 89.

49. See the thorough analysis of the 1948–49 experience in McLean and Haigh, pp. 160–173.

50. Shut-down topping capacity rose from 208,000 to 473,000 b/d (from about 3 per cent of the national total to about 7 per cent); shut-down cracking capacity from 76,000 to 88,000 b/d (from about 4.5 per cent to about 5 per cent).

51. *Petroleum Facts and Figures,* 9th ed., p. 258.

52. The accentuated impact of a refinery margin squeeze on refiners with insufficiently flexible equipment was far clearer in 1949 than during the two later squeezes. In that year, with a fairly well-sustained price of gasoline, refiners responded to market weakness in their heating oils by cutting down yields of both distillates and residuals while increasing the average gasoline yield to 43.7 per cent compared with only 40.1 per cent in 1948. In 1954, instead, it was gasoline prices that were weak, falling almost uninterruptedly

Inadequacies of refinery equipment may sometimes explain why some independent refiners have trouble in obtaining the crude oil they require. The hallmark of a modern refinery is its versatility—its ability to produce quality gasoline from a variety of crudes. A more primitive refinery, instead, may be able to obtain salable output only from special quality crude oils. Even though such a refiner may be able to purchase crude of the desired quality, he cannot ship by pipeline unless his particular crude is batched. But batched shipments involve minimum tender requirements that may be high relative to the independent's needs and may also necessitate sizable storage facilities to accumulate those minimum quantities at either end of the line. For "common stream" delivery, the corresponding practical requirements would be comparatively insignificant. So what masquerades as a problem of crude oil or pipeline availability on reasonable terms may instead be a problem of inadequate refinery equipment.

Appraisal: Conservation, Efficiency, and the Decline of the Independent

Thus it is possible to explain the decline in the number of independent refiners since 1935 very largely in terms of the operation of inexorable and socially beneficent economic forces. With rationally organized production most of the small refiners who sprang up in the field would never have come into existence. They were profitable, many of them, only because the temporary availability of cheap crude oil more than compensated for their gross processing deficiencies in deriving a mere token of the potential useful product from their raw material. However, to say that these small refineries were wasteful or uneconomic is to focus on the effect and ignore the cause. Any rational limitation of crude production to eliminate the perverse, uneconomic pressure of the law of capture would have removed (as

---

from a 1953 peak of 12.46 cents a gallon in July–August to 11.20 cents in October, 1954, with a monthly average not above 11.35 cents until August, 1955. The prices of the various fuel oils, in contrast, were relatively strong throughout this period. (Average refinery prices from *National Petroleum News*.) In consequence, gasoline yields in 1954 were slightly below the levels of both 1953 and 1955, while those of distillates increased moderately at the expense of residual fuel oil; and there was a tendency for shut-down cracking capacity to rise much more than shut-down crude. Again in contrast with 1949, the 1957–58 price slump was fairly indiscriminate, reflecting a general oversupply of products; and no dramatic shift in refinery yields could importantly evade its impact. The 1949 experience therefore may be a uniquely excellent example of the point made in the text.

prorationing did remove) their economic justification as well. They depended on waste for their existence, waste that should have been avoided, but their operations served to reduce rather than to increase the waste they built upon.

Production limitations by the states thus performed the function of economic catharsis. Prorationing to market demand involved serious wastes of its own but it increased beyond anything that had gone before the net economic value of future oil recovery. In so doing it eliminated relatively inefficient producers with no economic excuse for survival in a more rationally ordered industry. And if in consequence some refiners found themselves unable to survive, it follows that their disappearance was likewise required in the interest of the most economical use of national resources.[53]

If one adds to the impact of conservation measures the impartial objective effects of changing technology upon the competitive position of the independent refiner, one has a substantial explanation of the decline in his numbers.

STRATEGIC FACTORS AFFECTING THE
INDEPENDENT REFINER

Efficiency and conservation have clearly had much to do with the decline of the independent refiner but they are not the entire explanation. The technical and economic superiority of the huge plant will often be overcome by compensating counter improvements introduced by the imaginative smaller firm in selected locations. In contrast, the advantages of strategic market position may grow cumulatively without definite limit unless conscious social action is taken to curb its impact. The real problem therefore is not whether technology and conservation have bulked importantly in the disappearance of most independent refiners; they obviously have. The question is how serious are the additional, strategic handicaps that reflect not relative inefficiency but the mere size and integration of their larger rivals.

Three broad areas of potential strategic handicaps for the independent refiner (who, of course, may be partially integrated) have been

53. Thus Watkins, hardly an apologist for the major oil companies, declares: "If it be contended that there is evidence that many independent nonintegrated refiners were finding it difficult, if not impossible, to operate profitably . . . it may be inquired since when it has become a legitimate object of public policy to protect industrial investments, however improvidently made, uneconomically situated, and inefficiently operated, at the expense of the consuming public" (p. 160).

noted in this study and have formed the basis of innumerable complaints summarized in Congressional hearings and reports and in professional and popular literature: the problems of obtaining crude oil on reasonable terms, of securing transport of crude and of refined products via efficient media, and of access to markets for his refined products. In attempting an assessment of the merits in this controversial area, there can be no pretension to objectively demonstrable accuracy because judgment must rest on a qualified guess of whether things would have been appreciably different if the majors were not integrated.

The Price and Availability of Crude Oil

A plausible case can be made for the claim that, quite apart from comparative technology, independent refiners are forced to operate at substantially lower percentages of their operating capacity than the majors, especially in years of crude oil shortage, because supplies of crude are controlled by the majors who divert it to themselves through ownership of producing properties and through control of pipelines into the fields. The desire to secure assured sources of supply is a prime reason for backward integration, as asserted by the majors themselves, and if companies continue for decades to make investments for this purpose, it is hard to believe that their expectations have not typically been fulfilled.

When supplies of crude oil are short, the integrated companies as well as independents have trouble getting all they want. During the first six months of 1947, demand for products was pressing hard against available supplies, and production was at the limit of MER's. The Wherry Committee found that 113 nonmajor refiners were operating at only 69.5 per cent of capacity during this period, compared with 94.6 per cent for seventeen majors. Out of 108 independents who answered the Committee's inquiry, seventy-six alleged that difficulties, associated with their independent status, in procuring crude were in some measure responsible for their low rate of operations.[54] Table XXVI seems to confirm this contention. In 1947,

54. United States Senate, Special Committee to Study Problems of American Small Business, *Oil Supply and Distribution Problems*, Senate Report No. 25, 81st Congress, 1st Session (cited below as Wherry Committee), pp. 2–4. During the same period the 113 independents operated 20.5 per cent of their capacity for other refiners (i.e. primarily or entirely on crude processed for the account of others), compared with only 16.3 per cent in the corresponding period in 1946.

operating rates of majors (based on operating capacity) exceeded those of the "all other" group by 23.2 percentage points, a differential substantially greater than that of any prior (or subsequent) year shown.

The strenuous efforts of smaller refiners to integrate backward underscores their own recognition of strategic disadvantage. Every successful independent interviewed was trying to get into production, or, at least, to extend its own gathering lines in order to ensure more adequate supplies than it could count on acquiring in what remained of the open market. Generally, there is an inverse relationship between integration into production and crude-gathering systems: integrated companies almost invariably gather crude produced by others, but those with heavy production do proportionately less, and those with little production of their own do relatively more.[55] From the beginning, the investment in a crude-gathering system, whether by small or large refiners, has been motivated less by the profits in the operation itself than by the prospect of assured crude supply availability on which the entire enterprise depends.

Obtaining crude oil in a period of acute shortage tests the ingenuity of any buyer who does not have his own supply or a firm purchasing agreement with a major supplier. Many successful independent refiners had something of both and, in addition, a resourcefulness and flexibility in the use of direct and indirect premiums and other forms of assistance to producers that the majors—tied to their posted pricing system, restricted to "channels" by administrative precepts and vulnerable to charges of discrimination—could not match. Something of the stratagems of competitive shopping in tight markets is conveyed in the following composite paraphrase of the remarks of several successful independents interviewed.

> We had to go heavily into crude operations. We bought a drilling rig, and operated as a drilling contractor, in order to obtain the patronage of independent producers and get a first call on their supplies. We financed wildcatters. We bought interests in drilling ventures. We even made drills, to exchange for a first call on oil. Our company was the first to work out steel conversion deals; we bought steel scrap from friends and relatives in the scrap business, turned it over to steel companies for conversion into steel

55. McLean and Haigh, pp. 40, 45. Ashland is an outstanding example of a refiner, low on crude production, that has had great success in assuring itself of crude supplies through ownership of a comprehensive system of gathering lines.

casing; then we would turn the casing over to machine shops for threading and coupling, and then ship it to producers.

We have never been strapped for crude. For one thing, we've had a long term contract with ——— [a major company] that takes care of about half of our needs; the crude travels over ——— [the major's] pipeline to a terminal; from there we take it by barge right to our refinery. It is sour crude; that is all they were usually willing to sell us; but we've learned to handle it. Secondly, we really had to scramble until around 1949. We hired the chief scout of one of the major companies, and paid him a much higher salary than we would have paid anyone in our own organization; we set him up in an office in a producing region; we hired people he suggested and set them up in offices in other cities. These scouts are really a private espionage system of the majors; among themselves they'll disclose whatever information they have on wildcatting operations, but no outsider can get it. It was a real coup for us to hire ———; we got into that select circle.

Mr. ——— once came up with a wildcatter; we cornered him in a hotel room and got him signed up. We lent him and others large amounts of money for each added well. We paid black market prices for pipe. We bought a lot of cocktails and steaks to get producers to promise to sell to us. We paid fancy premiums. We offered independent producers, and even the major companies themselves, the very best service on trucking crude away from their wells. We would promise them trucks at any small well they named within twenty-four hours, some too small for them to bother with themselves, and we would cart it away. We became, in effect, the scavengers of the industry. We had crude coming from all over the country.

When we ran out of tank cars to carry the crude to the refineries, we combed the junk yards of the country, bought up a lot of old abandoned tank cars, repaired them, and built up a whole fleet in this way.

As a result, we not only had plenty of crude and products throughout the period of shortage; we were not only operating at 120 per cent of capacity in 1948 and never out of crude, but we brokered crude to other refiners. We made some 12 cents a barrel profit selling crude to other people in 1948. We practically ignored the cost; and we passed it on in the crude we sold to others.

The drama of the acute shortage, like that of 1947–48 when price was not a critical problem, has no counterpart in the slow, hard pressure that controlled production of crude oil, unalleviated by soaring product prices, can impose on the refiner who must purchase his oil; because here his economically feasible alternatives are more severely limited. To the extent that prorationing is economically questionable in holding production short of MER—and it is seriously questioned in Part II—the invidious consequences for the independent refiner dependent on purchased crude find no social justification.[56] When competition forces the majors to shade the profits of their integrated operations in weak product markets while the institutions of control hold the formal crude oil price firm, the price of crude may become a matter of business life and death to the nonintegrated refiner.

The experience of the Eastern States Petroleum Corporation, a large independent refiner on the Gulf Coast, indicates that the destructive impact of this situation is by no means confined to the inefficient refiner. Eastern States had a modern 12,000 b/d refinery with substantial cracking capacity at the beginning of 1938 (its capacity nineteen years later was 62,000 b/d). According to its vice-president, its equipment permitted it to produce gasoline to the standard specifications of several major companies which bought it to supplement their own supplies, and the company had never had any difficulty in obtaining crude or in getting it carried to its refinery in major-owned trunk pipelines. But Eastern States found itself so seriously squeezed in 1937–38 between the state-supported price of crude oil and high pipeline charges on the one hand, and declining prices of products on the other that it was forced to turn to Mexican crude in order to stay in business: "In other words, we had a refinery located in the very heart of the greatest producing and refining center of the world and were forced to go outside of the country to get crude." [57] Imported oil generally has not provided a feasible alternative even for independents

56. It is irrelevant for this concern to appraise the charge that such consequences were also purposeful, designed to curb the obstreperous activities of maverick independents in product markets. Assertions to this effect were not uncommon before the TNEC. See testimony of Karl A. Crowley, *Hearings,* Pt. XIV, pp. 7361–7387, 7591–7661, esp. pp. 7367–7368 and 7374–7375; also John E. Shatford, *ibid.,* Pt. XV, pp. 8522–8527, esp. 8538–8543.

57. TNEC, *Hearings,* Pt. XIV, p. 7340; also pp. 7336–7342.

so situated that they could use it.[58] In addition to the obstacle posed by the American import tariff, there was also the drawback that until after 1953 the price of foreign oil was based strictly on Texas Gulf quotations of United States crude. Increasing availability of Middle East oil, at discounts from posted prices, promised some respite until import restrictions limited this opportunity for smaller American refiners.[59]

While the pre-emption of crude buying and the practical monopolization of pipeline transportation by the majors in earlier days comprised devastating handicaps for independent refiners, it is generally agreed in the industry today that in "normal times" at any rate, those refiners that have survived have little trouble in acquiring crude.[60] Expansion of pipelines, closer federal controls, and the political nuisance value of outraged would-be shippers give credence to this opinion; certainly many independent refiners have no complaints to register, especially those who are equipped to use "common stream" crude. Furthermore, it is difficult to believe that crude availability would be much different if, at this late date, refiners were prevented from in-

58. The use of Mexican oil, because of the expropriation of American oil interests in that country, subjected the refiner to opprobrium and possible legal action. Eastern States avoided the import tariff by importing under bond and exporting all products refined from it. *Ibid.*, pp. 7348–7350.

59. The Delta Refining Company provides an illustration in point. The company had a five-year contract with Superior Oil to take 20,000 b/d of the latter's Venezuelan crude and the attempt to continue these imports brought it into conflict with the "voluntary program" of import restriction. The *Wall Street Journal* (January 20, 1958), p. 3, quoted a company official as explaining: "the contract . . . was undertaken after the company found it could not obtain domestically the oil it needed to increase the capacity of a Memphis refinery from 6,000 to 20,000 barrels a day. . . . The company 'looked all over' producing areas from which to draw oil in search for the kind of crude 'that would produce in our plant products of such quality and kind as would permit the sale of same at a price that would yield a profit,' " and turned to foreign sources only as a last resort. In applying for a liberal import quota, the president of Delta declared, "if he had to buy from domestic producers entirely . . . 'I'd be buying a ticket straight to the bankruptcy court.' " *Ibid.* (February 11, 1958), p. 20.

60. Whatever the actual facts of availability to established refiners, it is inconceivable that a new refiner would build even a moderate sized plant (say upward of 10,000 b/d) without assurances, through integration or its equivalent in long-term contracts, of an adequate crude supply laid down at minimum costs. Easy generalizations about the ready availability of crude oil do not conform with such practices or with the emphasis on security that majors themselves offer for their backward integration.

tegrating into crude. The majors, with a larger and more modern plant, established pipeline connections, greater buying power, and the widest public acceptance of their branded products, would still dominate scarce crude oil supplies in comparison with the independent.

The one important difference to be expected would be in the behavior of the crude oil price. If the big buyers of crude oil were not also the major producers thereof, it is difficult to believe that the price would remain so rigid in the face of weak product markets. Fabricators in other industries have some assurance that pressures on the prices of their products will be transmitted back to raw material levels, so that the independent enjoys some reasonable prospect of a remunerative margin. Crude oil markets are sheltered against such pressures.

The Price and Availability of Pipeline Transportation

For the refiner not located in the field, crude oil availability is economically inseparable from access to pipelines; and the competitive margin within which he must live will be vitally affected by the tariff he has to pay for transport. Historically, there can be no doubt whatsoever that this crucial fact has been used by the majors to confine their independent rivals to secondary locations in producing fields and to harass those with the temerity to challenge this fate.[61] The following facts are in general beyond dispute:

1. Crude oil trunk pipelines were constructed by major integrated companies primarily for their own use.

2. Early pipeline rates were set so far above cost, so close to alternative rail transport rates, that outside refiner-shippers were placed at a very serious disadvantage in competition with integrated, pipeline-owner refiners for whom such rates were nominal.

3. Although voluntary rate reductions were made in the 1930's, active intervention by the ICC and the consent decree of 1941 were needed to bring rates into reasonable relation with costs.

4. In addition to high pipeline rates, outside shippers have en-

61. The story of pipelines has been told many times. See, among others, the cited works of Prewitt; Cook; TNEC statements (*Hearings,* Pts. XIV, XV) of Crowley and Shatford; Wolbert; Rostow and Sachs; and the ICC, "Reduced Pipe Line Rates and Gatherings Charges," 243 ICC 115 (1940) and 272 ICC 375 (1948).

countered other discriminations in the form of unreasonably high tender requirements, refusals to carry, delays, and other obstructions.[62]

5. Access to pipeline transportation on reasonable terms is generally a critical determinant of competitive position.

The economics of pipeline operation and pricing, which explain if they do not justify this factual record, have been discussed at several points in this study and will not be repeated here. The superior efficiency of the crude pipeline as a transport medium enabled integrated refiners to pay producers a higher wellhead price for oil than nonintegrated refiners, whether located away from or in the fields. And the volume requirements for economic operation imposed a need for minimum tenders [63] and consequent storage facilities at points of shipment and of delivery that the independent shipper, unable to use common stream specifications, was often unable to provide.

The fact remains that the competitive handicap of the independent refiner was primarily a consequence of the integration of pipeline ownership. Independently owned and operated as a common carrier, the advantages of this transport medium would have been made available to all in a nondiscriminating fashion. The terms could not have been *equal,* for the costs of service to large and small shippers would vary, perhaps substantially, but the opportunity for use would have been equal at rates reasonably related to costs. The inherent superiority of the pipeline could not have been monopolized by certain refiners (integrated owners) to the competitive disadvantage of other refiners (the outside independents).

More effective regulation of common-carrier pipelines by the ICC, the consent decree of 1941, and high corporation taxes have greatly

62. Contentions in the late thirties that the ICC had not exercised its authority to correct abuses and that rates and returns remained so high as to seriously handicap nonintegrated refiners were not adequately answered. See, e.g., statement of Fayette B. Dow, TNEC, *Hearings,* Pt. XV, pp. 8596–8597; Farish and Pew, *Review and Criticism on Behalf of Standard Oil Company,* pp. 30–35; and other sources cited above.

63. It should be recalled here that pipeline operations and facilities (such as tankage) are adapted to defined specifications of crude that fit the volume needs of the customers, and that the pipeline company is responsible to the shipper for delivery of the volume and quality tendered with penalties for loss. Where shippers deal in qualities that will mix with those specifications on stream, the pipeline will usually accept very small shipments at designated intake points without regard to tender. Tender rules are protection against *special treatment* shipments otherwise likely to involve the carrier in loss.

mitigated the burden of excessive rates and service discriminations.[64] Some companies still complain; [65] many do not. Other than to point out that pipeline rates and service limitations to outsiders no longer pose anything like the competitive disadvantage they did in the past— and that a great deal of the damage was done before the situation was remedied—there is little basis for assessing complaints that persist.[66] That it may still be a handicap not to own production or a share in a pipeline, however, the experience of 1947–49 and the continuing urge of nonintegrated refiners to get into production and pipeline transportation by investment or by merger would seem to argue. McLean and Haigh found that, as a practical matter, the large oil companies do not often take advantage of the common carrier provisions of the law to force their way into lines owned by other companies; rather, they seek ownership participation in any lines they expect to use, despite the limitation of earnings. The significant reason stated was that they wanted "a voice in the allocation of capacity among shippers at times when the line was pressed to capacity." [67] These observations would apply a fortiori to product lines, the majority of which do not even pretend to be common carriers.

This confirmation of the attitude of nonintegrated refiners toward investment in and use of pipelines underscores the uncertainty of evaluation in this area. The rights of outsiders under stress may be com-

64. These matters were discussed in Chap. 13 (see above, p. 340, n. 35). Even apart from regulation, however, it would be foolish for a pipeline company today to earn high profits on carrying oil or products for its parent and thus incur a heavy tax liability and then pass on its dividends to the parent to be taxed a second time. See 243 ICC 115, 127, 139 (1940).

65. See the criticism by Michigan's Attorney General of the allegedly onerous minimum tender requirements imposed by the major common carrier products lines feeding the state. Pp. 102–103.

66. Rostow and Sachs, among others, have deprecated the benefits of these changes, though conceding that they have occurred, on the ground that they have produced no changes in the industry's structure or behavior. "Entry into the Oil Refining Business," pp. 857–858, 885–894, 902–903. Quite the contrary, behavior seems demonstrably improved but more effective regulation of pipelines certainly has not prevented the continuing decline of the independent refiner either in numbers or in industry share. Wolbert is an outstanding exponent of the view that improvements in regulation have largely eradicated the pipeline's threat to competition in refining, though even he would have the regulation more stringently applied.

67. McLean and Haigh, p. 421. The second reason—a probable residual value after full depreciation of the properties (usually fifteen to twenty-five years life)—suggests that regulated earnings under ICC control may not be as spartan as the 7 per cent limit indicates.

promised in many subtle ways by owners, in ways that regulation may be quite unable adequately to redress. The Wood River Refining Company, it will be recalled, though excellently situated with respect to common-carrier crude pipeline and barge transportation facilities and though possessing a modern refinery with ample catalytic cracking equipment, sold out to Sinclair in 1950 in part because it encountered such difficulty in obtaining crude oil at first, and because its margins had been so badly squeezed immediately thereafter. At that very time Sinclair was participating in the building of the Platte Pipe Line to provide an eastern market for its surplus production of sour Wyoming crudes—crudes that the Wood River Refinery was well adapted to process.[68]

Pipeline rates, however, would appear no longer to be a matter of life and death so far as the danger of a price squeeze on independent refiners is concerned. The real price-margin problem of the independent refiner arises out of production control in crude and from the fact that the major refiners are integrated into crude production while the independents are not.

Problems of Access to Markets

It is a common experience in industry that the expenditures required to develop consumer acceptance of the manufacturer's product may dwarf, both in amount and in the time required to build it, the investment in productive plant. The petroleum industry is no exception to this rule; it differs from some mainly in the fact that its major products must be purveyed through highly specialized facilities, along with a substantial amount of service, to mobile customers over an area as vast as the network of roads and streets that crisscross the nation. To develop patronage for their branded products, refiners have not been content to rely on advertising and the haphazard growth of distribution facilities in its wake; they have built, leased, and released facilities, and engaged the services of private owners as well, in a planned distribution system that would differentiate their name and help to tie the customer's repeat business to their brand. Forward integration is a sales weapon. Like all promotional expense, it is incurred in the hope of a profit; but the crucial profit to be gained is in the sale of product, not from the business of marketing as such.

In this light, there is no mystery in the unwillingness of integrated refiners to make their own marketing facilities available for the dis-

68. McLean and Haigh, pp. 308, 617–619.

tribution of competitors' products, nor in their refusal to renew the leases of dealers who handle competitors' gasoline and lubricants.[69] Apart from possible illegality, their power to insist on exclusive handling by contractor-retailers—a kind of vertical integration-by-contract —is limited by the freedom of the independent businessman to take his trade elsewhere, their success in doing so is striking evidence of either the mutuality of advantage in the arrangement or of the special inducements proffered. The reduction of split-pump stations to an oddity is certainly in part a voluntary recognition by contractors of the advantages of concentrated sales efforts and a single source of supply.[70]

69. In addition to explicit stipulations in rental contracts, the majors have always insisted that the pumps and tanks they provided be used exclusively for their gasoline, a practice upheld in *Federal Trade Commission v. Sinclair Oil Company*, 261 U.S. 463 (1923), and used by Standard of California after the Supreme Court decision prohibiting exclusive dealing (see above, pp. 475–476) to keep its dealers in line. Higher prices have usually been charged for deliveries to split stations, and lubricant-gasoline ratios are often set in requirements contracts at levels so high that it is impossible for the dealer to carry any other company's lubes—(see reproduction of such a contract in *Hearings* before Subcommittee No. 1 of the Select Committee on Small Business, 80th Congress, 2d Session, 1948, pp. 444–445).

These methods are hardly necessary when a mere cancellation of lease without explanation will suffice. Richfield's realistic claim that its lessees were not "independent businessmen," but to all intents and purposes part of the corporate organization, put the relationship in its true light. *United States v. Richfield Oil Corporation*, 99 F. Supp. 280, at 287–294 (1951). A survey made in 1939 (see TNEC, *Hearings*, Pt. XV-A), confirmed by another in 1950–51 (Howard, "The Marketing of Petroleum Products," appendix B), illustrates dramatically the reluctance of dealers leasing from their supplier to antagonize him or his sales representatives by prominently displaying or even carrying lubricants or other products that compete with the supplier's brands.

Sun Oil, in its defense in a current antitrust suit, while denying that it requires its dealers to handle its products exclusively, affirms that "a Sun dealer may freely prefer to push competitive products, but then Sun is equally free to sever business relations with a dealer not interested in promoting its products." See its *Brief* in *United States v. Sun Oil Company*, U. S. District Court, Eastern District of Pennsylvania, Civil Action No. 10483, filed October 11, 1957, pp. 130–131; also pp. 8, 32 ff., 245 ff.

70. Where not refused the right to purchase, split-pump operators have typically been penalized in the past by a higher (usually by ½ cent) tank-wagon price. Refiners sometimes justified the differential on the ground that dumps at such stations were smaller, hence more costly; but the penalty price, when employed, was applied to all split accounts and to no exclusive stations, regardless of the size and cost of deliveries to each. Cf. the Sun Oil Company *Brief* (see above note), p. 86, which also gives a very persuasive explanation of the disappearance of the split station in terms of the mutual interest of supplier

If a company develops a demand for its branded products, builds its own service stations, and requires them to handle its products exclusively, how has it foreclosed anybody from anything? Has it not created the business it is allegedly monopolizing? [71] It is apparent, of course, that the independent refiner, who is unwilling or unable to incur like expenditures to develop consumer demand for his branded product, will be forced to sell his output, whatever its quality, in bulk markets at lower prices, either to independent jobbers, to large industrial or commercial accounts, or to other refiners for their own distribution or, if quality is deficient, for further processing or blending. This is the fate of any manufacturer of a consumer product purchased by brand rather than on specification who prefers to remain a manufacturer only. Where, then, is the strategic handicap allegedly imposed on the independent refiner by vertical integration?

The possible exclusionary effects of integration may be grasped by considering the consequences of an alternative system in which refiners were not allowed to own service stations. In such a situation, large wholesalers would probably assume the role of the majors in service station development. Such jobber-retailers would be more free to shop around for motor oil and gasoline, possibly to handle more than one brand. If majors were prevented from binding independent marketers to themselves by exclusive agreements, some greater flexibility would be provided and somewhat less pressure would be imposed on the smaller refiner to build service stations in order to gain access to the market.[72] But would the consequences be markedly different? Would the dealer or the jobber-retailer, free of whatever coercion may now exist through forward integration,[73] forsake nation-

---

and dealer on pp. 24–28 and 79–88. See both Howard, "The Marketing of Petroleum Products," and the Senate Small Business Committee, "Gasoline Price War in New Jersey," *Report* (1956), pp. 12–13, for indications of the reasons why contractor stations may feel compelled to deal with one supplier exclusively.

71. This was Richfield's defense of its practice of requiring exclusive handling by its lessee dealers. See above, n. 69.

72. The discussion is confined to service stations and the sale of oil and gasoline, since this is the nub of the issue. The independent jobber is still the main distribution link for home heating oils and affords ample market access to the independent refiner. Heavier fuels, sold on specification, and commercial sales of gasoline are usually negotiated and delivered direct from refiner or terminal. In these areas, the impact of forward integration is minor.

73. There is no way of quantifying the scope of such coercion, but it is known to exist. See House Small Business Committee, "Alleged Coercive and Discriminatory Practices" (1955), pp. 6–12; and *ibid.*, "Distribution Practices in the Petroleum Industry" (1957), pp. 11–13.

ally established brands for private brands and junk concentrated brand promotion for mixed product retailing? It contradicts both common sense and marketing experience to assume that the broad picture of single brand distribution would be appreciably altered even if dealers were truly free to choose.

The distribution of Pennsylvania grade motor oils, paraffin-based lubes for which an early consumer preference was established in the days when good lubes could not be produced from Western crudes, provides a somewhat specialized illustration of some exclusionary effect of the current integrated system. Independent stations, not leasing from their major suppliers, have continued to carry oils like Quaker State and Kendall. The majority of lessee stations however are much more circumspect; they either refuse to carry Pennsylvania grade motor oils at all, or keep them out of sight unless a motorist requests them specifically. To counter the charge that Sun's alleged exclusion of such oils from its stations imposes a serious market limitation, Sun sponsored an intensive study of the products represented in the marketing areas surrounding a broad sample of its service stations. The study revealed that the Pennsylvania oils were sold in as many stations as the leading major company lubricants.[74] It is true, nonetheless, that the exclusion or suppression of Pennsylvania grade oils in major-controlled stations has restricted market volume for its independent refiners and, in some instances at any rate, this has been a factor in mergers with integrated firms, in part to gain more adequate market representation. Leading examples have been the merger of Vacuum Oil with Standard of New York, and Freedom-Valvoline with Ashland.[75]

74. The study was made in sixty-six market areas surrounding Sun stations. More retail outlets (352) handled Quaker State than any other oil; the next most frequently represented oils, in descending order, were five majors beginning with Mobil (322 outlets) and ending with Sun (210); then came Kendall, a Pennsylvania grade oil, with 180, next Shell, and next Wolf's Head, another Pennsylvania grade, with 136—and so on. On the basis of this evidence, the Sun *Brief* contended: "That it is not sold in a Sun station or in a number of Sun stations does not mean that Kendall oil is excluded from the *market*. . . . In fact Kendall is not foreclosed from the markets in which competing suppliers seek the business of motorists" (pp. 303–304; see also pp. 302–303).

75. Watkins has described some of the problems of Pennsylvania grade refiners created by a major company drive for exclusive dealing contracts (see pp. 68, 188–190). While the NRA Petroleum Administration delayed the promulgation of a rule prohibiting such contracts, "the refiners specializing in lubricating oils and greases were compelled to sit idly by for twenty months and watch the wanton destruction of their business by the major companies." *Ibid.,* pp. 241–242; see also TNEC, *Hearings,* Pt. XV-A.

It cannot be doubted, therefore, that the small refiner who tries to compete solely as a refiner will be seriously handicapped in rivalry with a major company. If this were not true, there would be no sense in the heavy outlays that the major oil companies have continued to make in marketing year after year. Whether or not these expenditures yield a marketing margin over cost, they have increased the returns of the majors as vertically integrated *refiners;* that is, they have improved their net refinery realizations by providing a more stable market, assuring closer to capacity operations, holding up the prices they could command. Without such expenditures, a refiner may find himself in difficulties no matter how good his product or how efficient his operations.[76]

If comments in the trade journals are to be credited, independent refiners have been encountering increasingly severe difficulties of this kind in recent years because of the general surplus of refinery capacity and weakness of gasoline prices, first clearly evidenced in 1954, recurring in 1956–58. Inland Texas and Texas Gulf Coast refiners, who had relied heavily on major companies as customers, have found that outlet dwindling as the majors themselves developed surplus refining capacity; and they have been faced with the alternative of expanding their own marketing investments or living within the skimpy margins that sales to unbranded jobbers permit.[77]

The strategic disadvantage of the independent refiner from the forward integration of the major, then, stems from the latter's development of consumers' adherence to its branded products, at an expenditure of resources that the independent refiner cannot hope to match, and for a purpose—the creation in the buyer's mind of largely imaginary differences between its product and that of others—of dubious social value.

How Independent Refiners Survive

There are many successful refiners in the United States outside the ranks of the so-called majors. How do they manage to survive and prosper?

76. Among the reasons which led Wood River Refining Company to sell out to Sinclair, McLean and Haigh stressed most prominently its failure to "develop an aggressive marketing program"—a condition of survival that the owners estimated would involve them in a capital expenditure of $6,500,000 on service stations, which they considered impractical in their existing financial situation (p. 616).

77. See esp. "An Independent Refiner Builds a Brand," *National Petroleum News* (June, 1956), p. 100; "Southwest Trend: Independent Refiners Move to Brands," *ibid.* (June, 1957), pp. 124–126.

The answer is in a way simple: they avoid most of the pitfalls so laboriously traced in this chapter, and/or compensate for them by capitalizing on some particular special advantage. It would be futile to attempt systematically to list either the pitfalls or the special sources of competitive strength. Detailed analysis would require a separate story for each successful refiner in the country, for each has achieved a distinctive blend of attributes that explains its success. However, their main sources of strength permit a few possibly illuminating generalizations.

First, it has been necessary to obtain a modern, efficient (though smaller-scale) plant to improve flexibility, increase yields of the more valuable fractions, and meet the high octane requirements of gasoline today. The smaller refiners in the country, as a group (still excepting the numerous extremely small firms), have substantially caught up with the larger in installation of cracking equipment—partly because of the weeding out of those that lacked these facilities. Improvement has been hastened by liberalization of major company licensing policies controlling thermal cracking [78] and by development of competing processes by independent research companies like Universal Oil Products and by engineering companies which build refineries under contract. Later—again after a period of restrictive licensing—Ethyl fluid became available to help the independent upgrade his gasoline. Many also, lacking a cracking plant, installed vacuum stills which permitted them to rerun residual fuels to lighter gas oils and asphalt. Still others, initially unable to afford the cost of catalytic cracking, put in catalytic reforming units through which they could markedly increase the octane rating of their gasoline. Indeed, until 1956 small refiners had a larger percentage of national catalytic reforming than of straight-run capacity, indicating that as a group they were using this less expensive method to compensate for their critical lack of catalytic cracking.[79]

In the last few years the smaller refiners have been catching up rapidly in catalytic cracking itself, those of intermediate size (say 10,000 to 50,000 b/d), almost completely.[80] They have been able to

78. See, e.g., Stocking, pp. 259–261; Bain, *Pacific Coast Petroleum Industry,* 2, 220; and Cook, p. 31.

79. The relevant statistics appear annually in the *Oil and Gas Journal*. As of January 1, 1954, refiners with less than 100,000 b/d capacity controlled 19.8 per cent of national distillation, but no less than 39.1 per cent of national catalytic reforming capacity.

80. See above, Table XXV. The Petroleum Administration for Defense was apparently instrumental in this realization. Construction authorizations by that

do so largely because of the substantial progress that has been made in adapting these processes for small unit refineries. Whereas catalytic crackers originally had to be designed for several thousand barrels a day capacity, efficient catalytic reformers have been developed with capacities as low as 600 b/d.[81] Both major oil companies themselves and engineering and research firms like Stone and Webster, Lummus, M. W. Kellogg, Universal Oil Products, Blaw-Knox, and others have played important roles in developing small package units and licensing them at royalties within the means of small refiners. The latter in some cases have done a great deal to help themselves.[82]

Second, every successful small refiner has put itself in a position to receive crude oil at the lowest possible laid down cost, while at the same time having access to large product markets. Unique are those near Los Angeles with a location that assures both. Others—important market factors like Derby Oil, El Dorado, Champlin, Ben Franklin, Deep Rock, Anderson-Prichard—with access to the crude oil supplies of the Midcontinent area, serve rapidly expanding local markets; but they can also ship their products via the common-carrier Great Lakes Pipe Line or by barge into the northern Midwest. Still others—like Taylor Refining, Crown Central, Eastern States, Pontiac Refining, Republic Oil Refining, Suntide—have located on the Gulf Coast of Texas, served by common-carrier trunk lines, and able not only to sell right in that phenomenally expanding economic empire but also to ship products by tanker at minimum cost to East Coast marketers and to major refiners with large East Coast marketing

---

agency at the end of April, 1952, were expected to raise the catalytic cracking capacity of refiners with under 20,000 b/d from 1.86 per cent to 6.54 per cent of the national total, while raising their proportion of crude throughput capacity only from 9.86 per cent to 10.87 per cent. PAD Release 412, June 27, 1952. Meanwhile, the larger refiners have been installing catalytic reforming capacity so rapidly that it has been they who have caught up with the smaller ones in this respect. At the beginning of 1954 companies controlling over 100,000 b/d of refining capacity had 80.2 per cent of national distillation, but only 60.9 per cent of national reforming capacity. Four years later the former ratio remained virtually unchanged, at 80.4 per cent, but these larger companies now controlled 80.4 per cent of national catalytic reforming plant as well.

81. *National Petroleum News* (August 12, 1953), p. 18.

82. Leonard Refineries installed the first small-scale catalytic polymerization unit in the industry in 1938, at a capital outlay of only $9,000. After the war, Leonard received a bid of $2,500,000 for a cat cracker; but by working closely with the engineering firm and making certain drastic alterations in the original plans, Leonard was able to have the unit completed at a total investment cost of slightly under $600,000. McLean and Haigh, p. 654; also p. 653.

requirements. Those like Northwest Refining in St. Paul, Ashland in Kentucky (now practically a major), Aurora Gasoline in Detroit, and International Refineries near Duluth can take barge deliveries of crude oil, or are hooked in with large common-carrier crude systems, sometimes with short pipelines of their own to take the crude from terminals to their own plants. They sell in markets that are more than adequate to take all they can produce.

In view of the importance of crude oil, cheaply and reliably laid down at the refinery, it is not surprising that the pipeline availability of Canadian crude in Superior, Wisconsin (mostly through Interprovincial Pipe Line), and of Williston Basin (North Dakota) oil in Minneapolis and St. Paul led to the construction and expansion of independent as well as major-company refineries in those areas.[83] The vigor of this response is evidence of a continuing virility of the independent refiner when conditions are propitious, and the apparent reliability of pipeline transport, even though all of these refineries are in some important fashion integrated—two of them in marketing, two of them with major companies.[84]

Many of these firms have the special advantage of being either the

83. International Refineries, a subsidiary of Western Oil and Fuel Company, theretofore a marketer and barge operator on the Mississippi River, completed a modern 11,000 b/d refinery near Duluth in 1953 using Canadian crude. Minnesota's first and for a long time its only refiner, Northwest Refining, has been expanding its capacity from around 8,000 b/d in 1953 (on January 1, 1957, it had 15,000 b/d operating and another 5,000 under construction). The Great Northern Refining Company, an even more recent entrant, had (on January 1, 1957) a modern 27,500 b/d refinery just outside of St. Paul, evidently running Canadian crude oil. Standard of Indiana has a 31,600 b/d refinery in Mandan, North Dakota, connected by a 200-mile crude line with the Williston Field in the West and by a products line connection eastward with Indiana's products line from Whiting. "An Oil Empire Is Growing in the Midwest," *National Petroleum News* (March 17, 1954), pp. 13–15; also *ibid*. (June 23, 1954), p. 7.

84. Western Oil and Fuel is an independent marketer which has pioneered in barge transport of products up the Mississippi; it has a large chain of service stations selling a highly respected "Mileage" brand, and in 1955 it purchased the Direct Service Company, a large independent marketer in the area. Northwestern likewise started in marketing. It owns an extensive chain of attractive "Erickson" stations and has a long term crude supply contract with Standard of Indiana. As for Great Northern, its two principal stockholders are producing companies with which it has signed long-term supply contracts; and it also apparently has an agreement with a subsidiary of Socony Mobil to supply a large quantity of its crude and to market the largest portion of its products. See *ibid*.

sole or the most important refiner in the substantial markets they serve: Aurora and Northwestern are notable examples. One of these has direct pipeline connections to deliver fuel oil to big nearby industrial customers; and both do a very heavy business in residual fuels with large steel companies near at hand. In these northern areas, location near the market has a substantial advantage for this trade, since the heavy viscosity of residual fuels make them extremely difficult to bring in either by pipeline or by barge especially in cold weather. Another substantial advantage of location near the market, which some have used, is the opportunity for exchange with other firms, including major companies that market in the area and cannot possibly lay down their products so cheaply. Full advantage of such exchange arrangements, of course, could be realized only by a refiner with fairly widespread marketing interests.

There are other factors that have played a significant role in the success of many small refiners. Many of them are fairly obvious and need not be discussed here. There is the vital and variable factor of managerial and technical ability, for example. A small refiner can apparently go far on the basis of skill in adapting, changing, tinkering with refineries. As an associate of one of them expressed it: "He plays a refinery the way you would play the piano." Obviously skills like these are unevenly distributed throughout the population of refiners: the outstanding ones succeed; many who lack these attributes fail. Many small refiners fall into particular geographical niches or specialize in particular products; some are "in and outers" who do very well at it; some concentrate on refining particular crudes; some find they can market more efficiently than their major competitors because they do not have to blanket an area with stations to sell their products but can pick and choose a few high volume locations. McLean and Haigh provide a very illuminating account of the kinds of interstices in which small refiners may be found prospering.[85]

One final factor deserves particular mention in this study. Almost every one of the successful independent refiners has also felt it necessary to integrate to some substantial extent in order to grow, if not to survive. The integration has taken many forms and operated in various directions: some own or have gone out to get crude production; some rely on long-term processing agreements with major suppliers or on long-term purchase contracts with them; many have gone into marketing very substantially, making heavy investments in service stations;

85. McLean and Haigh, Chap. 23.

others were originally marketers who felt it necessary to move backward into refining to assure their sources at reasonable price.[86]

As with the expansion of the majors, these integrations have been achieved through a combination of construction and merger. In the decade of the 1950's alone the merger of relatively small refiners like Kanotex into Anderson-Prichard, Wood River into Sinclair, Globe into Pure, Taylor with Delhi, El Dorado (after first having been acquired by the Atlas Corporation) and American Liberty into American Petrofina, Champlin into the Chicago Corporation, Deep Rock into Kerr-McGee, Derby into Colorado Oil and Gas, Republic with Plymouth, and Mid-Continent with Sunray was in every case a merger in the direction of a more completely balanced vertical integration. The growth of such "minor majors" to vie more effectively with the majors may be implicit evidence that only a vertically integrated firm can compete with a vertically integrated major in the oil industry.

The more successful the independent refiner has been in developing a gasoline comparable in quality with that of his major rivals, the better has been the opportunity and the stronger the competitive pressure to seek consumer brand acceptance through forward integration and to secure price protection on raw materials through backward integration. While the latter is made more urgent by the rigidities of prorationing and the former by the major's attempted preemption of consumer loyalties, it is not obvious that similar emphasis

86. It would involve excessive detail to document this final point that the successful "independent refiners" have made their way largely by abandoning the one attribute that is usually assigned to them—lack of integration. Most striking in recent years have been the extensive marketing programs put into effect, planned or merely contemplated by refiners who had until then sold largely to majors or jobbers: Texas Gas, Eastern States, Ingram Products, Republic, Delhi-Taylor, American Liberty (now part of American Petrofina), Derby Oil (now a subsidiary of Colorado Oil and Gas), and Crown Central are a few of the names that have been prominently mentioned. This pattern of development, so effectively pioneered by Frontier (Wyoming), Clark, and Leonard, has been accepted by a widening number of converts; one of the latest, Ingram Products, "Henry Ingram . . . [reports the *National Petroleum News*] . . . sees it as an unequal battle, so he's joined other independent refiners going branded. . . . 'The main goal now is to get our brand up,' says marketing vice president. . . . 'Get people acquainted with it, and get as much absolutely controlled business as possible.' . . . The company doesn't expect all of its salary stations to show a profit before three to five years. . . . Still . . . the advertising value of a station can be more important than its profits for a time."

Ingram has apparently learned his lesson; it was he who founded and sold out the Wood River Refining Company to Sinclair (February, 1958, pp. 132–135).

on branded distribution would not have grown inexorably as the market developed, whatever the organization of suppliers. What does seem evident is this: as long as the nether millstone of refinery margins is fixed by prorationing, the independent refiner must seek his salvation increasingly through vertical integration, both backward and forward. He must move backward to get under the millstone. He is under particularly severe pressure to move forward because it is precisely at times when markets are slack that he is subject to the most stringent margin squeeze, and is therefore most strongly impelled to stop selling his product unbranded, in the industry's most price-conscious market, in competition with the unbranded, dumped, surplus product of his major competitors. This tendency in turn threatens to alter the balance of competitive forces in product markets, most profoundly by imperilling the independent jobber, to whom the next chapter is devoted.

CONCLUSION

It is not necessary to choose between conflicting explanations of the so-called decline of the independent refiner. The complex historical process cannot even be called a decline unless one chooses to define the "independent refiner" as one who has gone out of business. Conditions of competition have changed, and continue to change, for the small and the non-integrated refiner: some are threatening, others are promising. There can be no simple explanation of the phenomenon.

The immediate task, however, is more modest—to weigh the impact of integration on the structure of the refining segment of the industry. It is reasonably clear that the combined size and integration of the major oil companies have impaired the competitive position of the non-integrated and the small, less integrated refiners beyond technical handicaps attributable to differences in the efficiency with which they serve the public.

The primary source of strategic, as opposed to economic, advantages that the large integrated refiner holds over the nonintegrated or small, less-integrated refiner stems from combining the competitive job of refining with other stages of the industry which are essentially monopolistic. In quasi public-utility fashion, the production of crude oil is limited to a reasonable market demand and price is thereby protected from the surges of an unruly supply. The critical importance of pipelines and the physical and economic limitations of competition in the provision of pipeline service have brought about an even closer approximation of the traditional notion of a public utility in that sphere. In the case of pipelines—more certainly of crude than of product lines —more effective public regulation and the natural growth of capacity toward a closer approximation to need in important market areas have substantially eliminated grossly discriminatory tactics. General awareness of the need for reasonable, nondiscriminatory treatment of all potential shippers, combined with regulatory powers now vested in the ICC, would seem enough to assure the desired kind of behavior.

But there is no such social control and no such expectation of socially desirable behavior in the case of crude oil supply. Quite the contrary. In the name of conservation, domestic crude oil supply is given a policy-determined scarcity and an enhanced value by action of the state. And yet no bar is set to the pre-emption of vital supplies of crude, thus arbitrarily restricted, by strong integrated private firms, and no social control is exercised over the disposition by them of the unearned value increment and high sheltered profits that such a policy tends to guarantee. It is in these areas—in the terms on which crude oil must be purchased in markets made thin by the presence of vertical integration and in consequent scarcity profits (only partially related to productive efficiency) that permeate and distort operations at *all* levels—that the independent refiner is most vitally prejudiced. Is it a reasonable public policy—can it possibly make for fair competition and economic progress under private enterprise—thus to limit supplies of the basic raw material of the petroleum industry and take no heed of its impact on competitive balance downstream?

Here then is the basic anomaly of competition in the presence of vertical integration in the petroleum industry. It has cropped up before in the analysis of conservation and it has dogged this study at every step. The problems of the independent refiner focus it more clearly because of the narrow margins, the instability, and the intensity of competition at this crucial stage. It is exactly because the decision-making process in the vertically integrated firm is essentially unitary that there is no wholly satisfactory way in which the costs and profits at one level of production can be separated and appraised relative to another, that the existence of integration, overlapping the ownership and production of crude oil, confounds analysis and confuses and distorts managerial motivations. Apart from the ownership and control of crude oil, vertical integration (like other forms of business organization) might more nearly justify itself by its relative efficiency in the ordering of production in competition with nonintegrated firms at each level of the industry.

Does mandatory unitization of production and freedom of imports, as recommended in Chapter 10, provide any hope for a fairer basis of competition than that established under current practice? Certainly, nothing short of a divorce of the ownership of crude oil from operations downstream would remove entirely the taint of an unearned increment in oil in the competition of integrated firms at other stages of the industry. It could not be expected that the paradoxical twist now given to private motivations, when leaders at user levels find it in their interests to urge output limitations and high prices for their essential raw materials, while product prices fall, would be completely dissipated as long as their ownership interest in crude oil remained inviolate.[87] Mandatory unitization, like prorationing, would banish the rule of capture and permit oil to be held below ground without serious penalty: would not the nonintegrated refiner suffer as much from the consequent stability of the crude oil price?

There is reason to believe that the situation in which the nonintegrated refiner finds himself would be substantially eased. Prorationing, as practiced by the Texas Railroad Commission, is not only a rigid unitary control which has effectively allowed for and therefore emasculated all supply sources governed by contrary public or private motives and policies; it is also a public regulation, a sanction imposed by the sovereign power of the people for the combined purposes of the state, in which conservation plays the most prominent role. Prorationing, therefore, must provide a more unyielding basis for price than any alternative that multiplies the number of decision-making bodies concerned with supply. At the same time, once state authority and state responsibility for the final decision are removed, not only is the practicability of effecting over-all supply limitation below MER to support a higher price destroyed; even the willingness to urge such action for private advantage is severely compromised by a situation in which policy responsibility is no longer cloaked in the inscrutabilities of public purposes.

Mandatory unitization would release for independent action separately administered low-cost domestic supply sources numbered in the hundreds. Even though they might be managed by representatives of

87. Even the refiner with very little production is often trapped into a perverted (from the public standpoint not necessarily from his) advocacy of higher prices for products rather than lower prices for raw materials as a solution for his competitive difficulties. See the conclusions of the so-called Blazer Committee in 1935, summarized by Watkins, p. 165, and the similar statement by Paul Blazer eighteen years later, before the Wolverton Committee, when a similar refinery squeeze was in the making.

the more important integrated companies, the interests of their smaller participants in current income (a combination of price and volume of production) could not be ignored, more especially when cut-backs in production were not required by MER and promised to be compensated by imports. Furthermore, although the dominant proportion of foreign oil may still be held by a few of the large international companies, a substantial amount has already come into the possession of smaller firms and, as the imposition of import quotas itself indicates, this foreign oil seeking domestic markets is already offering a truly independent competitive source of supply. Thus, although mandatory unitization would create some of the uncertainties of oligopolistic markets, the unyielding stability and upward bias formerly imparted by prorationing and import limitations would be significantly modified. Within the limits of MER, domestic and import supply alternatives should be available to an alert buyer that could be exploited at a favorable, that is a more flexible, price. Whether or not the profits of established, nonintegrated refiners would in the long run benefit by this possibility of a more flexible crude oil price, they would at least be freed of the incubus of competing with rivals enjoying more favorable and more discriminatory access to raw materials by reason of public cartelization. The ultimate consumer would be more fully assured the benefits of thoroughgoing competition.

CHAPTER 20

Integration and the Independent Marketer

THE OLD Standard Oil Company was thoroughly integrated into wholesale distribution. It had 3,573 bulk plants in 1906, distributing its products in almost every state in the Union. But the primary product was kerosene: there were only 79,000 motor vehicles registered in the United States in 1905. Accordingly there was no reason for refiners to own their retail outlets, and even five years later they controlled very few. But between 1910 and 1925 motor vehicle registrations jumped from 458,000 to 19,941,000, gasoline became by far the most important oil product, and the service station came into being.[1] With the hectic exploitation of this new market, the distribution of petroleum products took on its present aspect, and there were spawned problems, frictions, and complaints the intensity of which has in no way diminished to this day. In a very real sense this is the *noisiest* branch of the industry.

The reason for all the shouting is not hard to find. When a mammoth extractive and manufacturing industry comes to the point of distributing its products at every corner and highway of the nation with a strong emphasis on service on the spot, it must rely heavily on the talents of local businessmen. The big refiners, anxious to promote branded distribution of their products in order to help counter mounting supplies and sagging prices of oil and products, offered many inducements to independent wholesalers and retailers to come into the industry and sell their products.[2] Still, the tens of thousands who responded would probably have come without special inducements from their suppliers. The profit to be gained from soaring gasoline sales through the service station innovation, the relatively small amount of capital required to build either a station or a bulk plant capable of tak-

1. See McLean and Haigh, pp. 66, 71, 267–268.
2. The Standard companies sold mainly for tank-wagon delivery through their own bulk plants, making little use of independent distributors. Other refiners, however, particularly in the twenties and early thirties, relied more heavily on distributive facilities of outsiders. Swensrud, in DeGolyer, *Elements of the Petroleum Industry,* p. 384.

ing tank-car shipments from wholesale markets, and the chance to get into business for oneself were sufficient attractions.

The relations between suppliers and distributors could not possibly have remained purely complementary, for the former were under competitive pressure to go into marketing themselves as well. There were high profits to be gained in one's own distribution in the early days; while the performance of independently owned stations was inevitably spotty—too many were dirty, gave poor service, or even adulterated their products. Furthermore, with abundant open-market supplies and intensive competition for market outlets, the patronage of independent wholesalers and retailers was often unreliable. The safest course for a refiner was to own his distribution facilities.

The high profits of innovation and early entry began to crumble by the late 1920's under the heavy weight of excessive new facilities so hastily and unscientifically constructed. The mania of competitive construction and acquisition, however, did not abate until after the deepest depression years and the capping of the gushing wells. Only then could a real effort of rationalizing and streamlining be successfully undertaken.

This scramble of major companies for market outlets and the downward pressure on marketing profits generated first by competitive profusion, then by competitive rationalization, produced unceasing friction between independent marketers and integrated refiners. Independent jobbers found their more wealthy suppliers raiding their own dealers with all sorts of inducements, or constructing new strings of substitute bulk plants and service stations in their accustomed market areas. The more thorough the refiner's forward integration, the more it crowded the independent. Construction of a new refinery or terminal—the attempt to enter a new market—would typically create an opportunity for the jobber, whose patronage would be actively solicited in the effort to build up a market. But construction of new bulk plants and service stations, and direct distribution from the terminal when markets for the branded product had been developed, meant by-passing or competing with him, or making him a salaried employee or commission agent.

The dynamic, fluctuating fortunes of the industry would in any case have generated complaints. Shifting patterns of population, of driving habits, and of highway construction; extreme changes in the rate of expansion of supply and demand; innovations like the product pipeline and big transport truck; and the great disparities in the talents of the small businessmen attracted into the field inevitably would have produced many errors, a high incidence of failure, a continuous source of wasteful obsolescence of capacity. The large integrated firms became a suitable scapegoat for political attack and an object of genuine grievances as well. The marketers organized themselves into associations (whose number, membership, and influence seems to be increasing) to plead their case directly before the major supplier-competitors and, if necessary, before government agencies. An early fruit of these efforts was the application of state chain store taxes, which culminated in the almost complete withdrawal of major companies from direct service station operation. Controversy continues over such alleged practices as exclusive dealing, price discrimination, squeezing of jobber margins, and denial of supplies to independent marketers. And the question is constantly raised whether it is advisable to permit integrated refiner-producers to operate in marketing at all.

In a sense the vociferousness of independent jobbers, undiminished over a thirty-year span, attests the continuing vigor of competition and the dynamic character of the marketing of petroleum products. Yet the possibility of unfair leverage by the major companies requires more serious consideration. Would the public interest be better served by a complete segregation of functions than it is by the rather untidy and quarrelsome mixture of existing integrated and nonintegrated operations?

Since integration does not threaten a reduction of retailer numbers below the requirements of effective competition (see Chapter 15), this inquiry into the problems of the independent marketer will concern itself almost entirely with the fortunes of the wholesaler.

There are three general and interrelated sources of friction between the independent wholesaler and the integrated oil companies. First, there is the annoyance and insecurity that the former experience because of their dependence on the majors for the greater part of their supplies. There would seem to be no reason, a priori, why the dependence of marketer on supplier should be any more burdensome than that of the refiner on his distributor, and in fact it helps to retain a certain perspective if this mutuality of dependence is held in mind. The distributor may point out that his numbers are many and his potential suppliers few, so that the insecurity is greater on his side. But in each local market where the major is or wants to be represented, it is not clear that the alternatives available to the one are greater than to the other. Refiners bid against one another for wholesalers, and not only jobbers but branded distributors shift from one source of supply to another in response. Yet the relationship is not entirely symmetrical. The major supplier is big; and the individual distributor is far less important to the supplier's total operations than the individual supplier is to the jobber. Moreover, bulking large in the market, the major suppliers may follow essentially parallel market practices, further reducing the real alternatives available to the individual marketer. Size and integration will induce most majors to lay heavier emphasis on regularity of patronage, brand loyalty, and non-price competition than individual jobber customers may wish. The maverick who wants to shop around for supplies, use his own brand, rely more heavily on price than service to attract customers, therefore, may have trouble finding accommodation in times of shortage. Finally, the major has the capital to put his preferences into effect: he can tie up the service stations without which the jobber can hardly play an important role in the gasoline business. Thus he can reduce his dependence upon the jobber more readily than the latter by similar tactics can strengthen his own bargaining power.

This opportunity of majors to engage in direct marketing gives rise to the second group of grievances: the refiner-suppliers compete with their own distributors. Here is a condition more prominent in the oil industry than in most. Automobile, farm equipment, phonograph record, and hearing aid manufacturers do not try to take customers away from their own dealers. Since the oil company supplier thus has the option of deciding whether and where he will sell directly —an option allegedly exercised in the low-cost, high-density markets—the distributors complain that their suppliers skim the cream and leave them only with the less profitable business. And since the independent must operate within the essentially conventional margin his supplier provides while the latter has the wider spread between direct costs and refined product prices within which to operate, the integrated refiner-marketer can always undercut his own distributors regardless of their efficiency and exclude them from business he wants to handle directly. This fact leads, in turn, to the final omnipresent complaint: margins are always too low, and they are too often subject to unfair squeezes.

SUPPLY

An analysis of the supply problems of the independent wholesaler calls for describing a factual situation where the relevant facts do not exist in the organized fashion necessary to permit assured conclusions.

Nor are the issues clearly drawn: there is rather a feeling of uneasiness, punctuated with specific evidences of active discontent, the generality of which remains in doubt. Individual complaints issue, naturally, from the more vocal members of the jobber community, and primarily in periods of shortage. It is quite possible that the overwhelming majority of independent wholesalers neither feel nor have any basis worthy of serious attention for feeling discontented with their supply arrangements. Most important, although economists cannot be importantly concerned with the contentment (or lack of it) of any individual group of businessmen, they cannot ignore considerations of equity and fair dealing in shaping public policy. In brief, the cold economic facts are sketchy in this area and their implications for public policy are elusive.

It should be recalled that the oil industry necessarily places a heavy premium on continuity of flow and supply. Most businessmen on both disposing and receiving ends will demand it. Brand identification contributes to the realization of stable long-term arrangements. Investments in branded distribution are inherently less flexible than in the distribution of undifferentiated products: a distributor who has devoted years to the cultivation of good will for a particular brand will not easily shift to another. Within limits, the public is well served by these stable patterns—by the willingness to invest, the fuller use of capacity, the low costs of regularly scheduled, continuous deliveries, and the competition in product quality and service, to all of which they contribute.

The limiting consideration is the need to preserve effective alternatives for the independent businessman, and through him for the final buyer. The only effective check is the continuing possibility of price competition, which depends in turn on the opportunity for distributors to find open market supplies which they can buy at competitive prices with no strings attached and sell on whatever terms they choose. The adequacy of these opportunities, and consequently both the balance of bargaining power between refiner and wholesaler and the vigor of price competition, will depend fundamentally on the extent to which aggregate industry supply is calibrated with what the stable and orderly channels of distribution will absorb.

The wholesale marketer is supplied by both nonintegrated and integrated refiners, apparently more by the latter than by the former. That he gets most of his heating oils from the integrated companies is clear, for they account for nine-tenths of the supply and rely heavily on independents to distribute it. It is perforce true in the case of gasoline, again because that is where most of it comes from.[3] But though this is probably true even of unbranded heating oils, because major suppliers have pushed branded distribution less insistently here than in gasoline, it is less likely for unbranded gasoline. The truly independent gasoline jobber is heavily dependent on independent refiners.[4]

The changing fortunes of the independent refiners create problems for the independent jobbers as well. The thinner the open market to which the jobber can turn for supplies, the less independent a competitive role he can play. And the fortunes of the unbranded jobber reflect in turn the alternatives available to the branded distributors as well, their freedom to shift to unbranded distribution, or from one refiner brand to another, hence their bargaining position *vis-à-vis* the integrated suppliers as a group. The continuing tendency of independent refiners to merge with companies whose facilities make their integration more complete must narrow these alternatives.[5]

3. According to Cross, 33 per cent of the total national production of gasoline and 61 per cent of the distillate fuel oils in 1950 went to market (either to service stations or to final buyers) through nonrefiner channels. (See above, p. 388, Table XXI.) According to the 1954 *Census of Business,* something like 27 per cent of the total national bulk plant and terminal sales of gasoline, and 46 per cent of the distillate fuel oils, were made by nonrefiner-marketers. Computations from *Wholesale Trade,* Petroleum Bulk Plants and Terminals, Bulletin W-2-8 (1957), pp. 8–61, on the basis of reported product breakdown of sales, adjusted in proportion to the divergent sales coverages of the two groups reporting these details, in the manner explained below, Table XXVII, n. e. The 1954 Census omitted sales of unincorporated firms with no paid employees; their inclusion would doubtless raise the share of the non-refiner group slightly. See below, Table XXVII, n. a. Since integrated refiner-marketers accounted for over 90 per cent of national production of gasoline and heating oils in that year, obviously the major portion of distributors' supplies must have come from them.

4. However, this will depend on whether major refiners have large excess capacity, which varies from one time to another. Jobber purchases of "surplus" gasoline from majors have probably been on the wane, historically, but there are indications in the middle and late fifties that major company offerings to private branders have grown to such a point that they account for the larger proportion of their supplies. See above, p. 466, n. 33.

5. E.g., before its merger with Mid-Continent "Sunray sold most of its products to unbranded jobbers, several majors and sometimes to the open market." An important reason for the merger was to channel Sunray products through Mid-Continent's market outlets—*National Petroleum News* (February, 1956), p. 39. Similarly, Sunray Mid-Continent's planned acquisition of the remaining 50 per cent of Suntide Refining stock, with consequent full operating control over the refinery (Sunray had owned approximately 50 per cent ever

Independent refiners do not have to disappear to jeopardize the supplies of nonintegrated marketers. Through concerted purchases of distress gasoline by the majors (now outlawed) and through sales or processing agreements that turn over a large share of the output of independently refined products to the integrated marketing channels of other refiners when crude oil is scarce, the survival of the refiner may be assured while supplies to the jobber are constricted.[6] As already observed, it is common practice for some major companies to purchase a portion of their products from other refiners, mostly small, in some instances as a matter of continuing policy, in others as a result of temporary imbalances within their own organizations.[7]

To ascertain whether there is a trend in the supplies of major products to independents, a questionnaire was circulated to leading integrated refiners.[8] These data permit the conclusion that there has been no trend on the part of the major companies either since 1936 or since 1946 away from distribution through independent marketers, branded and unbranded considered together. On the contrary, in both gasoline and heating oils, more companies increased than decreased their percentage of total sales through such distributors.[9]

since it helped organize that company in 1952), is part of a program to expand the direct marketing of the D-X Sunray brand in Texas. It will thus eventually take out of the open market the output of this 65,000 b/d refinery, which has heretofore "been sold almost entirely in bulk lots" because Suntide had no marketing facilities of its own. *Wall Street Journal* (April 30, 1958), p. 27. In Kansas, "Drastic changes were taking place in the position of Independent refineries. . . . Three Independents closed down—Bay . . . Barnsdall . . . and Shallow Water. . . . This meant that three supply sources for private brand marketers were cut off. Three other Independent refiners merged with other companies. . . . Derby . . . Kanotex . . . and Champlin. . . ." *National Petroleum News* (May, 1955), p. 51.

6. See Wherry (Senate Small Business) Committee survey cited in above, p. 507, n. 54.

7. See above, pp. 393 and 434.

8. The object was to supplement McLean and Haigh's rather sketchy data for their seven-company sample (pp. 461, 688–696) by asking the remaining thirteen of the TNEC's twenty majors, plus Ashland, Deep Rock, Lion, Richfield, and Sunray, to supply the percentages of (a) their total motor fuels and (b) home heating oils sold in 1936, 1940, 1946, 1950, and 1953 through commission distributors, branded distributors, and unbranded jobbers. Replies of varying degrees of usability were received from eleven of them. Since that time several of these companies have been involved in important mergers. But only the one between Sunray and Mid-Continent might be expected to have altered substantially the marketing pattern of the predecessors. See above, n. 5.

9. The proportion of sales of gasoline through both branded and unbranded distributors (as always, commission agents are excluded) rose in seven instances

The statistics of the 1939, 1948, and 1954 censuses of business summarized in Table XXVII confirm this conclusion: neither in gasoline nor in heating oils is there any evidence of a decline in the market share of the independent wholesaler (the Census does not differentiate branded distributors and private brand jobbers). On the contrary, marketers unaffiliated with refiners increased their proportion of national bulk station and terminal sales of gasoline from 24.5 to 26.8 per cent, and of sales of all products even more, from 27.4 to 33.9 per cent.[10] The more rapid rise of the latter than of the former ratios doubtless reflects the more rapid comparative growth of national sales of heating oils, in the marketing of which independent wholesalers play a larger role.[11]

---

and fell in three compared with prewar. The maximum increase (except for Deep Rock, which had turned over its marketing almost completely to independent distributors) was 19.7 per cent of total sales, the maximum decrease, 8 per cent; but most of the changes in either direction were slight, and the median change for the nine companies for which data were available was an increase of only 1.8 percent, the arithmetic mean 8 per cent, of total sales. In the case of branded distributors alone, for which there were fuller data, the share rose for seven and fell for four; the median change (for fourteen companies, three of them showing no significant change) was +1 per cent, the mean +5 per cent.

In the case of heating oils more fragmentary data show rises in the percentages of six companies, declines for only one, with the median change a rise of 7.5 per cent, the mean a rise of 13 per cent, of total sales.

10. Incidentally, the trend apparent in these data diverges from the one shown in Cross' estimates for the 1946–50 period, when he found that total distributor-jobber sales of distillate fuel oil rose more rapidly and of gasoline less rapidly than the national totals. The respective percentage increases of jobber and total national sales were 78.1 and 69.5 in the case of heating oils and 28.1 and 39.0 for gasoline. *Harvard Business Review* (July–August, 1953), pp. 74–75. It also seems to contradict the assertion of the General Council of the National Oil Jobbers Association, Senate Judiciary Committee, "To Amend Section 2 of the Clayton Act," *Hearings* (1956), p. 482, and of the *National Petroleum News*. The latter observes that among the jobbers reporting to it that they handle gasoline, the average volume handled did not change appreciably between 1949 and 1957, and concludes that "the jobber's share of gasoline sales hasn't kept up with increases in national demand" (May, 1957), pp. 95, 102. The conclusion applies only to the average volume of sales by jobbers reporting they handled gasoline; *National Petroleum News* points out, however, that only 77.5 per cent of its surveyed jobbers reported handling gasoline in 1953 (it had no such information in 1949) compared with 93 per cent in 1957. Frank Breese, editor of *National Petroleum News*, kindly cleared up this question in private correspondence.

11. See above, n. 3, and pp. 386–387. The results of the above mentioned survey clearly reflect the greater importance of independents in the marketing of heating oils. The (thirteen company) median was 56.8 per cent of heating oils

TABLE XXVII

Sales from Petroleum Bulk Plants and Terminals by Type of Operation

	1939	1948	1954 [a]
BULK PLANT SALES: $000,000			
U.S. total	2,670	6,754	8,292
Independent stations [b]	564	1,630	2,510
Independents as % of total	21.1%	24.1%	30.3%
BULK PLANT AND TERMINAL SALES [c]			
All sales, $000,000			
U.S. total	2,943	8,914	13,041
Refiner-marketers	2,138	6,044	8,614
Others [d]	805	2,870	4,427
Others as % of total	27.4%	32.2%	33.9%
Gasoline, million gallons			
U.S. total			
As reported	20,854	32,288	39,313
Adjusted [e]	22,140	34,793	41,956
Other than refiner-marketer			
As reported	4,596	7,498	9,265
Adjusted [e]	5,425	9,479	11,230
Adjusted as % of U.S.	24.5%	27.2%	26.8%

[a] In the 1954 Census unincorporated firms without paid employees were not included. This group accounted in 1948 for 1,100 establishments and sales of $133 million.

[b] These are bulk plants owned and operated independently of other wholesale establishments. They therefore do not include the bulk plants of distributors who, though independent of refiners, own more than one plant.

[c] There is double counting in these totals, sales from terminals to bulk plants being included.

[d] These are bulk plants and terminals unaffiliated with refineries.

[e] All firms reporting product breakdowns accounted for 93.7 per cent of total national bulk plant and terminal sales in 1954, 92.8 per cent in 1948 and in 1939, when separate figures alone are offered, 92.2 per cent of terminal and 94.4 per cent of bulk plant sales. All nonrefiner-marketer firms making similar reports accounted for the following percentages of sales by all firms in that category: 82.5 per cent in 1954, 79.1 per cent in 1948, and in 1939, 74.6 per cent of terminal and 85.2 per cent of bulk station sales. The reported data are adjusted by dividing them by the respective percentages, on the assumption that the percentage distribution of total sales by all firms in each group was the same as for the reporting firms.

Source: U. S. censuses of business, Wholesale Trade, *Petroleum Bulk Stations and Terminals* (some variations in titles), 1939 (16th Census of the United States, 1940), 1948 (Bulletin N. 2-W-14) and 1954 (Bulletin W-2-8, 1957).

Nevertheless, there has probably been a long range trend from un-branded to branded distribution of major gasoline. Swensrud's sum-mary of "informed opinion" indicates it for the period up to the late thirties.[12] The questionnaire suggests a continuation of this trend until 1953, though the average change was slight.[13] The more striking fact was the unimportance, in most instances the insignificance, of un-branded gasoline distribution for the major companies.[14]

Moreover, though the figures show no historical trend, the fact is that even the branded distributor handles much the smaller per-centage of major company gasoline. Direct integrated wholesale dis-tribution is the general rule from refiner to service station or final in-dustrial or commercial buyer. Cross estimates that distributors not integrated with refiners handled 33 per cent of total national produc-tion (and 40 per cent of sales to service stations alone), and this figure is perhaps an overestimate.[15] The median percentage for the seventeen-

---

sold to jobbers and distributors, compared with (for fourteen companies) 23.6 per cent of gasoline. If one were to credit "independent" bulk stations in 1954 with the 1948 volume of sales of unincorporated firms excluded from the 1954 Census (see note a to the table), their share of national bulk plant sales would rise from 30.3 to 31.4 in that terminal year; a similar adjustment would increase the share of "others" than refiner-marketers in total bulk plant and terminal sales from 33.9 to 34.6 per cent in 1954.

12. TNEC, *Hearings*, Pt. XV, p. 8689. Contrast Warren Platt, *The Future of the Independent Oil Jobber* (Cleveland, National Petroleum News, 1941), pp. 20–21, to the effect that an increasing precentage of gasoline obtained by jobbers from major companies between 1933 and 1939 was for private brands. These years were unusually favorable for private brand jobbers because of the successive flows of cheap gasoline from East Texas, Michigan and Illinois.

13. See also the testimony to the same effect for the industry as a whole by Paul Blazer, chairman of Ashland, before the Wolverton Committee, *Hearings* (1953), p. 476, and McLean and Haigh, p. 470.

14. The median figure for fourteen companies was 1.5 per cent of total gasoline sales going to (unbranded) jobbers. It could be higher, if the com-panies reporting these sales as "very small" or "negligible" in fact sold more than 1.5 per cent through such channels. For only two companies (both bona fide, rather than borderline, majors) was the figure as high as 12 to 15 per cent; the next real major (i.e. passing by Ohio Oil, with 8.9 per cent) was Gulf, with 6 per cent (see McLean and Haigh, p. 461). In contrast the seventeen-company median for sales to branded distributors was 21.8 per cent of total gasoline sales.

15. See above, p. 389, n. 6. As explained more fully there, if McLean and Haigh are right when they report that 58 per cent of the total national service station sales were by stations controlled by refiners, Cross' estimate that 40 per cent of national service station sales are accounted for by independent distributors or jobbers would seem too high because majors sell a large pro-portion of their gasoline to contractor stations.

company sample showed 21.8 per cent of their total gasoline sales going to branded distributors, and the average would be lower if it were weighted on the basis of the relative importance of the companies surveyed.[16] The major companies generally concede that their policy is to distribute directly in areas of heavy concentrated demand, using distributors in essentially peripheral markets.[17]

In heating oils there appears to have been no trend toward branded distribution, although the figures are very skimpy here, and some specific major companies are known to have made substantial and successful efforts to have their jobbers handle branded product. Unbranded distribution is more important in heating oils than in gasoline, but even here it is not large according to the data for major companies as a group, and remains less important than branded.[18]

In the absence of detailed and comparable statistics it is impossible to say to what extent the foregoing observation about the declining and small relative size of major company sales of gasoline to unbranded jobbers must be qualified in the light of an apparent reversal of trend since 1953. There is no reason whatever to believe that company policies have changed significantly; but the appearance of some excess refining capacity since that date has apparently increased the availability of both independent and major refined gasoline to private brand sellers, who have been important in transmuting excess capacity into product price weakness. An apparent tendency of the major companies to curtail purchasing from independent refiners was remarked in the last chapter: "They have either had to decide to go the jobber route, or face the prospect of closing up shop."

16. The same is true among McLean and Haigh's seven companies (pp. 461–462). A few large refiners—notably Socony-Vacuum, Shell, and Phillips—seem to rely more heavily than most on distributors (Shell reported it moved 32 per cent, Socony Mobil 39 per cent, of their gasoline through independent wholesalers in 1956, *National Petroleum News,* June, 1957, p. 106); but the greater weight of the biggest companies was on the lower side of our median.

17. See McLean and Haigh, pp. 473–474.

18. Data are usable for only ten companies, and they have a very wide spread: hence their median (percentage of total sales to unbranded jobbers in 1950 or 1953) of around 10 per cent is most unreliable. Branded heating-oil distributors took a median of 28 per cent of total heating-oil sales from the fourteen company sample. It is simply the sketchiness of the sample, the inadequacies of the statistics supplied, and the difficulties of averaging so few observations when individual readings range from zero to 87 per cent that explain the apparent discrepancy between the 10 per cent and 28 per cent medians for unbranded and branded heating-oil distribution shown here, and the 56.8 per cent for the two combined, reported above, n. 11.

Actually, independent refiners have also been seeking to develop the other alternative—expanded marketing under their own brands. The other side of this coin is the one of interest here: "For unbranded jobbers, the independents' hunt for buyers is a blessing." [19] Meanwhile, the major refiners have also been selling increasing quantities of gasoline to jobbers under pressure of excess capacity. *National Petroleum News* estimated in early 1958 that the majors "probably supply about 75% of the private brand gasoline sold today," although with the clear implication that if the industry should succeed in bringing supply more closely in line with demand (at acceptable prices) major company gasoline would become less readily available to the jobber.[20] There are numerous indications that the share of the private brand jobber in leading markets is high and has increased significantly in recent years.[21]

19. "An Independent Refiner Builds a Brand," *National Petroleum News* (June, 1956), p. 100.

20. "Private Brander: He's Confident," *ibid.* (February, 1958), p. 137. In its 1957 survey, *National Petroleum News* found that not only did 17 per cent of the reporting wholesalers indicate they handled private brand gasoline, but an additional 5 per cent reported handling both major and private brands (May, 1957, p. 99).

21. Since available information is not systematic, only a few of the indications will be mentioned. In almost all cases the data or estimates of "private brand" sales really include not just the brands of nonintegrated jobbers but also of smaller refiner-marketers—almost all of which sell at about 2 cents below the major brands; the recently organized "Independent Brand Gasoline Marketers Association," e.g., includes prominently within its membership companies like Erickson, Clark, Western Oil and Fuel, and Gaseteria, which are refiners (or closely affiliated with them) as well as jobbers—*National Petroleum News* (August, 1957), pp. 94–97. *Business Week* cites an estimate that "the independents" accounted for 10 per cent of national gasoline sales around 1948, and "nearly 25 per cent" ten years later (May 17, 1958, p. 66).

A Shell Oil Company survey of the market share of "local brands" in 182 local retail markets for 1955 and 1956 showed thirty-two markets in which their share amounted to 30 per cent or higher in the latter year, with more increases than decreases compared with 1955. The median shares in 1955 and 1956 were 7.5 and 8.7 per cent in Shell's East Coast Division, 24.6 and 27.1 per cent in the Midwest, and 15.8 and 17.6 per cent on the West Coast (Computations from tables supplied by the Company). Heaviest concentrations of private brand sales were in parts of Illinois, Wisconsin, Indiana, and Minnesota in the Midwest, Georgia, and Tennessee in the East, and the Los Angeles area on the West Coast. For other estimates in individual areas see *National Petroleum News* (September, 1957), pp. 87, 156 (Los Angeles), 165 (Twin Cities); (January, 1957), p. 70 (a sharp rise in their market share in Michigan from 1950 to 1955); and House Small Business Committee, "Distribution Practices," *Interim Report* (1957), pp. 13–14.

Statistically, the independent jobber has done very well in the recent years of surplus, so far as access to supply is concerned, and there is no doubting that private brand jobbers, thus fueled, have played an important role in holding prices down.[22] In years of short supply, however, his sources are precarious, much more so than those of the branded distributor. Here again, the dealer in heating oil is better off than in gasoline. Companies like Sun, Texas, Amoco (the Eastern subsidiary of Standard of Indiana and completely different from its parent in this respect), and Sinclair, all extremely brand conscious in gasoline, turn over much of their heating oils unbranded to jobbers. But even a heating oil dealer in time of shortage may be unable to provide for his customers. His own lack of reliability as a customer is matched by the willingness of a Gulf Coast independent refiner to cut off supplies if he can get a better price elsewhere—perhaps from a major refiner. When oil must be rationed, old and steady customers of the major suppliers are in a preferred position.[23] Distributors that are taken care of during such periods are naturally loath to lose their status even when, in periods of looser supply, they might get lower prices by shopping around.

The inducement to stick to one supplier and carry his brand is even greater in gasoline because of the thinness of the open market. The threat of a squeeze-out, where the supplier refuses to take care of the jobber any longer and instead directly solicits customers in his area, often materializes.[24] So the unbranded jobber of gasoline lives danger-

22. It should be observed, however, that although the jobber must usually price his private brand below the majors to hold his market and will fight to preserve the differential, successful private-brand jobbers do not regard themselves as price cutters. "Maybe an independent can still go places on a strictly cut-rate basis, but Site Oil doesn't care to try. The company operated that way for 20 years, but times have changed—today Site is also quality-conscious. It's going places, too. . . . 'Until five years ago they were just a cut-rate operation,' says a major executive based in St. Louis. 'Since then they've become respectable.' " *National Petroleum News* (April, 1957), p. 101. With regard to the differential, however: " 'We'll go down to whatever their respective rock-bottoms are,' says a Site Oil Co. official." *Ibid.* (May, 1958), p. 82; see also the similar story about Spur, *ibid.,* pp. 88–89.

23. See Senate Small Business Committee, "Oil Supply and Distribution Problems," *Report* (1948), pp. 5–9.

24. "When they looked you in the eye and told you that they were definitely short, and you knew that they were taking on commercial accounts and building new stations and taking on every gallon they could get, everyone of them— *Mr. Forsythe:* That argument that there was a shortage did not impress you did it? *Mr. Morrison:* It did not impress me very much; no. The shortage just appeared to apply to us." Senate Small Business Committee, "Petroleum Market-

ously, except in areas like Kansas, Michigan, or the Los Angeles basin, or in regions fed by common-carrier product lines coming from such regions, where the persistence of independent refineries maintains a spot market.

Most major companies admit that they give preference to their own marketing departments and to branded distributors over open market sales to jobbers both when there is shortage and as long range policy.[25] They justify these policies on grounds partly of efficiency—the lower capital and operating costs of continuous, full utilization of capacity —and partly of equity: the jobber who wants to be free to shop around when products are in surplus and is unwilling to offer his supplier the assurance of his continued patronage has no right to expect the same treatment as loyal customers. Similarly, if the supplier uses distributors to break into a new market, later offering to buy them out,[26] the basic consideration is relative costs; the company will distribute direct whenever it thinks it can do the job more efficiently. The explanation is particularly convincing when the shift is part of a thorough rationalization of operations from refinery to customer, such as has occurred in so many instances in the last twenty years.[27] Finally, the refiner will claim the right to sell at the best price he can obtain. Since the private brand purchaser must ordinarily buy at a lower price and makes no contribution to advertising the supplier's brand, the refiner, major and independent alike, will naturally regard his patronage as the poorer alternative and give preference wherever he has the choice to the possibilities of expanding branded distribution.[28]

---

ing Practices," *Hearings* (1953), p. 108. For similar complaints on the West Coast during the Korean War period see these *Hearings, passim;* and *National Petroleum News* (April 30, 1952), p. 30, where major suppliers were reported to be refusing to renew contracts unless independents would use their brand name on resales.

25. Most also claim that they make an effort to extend fair treatment to regular jobber customers.

26. To what extent such offers are backed by the implicit threat to cut off supplies is of course impossible to know.

27. See the series of articles on "Direct Delivery," *National Petroleum News* (April 30, May 7, 14, and July 23, 1952), pp. 46–53, 42–51, 53–58, and 48–50, respectively. The third article summarizes estimates of cost savings amounting to 1.5 cents a gallon, resulting mainly from the elimination of the bulk plant operator's margin. Also above, pp. 364–365.

28. See, e.g., Sinclair's announcement of "efforts to upgrade sales into channels of highest price realization. This upgrading of sales means channeling more business directly through Sinclair facilities leading not only to volume increase but to stability and quality of business. . . . Stepped-up advertising, increased sales promotion, and intensified direct selling efforts are combined in pursuit of these objectives." *Annual Report,* 1952, p. 16. On the complaints of the inde-

The independent jobber, as a specialist in the nearest approach to a purely competitive market that the oil industry affords, competes strictly on a price basis with few hostages given or received in the interests of good will. In times of product surplus, he does well for himself; and the low price of the unbranded product he gets from integrated refiners—the surplus that they would find embarrassing to market through their regular channels—enforces an equally low price for the output of nonintegrated refiners, whose margins may thereby be squeezed against an unyielding price of crude. When product is short the integrated sources of supply tend to disappear, and the jobber is forced to bid a higher price for the output of the nonintegrated refiner, often in competition with the major. Thus his supply problems change radically over time and from region to region. His willingness to buy and the price he offers reflect fluctuations in total supply and demand for unbranded product under dynamic pressures from which vertical integration promises some surcease. Thus, as the independent refiner seeks to protect his margin under prorationing by forward integration, a protection that the independent jobber in no sense provides, the potential supply of unbranded gasoline for the jobber is further narrowed, more especially during periods of relatively short supply.

To bar refiners from replacing indirect with integrated distribution whenever they see an opportunity of either reducing costs or increasing realizations thereby would contribute neither to efficiency nor to competition. One company, often termed "brutal" and "ruthless," was alleged by distributors to "skim the cream" of the business, keeping for itself the big-volume, geographically concentrated markets and leaving for them only the more costly and less profitable job of "carrying the mail from door to door." Yet these tactics were part of a long-range program of drastically streamlining marketing operations; and even the company's critics conceded that costs had been sharply reduced as a result.[29] Certainly the competitive ideal is ruthless so far as the fortunes of participants are concerned; but whether this ruthless-

pendent refiner on the unreliability and excessive price-consciousness of some unbranded jobbers as customers see "Southwest Trend: Independent Refiners Move to Brands," *National Petroleum News* (June, 1957), pp. 125–126, 165.

29. See, e.g., the statement by the vice-president in charge of marketing of Standard of Ohio, which delivers about 95 per cent of its Sohio gasoline direct to retailers from its own terminals, because it sells almost exclusively in a highly cencentrated market area, and which is generally acknowledged to have been a leader in rationalizing its (direct) marketing operations. "Direct Operation vs. Jobber Operation," *National Petroleum News* (August, 1956), pp. 92, 94.

ness is compatible with public interest will depend precisely on the competitive character of the market itself. If the refiner enjoys a semi-monopolistic position, society is concerned that his ruthlessness be not employed for his own aggrandizement. But if the refiner must meet the effective competition of other refiners, society need not be concerned about the process by which each decides how to get his wares to market; competition will give to the distributors who can fulfill their functions efficiently the opportunity to do so, for one supplier or another.[30] And by the same token, mistakes that occur in the process will tend to be limiting and self-correcting.

Periods of shortage create particular problems for this kind of justification of the free exercise of the refiner's self-interest in the distribution of his product. Under normal conditions of shortage in competitive markets the processes of expansion in productive capacity are relied upon to redress temporary inequities. But in oil, short supply under prorationing has often been attributable to public policy or national emergency. Where this is in fact the case, as it was in World War II and the Korean conflict, rationing may appropriately be regarded as a public rather than a private function. And where crude oil production is curtailed below MER and refineries operate at less than capacity in the interests of stabilization, the pre-emption of a growing proportion of policy-limited supplies for branded distribution by vertically integrated firms may artificially threaten competition without hope for redress through increasing capacity. In this situation of government-created shortage there is a special responsibility on integrated suppliers to provide equitable treatment for independent jobbers who are thereby deprived of normal market alternatives. If this responsibility is not discharged voluntarily, it is the clear function of government to provide redress.

Furthermore, the expansion of direct or tied brand distribution by the vertically integrated firm is motivated only partially by cost reductions; it may seek rather to avoid competition, and the process, far from self-limiting, may be cumulative and self-sustaining, with decreasing emphasis on price. In this situation the distributor does not necessarily suffer. He loses his independence, but there is no reason to believe that he is typically any more addicted than the integrated major to independence per se when the sacrifice of some of it will free him from insecurities incident to open competition. The danger is, rather, that the jobber, and through him the ultimate consumer, may be de-

30. See the statement by the president of Richfield Oil of New York (Sinclair's subsidiary), which relies almost exclusively on branded distributors. *Ibid.,* pp. 93, 95.

prived of adequate and genuinely alternative sources of supply that are indispensable to effective price competition.

Many majors show a lively sense of responsibility in this area to be scrupulously fair in taking care of their distributors and jobbers in time of shortage, to offer them a fair purchase price for their facilities when embarking on direct distribution, and even in some cases to give them essentially unearned commissions on direct deliveries from the refinery or terminal. But it is not with the reasonableness of permissive behavior that this discussion is concerned but with inherent relative bargaining powers and resultant alternative opportunities. Society must rely, in an imperfectly competitive economy, on the sense of responsibility and fairness of its administrators, and will wisely use such pressures as public opinion and collective bargaining to influence the decisions reached. But a policy of competition is inherently distrustful of administrative discretion. When integration threatens to convey the power to make arbitrary, even antisocial, decisions (whether at the expense of nonintegrated firms or only of the consumer) and competition is ineffective to prevent it, this fact is significant, whether or not the power is ordinarily exercised in an arbitrary manner.

Supplier Competition

The prevailing system of distribution leads inevitably to conflicts between integrated suppliers and distributors, because their functions are not sharply demarcated. Thus the distributor may be refused product only to see his supplier take over his customers. The distributor's primary protection against such displacement is a direct hold on customer good will, which he may be able to transfer to another supplier. In the case of gasoline this means he must control service stations, and here he operates at a vital disadvantage, because the major has much more favorable access to capital. It is this, primarily, which relegates even branded distributors to outlying markets, and to a relatively small share of the total business.

Independent distributors often are forced into competition with their own [31] or other major suppliers. When the majors sell gasoline unbranded to jobbers or large retailers, they are engaging in indirect

31. Some companies refuse to engage in dual distribution, but, as with discriminatory price-cutting, they often feel forced to do so by the pressure of competition. Thirty-four per cent of those who responded to an extensive API survey of the 8,814 consignees of twenty-eight major companies reported direct deliveries by their suppliers to customers in their market territories. *Ibid.* (August, 1957), pp. 111–113.

price competition with distributors—sometimes their own.[32] Whole-salers are particularly critical of direct major competition for large industrial and commercial accounts, which is often an extremely competitive market. Obviously a distributor cannot compete for the business of a large commercial customer to whom his own suppliers may be offering prices no higher, and sometimes lower, than he himself has to pay. Pre-emption of service station locations on turnpikes by suppliers is another sore point. Jobbers contend that majors look on this business as advertising and bid up rentals to a point where they must be losing money [33] and it is impossible for independent marketers to compete.

Often such complaints mirror little more than a distaste for competition. More serious complaints, which we have already discussed at length, are price discrimination—special discounts either to certain (usually unbranded) jobbers or to big commercial accounts—and the charge that majors conduct their marketing "at a loss."

The attitude of distributors toward price differentiation is equivocal, to say the least. Their associations, apparently without exception, condemned the Federal Trade Commission in the Standard of Indiana case for seeking to protect retailers against the competition of price-cutting distributors who obtained concessions off the tank-wagon price. They argue that refiners should be encouraged to compete for distributor business with such discounts. But discounts to unbranded jobbers and large customers put the shoe on the other foot; here distributors would have the FTC suppress refiner discounts if the majors fail to do so voluntarily,[34] even though their menace to competition has not been convincingly demonstrated.

32. "Would you consider it cooperation when a supplier has one price to the jobber flying his flag and a lower price to his jobber's competitor?" Interview with Roy J. Thompson, Chairman, National Oil Jobbers Council, *ibid.* (April 8, 1953), p. 29.

33. See *ibid.* (January 6, 1954), p. 39; in "Stakes Getting Too High," *The Gasoline Retailer* (January 20, 1954), p. 2: "No small independent marketer could afford to bid in the neighborhood of 7 cents a gallon on gasoline and 10 per cent of gross receipts on all other sales." It was because of its refusal to take such "losses," according to Standard of Ohio, that its bids for stations on the Ohio Turnpike were uniformly unsuccessful. *National Petroleum News* (August, 1956), p. 94.

34. The National Oil Jobbers Council adopted a resolution in 1954 to turn to the federal government for assistance against "commercial account price-cutting." "Jobbers Demand Commercial Accounts Relief," *National Petroleum News* (December, 1954), pp. 35–37. For a striking illustration, see the testimony of Otis H. Ellis, General Counsel of the NOJC, before the Senate

MARGINS, COSTS, AND "SUBSIDIZED" COMPETITION

Both complaints registered above challenge the adequacy of distributors' margins (which are allegedly squeezed by major competition), the relative efficiency of integrated and nonintegrated marketing (since the adequacy of gross margins obviously depends on the costs of operation), and the profitability of major company marketing investments.

The distributor's margin, the difference between his purchase and his selling price, is set by the supplier (for branded distributors) at so many cents per gallon below the tank-wagon price. These margins are not necessarily uniform in a given area, and they are largely nominal. Since most distributor contracts are confidential, actual variations in terms may be very wide. Nominally, however, margins seem to have been around 1½ to 2 cents per gallon before World War II, and they have advanced since 1945 to around 3 cents on regular and a fraction of a cent more on premium gasoline.

The margin is a price for service rendered. It will therefore reflect the urgencies of refiner needs for distribution representation, especially great when he seeks to enter a new market; the availability of alternative open-market supplies of gasoline; and the competition of major refiners distributing directly and among wholesalers, branded and unbranded. And it will provide latitude for a kind of informal collective bargaining between the contracting parties with respect to what is fair or adequate.

In Table XXVIII the average spread between tank-wagon price to dealers and refinery realizations is compared annually with a computed index, the "marketer's cost of living," of the prices of inputs in the marketing process since 1940. These spreads include transportation from refinery to bulk plant as well as terminal charges; thus they exceed distributors' margins. It will be noted that regular gasoline spreads were relatively stable over the twenty years following 1935, exceeding the base period level by only about 10 per cent in 1954–55, while spreads on light fuel oils rose about 50 per cent—a striking contrast with the far greater rise in the marketer's cost of living. These data suggest a basis for the proverbial complaints of distributors about the inadequacy of their margins, which are said to have risen little above 2¢ per gallon for gasoline until sometime around 1950; but in the

Judiciary Subcommittee, "To Amend Section 2 of the Clayton Act," *Hearings,* (1956), pp. 317–344, 349–366. In the *Standard of Indiana* situation the jobbers feared that the proposed restriction on the major's right to grant discounts to jobber-retailers would cause them to abandon the use of wholesalers entirely.

absence of investment data and correlated sales volume associated with it they are compatible with either a squeeze on margins or a rise in marketing and transportation efficiency.

TABLE XXVIII

Marketing Spreads [a] *for Regular Gasoline and Light Fuel Oil: Total United States, 1935–55*

YEAR	REGULAR GASOLINE		LIGHT FUEL OIL		"MARKETER'S COST OF LIVING"
	CENTS PER GALLON	INDEX 1935–39 = 100	CENTS PER GALLON	INDEX 1935–39 = 100	1935–39 = 100
1935–39 Average	4.18	100.0	3.19	100.0	100.0
1945	3.54	84.8	3.75	117.6	140.1
1946	3.82	91.5	3.52	110.4	155.4
1947	3.93	94.1	3.58	112.3	181.4
1948	4.07	97.5	3.67	115.1	197.8
1949	4.42	105.8	4.12	129.2	203.2
1950	4.39	105.1	4.09	128.3	213.1
1951	4.23	101.3	4.24	133.0	229.4
1952	4.12	98.7	4.49	140.8	239.1
1953	4.26	102.0	4.62	144.9	249.3
1954	4.70	112.5	4.70	147.4	254.9
1955	4.63	110.9	4.81	150.9	267.2

[a] Marketing spreads are the difference between average selling prices and average refinery prices. In the case of gasoline the selling price is the average of tank-wagon prices in fifty cities, published by the API; the fuel oil selling price is the tank-wagon price to consumers, based for the most part on the BLS prices of Number 2 oil. The refinery price of both gasoline and fuel oil is from the census of manufacturers for 1935, 1937, 1939, and 1947—adjusted in the case of gasoline for ethyl gasoline—and in other years based on quotations in Platt's and the *Chicago Journal of Commerce.*

Source: economics department of a major oil company.

Whatever the merits of the controversy, the significant fact is that both the number of independent bulk stations [35] and the share of the business done by them and by nonrefiner-controlled bulk plants and

35. The Census listed 3,880 "independent" bulk stations in 1935, 6,422 in 1939, 7,241 in 1948, and something like 8,000 in 1954 (including 1,100 unincorporated firms with no employees as reported for 1948 but omitted in 1954). This damping in growth rate reflects the strong trend to direct distribution and consolidation of operations in larger plants and terminals during these years; e.g. the number of refiner-marketer bulk plants and terminals declined from 21,422 in 1939 to 17,837 in 1954, but their volume rose from $2,138 to $8,614 million.

terminals have increased over the past fifteen years (see Table XXVII above). Furthermore, available profit data, although skimpy, does not suggest a squeeze on independent wholesalers. Dun and Bradstreet data (summarized by Cross) shows gasoline distributors earning slightly less on tangible net worth in 1946–50 than integrated oil companies.[36] The Jobber Cost Survey conducted by the National Oil Jobbers Council showed that net profit was 16.5 per cent of net worth in 1946 and 14.8 per cent in 1950, before taxes, and 12.2 and 10.4 per cent respectively after taxes. Corresponding figures for the Chase Bank's thirty major companies after taxes were 10.3 and 14.6 per cent. The wholesalers' record is probably understated, since officers' salaries amount to no less than three-fifths of the net profits before tax in 1946, two-thirds in 1950, and over 70 per cent in 1955 and 1956.[37] More recent surveys by the NOJC report profits only in relation to sales. Although they seem to show a declining trend since World War II, one cannot be sure that this has not been fully compensated by improved capital turnover ratios. Dun and Bradstreet financial data (based, however, on an unfortunately skimpy sample of forty-four to fifty petroleum products wholesalers) show net profits on tangible net worth declining from an average of 10.61 per cent in the period 1948–52 to 6.98 per cent in the five years 1952–56, while comparable ratios for their thirty-four to forty-two integrated oil companies held up somewhat better, averaging 14.38 per cent in the first period and 11.63 per cent in the second. Despite this suggestion of a somewhat worsening financial situation, the *National Petroleum News* 1957 jobber survey disclosed aggregate planned capital expenditures of "upwards of $175 million," a figure that compares favorably with the $249 million the twenty majors spent on marketing investments in the

36. The gasoline jobbers surveyed earned 9.70 per cent on tangible net worth in 1941–45, and 13.87 per cent in 1946–50. Returns for oil companies (integrated) were 9.24 and 14.37 in the same period. Cross, "Vertical Integration in the Oil Industry," p. 74. Since oil jobbers have relatively little funded debt (The National Oil Jobbers Council, 1952 "Jobber Cost Survey," mimeographed, showed their fixed debt as about 5 per cent of total liabilities; while the Chase Bank—Coqueron, *Annual Financial Analysis, 1955*, p. 34—gives a comparable figure of 11.7 per cent for the thirty-four oil companies surveyed), their rates of return for these prosperous years are not inflated by heavy trading on equity.

37. "Results of Jobber Cost Survey" (mimeographed, 1952) by the Council, and *National Petroleum News* (August, 1957), p. 100. Officer salaries exceeded after tax profits in 1955 and 1956. Since the leading officers of these companies are usually their owners, some indeterminate portion of their salaries may be regarded as really part of the return on their investment.

same year, 1957.[38] The failure rate among distributors and jobbers is apparently well below the national average.[39]

With this over-all financial record it is difficult to see how much higher margins could be sustained, even if the majors chose to grant them, except by monopolistic restrictions on the entry of new firms and collusion on pricing tactics among those already in the business.[40]

Although it is not possible to identify the sources of wholesalers' profits, and although they improved their share of national gasoline business between 1939 and 1954, it is still a reasonable guess that their profits are derived disproportionately from heating oils. In gasoline, they distribute typically in less favorable areas and their share of national sales is much lower than in heating oils. Heating oils also provide a much higher percentage profit on sales.[41]

The real decline of wholesale margins in the last twenty years largely reflects increasing competition, in which both majors and wholesalers have made more use of direct deliveries from the refinery or terminal

38. (May, 1957), p. 103; and *National Petroleum News Factbook, 1958–59* (mid-May, 1958), p. 94.

39. Dun and Bradstreet, according to Cross ("Vertical Integration in the Oil Industry") lists twenty-two failures for oil jobbers during the years 1936–40, when the rate for failures per 10,000 in U.S. business was fifty-eight. From 1946–50 there were seven failures among oil jobbers, while the U.S. rate was twenty-one. The jobber population was over 5,000 in both periods. For 1951–55, Dun and Bradstreet data show an annual average of ten failures among petroleum product wholesalers, and 9,317 in all lines of business; with the number of businesses in the United States running at about 4,200,000, and the number of petroleum wholesalers running at 10,000 to 24,000 (the latter if we include commission agents, who are technically independent businessmen), the failure rate among the latter is at worst about one-half the national average.

40. In view of their own competitive propensities, many jobbers concede that even price agreements would not hold, and that, led by chiselers, all would sooner or later have to give away any higher margins granted by suppliers.

41. While the average nonrefiner-owned bulk plant and terminal sold just about the same amount of residual fuel oils, and markedly more kerosene and distillate fuel oils than the refiner-owned in 1954, it sold only about half as much gasoline. Computations from 1954 Census, "Petroleum Bulk Plants and Terminals," pp. 8–61. According to the NOJC surveys, profits from gasoline ranged between 0.4 and 1.1 per cent of sales in the 1953–56 period, while the respective annual low and high on heating oils were 2.4 and 3.2 per cent. On the other hand, gasoline apparently accounts for a somewhat larger amount of dollar sales than the heating oils, which compensates somewhat for a lower percentage profit. In 1954 the 10,482 nonrefiner-controlled bulk plants and terminals sold 9.3 billion gallons of gasoline and 9.0 billion gallons of the less valuable heating oils, according to the Census.

with savings that have been translated into the tank-wagon price.[42] At the same time wholesalers charge their exclusion from the areas of concentrated demand not to comparative efficiency but to major company conduct of their distribution at a loss. Since service station investments are incurred by the majors in part for market control, and the data available do not clearly show them profitable per se, the social economy of these outlays may not equal their worth from the viewpoint of the integrated refiner. Combined with superior access to capital, these special incentives give the integrated firm a competitive advantage over the independent marketer quite apart from differences in operating efficiency.

The problems of retail distributors of oil products are essentially questions of equity. Their difficulties were magnified by the early overbuilding of service stations and, more recently, by the onerous, sometimes devastating process of modernization, relocation, and concentration of outlets on potentially high-gallonage sites. The independent service station owner is hardest hit by these changes, but all established operators suffer somewhat from the impact of the added competition on their margins. These are serious consequences for the individuals concerned and, clearly, forward integration is partially responsible for them. But since the introduction of the Iowa Plan in the mid-1930's service station operators are not typically forced to compete with their own suppliers, and though the number of stations has declined in recent years there is no danger that independent retailers will lose enough ground, either in numbers or influence, to pose a threat to vigorous competition in this sector of the industry.

CONCLUSION

The position of the independent petroleum marketer seems to be both reasonably profitable and fairly secure. As a group, wholesalers appear to have increased their sales at least as rapidly as the industry as a whole in the last twenty years. And though the financial record of gasoline retailers is probably more spotty, there is no question of their numbers being so depleted as to menace the effectiveness of competition.

Nonetheless, the situation is mixed. Although definitive information is unobtainable and the unbranded jobber—the one true independent—seems to have enjoyed a renaissance during the surplus

42. See conclusions of Howard, "Interfirm Relations in Oil Products Markets," *Journal of Marketing, 20* (1956), 364–366.

gasoline production years of the late 1950's, the long-run position of the unbranded jobber seems to have waned. Prorationing and wartime shortages have contributed to this end; but the more important cause has been a reduction of nonintegrated refiners, a consequent drying up of spot markets, the by-passing of bulk plants, and increasing dependence of the jobber on more sporadic supplies from major refiners. There is no evidence of decreasing use of branded gasoline distributors by major companies. However, such distributors do seem to operate at the fringes of the better markets and at the sufferance of their suppliers, who control the more lucrative retail outlets, can always replace them with direct distribution, and can undercut them in soliciting large consumer and industrial accounts. Still, there are important exceptions to these generalizations; in many areas large independent jobber-retailers thrive and play a vital competitive role.

The consequence is a rather uneasy complementary competitive relation between marketers and integrated refiners, marked by continuous bickering, charges, and countercharges, but competition between them has contributed both to quality and service and to the development of more efficient methods of distribution. Rivalry has helped to compress jobber and retailer margins, and through their sales to big unbranded jobbers the integrated companies themselves have often supplied the fuel that undermined the price structure that a more rigidly stratified industry might more successfully have preserved.

Forward integration into wholesale distribution seems to have served the cause of efficiency on the whole, even though it has tended to diminish the availability of supplies to independent jobbers. Further integration into retail distribution has had somewhat more equivocal economic results. The emphasis on branded distribution, while not without value to the motorist, has imposed handicaps on both independent refiners and independent jobbers, and it has increased service costs at the expense of price competition. If this tendency has been relieved from time to time by outbreaks of price rivalry at both retail and wholesale levels, that relief has its source in the incompleteness of forward integration rather than in forward integration itself.

CHAPTER 21

The Impact of Integration on Competition

THE CRITERIA of desirable price behavior against which to test the impact of vertical integration in oil can only be vague and qualitative. The economics of this industry, rooted in the conditions of crude oil supply, offer no objective basis in costs for the orientation of competitive prices. And control, state or privately administered, is based on policy, not on costs. At present competition does modify policy in part through unplanned increments of supply (new discoveries of crude oil, new processing and distribution capacities that destroy balance or widen imbalance among horizontal levels of the industry), in part from uncertainties about the division of a growing, shifting market. In this precarious balance of programmed stability upset from time to time by conflict stemming from uncontrolled market forces, acceptable behavior must embody somewhat conflicting desiderata: stability and flexibility, long- and short-term downward pressures on cost and of price toward cost, standardization and uniformity on the one hand and variation and diversity on the other, and rivalry in quality and service but also rivalry in price. In brief, managerial discretion in planning and administration must be checked by market forces themselves conditioned by a lively diversity of competitive interests.

Both logic and observation confirm the judgment that the inherent thrust of integration is to foster the first of each of these alternatives and diminish the second. The dominant position of the large vertically integrated oil firm, combined with effective state controls of crude oil production and federal limits on imports, has achieved a measure of price stability in the industry. Not recurrent chaos but the prospect that petroleum product prices may be too high and too unresponsive to demand changes is the apparent threat to public interest today. The urgent question, then, is whether the structural organization of the oil industry may not have been too successful in quelling the competitive excesses of the pre-prorationing era.

Two important forces that work against the realization of this undesirable outcome have been stressed. The one is that vertical integration per se does not prevent competition even in price. Monopoly power is essentially a horizontal, not a vertical, phenomenon. As long as the number of sellers at each horizontal level of supply is large enough, whatever the scope of the vertical operations of each, active rivalry is not likely to be precluded even though the character of competition is altered. In fact, it was found that despite the growth of giant integrated firms, there has not been a strong tendency toward a higher degree of concentration in this industry; rather, the number of these large companies has increased with the years. Indeed, in the course of adapting themselves to a rapidly growing market the majors have not only been brought into strenuous market competition with each other but also, through inevitable imbalances in the process of growth, they have fed and helped to maintain open intermediate markets which are the life blood of nonintegrated and partially integrated producers, refiners and distributors. The strength and vigor of these open markets, which nourish opportunities for independent operators, is the second important force needed to assure the customer of an acceptable range of choices among alternative products, prices, and services.

Although the impact of these limiting forces has been attenuated in some important respects since 1935, the basic structure beyond the crude oil level remains essentially competitive. Even the tank-wagon price, the focus of the large firm's policy leadership, is not rigid. On it may be focused the policy consensus of a few leading firms, but its stability and its level depend on a complex of competitive tensions, reflecting the converging and divergent interests of a number and variety of sellers. In prorationing and import controls industry leaders have a powerful sergeant-at-arms—too powerful for workable competition—but beyond this floor of managed crude oil prices, managerial policy and administration have only limited effectiveness.

This tense balance of longer-term company leadership and short-run tension and disturbance is best demonstrated in the behavior of product prices through the 1953–54 and 1957–58 recessions, although the fact that the latter dip is so fresh in mind at the time of writing may impart a bias to these selected observations.

The crude oil price increase of June, 1953, was a policy increase, widely supported by general industry opinion, but in no sense required by the pressure of competitive forces. Market leaders had been sadly unsuccessful during the spring in obtaining the product price increases they felt their rising costs and declining profits justified. Only gasoline prices showed signs of strengthening in the month before the crude price was advanced; but within a week of Phillips' higher posting for crude oil product prices were raised all over the country.

The effort was something less than an outstanding success in the short run; it came on the eve of a recession and in the face of excess refining capacity and of an increasing availability of imported crude oil. All the persuasion and price leadership the industry could muster were not proof against accumulating finished-product inventories, and the price structure began to deteriorate. Two tables in Chapter 16 [1] trace the slide in product prices from their June, 1953, high. The Gulf low for 87-octane gasoline slumped, by stages, from 11.75 to 9.5 cents a gallon in March, 1954; Esso Standard's prices in New York followed, dropping from 16.2 to 15.0 cents in July of the latter year, and other East Coast prices moved in rough correspondence. The national weighted average price for the four principal products dropped from $4.22 a barrel in October, 1953, to $4.00 in May, 1954.

The influence of policy was far from negligible, however, even in the short run. Public authority initiated a succession of sharp cutbacks of crude production allowables, bringing national shut-in capacity within sight of 2,500,000 b/d; and the price of crude oil held almost completely firm. With some isolated reductions in postings, the weighted national average price, which had jumped from $2.63 to $2.83 in June, tapered only to a low of $2.81 in May and June, 1954. In consequence there was a tight squeeze on refinery margins: standing at $1.25 a barrel in January, 1953, when Korean War price controls were still in effect, margins rose to $1.36 in July and a monthly peak of $1.39 in October, after which they slumped to $1.19. Despite the refining squeeze and the net-purchaser status of most majors in crude oil markets, industry leaders urged production cutbacks on the control authorities of producing states.[2] Not the high rigid price of crude but lack of discipline among refiners who failed to cut back refinery runs enough was held to be the source of trouble. They were technically correct: product prices would certainly have sagged even further if crude oil production had not been cut back and its price sustained. Only refinery cutbacks could hold in line the burgeoning product inventories that played into the hands of price-cutters. The industry was relatively slow to respond to the frequent exhorta-

1. See above, pp. 395, 415, nn. 14, 67.
2. "H. S. M. Burns, president of Shell Oil Co. . . . said he thought the recent cutbacks were a 'step in the right direction' . . . Oklahoma crude purchasers threatened to reduce purchases regardless of what rate of output the corporation commission permitted. As a result, a 65,000-barrel-a-day dip was ordered. . . . The 10-day shutdown ordered in Kansas drew praise . . . 'Kansas did a magnificent job' said one major oil company head." "Most industry leaders agree oil production cutback must continue for 2 to 4 months to avert price break," *Wall Street Journal* (October 8, 1953), p. 18.

tions and bold announcements of reduced refinery runs [3] by its leaders; but refinery operations were finally brought into line. From close to 90 per cent of capacity in November, 1953, and an average of almost 92 per cent for that year,[4] utilization ratios fell to 87.9 per cent in December and to around 83 per cent by midsummer, where they stabilized until the following December. The *National Petroleum News* was able to comment approvingly that the cuts had apparently brought the industry over the hump so far as the threat to crude oil prices was concerned.[5] And in fact product prices soon firmed: "since mid-July, when refiners started to apply the brakes on crude oil throughput, markets have seen one of the fastest turn-arounds in years." [6]

On August 18 Socony-Vacuum led a tank-wagon price increase of 0.8¢ a gallon on the East Coast, and was immediately followed by other large marketers "to meet competition," as the industry so quaintly puts it, while leading refiners continued to hold back on runs to stills.[7] So gradually in 1954 inventories came under control, prices firmed, and industry opinion was vindicated, thanks to recovery of demand, the restraint of its leading members plus a crucial assist from the Texas Railroad Commission. Refinery spreads, which had averaged $1.24 per barrel in 1953, and had dropped to $1.16 for 1954 as a whole, were back at $1.26 in 1955: the crude oil price increase had been successfully passed on to consumers.[8]

3. "The president of a major oil company . . . will do his part this month by ordering a further reduction in crude oil runs by about 5 per cent or more at his company's big . . . refinery," *ibid.;* "L. F. McCollum, president of Continental Oil Company, commented that oil refiners should cut back operations further where needed to reduce excess inventories," *ESPA Weekly Letter* (December 31, 1953), p. 2.

4. Annual data in *Petroleum Facts and Figures,* 12th ed., p. 217. Monthly figures from *National Petroleum News.*

5. (July 28, 1954), p. 46.

6. *Ibid.,* August 11, 1954.

7. *ESPA Weekly Letter,* August 20, 1954. The price reductions during the winter and spring of 1953–54 apparently taught the industry a lesson about the penalties of being too slow to cut back on refinery throughput. The *National Petroleum News* reported in May, 1955: "As the second quarter opened, refiners recognized the need for larger-than-normal cutbacks. Companies individually have announced cuts in runs totalling more than 200,000 b/d, averaging 7.7 per cent. . . . This can check the build up in already high gasoline inventories . . ." (p. 12). Refinery runs were held well below 90 per cent of capacity during the spring of 1955.

8. See above, p. 421, Table XXII. Refining costs may well have increased in the interim, of course, but the profit data reflect no profit squeeze on refiners in 1955 compared with 1953.

During the first half of 1958, as during the same period four years earlier, it again seemed to be very much an open question whether the industry could succeed in holding the crude oil price line. Product prices had been slumping for a year, and dropped even more precipitously in February and March [9] despite stringent cutbacks in crude production allowables and somewhat less sharp and less disciplined reductions in refinery runs. Led as usual by the majors, particularly those with foreign production, refiners and producers induced state authorities to impose output restrictions that brought national crude oil production from its peak of 7.7 million b/d in March, 1957, at the height of the Suez crisis, to 6,240,000 b/d in April, 1958,[10] bringing shut-in reserves to a phenomenal 3,000,000 b/d at the beginning of the year,[11] probably higher in succeeding months.[12] Again, widely scattered reductions in price postings lowered the national average crude oil price from its $3.19 peak in 1957, where it had remained virtually constant through March, 1958, to $3.06 in June; but refinery product realizations (using variable weights) meanwhile fell to $4.09 per barrel in June, 1958, compared with their 1957 peak monthly value of $4.64. Once more, refinery margins absorbed the brunt of the price changes: from $1.46 immediately after the January, 1957, price increases, they plunged to 96 cents by March of the following year, recovering only to $1.03 by June.

Cutbacks in refinery runs had begun in October, 1956, as gasoline stocks mounted to disturbingly high levels, but were abated in the months following by the need to produce heating oils to meet anticipated winter requirements. They were again cut during the Suez crisis, partly to release crude oil for export to Europe and partly to reduce excessive gasoline inventories, but the deepest cuts were taken in the latter part of 1957.[13] Setting the example, and leading exhortations for cutbacks at both refinery and production levels, were the major

9. See above, p. 417, n. 71, for the crude oil and products price data and computations of refinery margins on which the following account draws.

10. Monthly production figures from *World Oil*.

11. J. H. Carmical, New York *Times* (January 5, 1958), sec. 3, p. 1.

12. Texas allowables were cut to new lows, of nine and then only eight days' production in March and April, respectively, and held at the lower level in May and June.

13. Averaging about 90 per cent in the first half of 1957 (compared with 93 to 94 per cent the year before), rates of utilization ranged between 87 and 90 per cent in the April to September period (compared with 93 to 95 per cent, excepting one month, in 1956), and then pressed down to 85.9 per cent in December (compared with 91.6 per cent the year before).

companies.[14] But while these efforts helped to support products markets, they were grossly inadequate. Pressures mounted and industry spokesmen and analysts berated refiners and the State of Texas for failing to cut back production more drastically: "differences of opinion between company management and proration authorities concerning the size of market demand have contributed to supply excesses. Another major cause is the refiners' preoccupation with the so-called incremental barrel in apparent disregard of the ultimate detrimental effect of such production." [15] Gradually, the campaign bore fruit. Refinery runs fell month by month, until in April, 1958, they had reached 78.2 per cent, well below the lowest monthly ratio of the 1953–54 recession. And month by month majors argued before the Texas Commission for contractions in crude production allowables greater than the severe reductions it was ordering. Even independent producers, reversing their normal role, eventually joined in the plaint, and the Commission responded with an unprecedented nine-day-a-month schedule for March followed by eight days of production for April.[16] Meanwhile, the federal government had been tightening its program of voluntary limitations on crude oil imports.

By late spring the worst seemed to have passed, and the Chase Manhattan Bank's *Monthly Review* for April could report a sharp reduction in inventories ("With each passing month the supply picture

14. Leaders in announcing cuts in runs to stills "in order to reduce top-heavy inventories" (*ESPA Weekly Letter,* July 26, 1957) were Esso Standard, Socony Mobil, Standard of Indiana, Sunray Mid-Continent, Continental, and Cities Service. At the September meeting of the Texas Railroad Commission that eventuated in a cutback of crude allowables to twelve days, "the lowest point in recent years," Humble, the state's biggest purchaser, "announced that unless the commission came down to the twelve-day level . . . the company 'reluctantly' would be forced to begin reducing its purchases below the prescribed level"; and Gulf, which was being sued by the State of Oklahoma for refusing to take all the oil proffered it under state production quotas, urged a cutback to ten days. Sinclair, Shell, Phillips, and Texas favored a thirteen-day rate (*Wall Street Journal,* September, 1957). This meeting was prophetic of those to follow with several majors urging on the Commission higher cutbacks than it was actually ordering.

15. Chase Manhattan Bank, *Monthly Review of the Petroleum Situation,* November, 1957.

16. "Independent producers, who usually urge high output, pleaded for the Commission to cut deeply to remove excessive stocks which several witnesses declared have caused a 'desperate' situation for domestic producers. Nearly all the major purchasers represented at the hearing agreed that a nine-day schedule would be satisfactory" (*Wall Street Journal*—February 21, 1958—p. 6). The hearing setting an eight-day schedule was reported March 21, 1958, p. 3.

continues to brighten"), along with a drop in the BLS index of product prices of 14.5 per cent from its 1957 peak. Product prices recovered steadily after June.

The crucial role of prorationing, and the monopolistic power which the state regulatory commission marshalls in its name to bolster and effectuate industry pricing policies, stands out stark in these episodes, softened only by the somewhat divergent interests and pressures of the independent producer, the integrated major with domestic production only, and the large importers. Here power is absolute, and without its sympathetic exercise there would be little room for price leadership in the domestic petroleum market.

In the price structure which is reared on crude oil, price leadership of the large integrated firm is more nearly barometric than governing. The dominant marketer, or the majors as a group, will try to lead by exhortation and by example in the contraction of their own refining schedules. However, industry refinery cutbacks are seldom effected promptly. If the leader's pricing policies do not properly reflect this incomplete adjustment of supply, competitive challenges will force his hand and sap not only the actual but the posted tank-wagon prices as well.

These upsetting market forces are not so strong as they once were. Prorationing has helped to thin the ranks of the independent refiner. Those that remain are not only technologically more competent but also bigger, better financed, more often partially integrated, and generally more adequately provided with some assured access to crude oil. And with this new status and these enlarged investment responsibilities, they are also more interested in stabilization, like their larger rivals, and more amenable to leadership. Thus the influence of policy at the product price level must not be underestimated.[17] The recent policies of the majors in scheduling refinery cutbacks in order to bring about a contraction in *industry* stocks and a firming of *industry* product price levels would have been almost unthinkable a couple of decades past. These are not competitive tactics (except as margins might drop below out-of-pocket costs); they are control stratagems, and they could not be undertaken unless there were good prospects that restraint would be emulated by the bulk of other refiners similarly

17. The preponderant position of perhaps ten major refiner marketers in most geographic markets, with their nationally advertised brands sold through owned or controlled market outlets and with their emphasis on service rather than price competition, plays some part, although practically impossible to measure, in market stabilization.

motivated by policy rather than strictly competitive market considerations.

Excess refinery capacity developed under the Defense Program has
been a recognized bane of the industry. In 1954 the *National Petroleum News* called upon the Deputy Petroleum Administrator for Defense to explain why there was too much refinery capacity.[18] Again in
1957 it attributed the sagging of product prices to the same influence.[19]
The percentage of total refinery cost that is direct, or out-of-pocket,
expense is extremely low, and it is toward this level that competition,
in the presence of excess capacity, would push refinery margins as
market demand contracted. The fact that petroleum product prices
have not typically fallen to any such extent in periods of recession
can only reflect collective self-discipline. Discipline is enforced largely,
but not exclusively, by state-imposed reduction in the supply of raw
materials—cutbacks that are themselves in large measure the product
of the nominations of leading refiners. Thus the conclusion still holds:
the large, integrated companies do manage, by their direct effort and
example, to maintain some discretionary control over price levels.

However, it has been shown how limited the power is of the price
leader and of vertical integration to hold price competition in check
where refinery supplies are inadequately controlled and the majors
cannot keep all supplies moving to market in strong hands. Illustrative
is the continuing vigor of the independent jobber, after years of evolving brand distribution through tied outlets by the integrated firm, who
is nourished largely through the continuing unbalanced operations of
the majors themselves. Thus although the majors, with their common
aversion to price wars and their control of the bulk of the product
flowing to market, undoubtedly exercise a substantial stabilizing effect
on product prices, their pricing policies can neither ignore nor stem
the force of competitive determinants.

In sum, although the price margins for refinery and marketing
services that are added to the price of crude oil do not behave like
purely competitive margins—in an industry so weighted with heavy
fixed costs and so dominated in each market area by a comparatively
small number of sellers this is not surprising; but they do not behave
like monopoly margins either. The stabilization that has been effected
through the vertically integrated firm has not raised profits above the

18. "Did the Government Push Oil Refiners into Overbuilding?" (July 21,
1954), p. 16.
19. "New Plants Add to Oversupply" (July 1957), p. 90.

average of other industries,[20] and, more important, it has not thwarted an essentially competitive behavior of product prices. Indeed, it is remarkable that petroleum, unlike steel (or railroads, with which economically it is more kin) and similar industries threatened by cut-throat price competition, has been so singularly impotent in eliminating periodic outbursts of destructive price rivalry. It too has tried, like steel, cement and other industries with essentially undifferentiated products from the viewpoint of knowledgeable consumers, to divert upsetting tendencies in price competition into less injurious channels, through basing-point pricing systems, for example. But apart from foreign marketing, where the circumstances have been uniquely propitious, these systems in oil have had no more than transient and qualified success.[21]

It is well beyond the purposes of this study to analyze comparative pricing practices of industries that are in many ways—degrees of concentration, importance of vertical integration, relation of fixed to variable costs—apparently so similar to petroleum. But some of the major differences help to characterize competitive forces in oil. The underlying question is really why the supply of refined products is so much more perversely inelastic than the supply of steel or cement from the standpoint of maximizing industry profits. Basically the supply of refined products cannot be so readily dampened by adverse market shifts, even when stocks rise, because refiners are loath to cut back on crude purchases. This is not just a matter of obligation to independent producers. Nor is it merely that an oil refinery would find it impossible to operate only on orders placed, even though continuity of flow is obviously a more crucial economic consideration in oil than

20. Little weight, however, can be accorded comparative profit figures. The prices extracted from customers could be exorbitant because of excessive costs and wasteful investment even though profit rates appeared reasonable.

21. "For years, oil economists have urged the oil industry to set its product prices as the steel industry does—on costs rather than on supply-demand factors." "Setback for New Oil Pricing," *Business Week* (July 20, 1957), pp. 45–48. This article attempts to explain Sinclair's failure in effecting a price increase to reflect the higher cost of a new wage agreement, following the cue of the steel industry. The increase was actually followed by major competitors, but within a few weeks prices were back to their earlier levels. See the sardonic, continuing commentary on the attempt in the *ESPA Weekly Letters*, concluding, after the experiment had failed: "Now that the smoke has cleared away, we hope that our industry may feel that there is considerable merit in being able to read the road signs and keep from going the wrong way on a one-way street" (July 12, 1957).

in steel or cement. It does not even seem that this reluctance to cut back crude purchases stems from difficulties in contracting refinery operations although the evidence is conflicting on this point: individual refinery units can be and are shut down, but the costs of shutting down a blast furnace or a steel furnace are probably as great or greater. The real reason for this phenomenon seems to be the greater pressure of the inelastic supply of crude oil as a raw material and of the costly wastes associated with its non-use once it is above ground. Here oil contrasts decisively with these other industries. Despite the elaborate regulations of crude oil production, state regulatory authorities are inevitably influenced by the interests of independent producers, whose insistence on volume and a quick pay-out is seldom sated; even some of the more powerful international producing companies cannot resist the temptation to avoid high domestic costs by importing the foreign crude oil it costs them so little to produce. And within the limits of domestic production allowables, the rule of capture still prevails against rational restraint. Heavy as are fixed costs in steel, the ratio in oil, from reservoir to service station, is even greater and productive operations within large segments are almost completely automatic. Until oil refining is much more closely concentrated than it gives promise of ever becoming "The famous 'last 10 per cent.' of a refiner's throughput which involves next to nothing in cost apart from chemicals, and can be sold at any old price without making the accountants blush, is firewood for kindling price-war conflagrations. Once a refinery is built its owners are prisoners in the hands of their investment . . ." [22]

The secret then of continuing product price competition in the petroleum industry, despite the rationality that size and vertical integration of its major participants may impart, is in this inexorable pressure to process the oil that is produced. It obviously dominates the smaller independent, especially the essentially nonintegrated refiners. But it also grips the large integrated firms themselves, especially in the presence of market growth potentials that can never be estimated precisely, and in which they are anxious to share, and it breaks out from time to time in rivalries that burst the bonds of policy-dictated individual self-restraint. From this viewpoint the exhortations for, and even the examples of, refinery cutbacks during the episodes analyzed above must be regarded primarily as political stratagems. The purpose was less to leave crude already produced to accumulate in storage than it was to organize the industry into a more compact pressure group to force state authorities to keep an even greater amount of the

22. Frankel, *Essentials of Petroleum,* p. 29.

oil safely underground by ordering more drastic cutbacks in production allowables.

Under these pressures, which operate over long time spans and broad areas with probably greater assurance than in the short run or in particular markets, the retail price of gasoline, excluding taxes, was roughly at the same level in 1955 that it had been in 1925, although it had dipped and recovered in the interim,[23] while the quality of the product improved substantially. The higher octane rating (one of the more obvious improvements in motor fuels) and the higher compression engines dependent on it have bettered the performance and increased the energy delivered to and by the automobile—whatever one thinks of the way in which the American consumer makes use of that potential. Compared to most other products, petroleum can probably give a favorable account of itself in both price and quality, an especially notable performance considering the problems of obtaining its raw material, the cost of which is a very high percentage of the final price.

Behind this price and quality record are notable advances in technology, substantial cost reductions,[24] and important service improvements. Benefits have been passed on, although not always at so rapid a rate as could be desired.

These considerations, more adequately detailed and supported in previous chapters, lead us to the conclusion that the structure and practices of the petroleum industry beyond the production level are —and provided something is done to improve the workability of competition in crude oil markets are likely to continue to be—workably competitive.[25] This optimistic judgment rests heavily not only on the

23. Price series, from 1918 on, in *Petroleum Facts and Figures*, 9th ed., p. 367; 12th ed., p. 305.

24. Corrected for changes in the purchasing power of the dollar, the long-run trend of oil products has been downward. See the interesting estimates in "Let's Look at the Oil Business," published in November and December, 1948, by the Department of Economics, Socony-Vacuum Oil Corporation, which has subsequently been keeping its estimates up to date. By comparing the trend in refining and marketing margins in the industry with a weighted index of changes in price of the relevant inputs, they attempted to show the extent to which these segments of the industry have progressed, in making more efficient use of inputs, and have passed the benefits on to the public. See above, p. 421, Table XXII.

25. This conclusion is apparently shared with Bain, whose detailed analysis of the West Coast petroleum industry leaves the strong impression that price leadership and group buying schemes establish at most a precarious balance in an inherently unstable market. He found the only power to charge monopolistic prices resided at the production level although he deplored excessive costs of

evidence of continuing price competition but also on the apparent virility of the independent refiner and jobber. It is not unconcerned, however, about the possible threat to the balance of existing competitive forces implicit in the observed tendency of smaller refiners to integrate forward into branded distribution and, along with crude-short majors, backward into crude oil. These defensive maneuvers under the aegis of prorationing threaten increasing pre-emption of crude oil supplies against non-integrated refiners and possibly higher distribution costs and prices for the consumer. The latter could result as forward integration further constricts an important supply source for the independent jobber, further narrows the significance of spot intermediate markets, and weakens the harassing function of nonrefiner private brands. But perhaps even more important is the possible change that the trend to integration may effect in the competitive psychology of refiner management as the firm becomes a smaller edition of its prototype rival, the major firm. As an investor in branded distribution facilities and as an investor in crude oil properties, the refiner finds the economic compulsions of refinery operations are modified and perhaps overridden by the demands of these other investments. His opposition to policies that raise the price of crude will undoubtedly wane, if his allegiance is not reversed entirely, and his concern for orderly marketing of his branded products could make him more receptive to administrative policies of refinery scheduling advocated by the industry's price leaders. Were this in fact the consequence, the hope for continuing workable competition would rest more heavily, possibly too heavily, on the rivalry of integrated firms themselves and the imbalances created by their respective rates of growth.

This threat reinforces a basic opposition from the viewpoint of public interest to state prorationing of domestic production of crude based on anticipated demand, and it underlies the proviso that optimistic predictions about the industry's competitive future depend on revising that system. The monopolistic shutting in of crude oil, which could have been produced without violating the principles of conservation, colors the competitive rivalry of vertically integrated companies at every stage of the industry with an aura of subsidy. It is forcing the nonintegrated refiner and the less well-balanced major as well, in self-defense, to procure for himself a financial stake in the production end of the business. Artificially frozen crude oil prices

wasteful distribution that a monopolistically competitive market had foisted on the consuming public (*Pacific Coast Petroleum Industry, 2*, 296–299).

menace the survival of the independent refiner through the margin squeeze. This cannot be in the public interest. The most serious accusations against vertical integration are that it compromises where it does not pervert the interest of the industry's most powerful firms in low crude prices, and that, by permitting those firms to merge monopolistic and competitive levels of the industry, less advantaged rivals are exposed to competitive pressures they cannot resist regardless of their efficiency.

A healthy oil industry demands some control of crude oil production, but it also needs incentives to a more efficient use of capital outlays at the extractive level and some flexibility in output below MER in response to market forces and world supply sources. Under present conditions the contribution that integration makes to the mobilization of capital for crude oil exploration and production is almost redundant; the problem is one of wasteful overinvestment and excessive domestic production capacity rather than the reverse. As elaborated in Chapter 10, the necessary combination of flexibility and basic stability is attainable through mandatory unitization of pools operating on natural drives, along with a more flexible national policy that permits imports to play their natural competitive function. Once the competitive fangs of the rule of capture are drawn and unitization is coextensive with each producing horizon, rational self-interest will be freed to develop the field potential with a minimum of investment and of public control.

Since the true source of monopoly profit in the oil industry is in the natural and artificial scarcity imparted to crude oil by control devices, it is tempting to some analysts to cut the Gordian knot by advocating a divorce of all crude oil properties from the control or ownership of the integrated refiner. Certainly in the absence of crude oil subsidy, especially now that inherent monopoly in pipelines has been softened by the growth and stabilization of markets, the multiplication of pipelines and the more effective regulation of their operations, vertical integration would be forced to justify itself in terms of its comparative efficiency in competition with nonintegrated or partially integrated forms of business organization. The elimination of that subsidy would go far to placate concern about the competitive plight of the nonintegrated refiner and marketer and about possibly socially wasteful overinvestment in branded distribution in the hope of "locking in crude oil profits." Apart from the practical problems that any such program of disinvestment would create—in foreign fields especially, these could add up to real national disadvantages—we do not believe that such a policy recommendation is warranted by our study of this industry and we find its economic and philosophical implications repugnant.

At many points this essay has emphasized the contributions that vertically integrated firms have made in the progressive development of this industry. It could not be said with assurance, nor does it seem likely that anyone could prove no matter how elaborate the facts at his disposal, that these contributions would not have been made or would not have taken place with equal rapidity and equal if not greater benefit to the consumer, if vertical integration had not existed. History has taken a particular course, and it does not provide clear-cut evidence of what the comparative results would have been had it taken some other. It is known, however, that oil companies undertook additional functions because managers believed that they could perform them better and more cheaply themselves; historically, this obligation was often imposed by then-existing inadequacies in market alternatives. Furthermore, there are advantages in vertical integration that have urged and supported more rapid conquest of obstacles to growth—in financing; in assumption of risk and its effective reduction; in the wider exposure of the firm to profit opportunities and its lower cost-threshold to acceptable propositions because a single investment could be made to serve several purposes; in the acquisition and use of specialized talents in a coordinated fashion; and in a closer and more efficient synchronization of the flow of oil and products from well to customer. These and similar advantages are often more properly the gains from size; but size and vertical integration are closely correlated in this industry and the latter is a clear inducement to the former. And they are advantages not lightly to be dismissed in the unforeseeable contingencies of the future.

In the modern market many of these advantages of vertical integration seem to have disappeared and all have been substantially narrowed by the spread of technology, the development of specialized talents, the mere growth of the market, and the dependence of the economy on that growth—the familiar process of evolving external economies. The probable social costs of dissolution seem smaller; the possible gains may therefore appear larger. But by the same token the need for dissolution to preserve a workably competitive structure in oil is less. In any experimentation with methods of business organization, experience cautions strict economy in arbitrary action and in direct controls. While proof may be impossible, a strong probability of social benefit is a necessary condition of responsible action.

Neither the easy criticism of monopolistic attributes nor the easy praise of competitive advantages of the integrated firm will suffice in this search for a desirable public policy. The advantages and the corresponding handicaps of independent operators are both monopolistic and competitive. They are monopolistic in the sense that they are in some measure strategic, arising out of the possession or control of scarce natural resources, crucial methods of transportation, strategic market outlets, or brand names. They are competitive in the sense that they reflect rival efforts which provide genuine services for the public—new sources of supply, superior methods of transportation, better quality and reliability of products and services. We believe that this study demonstrates a workable balance between monopolistic and competitive aspects of this industry's structure and performance—beyond the crude oil level. So long as there are other ways of eliminating the serious flaws at that stage, and with them the threat they pose to effective competition elsewhere in the industry, divestiture seems not merely unnecessary, but undesirable.

It is the crucial strength of a private enterprise system that it permits flexible adaptation to unknowable future problems as they evolve by permitting the individual and the firm to undertake whatever market function opportunity recommends without arbitrary disbarment, excepting only a clear transgression of the public interest. This study seems to demonstrate such a transgression of the public interest in the present organization and functioning of the crude oil stage of the industry. Without some hope of effective change in that area, we would feel compelled by our own analysis to explore more seriously the grave problems that would be posed by divestiture of crude oil ownership and control from other industry operations. But no such drastic step may be required: certainly none should be put in motion until much less onerous alternatives are found wanting. Mandatory unitization, combined with a freer import policy as outlined in Part II, promises enough diversity of competitive interests within a framework of discretionary private action to restore a goodly element of competition to the monitoring of industry practices. Even if majors qualified as managers of such unitized fields, the opportunity for competitive supply adjustment within field MER's seems good. Should this prove unduly optimistic, competitive pressure could be enhanced by restricting management of unitized fields to independent nonintegrated operators. Only if both alternatives failed should a curtailment of opportunities for private experimentation in industrial organization through divestiture be contemplated. Certainly, vertical integration itself is not incompatible with workable competition.

Bibliography

American Petroleum Institute (API), *Petroleum Facts and Figures.* 9th and 12th eds., New York, API, 1950, 1956.
—————— *Proved Reserves for Crude Oil, Natural Gas Liquids and Natural Gas.* New York, API, annually.
—————— *Statistical Bulletin.* New York, API, annually.
Attorney General, State of Michigan. *See below,* Kavanagh, Thomas M.
Ayres, Eugene, "Conservation and Motor Fuel—What's Ahead?" *Petroleum Refiner* (September, 1952), p. 83.
—————— and Charles A. Scarlott, *Energy Sources—the Wealth of the World.* New York, McGraw-Hill, 1952.
Bain, Joe S., *The Economics of the Pacific Coast Petroleum Industry.* 3 vols., Berkeley, University of California Press, 1944, 1945, 1947.
Baker, Hines H., "Achievements and Unsolved Problems in Oil and Gas Conservation." Statement and article in U. S. House of Representatives, Committee on Interstate and Foreign Commerce, *Petroleum Study,* 1953, *q.v. below.*
Beaton, Kendall, *Enterprise in Oil: A History of Shell in the United States.* New York, Appleton-Century-Crofts, 1957.
Burns, Arthur R., *The Decline of Competition.* New York, McGraw-Hill, 1936.
Cassady, Ralph, Jr., *Price Making and Price Behavior in the Petroleum Industry.* Petroleum Monograph Series, 1. New Haven, Yale University Press, 1954.
—————— and Wylie L. Jones, *The Nature of Competition in Gasoline Distribution at the Retail Level.* Berkeley, University of California Press, 1951.
Chase Manhattan Bank, *Monthly Review of the Petroleum Situation.* New York, Chase Manhattan Bank. *See also* listings under Coqueron; Coqueron and Pogue; Hill, Hammer, and Winger; Pogue and Hill; Terry and Winger.
Cook, Roy C., *Control of the Petroleum Industry by Major Oil Companies,* T.N.E.C. Monograph No. 39. Washington, D.C., 1941. *See also* Farish and Pew.
Cookenboo, Leslie, Jr., *Crude Oil Pipe Lines and Competition in the Oil Industry.* Cambridge, Harvard University Press, 1955.
—————— "Structure of the Oil Industry," in *Readings on the Petroleum Industry,* ed. R. S. Brown, Jr. New Haven, Yale Law School, 1950 (mimeographed).

Coqueron, Frederick G., *Annual Financial Analyses of the Petroleum Industry* (variously titled). New York, Chase Manhattan Bank.

———— and Joseph E. Pogue, *Capital Formation in the Petroleum Industry.* New York, Chase Manhattan Bank, 1952.

———— *Investment Patterns in the World Petroleum Industry.* New York, Chase Manhattan Bank, 1956.

Cram, Ira H., "The Outlook Offshore," address before the 36th annual meeting of the American Petroleum Institute, November 14, 1956. Continental Oil Company (mimeographed).

Cross, James S., "Vertical Integration in the Oil Industry," *Harvard Business Review, 31* (1953), 69–81.

———— and Robert F. King, "Channels of Distribution for Petroleum Products," reproduced in *Petroleum Facts and Figures.* 11th ed., New York, API, 1954. Originally dittoed, Massachusetts Institute of Technology, 1953.

DeGolyer, E., ed., *Elements of the Petroleum Industry.* New York, the American Institute of Mining and Metallurgical Engineers, 1940.

Dirlam, Joel B., "The Petroleum Industry," in *The Structure of American Industry,* ed. Walter Adams. New York, Macmillan, 1954.

———— and Alfred E. Kahn, *Fair Competition, the Law and Economics of Antitrust Policy.* Ithaca, Cornell University Press, 1954.

———— "Leadership and Conflict in the Pricing of Gasoline," *Yale Law Journal, 61* (1952), 818–855.

Dow, Fayette B., "Petroleum Transportation," T.N.E.C. *Hearings,* Pt. XV, 8583–8611. *See below* U.S., Temporary National Economic Committee.

Emerson, H. N., "The Place of the Tanker in the Transportation of Energy," *Proceedings,* 32nd annual meeting, American Petroleum Institute (November 10–13, 1952), Sec. V, 69–78.

Empire State Petroleum Association, *Weekly Letter.* Cited as *ESPA Weekly Letter.*

ESPA, monthly journal of the Empire State Petroleum Association, New York.

Fanning, Leonard M., *Foreign Oil and the Free World.* New York, McGraw-Hill, 1954.

Farish, W. S., and J. Howard Pew, *Review and Criticism on Behalf of Standard Oil Company (New Jersey) and Sun Oil Company of Monograph No. 39 with Rejoinder by Monograph Author,* T.N.E.C. Monograph No. 39A. Washington, D.C., 1941.

Federal Trade Commission, *The International Petroleum Cartel. See below,* U. S. Senate, Select Committee on Small Business. *See also below,* U.S., Federal Trade Commission.

Fleming, Harold, "The American Oil Industry—A Forty-Odd Thousand Company Enterprise," Oil Industry Background Information Bulletin No. 4. New York, API, n.d.

Fleming, Harold, "Oil Prices and Competition." New York, API, 1953.
Fortune: "Creating Tomorrow's Oil" (November, 1951), pp. 112–115, 139–149.
———— "The Oil Play" (August, 1948), pp. 69–74, 149–153.
———— "That Sinister Oil Cartel" (October, 1952), pp. 113–114.
Frankel, P. H., *Essentials of Petroleum.* London, Chapman and Hall, 1940.
Furcht, C. M., *Growth and Structure of U. S. Refining Industry, 1920–1950.* Coordination and Economics Department, Standard Oil Company (New Jersey), n.d. (mimeographed).
Gibb, George S., and Evelyn H. Knowlton, *The Resurgent Years, 1911–1927, History of Standard Oil Company (New Jersey).* New York, Harper and Bros., 1956.
Giddens, Paul H., *Standard Oil Company (Indiana), Oil Pioneer of the Middle West.* New York, Appleton-Century-Crofts, 1955.
Gonzalez, Richard J., "U.S. Not Running Out of Oil," *World Oil* (March, 1957), pp. 64–69.
Graber, Paul J., ed., *Common Carrier Pipeline Operations and Accounting.* Norman, University of Oklahoma Press, 1951.
Hansen, H. L., and Powell Niland, "Esso Standard: A Case Study in Pricing," *Harvard Business Review, 30* (1952), 114–132.
Hardwicke, Robert E., "Market Demand as a Factor in the Conservation of Oil," in U. S. Senate, Subcommittee of Committee on Banking and Currency, *Price Increases in Petroleum Products,* 1949, *q.v. below.*
Haslam, R. T., F. M. Surface, and J. R. Riddell, "Petroleum Marketing Cost and Cost Reduction," *National Petroleum News,* March 3, 10, and 17, 1943.
Heron, S. D. *See* Schlaifer, Robert.
Hidy, Ralph W., and Muriel E. Hidy, *Pioneering in Big Business, 1882–1911, History of Standard Oil Company (New Jersey).* New York, Harper and Bros., 1955.
Hill, Kenneth E., Harold D. Hammer, and John G. Winger, *Future Growth of the World Petroleum Industry,* pamphlet issued by the Chase Manhattan Bank, April 25, 1957.
Howard, Marshall, "Interfirm Relations in Oil Products Markets," *Journal of Marketing, 20* (1956), 356–366.
———— "The Marketing of Petroleum Products: A Study on the Relations between Large and Small Business," unpublished Ph.D. dissertation, Cornell University, 1952.
International Conference on the Peaceful Uses of Atomic Energy, Geneva, August, 1955, *Proceedings.* New York, United Nations, 1956.
Ise, John, *The United States Oil Policy.* New Haven, Yale University Press, 1926.
James, Marquis, *The Texaco Story.* The Texas Company, 1953.
Johnson, Arthur M., *The Development of American Petroleum Pipelines.* Ithaca, Cornell University Press, 1956.

Kahn, Alfred E., *In the Matter of Phillips Petroleum Company*. Federal Power Commission, Docket G-1148, Exhibit 390.

────── "Standards for Antitrust Policy," *Harvard Law Review, 67* (1953), 28–54.

Kaplan, A. D. H., *Big Enterprise in a Competitive System*. Washington, D.C., Brookings Institution, 1954.

────── Joel B. Dirlam, and Robert F. Lanzillotti, *Pricing in Big Business: A Case Approach*. Washington, D.C., Brookings Institution, 1958.

Kavanagh, Thomas M., Attorney General, State of Michigan, *Report to the Governor on the Gasoline Price Investigation, 1955–1956*, prepared by Stanton S. Faville. State of Michigan, 1956 (processed).

Kemnitzer, William J., *Rebirth of Monopoly*. New York, Harper and Bros., 1938.

Learned, Edmund P., "Pricing of Gasoline: A Case Study," *Harvard Business Review, 26* (1948), 723–756.

McGee, John S., "Price Discrimination and Competitive Effects: The Standard Oil of Indiana Case," *University of Chicago Law Review, 23* (1956), 398–473.

McLean, John H., and Robert W. Haigh, *The Growth of Integrated Oil Companies*. Boston, Graduate School of Business Administration, Harvard University, 1954.

Marshall, J. Howard, and Norman L. Meyers, "Legal Planning of Petroleum Production: Two Years of Proration," *Yale Law Journal, 42* (1933), 702–746.

Michigan, State of, Attorney General. *See above*, Kavanagh, Thomas M.

National Petroleum Council, *Petroleum Imports*. Washington, D.C., N.P.C., 1955.

────── *Petroleum Productive Capacity, A Report on Present and Future Supplies of Oil and Gas*. Washington, D.C., N.P.C., 1952.

National Petroleum News, a monthly trade journal (weekly before November, 1954). New York, McGraw-Hill.

────── *Factbook*, annually, mid-May.

Nelson, James R., "Prices, Costs and Conservation in Petroleum," *American Economic Review, Papers and Proceedings, 48* (1958), 502–515.

Nelson, W. B., "The Oil Industry: A Case Study in Imperfect Competition," unpublished Ph.D. dissertation, State University of Iowa, 1950.

Netschert, Bruce C., *The Future Supply of Oil and Gas*. Baltimore, Johns Hopkins Press, for Resources for the Future, Inc., 1958.

Nevins, Allan, *John D. Rockefeller*. New York, Scribner's, 1940.

────── *Study in Power*. 2 vols., New York, Scribner's, 1953.

Oil and Gas Journal, a monthly trade journal. Tulsa, the Petroleum Publishing Co.

Paley Commission. *See below*, U.S., the President's Materials Policy Commission.

Petroleum Industry Research Foundation, *United States Oil Imports, A Case Study in International Trade.* New York, by the Foundation, 1958.

Petroleum Press Service, a monthly. London, Ethelburga House.

Platt, Warren, *The Future of the Independent Oil Jobber.* Cleveland, National Petroleum News, 1941.

Pogue, Joseph E., *The Economics of Petroleum.* New York, Wiley and Sons, 1921.

―――― and Kenneth E. Hill, *Future Growth and Financial Requirements of the World Petroleum Industry.* New York, Chase Manhattan Bank, 1956.

Pratt, Wallace, "The Impact of the Peaceful Uses of Atomic Energy on the Petroleum Industry," in U. S. Congress, Joint Committee on Atomic Energy, *Peaceful Uses of Atomic Energy,* Report of the Panel on the Impact of the Peaceful Uses of Atomic Energy, II, Background Material, Joint Committee Print, January, 1956.

Prewitt, Roy A., "The Operation and Regulation of Crude Oil and Gasoline Pipelines," *Quarterly Journal of Economics, 56* (1942), 177–211.

Rostow, Eugene V., *A National Policy for the Oil Industry.* New Haven, Yale University Press, 1948.

―――― and Arthur S. Sachs, "Entry into the Oil Refining Business; Vertical Integration Re-Examined," *Yale Law Journal, 61* (1952), 856–914.

Schlaifer, Robert, *Development of Aircraft Engines.* Published together with S. D. Heron, *Development of Aviation Fuels.* Cambridge, Harvard University Press, 1950

Spengler, J. J., "Vertical Integration and Antitrust Policy," *Journal of Political Economy, 58* (1950), 347–352.

Stambaugh, A. A., "Below Cost Selling of Petroleum Products," Testimony before the Ohio Senate Committee on Financial Institutions, Commerce and Labor, April 11, 1951. Privately printed, Standard Oil Co. of Ohio, 1951.

―――― "The Marketer's Role in a Free Economy." Privately printed, Standard Oil Co. of Ohio, 1949.

―――― "An Oil Man Looks at Distribution." Privately printed, Standard Oil Co. of Ohio, 1951.

Stocking, George W., *The Oil Industry and the Competitive System, A Study in Waste.* Boston, Houghton Mifflin, 1925.

―――― and Myron W. Watkins, *Cartels in Action.* New York, Twentieth Century Fund, 1946.

Sun Oil Company, "History of the Sun Oil Company." By the Company, 1951 (multilithed).

Swensrud, Sidney A., "The Marketing of Petroleum Products," T.N.E.C.

Hearings, Pt. XV, 8671–8714. *See below,* U.S., Temporary National Economic Committee.

────── "The Relation between Crude Oil and Product Prices," *Bulletin of the American Association of Petroleum Geologists, 23* (1939), 765–788.

Tarbell, Ida M., *History of the Standard Oil Company.* 2 vols., New York, McClure, Phillips, 1904.

Taylor, Frank J., and Earl M. Welty, *Black Bonanza.* New York, McGraw-Hill, 1950.

Terry, Lyon F., "Petroleum Financing." Reprint of paper delivered at Financial and Accounting Group Session, 35th annual meeting of the A.P.I., San Francisco, November 15, 1955. New York, Chase Manhattan Bank, 1955.

────── and John G. Winger, *Future Growth of the Natural Gas Industry.* New York, Chase Manhattan Bank, 1957.

Till, Irene, "Gasoline—The Competition of Big Business," in Walton Hamilton and Associates, *Price and Price Policies.* New York, McGraw-Hill, 1938.

Thompson, Craig, *Since Spindletop.* Apparently published by the Gulf Oil Corp., Pittsburgh, 1951.

United Nations, Economic and Social Council, Economic Commission for Europe, *The Price of Oil in Western Europe.* Geneva, March, 1955.

U.S., The Attorney General's National Committee to Study the Antitrust Laws, *Report.* Washington, D.C., 1955.

U.S., Bureau of Mines, "Petroleum and Natural Gas," a chapter reprint from *Mineral Facts and Problems,* Bulletin 556, Washington, D.C., December, 1955.

────── "Petroleum Refineries, Including Cracking Plants in the U.S." An annual refinery survey.

U. S., Department of Justice, *Report of the Attorney General,* pursuant to Section 2 of the Joint Resolution of July 28, 1955, consenting to an Interstate Compact to Conserve Oil and Gas. Washington, September 1, 1956.

────── *Second Report of the Attorney General,* as of September 1, 1957, pursuant to Section 2 of the Joint Resolution of July 28, 1955. Washington, D.C., 1957.

U.S., Federal Trade Commission, *Petroleum Industry, Prices, Profits, and Competition.* 70th Congress, 1st Session, Senate Document No. 61, 1928.

────── *Report on Distribution Methods and Costs,* Pt. IV, 1944. Cited as FTC, *Distribution Methods.*

U. S. Congress, Joint Committee on the Economic Report, *Federal Tax Policy for Economic Growth and Stability.* 84th Congress, 1st Session. Joint Committee Print, November 9, 1955. Papers on "The Impact of Federal Taxation on Natural Resources Development" by Gray, Harberger, Lambert, Nelson, Stanley, and Smith.

U. S. House of Representatives, Committee on Interstate and Foreign Commerce, *Fuel Investigation.* House Report 2342, 80th Congress, 2d Session, 1948.

———— *Petroleum Study.* Hearings, 83d Congress, 1st Session, 1953. (Cited, Wolverton Committee, *Hearings.*)

———— *Petroleum Survey, Oil Lift to Europe, Preliminary Report.* Union calendar No. 101, 85th Congress, 1st Session, House Report No. 314, 1957.

U. S. House of Representatives, Select Committee on Small Business, Subcommittee No. 1, *Monopolistic and Unfair Trade Practices.* Hearings, 80th Congress, 2d Session, 1948.

U. S. House of Representatives, Select Committee on Small Business, Subcommittee No. 5, *Alleged Coercive and Discriminatory Practices against Retail Gasoline Operators by Oil Company Suppliers, Interim Report.* House Report No. 1423, 84th Congress, 1st Session, 1955.

———— *Distribution Practices in the Petroleum Industry, Interim Report.* House Report No. 1157, 85th Congress, 1st Session, 1957.

U. S. House of Representatives, Select Committee on Small Business, Subcommittee on Oil Imports, *Effects of Foreign Imports on Independent Domestic Producers.* House Report No. 2344, 81st Congress, 2d Session, 1950.

U.S., Interstate Commerce Commission, "Reduced Pipeline Rates and Gathering Charges." 243 I.C.C. 115 (1940), and 272 I.C.C. 375 (1948).

U.S., Office of Defense Mobilization, *Report of the Special Committee to Investigate Crude Oil Imports.* July 29, 1957.

U.S., the President's Materials Policy Commission, *Resources for Freedom.* Washington, D.C., 1952. Cited as Paley Commission.

U.S., Senate Committee on Banking and Currency, Subcommittee, *Price Increases in Petroleum Products.* Hearings, 81st Congress, 1st Session, 1949.

U. S. Senate, Committee on the Judiciary, Subcommittee on Antitrust and Monopoly, *To Amend Section 2 of the Clayton Act.* Hearings, 84th Congress, 2d Session, 1956.

———— *Petroleum, the Antitrust Laws and Government Policies.* Report No. 1147, 85th Congress, 1st Session, 1957.

———— and Committee on Interior and Insular Affairs, Subcommittee on Public Lands, *Emergency Oil Lift Program and Related Oil Problems.* Pt. II, 85th Congress, 1st Session, 1957.

U. S. Senate, Select Committee on Small Business, *Gasoline Price War in*

New Jersey. Hearings, 84th Congress, 1st Session, 1955. Report No. 2810, 84th Congress, 2d Session, 1956.

———— *The International Petroleum Cartel.* Staff Report to the Federal Trade Commission, 82d Congress, 2d Session, Committee Print No. 6, August 22, 1952.

———— *Petroleum Marketing Practices.* Hearings, 83d Congress, 1st Session, 1953.

U. S. Senate, Special Committee to Study Problems of American Small Business, *Oil Supply and Distribution Problems.* Senate Report No. 25, 81st Congress, 1st Session, 1949.

U.S., Temporary National Economic Committee, *Investigation of the Concentration of Economic Power.* Hearings, Pts. XIV–XVIIA, 76th Congress, 2d Session, 1940.

———— *Monograph No. 39. See above,* Cook, Roy C.

———— *Monograph No. 39A. See above,* Farish and Pew.

Watkins, Myron W., *Oil: Stabilization or Conservation?* New York, Harper and Bros., 1937.

Wilson, Robert, *Oil Competition in the Midwest, A Case History.* Washington, D.C., National Petroleum Association, 1950.

Wolbert, George S., Jr., *American Pipelines.* Norman, University of Oklahoma Press, 1952.

Wolverton Committee, *Hearings. See* U. S. House of Representatives, Committee on Interstate and Foreign Commerce, *Petroleum Study.*

World Oil, a monthly trade journal. Houston, Gulf Publishing Co.

Wright, Willard M., "Keep Pace with Change," address before the Ohio Petroleum Marketers, September 15, 1952 (mimeographed by the Sun Oil Co.).

Zimmermann, Erich W., *Conservation in the Production of Petroleum.* Petroleum Monograph Series, 2. New Haven, Yale University Press, 1957.

New Jersey Hearings, 84th Congress, 1st Session, U. S. Senate, No. 2810, 84th Congress, 2d Session, 1956.

———. The International Petroleum Cartel, Staff Report to the Federal Trade Commission, 82d Congress, 2d Session, Committee Print No. 6, August 22, 1952.

———. Emergency Machinery Fuels for Distribution and Oklahoma, 1955.

U. S. Senate, Special Committee to Study Problems of American Small Business, Oil Supply and Distribution Problems, Senate Report No. 25, 81st Congress, 1st Session, 1949.

U. S. Temporary National Economic Committee, Investigation of the Concentration of Economic Power, Hearings, Pt. XIV-XVIIA, 76th Congress, 3d Session, 1940.

———. Monograph No. 36. See above, Cassady, Ralph C.

———. Monograph No. 39. See above, Frisch and Pitts.

WATKINS, MYRON W., Oil: Stabilization or Conservation? New York, Harper and Row, 1937.

Welcome Refiners Oil Company, in the Midwest, A Case Study, Washington, D.C., National Petroleum Association, 1950.

Wolbert, George S., Jr., American Pipelines, Norman, University of Oklahoma Press, 1952.

Watchdog Committee. Wanless, See U. S. House of Representatives, Committee on Interstate and Foreign Commerce, Petroleum Study.

World Oil, a monthly trade journal, Houston, Gulf Publishing Co.

Wright, Wilbur M., "Keep Pace with Changes," address before the 14th Petroleum Mechanics, September 15, 1952 (mimeographed), Los Angeles.

Zimmermann, Erich W., Conservation in the Production of Petroleum, Petroleum Monograph Series 2, New Haven, Yale University Press, 1957.

Index

Authors cited in footnotes are indexed on first reference to each publication only.

Continental Oil Co. (*continued*)
172; *1956* production and refining operations and self-sufficiency ratio, 224; appreciation of security prices, 326, 327, 331; mergers and new construction, 348 n.; builds pipeline, 460 n.; no refining capacity in *1920*, 487 n.; announced *1957* cut in runs to stills, 558 n. *See also* Conoco plan

Cookenboo, Leslie, Jr., 18 n., 28 n.

Coolidge, Calvin, 142

Coqueron, Frederick G., 4 n.; and Joseph E. Pogue, 315 n.

Cosden and Co., 488 n., 489 n.

Coumbe, A. T., and I. F. Avery, 12 n.

Cram, Ira H., 176 n.

Creole Petroleum Co., 108

Cross, James S., 267 n.; and Robert F. King, 13 n.

Cross process, 296 n.

Crown Central Petroleum Co., 33 n., 521, 524 n.

Crude oil: ingredients, 63; "pressure," as explanation of integration, 104–6; pricing, 166–229
    Alberta, 460; Bahrein, 212 n.; California, 114, 138 n., 139 n., 149; Canadian, 522 n.; Caribbean, 214; Indiana, 44; Lima, 294; Mexican, 510; Michigan, 227 n.; Midcontinent, 67, 83 n., 105 n., 155, 418 n., 460, 496 and n.; Middle East, 214; Oklahoma, 226 n., 555 n.; Pennsylvania, 66, 80 n., 84, 184, 293 n., 294 n., 300, 338 n., 415; Texas, 114, 193, 195; United States, 123, 137; Venezuelan, 511 n.; Williston Basin, 104 n.; Wyoming, 271

Cullinan, J. S., 86

Cunningham, A. R. *See* Murphree, E. V.

Cushing Pool, 130 n.

Daniel, G. H. *See* Robinson, E. A. G.

Davies, Ralph K., 206 n.

Deep Rock Oil Corp., 170, 206 n., 217 n., 521, 535 n.; absorbed by merger, 349, 524; marketing turned

over to independent distributors, 536 n.

Defense Production Act (*1950*), 346 n.

DeGolyer, E. E., 284 and n., 285

Delhi-Taylor Co., 524 and n.

Delta Refining Co., 511 n.

Demand: nature of, 64–6; major changes, 87, 136–42, 146–63, 461 n. *See also* Prices

Department of: Agriculture, 282; Defense, 202; Interior, 181 n., 194, 195; Navy, 212 n.; State, 40, 121, 202, 248. *See also* Attorney General, Secretary of

Derby Oil Co., 521, 524 and n., 535 n.

Deterding, Henri, 116

Detroit: price fixing, 412; price war, 480 n.

Dewar and Redwood, 295

Direct Service Co., 522 n.

Director of Defense Mobilization, 203

Director of Price Stabilization, 191

Dirlam, Joel B., and Alfred E. Kahn, 46 n., 278 n. *See also* Kaplan, A. D. H.

Doherty, H. L., 89, 142, 241

Douglas, Paul, 11 n.

Dow, Fayette B., 333 n.

Drake, Edwin L., 75, 284

Dubbs, Jesse A., 296 n.

Dubbs process, 295

Duff, Dahl M., 208 n.

Dun and Bradstreet, 549, 550 n.

Du Pont. *See* E. I. du Pont de Nemours and Co.

E. I. du Pont de Nemours and Co., 296, 306 n.

East Coast area, 82, 94, 97, 161, 197 n., 203, 204 and n., 211 and n., 229, 245, 394, 395 n., 403, 413 n., 459 n., 521; outstrips Pennsylvania capacity, 83; Standard of California enters, 93, 456 n.; invaded by Standard of Indiana, 95; Shell enters, 97; residual fuel imports increase, 201; tank-wagon